Microsoft® Office 2000
Developer's Guide

Microsoft® Office 2000 Developer's Guide

D. F. Scott

An imprint of IDG Books Worldwide, Inc.
An International Data Group Company

Foster City, CA ◆ Chicago, IL ◆ Indianapolis, IN ◆ New York, NY

Microsoft® Office 2000 Developer's Guide

Published by
M&T Books
An imprint of IDG Books Worldwide, Inc.
919 E. Hillsdale Blvd., Suite 400
Foster City, CA 94404
www.idgbooks.com (IDG Books Worldwide Web site)

Library of Congress Catalog Card No.: 99-62414

ISBN: 0-7645-3330-4

Printed in the United States of America

10 9 8 7 6 5 4 3 2

1B/TQ/QW/ZZ/FC

Distributed in the United States by IDG Books Worldwide, Inc.

Distributed by CDG Books Canada, Inc. for Canada; by Transworld Publishers Limited in the United Kingdom; by IDG Norge Books for Norway; by IDG Sweden Books for Sweden; by IDG Books Australia Publishing Corporation Pty. Ltd. for Australia and New Zealand; by TransQuest Publishers Pte Ltd. for Singapore, Malaysia, Thailand, Indonesia, and Hong Kong; by Gotop Information, Inc. for Taiwan; by ICG Muse, Inc. for Japan; by Norma Comunicaciones S.A. for Colombia; by Intersoft for South Africa; by Le Monde en Tique for France; by International Thomson Publishing for Germany, Austria and Switzerland; by Distribuidora Cuspide for Argentina; by Livraria Cultura for Brazil; by Ediciones ZETA S.C.R. Ltda. for Peru; by WS Computer Publishing Corporation, Inc., for the Philippines; by Contemporanea de Ediciones for Venezuela; by Express Computer Distributors for the Caribbean and West Indies; by Micronesia Media Distributor, Inc. for Micronesia; by Grupo Editorial Norma S.A. for Guatemala; by Chips Computadoras S.A. de C.V. for Mexico; by Editorial Norma de Panama S.A. for Panama; by American Bookshops for Finland. Authorized Sales Agent: Anthony Rudkin Associates for the Middle East and North Africa.

For general information on IDG Books Worldwide's books in the U.S., please call our Consumer Customer Service department at 800-762-2974. For reseller information, including discounts and premium sales, please call our Reseller Customer Service department at 800-434-3422.

For information on where to purchase IDG Books Worldwide's books outside the U.S., please contact our International Sales department at 317-596-5530 or fax 317-596-5692.

For consumer information on foreign language translations, please contact our Customer Service department at 800-434-3422, fax 317-596-5692, or e-mail rights@idgbooks.com.

For information on licensing foreign or domestic rights, please phone +1-650-655-3109.

For sales inquiries and special prices for bulk quantities, please contact our Sales department at 650-655-3200 or write to the address above.

For information on using IDG Books Worldwide's books in the classroom or for ordering examination copies, please contact our Educational Sales department at 800-434-2086 or fax 317-596-5499.

For press review copies, author interviews, or other publicity information, please contact our Public Relations department at 650-655-3000 or fax 650-655-3299.

For authorization to photocopy items for corporate, personal, or educational use, please contact Copyright Clearance Center, 222 Rosewood Drive, Danvers, MA 01923, or fax 978-750-4470.

 is a registered trademark or trademark under exclusive license to IDG Books Worldwide, Inc. from International Data Group, Inc., in the United States and/or other countries.

 is a trademark of IDG Books Worldwide, Inc.

ABOUT IDG BOOKS WORLDWIDE

Welcome to the world of IDG Books Worldwide.

IDG Books Worldwide, Inc., is a subsidiary of International Data Group, the world's largest publisher of computer-related information and the leading global provider of information services on information technology. IDG was founded more than 30 years ago by Patrick J. McGovern and now employs more than 9,000 people worldwide. IDG publishes more than 290 computer publications in over 75 countries. More than 90 million people read one or more IDG publications each month.

Launched in 1990, IDG Books Worldwide is today the #1 publisher of best-selling computer books in the United States. We are proud to have received eight awards from the Computer Press Association in recognition of editorial excellence and three from Computer Currents' First Annual Readers' Choice Awards. Our best-selling ...For Dummies® series has more than 50 million copies in print with translations in 31 languages. IDG Books Worldwide, through a joint venture with IDG's Hi-Tech Beijing, became the first U.S. publisher to publish a computer book in the People's Republic of China. In record time, IDG Books Worldwide has become the first choice for millions of readers around the world who want to learn how to better manage their businesses.

Our mission is simple: Every one of our books is designed to bring extra value and skill-building instructions to the reader. Our books are written by experts who understand and care about our readers. The knowledge base of our editorial staff comes from years of experience in publishing, education, and journalism — experience we use to produce books to carry us into the new millennium. In short, we care about books, so we attract the best people. We devote special attention to details such as audience, interior design, use of icons, and illustrations. And because we use an efficient process of authoring, editing, and desktop publishing our books electronically, we can spend more time ensuring superior content and less time on the technicalities of making books.

You can count on our commitment to deliver high-quality books at competitive prices on topics you want to read about. At IDG Books Worldwide, we continue in the IDG tradition of delivering quality for more than 30 years. You'll find no better book on a subject than one from IDG Books Worldwide.

John Kilcullen
Chairman and CEO
IDG Books Worldwide, Inc.

Steven Berkowitz
President and Publisher
IDG Books Worldwide, Inc.

*Eighth Annual
Computer Press
Awards ≥1992*

*Ninth Annual
Computer Press
Awards ≥1993*

*Tenth Annual
Computer Press
Awards ≥1994*

*Eleventh Annual
Computer Press
Awards ≥1995*

IDG is the world's leading IT media, research and exposition company. Founded in 1964, IDG had 1997 revenues of $2.05 billion and has more than 9,000 employees worldwide. IDG offers the widest range of media options that reach IT buyers in 75 countries representing 95% of worldwide IT spending. IDG's diverse product and services portfolio spans six key areas including print publishing, online publishing, expositions and conferences, market research, education and training, and global marketing services. More than 90 million people read one or more of IDG's 290 magazines and newspapers, including IDG's leading global brands — Computerworld, PC World, Network World, Macworld and the Channel World family of publications. IDG Books Worldwide is one of the fastest-growing computer book publishers in the world, with more than 700 titles in 36 languages. The "...For Dummies®" series alone has more than 50 million copies in print. IDG offers online users the largest network of technology-specific Web sites around the world through IDG.net (http://www.idg.net), which comprises more than 225 targeted Web sites in 55 countries worldwide. International Data Corporation (IDC) is the world's largest provider of information technology data, analysis and consulting, with research centers in over 41 countries and more than 400 research analysts worldwide. IDG World Expo is a leading producer of more than 168 globally branded conferences and expositions in 35 countries including E3 (Electronic Entertainment Expo), Macworld Expo, ComNet, Windows World Expo, ICE (Internet Commerce Expo), Agenda, DEMO, and Spotlight. IDG's training subsidiary, ExecuTrain, is the world's largest computer training company, with more than 230 locations worldwide and 785 training courses. IDG Marketing Services helps industry-leading IT companies build international brand recognition by developing global integrated marketing programs via IDG's print, online and exposition products worldwide. Further information about the company can be found at www.idg.com.   1/24/99

Credits

ACQUISITIONS EDITOR
Greg Croy

DEVELOPMENT EDITOR
Barbra Guerra

TECHNICAL EDITOR
Allen Wyatt

COPY EDITORS
Richard Adin
Anne Friedman

PRODUCTION
IDG Books Worldwide Production

PROOFREADING AND INDEXING
Publication Services

About the Author

D. F. Scott has one of the longest-running bylines in the history of computing journalism, having inaugurated his first programming column in 1984. For more than two decades, Scott has made significant contributions to the way people work. His published analyses and tutorials date back to when the 6502 was a popular processor and when hard disk drives were referred to as "Winchesters." Scott's articles on programming and new technologies have appeared in such prominent publications as *Computer Shopper* and *Computer Monthly*, as well as in one of the 1980's most prolific journals for computer enthusiasts, *ANALOG Computing.* One of the world's first online moderators, Scott co-founded the *Computer Shopper Information Exchange* in 1987, which was among the first to publish electronic articles from a major magazine publisher for public download, and only the second (after *Byte*) to publish original articles with the publisher's brand name and staff. Today, Scott continues to diligently work to extend, revise, and perfect the systems with which the world disseminates digital information.

*For Jennifer, the keeper of my heart and gardener of my soul;
and for Katerina, my magnificent daughter – and our gift to God and to the future.*

Preface

The best programming books I've ever read work in two ways: You can read them front to back, and everything makes solid sense in that sequence. Also, you can find what you need to know from anyplace in the book, and whatever you read from the middle of the book makes some degree of sense on its own.

Why You Should Read This Book

This is how *Microsoft Office 2000 Developer's Guide* works: The primary purpose of this book is to show you how to remodel the Office 2000 (O2K) applications into more effective, more efficient, and more pertinent programs for your business. There are a number of ways to go about this, and I'll show you as many as I can in the space here. This book opts to present examples in a slow and richly detailed manner. I'd rather show you one way to work that you'll understand rather than eight ways without enough space to adequately explain them.

Only the most important terms are thoroughly explained

Learning how to program a computer is in many ways like learning how to manage a staff of employees. You can't possibly memorize beforehand what to say or do in every conceivable situation. There is no step one, step two, or step three for any one problem. What you learn from this book is how to figure out what you need to do after a thorough assessment of a problem. I know better than to throw a bunch of terms at you and expect you to figure everything out for yourself. With this book, I try to help you with the "figuring out" part of programming.

There are, of course, thousands of terms, or *keywords*, in the vocabulary of Visual Basic for Applications (VBA) and O2KOM. Although you need to know about them, you needn't memorize all of them to be a fluent O2K programmer. If you understand the context in which these keywords are used, and the way the VBA interpreter works when it sees these keywords, you will know all that you need to know. You can then rely on this book to remind you of the details or the specific syntax when the need for a particular keyword comes up.

Although I want this book to be a trusted reference, it is by no means a dictionary. I doubt the person exists who learned the English language by reading Webster's from A to Z. This book requires some of the new lexicon of computer programming, plus the lexicon of Microsoft. I have elected not to use terms that are confusing, ill chosen, products of mixed metaphors, or that simply do not adequately describe their functions. In such situations, this book uses terms that are more generally accepted or that are simply *correct*.

Examples have depth and comprehensibility

This book utilizes two types of example source code: *Fragments* are examples that appear to be extracted from a much larger VBA project. You don't need to see the whole project to understand what a fragment means. Many times the role of an individual keyword is small or localized enough that it can be adequately depicted in a fragment. *Listings* are larger examples and generally consist of complete procedures or modules, if not entire programs. Listings are numbered and at times segmented, so that you're not inundated with code without enough explanation to guide you. Between the listing segments, I sometimes break away to explain in English what's happening within those segments. I believe it is unreasonable to expect you to learn to program by typing in reams of source code listings and waiting for their meanings to manifest themselves magically within your subconscious. Programming is a practical, not a mystical, process. I explain in practical terms what is going on.

Later in the book, as the focus shifts toward managing the programming process, not every example demonstrates The Way Things Should Work. In some cases, I show the construction of a VBA program in its beginning and intermediate stages, indicating how some ideas eventually are dropped as a program's development progresses. You also see how some things *don't* work, and hopefully gain an understanding of why.

Goals of this book are described by "the five R's"

With every paragraph, this book strives to fit the five essential R's:

1. **Rational.** This book focuses on problems and their solutions. Sometimes the logic of programming is a bit convoluted. Just because it sometimes conflicts with the way you work in the real world should not mean there's something wrong with *you*. This book is really about how you improve the way computers work, as much as it is how computers help you. So the logic I employ in describing and explaining what's going on and what to do is more practical and sensible than mathematical.

2. **Reliable.** You can trust that the information provided here has been thoroughly engineered, tested, and reviewed by the most experienced team in the business. It is not a rewrite of the existing documentation or the Help system. If I say something works, it's because I've seen it work, not just because Microsoft promises that it will someday.

3. **Reasonable.** VBA programming is a very difficult subject; don't think I'm not mindful of that fact. Although the methodologies portrayed here are probably not "simple" compared to, say, a recipe for lasagna or a blueprint for a covered patio, as computing standards go, they aren't outlandish. I believe that a thorough comprehension of the *basic* techniques of O2K programming will take you further than a poorly guided tour of the most extreme examples.

4. **Responsible.** I have a duty to you, the reader, to be fair, objective, and balanced in my assessment of any process, program, technology, or methodology. You'll read my professional opinion from time to time; these opinions are mine and are not necessarily those of IDG Books Worldwide. Sometimes I go out on a limb, but I promise it's a solid limb.

5. **Realistic.** Each process demonstrated is indicative of a real-world problem, and is approached from the perspective of a programmer in a business situation. It presents a situation in which I feel you are likely to find yourself. It does not play "Advanced Dragon Master"; with respect to my colleagues who have written some great dragon games, this book is about getting work done.

How This Book Is Organized

Microsoft Office 2000 Developer's Guide contains two parts. Part I, "Adopting Visual Basic," contains the first eleven chapters, and Part II, "The Office 2000 Platforms," holds the remaining seven chapters. Here are descriptions of the chapter contents and how they are sequenced.

Chapter 1, "An Overview of Office 2000 Programming," spells out in detail the capabilities of Visual Basic for Applications and gives you a clear concept of the nature of the changes you can, and should, make to O2K components. It is foolish to pass off VBA as a mere customization tool. On the other hand, although you can use VBA to write stand-alone applications, that isn't what the system was designed for.

In Chapter 2, I introduce "The Office 2000 Object Model" (O2KOM). Every addressable part of the O2K applications has a name, and many of these named objects have their own named properties and functions (methods) as well. In order that these objects might make more sense to you, the human programmer, they have a sort of rank-and-file hierarchy that is, in most instances, sensible. In the same respect that a paragraph belongs to a document, in the Word 2000 object library a `Paragraph` object belongs to a `Document` object. The main Office 2000 Object Model names those aspects of the applications that can be directly addressed, and thus can be instructed to make a change or be changed.

In Chapter 3, "Comprehending Visual Basic Symbology," I expand on the topic of representative terms. In VBA, as in nearly every programming language ever conceived, arbitrarily named terms called *variables* represent the values stored in locations within a computer's memory. While the object models provide VBA with access to data belonging to an application, variables are ways to create and manage data outside of an application.

Chapter 4, "The Contributions of the BASIC Language," starts to view the language for its own merits. BASIC was a programming language long before the advent of Microsoft's applications suite. When you master the instructional syntax of Visual Basic, you are able to perceive in your mind a program for an Office 2000 function before you actually start to develop it.

In Chapter 5, "Utilizing Forms Controls as Display Devices," I examine the graphical controls used by VBA, which include the many so-called ActiveX controls. All of the familiar Windows gadgets used to devise the graphical part of an application – scroll bars, radio buttons, check boxes, drop-down combo boxes, and the like – are provided to VBA by ActiveX controls rather than by the Windows 32-bit API, which historically provided these features to other programming languages. The result of this is that the structure of the VBA module becomes far more modular, and the overhead necessary for the computer to execute the module is reduced tremendously.

Chapter 6, "The Common Terminology of Controls," concentrates on how to use the forms controls introduced in Chapter 5 in the development of onscreen devices that elicit information from a user. VBA makes use of a platform that is, in its own right, an ActiveX control – namely, the UserForm object that is a part of the Forms 2.0 library. The other ActiveX controls adhere to this platform like blocks in a Lego set. The functionality of all of these devices thus becomes accessible to you, the programmer, through the VBA console.

With the groundwork laid out in Chapters 5 and 6, you can then make use of Chapter 7, "Extending Office 2000 with ActiveX Controls," to help you make sense of the individual controls. The label control, for instance, behaves differently from a text box; the former is designed to display text, whereas the latter provides the user with a place to type text. Yet you might be surprised to know that the label control behaves quite similarly to the command button, which is generally reserved for "OK" and "Cancel."

With Chapter 8, "Why the Component Object Model Matters," I shift my focus to how the Windows platforms handle communication between processes. As you know, Windows can run more than one program at a time. Through multitasking, multiple applications that do run at the same time can, conceivably, share the same data processing workload. When they do, the borderline between these applications starts to blur, especially when a VBA module is communicating with all of them.

Chapter 9 builds on the information framework developed in Chapter 8 to demonstrate "Devising Runtime Objects." Here is where you put to use all the tools of both VBA and Windows programming to develop functionality that can be put to use in any or all of the O2K applications. You begin to see how to alter or mold all of Office 2000 to suit the specific requirements of your own business.

In Chapter 10, "What Windows Knows That VBA Doesn't," I shift from narrowly addressing Windows applications to broadly addressing the Applications Program Interface (API) of 32-bit Windows. There are fewer reasons than ever before to directly address the API, but the reasons that remain are quite compelling. Through the API, you can track such intricate functions as what the mouse pointer is doing, or whether portions of a particular window are being overwritten by another.

Chapter 11, "Packaging and Distributing the VBA Application," discusses a subject that isn't covered in other programming books, because it isn't applicable to other programming books. You may find yourself deploying your VBA module or project on multiple systems or networks, perhaps in different companies, depending on what wing of the programming business you find yourself in. Getting your VBA module deployed so that it runs flawlessly despite your users' personal Office 2000 preferences (and there are many to consider), brings up distribution issues that you don't have to consider with any other type of program.

Moving into Part II, "The Office 2000 Platforms," Chapters 12 through 18, I look at the object models of the four key Office 2000 applications and build extensive examples of VBA projects that feature those applications. Included in this part of the book is Chapter 16, "Comprehending Databases," in which I deal with a component of Office 2000 that isn't directly visible to the general user: Jet. It is a database engine that provides services to all the more visible Office 2000 applications, most prominently Access and Excel.

Special features in this book

Most of the sidebars in this book are specifically focused and fall into a few categories.

ON POINT

From time to time, text pauses for a clearly marked summary capsule called *On Point*. Each capsule is a summary of the paragraphs leading up to it, as well as a reminder of any earlier information you might need to recall in order to comprehend the paragraphs that follow. This way, you don't have to try to read this book all in one session just to ensure that all the information is fresh in your mind. You have places to stop and insert your bookmark. When you come back, your mind can catch up quickly, and you won't be thumbing back through previous pages trying to remember where you saw some term.

In the *Guide,* I resurrect a once-prominent feature of programming books in the 1970s and 1980s. **The most important sentences are boldfaced, like this.** This way, if you scan pages for the gist of the information contained therein, you can see the main points clearly and distinctly.

AT PRESENT

Because you will write VBA modules that change how Office 2000 works, from time to time you need to know something about how something works now before you change it. I present brief sidebars called *At Present* that explain to you, or remind you of, some feature of O2K and how it works *before* you make changes to it.

IN DEPTH

On occasion, it is prudent to narrow the focus for a few extra paragraphs on a particularly difficult or esoteric topic. The *In Depth* sidebars enable you to step aside from the main topic of the chapter in order to dedicate some space to make some concept clearer and more comprehensible, or explain some practice that contributes to the overall context of the chapter.

IN THEORY

Each chapter closes with an essay. The reason why this book allocates such valuable space to mere prose is because programming, in and of itself, does not induce thinking, and thinking is heavily required for one to truly program. The In Theory segments examine the chapter topic on a more personal, sometimes philosophical level. They attempt to extricate from the technical quagmire some quantum of pertinence that may, unencumbered by the delicate illusion of technocratic efficiency amid the business of programming, inspire you to continue.

IN BRIEF

Because the *On Point* sidebars serve to summarize segments throughout the chapter, the usual closing summary segment has been remodeled and made more succinct. Now, an *In Brief* segment presents the five most important points to take with you as you move from one chapter to the next. You'll probably find them most useful during the periods in between chapters when you insert your bookmark, put the book down, and do something else – such as make a living. Now you can flip to the page before your bookmark and remember what you learned in the previous chapter.

Conventions used in this book

This book assumes that Visual Basic for Applications is your first programming language. If I refer from time to time to VB Standard Edition, or to Java or C++, my intention is to give you a better understanding of VBA's approach to a job by means of comparison. Just because you learn to program using VBA does not mean that you are locked into the Visual Basic suite for the remainder of your career. And VBA's approach to object orientation or procedural logic can certainly be original, though that does not necessarily make it optimal in comparison to the approaches taken by other programming languages. This book does not preach the gospel of VBA, as it were. If you have studied Java, and you like some of its approaches better than VBA's, well, you might be right.

SYNTAX TABLES

When I introduce a new keyword, I want to represent to you as completely and comprehensibly as possible the rules of how to form an instruction using that keyword. Experience has taught me that the symbolic tools generally used to show newcomers how to form a program instruction are often more confusing than the construction itself. So the tool I use here is something called a *syntax table*. This device breaks down a keyword element into its constituent parts, both required and optional. The intention is to show you what to type, step by step. Syntax tables are set up to show you the numbered parts and then describe them in the table that immediately follows the figure portions.

Here you see the syntax table for the term Selection, part of the Word 2000 object library, used in the formation of VBA instructions. When you write an instruction that pertains to Word's cursor, some part of that instruction uses the Selection term. This table specifies the rules that come into effect when you use that term in an instruction. At the top are five numbered boxes that represent all possible parts of the Selection term when it is employed within an instruction. The parts *before* Selection answer the question, "Whose cursor is this?" while the parts *after* Selection answer the question, "What parts of the cursor are we talking about?" Some parts are required (bold, solid boxes), others are optional or are used only in certain conditions (dashed boxes). The following table explains each of these five parts in order.

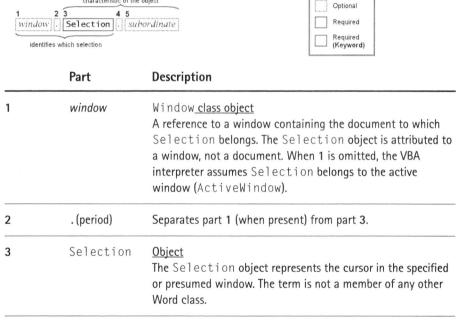

	Part	Description
1	*window*	Window class object A reference to a window containing the document to which Selection belongs. The Selection object is attributed to a window, not a document. When 1 is omitted, the VBA interpreter assumes Selection belongs to the active window (ActiveWindow).
2	. (period)	Separates part 1 (when present) from part 3.
3	Selection	Object The Selection object represents the cursor in the specified or presumed window. The term is not a member of any other Word class.

Continued

| 4 | . (period) | Separates part **3** \|from part **5** (when present). |
| 5 | *subordinate* | <u>Object, method, or property</u> A term associated with the `Selection` object. For instance, `Selection.Range` represents the area of text currently highlighted by the cursor. |

Notice how the numbers in the left-hand column correlate to the numbered boxes at the top. This way, you can use the table to determine which part means what, when to write that part, and whether you should write that part in certain circumstances. If a part of an instruction may be repeated, a long arrow in the diagram leads you back to the point where repetition begins. Exactly *why* you'd want to repeat that part is explained in the Description column of the table. Each syntax table is followed by further explanation, and then by some examples of the instruction put to use in a program. When a certain phraseology requires a longer explanation, the description in the table refers to an *In Depth* sidebar that goes into greater detail.

An Office 2000 object often is a member of some broader class of object and usually contains a lexicon of its own terms. For example, in Excel, the object term `Range` represents a grouping of cells in a spreadsheet. It "belongs" to an object of the `Worksheet` class, which makes sense for the same reasons that a range of cells belongs to a worksheet when you use Excel every day. Within a VBA program you may assign a name such as `Invoice` to the worksheet containing this range; or the worksheet may have a number such as `Worksheets(1)`; or the worksheet may simply be whichever one is in the active window at the time, represented by the term `ActiveSheet`. All three of these are valid `Worksheet` class objects. In a syntax table you find a dashed box around the italicized word *worksheet* to represent the class of object to type at that point in the instruction. Here you don't actually type "w-o-r . . ." In this particular instance, you might type nothing at all; the VBA interpreter can accept an *absence* of a term as though you typed `ActiveSheet` — this is why our box is dashed. A solid box indicates that something must be typed in that spot.

You may be wondering why not to include all of these syntax tables in an appendix. The facts contained in these syntax tables are more important as tools in the explanation of O2K programming than as mere background data. The syntax tables provide information you need to see now — not to memorize, mind you, just to read and digest so the meaning becomes clearer. Making you turn to some other page all the time only adds busy work to what already is a busy enough subject. *Microsoft Office 2000 Developer's Guide* shows you what you need to know now and explains to you what it all means now.

THE USER AND THE PROGRAMMER

Frequently during the course of the book, I refer to somebody in the third person —
"the user." This is the person who will use the programs that you build with VBA.
To reduce confusion, I make distinctions between the programmer (you) and the
user. You may be the user of the programs you build; but even if that is the case, it
always makes sense for you to consider the user of your programs as someone *else*
besides yourself. When you think of yourself as both programmer and user, you
might tend to build assumptions into a program, such as completely knowing what
the program does. As a result, you might place a feature in a location that only you
might be able to find, or craft that feature in such a way that only you might be
able to interpret it. **Assuming that the user has your preconceptions about a task
your application performs is not good programming.** (There's that boldface put to
use.) The best way to make a feature self-explanatory to its user, even if it's you, is
to assume the user is someone else. I make that same assumption during the course
of this book.

UNIVERSAL PUNCTUATION

Something I do in this book that Microsoft does not do with respect to its own documentation follows a more universal convention: The categories of certain VBA
and O2KOM keywords are easily identifiable by the punctuation that precedes or
follows them. To maintain that ease of identification, I include that punctuation
when referring to the keyword by itself, as part of a sentence. For example, there's
the `Int()` function, the `_Initialize` event, the `.Text` property, and the `.Show`
method, all of which include punctuation that helps identify their purpose.

ICONS

And of course I've included icons, as described here.

To draw your attention to an interesting or noteworthy piece of information.

To provide you with a little "extra" that will ease your way.

A warning that could prevent problems that you might typically encounter.
This, from the voice of experience.

To guide you to more information or another part of the book.

 Directs you to sample code that you'll find on this book's CD-ROM.

Now that you have some idea of the ground rules, it's time to get started. It's good to have you along for what promises to be a challenging, invigorating, and perhaps enlightening journey. Let's make things work.

Acknowledgments

My partner in this effort, as he has been for nine of my 13 books thus far, is Greg Croy. He is a true gentleman in this business and, in my view, the most sensible and wise editor in the computing book press. While mountains have fallen, he has remained standing; and where the fearful have scattered, he has stood fast.

I owe Greg this paragraph, because it was cut from the previous edition by someone who perhaps thought I didn't mean it: The business of publishing computing information in bound form is tumultuous. It has become a news-gathering operation, and we in this industry are just now adapting to the new schematics of this business. Greg is better at adapting than most. He has acted as my liaison and representative and, as a result, has fought the most effective two-front war since the Battle of the Bulge. I owe a lot to this man for his generosity, his persistence, and at times his forgiveness.

Joining Greg and me in the effort to bring you the most accurate and pertinent information available is Barbra Guerra. There is no nonsense about her; and in this industry, that is a high compliment. It is good to have a development editor on a project who knows how to fight the good fight.

Also joining this project as technical editor is a fellow named Allen Wyatt. If his name rings a bell, it is because you've probably seen it on the front of a few dozen books published since the mid-1980s, including the groundbreaking, standard-setting *Using Assembly Language*. Without a doubt, Allen is the finest technical editor I have ever worked with. I'm not saying that because he told IDG Books Worldwide he liked my work (although that was quite nice of you, Allen, and thanks again). I have always stated that the best editors are themselves authors, and the best authors are editors. Allen Wyatt proves my point.

I'd also like to take this opportunity to thank IDG Books Worldwide's Andy Cummings for his faith and support, especially during this most trying period in the history of this industry.

Portions of this book, some of which may have appeared in other editions, also were edited by the following: Nancy Albright, Susannah Pfalzer, Matt Lusher, Lothlorien Baerenwald, and Laura Brown. All have contributed concepts and guidance to this work.

Special thanks go to my IDG Books Worldwide colleague, John Walkenbach, who provided some of his finer material for the CD-ROM. Look for *Excel 2000 VBA Power Programming* by John Walkenbach from the same source of this book.

Thanks also to Jerry Pournelle, whose published idea for a useful Word 2000 utility appears in Chapter 14. His idea and his likeness appear here with his permission. Whether the results of my attempt to address his idea meet with his approval remains to be seen.

Contents at a Glance

Contents

Introduction

This is a story about making your computers perform the tasks you need, and expect, them to perform, in precisely the manner you require. Because you have Microsoft Office 2000, you have at your disposal a real programming language: Visual Basic for Applications. While this news is gratifying to me and my colleagues who have been programmers and authors for more than two decades, and who are more than happy to welcome you into the fold, you may or may not be as enthused. You see, we've grown accustomed to people getting into the business of programming because that is what they *want* to do with their lives. Who would willingly march into the esoteric realm of algorithmic optimization, derivative instantiation, and virtual classes, but someone intentionally headed in that direction? Programming, like ice sculpture, is a voluntary craft . . . generally.

In today's digital offices, this is not necessarily the case. People such as you may have been thrust into the position of programmer out of sheer necessity rather than interest. The reasons why have to do with the circumstances with which countless businesses worldwide – perhaps including yours – currently find themselves.

The Situation at Hand

Microsoft Windows is the operating system that marshals the data for a large and growing number of the world's businesses – a considerable plurality, if not yet a majority. Windows 98 and Windows NT 4.0 were intentionally designed to accommodate Microsoft Office. Although Microsoft does not keep all of its software design techniques and methodologies entirely secret, it is the Office suite that makes full use of them first and foremost. As a result, Microsoft Word has become the world's document generator, Microsoft Excel the world's data analyst, and Microsoft Access the world's data entry system.

Visual Basic for Applications is the system devised by Microsoft for enabling users to customize and extend the functionality of Office 2000. VBA is not a separate product; it is an integral part of every installed O2K suite, regardless of whether just one, some, or all of its components are installed. Any logical functionality built into a document or worksheet, any changes in the operating characteristics of an O2K application, and nearly all of the functionality built into a stand-alone Access program are made possible by VBA.

Millions worldwide depend on Microsoft Office for the integrity of their own businesses' information, and in many cases for their own livelihood. A few years ago, you could say the main Office application components – Word, Excel, PowerPoint, and Access – were faring respectably well in their respective markets, or enjoying respectable leads, or at least holding their own. Today they are almost without competition in those markets; one report gives PowerPoint a 93 percent stake of the presentation graphics software market and its nearest competitor 4 percent. How did this happen? If such dominance truly came about more by accident than design, then whose accident was it?

The choice made by any large business to deploy Office 2000 on its network of hundreds of processors is most likely made not by everyone in that business, but by a mere handful of people after studying what few choices there are in the software suite department (many catalogs list Office alone). Employees generally use whatever applications are installed on their workstations through no choice of their own; and most often, the statistics show, they come to work and launch Microsoft Office. Before you start thinking this is a commercial, there is this spoiler to consider: Many businesses' IT divisions admit believing the choice of Microsoft Office was practically made for them. After all, Office is, like Windows, a Microsoft product, and it's plain to see that one was designed to accommodate the other. Businesses trust Microsoft to be better able to write a critical applications suite for a Microsoft platform, for the same reasons they wouldn't dare install Chrysler parts on their fleet of Fords.

But Microsoft has, throughout its history, manufactured operating systems and core applications through separate divisions. Why has Microsoft Office only now become such a dominating factor in the business world? The answer involves a critical shift in the nature of business applications.

In the late 1970s and throughout the 1980s, custom business applications wrote their own reports, analyzed their own data, and managed their own transactions, all within the comfortable sarcophagi of their private memory spaces. Back then, a product called dBASE did help standardize the format of their data; many custom programs were, in fact, dBASE applications. dBASE could be relied upon by custom applications not because the two co-existed in memory, but because the process of compilation literally grafted them together into the same program. The most popular compiler for such tasks was called Clipper. (Today, dBASE and Clipper are historical relics.) Businesses at that time also trusted WordPerfect to generate business documents and correspondence, because nothing before (and perhaps since) turned out crisper, cleaner copy. But there was nothing to graft WordPerfect onto any custom report generator, so custom applications couldn't make direct use of that capability. They could, conceivably, produce WordPerfect-format documents, but that was about it. You see, programs back then did not truly multitask. In other words, a custom program couldn't "call" WordPerfect and say, "Here, typeset and print *this*."

The fact that custom applications could not perform critical data processing functionality as efficiently as packaged applications drove the custom software market to near-extinction by 1992. At about that time, the critical shift came about: As Windows 3.1 introduced the world to component software architecture – where programs are capable of sharing data and even processing jobs with other programs – Microsoft Office became that new methodology's standard bearer. The results were faster, more capable, more expandable applications. Because independent developers could now build programs that literally communicated with Office components – especially Access and its Jet database engine – it was no longer incumbent upon custom applications to perform the entire processing job by themselves. Compilation such as the type performed by Clipper became unnecessary. Now, custom programs could play a role in generating real Word documents, real Excel spreadsheets, real Access data reports, without having to be grafted onto them. While their competitors tried desperately to keep up, the Office applications always managed to take advantage of Microsoft's innovations first.

Add to these facts the most successful strategic marketing campaign in the history of software: Having put these applications together in one package and slapping a low price on it, Microsoft made them desirable as a *coalition*, not just a bundle. Users who wanted the best word processor for Windows purchased Word . . . and also got Access. Those who wanted the fastest, most capable spreadsheet purchased Excel . . . and also got PowerPoint. When these users discovered they needed a product in some other category, they were often surprised to learn they already owned it. By 1994, some of the world's most powerful software names – 1-2-3, Quattro Pro, Harvard Graphics, WordPerfect, Paradox – already had become inhabitants of the bargain bin.

Today, businesses are returning to the principle of custom, even proprietary, software; and the IT divisions of even the smallest companies are now undertaking the difficult task of designing and implementing their own applications. Law offices, biochemical laboratories, industrial engineering firms, advertising agencies, government accounting offices – all of these unrelated divisions of industry utilize work processes that are highly specialized, resistant to outside influence, and often proprietary. Such industries are looking to their own resources to provide the programs they need to manage their information. Yet a great many of these types of businesses also have chosen Microsoft Office to format their documents, forecast their figures, and manage their transactions. So the issue of integrating proprietary tasks with general applications becomes critical, not just for these businesses to remain competitive, but for them to survive. For this reason, many individuals – perhaps including yourself – are being drafted into the role of programmers.

In Want of Enthusiasm

So in recognition of the fact that you might not be taking up the job of programming by your own volition, I can't count on your own personal interest and excitement to carry you through this book the way I might for a book about C++, Java, or Visual Basic 6.0. Of course, I'd love it if you genuinely are interested in or intrigued by this subject matter. Even if you aren't now, perhaps you will be midway through this book.

For me, programming is a form of personal expression. Writing a book, writing a program, and painting a canvas all belong – at least from my perspective – to the same genus of creation. Sometimes modern programming reminds me of painting on a low-grade canvas, and from time to time, as my wife will attest, I have expressed myself in a nonappreciative manner whenever that canvas starts to rip open, analogously speaking. But amid the shortcomings of programming platforms since the advent of the TRS-80, I have remained a programmer; and for all of that time I've used a language not too different from what this book teaches you. During that time, I have come to realize, and even to accept, that not everyone is as enticed by the idea of making digits work miracles as I was in the beginning. Back then, I looked at a blank screen and saw opportunity. Today, taking into account the chaos in which this industry presently finds itself, I wonder how it is that anyone gets the courage to even start.

Yet I look at those who have managed to start, and who have even jumped head-long into the raging rapids of the craft of programming, and I notice that many of them carry at least one good book. Perhaps its cover is well worn, taped along the spine two or three times, and has fading pastel sticky notes hanging off every page. I think of how good the author of that book must feel to know that his own book, in the midst of computing's current corporate political quagmire, is from one other person's point of view a reliable, calming, sustaining influence. I can hope to be as well worn.

You might *want* to know how to customize Microsoft Office with VBA. But I have to understand that you might be in the uncomfortable position of simply *needing* to know VBA. Want might come later, after the subject matter starts to seem bearable. I don't use cartoons in this volume, and not all paragraphs have their own punch lines. (I have been known to make the accidental pun from time to time, and often my alliteration is a side effect of waiting for Web pages to load from Microsoft's server.) However, I do want to speak English to you and be at least as sensible in communicating my message to you as you would expect me to be if I walked into your office right now and sat down at your desk.

I want this book to be a positive influence. I can achieve that goal by making a very turbulent, incongruous topic start to come to order.

Office 2000 Programming Is Real Programming

I can start by clearing up the single greatest, and most proliferated, misconception about the topic of programming with VBA: It is not a macro language. I explain why in detail in the chapters to come; for now, keep in mind that **a macro is an automatic sequence made up of a program's existing commands.** I do not write macros in this book. I do write applications, and there is a huge difference.

A VBA program is a set of instructions that takes control of an O2K application and gives it functionality it did not have before. You will write VBA programs that consist of VBA modules, which are in turn comprised of VBA procedures. These programs add features and functions to the Office 2000 applications. Here are the types of VBA programs with which this book is concerned:

* The most conventional and well-known type of VBA program — a derivative of the macro — is the extension command. Such a command can be as small as a single VBA procedure. It makes itself available through the menu bar, or one of the toolbars, or a specialized keystroke. Because VBA is not a macro language, this extension command can give the O2K application user the capability to perform some task that the application itself does not offer.

* You can "embed" functionality into an O2K document (a product of one of the Office 2000 applications). In the simplest example, a set of buttons can be deployed within a document. When a user clicks on one of these buttons, the content of the document can be made to change somehow, or a command is given to the application supporting the document. This makes obvious sense in the case of an Excel spreadsheet, which can obviously benefit from the addition of interactive features or conditional logic. What is not so obvious is that similar functionality can be embedded directly into a Word document. Of course, the usefulness of interactive features within a document is limited to the screen and not the printed page; but Microsoft has made the case of late that digital documents truly belong on the screen anyway.

* Functionality that pertains to a specific class or category of document that you or your company produces can be programmed into the template for that category. So a VBA module with procedures that pertain specifically to generating an invoice can be attached to an invoice template for Word or Excel.

* Because all O2K component applications (except Outlook) use the same VBA interpreter — albeit within their own respective environments — a VBA program can be developed that involves two or more O2K applications. Later in the book you see one example of how a VBA module can channel a Word outline into a PowerPoint presentation.

* A robust application made with Access is a VBA program. The most fundamental Access programs are written using the so-called "macro language," which is neither VBA nor truly a macro language. But stand-alone programs with any depth of functionality, and which also must utilize databases from outside their own local namespace, are written with VBA.

Because O2K applications are designed to communicate with other components in the outside world (if you go so far as to consider Windows a "world"), they each utilize a type of lexicon that enables them to give names to their various features and to the elements of data with which they work. The collective lexicon of O2K is called the Office 2000 Object Model, or O2KOM. This lexicon is not Visual Basic for Applications. O2KOM is like a glossary that Office 2000 hands out to prospective programming environments — VBA among them — that wish to make contact with its applications. There are so many terms in the full O2KOM that, if I granted one paragraph for each term, I estimate that IDG Books Worldwide would need to publish at least three volumes of this book's size to cover them. Luckily, not all the terms in O2KOM are of tremendous importance, and some are not even pertinent. This book covers what I feel is all you need to know about O2KOM — comprehensively, but selectively.

Part I

ADOPTING VISUAL BASIC

Chapter 1

An Overview of Office 2000 Programming

IN THIS CHAPTER

- ◆ An example of a complete VBA procedure

- ◆ An introduction to the Office 2000 Object Model

- ◆ The parts of speech used in VBA programming

- ◆ An outline of the makeup of a project, a module, and a procedure

- ◆ How a procedure or module differs from a macro

- ◆ The new and burgeoning concept of Windows components, in the context of VBA programming

WITH MOST PROGRAMMING LANGUAGES, you start with a blank slate. You build a program gradually, incrementally, adding new objects and functions that follow rules that are defined by you. A programmer, like a poet, loves a blank slate, an empty page. It rings with possibilities, and has yet to encounter imperfections.

On Point

In the Introduction, I demonstrated how syntax tables are used in this book to demonstrate the most important Visual Basic for Applications and Office 2000 Object Model keywords. I briefly mentioned a few facts that are reintroduced here in greater detail: First, I noted that some terms represent objects that are "members of" — or that reasonably belong to — other objects. Second, I noted that there are other terms used to describe the characteristics of some objects, and that these other terms are written after the object terms themselves, separated by a period. This chapter covers these rules from the beginning.

With Visual Basic for Applications (VBA), you are writing stanzas that someone else has already begun, with epic characters that someone else has created, and situations that someone else expects you to fill in. You cannot presume the slate is blank, or, for that matter, in one piece. Data is already being processed, and the body of a data document is already being constructed. Worksheets, databases, presentations – all of these items, and the tools that create them – are already in business, and you don't have much authority over how they work. Your job as programmer becomes less like a poet and more like a building inspector. You're watching a work of construction in progress, and barking orders over the shoulders of foremen. Not at all a subject for an epic poem, it seems. But while you are, politically speaking, in charge, not every event that takes place is directly under your control.

What Visual Basic for Applications Does

It would be technically correct to state that VBA provides the Office 2000 (O2K) applications with a means for crafting functionality that they would not possess on their own. But that might give some the impression that O2K is somehow lacking. I'm reminded of the old argument that Macintosh users proffered back in 1984, after the first closed-box Macs were shipped: Why would a system that does everything anyway *need* to be extensible?

The answer is because nothing in business is generic. When businesses were first introduced to the desktop computer, they began training their employees to work the way the software mandated them to work. When the software changed, so did they; and when the software manufacturer went out of business (case in point: WordStar), chaos ensued. Yet this dependence upon the process model of the software was not a product of history. Before the advent of desktop computers, legal briefs weren't considered "IBM Selectric documents," and transparencies weren't considered "Pitney-Bowes presentations."

By definition, the information a computer user conceives should not be locked into the machine that generated it, especially if that machine is made up of mere software. A business succeeds through adopting its own strategy, rather than conforming to someone else's; and simple work processes are part of a business's overall strategy. Businesses don't have time to adapt to new software; software must adapt to them.

So with Microsoft Office being the world's single most-deployed office suite on desktop computers, all of those businesses must be capable of changing Office 2000 to suit their particular needs. Visual Basic for Applications is the vehicle for that change.

The interpreter is in charge of processing instructions

VBA is a Windows component that plugs into the Office 2000 applications and, to varying degrees, coexists with them. Yet, while VBA is designed to be cohesive to each application, it is its own application. VBA is an interpreter that executes instructions as part of its own independent Windows process. Think of "interpreter" in this context the way you'd think of a foreign language interpreter on a diplomatic mission. The VBA interpreter reads a message in one language – BASIC – and renders that message in another language – the binary executable code of Windows. So when we say the interpreter *executes* instructions, what we're referring to is the broader concept of converting the message you've written into your source code from something that looks partly like English, into something that looks mostly like binary, and then directing the computer to process that converted code.

An interpreter reads instructions written in a strictly defined language, and executes these instructions immediately after it has determined what they mean. This is different from a *compiler* like Visual C++, whose job is to convert language instructions into binary instructions that are run from an executable file later. Most computer applications run from compiled executable files; all of the O2K applications, for instance, were compiled using Microsoft's in-house C++ compiler. VBA, on the other hand, loads its instructions from a VBA module file, deciphers the meaning of those instructions, and executes its orders immediately based on what they say. (Most implementations of Java are also interpreters.)

As is shown throughout this book, a program such as the kind you build using VBA is not really a list of things to do. In other words, when you read the source code of a VBA program, the instructions won't appear to you to be saying, "Do this, then do this, then do this. . . ". Instead, a VBA program reads more like a thesis. It puts forth propositions, then acts on those propositions to prove an underlying point – the point being the form and format of the data it creates or builds onto. All computer programs work in very much this same way, though perhaps without the rhetorical flourish you would expect from a real thesis. The terminology is more limited, and choice of syntax is often made for you. But more than one programmer has likened the process to writing haiku. Not that I intend to teach you to be a poet; I merely want to give you some cause for hope.

Object libraries supplement the VBA vocabulary

The reason a VBA program can affect the operation of O2K applications is because VBA has a built-in line of communication with components that have links to those applications. These components – the "mutual friends," if you will, of VBA and the O2K applications – are the *object libraries*. They provide everyone with the common language they need to speak to one another, by defining O2K's data parts and the ground rules by which they operate as *objects*.

In Depth: What is an object, really?

You will see the term *object* used throughout this volume. Perhaps you've noticed that professional programmers tend to use this term as though it were a mantra that conjures the spirit of order and clarity from their subconscious. Truth is, a computer object is more a creature of pragma than dogma. In current usage, **an object is a pairing of program code and internal data, that presents a limited set of its own functions to other programs using a discrete and accepted language.** This way, the program code belonging to the object can utilize its own internal functions privately, without "exposing" them to program code outside of itself. One purpose for this design is to give the programmer a way to replace one version of an object with a newer version whose external functions use exactly the same names. This is so other programs that attempt to contact the new object will not need to "know" that the object is new, and will not need to change the way they contact that new object.

There are many variations on this concept of "object," and there does exist a minority of programmers who would disagree with the previous paragraph altogether. Others, who are rapidly becoming a majority, have adopted a far more detailed definition, and tend to spurn so-called "object-oriented languages" whose concept of objects differs. This book will go into greater detail about Microsoft's concept, as embodied in Windows and Office 2000. For now, in an upcoming example in this chapter, look for the term `ActiveSheet`. This is one instance of how Excel presents an open worksheet as an object.

The Office 2000 Object Model (O2KOM) is a compilation of all of the object libraries of the O2K applications. Technically, O2KOM is not a part of Visual Basic for Applications, but it is a major part of VBA *programming*. You could write an entire VBA application without O2KOM. Why you would want to, though, is a mystery. You would be better off crafting a stand-alone Visual Basic application using Visual Basic Standard, Professional, or Enterprise Editions; all of these versions of VB have faster interpreters and the option of full executable code compilation. VBA was designed to communicate with Office 2000, but it can also work in conjunction with any Microsoft Windows Component Object Model (COM) application. In short, VBA does a poor solo act.

VBA provides you with the grammar for changing or supplementing Office 2000, and the object libraries of the applications they work with provide you with a majority of the vocabulary. In effect, you're using two languages, each entirely dependent upon the other to make sense to the computer – or to you.

On Point

Visual Basic for Applications is an interpreted procedural programming language. Interpreted languages differ from compiled languages in that their programs' source code is designed to be executed at the same time that a program in the background is trying to determine just what that code means. By contrast, for compiled languages, the meaning of the source code from the computer's point of view is already spelled out beforehand in the executable code that it already understands.

All VBA programming in Office 2000 blends the native vocabulary of VBA itself with the terms provided by the Office 2000 Object Model. The VBA vocabulary provides you with the terms you need to define, and make sense of, the program, the modules and procedures contained within them, and the order of execution. The O2KOM vocabulary provides you with the terms you need to address the data elements used by the O2K applications.

What is a program?

At the risk of making you feel a bit nervous, I want to show you a complete VBA procedure. **A procedure is a single, simple sequence of instructions**; like a macro, it has a clear beginning and an end, and the sequence starts at the top and heads toward the bottom. I won't try to explain every nuance of this procedure now, though we will come back to it from time to time later in the book. My intention here is to begin to give you a clearer idea of what VBA does when it executes a procedure. There's really no good way of giving you the tour of the factory floor, if you will, without turning on the machinery at least once.

If you're a veteran user of Excel, you'll recall that when you indicate a range of cells and select Edit → Cut or Edit → Copy prior to the paste (and even after a paste during a copy operation), the original range is demarcated with a moving marquee. This is a signal to the user of a cut/copy in progress. If a user presses Esc at this point, the marquee goes away and the process is aborted.

Here's the scenario: Microsoft Excel presently only lets you *paste* a group or range of worksheet cells whose collective size is equivalent to the size of the range you cut or copied. Suppose you want the Excel user to be able to copy the contents running down one or more columns into one or more rows, regardless of the fact that the destination area may not have equivalent geometry to the source area. Listing 1-1 presents a single Excel VBA procedure that makes it possible for the user to indicate any range of cells, and designate any range of any size as a copy destination. The copied cells simply flow into their new range, one-by-one. This is a crude form of this procedure, for reasons which you'll certainly understand by the time you reach the end of this book; for now, consider it simple enough to examine in this context.

Listing 1–1: A procedure that "flows" Excel cell ranges into new areas, regardless of shape.

```
Public Sub MoveWrapRight()
    Dim rngSrc As Range, rngDest As Range
    Dim strDest As String
    Dim lMax as Long

    Set rngSrc = _
     ActiveSheet.Range(ActiveWindow.Selection.Address)
    strDest = InputBox("Enter a destination address:")
    Set rngDest = ActiveSheet.Range(strDest)

    If rngSrc.Cells.Count < rngDest.Cells.Count Then
        lMax = rngSrc.Cells.Count
    Else
        lMax = rngDest.Cells.Count
    End If

    For lCtr = 1 To lMax
        rngSrc.Cells(lCtr).Copy
        ActiveSheet.Paste Destination:=rngDest.Cells(lCtr)
    Next lCtr

    Application.CutCopyMode = False
End Sub
```

In its current state, this procedure requires two items of input data from the user. The first item is the range of cells to be copied, which the user selects prior to invoking this procedure as an Excel macro. The second is explicitly requested by the procedure: a destination address where the indicated range is to be copied — this is a standard Excel range address in the "A1" format. Perhaps you've spotted the cue.

The procedure is an enclosure of instructions that begins with the first line marked `Public Sub`, and ends with the final line `End Sub`. The name we gave the procedure, `MoveWrapRight`, was entirely arbitrary; we could have named it something else. The closed parentheses `()` is an indicator that this procedure needs no incoming data from some other program or from the application that calls it; the procedure can work entirely with what data it can gather for itself.

Before we go on, allow me to point out the use of the underscore (_) character in the instruction that begins `Set rngSrc =`. The sole purpose of this character is to instruct the VBA interpreter — as well as the human reader — that the remainder of this instruction continues on the next line. Think of it as VBA's version of hyphenation.

Variables are symbols that represent units of memory

For the procedure in Listing 1-1 to work, it has to keep track of four items:

- ◆ The range of cells being copied

- ◆ The range where the copies are to appear

- ◆ The cell range address that the user designates for the copies

- ◆ The total number of cells to be copied

This procedure represents these four items as *variables*. **Variables are arbitrarily named symbols that represent certain contents of memory.** These contents are generally either numerical values or groupings of textual characters, which the BASIC programming language calls "strings." The symbols this procedure uses for variables are foreign to the VBA vocabulary — in fact, it's a rule that these symbols *must* be foreign. The VBA interpreter recognizes its keywords as terms that are not variables; if it comes across a term that is not in its vocabulary, it tries to treat that term as a variable. VBA will try to recognize `rngSrc`, `rngDest`, `strDest`, and `lMax` and, not finding them among its vocabulary, will try to process them as variables. So the purpose of the first three `Dim` instructions (indented following the initial line `Public Sub MoveWrapRight()`) is to formally introduce the four variables to the procedure, and specify — or *declare* — what type of variables these are. This is important, because VBA cannot ascertain the *type* of a new variable just by looking at what you chose to name it. In other words, VBA can't look at `lMax` by itself and determine it's a *number*. You can do so, provided you name the variable in such a way that readily identifies itself to you, but the interpreter cannot.

The object library provides an application's lexicon

The logical part of this procedure begins at the part marked `Set rngSrc`. What the procedure does, in English, is as follows: It first determines the range being copied by polling the user's selection (`ActiveWindow.Selection.Address`), and assigns `rngSrc` to represent that range. Then the user is asked to enter the destination range – by hand for now – and then the range that the address points to is assigned to `rngDest`. Now VBA knows the two critical worksheet areas in this task.

The object library of Excel 2000 plays a crucial role here. The terms `Selection`, `ActiveWindow`, `Address`, and `Range` are provided by the Excel 2000 object library. The VBA interpreter recognizes them because the program in Windows that runs the object library is in constant communication with VBA. So unlike the way one would write a C++ program, these terms don't need to be declared someplace, or defined by some outside file that is referred to with an `#include` statement and linked in later. Simply because Excel 2000 invoked VBA to start with, these terms are automatically recognized, as though they were an intrinsic part of the VBA language.

Conditional instructions are bound by clauses

The purpose of the next section of the procedure – the one that begins with `If` and ends with `End If` – is to determine how many cells are to be streamed into the new range by judging which of the two ranges is the *smallest*. The number of cells in the smallest range is assigned to variable `lMax`.

I'd like to borrow an example from outside programming. Think about, if you will, the way some legal contracts are written, in which clauses that are subordinate to others are slightly inset. One reason for this typography is so that your eyes easily discern which paragraphs are dependent on others. VBA instructions are inset for exactly the same reasons. Notice the `If...Then...Else` comparative clause in Listing 1-1. `If...Then...Else` is called a *clause* because it constitutes a part of the procedure rather than the whole, yet it states a set of rules completely, making it a unit unto itself. It's fairly obvious that either one group of inset instructions or the other gets executed, but not both. The `Else` separates the two sets, and which one gets read depends on the result of a comparison: whether there are fewer cells in the source range than there are in the destination range.

In this code fragment, you see several instances of familiar mathematical operators, mainly the equal sign (=). In programming, you need to refrain from thinking of = in the same respect as you would think of the equal sign in common math or algebra ($E = mc^2$). Here, the operator can be used in either of two respects: to assign some value or memory contents to a variable, or to compare one value with another for equality. In Listing 1-1, you see = used in the first respect only. For instance, the number of cells in the source cell range is assigned to variable `lMax` with the instruction `lMax = rngSrc.Cells.Count`.

There is, however, one instance of comparison involving the `If...Then...Else` clause. Here, the lesser-than operator < is used to compare the number of cells in the source range `rngSrc.Cells.Count` to the number of cells in the destination range `rngDest.Cells.Count`, to see if the source count is lesser than the destination. The result of this comparison — as with literally every other such *binary comparison* you'll ever write in the course of VBA programming — is true or false. The instruction that gets executed next is dependent upon the result of that comparison.

Repeated instructions are also bound by clauses

Below `If...Then...Else` is another clause, which is bordered by `For` and `Next`. This is a repetitive clause, which tells the interpreter to execute that clause's subordinate instructions for the number of repetitions, or *iterations*, recorded by variable `lMax`. The instructions within this `For...Next` clause copy *one* cell to *one* new location. But each time the clause is repeated, the value of variable `lCtr` is increased by 1. In programming terms, we say `lCtr` is *incremented*. After that happens each time, the term `Cells(lCtr)` points to a different cell. This is how repeated instructions can be made to do *different* things with each iteration; very rarely will you find it necessary to repeat the same task even though you're repeating the same instructions. `If...Then...Else` and `For...Next` are staples of the BASIC programming language; some form of them appears in every true version of BASIC ever developed since the very first edition in 1964.

This little procedure is indicative of a lot of the programming you'll encounter with VBA — not saving the world so much as your own little corner of it. This procedure will be revisited elsewhere in the book, especially because it's not yet done. For now, it doesn't take into account such circumstances as wrapping copied cells from top to bottom rather than from left to right, nor does it gather input from the user with a less arcane tool than typing characters into a text box. In the context of this book's first chapter, the task covered by this particular example might appear a bit mundane. However, for many information technology personnel who write procedures like this one several times per day, this is like emergency medicine. Remedial work is always part of the job.

In these last few paragraphs of description, I allowed many of the details to remain knowing that at first they might appear foreign, but also that they may serve to provide a picture of the types of considerations that will go through your mind as you program with VBA. Something you have to understand as a programmer is that details are important. If something as fundamentally mundane as the direction in which cells in a worksheet range are counted is truly an issue with the user of a program, then there is something wrong with the program. In the real world, outside of the cool logic of the computer, that sort of detail is immaterial. But in the *very* real world of computing, that detail is a fundamental dynamic. Without it, there is a gap that needs to be filled. VBA programming is an exercise in strategic and creative gap-filling.

The Characteristics of VBA Objects

Think of the Object Model as the "Radio Shack catalog" of the Office 2000 programmer. It lists the transistors, resistors, and capacitors that, when soldered onto the logic board, empower a functional device (or just another cheap radio, depending on your point of view).

It's easy enough in your mind to consider an ordinary machine as being made up of interconnected parts, even if you have never seen inside that machine or gazed at its blueprints or schematics. A computer program is a logical form of a machine. Objects, therefore, are logically interconnected parts. The characteristics that VBA programming gives to objects resemble the characteristics of parts of a physical machine:

♦ **Properties are the characteristics of an object that you can change.**
Whether a feature of the program is turned on or off, whether the text you're about to type is black or red or some other color, what the coordinates are for an open window – all of these factors that can be associated with objects are represented as properties. "Specifications" might be a suitable synonym.

♦ **Methods are actions that are associated with an object.** They are generally phrased as verbs, and may represent something the object does, or something that can be done to the object. A method is generally a command to the object. Don't confuse the computing term "object" with the grammatical term "object"; sometimes the computing object is really the *subject*, grammatically speaking.

♦ **Events are terms that represent some occurrence registered by the object.** When a button object is pressed, when the mouse pointer passes over a graphic, when the answer to a calculation has been reached, whether a download is completed – anything that can reasonably serve as a trigger that launches a procedure, is represented as an event. When we say Windows uses an "event-driven model," we mean that most of its programming is geared to be sensitive to things the user does, and to respond to those events.

♦ **Constituents are objects in and of themselves that are contained by another object.** A dialog box contains buttons; a document contains characters or sequences of characters; a database contains records. The object that contains a constituent is often referred to in VBA as a *parent*, and by programmers from other genres as an *antecedent*.

Properties represent characteristics of objects

Think of a property as an element of vital data that describes, in terms of *value*, some quality or asset associated with an object. When you build your own objects (which you can with VBA), you will want to conceive ahead of time those aspects of your objects that are best described with numbers. You can then devise properties to represent the numeral values you've come up with. In the Office 2000 Object Model, applications' objects already have properties. Even though you may at times refer to those property settings with terms, these terms represent numbers. All properties are, at their root, numeric.

When you change a setting of one of the properties of an object in O2KOM using VBA, you write an instruction that looks like an algebraic equation. For instance, in Listing 1-1, you saw this instruction:

```
Application.CutCopyMode = False
```

Here, there's a simple one-to-one relationship between an object and its property. The object is `Application`, which here represents the embodiment, if you will, of all the addressable or accessible parts of Excel. The term `.CutCopyMode` is the property. The purpose of this instruction is to tell Excel that the user is no longer cutting or copying cells. In effect, VBA addresses the *application* directly, asking it to flip one of its "main toggle switches." A true/false property of the `Application` object is, by definition, one of those "main toggle switches." The period between the two terms is VBA's way of indicating that the latter term is associated with the former term; otherwise, it might not be clear to VBA what `.CutCopyMode` refers to.

Property settings can have wide ranging effects

A common type of property in VBA is called `Boolean`, after the British mathematician George Boole who introduced the binary system to Western mathematics. A Boolean value is either `True` or `False`; digitally, these two are translated into -1 and 0, respectively. In the instruction `Application.CutCopyMode = False`, the value of 0 is assigned to the `.CutCopyMode` property. The property retains this value the way a variable retains it; for instance, your program could declare a variable `bOn` as type `Boolean`, with the instruction `Dim bOn As Boolean`. Later, you could assign a value to the variable with an instruction `bOn = True`. But the assignment of `True` to a variable doesn't immediately affect anything in the program except for the variable; whereas, when you assign a value to a property of an object, you could be changing the state of that object directly, in perhaps more than one way. When you assign `False` to Excel's `Application.CutCopyMode`, the immediate effect is a change in one operating condition of the application.

For another example, suppose an object represents a push-button that belongs to a toolbar control. If you write an instruction that sets the `.Value` property of that button to 1, you are in effect telling the program to press the button. On literally the other side of the equation, if you have a conditional clause that begins and ends with these lines:

```
If btnAccept = 1 Then
        .
        .
        .
End If
```

then the VBA instructions between these lines are executed only if the button represented by btnAccept is pressed. Alternately, we could have used a VBA constant tbrPressed to represent the numeral 1, if we might have forgotten whether the "pressed" value for the button is 1 or -1 — which is sometimes a problem among Microsoft objects. But what's the likelihood of us remembering the proper spelling of tbrPressed as opposed to remembering a simple number? When you're assigning a value to a control, the VBA environment brings up all the possible settings for a property in a little list box as you're typing the equation, so you can simply choose the constant from the list rather than look it up in the manual. Of course, this does mean you have to recognize the proper constant among the others in the list box, but the Pressed part is fairly easy to spot.

Methods are functions applied to or by objects

What distinguishes a method from a property is the emphatic nature of the method. In a less politically correct period, we would call these "commands." Methods are, after all, terms that an object recognizes and to which it responds, the way a dog knows certain sounds but ignores others.

One of the most common methods you'll find with respect to any object is .Open, which brings an object into the workspace of an application. Say, for instance, our active application is Word 2000. The procedure you're writing already has the name of the file it wants to open, symbolized as a variable strFilename. (A variable of type String, by the way, refers to text rather than a value.) I'll assume that you've taken steps earlier in the procedure to verify that the file represented by strFilename actually exists and that its contents actually point to a valid, existent Word document path and filename. So you would have Word open the file with this instruction:

```
Documents.Open strFilename$
```

The Documents term used here is a unique type of object. It's called a *collection*, and it represents a plurality of member objects. A collection object is not equivalent to all of its members taken as a whole; instead, it represents the single object that actively brings together those members. It's similar to a class in C++, except in this instance, you're actually addressing the collection as a whole, rather than a specific member of that collection. Here, `Documents` represents the totality of open document files in the Word application. Before opening any files at all, `Documents` could conceivably represent an empty collection, the way an italicized capital letter in algebra such as *A* can represent an empty set {}.

Obviously, at the time the VBA interpreter encounters this instruction, the file represented by `strFilename` isn't open yet; so we're not addressing `strFilename` as an object, but as a parameter of the `.Open` method. The file whose name is symbolized by `strFilename` is not a member of the `Documents` collection until it is open; and once it is open, `strFilename` doesn't symbolize the object representing the open document. It merely represents its filename. But it still serves as a tag for that document, so the identifier `Documents(strFilename)` symbolizes the newly opened file.

Why is this type of command called a *method*? It seems that in ordinary discussion, a "method" describes the *way* you do something, rather than something that you might do. The term's use in computing was coined in 1970 by Alan Kay, the inventor of a breakthrough object-oriented language called Smalltalk. In the Smalltalk language, a part of the program that really does describe the *way* something is done is, reasonably enough, called a method. Rather than use the traditional command structure (which was finding itself against a developmental brick wall in 1970), Kay had the Smalltalk programmer address functionality in the form of verbs that could each be defined in more than one way — thus the idea of applying real methods. Visual Basic is a far less abstract, less aesthetically ornate, language than Smalltalk; but to substantiate its standing as an "object-oriented language," it has had to borrow some of the lexicon of other languages whose object-orientation was never in doubt.

Some method instructions require arguments

In Listing 1-1, the `.Paste` method of Excel's `ActiveSheet` object was invoked. It isn't always clear from the way a method instruction is phrased whether the object associated with the method represents the thing that is *doing* the method, or the thing that the method is *done to*. The rules of method syntax are not that specific. (The Latin language is difficult to learn because of its many syntax rules; the VBA language is difficult to learn because of its lack of them.) In this case, `ActiveSheet` is to be the locale of the paste operation. The specific destination of the paste is denoted by `Destination:=rngDest.Cells(lCtr)`. Here, `Destination` is one of the named *arguments* recognized by the `.Paste` method. The term `rngDest.Cells(lCtr)` refers to the cell that is the next paste recipient in the queue. That term serves to answer a "Where?" question on behalf of the `.Paste` method. The argument name and the assignment to that argument are separated by the curious-looking `:=` operator, which is actually a derivative of the Pascal programming language, not BASIC. (The Latin language is difficult to learn because of its singular, nomadic origin; VBA is difficult to learn because it has about 18 or so origins, only a few of which anyone still remembers.)

Here's a more complex example of a method instruction, taken from the object library of Word 2000:

```
Selection.HomeKey Unit:=wdStory, Extend:=wdMove
```

In Microsoft Word, the Home key on the keyboard has different meanings depending on the context in which it is used. But the purpose of the Home key is, in any context, to move the cursor to the beginning of *something*. In the Word 2000 object library, the `Selection` object actually refers to the cursor, but in a broader sense; the cursor can be indicating either where typed text will appear, or an area of text that you're about to operate on with some Word command. So `Selection` takes into account the cursor's dual role, and the `.HomeKey` method represents an action similar to the user pressing the Home key. The difference here, however, is that with the `.HomeKey` method, you can state the *context* in which the Home-key-press-like action takes place. You do that by stating *arguments*, which are values representative of how something is supposed to be done – values that really do specify the method.

In the case of `Selection.HomeKey Unit:=wdStory, Extend:=wdMove`, the `.HomeKey` method tells the `Selection` object (the Word cursor, in its dual role) to move itself to the beginning of the main body of the document. Microsoft Word now uses the term *story* (though not consistently) to refer to the main body of the document – meaning, not including the headers or footers. For this instruction, we used a relatively new process for specifying arguments, which looks a bit like something out of Pascal rather than BASIC: In this process, arguments are *named*, and their settings are assigned using the new `:=` operator. Here, `wdStory` and `wdMove` are *constants*, that are representative of numeral values. As in algebra, unlike variables, **constants are always representative of the same values.** The point of having them on hand is so you don't have to look up the numbers they represent.

Naming the arguments in the manner shown in the previous two examples helps instructions to appear more interpretable to the *human* reader; the VBA interpreter couldn't care less about what the names specifically are. In fact, the method instruction could be specified using the old Visual Basic method, as follows:

```
Selection.HomeKey 6, 0
```

This is exactly the same instruction as the previous `.HomeKey` example, except without the named arguments and without the substitute constants. The interpreter knows that 6 means "top of the story," and 0 means "just move the cursor and don't highlight any text along the way," simply because the 6 comes first and the 0 comes second. **When arguments are not named, the VBA interpreter determines their pertinence from their ordinal position in the arguments list.** When you do apply names to the arguments, the interpreter won't care about the order in which they appear, as long as you name all the arguments. I'll discuss this subject in further detail later.

Events are exclusive procedures triggered by objects

One aspect of objects with which Listing 1-1 is not concerned is the *event*. It doesn't show up too often, except in a very crucial location: **An event term helps to name a procedure that is executed in response to that event.** The one procedure you've seen thus far is `Public Sub MoveWrapRight()`, whose name was chosen arbitrarily. Excel 2000 can invoke this procedure as though it were a macro, by having you assign its name to a menu command, a toolbar button, or a command button placed inside a worksheet. In a larger VBA program comprised of multiple procedures, you can make one procedure can be made self-executing by simply giving it the name of the event to which the object is responding.

Only a few of the objects in O2KOM utilize events; but practically all of the ActiveX controls you use in building custom dialog boxes make use of events. Here's a simple procedure that "belongs" to an ActiveX command button inserted in a dialog box, that reads a filename from an ActiveX text box and instructs Excel 2000 to open that filename as a workbook:

```
Private Sub OpenFile_Click()
   Workbooks.Open AddThisFile.Text
End Sub
```

The `_Click` event is associated with ActiveX command buttons, and is recognized by a button when it is clicked on once. In this instance, `OpenFile` is the arbitrarily chosen name – or more accurately, the `.Name` property – of the command button in this dialog box. By naming the procedure with the name of the button receiving the event, and following the button's name with an underscore `_` character and the name of the event, a procedure is automatically set up that responds to that specific event. So you don't need a macro trigger or another instruction to call `Private Sub OpenFile_Click()`; the interpreter takes care of triggering the procedure at the appropriate time.

As you'll see throughout this book, certain objects such as `Document` in Word 2000 have their own "lifetimes," during which they experience certain common events – being invoked for the first time, being opened from disk storage, being saved, being closed, being deleted. These events have terms in the object libraries to which the objects respond; and using the same methodology I described earlier, you can craft procedures that specify the behavior not only of those objects but also the entire application, whenever those events take place.

Constituents are objects attributed to other objects

Throughout Windows programming, the trend at Microsoft has been to present objects in a respectable, family atmosphere – referring to the parent/child relationships established between objects. For instance, in Word 2000, the `Find` object is the hub of a complex system representing a search for a passage of text. The way this works, the `Replacement` object is the child of the `Find` object; so any text to be substituted for a located passage is identified as `Find.Replacement`. It would appear, based on the rules of our earlier discussion, that `.Replacement` is a property of the `Find` object. If you ask Microsoft, your suspicion would be confirmed — at least for the time being. But if you investigate further, you'll find that `Replacement` is itself an object. It has properties such as `.Text`, which represent the text that is being substituted. Microsoft explains `Find` and `Replacement` as having a parent/child relationship, where `Find` is the parent object and `Replacement` the child. But if you look up `Replacement` in the Help system, you'll find it under Properties. Furthermore, `Find` doesn't stand by itself; it needs to be attributed to some document or part of a document, otherwise Word 2000 will not know what body of text is being searched. As a result, `Find` has *three* parents — namely `ActiveDocument`, `Selection`, and `Range`. We don't want this book to have to be shelved behind the counter, so we won't go into too much detail about this relationship.

So if `Replacement` is both a property and an object, which takes precedent? This book says the latter: `Replacement` is first and foremost an object and not really a property. Why? Because of a technicality of programming: **A property, by definition, has a discrete value or represents discrete textual or memory contents.** An object, by definition, is not discrete; if it were, it actually would not be an object. An object, by definition, is abstract, and representative of a collection of different aspects, characteristics, and actions that the object may either undertake or be subject to. This standard was not adopted arbitrarily; over time, in the context of programming, you will find it's simply easier to deal with in an abstract manner.

Why this book addresses constituents differently

This book uses a few terms that Microsoft does not use in describing the relations between objects. I've brought in some help from outside the realm of Visual Basic, because, to be honest, all this parent/child stuff is confusing, especially when you find out some parents are the children of their own children. So rather than pollute this book with a bad analogy, I decided to use more practical terminology. I say that one object is the *constituent* of another when it is associated with that other object in the context of an instruction.

Here's an example that demonstrates why I use this terminology: In VBA, the object that represents the application being addressed is, reasonably enough, `Application`. When a procedure needs to address the Word document that currently has the cursor, or the *active document*, O2KOM has you use this pairing:

```
Application.ActiveDocument
```

This pairing makes perfect sense – it refers to the currently active document in the application that the procedure is addressing. Now, say we need to address the first paragraph of this document. O2KOM has you use this concatenation:

```
Application.ActiveDocument.Paragraphs(1)
```

The part in parentheses is what we call a *subscript.* A subscript is used to identify **a specific member of an array or collection.** When dealing with a collection such as `Paragraphs`, or an array (which in VBA is a variable that represents a *list* of values rather than just one), the subscript (1) refers to "member #1." Here the object grouping is referring to paragraph #1.

It's obvious here that `ActiveDocument` is a constituent of `Application` and the `Paragraphs` collection is a constituent of `ActiveDocument`. Suppose you have a situation where a separate procedure searches through each consecutive paragraph of a Word document. The strategy you'd use to accomplish this is to allocate an *object variable,* and then make that variable point to each of the paragraphs in sequence. You'd allocate the variable with an instruction such as this:

```
Dim paraWhat As Paragraph
```

In VBA, `Dim` is the main declarative instruction. The term is used exclusively to bring arbitrarily named variables into existence. `Dim` is short for "dimension," which was the 1964 term for memory allocation – imagine a sequence of memory bits in a one-*dimensional* row, and you'll have a better picture of what the originators intended. The attribute `As Paragraph` sets a type for the new variable; when it comes into existence, `paraWhat` will be empty, but at least it will be an empty paragraph.

When you declare a new variable such as `paraWhat` with a type that is an *object class* (such as `Paragraph` in this context), you give this new symbol the same properties and methods as any other symbol that VBA recognizes as a paragraph. Here, `paraWhat` is, for all intents and purposes, an object of class `Paragraph`. **You cannot declare a variable as a property.** Even though a variable can represent a value and a property can represent a value, a property is by definition attributed to some object. For VBA to address a property, it must know the object to which the property is attributed.

This is one similarity between a constituent and a property: In VBA, you cannot address a constituent unless VBA knows the object with which it's associated. But a constituent is an object; and the same term that represents a constituent may also represent a class of object. Such is the case with `Dim paraWhat As Paragraph`. After the variable is declared, it does not point to any specific paragraph, though it has all of the qualities of a paragraph that matter to VBA.

To set `paraWhat` to point to a specific paragraph in a Word document, you'd need an instruction such as this:

```
Set paraWhat = Application.ActiveDocument.Paragraphs(x)
```

Here, `x` is an integer variable that can be set to any whole number, so `x` can count from 1 to the last paragraph in the document. Each time the interpreter encounters this instruction, `x` can be incremented so that the instruction steps through the document paragraph by paragraph.

When this instruction first assigns a paragraph to `paraWhat`, the procedure that contains that instruction acquires all of that paragraph's vital data. So suppose the procedure needed to know the filename of the file that contains the paragraph to which `paraWhat` points. The procedure could use this instruction:

```
strParaFilename = paraWhat.Application.ActiveDocument.Name
```

You can see that the chain of constituency can come full circle. Variable `paraWhat`, which was rooted in the `Application` object, here has `Application` as one of its own constituents. Yet it makes sense, because constituency does not necessarily mean containment. The application that generates a paragraph is certainly one of that paragraph's defining attributes; and we can access some element of that application — such as the filename of its active document — by having the object variable `paraWhat` point back to its own `Application` constituent.

Now, Microsoft has managed to confuse matters somewhat, by equating constituents with properties. If you look in the VBA Help system, you'll see that it defines a `Document` object and a `Document` property separately. But even in its role as a "property," from Microsoft's point of view, `Document` is still an object that has its own attributes and even its own constituents. `Document` and `Document` are never two separate terms, nor are their two aspects — that of constituent and antecedent — ever too far detached from one another.

Finally, to validate my point, one need only refer to Microsoft's own programmers' tool called OLE View (part of Visual Studio, but also available for download from Microsoft's Web site). This program is capable of "decompiling" the Office 2000 object libraries into the language in which they were originally written, which is called Interface Definition Language (IDL). Actually, IDL is a slightly modified version of the declarative portion of C++ — modified in such a way that both a C++ compiler and an IDL compiler can make sense of it. If you look closely at one of these decompiled libraries, you'll notice that any object that the Help system qualifies as a "property" is declared as having a type that is equivalent in size and structure to a *pointer* to another object. Here, a pointer is a kind of link between something container and something contained. So the concept of constituency is exhibited in Microsoft's own IDL-language libraries. Thus, this book chooses to call things what they are rather than how someone else has re-interpreted them to appear.

In Depth: ActiveX controls are represented as objects

The "other" category of pre-existent object in VBA – besides those objects that are supplied by O2KOM – is the ActiveX control. ActiveX is the trademark applied by Microsoft to all of its component-based software, which includes what used to be called Object Linking and Embedding (OLE). VBA lets you build dialog boxes and other forms by dragging and dropping controls from a toolbox onto a construction window, and then attaching code to those controls. In this process, the controls you drop, as well as the form you drop them onto, are all ActiveX components. In VBA, the components and their attributes are represented as objects.

What is distinctive about the way ActiveX objects are programmed, as opposed to any other kind of object, is that ActiveX objects have default, or startup, property settings. You specify these settings through the Properties window in the VBA workspace. **You do not need to specify startup settings for ActiveX controls with VBA instructions.** Instead, you indicate the control on the form under construction whose startup properties you intend to set, then you choose its properties from the list in the Properties window, and type or click on the setting you need.

Once the startup settings have been made, your VBA instructions do specify the behavior of the ActiveX controls. These controls rely almost entirely on events for their livelihood. For instance, for the `UserForm` object, which represents the platform on which the ActiveX controls are placed, there is an `_Initialize` event which takes place when the interpreter first recognizes its existence, a `_QueryClose` event which takes place when the form is about to be removed, and a `Terminate` event which takes place just before the form leaves the screen. VBA automatically runs the form's event procedures, such as `Private Sub UserFormTerminate()`, assuming these procedures exist, when the events are recognized. So `Private Sub UserFormQueryClose()` might be a procedure that pops up a dialog box to ask if the user meant to close the form, or if the form really does contain the changes the user intends to make.

Visual Basic's Parts of Speech

Besides the object terminology that we've just discussed, Visual Basic adds a few parts of speech of its own to the mix. Thankfully, there are only three, and they're easy to explain.

Statements are indications of change

The way BASIC languages work, the instructions you write are not phrased like requests, or for that matter even like commands. Instead, most BASIC *statements* read like observations of the way things are. The VBA interpreter that reads these statements has the task of playing catch-up with your source code's observations.

As a general rule, **a statement specifies an action to be taken by the program.** In Listing 1-1, we used this conditional clause based on the VBA If...Then statement:

```
If rngSrc.Cells.Count < rngDest.Cells.Count Then
    lMax = rngSrc.Cells.Count
Else
    lMax = rngDest.Cells.Count
End If
```

If...Then is easily the most often used statement in all of Visual Basic. In the form it takes in the code fragment above, it gives you the opportunity to state how your program responds to something being true, *or* how it responds otherwise (the Else part). The interpreter expects to see an expression between the If and the Then keywords.

The If...Then term is treated by VBA as a statement because it isn't asking anything, or making requests. It's saying, "This is the way things are: *If* this, *so* this." Other statements, such as Dim, do sound like commands, if you think of "dimension" as an active verb (and few do anymore). VBA statements don't employ any punctuation – no commas, no parentheses, no separating periods or underscores. They're made up of words set off from the rest of the text (or *delimited*, to use the computing term) with spaces, just like an English language word.

Expressions are logical operations with discrete results

Notice how VBA uses equations (Application.CutCopyMode = False, bOn = True, btnAccept = tbrPressed) not in the way that mathematicians use them – to express solutions or postulates that are presumed to be true beforehand – but instead to change the state of something in the program. Equations used in VBA instructions are called *expressions*. In their capacity as terms of assignment – for instance, within comparison instructions using the If...Then statement – expressions serve to compare the value on the right to the symbol on the left. The results of these comparisons are True/False (Boolean) values that act as switches, directing the VBA interpreter as to where to go next. (By the way, you'll notice True and False are capitalized when referring to them as Boolean states.)

Most expressions have two sides, separated by a mathematical *operator* such as =. These are called *binary expressions* not because the computer uses the binary numeral system, but because they have *two* parts. Those "parts" are the two values represented on opposite sides of the operator. No matter their length, both sides of a binary expression must evaluate, or reduce, to a discrete value or datum in memory. By contrast, a *unary expression* has one part. Unary expressions are rare, and are exclusively used to represent the result of an evaluation in an expression that generally expects to perform that evaluation and obtain that result for itself. You'll see an example shortly.

The two types of binary expression in VBA (and Visual Basic, for that matter) are called *assignment* and *comparison*. An expression of assignment attributes a value or the contents of some portion of memory, to a variable. It assigns the value positioned to the right of the = operator, to the symbol (the object or the variable) positioned to the left of the = operator. An assignment expression can take any of the following forms:

- ◆ **Direct.** In the simple case of the instruction `iNum = 5`, the numeral value 5 is directly assigned to the (integer) variable `iNum`. In the instruction `strWarning = "Stop"`, the text between the quotation marks is assigned to the string variable `strWarning`.

- ◆ **Indirect association.** Here, one variable is given the value or contents of another, as in `strCompare = strWord`. In this and all other instances of such an expression, the two symbols are not made identical symbols. Instead, a copy of the contents, symbolized by the part to the right of the operator, is given to the variable to the left of the operator. The left part should be comprised of one variable *and nothing else*; this variable is the "subject," if you will, of the expression.

- ◆ **Indirect evaluation.** Here, the results of a mathematical or logical operation are assigned to a variable. In the conversion expression `dRadians = dDegrees * 0.9`, the result of the mathematical operation to the right of the operator is assigned to `dRadians` to the left of the operator. In `strDest = InputBox("Enter a destination address:")` — from Listing 1-1 — the result of an intrinsic VBA function (defined momentarily) is assigned to `strDest`.

An expression of comparison always has two parts, again separated by an operator. But this time, the operator is not always =; it can be <, >, <=, >=, or <> (not equal to). The type of operator used designates the type of logical comparison that takes place, and the result is always True or False. (It has become customary to capitalize "True" and "False" when referring to a Boolean logical result.) So an expression of comparison is said to *evaluate to* True or False.

By itself, a single variable or even a single numeral can be considered a *unary expression*, representative of its own value. At this moment, that probably makes about as much sense to you as an Army Colonel being named an Honorary Colonel. But in a conditional statement (we'll talk more about statements in a moment) that is dependent upon a certain value being *positive*, a single variable can be the subject of the test.

If...Then blends statement and expression

A conditional clause is bound by two main parts: the statement and the expression. If...Then forms the statement part, while the expression part describes the critical comparison. However long the clause becomes, the If...Then statement binding it tests an expression for logical truth – which, in VBA, is -1. So if variable iCmp were equal to 5, and a statement tested If iCmp = 5, the test would evaluate to -1 (or True).

Whatever the subject expression of the condition in an If...Then statement may be, and however it may be phrased, VBA reduces that expression to True or False through evaluation. So if a variable bEOF is declared As Boolean, in order that its value is always True or False, the variable alone can act as the entire expression. Thus, a conditional clause phrased If bEOF Then... is both logical and legal in VBA. Here, the expression bEOF happens to be equivalent to the value of variable bEOF. As a general rule, **all unary expressions evaluate to their own representative values, whereas expressions with more than one expression evaluate to either Boolean** True (-1) **or** False (0). Since VBA employs full *type checking*, a Boolean variable such as bEOF cannot accidentally equal something else. So the test If bEOF Then... can yield only True or False.

Functions are applied mathematical actions

The rule for functions is this: **A function specifies a change to be made to a value or other contents of memory.** The contrast between a function and a statement is that a function affects your *data*, whereas a statement affects your *program*.

A VBA *intrinsic function* is like a mathematical function applied to a value or an expression; more figuratively, its effect is similar to what happens to a value in a calculator's display when you press one of its function buttons. Generally, a VBA function consists of a short term, immediately followed by one or more arguments within parentheses. Sqr() is among the simplest functions; it evaluates whatever is between the parentheses and then yields the square root of that value. The result is then usually assigned to a variable, with an instruction such as dSideLength = Sqr(iSquareArea). The interpreter evaluates what's between the parentheses before it applies the function; so Sqr(9 + 16) would yield 5, not 7.

You can build your own function terms into a VBA program by means of a *function procedure*. As you'll see shortly, such a procedure – unlike a Sub procedure – receives input data, performs operations on that data, and yields a discrete result. After you've added a function procedure to a module, expressions within other procedures in this module can utilize that new function by invoking the name of that function procedure, just as though it were a VBA intrinsic function. So if VBA comes across what seems to be a function, it first tries to match its name against its own list of internal functions. If it doesn't find the name there, it tries to match the name against its list of added function procedures.

The Structure of a VBA Project

VBA calls a program under construction a *project* – a term gleamed from the realm of C++ compilers. The beauty of programming in BASIC, historically, has been that you are capable of testing a routine immediately, and just as easily discarding it if you find out it doesn't work or it's insufficient. A VBA project at any one time may contain quite a few procedures that you'll simply cast aside later. But that's fine, because VBA gives you plenty of tools with which to manage your work in progress.

The VBA environment manages multiple projects

With VBA, the concept of a project is slightly stratified. Most Office 2000 documents, including Word pages, PowerPoint presentations, and Excel worksheets, are based on at least one, if not two, templates. The Normal template contains all of the functionality that is supposed to be shared among all documents in an application. Specialized templates contain other functionality that is specific to a document of a particular type – say, a military briefing, a stochastic chart, or an LCD projector presentation. Aside from that, each individual document may contain functionality specific to it and to no other document. At any one time in VBA, you could be programming as many as three projects, pertaining to the two active templates and the individual document. What you might perceive to be one project, VBA interprets to be three. This can be confusing, especially when it comes time for you to "save your project."

Procedures are collections of instructions

I've used the term *procedure* frequently throughout this chapter, but have yet to formally define it: **A procedure is a grouping of VBA instructions whose objective is to manage at least one element of the final module's functionality.** Imagine how you would delegate a job's component tasks among individuals that you manage. As the programmer of a VBA module, you delegate responsibilities to procedures. This helps divide a complex job into manageable units.

A language interpreter executes its instructions in sequence, but this doesn't mean that the program it's running can be laid out on a scroll and executed from front to back. With a VBA program, as with most other types, execution starts with one instruction, but from there may branch to any set location, based on what the programmer has determined it is logical for the program to do at the time.

The way *branching* is handled in modern programming languages such as VBA is by building clusters of code – VBA calls them procedures, other languages call them functions – which have definitive boundaries that mark their entry points and their absolute conclusions. Listing 1-1 demonstrated the most common start and finish to a VBA procedure: Sub and End Sub. Again, Sub is a vestigial term that dates back to when some BASIC routines were set off from the rest of the source code by way of *subroutines*; although a Sub statement marks most procedures, they're not really subroutines anymore. Frequently, procedures contain calls to other procedures. A *call* is how a VBA statement cues the functionality provided by some other body of code. Often, a procedure call will contain *arguments* (also called *parameters*) that provide the procedure that's picking up the cue with some elements of data that are particular to the job at hand. The receiving procedure can perform functions on these arguments. A simple example involves a procedure that draws a rectangle. The procedure itself should not specify the location of that rectangle; those coordinates should instead be provided by the calling procedure, so that the rectangle procedure is told "where" and doesn't have to presume "where."

A procedure is generally given a name so that other procedures in a module (or elsewhere in the project) have a way to contact it, and so that it can represent the functionality of that procedure. The meaning of Public Sub MoveWrapRight() may be easily ascertained by a person looking up procedures in Excel's list of "macros." But MoveWrapRight as a term by itself also works like a command whenever Public Sub MoveWrapRight() shares the same module.

The second most common type of procedure in VBA is the Function procedure mentioned earlier. **A function procedure is as close as VBA comes to the phraseology of an algebraic equation.** You may be able to spot some of the similarities in this example, which finds the area of a triangle based on its height and width:

```
Public Function TriangleArea(dHeight as Double, _
  dWidth as Double) As Double
    TriangleArea = dHeight * dWidth / 2
End Function
```

The inputs, along with the type or class of the function's own result, are explicitly named and declared in the first line of the function. That result is intentionally assigned to the *name* of the procedure TriangleArea, just as though it were a variable. With this procedure in place, another instruction in another procedure can utilize the function in the middle of an expression, like so:

```
dThisArea = TriangleArea(dThisHeight, dThisWidth)
```

Notice the arguments to the function inside the parentheses. Whatever value or variable is written into the first and second slots will be treated as the height and width of the triangle, respectively.

Modules are collections of procedures

A *module* is a grouping of VBA procedures within a single file and that can pass control to one another. To better understand what is meant by "pass control," imagine reading a book where the chapters refer to one another frequently. For example, assume Chapter 1 says "See Chapter 27 for more," while Chapter 27 says, "As explained in Chapter 3," and so on. Or, better yet, imagine using a Web site, where the hyperlinks have you leaping from page to page and back. Procedures in a module are analogous to chapters in a book. When a procedure includes the instruction `MoveWrapRight`, it passes control to `Public Sub MoveWrapRight()`. The "cross-reference," if you will, has the VBA interpreter going back to read the same functionality over again.

Another procedure within the same module can pass control to this one by calling it by name. If this procedure needed any data from the procedure that called it, that data – those arguments – would be "passed" to it in the area between the parentheses. Chapter 4 discusses this in greater detail (what you just read is the publishing equivalent of a procedure call, "passing the buck" to some other part of the work).

The term `Public` in this declaration refers to the accessibility of the `Sub` procedure outside of the module that contains it. When a VBA project contains more than one module, a procedure in one module may contact a `Public` procedure in another module. Meanwhile, a procedure declared `Private` is only accessible from within a procedure that shares the same module. Furthermore, a `Public` procedure in an active document or template in Word, Excel, or PowerPoint shows up in its "Macros" list, so the user may choose that macro manually. Notice that an event procedure – which is triggered whenever a certain event takes place that's attributed to an active object – is always declared `Private` by default. There is no valid reason for the user to contact an event procedure directly, and there certainly is no good reason for another procedure in another module to try to contact an event procedure directly. (There is one more good reason, which is illustrated in the chapters to follow: If a VBA program uses two dialog boxes, the code for those dialog boxes will reside in separate modules. Since the code that sets up a dialog box must reside within an event procedure named `Private Sub UserForm_Initialize()`, it's quite possible that there may be two procedures so named within the same project. This is legal, because both procedures are declared `Private`; but if one could be declared `Public`, then two procedures of the same name would be visible to one module – which cannot be allowed.)

On Point

Objects are terms that represent the content and functionality of addressable units of data. Objects in Windows programming, which includes VBA, are characterized by their association with properties, methods, events, and what we choose in this book to call constituents. A property describes a value or a term that describes an attribute of an object. A method is a command to which the object "responds," as though you're addressing the object in a conversation. An event is an occurrence that an object deems of significance to it; an object can be programmed to respond to events, such as mouse button clicks or file download completions, when they occur. A constituent, as I've defined it, is an object itself that is associated with an object at a higher level, perhaps to suggest containment, or to imply a component relationship, or some other type of belonging.

Visual Basic provides three other parts of speech to the grammatical mix: An expression is a sequence of values, symbols, and mathematical operators that can be reduced through calculation to a single value or a single textual string. A statement specifies a state of change that is to take place at the point when the interpreter executes the instruction containing the statement. A function performs a mathematical calculation or logical operation upon a value or expression.

A clause is a compound instruction that is bound to a statement, such as If...Then or For...Next, and that encloses several dependent instructions. These dependents are generally indented, so that the human reader can infer their dependent state in the clause. A procedure is a grouping of instructions named in such a way that its name represents its functionality to instructions outside of the procedure. A Function procedure is special in that it returns a discrete result to the expression that makes reference to it.

Comparing Procedures to Macros

The veteran user of computer applications has become accustomed to the idea that the functionality of applications is customizable through macros. VBA is not a macro language. It is, instead, an independent component that addresses all of the Office 2000 applications on a relatively equal footing. The programs you write with VBA instruct all of these applications as to how to construct one or more of the objects that comprise an Office 2000 document.

What a macro is and VBA isn't

The differences between a VBA module and a macro are not just esoteric. Perhaps the most extensive example of a true macro language ever developed belongs to WordPerfect version 5.1 for DOS. A WordPerfect 5.1 macro is a sequence of that program's own commands, recorded and played back using a process maintained entirely by the WordPerfect application. Anything you could instruct WordPerfect to do using a keyboard command, could be recorded as part of a sequence of such commands; later, with a single keystroke, you could have WordPerfect play back the entire sequence. When you recorded or constructed a macro, all of your facilities were provided by WordPerfect. The word processor was solely responsible for your content.

Macros are a convenience feature of applications, but they are not programs because they are not written with real languages. Why is that important? Because a language can instruct an application to do something it wasn't previously capable of doing. A VBA module isn't just a set of recorded commands played back in sequence. It is instead a complex set of rules and procedures written using an independent language.

Why is independence important here? Because an application is responsible for the maintenance and execution of its own macros. Although you call up VBA from within an Office 2000 application, it is not an intrinsic part of that application, but its own component. You have freedoms within VBA that you do not have with the application you're operating on. VBA is responsible for the maintenance and execution of VBA modules. It is its own entity. The limitations of an application imposed by the finiteness of the commands it can execute are of no consequence to VBA. VBA has connections with everything else in Windows; all VBA truly needs from an Office application is a hook to a menu command or toolbar button, or some other switch that the user can push to make the module run.

But didn't I say earlier that VBA makes a poor solo act? Sure, for why would a programmer use VBA for a stand-alone application when Visual Basic Enterprise Edition is available? As an extender to Office 2000, though, VBA has an unlimited license, granted it exclusively by Microsoft Corp., to go off the board entirely and define new functions, new processes, new ways for Office 2000 to work. That none of these new processes are rooted in the existing Office command structures does not concern VBA in the least. You could use VB Enterprise Edition to write entirely new object libraries (Windows' own definitions for objects) or new ActiveX controls. But Office 2000 cannot make the leap from the structure of its documents to the structure of these objects or controls without a go-between. On the other hand, VBA cannot write new ActiveX controls or object libraries for Office 2000; it needs Visual Basic, or Visual C++, or some other *lower-level* Windows development tool. But once those new objects are in place, Office imposes no rules upon VBA as to how it can make use of them. So VBA is given free reign over its limited domain.

The template as document "class"

Most long-time Microsoft Office application users are familiar with the concept of templates. Basically, a template provides a framework or standardized format for a document. Whatever data is contained within a template when a user begins a new document based on that template is copied into it and saved along with it, if it's not deleted. By definition, **a template provides boilerplate functionality to a document.** You can write VBA modules that are designed to provide exclusive functionality to a particular type of document – for instance, modules exclusively for legal briefs, or for stochastic data sheets, or for intra-application tools such as importing form-based Access data into a Word-based report. It's important to note, though, that while boilerplate text or other data provided to a document by a template is copied into that document and saved along with it, VBA procedures that are part of a template remain in the template. You can't distribute these modules unless you distribute the template. If you were to change templates for a document in mid-processing, the document wouldn't lose the boilerplate data that came from the template, though it would lose any modules or macros that are not specifically associated with the document. You can, however, in certain cases (and they are admittedly rare) write modules specifically for a single document, that will be saved with that document file.

As a result, unlike any of the other Visual Basic environments, VBA is capable of managing three tiers of projects, and more than three projects, at one time. The tier categories are as follows:

- ◆ **The Normal project** contains modules and procedures that are available to all documents in an application at all times. There is only one Normal project for an application, because there is only one Normal template for an application.

- ◆ **The template project** contains code that pertains to a particular class of document generated by an application. At any one time, there are as many template projects open as there are active templates within an application. If Excel has three worksheets open, with two of those worksheets using the same exclusive template and the third using a second template, then there are two template projects active in Excel's VBA window.

- ◆ **The document project** contains code and attribute data specific to an open document. VBA automatically generates as many document projects as there are open documents, even if that document project contains no VBA source code.

VBA doesn't bear all the features of a full-fledged object-oriented language; but in a figurative sense, the way it handles templates could be likened to the object-oriented concept of inheritance – if you don't mind stretching its definition a bit.

The Normal template for an Office 2000 application defines the primary "class," if you will, of functionality for that application on the system in which it's installed. Every document produced with that application bears the functionality of Normal. The exclusive templates add functionality to that already provided by Normal; so in a limited but still arguable way, a document produced with an exclusive template is the beneficiary of so-called *multiple inheritance.* It inherits the functionality of two classes of documents, defined by two templates. From there, the document can extend this functionality with some of its own.

Whose macros are really macros?

Now that it appears the matter of macros and modules has been straightened out, we're going to wrinkle it all up again. Each of the Office 2000 applications was mainly written within different divisions of Microsoft. As a result, although there was some modicum of collaboration, the different authorship groups did not come to complete agreement as to how the applications would present their functionality to the world. As a result, all four of the main applications claim to have macro capabilities, but some are macros by the technical definition and some are not. *This is your official confusion warning. The following material deals with the products of inter-office corporate politics in the software industry, and may not be suitable for sensitive readers.* Here's the rundown:

♦ **Word 2000's macros** *are not* **macros.** When you "record a macro" in Word, the functions you record are translated into VBA procedures. They may not be translated very well, but what does get translated does run through VBA. Now, Word does contain macro commands; whenever you try to customize a toolbar or menu bar, you'll see a list of them. There they are, plain as day, macro commands. But strangely enough, these commands are not a fundamental part of the language you use to write the procedures that are called "Word macros." Another wonder of computing science!

♦ **Excel 2000's macros** *are* **macros.** Excel distinguishes between VBA modules and worksheet macros. In Excel, a worksheet macro is a single VBA `Function` procedure that evaluates the content of the worksheet without having any direct affect on that content. In other words, the macro produces a result, but it isn't directly responsible for displaying that result or for changing the appearance of the worksheet in any other way. This way, your Excel worksheet formulas can include your custom function macros by name. But here's the clincher: **When you have Excel "Record Macro," what gets recorded is not an Excel macro.** (*What?*) Instead, Excel records a VBA procedure that is not responsible for evaluating content, but that can and often does change the appearance or content of the worksheet. This recorded procedure – unlike a true Excel macro – may be enrolled in the menu bar or toolbar of the application.

- ◆ **PowerPoint 2000's macros** *are not* **macros.** Like Word 2000, what gets recorded is a VBA procedure.

- ◆ **Access 2000's macros** *are* **macros.** The use of true macros is extremely important to Access, because a macro is the only way to express certain complex database queries. Although you can use VBA modules to automate processes that utilize Access, you don't write database queries with VBA; instead you use Access' own macro system. Here, commands that are used to generate queries are organized in a three-column table, arranged as a sequence of commands rather than as a set of linguistic instructions. By contrast, you write so-called Access *modules* using VBA. Most users of the "other three" Office 2000 applications aren't expected to be programmers; an Access user, on the other hand, is a person who manages information directly. The user of the Access module – the product of the Access programmer – is expected to be the same "end user" who does not program the other applications.

If you're keeping score at home, you might be wondering, how does Microsoft Internet Explorer fare in the macro/non-macro squabble? IE 4.0 is, as you probably know, currently built into Windows 98; and Office 2000 is designed to upgrade it automatically to IE 5.0. IE doesn't pretend to use macros, but the HTML-based Web pages that IE is designed to interpret, may contain two scripting languages. One of these languages is called Visual Basic Scripting Edition, or VBScript for short. **VBScript is not VBA.** VBScript is a lighter-weight version of Visual Basic than VBA. The other language IE supports is JScript, which is based on Netscape's JavaScript, which is itself a lightweight language inspired by Sun Microsystems' Java language – though JavaScript is not Java.

On Point

Due to the complex nature of the Office 2000 applications, there ends up being more than one tier of project, and thus more than one project may be open in the same VBA environment at any one time. A single project contains one or more modules, which are sets of VBA procedures generally designed to reference one another. The fact that an open document in one of the applications can have contents and functionality based on a global Normal template, plus an exclusive document type template, plus some extensions of its own outside of templates altogether, mandates that three tiers of project types be maintained by VBA for all three sources of a document's functionality.

The Component Object Model of Windows

Over the past decade, Windows has made a slow but steady migration from an environment that supports behemoth applications, to a society of components that collaborate to compose an environment. All of Office 2000 is now component-based. What this means is that its core functionality is presented almost entirely by library programs, such as .DLLs, rather than stand-alone applications.

In Chapter 8, I'll discuss in greater depth how the component model works.

Suffice it to say that the programs users call up when they choose their listings from the Start menu, are really *container* programs which, through an elaborate system of interprocess communication called (at the time of this printing) the Component Object Model (COM), ignite the separate components that make Word, Excel, and PowerPoint look and act like conventional applications.

As a result of this trend, many features of the Office 2000 applications are actually provided by outside components. All of the Internet-based functionality, for example, is provided through Internet Explorer. The spelling checker in Word 2000 and the spelling checker in Excel 2000 are now, thankfully, the same spelling checker, called Proof. Both applications and Proof are brought together by a system of interapplication communication that follows the guidelines of COM. The Equation Editor, the organizational chart generator, all of the format converters, every ActiveX control, ActiveX Data Objects (ADO), and, finally, Visual Basic for Applications are all self-maintaining COM components.

A component object has a distinct identity

So is COM a model for component objects, or an object model for components? The answer depends on whom you ask, ("What do you want to hear today?") but let's assume that you asked me. A *component object* is a program that is addressable by another program, while both programs are running, with the same object-oriented syntax that the program would use to address parts of itself. When a program does contact another program in Windows, a *third* program (known historically as Object Linking and Embedding, but known at the moment . . . well, strange as it may seem, it doesn't *have* an official name at the moment, so we'll just call it OLE) acts as the facilitator, providing the channel for the initial contact to take place and for the contacted program to respond. The goal is to make components address each other as though they were actually part of the same, seamless program.

The Word 2000 object library is the file that OLE uses to enable other applications, such as Excel, to contact and exchange data with Word. Likewise, the Excel 2000 object library is used whenever Word needs to contact it through OLE.

How documents are distinguished from mere files

In Microsoft's model of the computer application, the main data product generated by that application through user interaction is the *document*. This is important because a document in Windows isn't really a file. In many cases, thanks to the advent of drop-in components and embedding of other documents' data, a document can be comprised of the data from several files. To maintain some continuity, Windows still attributes one filename to each saved document, because an application still needs a tag to know what to pull up when a user requests something. But recently, a Windows file has become like a World Wide Web page that is subdivided into frames. The contents of the frames are actually separate Web pages. Likewise, many drop-in objects in a document, especially graphics and controls, are products as well as contents of other files. When a user double-clicks on a single filename, it's quite possible for the application to respond by loading several files.

For many users who have become accustomed to the way desktop computers have traditionally worked, the relationship between an application and a document and a file seems sacrosanct. To them, a document file seems to be defined by its file format. And the quality of the data product is judged by how it performs within the context of its native application. (I remember when sorting a column of spreadsheet cells in ascending order was a feature with a gold bullet attached to it on the back of the box.) So why should Microsoft want to divorce data documents from the two pillars that have historically supported them, the application and the file format?

Well, if you ask Microsoft's marketing officials, the answer is that they really don't want to divorce data documents from the application and the file format. Word, Excel, and Outlook each has its own markets as independent products, so Word 2000 still needs to create and save a Word 2000 document, for the benefit of a few million people who use Word 2000 and no other part of Microsoft Office. But for almost a decade, Microsoft's programmers have been working in another direction. Their goal has been to build Windows into a platform where a user sees a document in the center of the screen, and all the applications installed on the user's system collaborate in building the data for that one document. With every release of the Office suite, Microsoft's programmers move closer and closer to this goal. To even the score, though, Microsoft's marketers move just as far in the opposite direction. For Microsoft to maintain Office as a premium product, the Office components must continue to be sold separately to sustain the "regular" end of its customer base.

On Point

Because of its abstract procedural nature and because it can declare its own symbols for values and data, a VBA procedure is not a macro. This does not exempt VBA procedures from being called macros by Word 2000 and PowerPoint 2000. Excel 2000 and Access 2000, however, do distinguish macros from procedures properly, especially because they both also employ true macros.

The Microsoft Office 2000 applications are no longer comprised of single, gargantuan blocks of executable code that is uncommunicative with programs outside of it. Instead, they are now comprised of multiple, gargantuan components whose job it is to communicate their purpose to one another. As a result, the main applications are now divided into containers and engines. It is the engine that provides the functionality that a user of the application expects to see; the container is just a shell in which that functionality can be housed. But because an engine is not exclusive to any one container, the core functionality of any of the Office 2000 applications could show up in other container programs, including Internet Explorer, Microsoft Exchange Client, Outlook, and Binder.

As a result of a sound business decision, the Office 2000 components must be as capable of operating independently as they are cohesively. This means that, for now, the ultimate goal some programmers have of an "Office document," comprised of one or more objects gleaned from the individual components, remains on hold. A file that begins its life *in Excel* must therefore be a worksheet first and foremost. Likewise, when you import or embed objects into a Word 2000 document, the saved file for that document still bears a capital "W" icon.

In Theory: VBA Is Still BASIC

The BASIC programming language on which all versions of Visual Basic are based is one of the oldest such languages in current use in some form; only FORTRAN and COBOL are older. BASIC is an acronym for Beginners' All-purpose Symbolic Instruction Code. Of course, the breadth of usefulness implied by the term "All-purpose" has widened considerably since 1964 when the language was first developed. It was first introduced as, for most intents and purposes, the operating system of the computer.

The lessons of experience

When microcomputers first became publicly available in 1977, and businesses began embracing the idea of at least keeping some of their records electronically, the operating system of these new machines was BASIC — which was already 13 years old. The company that transferred BASIC from the mainframe to the microcomputer was Microsoft, first for the Altair 8800 in 1976, then the following year for Radio Shack's revolutionary TRS-80. When you turned on a TRS-80 Level I computer, what you saw within a few seconds was the word "READY," followed by a blinking cursor. What the TRS-80 then expected to see from its user was BASIC. So when the manufacturers dreamed of millions of willing citizens of a new electronic village becoming computer literate, they saw us all as BASIC programmers.

Well, it never happened. Early on, the computer literate public became divided into two sects: programmers and general users — with the latter group greatly outnumbering the former. To be computer literate suddenly meant being familiar with the operation of packaged software. Computer users had their first opportunity to become *de facto* programmers, and they turned it down. Four years later, IBM and Microsoft gave users their second chance by embedding BASIC in the IBM PC's ROMs. This time the opportunity wasn't just turned down, it was altogether ignored.

Lo and behold, Office 97 arrives (for once, in the year of its name), and it appears Microsoft has done away with the old-fashioned macro. In its place is the more procedural, more English-like Visual Basic for Applications. BASIC once again finds its way to the desktop of the general user. Why?

VBA resurrects the BASIC-driven application

VBA is the product of Microsoft working to make good on a promise it made to users some years back, before the introduction of Windows 95 — to "make it all make sense." As much as we'd like to believe that every real-world office information procedure can be managed through one of the Office 2000 applications, the truth is that, for most people, Office 2000 is a foreign entity intruding on their everyday work. These people find themselves begrudgingly readapting their work processes each time Office or some other major application undergoes a revision.

While not everyone wants to be a programmer, not everybody wants to be a guinea pig either. Remember what happened in offices worldwide when WordPerfect made its most sweeping revision, from the trusted and respected Version 5.1 for DOS to the altogether foreign 6.0 for Windows. WordPerfect promised users the world, but was only able to deliver what it could after a delay of nearly a year and a half. When 6.0 hit the shelves, it stayed there. Users had finally conquered the eccentricities of version 5.1, and had come to rely upon it, staked their businesses on it, and depended on it to stay the same. When WordPerfect Corp. dropped its support for 5.1, its users dropped their support for WordPerfect Corp. The resulting shock wave decimated not one, but two companies:

WordPerfect Corp. and Novell Applications Group that took over the product line in 1994. Today, Corel has made some headway in its attempt to restore WordPerfect's former luster, knowing full well that Version 5.1 is still the world's most installed and most used word processor brand. But its current market share, in terms of present-day sales, remains in the single digits.

Individuals and businesses have a need for computers to work the way that they themselves work. WordPerfect 5.1 met those users halfway, and then WordPerfect Corporation abandoned them with the release of version 6.0 – the single most fatal mistake in the history of desktop computing. Today's best selling word processor is Microsoft Word, part of the Office 2000 suite. But it hasn't yet earned the level of respect that WordPerfect commanded in its heyday, and Microsoft recognizes that fact.

VBA is part of Office 2000 because, if for no other reason, no business is defined by some cookie-cutter conformation imposed on it by the software on which it depends. Software must change to fit the user. As Microsoft has proven – by accident or by design – the people who use software cannot rely solely upon its manufacturer to make that software change. Instead, software must be . . . well, *soft*, pliable, extendable. VBA is the part of Office 2000 that is, from your point of view, an open book.

In Brief

- ◆ Visual Basic for Applications is an interpreted language, which means that its instructions are executed by a separate component at the same time that they are read in from the program source code file.

- ◆ The lexicons for each of the Office 2000 applications are provided by object library files independent of VBA, though made available to VBA by means of Windows' Object Linking and Embedding.

- ◆ A program is a sequence of instructions whose order of execution can be altered by the instructions themselves.

- ◆ Through the use of conditional clauses such as If...Then, the execution of instructions can be made contingent upon the evaluation of a mathematical expression.

- ◆ A procedure is a formal grouping of instructions that can be called by name, and whose name represents the functionality of that procedure to both instructions outside the procedure and people outside the computer.

Chapter 2

The Office 2000 Object Model

IN THIS CHAPTER

- ◆ The logic behind representing data as objects

- ◆ Why there is a hierarchy for objects in the Office 2000 Object Model

- ◆ The `Application` object, common among the individual applications' object libraries

- ◆ The globals, which are the chief objects in the Object Model

- ◆ The `Dim` statement, which calls new object reference variables into existence

- ◆ How the `Set` statement is used to assign new object references

AN OBJECT IN COMPUTING is not necessarily a "thing," the way we think of "things" in the *objective* world. Commonly, it is the program itself that defines just what objects are for the sake of the computer running the program – what the objects look like (if they're graphical), what their properties or parameters are, what other objects share their same class membership. With Visual Basic for Applications (VBA), the objects used by Office 2000 are already defined. You can still program your own objects, and Chapter 9 will show you how. But efficient VBA programming is mainly achieved through a mastery of the objects that already exist when you first bring up the VBA editor window – the objects that comprise the Office 2000 Object Model.

Life in a World Full of Objects

In any computing language, an object represents the characteristics of some feature of the program, or some element of data produced by the program. As a representative, an object term symbolizes data, but it also acts as the proxy for that data. Changes to be made in the data's constitution, or in the way data is processed, stored, or displayed, are addressed as requests made to the object, acting as the appointed representative of the data.

Think of any part of a computer program that you currently use that you can actually see; forget for now those parts you can't see. Anything you can isolate that you can reasonably consider in your mind as a *thing* – a toolbar, a character on the page, perhaps something more abstract like a color, perhaps something more truly abstract like a database record – is probably considered by the program as an object. If not, perhaps it should be.

The objects, or component parts, that make up a machine or mechanism have characteristics that are peculiar to that mechanism. They have other aspects that may be of interest to an outside observer, such as whether they're copper or plastic, or whether they were manufactured in Shanghai or Singapore; but those aspects are unimportant to the engineering and design of the mechanism. Perhaps they're important to its quality, but that's another issue. From an engineering standpoint, the characteristics of a component in a mechanism that are directly applicable to the working dynamics of that mechanism can always be described as *finite*. To qualify the utility of a component part, all an engineer needs to do is define that finite set of dynamics – Where does it fit? What work does it produce? Where does it produce the work? What does it need in order to go? To the engineer, the answers to those questions *are* the component part; everything else is aesthetic, which doesn't make it bad, just not fundamental. To an engineer, a component part in a machine is qualified by its fundamental dynamics.

To a programmer, as well as to a computer, an object in a program is defined by its fundamental functions. There is nothing aesthetic about an object that would make it some day pleasing to, for example, an antique collector. When a programmer builds objects, all he needs to define are its *dynamics* with respect to the program. An object from the programmer's point of view has no "face," no mass, no volume, no manufacturer's label. The only sketch the programmer has to render for his interpreter (or compiler, if he isn't using VBA) is an outline, a formless description of logic and function.

Calculus – to borrow some ideas from another branch of science – can describe so much about what can be directly observed in nature. But by itself, as a textbook borrowed from a library shelf, it describes nothing about nature whatsoever. If the association between calculus and nature is never introduced to the initiate to calculus, then the whole point of it is lost. Programming describes so much about work processes and the dynamics of information. But by itself, it's a jumble of variables, operators, and symbols whose bearing or importance with regard to how people actually work is lost somewhere in the passing of parameters. To properly associate the realm of programming with the realm of everyday work, you first realize that the process of programming is truly a scientific one, in that it involves *observation*. Like any other science, programming is a recording of observations. Every program is a model of the dynamics of information, and has some bearing upon the true nature of information in the real world outside of the computer.

Which all sounds so lofty and profound, especially with regard to the procedure that streams cells from one size of range to another size of range that you saw in Chapter 1. It's nice to have these grand goals of the cohesion of information and everyday work in a seamless environment; but just how do those goals guide one through the task of modeling the mundane? All scientific observations are, in and of themselves, mundane from someone's point of view. As the brunt of jokes on late night television monologues, a multimillion dollar federal grant for the study of the secretions from the skin of frogs seems, in and of itself, entirely ludicrous. Yet to the scientist who sees this as a natural process that may have been an evolutionary solution to the spread of disease from free-growing fungi, it has a broad-ranging importance that few can see when it's isolated and scrutinized under a spotlight.

Massive applications such as Word 2000 are products of the amalgamation of thousands of mundane processes. The extensions to those processes made through VBA programming may have a limited appeal, even to a comedy writer working for late night TV. It is the collection of these processes and extensions into a single cohesive engine of information management that validates and gives value to each microcosmic process contained within it.

The Roots of the Object Model

A VBA instruction cannot directly address an object in the Office 2000 Object Model (O2KOM) without having some prior concept of what that object belongs to. **Every object in O2KOM is rooted to a primary object.** If that primary object cannot be presumed by a VBA instruction, then it must be stated outright.

If you were to look in a reference guide in a public library for magazine articles that pertain to a given subject, the citations you would find would be organized in terms of larger "containers" that get progressively smaller – magazine title, volume number, edition number, page number, column number, paragraph number. Any of these latter numbers would be pointless without the one before it to substantiate it. In O2KOM, a similar progression of successively more specific objects takes place each time an object is referenced. The name of the broader "containing" object, what is called the *antecedent*, can be omitted if the interpreter considers it to be the default object. But even when a default object isn't explicitly spelled out in the source code, it plays a role in identifying the object stated in the instruction.

As a practical example, VBA cannot directly address a Document object out in open space. You can declare a VBA object variable for it, which would have a Document type, designed to represent some document that is later assigned to that variable. But you can't do anything functional with that object variable until you assign it to represent a real Document object. What all this comes down to is this: You can't address a Document object that doesn't have an association with a real document. For VBA to make that real association between the Document object and the document, the Document object must be rooted to a primary object that belongs to a running Office 2000 application.

The object library names are the primary objects

When you start VBA from within any of the Office 2000 applications, the VBA windows you see are exclusive to that application. Word, Excel, and PowerPoint all bring up the separate VBA window; Access brings up VBA's editing features within its own workspace. At that time, the VBA interpreter assumes the primary object — the highest-ranking member of the hierarchy — is the name of the object library associated with that application. The address for that library is, easily enough, the name of the application itself. Table 2-1 lists the primary objects for each of the four main Office 2000 object libraries.

TABLE 2-1 PRIMARY OBJECTS FOR THE OFFICE 2000 OBJECT LIBRARIES

Object library	Primary object
Word 2000	Word
Excel 2000	Excel
Access 2000	Access
PowerPoint 2000	PowerPoint

All the constituents of these primary objects represent all of the addressable parts of the programs, and all of the addressable data produced by these programs.

While you're working in the VBA editor for an application, you do not need to specify the primary object each time you make a reference to one of that application's own objects. For example, here's the object term for the document in Word that currently has the *focus* — in other words, that is currently the recipient of user input:

```
Word.ActiveDocument
```

Yet, while you're working in Word's VBA editor, Word is presumed to be the *default object*. So if you were to write instead:

```
ActiveDocument
```

then VBA would know that you're referring to the same thing as Word. ActiveDocument. In the Word 2000 object library, ActiveDocument is one of its *globals*, which means it can get away with being validated automatically without having to show the interpreter its credentials, if you will.. A global, as you'll see, is a term that receives automatic recognition for being a primary object of the application.

When would you use the primary object names in VBA programming? Mainly when you are referring to an application's globals from within *another* application's VBA editor. Let's assume your Excel procedure referred to your Word document using an object variable. The procedure would *declare* that variable – in other words, it would introduce the variable term to the program – with this instruction:

```
Dim objWordDoc As Word.Document
```

This instruction would only work, by the way, if you've set Excel's VBA editor to recognize the Word 2000 object library; it's a simple process, and you'll see how to do it a bit later. What this instruction does is declare a new term objWordDoc that will act exclusively as a reference to a document currently open within Word. Variables that serve in this manner are called *object references*. Word.Document is the *object type* for this new object reference. An object type term, such as Document, tells the interpreter to fashion this new variable so that it has all the characteristics of a Word document object. For Excel, for the convenience of the human reader, I specified Word.Document explicitly, even though no other object library in O2KOM has a Document type but Word. With the Word 2000 object library loaded into Excel's VBA editor, the explicit reference to Word can be omitted because Document is exclusively Word's own global.

In Depth: Making one application's VBA recognize another's library

You may not realize it, but there are several object libraries installed in your particular copy of Windows at any one time. Those libraries become part of Windows, from Microsoft's perspective, the moment they're installed. An object library acts as a dictionary for the VBA interpreter. All of the object terms and many of the functions used in VBA programming are provided by object libraries. When the VBA editor first comes up in an application's workspace, the VBA interpreter recognizes these object libraries:

Visual Basic for Applications object library, which provides VBA with many of its own keywords

The application's own object library

OLE Automation, which provides the facilities for VBA to contact other applications besides the Office 2000 suite

Microsoft Office 9.0 Office Library, which contains objects common to all of the Office applications, such as toolbars and dialogs.

ActiveX Data Objects 2.0, in the case of Access

Continued

In Depth: Making one application's VBA recognize another's library *(Continued)*

A library for each active document template, especially in the case of Word

To make the VBA programs you write capable of addressing the functionality of more than one Office 2000 application, the VBA editor for the source application must be set to reference the collaborating applications' object libraries. **Object terms peculiar to an application other than the one to which a VBA editor belongs are, by default, unavailable from that editor.** Most notably, you'll want to invoke the Forms 2.0 object library so that your VBA application can build its own dialog boxes with ActiveX controls. To make an outside object library available to a VBA editor, follow these steps:

1. Select References from the Tools menu of the VBA editor window. VBA will bring up the References dialog box shown in the figure below. Of course, the particular references shown here may vary from what you will see.

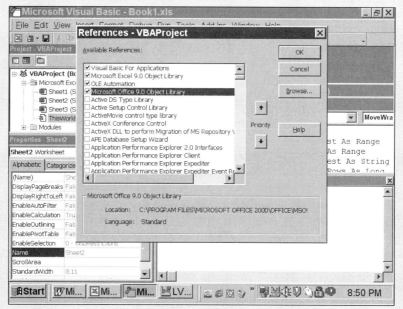

2. The list shows the explicit names of each of the available object libraries in your Windows system. Those that VBA currently recognizes have been shifted to the top of the list, and are marked with a checkbox. To add a new library to this list, check the box beside the library title. You may add as many libraries as necessary for your current project. You may also remove a currently active library by unchecking its boxes.

3. Click OK to finalize your choices.

Once Excel's VBA interpreter has executed this instruction, `objWordDoc` will be a valid reference, but thus far it is a reference to nothing — it isn't pointing to a real document just yet. To accomplish that, we need another instruction:

```
Set objWordDoc = Word.ActiveDocument
```

In this case, `objWordDoc` has been assigned to "point to" whatever Word document currently has the cursor. In the VBA source code, variable `objWordDoc` represents whatever document is active at the time the `Set` instruction is executed; at run time, we can say `objWordDoc` "points to" that document. It is not a substitute term for `ActiveDocument`; there'd be no point in having one when you can just as easily type `ActiveDocument`. The point of making this assignment is so that `objWordDoc` can continue to point to the same document even after it's no longer active. (It does have to be loaded, however.) So if later on, the procedure needs to determine the filename of this document that `objWordDoc` points to, it can use this instruction:

```
strDocFileName = objWordDoc.Name
```

Here, variable `strDocFileName` is assigned a filename, by way of the `.Name` property. `.Name` is a valid property for `objWordDoc` because, either by virtue of having been `Set` to point to `ActiveDocument` or having been declared `As Document`, variable `strDocFileName` is a `Document` class object, and `Document` class objects have `.Name` properties. In fact, they have `.Name` properties even when they don't point to real documents yet.

On Point

Every object in the Office 2000 Object Model is rooted to a primary object. This rooting is Windows' way of uniquely identifying any data object, among others of like or similar classes. VBA uses the primary object in performing a lookup process each time an object instance is stated in an instruction. The interpreter may chain through several classes of objects in succession, with each class progressively more specific than the previous one, until the object term at the end of the chain can uniquely identify it.

For the four main Office 2000 (O2K) applications, the name of the application itself serves as the primary object. In very few circumstances will you find it necessary to use these primary object names in an instruction, because VBA generally considers them to be default objects. The exceptions are when two or more O2K object libraries are being referenced by the same VBA module.

Addressing the central object

The central object of all of the main Office 2000 applications' object libraries is `Application`. The reason for having one object term that is common to all object libraries and to which all the subordinate terms are inexorably tied, is because much of constituency in O2KOM is a two-way street.

You see, `Application` has a reciprocal relationship with each of the subordinate terms under its wing. These subordinate terms are the *global objects*, named for the fact that they are uniformly accessible from anywhere in the VBA module; there are no scope limitations for these terms. The globals are like tall transmission towers visible from fifty miles away, from behind every hill. The network that ties these towers together is `Application`. Although the globals are constituents of `Application`, in situations where an instruction needs to determine the source of one of the globals, `Application` acts as a constituent of the globals. It follows that if a procedure needed to know the name of the file that contains the active VBA procedure at the moment, an instruction could be phrased like this:

```
strActTpltName = _
  Documents("CONTROL.DOC").Application.MacroContainer
```

Note once again the underscore (_) character, which allows the instruction to skip to the next line where it has more room. Here, the `Application` term plays a dual role. Positioned to the right of `Documents("CONTROL.DOC")`, it acts as that global's constituent. Meanwhile, positioned to the left of `MacroContainer`, the `Application` term simultaneously acts as this other global's container or antecedent. The reason `Application` plays this dual role is so that the instruction may retrieve an object using unrelated data as a source. The `Documents` global here has no `MacroContainer` object. So when we want to find the macro container (the Word document template that manages the main body of VBA procedures) for a particular document, we use the `Application` object as an all-purpose connector.

By the way, the `MacroContainer` global has a generic `Object` type, because Word can't know beforehand whether the container of any one macro (module) is a text document (.DOC) or a template (.DOT). The default property of this generic object is a character string, which is returned in our example instruction to a string variable `strActTpltName`.

Figure 2-1 depicts the relationship between the core objects in the main object libraries. The names for the object libraries themselves – the default terms – are at the top of the order. Here, `Application` quite literally plays a pivotal role; any information about the environment in which a global object exists must pass through the object that represents that environment; in this case, that object is `Application`.

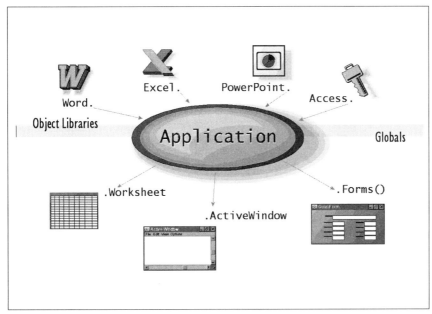

Figure 2-1: The relationships between the primary objects and Application.

Here is how you construct a reference to the Application object.

Application
All Office 2000 object libraries

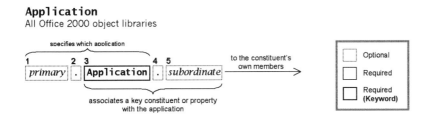

	Part	Description
1	primary	**Object** Any of the following: a global object, a valid object reference for a global object, or the name of one of the Office 2000 object libraries. When you use a reference to a global here, `Application` ties the constituent or property represented by *subordinate* (part **5**) back to the global, creating an *indirect reference.* An example of an indirect reference translated into English is: "The name of the document in the active window of the `Application` that is responsible for *this cursor.*"
2	. (period)	Separates the antecedent object (part **1**, when present) from the key object (part **3**).
3	Application	**Object** The `Application` object represents the engine component of an Office 2000 application, and is the primary object in all of the object libraries in the Object Model. You may not need to write `Application` into your instructions if the application it refers to is the same one you're working in; for example, the VBA console in Excel 2000 knows that `Application` refers to Excel, so it may be omitted in references to Excel's own globals.
4	. (period)	Separates the object term from any subordinate term (part **5**, when present).
5	*subordinate*	**Constituent or property** Either a valid global object term for `Application` recognized within the currently active object model (such as `Worksheet` or `Document`), or one of the current list of properties recognized for `Application` within that object model.

For a global to be able to recall `Application` as though it were one of its properties, is like "backing up one" in the Object Model. In a situation where the only data that you know you have doesn't have a direct relationship with the data you need to acquire — such as the example with the active document and the name of the file that's running its procedures — you use the `Application` object as a go-between.

Spending time with the globals

The *globals*, as I've grown fond of calling them, form the center of activity of the O2KOM object libraries. These are the objects that don't need to be bound to their respective libraries' primary object terms in order to be recognized, even when they're imported into a foreign editor. **Every O2KOM instruction you write involves a global object in some way, even if it is the default object and its term is omitted.**

The rule for globals is this: **If it's a constituent of** `Application`**, it's a global.** It can then be a root object in an expression. You don't have to write out `Word.Application.ActiveDocument.Range.End` to find the number of the last character in the active document; you can just write `ActiveDocument.Range.End` from within Word VBA.

For each of the O2K object libraries, every object term used in a VBA instruction must somehow answer the question, "Just what is the subject of this instruction, specifically?" It's ironic just how much this type of object depends on a subject. Whether it's mentioned in the object term or not, the "subject" of each O2KOM term is one of the globals listed in Table 2-2.

TABLE **2-2 GLOBAL OBJECTS FOR THE FOUR MAIN OFFICE 2000 OBJECT MODEL LIBRARIES**

Word 2000		
	ActiveDocument	FileSearch
	ActiveWindow	FindKey
	AddIns	FontNames
	AnswerWizard	GetSpellingSuggestions
	Application	HangulHanjaDictionaries
	Assistant	KeyBindings
	AutoCaptions	KeysBoundTo
	AutoCorrect	LandscapeFontNames
	Browser	Languages
	CaptionLabels	LanguageSettings
	COMAddIns	ListGalleries
	CommandBars	MacroContainer
	CustomDictionaries	MailingLabel
	CustomizationContext	MailMessage
	DefaultWebOptions	NewWindow
	Dialogs	NormalTemplate
	Documents	Options
	EmailOptions	Parent
	FileConverters	PortraitFontNames

Continued

TABLE 2-2 GLOBAL OBJECTS FOR THE FOUR MAIN OFFICE 2000 OBJECT MODEL LIBRARIES *(Continued)*

	RecentFiles	NextLetter
	Selection	ODBCErrors
	SynonymInfo	OLEDBErrors
	System	Parent
	Tasks	Range
	Templates	RecentFiles
	VBE	Rows
	Windows	Selection
	WordBasic	Sheets
Excel 2000	ActiveCell	ShortcutMenus
	ActiveChart	ThisWorkbook
	ActiveDialog	Toolbars
	ActiveMenuBar	Union
	ActiveSheet	VBE
	ActiveWindow	Windows
	ActiveWorkbook	Workbooks
	AddIns	WorksheetFunction
	AnswerWizard	Worksheets
	Application	Access 2000	AnswerWizard
	Assistant	Application
	AutoCorrect	Assistant
	Cells	CodeContextObject
	Charts	CodeDb
	Columns	COMAddIns
	COMAddIns	CommandBars
	CommandBars	CodeData
	DefaultWebOptions	CodeProject
	Dialogs	CreateControl
	DialogSheets	CreateControlEx
	Excel4IntlMacro	CreateDataAccessPage
	Sheets	CreateForm
	Excel4MacroSheets	CreateReport
	FileFind	CreateReportControl
	FileSearch	CreateReportControlEx
	Intersect	CurrentData
	LanguageSettings	CurrentDB
	MenuBars	CurrentProject
	Modules	DataAccessPages
	Names	

```
DBEngine                         PowerPoint 2000  ActivePresentation
DefaultWebOptions                                 ActiveWindow
DefaultWorkspaceClone                             AddIns
DoCmd                                             AnswerWizard
FileSearch                                        Application
Forms                                             Assistant
LanguageSettings                                  COMAddIns
LoadPicture                                       CommandBars
Modules                                           DefaultWebOptions
Parent                                            DialogsFileDialog
References                                        FileFind
Reports                                           FileSearch
Screen                                            LanguageSettings
VBE                                               MsoDebugOptions
WizHook                                           Presentations
                                                  SlideShowWindows
                                                  VBE
                                                  Windows
```

For all of these applications, most of the globals fall into two major categories: First, the *collections* are objects that refer to a series of items that belong to a single class. For instance, in Excel 2000's list of globals, Cells represents all of the cells in any given worksheet range. To refer to a specific cell in a long range, you address it using a pair of row/column indexes, as in Cells(41, 16), or with either argument represented by an integer variable. A collection object is generally identifiable by the plurality of the noun that names it.

The second major category of globals is the *persistent instances* (say that three times real fast). They're persistent because they are presumed to exist as long as the application is active. At some point you may declare your own variables to point to a particular Word document and a particular Excel worksheet. Those variables will be of classes Document and Worksheet, respectively. Meanwhile, Active Document and ActiveSheet are persistent instances of those same classes. These instances and their properties are addressable even when their respective applications do not have any documents active.

Normally, circumstances beyond the direct control of your source code cannot influence the values of your variables inside your source code. A string variable just doesn't contain "Netscape" one moment and "Microsoft" the next without some instruction to make that happen. But because the objects represented by ActiveDocument and ActiveSheet are indeed "active," they can be changed by the user without anyone or anything having to give notice to your VBA module. For this reason, these objects are represented not by variables but by reserved words in O2KOM. To get a handle on whatever it is the persistent instance represents at the time, you should declare an object variable and assign it to point to the active document. This way, if the user flips between documents in mid-execution, the document that your VBA program is analyzing doesn't suddenly appear transformed, rendering your analysis data meaningless.

As I'll demonstrate shortly, a collection object may bring together a set of persistent instances. The trick is in knowing how to address the specific instance you want.

Singularities are instances of single objects

A minority of the global objects in Table 2-2 are what this book calls *singularities* (Microsoft actually does not have a name for them). Simply put, a singularity is a persistent instance of a single object, as opposed to a set of objects. Selection is a prime example of a global singularity. It is a valid constituent of Application (among other objects). So Selection by itself refers to the active cursor in the active window.

What mainly distinguishes singularities is the fact that they are not collections. A singularity term represents *one* object. In the case of key instances, a singularity such as ActiveWorkbook is a persistent instance of a class like Workbook. Its characteristics may change as the user continues to operate the application, but the object itself can be counted on to exist. The syntax of a global singularity appears below:

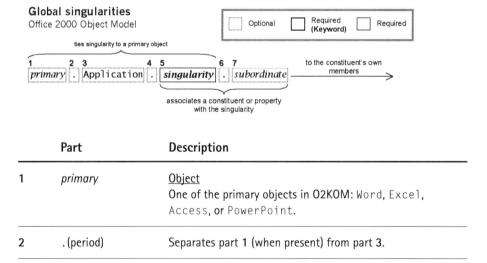

	Part	Description
1	*primary*	Object One of the primary objects in O2KOM: Word, Excel, Access, or PowerPoint.
2	. (period)	Separates part 1 (when present) from part 3.

3	`Application`	<u>Object</u> Ties the singularity (part **5**) to a primary object (part **1**) in situations where the singularity is a member of an object library of an application other than the one hosting the VBA interpreter. **Example:** `Excel.Application.Selection` Here, `Application` ties the `Selection` singularity back to `Excel`. This syntax is used within a Word VBA procedure to address the active cursor in Excel.
4	`.` (period)	Separates part **3** (when present) from part **5**.
5	*singularity*	<u>Object</u> A persistent instance of a single object of a recognized class.
6	`.` (period)	Separates part **5** from part **7** (when present).
7	*subordinate*	<u>Constituent, property, or method</u> One of the terms recognized as a member of the singularity.

Collections represent multiple instances of one class

Notice that most of the objects listed in Table 2-2 have names that are plural nouns. Apparently these objects are collections. **A collection is the set of all operative instances of a given class within an application.** In English, that means that whenever an Office 2000 application manages more than one incarnation, or *instance*, of some element of data – most notably, documents – those elements are addressable collectively. The rule that Microsoft imposed upon itself is to name its collection objects after the class to which all objects in the collection belong. So `CommandBars` – a collection that the four main O2K applications share – is evidently a collection of objects that are of class `CommandBar`.

All collection objects, thankfully, share the same syntax, which is spelled out here:

Global collections
Office 2000 Object Model

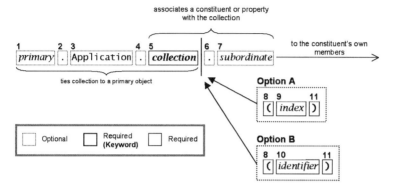

	Part	Description
1	*primary*	<u>Object</u> One of the primary objects in O2KOM: Word, Excel, Access, or PowerPoint.
2	.(period)	Separates part **1** (when present) from part **3**.
3	`Application`	<u>Object</u> Ties the singularity (part **5**) to a primary object (part **1**) in situations where the singularity is a member of an object library of an application other than the one hosting the VBA interpreter.
4	.(period)	Separates part **3** (when present) from part **5**.
5	*collection*	<u>Object</u> A set taking into account all active instances of a given class.
6	.(period)	Separates part **5** from part **7** (when present).
7	*subordinate*	<u>Constituent, property, or method</u> One of the terms recognized as a member of the collection.
8	((left parenthesis)	When specifying an individual member of the collection, this begins a subscript.

9	*index*	Integer For Option **A**, this numeral is used to identify an object within the collection, with respect to its ordinal sequence in the collection. **Example:** `Documents(2).Name` In Word VBA, this represents the filename of the second document in the collection. Here, 2 is said to be the *subscript* of the collection term.
10	*identifier*	String For Option **B**, this evaluates to the name or `.Name` property of the specific object within the collection. **Example:** `Documents("990205` `Invoice.doc").Characters.Count` In Word VBA, this represents the number of characters in the member of the `Documents` collection that is named `"990205` `Invoice.doc"`. If no such document is currently loaded in Word (even though it may exist in storage), this instruction will generate an error.
11	)(right parenthesis)	Closes the subscript.

The Immediate window presents instantaneous results

As a workbench for testing how you address objects in VBA, perhaps the least appreciated tool in VBA programming is the Immediate window. As Figure 2-2 shows, its location in the VBA environment is generally near the bottom of the screen, and contains nothing but a somehow familiar looking blinking prompt.

Even when your VBA module isn't running or is in "Pause mode," the Immediate window is active. This means you can use the Immediate window at any time to run any *dynamic* VBA instruction — in other words, not a procedure header and not a variable declaration, but something that will yield results the moment you press Enter. The Immediate window forgives the invocation of a variable that you haven't declared; it simply calls it into existence by default as one of VBA's Variant type variables.

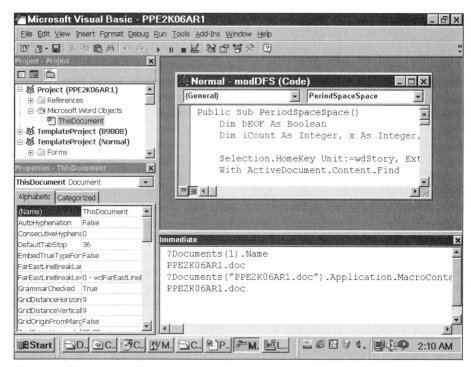

Figure 2-2: The standard VBA operating environment, with the Immediate window on the bottom.

The reason I'm bringing this up now is this: You can use the Immediate window to test how you address any given object, including collections. I tend to use the old ? symbol as an abbreviation for Print, which is an ancient BASIC statement that today applies to nothing else but the Immediate window. Using that old statement, I have the window "print" the current value of an object or object reference, by simply typing ? followed by the reference. On the line below, just like an old DOS prompt, the Immediate window responds with the reference's current setting. Here's the "transcript," if you will, of one of my recent sessions with the Immediate window:

```
?Documents(1).Name
Document6
?Documents("Document6").Application.MacroContainer
b9808.dot
```

The lines that start with ? were my commands to the Immediate window, and the lines that follow them are the window's responses. These lines tested how VBA interprets Documents(1).Name, and how it responds to Documents ("Document6") .Application.MacroContainer. In both cases, the interpreter returned valid responses; had I not phrased these objects properly, a dialog would have popped up explaining my error.

While I was typing these references, the VBA environment was helping me along by popping up, on the very line where I was typing, a list of valid objects and subordinates. This window, which Microsoft calls an "auto list," pops up into the Immediate window or into a code window whenever I'm in the middle of typing a subordinate object term whose antecedent is recognized by the interpreter. Figure 2-3 shows this auto list in the middle of my typing into the Immediate window.

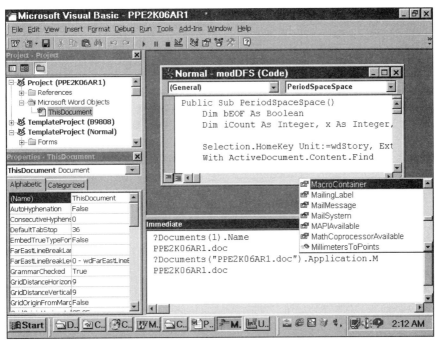

Figure 2-3: VBA's object term auto list.

Now, I could double-click on one of these terms to have it automatically typed in and spelled properly, but I type rather fast and I don't want to take my hands off the keyboard. So I could operate the auto list using keystrokes instead:

First down-arrow   Brings the highlight into the list keypress

Successive up/down arrows   Navigate through the list

Shift+Space   Types the highlighted item and adds a space

Ctrl+Enter   Types the highlighted item

Using numerals, literals, and variables as subscripts

When I addressed the `.Name` property of the first `Document` class object in the collection in my test with the Immediate window, I used Option A as demonstrated in the syntax table for global collection objects earlier. `Documents(1)` represents the first document in the collection; luckily, `1` here does mean "first." (Not every object consistently uses `1` as the numeral for "first;" some use `0` instead.) In my second test instruction, I used the syntax for Option B, substituting the name `"Document6"`, which I already knew to be valid because it was the results of the first test instruction. Notice I used quotation marks around the document name; it's not the name of an object term but instead the title given to an open document. When that document is saved, the generic `Document.x` title will be replaced with the document's filename. So the title is a string, not an object reference. Now, if I had earlier assigned `strName = "Document6"` then I could phrase a valid instruction with `Documents(strName)`. Here, the string variable name stands in place of the text, so I don't need quotation marks. **Characters passed directly as an argument to a function or used as a subscript, without being represented by a string variable, are collectively called a** *literal.*

On Point

The `Application` object is central to all of the Office 2000 object libraries. The terms that are constituents of `Application` in these libraries are considered globals and may be referenced from any point within the application without the need for antecedents to qualify them. `Application` is unique in that it has a reciprocal relationship with its constituents; for the globals, `Application` may also act as a constituent itself. This permits two objects that don't otherwise bear any relation to one another to be connected to each other using `Application` as a conduit. `Application` acts as a constituent for one object term and as an antecedent for the other object term.

Among the global objects are the collections, which represent the sets of any number of objects of a given class. The name of a collection in O2KOM is the plural of the name of its members. The other major category of object among the globals is persistent instances, whose characteristics' settings are subject to frequent change as their applications continue to be used, but whose characteristics' identifying terms may be relied upon to be present at all times. Persistent instances are frequently identified by the use of the prefix `Active-`.

Putting all this information into practice

I promised in the Introduction not to bombard you with a lot of esoteric data and terminology without at least buffering it with some real-world examples. So here's a Word 2000 procedure that deals with a commonplace editing dilemma:

Many people type two spaces in-between sentences, because that's the way secretarial courses have taught them to type. Certain authors (who shall remain nameless) type two spaces between their sentences, but certain publishers balk at seeing this extra space of separation, because it can jam their typesetting machines. A VBA procedure is needed for Word 2000 that examines a document and changes every sequence of one period and two spaces to one period and one space. But we need to take this idea one critical step further: Because certain authors' macros look for pairs of spaces to determine where some sentences end and others begin, the process of contracting the sentence separation needs to be reversible. If the document contains sequences of one period and one space already, we want the procedure to replace those sequences with one period and two spaces. Implied in all of this is the need for VBA to ascertain whether the document is full of one sequence or the other.

Listing 2-1 shows one version of the procedure that takes a speculative approach to this problem. It analyzes the front of the document to determine whether the document is likely to be full of single or twin spaces and, based on what it finds, corrects the rest of the document accordingly.

Listing 2-1: Implementing raw searches for single spaces or space pairs.

```
Public Sub PeriodSpaceSpace()
    Dim bEOF As Boolean
    Dim iCount As Integer, x As Integer, iCmp As Integer

    Selection.HomeKey Unit:=wdStory, Extend:=wdMove
    With ActiveDocument.Content.Find
        .Text = ". (<[A-Z])"
        .Forward = True
        .MatchWildcards = True

        For x = 1 To 5
            If .Execute Then
                iCount = iCount + 1
            Else
                bEOF = True
                Exit For
            End If
        Next x
    End With

    If bEOF Then
```

```
        iCmp = x
    Else
        iCmp = 5
    End If

    With ActiveDocument.Content.Find
        .Forward = True
        .MatchWildcards = True
        Selection.HomeKey Unit:=wdStory, Extend:=wdMove

        If iCount = iCmp Then
            .Text = ".  (<[A-Z])"
            .Replacement.Text = ". \1"   'replace two for one
        Else
            .Text = ". (<[A-Z])"
            .Replacement.Text = ".  \1" 'replace one for two
        End If

        .Execute Replace:=wdReplaceAll
    End With
End Sub
```

To give you a general idea of what's happening: The procedure is an enclosure of instructions that begins with the first line marked `Public Sub`, and ends with the final line `End Sub`. The name I gave the procedure, `PeriodSpaceSpace`, was entirely arbitrary; I could have named it something else. The closed parentheses `()` is an indicator that this procedure needs no incoming data; it can work entirely with what data it can gather for itself.

The logic behind this procedure is as follows: To determine with relative certainty whether the document is full of period-space-space sequences, the procedure looks for five such sequences in the document. If there are five, or at least if there are as many sequences as there are sentence separations, then that's enough to conclude the document needs to be changed for single spaces between sentences. But if the procedure can't find five period-space-space sequences, the procedure changes the document the other way instead, changing single-space separations to double-space separations.

After the first line, the procedure introduces the interpreter to variables that will be used to represent numeral values. The `Dim` instructions tell the VBA interpreter what types of numeral values are being represented. The variables are used later in the procedure to count and to make comparisons.

The object library of Word 2000 plays a crucial role here. The Word 2000 object library provides the terms `Selection`, `ActiveDocument`, `Content`, `Find`, and all of the terms adjacent to these four. The VBA interpreter recognizes them because, in this instance, it was invoked by Word, and is running in conjunction with Word. So unlike C++, these objects don't need to be declared someplace, or defined by some outside file that is referred to with an #include statement and linked in later, the way a C++ compiler works. Simply because Word invoked VBA to start with, these terms are automatically recognized, as though they were an intrinsic part of the VBA language.

Listing 2-1 contains our first two examples of VBA's With clause. The purpose of With is to name one object as a *subject* (please forgive the flip-flop) for the instructions contained within the clause. The resulting convenience is that certain long objects, such as ActiveDocument.Content.Find, don't have to be typed out each time. This certain long object – which is part of the Word 2000 object library – represents a search operation for a sequence of characters in a document. Within a With clause, any terms you write that begin with a period are presumed to be properties, constituents, or methods of the subject object. So in .Forward = True, VBA fills in the missing antecedent with ActiveDocument.Content.Find.

Notice the three If...Then...Else comparative clauses above. The way these clauses are constructed, it's fairly obvious that either one group of inset instructions or the other gets executed, but not both. The Else term separates the two sets, and which set is executed depends on the result of the dependent True/False expression. Notice also how the first If...Then...Else clause is subordinate to another clause, which is bordered by For and Next. This is a repetitive clause, which tells the interpreter to execute that clause's subordinate instructions 5 times. Here, the entire dependent expression is .Execute – a method. Why does this qualify? Because this particular method *returns* a True/False value. So from VBA's perspective, writing .Execute is just as good as writing True or False. It will evaluate to one or the other anyway. The True/False result of .Execute is a success/failure signal; in fact, that's generally what a True/False result means for any method that returns a Boolean value. It's the method's way of indicating to the procedure that calls it, whether or not its own task worked.

So what is the procedure in Listing 2-1 actually saying? Let's read this procedure's instructions to the interpreter from the top, as though they were written in English, and as though we're talking directly to the VBA interpreter:

We'll be using three variables over the course of the procedure. Three of them are whole numbers (Integer), while the fourth is a True/False value (Boolean). Starting at the beginning of the active document, preset a search operation so that it looks for a period, followed by two spaces, then any word that begins with one of the capital letters A through Z. Using this as the active search, try to find five of these character sequences, or at least as many as the document allows. For each successful search, add one to the running tally; otherwise, set the signal that the end of file was reached. Now that we're in the homestretch, let's reset the search. If all the successful searches returned the sequence we wanted, set the new search parameters to replace two-space sequences for one-space sequences. Otherwise, set the search parameters to replace one-space sequences for two-space sequences. Finally, execute the final search and then exit the procedure.

In Depth: How many cursors are there in Word 2000, really?

The two Word globals with which the procedure in Listing 2-1 is concerned are `ActiveDocument` and `Selection`. These two are actually constituents of `Application`; but as the rule states, you can omit `Application` when you're programming Word globals within Word VBA. As a global, `Selection` represents the point in Word where the cursor is blinking. That's a crucial test for this reason: **Each open window in Word maintains its own cursor.** It's something you might know without actually knowing that you know it: When you leave one window, go into another, and then go back into the first one, the blinking cursor goes back to the place where you left it. From VBA's perspective, however, the cursor doesn't leap from window to window. Instead, windows have their own constituent cursors; so the cursor for the document in the second window, whether or not it's active, is represented by `Windows(2).Selection`.

So if every Word window has a `Selection`, why does `Word.Application` have its own `Selection` also? Because the real purpose of `Selection` as a term in the object library is to provide you with a way to address where the next incoming letter will go, or where a block of text has been indicated. Since you will want to know this information in many different contexts, Word provides as many ways of addressing that information as there are contexts. Thus, Word's cursor, the cursor in the active window in Word, and the cursor in the first Word document, are all addressed in different ways. The Word object library could have given each object representing the cursor in these three contexts a different name, but imagine how difficult it would be to explain why there are three names for the cursor, as opposed to why there are three object paths to address the cursor.

Implementing Object References

Many of the paragraphs you read these days amongst the multitude of manuals on the subject of programming begin with the words, "You can." "*You can,*" one might read, "declare a variable as an object, and set it to refer to an existing object." The discourse might proceed, "To declare an object variable, use the `Dim` statement to name your variable, then give it the object type of your choice." *You can* declare about 80 variables, and name them all after admirals of the British Royal Navy. *You can,* if you so choose, pick up your computer and throw it out the window. The question that so oftenfails to be answered in paragraphs like these is this: *Why* would you use this technique? Evidently the programmers who do declare object references have goals in mind, so what are they?

Among the reasons one would want to declare your own variable as an object reference are these:

◆ A procedure might receive an object variable as one of its parameters. For instance, you may write a function procedure that returns statistical information about a given document. The call to this procedure could pass this object's `Document` class reference, or perhaps `ActiveDocument`, as an argument to this function procedure. In the heading of the procedure, you would name the received argument and declare its type all on the same line. For example, a valid procedure name would be `Public Function DocStatistics(docExamine As Document) As String`. In this example, `docExamine` represents the incoming `Document` class argument. By stating `As Document` explicitly, you're allowing the VBA interpreter to perform *type checking* to make certain that the incoming argument is indeed of `Document` class. While type checking is active, you won't be able to even *program* a procedure call that doesn't use a `Document` class reference without the interpreter notifying you that such a procedure call would be erroneous.

◆ You may require an object reference that can refer to one object in a succession or collection of objects of a like class. This would be necessary in a situation where you're collecting a list of information about all or some of the objects in a collection, such as `Paragraphs` or `Cells`. You cannot assign the characteristics of a collection to an object reference in one fell swoop, even if your object reference is declared `As Collection`. You can only gather information about each object in the collection one at a time, and then add that item to your list or to your `Collection` class object. Listing 2-2 later in this chapter will present an example of this common use of a single object reference in gathering information about a collection.

◆ You may use an object reference to create an entirely new object — one that doesn't represent a pre-existing object. For example, in Word VBA, *you can* declare a `Document` class object `As New Document`, and then use the methods attributed to the `Document` class to build that document. (Some documentation sources incorrectly claim that you *cannot* do this.) For example, say you declared a variable with the instruction `Dim docCyberDoc As New Document`. At this point, the document would not exist in Word, although the object from VBA's perspective has all of the characteristics of any other `Document` class object. You could bring text into a processed document using the method `docCyberDoc.Application.Selection.TypeText "Insert your text here."` Notice the dual role being played again by the `Application` object, as it links the reference `docCyberDoc` to the `Selection` object. To bring the document into a Word window (i.e., to make it *real*), you could use the method `Application.ActiveWindow = docCyberDoc.ActiveWindow`.

Using the tools of modern book typesetting, let's demonstrate precisely how a `Dim` statement is constructed:

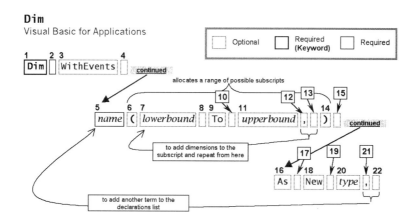

	Part	Description
1	Dim	**Statement** The `Dim` statement allocates memory for at least one variable of the stated *type* (part **19**, when present), and gives this variable the name *term* (part **4**). This name will be recognized as representing the allocated unit of memory throughout the same body of code where the `Dim` statement appears.
2	(space)	
3	WithEvents	**Qualifier** In the context of a VBA class module (discussed in Chapter 9), `WithEvents` is used to state that the object reference declared with `Dim` may recognize its own events.
4	(space)	
5	*term*	**Variable** An arbitrarily (though sensibly) chosen name that will be reserved by the VBA interpreter to exclusively refer to the allocated unit of memory, up until execution of the body of code containing the `Dim` statement is terminated.
6	((left parenthesis)	Begins the subscript portion of the statement.

7	*lowerbound*	<u>Integer</u> When declaring arrays whose members will be referenced by number, *lowerbound* sets the index number of the first member of the array. If *lowerbound* is omitted (as is usually the case), the interpreter assumes this initial index to be 0 by default.
8	(space)	
9	To	Separates lower bounds of array range from upper bounds.
10	(space)	
11	*upperbound*	<u>Integer</u> When declaring arrays, *upperbound* sets the index number of the final member of the array. Members of the array will be numbered consecutively from 0 or *lowerbound* to *upperbound*. The index number for an array is also called its *subscript*. If *upperbound* is omitted, the array is considered *dynamic*, and bounds must be specified later using a ReDim statement before it can be used.
12	, (comma)	When declaring arrays with more than one dimension (for instance, a table as opposed to a set or sequence), a comma is used to separate the index subscripts for different axes of the array. In the case of multidimensional arrays, each subscript acts as a reference for its associated axis. VBA recognizes arrays with up to 60 dimensions.
13	(space)	
14	) (right parenthesis)	Closes the subscript.
15	(space)	
16	As	Begins the specification of the new variable's type.
17	(space)	
18	New	<u>Qualifier</u> If New is used when designating an object class as the type for the variable (part 20), the variable will refer to a newly-formed object entirely independent of any existent object. This allows a module to construct a new object from the ground up. This process is known as *early binding*, as opposed to *late binding* defined below.

Continued

	Part	Description
19	(space)	
20	*type*	<u>Type or class</u> States the type and structure of the new variable. Designating a standard type states in turn how much minimum memory is allocated for storing its represented value. Designating a defined object class declares the variable to be an object reference, with all of the characteristics and constituents of that class; for example, a variable declared As Workbook will have all of the characteristics of an Excel Workbook object. Declaring a variable As Object allows the structure of the object to be specified later in the program — a process called *late binding*. Omitting an object type allows the interpreter to declare the variable as type Variant, which results in a variable that may be assigned a value of any standard type, or a character string, without violating type checking.
21	, (comma)	
22	(space)	
23	(Enter)	Closes the declaration statement.

Variables declared using Dim have a *scope*, or term of existence. Whenever the body of code containing a variable's Dim statement is terminated, the memory for that variable is released, and the variable ceases to exist. Variables declared within a procedure, therefore, are said to have procedural scope. Variables declared outside of a procedure are called *module-level variables*, and may be used reliably anywhere within the module.

Why would you want variables to terminate themselves when they're done? After all, with the financial crisis in Asia at the time of this writing, memory is dirt cheap. As you'll see when you gain more experience writing your own longer programs (longer than the examples shared thus far), the more variables you use for a longer period of time, the more you tend to forget what you called them. With procedure-level variables in place, one procedure can declare a variable iThis, and another procedure can declare a variable iThis, and both variables will never be the same. They share names, but since they don't share the same body of code, it doesn't matter.

In Depth: Using Dim to declare arrays

An *array variable* is VBA's way of referring to a set, a sequence, or a table using a single name. **An array is a list or table of values or string contents, each of which is addressable by its index numeral.** You give this sequence a name with the Dim statement. When you specify an upper bound for the array (part **11** in the previous syntax table), an integer (whole number) is used as an index for the elements that are members of the array. This index is the *subscript*. Its own value ranges from zero or whatever you may have specified for the lower bound (part **7**) to the upper bound. The index represents the relative place of a unit of data within the array. Expressions that involve the array variable will use this index.

If you don't specify an upper bound, the variable is said to be a *dynamic array*. Think of this as a "rubber array," whose length can be set and altered as needed. Its lower and upper boundaries may be specified later in the script using the ReDim statement. I'll discuss that statement in much greater detail in Chapter 3.

A one-dimensional array, or list, is generally declared using a single integer (or integral expression) between the parentheses. A two-dimensional array, or table, is declared using two integers between the parentheses, each separated by a comma. These integers represent the furthest column and row, or x-axis and y-axis values, in the table. A two-dimensional array in VBA is like a two-axis table in Excel. A three-dimensional array is declared in the same manner, only with three integers or integral expressions separated by commas. You would need an array with more than one dimension if the indexes of your array were to serve as references; for example, if you're retrieving the name of the person who lives in city 5 who drives car 14. Both integral indexes that apply here, are candidates for references for a two-dimensional array.

As you might surmise, there is a far more important reason for variables to have different scopes of existence: Procedures in a long modular program are designed to be executed more than once. Each time the same procedure is executed its local variables get declared again. Localizing a variable's scope so that it terminates itself is one way for a procedure to pick up after itself, especially so memory will be "clean," if you will, when it comes back. Because source code does not change during the course of execution, a procedure will always redeclare the same variables. Generally, you will want these redeclared variables to be new each time, *unless you specify otherwise* (and there's a way to do that, which I'll discuss later).

DIM EXAMPLE

Here's a two-procedure example that demonstrates one common use of the Dim statement: Let's assume that a Word VBA module uses its own dialog box. To run that dialog box, VBA employs a *form module*. Within this form, there is a list box that displays the filenames for all of the active documents in Word. When the user double-clicks on the filename, the form responds by bringing up that document in Print Preview mode, which isn't readily available from Word's View menu. First, we concentrate on using the list box to bring up the document. Listing 2-2 shows the instructions that bring the documents' names into the list:

Listing 2-2: Bringing a list of active documents into a list box control.

```
Private Sub UserForm_Activate()
    Dim docThisDoc As Document
    '
    ' Imagine there are other instructions here
    '
    For Each docThisDoc In ActiveDocument.Application.Documents
        lstTitleList.AddItem docThisDoc.FullName
    Next
End Sub
```

This procedure will be automatically executed the moment the form enters the screen. The reason why is because of its name: Whatever the form's name (or .Name property) actually is (in our example, PreviewForm) the name of its *class*, UserForm, is what VBA expects to find here. One of the events recognized by this class is _Activate, which takes place when it has been made the active form — which means, it's on the screen, it's visible, and its contained controls are, by default, made active. By naming this procedure Private Sub UserForm_Activate(), we've ensured that it will be executed at the proper time.

The procedure starts by declaring a variable docThisDoc whose purpose is to act as the single object reference for all of the open documents in succession. The same reference will cycle through each document object, pull up the name of that document, put that name in the list box, and move on to the next document.

Let's assume that this isn't the only purpose for this form procedure and that there are other instructions in the marked area of Listing 2-2 that fulfill some other purpose. The For Each...Next loop clause shows how docThisDoc is used as a pointer that counts through the documents belonging to the Documents collection.

With docThisDoc pointing to one in the Documents collection, the object reference has all of the characteristics of a specific Document object. So we can poll docThisDoc for its .FullName property and can retrieve a string containing the document's filename that can be added to the list box lstTitleList. Each time the interpreter encounters the Next instruction, it ticks off one more document in the Documents collection, and assigns docThisDoc to point to it. The instruction lstTitleList.AddItem docThisDoc.FullName will be executed exactly as many times as there are open documents in Word. Each cycle of a loop clause is called an *iteration*.

At Present: Open documents in Office 2000 have their own windows

Historically, every one of Microsoft's own Windows applications has possessed something called a *workspace*. Each Office 97 application had its own exclusive window. The workspace for each window was a sort of corral within which its documents and other data windows shared space. When you minimized a document window, its icon dropped to the lower left portion of the workspace. This behavior was at one time a formal programming methodology, to which Microsoft gave the name "Multiple Document Interface" back in 1985.

Beginning with Office 2000, all document windows share the same workspace — namely, the Windows Desktop. Now each document window has its own icon on the Windows Taskbar, along with its token slot in the Window menu. Because of this new behavior, it's a bit more difficult now for the VBA programmer to ascertain which window is the "active window." You see, the Taskbar recognizes one active window among all windows currently in use. After the user has been operating another program, the "active window" in Word or Excel becomes whichever document the user clicked on in the task bar to bring that application back up. We'll encounter the problem of the "active window" throughout the upcoming chapters. For now, the example we're currently demonstrating makes the chosen window the "active window" by changing its view mode.

Part 2 of this demonstration comes in the form of a procedure shown in Listing 2-3. This procedure has Word 2000 pull up the chosen document in Print Preview mode when the document is double-clicked on in the list:

Listing 2-3: Bringing the chosen document into Print Preview mode.

```
Private Sub lstTitleList_DblClick(ByVal Cancel As _
 MSForms.ReturnBoolean)
    Windows(Documents(lstTitleList.Text).ActiveWindow.Index) _
    .View.Type = wdPrintPreview
    Unload PreviewForm
End Sub
```

The first two lines and the next two lines in Listing 2-3 each constitute a single instruction. In VBA, when an instruction is so long that it has to be broken up over more than one line, a lone underscore _ is used to tell the interpreter, "Continued on next line." `Private Sub lstTitleList_DblClick()` is an event procedure attributed to the `lstTitleList` object that represents the list box control. The event that triggers this procedure is _DblClick, which occurs when the user double-clicks on the list box. The argument within the parentheses is mandatory for the interpreter, but not relevant to this procedure. VBA actually generates this argument automatically; even if you don't use it, the interpreter might balk if you remove it.

The first real instruction in this procedure, following the `Private Sub` declaration, begins with the word `Windows`. Not as in "Microsoft Windows," mind you — this is one of Word's global collections. What this myriad of gobbledygook is saying, when translated into English, is this: "Word, take the window whose index number is the same as that attributed to the window of the document whose name is the same as the one the user just double-clicked on, and change its view mode to Print Preview. Please."

The text of the chosen line in the list box is always `lstTitleList.Text`. Even when the list box has multiple lines, the `.Text` property of the list box is always retrieved from the line that contains what Windows calls the *focus*. Since the line contains only the document's filename and nothing else, the text of that line can be used as an index to identify the document in the `Documents` collection. Remember that a specific document can be addressed in `Documents` by either its index numeral or its filename.

In the Word 2000 object library, `View` is a constituent of `Window` class objects, and represents all of the visual characteristics that Word applies to the window, such as whether it's in Normal view or Print Preview mode. Here, `wdPrintPreview` is a constant that stands for Print Preview mode when assigned to the `.Type` property of the `View` object. Assigning this constant to the property (assuming you've ascertained the right window in the first place) switches that document's window into Print Preview.

When to specify the class and when not to specify it

The `Dim` statement is used to call forth a new object reference variable for a module or procedure. Hopefully, the name you give to this reference variable conveys its meaning appropriately to you as well as other human readers; the VBA interpreter's only care is that the name you choose is *unique* — one that it hasn't seen before.

Generally, the `Dim` statement (or one that may be used in its stead, such as `Public` or `Private`) is used to specify the term's unique object class. However, you may choose instead to assign to the declared variable the generic `Object` class in either of two circumstances:

1. If the class of object that the variable will represent is indefinite at the point in the code where you declare it; or,

2. If the class is to be assigned to the variable later by virtue of the `CreateObject()` or `GetObject()` VBA function. (Both of these functions involve looking up the object's class in the Windows System Registry.)

A declaration statement such as `Dim` is not necessary for variables representing incoming arguments for a procedure; in such cases, their names are included as symbolic placeholders for the incoming arguments, and their types are specified within the procedure declaration. `Dim` may be used to declare an array of one or more dimensions, or axes, to be represented by a single term with one or more subscripts (this was the original purpose of the `Dim` statement in BASIC).

Set assigns an object's characteristics to a variable

As I outlined in Chapter 1, when you assign a single value to a variable, you use a simple equation called an *assignment expression*. For instance, you might use this instruction to assign a filename to a string variable:

```
strFileName = "K:\NetDocs\Invoice\Invoice.dot"
```

Assignment expressions such as this one can only assign *one* datum (one value or one string) to one variable. To assign an object to an object reference variable, since that object has more than one characteristic, the simple assignment expression will not work. Instead, you invoke a `Set` statement, which looks like an ordinary assignment expression but for the presence of the statement keyword itself. For example:

```
Set wkbThisWorkbook = Excel.Application.Workbooks(1)
```

Here is how you construct a Set statement:

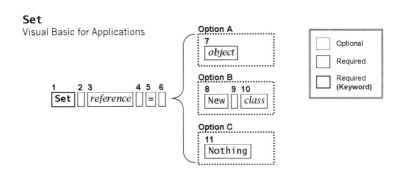

	Part	Description
1	Set	<u>Statement</u> When a variable has been declared with an explicit object class, Set either assigns to that variable the characteristics of an existent object (by means of an active object library or some other existent object reference), or allows a new instance of a specified class to be generated and assigned to the variable. The newly assigned variable is considered an object reference, although it does not necessarily substitute for the object to which it refers. Instead, an object reference should be considered a "snapshot" of an object, representing the object's characteristics at the time of assignment.
2	(space)	
3	*reference*	<u>Variable</u> The name of a variable previously declared with an object class. This class could be one that is recognized by any of the active object libraries (such as Document or Workbook) or it could be VBA's generic Object class.
4	(space)	
5	=	<u>Operator</u> Separates the object reference from the object or object class being assigned to it.
6	(space)	

| 7 | *object* | Object specifier |
| | | For Option **A**, a term that represents a valid object. This term could be provided by one of the active object libraries, or it could be another object reference previously assigned by another `Set` statement elsewhere. |

| 8 | New | Qualifier |
| | | For Option **B**, this term tells the interpreter that the reference (part **3**) is not to point to an existing object, but instead is to refer to a new instantiation of the stated class (part **10**). |

| 9 | (space) | |

| 10 | *Class* | Class identifier |
| | | Specifies the class of object being instantiated by the `Set` statement. |

| 11 | Nothing | Constant |
| | | For Option C, it clears the object reference of all of its attributes and constituents and releases it from memory. The term reference may then be used later for any purpose. |

In Depth: Instantai. . . Wait. . . Could you spell that again, please?

Throughout the last few paragraphs and in the last syntax block, I used the term *instantiate* as though it's something the doctor reminds us to do three times a day before we go to bed. Pronounced "in·stahn·chee·eight," it means to call into existence a member of a specified class. Imagine the US Mint instantiating a run of twenty-dollar bills. Obviously, they're all cut from the same mold.

So why the fancy term? Because an *instance* of a class goes on to become its own unique object. The fact that it has the same properties as any other instance of a class makes it no less a member. But it's the properties of an object that allow its characteristics to be defined. My wife and I both have hair. Hair is a property for both of us. But hers is blond and mine black. Those are different characteristics, as well as the fact that hers is in somewhat greater abundance than mine. In VBA, differing characteristics are made possible by varied property settings.

Assigning an object to an object reference with the Set statement does not change the scope of that reference. So if you declared the reference outside of all procedures in the Declarations section of a module so that all procedures in the module have equal access to that reference, then after the Set statement for that reference is executed, it will retain its modular scope. However, the way VBA is structured, a problem arises: You cannot write statements other than declarations outside of procedures, because there's no way to specify where the interpreter would begin executing any instructions that would lie outside of procedures. **All *active* statements and functions in VBA must be written within procedures, because procedures have clearly marked entry points.** Therefore, since Set statements are active instructions and not declarations, they must appear within procedures, even if the objects to which those Set statements refer were declared outside of procedures. Again, the scope of the reference is retained, even when the declaration is module-level and the Set statement is in a procedure.

Variables are controlled entirely by your code

Once an object variable is declared using Dim (or Static, as will be demonstrated later in the book), the object data to which that variable refers is assigned directly by your VBA instructions only, and by no one or nothing else. This is important, because if you were to use this instruction:

```
Set docThisDoc = ActiveDocument
```

and for some reason ActiveDocument were to change by virtue of what the user is doing with respect to Word, the object referred to by variable docThisDoc would stay as it was. The Set instruction does not make any given variable an alternate reference to the same single object. Rather, it takes a snapshot, if you will, of the characteristics of that variable at the time the Set statement is executed, and stores those characteristics within docThisDoc as a separate object. The equation above is not to be taken entirely algebraically; just because *A* equals *B* now, does not mean that *A* will continue to equal *B* by the time the interpreter sees the next instruction.

A declared variable is assigned to refer to a specific object by means of the Set statement. This object is generally pre-existing, especially in cases where it is supplied by O2KOM. However, Set may assign a variable to point to a new instance of a specified object class. In such cases, the module itself, and not the user, constructs the contents of the data represented by the object. Once a reference variable is assigned to an object by Set, the variable does not act as an alternate identifier for that object; instead, it acts as an indicator or "snapshot" of the object's characteristics at the time the Set statement was executed.

In Theory: Whose Object Model Is It Anyway?

The Visual Basic language, on which VBA is based, is the product of many varying methodologies meshed together over three and one-half decades. The BASIC programming language is about twice as old as the idea of object orientation. BASIC was originally designed as a purely procedural, algebraic language. By that, I mean that all of the variables the language used, despite the fact that they were symbolic, represented discrete values. The processes that perform operations upon those variables were purely formulaic.

The reason for objects in computer languages is to introduce a level of abstraction in the way processes are addressed. By addressing processes as "things" that have their own inherent capabilities, rather than as formulas, the act of conceptualizing what it is a program is supposed to do is made simpler for some programmers. They can start to envision the dynamics of their programs as though they were mechanical devices. But not all programmers favor the ideal of abstraction. If they're mathematicians as well, they perceive procedures as formulaic structures rather than commands that a manager gives his subordinates.

Object orientation never has, and never will, make matters easier for computers. It is the job of compilers such as C++ and interpreters such as VBA to work through the abstraction level and rebuild the programmer's conceptualizations into a firmly logical, tightly regulated machine code. Because it's up to the computer to sift through all this, perhaps no compiled or interpreted object-oriented program will ever be as well optimized or as logically precise as code crafted by an assembly language (machine code) programmer, who never deals with "objects" on this level. For the assembly programmer, "object code" is the product of a proper assembly operation. Strangely, assembly programmers and those who program compilers themselves, call it "object code" because it's logically reduced and unabstracted – the exact opposite reason why high-level language programmers name their abstract work "object code."

But neither Visual Basic nor VBA are truly object-oriented languages as is evidenced by the need for the Set statement in the first place. In VBA, as you learned in this chapter, many component objects are assumed to preexist. VBA can access such an object directly, using the name given it by one of the object libraries. But in order for VBA to perform certain operations on multiple members of a set of such objects, such as Documents and Worksheets, it has to merge a procedural method with an objective method. First, using Dim, you declare a procedural variable with the same object class as those members you seek to address. Then you write a program which in effect says to VBA, "See this symbol? If this were the same as the first member of this set, I would want you to do *this* to this symbol. Now if this were the same as the *second* member of this set, I would want you to do the same thing. And if this were like the *third*..." This association of a preexistent object with a procedural variable is undertaken by the Set statement. Set is but one of many examples of tools made necessary by the changes in programming methodology so that Visual Basic and VBA can still be BASIC.

In Brief

♦ The primary object refers to the object library from which a global or other term is derived. While working in the native VBA environment of an application, however, the primary object name for its own library may be omitted.

♦ Application is a central term common to all of the O2K object libraries, giving all of them a common, centralized axis to which other terms, such as the globals, can relate.

♦ A global is a single preexistent object (*singularity*) or a *collection* of preexistent objects that always exist, are maintained by the Office applications, and are subject to change by the user — from outside of VBA control.

♦ Dim is the most-often used VBA statement for calling a variable or object reference into existence. Technically speaking, its true purpose is to reserve memory for the purposes of representing data.

♦ An object variable can be made to point to a global (pre-existent object), or to some other object variable, by way of the Set statement.

Chapter 3

Comprehending Visual Basic Symbology

IN THIS CHAPTER

◆ The different types and uses for variables in VBA modules

◆ How and why variables are *declared*

◆ The weird and wonderful practice of utilizing "Hungarian notation"

◆ The use of array variables to represent sets or tables of values

◆ The string variable – its purposes and limitations

◆ How expressions are crafted in VBA

◆ The procedure/module structure of VBA programming

◆ The declaration and construction of `Sub` and `Function` procedures

◆ The definition of *scope* with respect to both variables and procedures

TRADITIONALLY IN VISUAL BASIC (VB), a program accomplishes practically nothing without the frequent use of variables. This is because in most cases, the VB application defines and constructs on its own all the data that it will ever use. The main Declarations section of a VB application is generally overflowing with `Dim` or `Public` statements, looking like one of Daniel Webster's notebooks, redefining the language at the same time it makes use of the language.

Because Visual Basic for Applications (VBA) was mainly constructed around the principle of using some other application's data rather than its own, the use of variables seems to take a back seat to the Office 2000 Object Model (O2KOM). Yet any module you intend to write whose functionality exceeds what was previously capable with a mere macro, will rely at least partly on the use of arbitrarily named variables as symbols for values.

In Chapter 2, I introduced you to the `Dim` statement, but my examples focused mainly on its relevance in generating new object references. In this chapter, I'll expand the breadth of information on this topic, and also introduce you to three other statements that can be used in certain conditions in its stead: `Public`, `Private`, and `Static`.

Variables As Symbols for Values

In an allegorical, but not too unrealistic, sense, memory within a computer is like a loom, weaving threads together in precise, arithmetic, symbolic patterns. Nearly all of the greatest Indian mathematicians throughout history have been weavers themselves, or have at least been inspired by the mechanism of the loom. Both of the key inventors of digital computing, Charles Babbage and John von Neumann, have likened the process of symbolizing values mechanically to operating a loom.

The placement of colored threads along a line in such a way that successive lines form a pattern on a grid, is indeed a digital process. In the fifteenth century, English barbers, known for the cleanliness of their linens, were also known as *rasters*, the term actually referring to the small sideways blades they used. The tightly woven cloth these barbers used on their customers' faces, and later wore as their own uniforms, came to be known as "raster cloth" (or, in the Middle English spelling, *Raster clathe*). Sometimes raster cloth wasn't all white; as time passed, it became decorated, either by patterns woven into the cloth itself, or stitched onto it by needlepoint. As the term grew to become a colloquialism, "raster" referred less to the barber and more to the cloth, the way "cheese cloth" has little to do anymore with cheese. So several hundred years later, when the idea of electronic memory was first conceived, and was first likened to the process of using a loom, the individual rows of signal carriers that comprised these memories – whether they were tubes, transistors, or magnets – were lovingly dubbed *rasters*. Today, the process of arranging graphical data byte-by-byte in symbolic rows is called *rastering*, after the cloth whose name came from a barber whose name came from a blade.

The symbolism employed by all digital computers – representing procedural math in memory using binary values – is more ancient than you may think. If you've ever studied the mandala-like patterns associated with the time-honored Chinese philosophy *I Ching* (loosely translated into English as "book of changes"), you may have noticed the wheel formed by the progression of patterns of six stripes divided into two groups of three, some stripes broken, some solid. If you look closely at the arrangement of solid and broken stripes through the wheel, and take note of how with each successive hexagram, the grouping of broken lines migrates in distinctive "on/off" patterns from the inside to the outside of the wheel, you might discover something profound: An *I Ching* hexagram is a byte, albeit with six bits instead of eight, yet with the key "nybble" division in the middle that characterizes a byte. And the mystical actions these hexagrams perform on one another, translated into English as "fire over water" and "earth over wind," are in reality mathematical operations very similar to the Boolean arithmetic today used in all electronic computation. So while some Western scholars have dismissed this ornate symbology as mere mysticism, it may actually serve to explain why the ancient farmers, engineers, and stone masons were so adept at managing complex figures in their heads. They evidently had taken up rastering long before the English barbers did.

A variable represents a unit of memory

Tomorrow's esoteric mystic symbolism is busy at work today processing our business documents for us. All modern programming is an elaborate process of memory management. No matter how a programming language approaches the subject of producing information, from a mechanical perspective, its job is to instruct the processor to move memory contents and perform logical operations. The number of types of these logical operations is startlingly few, and the breadth of these operations is shockingly narrow. But the fact that a single processor can now manage literally trillions of permutations of these narrow operations, is why simple logical comparisons such as "this OR that" become the progenitors of elaborate processes such as Office 2000 and VBA.

The first BASIC language variables came in three flavors, and VBA carries on the legacy of these three traditional variable types:

- ♦ **An integer** is, simply put, a whole number.

- ♦ **A floating-point value** may have a fractional portion, expressed with digits following a decimal point; the term "floating-point" refers to the strategic method used to encode the placement of the decimal point within the value in memory.

- ♦ **A character string** is a sequence of one or more 8-bit ANSI symbols representing all the displayable characters in the system.

All of the Visual Basic-brand interpreters, including VBA, manage several different variable types, which are listed in Table 3-1.

VBA variables are declared by their first reference

It's a dirty little secret among us BASIC programmers, but the interpreter actually accepts a variable as a variable the first time it runs across that variable in an instruction. The interpreter knows that this new term must be a variable because, first of all, it's not a reserved word (one of the words used in VBA instructions or O2KOM terms), and secondly, because it's used in an instruction whose syntax designates that the term belonging in its position in the syntax should be a variable. So the interpreter *dynamically* declares the variable as a *variant*, which is defined in Table 3-1 below as the default "one-size-fits-all" variable type. When the interpreter sees the variable for the first time, it may or may not know what type of value it will represent, so it sets aside a larger chunk of memory than it normally would even for the average double-precision decimal value. This chunk of memory acts as a table of sorts that will help point the interpreter to the actual type of the variant's contents, whenever those contents are later referenced.

TABLE 3–1 VARIABLE DATA TYPES SUPPORTED BY VBA

Type keyword	Identifier character	Value range	Memory consumption	Description
Boolean	(none)	-1, 0	16 bits	Stores True/False values
Byte	(none)	0 – 255	8 bits	Identifies attributes or properties from a short, enumerated list
Integer	%	-32,768 – 32,767	16 bits	The most common whole number storage type
Long	&	-2,147,483,648 – 2,147,483,647	32 bits	Can enumerate large lists, such as attendees or total sold tickets
Currency	@	-922,337,203,685,477.5808 – 922,337,203,685,477.5808	64 bits	Perfect for monetary values, which may be fractional, though with low precision
Single	!	$-3.402823 \ 10^{38}$ – $-1.401298 \ 10^{-45}$, $1.401298 \ 10^{-45}$ – $3.402823 \ 10^{38}$	32 bits	The most common fractional data type
Double	#	$-1.79769313486232 \ 10^{308}$ – $-4.94065645841247 \ 10^{-324}$, $4.94065645841247 \ 10^{-324}$ – $1.79769313486232 \ 10^{308}$	64 bits	Usually reserved for scientific operations
Date	(none)	1 January, 100 – 31 December, 9999	64 bits	Represents a period in time, including hour, minute, and second
String	$	"" (null string) – (2 billion characters +)	10 bytes + length in characters	Represents character codes, words, passages, citations, without formatting
Variant	(none)	Dependent on content	16 bytes + value storage size, or 22 bytes + character length	The default variable type in VBA, few variables are ever purposefully declared As Variant

Listing 3-1 presents an example of dynamic declaration in the form of a small procedure. This procedure assumes you format your Word document using headings that contain the explicit text, "Section *x*," where *x* is a section number or letter.

Listing 3-1: Dynamic declaration of a unit string variable.

```
Public Sub FindSection()
    strResponse$ = InputBox("Find what section?", _
      "IDG Books Office 2000", "1")
    Selection.HomeKey Unit:=wdStory, Extend:=wdMove
    With Selection.Find
        .Text = "Section " & strResponse$
        .Forward = True
        If .Execute Then
            Beep
        End If
    End With
End Sub
```

This procedure doesn't take any arguments, which means that it doesn't receive any input values from the instruction that calls it. The procedure has been declared `Public` so that it shows up in Word's Macros dialog box. Yet without any declaration between the parentheses or thereafter, variable `strResponse$` still gets assigned the results of the `InputBox()` function, which displays a generic dialog box with the question, "Find what section?" and a text field at the bottom for entering a response. We could have used the statement `Dim strResponse$ As String`; but for these admittedly meager purposes, where the variable is only referenced twice anyway, such a formality would frankly be silly. It wouldn't affect the performance of the procedure in the slightest. Although the VBA manual and help system states that a variable declared dynamically is declared as a variant, **if you remember to write in the type identifier character, the interpreter will recognize the new variables not as variants but as the types they truly are.** The type identifiers in Listing 3-1 are $ for the string variable and % for the integer variable. For these purposes, dynamic declaration is just as good as explicit declaration. (By the way, because we used the type identifier character for strings $ in the name of the variable, we could have left off the `As String` portion of the declaration statement and gotten away with it.)

Is there a need to explicitly declare variable types?

The true purpose of stating variable types explicitly in declarations, or with type indicator characters at the end of variables' names, isn't always entirely clear with respect to BASIC programming. With the very first interpreters, only arrays (sequences of variables) were ever explicitly declared. As a result, unit variables were allowed to declare themselves whenever they were first used in an instruction, such as `50 P = 3.1415926` or `1290 X$ = "BYE"`. It wasn't that these first BASIC interpreters were breaking any rules. There simply weren't any rules yet on this matter to be broken. It was the pervasive influence of the C programming language (named, by the way, simply for the fact that it was the successor to "B") that started the trend in all programming toward explicit declaration.

The reason C is such a stickler about explicitness of types is that its variables are symbols for specific memory addresses, and nothing else. There's no extra baggage involved and no complex interpreter that generates memory blocks for data on the fly as in BASIC. When the C program is compiled, the memory contents *are* the values, with no representative symbols as their go-between. Visual Basic has become a truly compiled language like C; and while its descendent, VBA, is not yet a compiled language, it has to maintain that certain expected degree of compatibility with its parent in the product line. Although the way VBA addresses memory is somewhat more elaborate than C, the broader VBA programming methodology has benefited from what C and its successor C++ has taught us: A program is a digital form of a machine, and a machine works best when its parts are engineered to fit together, to maximize output, to distribute the workload, and to conserve its own energy.

The benefit of giving variables defined types is realized through the establishment of working rules for your VBA module. For explicitly declared variables that are given types, the interpreter employs *type checking* to make certain that no value assigned to a variable, or no value passed as an argument to a procedure, is of an incorrect type. But isn't type checking for correctness only significant when explicit type declaration is in effect — in other words, isn't this system self-serving? The answer, in a sense, is yes. You can, if you wish, construct an entire VBA module without any explicit type declaration for variables. When you're writing a simple single-procedure macro substitute, or a custom function procedure for Excel, omitting the explicit declarations is just a time-saver that doesn't really affect the performance of the final product to any noticeable extent. Also, even if you leave out the type identifier character, and the dynamically declared variable does start out life as a variant, **the type of a specific variant is automatically reset by the interpreter once the variant is assigned a value or a string.** If you assign an integral value to a variant, then that variant becomes an integer, albeit with several extra bytes of baggage in the storage department, retained from when the variable was a variant like skin not quite shed from a desert rattlesnake. A VBA procedure or module that requires explicit declaration is not required. (It wouldn't be BASIC if it were.)

But a program where explicit declaration is used and enforced conserves memory, and reduces the possibility of erroneous results. Plus, especially in an environment such as VBA where a multitude of object classes are employed over and above the existing variable types, it becomes important for procedures to distinguish objects used as arguments from variables. On the surface, it seems the distinction couldn't be clearer; one datum has constituents, has properties, recognizes its own events, and responds to its own method calls; whereas the other datum is 5 or $12.95 or "Hi, there." But those are the conceptual differences between objects and variables; in the computer, both take the form of stored data in memory, so it becomes important to be able to inform the interpreter of how it is to perform the job of interpretation. For this reason, declaring variables As Integer, As Boolean, and `As Single` becomes far more important now than it was back when all the BASIC program had to do was ask for input numbers, apply them to a formula, and chart the solution on 17-inch quadrille-line printer paper.

Distinguishing variable types for our own sake

For the extent of their careers, some of the finest programmers in the business – Dennis Ritchie, Bjarne Stroustrup, and P. J. Plauger among them – have written extensively about the need for programmers to produce code that was legible by human beings as well as by computers. Despite my admiration of their contributions to the art, I have gone on record stating that for amateur programmers, it is more important to produce computer-legible code than human-legible code – let matters of style come later.

Since then, I've written a few more applications in C++. In the midst of so doing, I've caught myself more than once referring to the writings of a certain Charles Simonyi, and I have to admit, I have given in. Simonyi developed what we in the software business, gifted with near-perfect hindsight, now consider the first truly integrated computer application, Multiplan. (He began developing it for Xerox PARC; but since Xerox didn't see the potential value in it – nor in PARC's other inventions, which include the mouse, the icon, the toolbar, and the help button – he ended up completing the product at Microsoft.) Multiplan's many integrated elements were so well-integrated with one another that most observers didn't even notice that they were separate components. Often cast aside as just another spreadsheet (which it wasn't), and repudiated for not fully mimicking Lotus' 1-2-3 (which it never tried to do in the first place), Multiplan included the first database manager that determined its own structure based on its own assessments of the data input by the user.

One of the virtues that Microsoft saw in Multiplan – as well as most anything else that Simonyi wrote – had to do not with the finished application as much as with the raw source code. Neither assembly languages nor C had any absolute method that enabled a programmer to ascertain, by looking at a variable in a function out of context, just what structure the variable has. In BASIC, whose string variables always ended with a $, there had begun a trend in the late 1970s to suffix integers with a % and floating-point variables with a #. But with C, you couldn't tell a pointer-to-character (the next best thing to a string) from a long integer without looking up the headers of the source code files; so Simonyi conceived a simple system for prefixing variables with letters that denoted their types. Thus names for pointers-to-character were prefixed with `pchr`, and names for global pointers to groups of such pointers were prefixed with `vbchrMac`. Problem was, it was up to Simonyi's associates at Microsoft to have to keep up with all these seemingly free-flowing prefixes. It had become an inside joke at Microsoft that Simonyi must be embedding choice words from his native Hungary into his code (indeed, some of his chosen abbreviations were from Hungarian when their English alternatives had already been used). In keeping with the good spirit of the joke, Simonyi claimed it for his own, and published internal documents that served as "dictionaries of Hungarian notation."

In Depth: Voluntary (and involuntary) type enforcement

When your VBA modules grow to become elaborate operations with multiple procedures that pass arguments between each other frequently, you may want to set up a situation where you have the interpreter enforce rigorous type checking for your own sake. For this reason, for Word, Excel, and PowerPoint, you can add this statement to the very front of your module's Declarations section:

```
Option Explicit
```

It's a very unassuming statement, whose syntax is exactly as you read it above and no other way. With this statement in your Declarations section, VBA will not execute a single instruction in a module whose variables have not yet been explicitly declared. Why is this a good thing? Before you run a program, the VBA interpreter checks all of your instructions using variables, to make certain they're phrased properly. With `Option Explicit` in place, the interpreter will also check to make sure that all your variables are *spelled* properly. The interpreter can't know what "properly" is unless you include instructions that specify the correct spelling. Your variable declarations can act as those specifications as long as you've written `Option Explicit` into your Declarations section. Otherwise, the interpreter will dynamically declare any misspelled variables it finds as separate variables, which will mess up your math.

Thus one of the most common programming practices – the use of Hungarian notation in giving titles to variables – became named for a country; and to this day, I can't use the term "Hungarian notation" in a book without my editors raising eyebrows. Yet the person who is indeed the cause for the name itself, accepts it as he should, as a badge of honor. Today, all of us who use Microsoft Word appreciate the beauty of the core textual processing engine that he designed, which still survives intact into the latest version. Simonyi remains a Senior Programmer at Microsoft.

A single suffix character may denote a variable's type

There are a number of ways to name a variable in VBA. You could declare an integer, for example, using the conventional BASIC notation that emerged in the 1970s:

```
Dim B%
```

Here, the variable takes the nomenclature that was prominent around 1978. It is a single letter, capitalized, with a type identifier % to denote that the term is an integer. Now, if you really wanted to be old-fashioned, you wouldn't use the Dim statement at all to declare this unit variable; you could just assign to it an initial value:

```
B% = 100
```

and the interpreter, upon seeing B% for the first time, would conclude on its own that it was a variable, enroll it as such dynamically, and assign to it the appropriately integral value 100. VBA allows this old method and puts up with some of its eccentricities. For instance, the % part, although it serves to identify a variable's type, is not considered part of the variable's name. So if B% = 100, then the value of B *without* the % is also 100. Furthermore, because **VBA variable names are not case sensitive,** the value of b and of b% would also be 100. Any ideas that you may have had about employing the same algebraic variables as your favorite physicists — for instance, the way Erwin Schrödinger used *t* for time and *T* for temperature — flies out the window along with his cat.

The way Microsoft suggests that you declare variables is by naming them using words that give some clue to you, or any other human reader, as to their meaning — even if you have to use abbreviations to go about it. Their suggested declaration method looks something more like this:

```
Dim bushels As Integer
```

Part of the recommendation is that you use a lower-case letter as the first character of the variable so that object names, whose initial letters are generally capitalized, stand out as objects. (A digit or punctuation may not begin a variable, although both may be used in successive positions.) But here, Hungarian notation can help further by identifying the type of the variable *for your purposes.* So using some of the accepted notation, the declaration looks more like this:

```
Dim iBushels As Integer
```

This way, when you write an assignment expression such as this:

```
iBushels = 100
```

the initial lower-case i reminds you, as you write it as well as afterward, that the variable is an integer. This may become important when you assign to this variable the result of a long mathematical expression. If the expression yields a fractional value, and you assign that to the integer variable, your instruction won't generate an error. Instead, the interpreter will round the value to the nearest integer before assigning that to the integer variable. Perhaps that may be what you want, but you won't know for sure unless you know precisely what's going on — and that is what the little i reminds you of.

There is no absolute consensus on the content of Hungarian notation—even Microsoft's and Simonyi's versions tend to differ. Table 3-2 below shows the notation I use in my own work, and that appears throughout this book.

TABLE 3-2 HUNGARIAN NOTATION CONVENTIONS USED IN THIS BOOK

Type keyword	"Hungarian" prefix
Boolean	b-
Byte	by-
Integer	i-
Long	l-
Currency	cur-
Single	s-
Double	d-
Date	dat-
String	str-
Variant	v-

On Point

The VBA interpreter actually declares a variable the first time it encounters that variable in the source code. Formal declaration of variables with exclusive statements like Dim are not required, although this practice becomes more convenient and relatively necessary as the complexity of the VBA project grows. Formal declaration is necessary in order to set the scope of a variable to something broader than procedure-level or "local" scope. In the absence of formal declaration, the interpreter can dynamically declare a variable the first time that variable is used in an expression.

During formal declaration, a variable's type or object class may be stated explicitly using the As modifier of the declaration statement. For dynamic declaration, the type of a variable may be set using a type identifier character at the end of the variable name. Although not formalized or in any way required, Hungarian notation is a practice among programmers that proves to be a convenience in cases where many variables are in use, and the programmer or other human reader needs some indication of each variable's declared type. This notation uses an abbreviation prefix, often of the programmer's own choice, in all lowercase, prior to the actual name of the variable, whose initial letter is then capitalized.

The variant type is the default type for VBA variables; if a variable is declared explicitly or dynamically, and a type is not stated for it, then the interpreter gives it the variant type. With variants, the actual variable type is determined when it is first assigned data contents.

The next segment deals with the concept of arrays, which are VBA's way to concatenate data being represented by the same type of variable. In order that you may distinguish between an array and a collection, please review our discussion of collections in the context of Office 2000 globals in Chapter 2.

Variables As Sequences or Tables

In Chapter 2, we glossed over the use of the `Dim` statement to declare *arrays*, or sets and tables of variables with the same group name and the same type. Traditionally in Visual Basic programming, arrays have been used to house small, temporary databases in memory. A set of several linear or one-dimensional arrays, each of which have an identical number of units, could be used to support a record-style database. In this simple schema, a single numeral could be employed as an index for all of the arrays, so that the index serves as a *de facto* subscript for the entire record. Figure 3-1 depicts this mechanism.

Here, the arrays are depicted as vertical stacks of equal length. The *de facto* record is represented as the horizontal bar; changing the single array index moves this "bar" and reveals a new record. So `strFirstName(423)`, `strLastName(423)`, `strMiddleInit(423)`, and `strStreetAddress(423)` would all obviously be members of the same record. You could process this in-memory database using a `For...Next` loop clause that counts from 1 to the total number of records in the stack, then you could employ that count as a variable x for addressing each record within the clause, as in `strLastName(x)`. Granted, this is not how you manage a database when you're programming an Access module; but this process makes a reliable short-term method in a pinch.

Arrays can also be used for completely different types of symbology that have little or nothing to do with common record-style databases. I've programmed many board games using an eight-by-eight chessboard, and a two-dimensional integer array such as `board(x%, y%)`, whose values are symbolic of which pieces are sitting on the squares. Say a white king is symbolized as a 1. For an opening position, I would assign the king to his opening square:

```
board(5, 8) = 1
```

where `board(1, 1)` is the square in the upper-left corner, where a black rook sits at opening position. The coordinate system used here counts squares across (rank) first, squares down (file) second. Obviously, this type of symbology doesn't exist in O2KOM, which is in a sense why we have VBA. You can construct symbology that hasn't previously existed.

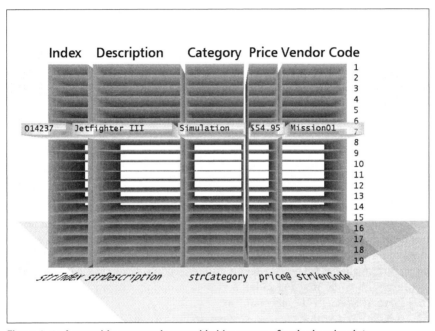

Figure 3-1: A record in memory is assembled by means of a single subscript.

Object arrays versus collections

One way of working with a series of objects of the same class is to declare an array whose type is set to that class. You could, for instance, declare a series of documents using the statement `Dim docSeries() As Document`, where the missing subscript between the parentheses would be filled in later by a `ReDim` statement (whose purpose I'll explain later in this chapter). But declaring arrays of O2KOM objects is generally unnecessary. Collections for most important classes of objects are already part of O2KOM, and their mode of address is the same as for arrays. For Word 2000, `Documents(1)` represents the earliest open document in the sequence; and through a trick of property addressing, `Documents(Documents.Count)` represents the most recent document. So `Documents(Documents.Count).Name` represents the filename of the most recently opened file because `Documents.Count` represents the number of open documents, and new documents are added to the collection in the order that the user opens them.

If you were to use a conventional VBA array instead, you would first declare the array using a statement such as `Dim docArray(Documents.Count)`. Notice we still need to refer to the collection property `Documents.Count` to find out just how many open documents there are. Next, we would set each member of `docArray()` to point to each individual member of the `Documents` collection; so obviously declaring the array in the first place is redundant.

Redundant, yes, but could there be a case where such redundancy is necessary? You already know that an O2KOM collection such as `Documents` or `Worksheets` cannot be directly manipulated; most of its properties are *read-only*, which means that you can check or *poll* its values but you cannot change them. But a VBA array is yours to tinker with; the order of members in the array, the settings of shadow properties you create for your array — all of this is yours to design. Give you any ideas yet? Suppose you needed a list of the names of open Word documents, not just in the order in which they were opened (which is the natural order of the `Documents` collection, and cannot be changed through VBA code), but instead *sorted alphabetically.*

Organizing an array around a collection

In Chapter 2, we demonstrated an example where a list of open Word documents was placed in an ActiveX list box in a `UserForm` container. The list of open documents' names was taken directly from the `Documents` collection; so the order in the list was exactly the order in the collection, and that is the order in which the documents were brought onto the Windows Desktop, or the same order that the documents are listed in Word 2000's Window menu. In Listing 3-2, we've rewritten this example so that the list contents are alphabetically sorted — or, more accurately, sorted by order of ANSI characters, where digits precede letters.

Listing 3-2: Building a shadow array around the Documents collection.

```
Private Sub UserForm_Activate()
    Dim strDocName() As String, x As Integer

    ReDim strDocName(Documents.Count)
    For x = 1 To Documents.Count
        strDocName(x) = Documents(x).Name
    Next x

    BubbleSort strDocName()

    For x = 1 To Documents.Count
        lstTitleList.AddItem strDocName(x)
    Next x
End Sub
```

This procedure is triggered whenever the form is called into the workspace, so it is dependent on some other procedure to provide the trigger. If you compar this rendition to Listing 2-2 in the previous chapter, you'll notice that it's somewhat busier, and that the Document class reference is missing. In its place is a simple string array; but in the first instruction, the length of this array is also missing. This is because we require the procedure to find out for itself how long to make the array. The Dim statement normally requires a *constant* for its array length. Although VBA officially considers Dim a statement, it is actually a definition rather than an active instruction – it sets the stage for the active instructions that come *later* in the procedure. As a result, Dim cannot set up an array based on an indefinite length, or a length determined by the result of an expression – to do so would require an active instruction, which Dim is not. So we declared strDocName()without any definite length at first as a *dynamic array*. We later invoked the ReDim statement to set the length of strDocName() to the same number of units as there are documents in the collection – which is determined by Documents.Count.

The For...Next loop clause is a control structure that counts by one, from 1 to the number of documents, and it keeps track of that count within the variable x. The variable is then used as a uniform index for both the strDocName() array and the Documents collection; the array becomes a mirror of the .Name properties stored in the collection. The objective here is to sort this array because we cannot sort the collection. We can look into the array, but we can't manipulate the order of documents in the Documents collection without shutting down some documents and reloading them – which is way too much hassle for just a simple sorted list.

An algorithm is used to sort array elements

BubbleSort is not a keyword, but a procedure call we've written exclusively to handle the sorting of this short list. It uses the common BubbleSort algorithm, respected in the programming community for handling short lists. The single argument passed to the procedure Private Sub BubbleSort() is the array strDocName(). It hasn't been for very long in the history of Visual Basic that we've been able to pass an array as a parameter, especially a dynamic one. The sorting procedure picks up the array and, once it's finished, the array is properly sorted. The second For...Next loop then takes the names in the sorted list and one by one places them in the list box control named lstTitleList.

The BubbleSort procedure is, while small, quite complex, although it is a brilliant example of the proper use of arrays in BASIC programming. (I can write "brilliant" without appearing egotistical because I didn't invent this algorithm myself.) Listing 3-3 shows the procedure:

Listing 3-3: A simple form of the most common sort algorithm for short arrays.

```
Private Sub BubbleSort(strArray() As String)
    Dim j As Integer, k As Integer, l As Integer, n As Integer, t$

    n = UBound(strArray)
```

```
    For l = 1 To n
        j = l
        For k = j + 1 To n
            If strArray(k) <= strArray(j) Then
                j = k
            End If
        Next k
        If l <> j Then
            t$ = strArray(j)
            strArray(j) = strArray(l)
            strArray(l) = t$
        End If
    Next l
End Sub
```

To keep this procedure looking simple, I've retained its classical single-letter variables, with the exception of `strArray()`. This is the array whose contents will be sorted. Wait a minute, what happened to `strDocName()`? This is the same array, except that for the purposes of `Private Sub BubbleSort()`, it's called `strArray()`. The variable name of a received argument does not have to be the same name as that used by the procedure call. Why? Because several procedures elsewhere in the module might like to make use of this sorting procedure, especially if they're sorting different arrays from one another. Whatever name an array uses outside the scope of this procedure, `strArray()` is the name given to it when it's received as an argument. This is a separate variable, operating on a separate copy of the array data; though once the procedure successfully concludes, the results of `strArray()` being sorted are automatically reflected in `strDocName()` outside the sorting procedure. This is the standard mode of operation for VBA procedures: **Changes made to arguments are reflected in the variables used to pass those arguments.** However, it is not the way all argument passing has to work, as you'll see.

To explain what is happening in this sorting procedure is a bit complex, especially when all of our terms haven't been defined yet. I will define those terms over the course of the chapter; and as I do, I'll come back to this procedure to show you these new principles in practice. In short, here is how the procedure does its job: When the procedure begins, the array `strArray()` is considered unsorted. Variables j, k, and l are indexes for items belonging to the array. Variable l is a partition that sweeps gradually from the beginning to the end of the array, leaving everything in its wake sorted. As l proceeds, k sweeps faster from wherever l is now to the end of the array, searching for text that belongs earlier in the array — or, from its point of view, for "lower values." When k finds one, it hands that index over to j and moves on. By the time k has reached the end of the array, it should have the lowest (earliest) known value it's ever seen, so that value is swapped with the one pointed to by l, the slower-moving sweeper. Variable l moves to the next position, and the whole process starts over again, until l runs out of array in which to move.

The procedure can ascertain "value" with respect to textual strings by assuming that, for instance, "b" is "lesser than" "n," and "z" is "greater than" "n." With these assumptions in place, it becomes as easy for a VBA procedure to sort text as it is for it to sort numbers.

We'll come back to the BubbleSort procedure from time to time. This may be your first example of an algorithmic process. It's a part of programming that isn't taught much anymore, because many programming environments offer their own algorithm libraries for jobs such as complex sorts and binary searches. But quite a bit of real-world programming involves algorithms such as BubbleSort – if you're not crafting your own, perhaps you're adapting one to your own purposes. Even in the latter case, it helps for you to understand what's going on in an algorithm procedure. In this one, there are a lot of expressions, both of comparison and of assignment; as this chapter proceeds, I'll show you how they both work.

When the list is sorted and on the screen, we have a new problem: The index number of the items in the list box control no longer correspond to the index number of the Documents collection, and we still need to address the collection to tell it what document to bring up. Listing 3-4 shows our solution, which involves polling the collection's contents.

Listing 3-4: Re-associating the list box's filenames with the Documents collection's names.

```
Private Sub lstTitleList_DblClick(ByVal Cancel _
   As MSForms.ReturnBoolean)
     Dim docThisDoc As Document

     For Each docThisDoc In Documents
         If lstTitleList.List(lstTitleList.ListIndex) _
           = docThisDoc.Name Then
             docThisDoc.Activate
         End If
     Next
     Unload UserForm1
End Sub
```

Here, we're using the same method as in Listing 2-2 for declaring a pointer document docThisDoc, and then having it run through each document in the collection using a For Each...Next loop. The embedded If...Then clause checks to see if the text of the list box item the user double-clicked on (the text being the .List property whose subscript is given its own .ListIndex property) is equivalent to the name of the document currently being perused by the loop clause. There's no fancy algorithm to this process; since Documents is unsorted, it can only look through each document name in the collection, starting at the top. When a match is found, then the .Activate method for the found document brings it to the fore, and the form (dialog box) is unloaded from memory.

Variables As Words or Text

The string variable has been an integral part of all BASIC languages since its origin. Assigning text to a variable, using an expression like `strName$ = "Word 2000"`, might seem a bit awkward to the mathematically trained eye. As a programmer, you must consider variables as symbols for memory contents, not as representatives of observed statistics or empirical data.

How strings represent "raw" text

When we say that a string represents text, we're referring to a far more crude mode of representation than that used by `Word.Application.ActiveDocument.Paragraph(1)`. A string variable represents no formatting, no fonts, no embedded fields or hyperlinks. Instead, it contains just a chain of characters.

The most "raw" representation of characters in Windows is called the ANSI code, after the American National Standards Institute. The Institute adopted the original 7-bit form of this code, called ASCII (pronounced *as'-key* and standing for the American Standard Code for Information Interchange), and then found a purpose for the eighth bit to round out the byte. The ANSI code uses an 8-bit (1-byte) pattern to represent each typeable, displayable character in Windows. Each pattern translates into a decimal (base-10) value, but the code itself was designed to symbolize characters using binary (base-2) values. Table 3-2 illustrates how the ANSI code represents the base-2 *bitwise* pattern for the word "Visual."

TABLE **3–2** THE CHARACTER STRING FOR "VISUAL," STRUNG OUT IN ANSI

Character	ANSI Decimal	ANSI Binary
V	86	01010110
l	105	01101001
s	115	01110011
u	117	01110101
a	97	01100001
l	108	01101100

When you make an assignment expression like `c$ = "Visual"`, you're really telling the VBA interpreter to load six bytes (the length of the string) with the values in Table 3-2, and to treat those values not as numeric data but as codes for characters. It's important that the interpreter make this distinction, otherwise it could confuse the memory region that holds the characters `Vi` for the integer value `-26966`, which uses the same bitwise pattern as shown in the right column above for those two characters.

Expressions of assignment using strings

String-based textual storage is unsophisticated. As such, you cannot expect a string variable to hold the contents of a Word document, and then be able to spill those contents onto a fresh Word page and have them appear properly formatted. The purposes of Word textual objects and VBA strings are altogether different from one another.

However, the text-based properties of ActiveX controls, such as text fields and drop-down list boxes, are of the same type as VBA string variables. You could therefore use an instruction such as this:

```
strChoice$ = lstSelection.List(lstSelection.ListIndex)
```

to assign the textual contents of the item in a list box `lstSelection` that the user has just chosen, to a string variable `strChoice$`. There is no type mismatch in this case, for the `.List` property of a text box control uses the same raw text as a string variable. In fact, **the current settings for all textual properties of ActiveX controls and O2KOM objects may be assigned to string variables.** In turn, those properties may be assigned the contents of string variables, if those properties are not *read-only*; in other words, if they allow "writes." The `.Name` property for Excel 2000's `ActiveWorkbook` global object, for instance, cannot be assigned the contents of a string, not because the property and the string are incompatible, but because the object designers deemed it prudent that only the user be capable of changing the filename of an open document.

Here's another example that assigns the contents of an ActiveX text box control to a variable:

```
strLastName = txtLastName.Text
```

The `.Text` term is common to most ActiveX controls and refers to their textual contents. What's the purpose of making this type of assignment? The main purpose is so that a procedure may have a reliable "collection agent." Variable `strLastName` can "absorb" the textual contents of the ActiveX control *at the time the instruction referring to it is being executed.* If the user changes the text box's contents, `strLastName` remains the same. (In VBA, there are no formal "pointer" variables like in C or C++.) Later on in the module, the assignment can easily work in reverse; after `strLastName` has been doctored or corrected, its changed setting can be written right back to the text box control, by just reversing the order of terms:

```
txtLastName.Text = strLastName
```

A **string variable is a tool for the manipulation of characters.** The last two assignment expressions are examples of what might take place at the beginning and the end, respectively, of this manipulation process. In between, you may be applying VBA intrinsic functions or performing other operations on the string. For instance, you might want to remove any leading spaces from the beginning of the string, with a function instruction like this:

```
strLastName = LTrim$(strLastName)
```

With an assignment expression, the result of all the operations and functions stated on the right side of the equation, are assigned to the single variable on the left side of the equation. This holds true even in cases like the instruction above, where `strLastName` is being assigned another form of itself. As long as the symbol on the left is valid, VBA will accept the assignment. So the above assignment is truly telling VBA to replace the current contents of `strLastName` with a copy of it that doesn't start off with any space characters. `LTrim$()` is one of VBA's intrinsic functions.

Listing 3-2 showed you earlier how a string array could be used in a very sophisticated process to mirror the `.Name` properties of a `Documents` collection, and then sort those property settings so they could be presented to the user in some kind of order. Even though that process was relatively sophisticated, the same order of three events held true: initial assignment, logical operation, result rendering. This particular process did not represent the objective of the entire VBA program, though it was an important dependent process.

In Depth: Of prefixes, suffixes, and neither

You may be wondering at this point, "Do I use the $ *with* the `str` prefix, or leave one or the other out, or what?" Both the `str` prefix (which was attached to many of the previous example variables) and the $ type identifier character at the end, are optional. The VBA interpreter doesn't recognize the `str` prefix formally as having any meaning at all; it's simply a bit of common Hungarian notation, for the express purpose of the human reader of the source code. The interpreter does recognize, however, the $ character as an exclusive indicator of the variable's `String` type. If you were to simply declare a string with `Dim s$`, the interpreter would recognize `s$` as a string and not a variant. This is a good thing. So the type identifier may be of greater overall use than the Hungarian prefix. But you could also declare `Dim strName As String` without the identifier, and let the prefix serve to remind you of the variable's `String` (non-`Variant`) type. Or you could forget both and declare `Dim s As String`, though it might be more difficult in such an instance for you to recall whether `s` is your string and `b` your double-precision decimal.

The Mechanism of Mathematical Expressions

The major similarity between variables in a computer program and variables in a scientific treatise is the fact that they're both called "variables." With VBA you have to break the habit of thinking of a variable only in the context of a formula. VBA equation instructions are not formulas. A formula in math symbolizes a balance between the expression on the left side of the equality sign and the expression on the right.

Expressions stand for real values or real data

In scientific math, a formula expresses a relationship or proportion between observable elements. However, a formula does not necessarily solve a problem at hand in terms of real values. $E = mc^2$, for instance – perhaps the most famous formula in the world – expresses a relationship between three observable elements of physics: energy, mass, and light. Given a real value for one, if not two, quantities of these elements, you might be able to solve for the rest.

But a VBA equation is not a formula. (I used to call Visual Basic equations "formulas" myself, and got into trouble for it. So I've learned my lesson, and intend to teach it here.) Unlike a scientific formula, a VBA equation, or an *expression of assignment*, utilizes terms that, to the right of the equality operator, stand for real values. For instance, if the interpreter were to see an instruction like this:

```
E = m * c ^ 2
```

there would need to be real values represented by variables m and c, which are brought together in the assignment expression above to arrive at a true value for E. Variable E does not yet have to have a value; in fact, it doesn't even need to be declared. But m and c do require declaration, if only dynamically during the course of another expression of assignment earlier in the module. So the purpose of this particular expression is not to express a relationship, but to find something to assign to E. In other words, if E already had a value, then it would not in turn solve for m and c. Whatever value is already in E will be replaced with the solution to m * c ^ 2. If m and c are uninitialized (i.e., they equal 0), then when E = m * c ^ 2 is evaluated, E too, Bruté, will equal 0.

The operators used to build expressions

The example above is probably not practical for anything other than to demonstrate the difference between a VBA expression and a formula. To do the concept of the expression some justice, I should formally define it:

An expression is a combination of at least one datum (value, variable, object), and any number of operators, which, when evaluated by the interpreter, yields a real — not a symbolic — result. You may recall from Chapter 1 that an expression *evaluates* to a result. In an expression of assignment, that result can be given to a variable, stated to the left of the = operator. Whatever value is currently represented by that variable will be overwritten.

The same variable may be used on both sides of an expression of assignment. For example:

```
i = i + 1
```

Obviously, as a real world formula, this would not be valid at all. It would not, to use the algebra term, "solve for" i. As a VBA expression of assignment, though, it works perfectly well: The value 1 is added to whatever i currently evaluates to, and the result is stored back in variable i. In a sense, the right side of this expression is the "before" side, and the left side represents "after." (This adding of 1 to things is what we frequently call *incrementation*, out of the need to give simple processes five-syllable names.)

In an interesting sense, expressions with equality operators can themselves evaluate to real values. The conditional clause If...Then (which I'll profile in the Chapter 4) expects to receive an *expression of comparison*, whose real value is either True or False. The If...Then statement needs a True value in order for the instruction that follows it to be executed. So although i = i + 1 as an expression of comparison would evaluate False in all cases (it's a logical impossibility that a variable could equal itself plus one), other similar-looking expressions where the same variable does not appear on both sides of the operator, can be used in expressions of comparison.

For example, if a procedure receives an argument that you've determined in advance to be too high, you could have it trimmed to a maximum value using a conditional clause that utilizes an expression of comparison, like this:

```
If sFuel > 14000 Then
    sFuel = 14000
End If
```

The If...Then statement contains the expression of comparison, sFuel > 14000, which can evaluate to either True or False. The interpreter needs a True value for the expression of assignment sFuel = 14000 to be executed; otherwise, it will be skipped over. There are several more examples of conditional clauses in Chapter 4.

Expressions of comparison tend to contain other expressions, but only on the right side of the comparison operator. On the left side is a single variable — not a literal value or a string, but a variable. Assuming you have real values for m and c, you could phrase a comparison E = m * c ^ 2, and in an If...Then statement like the one above, it could evaluate to either True or False.

All of the operators used by VBA in building expressions are listed below in Table 3-3:

TABLE 3-3 VBA OPERATORS

Operator	Category	Description
=	Assignment	**Comparison Equality.** Used in expressions of assignment to render a result value and assign it to a variable, and in expressions of comparison that yield a True/False result if the solution to the expression to its right equates with the variable to its left.
<	Comparison	**Lesser than.** Used in expressions of comparison to determine whether the value of the variable to its left is lesser than the expression to its right.
>	Comparison	**Greater than.** Used in expressions of comparison to determine whether the value of the variable to its left is greater than the expression to its right.
<=	Comparison	**Lesser than or equal to.** Used in expressions of comparison to determine whether the value of the variable to its left is lesser than or equal to the expression to its right.
>=	Comparison	**Greater than or equal to.** Used in expressions of comparison to determine whether the value of the variable to its left is greater than or equal to the expression to its right.
<>	Comparison	**Not equal to.** Yields a True result if the expression to its right does not equate with the expression to its left.
+	Arithmetic	**Addition.** Adds the value of the expression to its right to the value of the expression to its left. Also, the + operator can be used in textual operations, to join the string to its right to the string to its left. (The & operator may also be used for joining strings.)
-	Arithmetic	**Subtraction.** Subtracts the value of the expression to its right from the value of the expression to its left.
*	Arithmetic	**Multiplication.** Yields the product of the value of the expression to its left and the value of the expression to its right.

Operator	Category	Description
/	Arithmetic	**Division.** Divides the value of the expression to its left by the value of the expression to its right, and yields a precise result.
\	Arithmetic	**Integer division.** Divides the value of the expression to its left by the expression to its right, and yields only the integer portion of the result, without any fractional or remainder portion.
Mod	Arithmetic	**Modulo division.** Divides the value of the expression to its left by the expression to its right, and yields *only* the remainder portion. For instance, to determine what hour it would be on the clock 38 hours past 2 o'clock, you would use this instruction: `hour% = (2 + 38) Mod 12`
^	Arithmetic	**Exponentiation.** Raises the value of the expression to its left to the power of the value of the expression to its right.
-	Arithmetic	**Negation.** Negates the value of the expression to its right. For example, if `iAccum` is equal to 38, then `-iAccum` results in –38.
&	Textual	**Concatenation.** Joins the character string to its right with the character string to its left. (May be rejected in certain circumstances with Excel, where & is used in cell addressing.)
Like	Textual	**Similarity.** Yields a `True` result if the string to its left bears resemblance to the string to its right.
Is	Object-oriented	**Correlation.** Yields a `True` result if the object term to its left refers to the same object as the term to its right.
And	Logical	Yields a `True` result if the expression to its left and the expression to its right both evaluate to `True`.
Or	Logical	Yields a `True` result if either the expression to its left or the expression to its right, or both, evaluate to `True`.
Xor	Logical	Yields a `True` result if either the expression to its left or the expression to its right, *but not both*, evaluate to `True`.

Continued

TABLE 3-3 VBA OPERATORS *(Continued)*

Operator	Category	Description
Not	Logical	Reverses the logical result of the expression to its right.
Eqv	Logical	Yields a True result if the expression to its left evaluates to the same True/False value as the expression to its right.

Assessing the order of evaluation

The VBA interpreter does not evaluate every expression it sees from left to right. Instead, it picks out certain preferred operators and works with the terms to either side of them first. The reason for this is to coincide with the rules of real-world algebra, which also isn't exactly a left-to-right affair. Table 3-4 lists the precedence of operators in an arithmetic expression:

TABLE 3-4 ARITHMETIC OPERATORS' ORDER OF PRECEDENCE

	Operator(s)	Purpose
1.	^	Exponentiation
2.	–	Negation
3.	*	Multiplication
	/	Division
4.	\	Integer division
5.	Mod	Modulo division
6.	+	Addition
	–	Subtraction

The reason that exponentiation comes first is due to our expectation that VBA have *some* bearing upon real-world algebra. The algebraic value x^2 is considered a whole, single term — as whole as x alone — and xy is considered one term in many kinds of equations. Not even the novice to algebra considers $-x$ to be two terms and x one term. So because we expect exponentialized, multiplied, negated, and divided

(1/2, 3/8, etc.) terms to be whole, the VBA interpreter handles the operators upon which those terms depend, first and foremost. The algebraic expression $x + y$ is clearly made up of two terms and one operator; because VBA makes expressions with combining operators look similar to expressions with separating operators, VBA treats these operators the way we expect them to be treated in an algebraic setting.

Parentheses alter the order of an expression's evaluation

As in algebra, the order in which terms are evaluated is changed through the use of parentheses to designate the terms that should take precedence. A real-world example I like to cite involves the commonly used formula for depreciation of an asset, necessary for figuring out the personal income tax returns of many citizens. As I stated earlier, a VBA expression is not a formula. However, a formula can be used as the model for an expression of assignment. Here is a valid VBA `Function` procedure that yields a dollar amount of depreciation, given a set number of depreciation periods and a fixed rate:

```
Function DepAmount(curInitValue As Currency, curPriorDep _
   As Currency, sngFactor As Single, iLifeOfAsset As Integer) _
   As Currency
     DepAmount = ((curInitValue - curPriorDep) * sngFactor) / _
       iLifeOfAsset
End Function
```

Had we not used parentheses in the assignment for `DepAmount`, the portion `curPriorDep * sngFactor` would have evaluated first, with the result being divided by `iLifeOfAsset` and then subtracted from `curInitValue`. This would be entirely wrong. For the formula to work, the subtraction must take place first. So in the three tiers of parentheses created by this expression, the tightest and furthest "inside" gets evaluated first. In this case, that's the subtraction, the result of which gets multiplied, and the result of that gets divided. The result is a dollar amount that represents how much an asset gets devaluated for one period, given `iLifeOfAsset` number of periods. This result is assigned to `DepAmount` and passed back to the instruction that placed a call to this function. You'll see how `Function` procedures work in depth later in this chapter.

The Pythagorean Theorem, which predates VBA by quite some time (and whose patent holder is, unfortunately for Microsoft, unavailable to take calls), states the relationship in length between the hypotenuse of a right triangle and the lengths of its two adjacent sides. In the algebraic form of the equation, parentheses are not necessary to change the order of operation:

```
c = √a² + b²
```

On Point

An array variable represents a list, sequence, or table of data elements of the same type. A standard list is described as a "one-dimensional array," and employs an index numeral or subscript as an exclusive identifier of which element in the list is being addressed. A table of data, employing rows or columns, can be stored in a two-dimensional array, where two subscripts are employed.

An expression in VBA is a combination of one or more values, or symbols for values or data, combined with any number of operators that perform mathematical or other functions on that data, to produce a single real result. By "real result," we don't mean a symbol for a possible result, or a variable name, but something tangible to the interpreter, such as a numeral value, character string, or object reference.

A VBA expression is not a formula because it is not designed to characterize relationships between observed elements. Instead, its purpose is to calculate real results and assign those results to a single variable. Operators are symbols, ranging from one to three characters in length, which perform functions on the data or variables to either side of them in an expression.

VBA recognizes a natural order of execution, or precedence, among operators in order to meet the expectations of programmers trained in algebraic notation. As a result, the interpreter does not execute arithmetic functions as they are written from left to right, because some operators in the middle may take precedent. To alter the order in which an expression's operators are executed, parentheses may be used to enclose the data and operators whose functional order should take precedent over the others.

For the VBA version of the equation, parentheses aren't necessary to the expression portion:

```
c = Sqr(a ^ 2 + b ^ 2)
```

The parentheses that do appear here are for the sake of the `Sqr()` square root function. Here, the expression `a ^ 2 + b ^ 2` evaluates to a real, single value, which is passed to the `Sqr()` function as its single argument. The results of that VBA intrinsic function are then assigned to `c`.

Building a Procedure-Based Program

What makes a complex VBA module work well is how it delegates its workload among multiple procedures. I've stated up to this point that a module is made up of procedures, but I haven't really focused yet on *why*.

Computer programs no longer run like scrolls from front to back. Instead, they spend a majority of their processing time waiting for the user to do something. When the user finally does do something, this triggers an *event* in the program, to which it responds by executing code designed to handle that event. The majority of processor time for today's programs is spent in repetitive, nonproductive cycles, waiting for the user to do something. But this architecture is necessary precisely because processors have become so fast. The alternative would be for a computer to run a true *program* in the original sense of the word – a massive series of steps where user and computer exchange prompts and data in a predefined sequence, not unlike a NASA checklist for a space shuttle launch.

In NASA terminology, "the next event" is generally a prescribed activity that takes place at a certain point on the clock, is estimated to last for only so long, and involves a predetermined exchange of data. NASA's checklists work, because, for astronauts escaping the bounds of Earth's gravity, *anything can happen*, and it is up to the astronauts to know in advance precisely how to respond – what program to engage for a certain event. In modern Windows applications (which are surprisingly no less sophisticated than some NASA checklists I've read), the tables are turned, and it is the computer that is responding to the event coming from the user. From the perspective of the computer application, *anything can happen*, and it is up to the program to know how to respond. For this reason, among others, procedures are segmented and modular.

Why we have procedures in the first place

The original purpose for procedures in the BASIC language (at first, they were called "subroutines") was to gather instructions together that needed to be executed repetitively. This is still a valid reason to use procedures in Visual Basic and VBA; yet the other reason – which is certainly more important – is that you really have no choice. All VBA instructions are executed from within procedures.

Generally, there's little point in touting the benefits of adopting a principle when one is faced with no other readily available choice – case in point, Russia, communism, 1917.. On the other hand, if a principle is something we have to live with, we might as well find the time to seek the sensibility in it. Procedures were developed more for the programmer's benefit than for the computer's. Although dozens of programmers and programming languages lay claim to the invention, it was probably Prof. Niklaus Wirth who gave life to the modern concept of procedures in the Pascal programming language that he invented.

Visual Basic and VBA uses the term "procedure" to mean what Prof. Wirth refers to as a "module" and what C/C++ programmers refer to as a "function." However you choose to refer to it, the concept is still very much the same. There are two key purposes for procedures: First of all, they give programmers a mechanism for tackling the greater programming problem in smaller, bite-size chunks. A program can be made to work piece-by-piece; if one part fails, it doesn't take down the entire structure of the program. Secondly, procedural construction adds something to the art of programming borrowed from the science of mathematics. A **procedure** becomes a symbol for a function, such that writing the symbol within an expression is as good as having written the entire body of the function.

As you'll see later in this chapter, VBA's implementation of this principle of symbolism is actually a bit more difficult than that of C and C++, although it is not altogether insensible. To begin with, let's examine a highly simplified example of the VBA procedure concept. We want you to get a clear idea of the *concept* of procedures first, before we go on to deal explicitly with their syntax.

Why procedures have penetrable boundaries

Assume for the sake of this example that the VBA program you are writing is for Word 2000. From time to time, your program will need to record several passages of text with information based on named sources catalogued elsewhere in the document, like a bibliography. The act of recording these textual passages may not be the primary purpose of your program, although this is one of the jobs it will need to perform from time to time. One way to have your VBA program go about this task would be to write a procedure whose sole and exclusive job is to add a text passage to the ongoing array. This procedure might have a name written like this:

```
Private Sub CatalogPassage()
```

The term `Private` in this context means, only the program can see it; the user cannot. Meanwhile, the term `Sub` identifies `CatalogPassage()` as the name of the procedure. The term is a throwback to the days when procedures in BASIC were "subroutines." Nowadays, VBA procedures are not necessarily subordinate to anything; in fact, the startup procedure of a large program is generally marked with `Sub`.

A procedure named like this might be able to ascertain the text that it's supposed to record by looking at whatever the user has indicated with the cursor at the time. It might have to go that route because the procedure is receiving no data explicitly from the rest of the program to help it out. Variables that a procedure generates and uses for its own purposes generally belong exclusively to that procedure, and are discarded once it stops execution. Keep that in mind for a moment. When an instruction outside the procedure requests that VBA move execution to a named procedure, we say that it *calls* that procedure. Thus, the name we use for that type of instruction is a *procedure call*, or simply "call." (In fact, VBA does support the `Call` keyword, though because it uses an arcane syntax, few choose to use it in everyday work, including this author.) When a procedure call takes place, the execution of the VBA program, in a figurative sense, exits one world and resumes inside another. This is because the procedure where the call is contained generally maintains its own exclusive variables, which are not in play once execution resumes inside the procedure that was called. Each procedure has its own exclusive definition of "the world" or, to speak less in hyperbole, the problem at hand. Usually when VBA moves from one procedure to another like `CatalogPassage()`, it crosses a critical threshold, and its perspective on the world changes in so doing.

The reason for this almost philosophical mode of construction is simpler than you might think: It is easier for you, the programmer, to develop a procedure that can perform its job under *any* circumstances than it is for you to develop one that can perform the same job under some specific circumstance. That's why there are variables: so that you have symbols to represent current circumstances – the number of people in the data table, the mass of the object, the area of the text box control, the number of recorded text passages in the array. By contrast, a program developed using the old, "monolithic" model of the late 1960s and early 1970s utilized one large set of data for all of its instructions. All of this data was explicitly representative of the jobs performed by each division of the program at all times. So any one task undertaken by that program, even if it was repetitive, was contingent upon this massive data set, whose values at any one time grew more unpredictable as the program grew more massive.

Imagine if all machine tools specialists everywhere had to work in the same huge, collective factory, even if they had the right amount and the right types of machinery and tools there on site. Never mind the commute. Put yourself in the role of plant manager. (Before you dismiss this idea as fantasy, remember that there are companies and even countries that have tried this idea – Russia, communism, 1917.) The mindset you might choose to invoke as the manager of a megafactory is that you should apply the same management principles to one large group as you would to dozens of smaller groups. Notice that I said "might." As a result, you might not choose to subdivide your workgroups; besides, if you needed divisions, you wouldn't have made the effort to consolidate in the first place. But if you're thinking, "How undemocratic," recall that it was America that championed the principle of consolidation in business throughout the 1980s that led to the principle of downsizing in the 1990s. The human resources manager of today's postmerged conglomerate corporation is faced with the same type of debacle as the COBOL programmer of 1968 deciding how many digits to use in the date column.

Am I digressing? Not too much, really: Smart programming and smart management are often based on the same principles, one of which is *sensible distribution of resources*. A program is a machine built out of logic rather than steel, whose resources are procedures rather than people. If this machine can be engineered to function almost autonomously – to be given just enough functionality to perform its simple job with limited resources in abstractly defined conditions – then the procedure in a program, like a well-trained factory worker, becomes a flexible tool that can be easily reassigned to perform its job elsewhere. This is one of the principal ideas of object-oriented programming, which we revisit frequently over the course of this book.

There is one more reason for invoking this discussion of twentieth-century factory floor management principles: I just did what a well-written program does all the time. I exited one world and resumed inside another, but I performed the same basic job. Both worlds had their own exclusive contexts, but they also shared one broader, mutual context that allowed a seemingly unrelated topic to relate to a broader principle, and therefore help me make my point. A programmer frequently thinks in terms of *analogy*. Some mathematical and logical jobs that you will program within single and multiple procedures may not appear to have direct bearing on the overall problem at hand. But symbolism, of the type that variables provide, enables a foreign procedure to link with a module that performs a vastly different job.

An argument is data explicitly handed over to a procedure

The beauty of procedural construction is that a procedure can be made to take from the outside world what it needs, while the rest of its job is defined under its own rules and terms without interference from outside. Our bibliography referencing example procedure can be made more flexible by having the procedure call hand over its textual passage on a plate, as it were, as an *argument*, rather than making the procedure fetch the thing for itself by examining the current cursor location. This way, the passage recorder isn't relegated to working within a specific, defined task; if there are three or four similar tasks at work within the VBA program, the same procedure could be utilized by all of them. The first step to achieving this is by adding an element to the procedure's declaration, like so:

```
Private Sub CatalogPassage(rngThis As Range)
```

Now the procedure knows exactly what it is supposed to receive from the outside world, and in turn what it can retain responsibility for in its own right. The outside procedure can be responsible for determining what gets recorded, and the procedure can be responsible for *where* that gets recorded. We could take this one step further: Suppose the procedure keeps track of more than one array, each with its own exclusive purpose. We could make *which* list gets the recorded range dependent upon an index number given to the procedure as an argument:

```
Private Sub CatalogPassage(rngThis As Range, iWhich As Integer)
```

Outside, a call to this procedure could hand over the text currently indicated by the cursor, using this instruction:

```
CatalogPassage ActiveWindow.Selection.Range, 1
```

Or it could hand over some other range belonging to some other job, and have that range be recorded at a point indicated by an independent integer variable, like this:

```
CatalogPassage rngWherever, iHere
```

When the VBA interpreter encounters either of these instructions, it immediately proceeds to the procedure `Private Sub CatalogPassage()`, which will receive these arguments in exactly the same way in both cases. At this point in the process, VBA initiates two new elements of data representative of the textual range (in Word

2000, a `Range` class object) and an index number, which is a whole number or `Integer`. No matter how often this procedure gets called, these new elements will be called into existence fresh each time. The part of a program to which a variable belongs is extremely important. It serves to establish a guardrail of sorts around the area of the program where the variable is presumed to exist, thus establishing what we call the *scope* of that variable.

Now, suppose the second argument of the calling instruction uses a variable `iHere` rather than a numeral 1. If for some reason, `Private Sub CatalogPassage()` were to make some change to the value of `iWhich` – the variable that received the value passed to it by `iHere` – then by default (meaning, unless you say otherwise) the value of `iHere` is changed accordingly. For example, if the procedure were to contain this instruction:

```
iWhich = 0
```

then after the procedure ends and execution proceeds back to the instruction following the procedure call, `iThis` will equal 0. When we just got through understanding that variables within procedures have their own separate worlds, why must there now be some link between them? Because the purpose of a procedure may very well be to make some change or cause change to happen; if that procedure were *totally* exclusive unto itself, no such change could occur. It's important, therefore, that certain changes made within a procedure – though not all of them – be *reflected* somehow in the world outside the procedure.

There may be circumstances, however, where you specifically do not want the called procedure to change a specific element represented by an argument passed to it. The way you could reverse this behavior is to change the way the procedure heading is phrased, by adding one word:

```
Private Sub CatalogPassage(rngThis As Range, ByVal _
  iWhich As Integer)
```

The change worth noting here is the addition of `ByVal`, which is a directive to VBA to make a copy of the argument data, and only have the called procedure make changes to the *copy* of the data, not to the original. The underscore _ is there only because we had to break the instruction up to make it fit on two lines; it actually doesn't affect how the instruction is interpreted in the least.

By the way, it just so happens that if `Private Sub CatalogPassage()` makes any changes to the constituents or properties of `rngThis`, then `ActiveWindow.Selection.Range` gets changed, and in turn the location of the cursor in Word 2000 or the contents of the text being indicated are also changed. This behavior is also neutralized by the use of `ByVal`, in this case before `rngThis` in the procedure declaration:

```
Private Sub CatalogPassage(ByVal rngThis As Range, _
  ByVal iWhich As Integer)
```

A Function procedure hands data back to the caller

Suppose the VBA program you are writing needs to know the approximate length of each passage of text that is being recorded, not involving an obvious attribute like character count but instead a typesetting attribute not native to Word. You want to know the length of the passage in "ens," a typesetter's measurement of character width in the current typeface, where an "en" is equivalent to the width of one letter "n" in the current font and point size. This type of measurement would be something for which you'd need a separate procedure – because you require this measurement often – but also for which you'd need what VBA calls a Function procedure, as opposed to a Sub. The difference here is that a Function procedure returns a value to the instruction that called it. As a result, the name of the Function procedure is symbolic of that future return value.

The heading for your "en" counting procedure might look like this:

```
Public Function EnLength(ByVal rngThis As Range)
```

You would use the term Public here instead of Private because you want this procedure to be addressable by any and all modules (source code files) that you have open in your VBA project. But the Word 2000 user won't see this procedure in its Macros dialog box because it's a Function and not a Sub.

Unlike with a Sub procedure, the name of a Function procedure in VBA is treated as though it represents a value – almost like a variable, except that it generally accepts argument data within parentheses. (Parentheses used beside a variable are for other purposes.) Because you would expect Public Function EnLength() to be representative of a value, you would write its procedure name within an expression where that value is required. Suppose you want the size of a rich text box control to be stretched just wide enough to fit a given passage, plus a little extra margin. An expression that sets the width of the control might look like this:

```
RichText1.Width = EnLength(rngThat) + 2
```

This expression places a call to Function EnLength(). Once the procedure returns a value, that value stands in place of the entire function call. The value gets 2 added to it, before being assigned to the .Width property of the rich text box control named RichText1. Notice how events ended up being scheduled here: The above line is an entire instruction, but Public Function EnLength() was executed in its entirety when this instruction was only halfway finished. The VBA interpreter puts this instruction on hold while it waits for a final result value from the Function procedure. This is an example of what I mean when I say that **the name of a Function procedure is symbolic of its value.**

Taking advantage of procedure-based construction

The Visual Basic genre of programming languages are called *high-level* languages, largely because you don't have to program low-level affairs for the computer such as *how to* move the mouse pointer, or *how to* display a window (first the computer decides how big the window is, then where it goes, then it mirrors in memory the portion where the window is going to overwrite, then it starts drawing the border...). This is especially beneficial to you, the programmer, because when a VBA program is initiated by one of the Office 2000 applications, the processor code executed by the interpreter really does dictate for Windows such things as what to do while the user is doing nothing, and what user events to look out for. The interpreter has the processor perform these tasks because that's part of the interpreter's job; but you don't have to program those tasks for the interpreter, because it already knows how to manage the processes of sitting and waiting and watching. All you have to program are the high-level functions — what figures are being input by the user, what is supposed to be done with those figures, what does the user need to see at this point, what is the output supposed to look like? The matters of handling the computer are managed by the interpreter and by Windows, leaving handling the user entirely to you.

How you handle the user (mark me well, I will tell you, sir) is to build your complex VBA program in the following stages:

◆ First, build the core of your code that handles the main data processing tasks.

◆ Next, delegate a startup procedure to bring your controls into the workspace, or execute whatever plan you have to elicit information from the user — perhaps from a dedicated window, perhaps from the active document.

◆ Design the appearance of your controls and dedicated windows, if there are any.

◆ Build the procedures that respond to the crucial user events, and link to the core functionality that you have already built.

◆ Finish the program with any housekeeping procedures that are required, such as online help, user preferences maintenance, and the About Box for your logo.

Figure 3-2 depicts the relationship between these four parts of a VBA program in the order of its execution. All VBA modules end up being *event-driven* programs, even if they're single procedures that respond to button presses in an O2K toolbar.

In a complex program that utilizes general, form, and often class modules, a startup procedure in one of the modules gives variables their initial values, sets object references, loads whatever stored data the program will require from a database, and initiates whatever controls are to be employed. Once the startup procedure ends, and the main window or UserForm object is inhabiting the workspace awaiting user input, the VBA program enters a phase where nothing appears to be happening. It executes no instructions, and yet the program is still officially running.

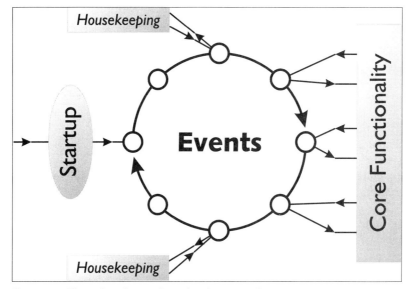

Figure 3-2: The order of execution of major parts of a VBA module.

A user event that triggers a core procedure may be a button click (especially OK), or the movement of the cursor from one text box to another, or a menu command selection. Once its response to the event is complete, an event procedure commonly passes execution back to the event waiting cycle, unless its job is to shut down the program. This waiting cycle is the part of a VBA program you know is there, even when there is no source code for it. The interpreter window reads "[running]," yet there's no instruction being executed. The waiting cycle is actually handled by Windows, not VBA. Once an event occurs, VBA takes over – or, more accurately, is told to take over by Windows.

How the VBA interpreter knows where to start

With VBA, the rules governing which procedure is the startup procedure are not as simple as they are for Visual Basic Standard Edition. When a procedure works in place of a macro – especially for those Office 2000 applications that don't use real macros anyway – the name of that procedure acts as its own startup point. *All*

WordBasic procedures were at one time named `Sub MAIN`; only in later editions were they allowed to have other names – although all WordBasic startup procedures were named `Sub MAIN`. The macros containing these procedures had their own names, independent of the names of their procedures. By contrast, with VBA and Word 2000, the name of the macro, from Word's point of view, and the name of the startup procedure are the same.

When the Word 2000 user selects Macros from the Tools menu, the dialog that comes up lists all the `Public Sub` procedures in all the general (non-form) modules. Obviously, in the case of any chosen single-procedure Word "macro," its entry point is at the top. For a macro whose startup procedure may call another procedure, it's important that the name of that other procedure not show up in the Macros list. If it could, the user could start his macro in the middle rather than at the beginning – which is, when you think about it, actually quite dangerous. After all, how is the *user* supposed to know which is the startup procedure for any given module?

The solution involves the nomenclature you give to a `Sub` or `Function` procedure. Assume you want the startup procedure for a module to be called `Sub Main()`, in keeping with Visual Basic tradition. You should add one crucial word to the front of the declaration: `Public`, which makes the declaration formally `Public Sub Main()`. Other procedures which you don't want the user to see in the Macros list should be given the `Private` declaration, as in `Private Sub Cleanup()`. The `Private` nomenclature is given by VBA automatically to event procedures, or to those procedures such as `Private Sub UserForm_Activate()` that VBA executes in response to user-generated events. This way, the user doesn't see these same procedures in the Macros list, and doesn't execute them out of turn or, worse yet, out of curiosity.

However, the word `Main` by itself doesn't exactly stand out to the *user* and say, "Here's the start of the module, pick me!" For that reason, refrain from using the name `Main` or `MAIN` for any macro you write for execution directly by the user, by name. But better still, you may find it a more efficient and expedient design decision to make a toolbar button that executes `Public Sub Main()`, or whatever you choose to call it, as its startup procedure. This doesn't necessarily involve any programming on your part; but as you'll see later in the book, it can if you require a detailed toolbar rather than just a simple "Start" button. You can add a button to any Office 2000 application's toolbar by right-clicking on that toolbar, choosing Customize from the pop-up menu, dragging a button from the palette onto the toolbar in question, and setting it to point to the "macro" in the list called **Main**. Remember, though, that `Public Sub Main()` must exist at this point to augment any toolbar, even if you're not done debugging the procedure. Using a toolbar button relieves the user from having to fish through the Macros list; and using your VBA program should never at any time resemble fishing, even if your user just happens to enjoy fishing.

For reasons that are not entirely associated with the fact that files containing VBA procedures are called "modules," the type of programming I've just described is called *modular*. You build a VBA module one working part at a time. This is a very efficient way to program; it had better be, because for VBA, it is the *only* way to program. The "working parts" that are referred to here are the procedures.

The case against modules

My technical editor raises an issue at this point; and because I value his input, I'd like to share it with you: The true value of modular programming can only be appreciated in complex situations. VBA is the language Microsoft chose to assume the role of WordBasic for Microsoft Word, and XLM for Microsoft Excel. In doing so, VBA became the company's "macro" language, even though we've already established that it doesn't do macros. By definition, a macro is a recitation of some sequence of commands that a user may frequently require. For a VBA procedure to take over the role of a macro, it must work in the macro's old microcosmic realm where very little of the tools and resources of a programming methodology such as Visual Basic may ever be appreciated. In fact, these conveniences of macrocosmic programming may introduce an unnecessary degree of overhead, when the entire business of your single-procedure wonder might be to move a character over one space, or place the dollar sign where it belongs. So a great deal of my earlier grandiose discussion featuring lessons borrowed from The History Channel might not have much bearing on about half of the work you perform in VBA, other than to simply weigh you down with resources you won't use. My technical editor recalls a friend who, to this day, swears by the methodology of QuickBasic, the Microsoft BASIC that preceded Visual Basic and ceased to be supported by Microsoft in 1993. The reason, that friend contends, is that Visual Basic is far too complex for the type of jobs for which most people use computers.

Because this is my ninth book (in North America) that has anything to do with Visual Basic, you might hope I would disagree with that last point. I would agree that general users might welcome from Microsoft (or perhaps any other software company) a simpler programming environment whose usefulness is limited to simpler tasks. I have made the point in print that I believe some aspects of Visual Basic are far more esoteric and difficult to comprehend than their counterparts in C++. But it only makes sense that Microsoft offer a programming environment, and a methodology to go along with it, that addresses the entire wealth of Windows programming concepts, from moving that dollar sign around a text range to the Distributed Component Object Model. Whatever "more basic than BASIC" language may come about, Visual Basic should always play a welcome role in any Windows programming situation, including Office 2000. That any form of Windows programming brings with it an overwhelming amount of conceptual overhead is a fact that none of us can do anything about.

The foundations of Sub and Function procedures

You've already seen several examples of the formation of the `Sub` procedure statement, and a few examples of the `Function` statement. Using this book's syntax table tool, let's spell out for you precisely how these two statements are formed to create procedure components for a VBA module. I'll begin with the `Sub` statement:

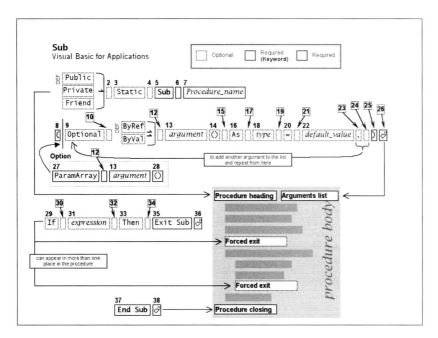

Part		Description
1	Public Private Friend	**Attribute** Specifies whether the Sub procedure may be called by procedures in other modules. By default, a Sub procedure is *public,*which means that other modules in the current project may make calls to the procedure. If part 1 is omitted, the VBA interpreter assumes that the declared procedure is to have public scope. If you write Private instead, the procedure may only be called from other procedures within its native module, but not by any procedures in any other modules in the project. This is so a module may be free to implement its own methods with its own names, without you having to worry about using a name already in use by another module. Private procedures are also *not* included in the Office 2000 application user's Tools	Macros dialog box, so the user cannot invoke one of these procedures accidentally.

Continued

Part		Description
		In the context of class modules (discussed in Chapter 9), the term Friend is used to declare a procedure that may be called by a procedure in any module within the class module's own native project (like a Public procedure), but may not be called by a module in some other project in which the module's class is invoked (*unlike* a Public procedure). This is so the native project may change the class module's run-time characteristics as warranted in order to fully test its capabilities, but also so those characteristics can be off-limits to other modules once the class module is completed and deployed. More importantly, though, procedures declared as Friend within a class module are not considered methods of the object being defined by that class. The real point of the Friend declaration is to provide you with a way to build procedures within a VBA class module that are not "exposed" to programs that instantiate that class.
2	(space)	
3	Static	Attribute Directs the interpreter to maintain the values of all local variables declared within the Sub procedure after it is exited for use later when the procedure is reentered. If you don't write Static, the interpreter discards the procedure's local variables upon reaching End Sub (part **36**).
4	(space)	
5	Sub	Statement Denotes the beginning of a standard procedure. By definition, a Sub procedure may alter the values of arguments passed to it by reference, although it does not return a value to the body of the program that contains the procedure call. As a result, when the procedure name (part **7**) is used in the body of a program, that name is representative of the job performed by the procedure, not some value or data returned by the procedure. A Function procedure, by contrast, returns a value or some data to the instruction (actually, to the *expression*) that calls it.
6	(space)	

	Part	Description

7	*Procedure_name*	<u>Literal</u>
		A name that identifies the procedure. This name should be unique among all procedures in the module, regardless of whether the procedure is `Public` or `Private` in scope. The name should also be unique all procedures in the current VBA project if the procedure is declared `Public` (part 1). This name will be used outside of this procedure within expression instructions.
		
		Rule: The name of a procedure must begin with an alphabetical character, although it may be followed by up to 254 characters, including alphanumerics and the _ underscore character.
		
		Rule: The name you choose for a variable is also used outside of the procedure as the *parameter name* for the argument passed to this procedure. So for a procedure declared thus:
		
		`Sub Organize(Index as Integer)`
		
		the following procedure call is legal:
		
		`Organize Index:=12`

8	((left parenthesis)	Begins the `Sub` procedure's grouping of arguments.
9	`Optional`	<u>Attribute</u> Written before an argument that the interpreter is to treat as optional. A call to this `Sub` procedure may either include the optional argument or omit it. **Rule:** After the first argument variable you declare `Optional`, all other successive arguments between the parentheses are also treated by the interpreter as optional, and must also include the `Optional` attribute. **Rule:** `Optional` cannot be used within the same arguments list as `ParamArray`.
10	(space)	

Continued

	Part	Description
11	ByRef ByVal	**Attribute** States the relationship between a variable passed as an argument to the `Sub` procedure, and the variable declared within the `Sub` procedure that receives the argument. When the VBA interpreter makes changes to the value or contents of an argument variable, by default those changes are reflected in the variable outside of the procedure that passed the argument (unless the argument was passed as a literal). `ByRef` can be included to make this default state clearer. If you write `ByVal` before an argument instead, the procedure receives a *copy* of the value or contents of the variable used as an argument, and the original variable is unaffected. (See the *In Depth* sidebar that follows.)
12	(space)	
13	*argument*	**Literal** An arbitrary name that is used to represent the argument being received from the calling body of the program. All rules for variable names apply here. This variable is local in scope, and is dropped from memory at `End Sub` unless `Static` (part **3**) is written at the front of the `Sub` statement.

14	( )	Denotes that the argument is an array, containing any number of elements. An array may be declared at any position in the arguments list – in prior editions of VB, an array could only be declared at the end of the list.
		
		Example: Suppose you declare a procedure like this:
		
		`Public Sub Sort(strList() As String)`
		
		Variable `strList()` is understood to be an array. No matter how many elements the array for the passing argument may contain, an entire array called `strPeople()` may be passed to this procedure using an instruction like this:
		
		`Sort strPeople()`
		
		Here, the VBA interpreter performs type checking to ensure that the passed argument is indeed an array.

15	(space)	
16	As	Denotes that the incoming argument should be of the type or class stated in part **18**.

Part	Description
17	(space)	

Part	Description
18	*type*	<u>Type or class</u>
	Variant DEFAULT Byte Boolean Integer	States the data type of the variable that receives the incoming argument. At run time, the interpreter will check the data type of the incoming argument against that of the variable declared here and, if they are not compatible, an error may be generated.
	Long Currency Single Double Date String Object	Commonly recognized object types are listed at left, although the name of an Office 2000 class or one defined by VBA as a class module may be used instead. A composite variable type name may also be used, but only if its Type declaration appears within the same module, and if Optional (part **9**) is omitted.

Part	Description
19	(space)	

Part	Description
20	=	Assigns the named argument a default value (part **22**).

Part	Description
21	(space)	

Part	Description
22	*default_value*	<u>Expression</u> In cases where Optional (part **9**) is stated for the given argument, and this argument is not supplied by the procedure call, this serves as the value for the variable represented that argument when the procedure begins. This way, if the function call omits this argument, the interpreter can assign *default_value* to the argument's corresponding variable, rather than initialize that argument to Nothing or 0. This only works if *argument* is a standard VBA type, not a class. The standard type of *default_value* must match the stated *type* (part **18**).

Part	Description
23	, (comma)	Separates two arguments in a group.

Part	Description
24	(space)	When the Sub procedure contains multiple arguments, a comma and space are used to separate them.

Continued

	Part	Description
25	) (right parenthesis)	Closes the arguments list.
26	(Enter)	Terminates the header and formally begins the procedure.
27	ParamArray	As an option, ParamArray *argument*( ) may be written as the final argument for the Sub statement. ParamArray directs the interpreter to accept an indefinite number of incoming arguments from this point in the sequence forward, from the list of arguments passed by the calling body of the program. In such a case, *argument* should be followed by empty parentheses (part **27**). These arguments are of type Variant; the type specifier (part **17**) is omitted here.
		Rule: ParamArray cannot be included in an arguments list that contains Optional (part **9**).
28	( )	When ParamArray (part **27**) is included at the end of the arguments list, then the empty parentheses ( ) are used to emphasize that the argument is an array whose purpose is to collect all the incoming arguments, however many there may be, in order of their appearance in the procedure call. In this case, the interpreter will perform type checking at run time to ensure that all of the incoming parameters are *not* arrays in themselves, but unit values.
29	If	Statement Used in a situation where execution of the Sub procedure may need to be exited prior to reaching End Sub.
30	(space)	
31	*expression*	A mathematical test that returns a Boolean True/False value. If the test returns True, then the statement following Then is executed — in this case, Exit Sub (part **35**).
32	(space)	
33	Then	Separates the expression (part **31**) from the directive (part **35**).
34	(space)	

Part	Description
35	Exit Sub
	<u>Statement</u> Forces execution of the Sub procedure to be terminated immediately. Execution proceeds to the instruction immediately following the procedure call.
36	(Enter)
37	End Sub
	<u>Statement</u> Denotes the formal close of the Sub procedure. Upon reaching this line, execution proceeds to the instruction immediately following the calling instruction outside the procedure.
38	(Enter)
	Ends the procedure.

In Depth: Passing arguments by reference or value

By default, arguments are passed to VBA procedures by *reference* rather than by value. This means that, when a procedure makes alterations to the value or contents of a variable used to receive an argument that was passed to the procedure, the original variable used in the procedure call is likewise altered. This behavior can be made clearer by including ByRef before the variable name for the argument in the Sub or Function procedure declaration. Alternately, the ByVal attribute may be used to disassociate the variable used in the procedure itself from the variable in the procedure call. This way, only the value or contents of the original variable are received by the procedure, and any alterations made to the variable in the procedure are not reflected in the original variable used in the procedure call. When ByVal is stated before the receiving variable, the argument and the original variable are considered separate, and changes made to one are not reflected in the other.

For example, suppose you declare the following:

```
Public Sub PassTrial(ByRef x, ByVal y)
```

If a is currently 5 and b currently 15, a call to this procedure could be placed as follows:

```
PassTrial a, b
```

Upon receiving the arguments, the procedure will set x to 5 and y to 15. If the procedure changes x to 6 and y to 25, then outside of the procedure, a will be 6 but b will still be 15.

The name of a procedure symbolizes its task

The `Sub` statement is the primary procedural declarative instruction in the entire Visual Basic vocabulary. Paired with `End Sub`, the statement encloses a procedure of a given name. This name is used to identify the body of code in procedure calls elsewhere in the program. **A procedure is a body of code designed to be executed more than once, and to perform a regimented set of instructions when called upon by name, generally upon data that is passed to the procedure by the calling instruction in the form of arguments.** The key here is "more than once." VBA source code is not written in one long scroll, mainly because it's more prudent to be able to reuse portions of that code more than once in the program.

When a procedure is called by name, program execution branches to the `Sub` statement that bears that name. A procedure call is placed to `Sub` *ProcedureName( )* from any point in the program by stating this procedure name *ProcedureName* just as though it were a statement, along with any arguments that are to be passed to the procedure, separated by commas. Here's how a standard procedure call is constructed:

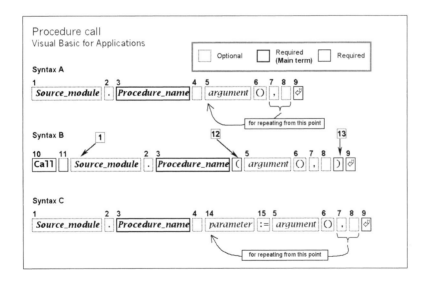

	Part	Description
1	*Source_module*	Literal In situations where more than one module in the active project may contain a Sub procedure with the same name (part **3**), regardless of whether their types or number of arguments differ, it is necessary here to specify the name of the module that contains the specific Function procedure being addressed. If more than one project inhabits the VBA workspace, due for instance to more than one Office 2000 document template being open simultaneously, it may be necessary to specify the name of the project containing this module, often as its filename contained in square brackets; for example: [legal.dot]. The project name, when stated, is separated from the module name by a period (part **2**).
2	. (period)	Separates the name of the Sub procedure (part **3**) from the name of its source module (part **1**), when included.
3	*Procedure_name*	Literal Matches the name given to the Sub procedure. This name should be within the scope of visibility of the instruction placing the procedure call; in other words, the Sub procedure should make itself available to the point in the module containing the procedure call if execution is to be transferred to that procedure.
4	(space)	Separates the arguments from the procedure call name (part **3**) for syntax **A** and **C** only.

Continued

	Part	Description
5	*argument*	<u>Data</u> An element of data that the called Sub procedure receives and utilizes. For syntax **A** and **B**, the contents of the data passed here are received by a variable in the same position within the Sub procedure header as the *argument* holds within the procedure call. For instance, the third datum in the procedure call is picked up by the third variable in the procedure header. For syntax **C**, the contents of the data passed here are received by a variable with the same name as the *parameter* (part **11**), which points to it in the procedure call, regardless of where this argument may appear in the arguments list.
6	( )	Denotes that the variable mentioned in *argument* (part **5**) is an array, and that the contents of that array are to be passed whole to the Sub procedure. The passing of arrays is always done by reference in VBA, which means that as the called Sub procedure makes changes to its receiving array, the called array is changed as well.
7	, (comma)	Separates two arguments in a group.
8	(space)	
9	(Enter)	Ends the procedure call.
10	Call	<u>Statement</u> Designates that the instruction is a call to a Sub procedure. Syntax **B** is an archaic, though still supported, construction for procedure calls. Note the use of parentheses (parts **12** and **13**) to enclose the arguments list; these are only necessary for syntax **B**.
11	(	Begins the arguments list.

	Part	Description
12	)	Closes the arguments list.
13	*parameter*	Symbol The name of the parameter that points to the given argument (part **5**). This is also the corresponding name of the variable that represents the argument in the Sub procedure.
14	:=	Operator Used to separate the argument being passed (part **5**) from its corresponding name (part **14**).

In Depth: The finer points of posing arguments

For syntax **A**, precisely as many arguments need to be placed in the procedure call as there are within the declaration of the procedure. This way, the first argument passed corresponds to the first variable receiving the argument, the second argument passed corresponds to the second variable, and so on. For arguments stated within the Sub procedure to be Optional, you can pass a *null argument* to the procedure, though you need to leave the commas separating the arguments in the procedure call. For example, in this procedure call:

```
GoThere docThis, , 12
```

the second argument is presumed optional and could thus be omitted, though the comma needed to remain so that the interpreter could ascertain that the argument indeed was omitted. For syntax **B**, these same rules hold true, although arguments are listed in parentheses.

For syntax **C**, arguments are passed to the Sub procedure by stating their variable names (part **14**) explicitly, then separating the variable name from its corresponding argument using the := operator (part **15**), VBA's first obvious "borrowing" from Pascal. No amendments have to be made to the Sub statement itself in order to facilitate naming of arguments, although it may be a good idea to name argument variables using words that another programmer might expect to see — for instance, Name rather than strNm$. When using syntax **C**, optional arguments can be left out altogether (no commas need mark their places), and arguments can be written in any order — not necessarily in the order in which the receiving variables are listed in the Sub statement. However, ParamArray may not be used with syntax **C**, because it is impossible for the interpreter to give specific names to an unknown number of variant arguments.

PROCEDURE CALL EXAMPLE

To invoke this procedure:

```
Sub DeployDialog(iType As Integer, strTitle As String)
```

the procedure call may take any of the following forms:

```
DeployDialog 12, "Banjo types"
```

```
Call DeployDialog(12, "Banjo types")
```

```
DeployDialog strTitle:="Banjo types", iType:=12
```

Only in syntax **B** of our Procedure Call syntax table do parentheses need to be used in calls to a `Sub` procedure. Besides, you'll find few programmers use the `Call` statement because it's seven more characters (if you count the space and parentheses) that add no substantive value to the source code. However, the `Call` statement syntax does make the part of the procedure call that follows the `Call` statement itself look more like a C/C++ function call, for programmers who expect to see parentheses used for these purposes.

On Point

A procedure is a collection of VBA instructions designed to be executed more than once, to be called upon by name, and to perform instructions on data passed to it by a procedure call. The data given to a procedure are its arguments. In the conventional syntax for VBA, the arguments to a procedure are passed to it in sequence, and are accepted by the procedure in the same sequence and assigned to freshly declared variables.

A `Sub` procedure may receive values from the instruction that calls it. It doesn't have to, though it generally does. Those values, called *arguments*, are passed to the procedure either by way of variables or literal values. Arguments to be passed are listed in sequence beside the procedure call. The variables that receive the arguments are declared within the `Sub` statement, and are considered by the interpreter to be local to that procedure. These values are normally discarded when the interpreter reaches `End Sub` or `Exit Sub`, unless they are explicitly marked with a `Static` term.

What this means is, a Sub procedure is free to use whatever variable names it wants within its own boundaries without fear of an error-generating conflict. Granted, long variable names these days are less likely to conflict with one another within the same VBA module. Still, there is always the possibility that if more than one person is working on the same module, and you import some procedures written by someone else into your module, the two of you might have chosen the same names to refer to altogether different types of variables. This is one reason why there is the so-called *local scope*. When a variable doesn't have any bearing on any instructions outside of the procedure that originated it, there shouldn't be any need for the interpreter to be maintaining that variable while it is executing code outside of its home procedure. Later in this chapter, we'll concentrate on the concept of scope and how it helps define a program's multiple simultaneous contexts.

A Function procedure yields an explicit result

What is distinctively different about the Function procedure with respect to the Sub procedure is that the instruction that calls the Function procedure (the *function call*) expects an answer. This answer comes in the form of result data, which is put to use within the expression that calls the Function procedure. Unlike a call to a Sub procedure, a Function procedure call is part of a mathematical expression. Here, in explicit terms, is how you phrase the statement governing the Function procedure:

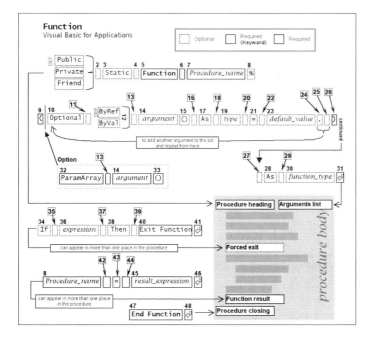

	Part	Description
1	Public Private Friend	**Attribute** Specifies whether the Function procedure may be called by procedures in other modules. By default, a Function procedure is *public.* If part 1 is omitted, the interpreter assumes a public scope, making the procedure callable from all modules in all currently loaded projects within the Office 2000 application. If you write Private instead, the procedure may only be called from other procedures within the same module. For Function procedures within a class module, declaring the procedure as a Friend makes it visible to other procedures within its native project, but shields it from code that may instantiate that class.
2	(space)	
3	Static	**Attribute** Tells the interpreter to maintain the values of local variables within the Function procedure after it is exited, for use later when the procedure is reentered. If part 3 is omitted, the interpreter discards the procedure's local variables upon reaching End Function (part **47**).
4	(space)	
5	Function	**Statement** Tells the interpreter that the procedure enclosed by this statement is meant to return a value, or another datum such as a string or object, to the instruction or expression that calls it.
6	(space)	
7	*Procedure_name*	**Literal** A name that identifies the procedure. This name should be unique among all procedures in the module, and to all procedures in the entire project if the procedure is declared Public (part **1**). This name will be used outside of this procedure to refer to the functionality embodied by this Function procedure. The same rules that apply to naming a Sub procedure, apply equally to a Function procedure.

	Part	Description
8	! # $ % &	<u>Type-specifier character</u> (No default) Restricts the data type of the value returned by the function procedure to any of the following: ! Single precision floating point # Double precision floating point $ String % Short integer & Long integer **Rule:** This character takes the place of As *type* (parts **17** through **19**); both explicit type and type character may not be used within the same declaration.
9	((left parenthesis)	Begins the Function procedure's grouping of parameters.
10	Optional	<u>Attribute</u> Tells the interpreter to treat the next argument (part **14**) as optional. If the call to the Function procedure omits this argument, the interpreter will not generate a fault. **Rule:** After the first parameter variable declared Optional, all other successive parameters between the parentheses are also treated by the interpreter as optional, and also require the Optional attribute. **Rule:** Optional cannot be used within the same parameters list as ParamArray.
11	(space)	
12	ByRef ByVal	<u>Attribute</u> States the relationship between a variable passed as an argument to the Function procedure, and the variable declared within the Function procedure that receives the argument. If ByRef (default when omitted), argument passing is assumed to be *by reference*, so any changes made by the Function procedure to the receiving variable will automatically be reflected in the passing variable (assuming the argument has not been passed by a literal). If ByVal, argument passing is assumed to be *by value*, so changes to this variable will not be reflected in the passing variable.

Continued

	Part	Description
13	(space)	
14	*argument*	Symbol An arbitrary name that represents the argument being received from the calling body of the program at this position in the sequence of the arguments list. All rules for variable names apply here. This variable is local in scope, and will be dropped from memory when the interpreter encounters `End Function` (part **47**) or `Exit Function` (part **40**) unless `Static` is specified (part **3**).
15	( )	Denotes that the argument is an array and may contain any number of elements. The interpreter will perform type checking at run time to ensure that the incoming argument at this position is indeed an array. A fixed or dynamic array may be used in the instruction that passes this argument.
16	(space)	
17	`As`	Denotes that the incoming argument should be of the type stated in part **19**.
18	(space)	

19	*type*
	`Variant`
	`DEFAULT`
	`Byte`
	`Boolean`
	`Integer`
	`Long`
	`Currency`
	`Single`
	`Double`
	`Date`
	`String`
	`Object`
		Type or class
		States the data type of the variable that receives the incoming argument. The interpreter checks the data type of the incoming argument against that of the variable declared here and, if they are not compatible, an error may be generated. A class name used here may be a class recognized by the Office 2000 object library, or any other active object library that the VBA interpreter may currently reference; or it may be the name of a class defined by an active VBA class module.

20	(space)	
21	=	In circumstances where a given argument (part **14**) has been declared `Optional` (part **10**), the equal sign attributes a default value (part **23**) to the argument.

	Part	Description
22	(space)	
23	default_value	<u>Expression</u> Sets the default value of the argument (part **14**) in cases where it is declared Optional (part **10**). This way, if the procedure call omits this argument, the VBA interpreter will assign default_value to that argument, rather than initialize it to Nothing or 0. If a type is specified for the argument (part **8** or **19**), then the interpreter employs type checking to ensure that the type for default_value matches the argument's type.
24	, (comma)	Separates two arguments in a grouping.
25	(space)	When more than one argument is being declared, the comma and space are used to separate them.
26	) (right parenthesis)	Closes the arguments list.
27	(space)	
28	As	Denotes that the result value of the Function procedure should be of a given type (part **30**).
29	(space)	
30	*function_type*	<u>Type or class</u> Denotes the data type of the value or data returned by the Function procedure. A specific object class name may be used in place of *type*, if that class belongs to one of the active Office 2000 object libraries or other such libraries, or if its class module belongs to the current VBA project. A composite variable type name may also be used, but only if its Type declaration appears within the current module, and if Optional (part **10**) is omitted. Rule: All Function procedures return a value, a string, or an object reference to the instruction that called it. This returned item represents the result of the function represented by the procedure, given its specified arguments.
31	(Enter)	

Continued

	Part	Description
32	ParamArray	Indicates to the interpreter that the procedure is to accept any number of arguments from this point forward, and to assign those arguments in sequence to an array variable of type Variant, to be named by part **14**. By protocol, a ParamArray argument is the last in the declared arguments list for a Function procedure.
		Rule: ParamArray cannot be included in an arguments list that contains Optional.
		Rule: All ParamArray arguments are considered to be of type Variant. The interpreter performs type checking to ensure that all of the incoming parameters are *not* arrays in themselves, but unit values. However, this type checking does not extend to the specific type of the argument; as with all newly declared variants, types are assigned to them upon receiving initial values. If ParamArray is stated, parts **16** through **19** must be omitted.
33	( )	Underscores the use of the argument (part **14**) as a parameter array.
34	If	Statement Used in a situation where execution of the Function procedure may need to be exited prior to reaching End Function.
35	(space)	
36	*expression*	A mathematical test that returns a Boolean True/False value. If the test returns True, then the statement following Then is executed — in this case, Exit Function (part **40**).
37	(space)	
38	Then	Separates the expression (part **36**) from the result statement (part **40**).
39	(space)	
40	Exit Function	Statement Forces execution of the Function procedure to be terminated immediately. Execution proceeds to the instruction immediately back to the instruction line where the Function procedure was called, and may complete the expression that contains the call.
41	(Enter)	

	Part	Description *(continued)*
42	(space)	
43	=	Separates the result of the `Function` procedure (part **45**) from the name that represents that result (part **8**).
44	(space)	
45	*result_expression*	Expression Specifies a return value for the `Function` procedure, by assigning a final value, or an expression that evaluates to a final value, to the *Procedure_name* (part **8**), repeated here from the `Function` procedure's declaration line. The name of the `Function` procedure in VBA serves a dual role as a variable to which the result of that procedure is assigned. Such an assignment may appear more than once within the procedure; for instance, a clause that checks for three or more conditions may result in three or more final results.
46	(Enter)	
47	End Function	Statement Denotes the formal close of the `Function` procedure. Upon reaching this line, execution proceeds back to the instruction line where the `Function` procedure was called, and may complete the expression that contains the call.
48	(Enter)	Ends the `Function` procedure.

The `Function` statement acts as a header for a procedure that is designed to return a value to the body of code that called it. Paired with `End Function`, the statement encloses a procedure whose name is presented within the `Function` header. This name is used to identify the body of code within instructions or expressions elsewhere in the program.

A return value is denoted in at least one point in the `Function` procedure by assigning the result of an expression – simple or complex – to the procedure name itself using an equation instruction such as the one in this procedure:

```
Private Function Hypoteneuse(dSide1 As Double, dSide2 As Double) _
  As Double
    Hypoteneuse = Sqr((dSide1 ^ 2) + (dSide2 ^ 2))
End Function
```

An instruction that assigns a result value to the Function procedure's own name – such as Hypoteneuse above – does not formally denote the end of the Function procedure, though it generally falls close to a terminating End Function or Exit Function statement.

The Function procedure receives arguments from the calling equation instruction either by way of variables or literal values. The interpreter views the variables that receive these arguments as local to the Function procedure. This means that, unless a variable has been explicitly marked with the Static term within the arguments list between the parentheses of the Function statement, the interpreter will drop these local variables from memory once it has processed the End Function instruction.

A call to a Function procedure is often treated as part of an expression. In this context, it is called a *function call*. Like every other expression in VBA, an expression containing a function call evaluates to a real value, or to some other real data, not to a variable. A function call takes the following form:

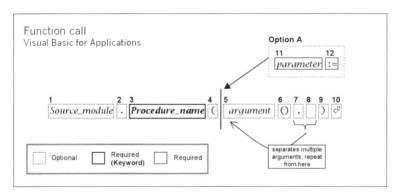

	Part	Description
1	*Source_module*	<u>Literal</u> When more than one module in the active project contains a Function procedure with the same name (part 3), regardless of whether they have different types, classes, or arguments, it is necessary here to specify the name of the module that contains the specific Function procedure being addressed. If more than one project inhabits the VBA workspace, due, for example, to more than one template being open simultaneously, it may be necessary here to specify the name of the project containing this module, often as its filename contained in square brackets; for example: [legal.dot]. The project name would be separated from the module name using a period.

	Part	Description
2	. (period)	Separates the name of the `Function` procedure (part **3**) from the name of its source module (part **1**), when included.
3	*Procedure_name*	Literal Matches the name given to the `Function` procedure. The procedure being called should be within the scope of the function call.
4	((left parenthesis)	Begins the arguments list.
5	*argument*	Expression Evaluates to a real value or other real data that is passed to the `Function` procedure, to be received by a variable declared by the `Function` statement. This variable either corresponds in position to that of the argument (part **5**) in the function call, or has a name equal to its parameter name (part **11**) in the function call, when present.
7	, (comma)	Separates two arguments in a grouping.
8	(space)	
9	) (right parenthesis)	Closes the arguments list.
10	(Enter)	Terminates the function call when it stands on a line by itself. When the function call appears in the midst of an expression within an instruction line, the carriage return is not required here.
11	*parameter*	Symbol Matches the name used for the argument's associated receiving variable in the declaration statement for the `Function` procedure being called.
12	:=	Operator Used to separate the parameter name (part **11**) from its associated argument (part **5**).

FUNCTION CALL EXAMPLE

For a procedure with this declaration:

```
Private Function dHypoteneuse(dSide1 As Double, _
 dSide2 As Double) As Double
```

you would use the following function call:

```
dSide = dHypoteneuse(dSide1, dSide2)
```

Notice the use of parentheses to gather the arguments together, and also the variable on the left side of the equation that will receive the result from the Function procedure.

Regulating and Managing Scope

The necessity for the concept of scope does not readily make itself known in programming. After all, BASIC got along quite well for more than two decades without "scope" even entering into its vocabulary. When BASIC became a modular language, it began to follow the trend set by C and Pascal of encouraging programmers to build reusable code. Common procedures could easily be imported into projects and seamlessly entered into the source code of whatever program was being worked on at the time. But in order for that goal to become reality, the BASIC interpreter needed a way to distinguish variable names from the main program, from those from the imported portion that may have the same names. So the concept of "local" and "global" scopes was introduced.

The four scopes of variables in VBA

In VBA, the stratification of scopes has gone about as full-tilt as it can go. Here is a list of the recognized scopes in VBA, and the extent of the visibility of variables and procedures with those scopes:

♦ Local scope (also called *procedure-level scope*) describes the relative visibility of variables declared within a procedure. Between Sub and End Sub, and between Function and End Function, any variables you may declare with the Dim statement or with the Static statement (profiled a bit later) are considered local to that procedure. These variables will not be recognized outside of their native procedures as symbolizing the same values or data.

◆ **Modular scope** describes the relative visibility of variables declared *outside* of a procedure, within the Declarations section of a module (at the top of its source code listing). Variables declared here are recognized uniformly by all of the procedures in the module in which they're declared. That said, **local scope takes precedent over modular scope within a procedure.** So even though the VBA interpreter reads module-level declarations first, if a `Dim` statement within a procedure declares a variable with the same name as an existing module-level variable, the local declaration will conveniently obscure the modular declaration. Instructions within that procedure will recognize the local variable and ignore the identically named modular variable; they will not affect or alter the modular variable in so doing, they'll just ignore it. Why would such a condition ever crop up? If you're importing procedures written by someone else into your project, you want some assurance that you won't need to edit that other person's procedures just to make them compatible with yours. With local scope boundaries maintained, the chances of you having to do that are averted.

◆ **Public scope** describes the visibility of procedures' names to procedures in other modules in the same project. Here we have to be careful, because "project" in VBA doesn't mean exactly the same thing as "project" in other editions of Visual Basic. In VBA, because more than one document may be open, more than one template may be open as well; and because in Office 2000 there is a correspondence of one project to one template, multiple projects may be open simultaneously. Public procedure names are addressable by other modules within the same project, but not outside its own module. Procedure names are, of course, visible to other procedures in the same module, otherwise, what would be the point? By default, `Sub` and `Function` procedures are public, making them accessible to other modules in the same project. By contrast, when a procedure is explicitly declared `Private`, or if the Declarations section of a module is headed with the `Option Private Module` statement, then that procedure is only visible to other procedures in its own native module.

◆ **Global scope** describes the accessibility of objects in the currently referenced object libraries, to any and all procedures throughout the VBA workspace. By default, when VBA is brought up within any of the O2K applications, the object library for that application is automatically made referenceable, placing its objects in global scope. ("The Globals," a decent, wholesome family that I'll introduce to you down the street in Chapter 2, are common examples.) Making another object library referenceable places its objects in global scope as well.

There are certain other statements in the VBA vocabulary that declare variables with different scopes and accessibility rules than would normally be set for them with the common Dim statement. Within procedures, for instance, the Static statement is used to declare local scope variables whose values are *not* dropped when the procedure is exited; in other words, their values or other data is retained. Here's how the Static statement is constructed:

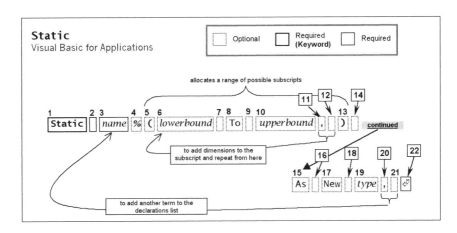

	Part	Description
1	Dim	**Statement**
		The Static statement allocates memory for at least one variable of the stated *type* (part **18**, when present), and gives this variable a unique name (part **3**). This name will be recognized as representing the allocated unit of memory throughout the same body of code where the Static statement appears.
2	(space)	
3	*term*	**Variable**
		An arbitrarily (though sensibly) chosen name that will be reserved by the VBA interpreter to exclusively refer to the allocated unit of memory, up until execution of the body of code containing the Static statement is terminated.

	Part	Description
4	! # $ % &	<u>Type-specifier character</u> (No default) Restricts the data type of the value returned by the function procedure to any of the following: ! Single precision floating point # Double precision floating point $ String % Short integer & Long integer **Rule:** This character takes the place of As *type* (parts **15** through **19**); both explicit type and type character may not be used within the same variable declaration.
5	((left parenthesis)	
6	*lowerbound*	<u>Integer</u> When declaring arrays whose members will be referenced by number, lowerbound sets the index number of the first member of the array. If lowerbound is omitted (as is usually the case), the interpreter assumes this initial index to be 0 by default.
7	(space)	
8	To	Separates lower bounds of array range from upper bounds.
9	(space)	
10	*upperbound*	<u>Integer</u> When declaring arrays, *upperbound* sets the index number of the final member of the array. Members of the array are numbered consecutively from 0 or *lowerbound* to *upperbound*. The index number for an array is also called its *subscript*. If *upperbound* is omitted, the array is considered *dynamic*, and bounds must be specified later using a ReDim statement before it can be used.
11	, (comma)	When declaring arrays with more than one dimension (for instance, a table as opposed to a set or sequence), a comma is used to separate the index subscripts for different axes of the array.

Continued

	Part	Description
12	(space)	
13	) (right parenthesis)	Closes the subscript.
14	(space)	
15	As	Begins the specification of the new variable's type.
16	(space)	
17	New	Qualifier If New is used when designating an object class as the type for the variable (part **19**), the variable will refer to a newly-formed object entirely independent of any existent object. In other words, the statement *instantiates* an object.
18	(space)	
19	*type* Variant Byte Boolean Integer Long Currency Single Double Date String Object	Type or class States the type and structure of the new variable, and in turn designates how that variable will. be stored in memory
20	, (comma)	Separates two arguments in a grouping.
21	(space)	
22	(Enter)	Closes the declaration statement.

A procedure declared Static, or one that contains variables that are declared with the Static statement, can be its own self-contained world. Suppose, for instance, an Excel procedure represents a "shadow cursor" of sorts, that returns an

Excel cell range address (such as A1:C15) to other procedures – sort of a floating reference point. Excel formulas or macros might need to reference this shadow cursor directly; and because its address point for a VBA module is a procedure name, the shadow cursor only needs to be "known" by the procedure. The variable that holds this shadow cursor Static could be declared like this:

```
Static rngShadow As Range
```

Because the procedure will be executed more than once, the declarations within the procedure, including the Static statement, will be seen more than once. When Static is encountered for the second time and thereafter, what happens to rngShadow? Thankfully, nothing. The interpreter will see that variable rngShadow is already present, already running, and will leave it alone with respect to this statement.

Public is used to declare module-level variables

When you use the Dim statement to declare modular scope variables, no other module in the project has access to those same variables. (If other modules declare private variables with the same names, they will point to different values or data.) To build variables – especially references to objects – that are visible to all modules in a project (public scope), you would instead use the Public statement in the module's Declarations section.

Because Public and Dim don't have the natural symmetry you might expect from statements whose restrictions are quite the exact opposite of one another, VBA utilizes an alternative statement Private, which works the same way as Dim in the Declarations section of a module and which has a more sensible correlation with Public to the human reader. Both Private and Public, besides their own names, use the same syntax, as defined below:

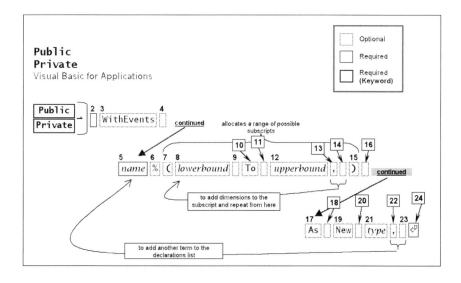

	Part	Description
1	Public Private	**Statement** The Public statement is reserved for the Declarations section of a module, and is not used within procedures. It allocates memory for at least one variable of the stated *type* (part **20**, when present), gives this variable a unique *name* (part **5**), and makes this variable available to its native module, as well as all others in that module's native project. Variables declared at the module level with Public are retained even after that module has ended its execution. This way, portions of a VBA program do not have to be kept artificially active to maintain variables while the user is operating the Office 2000 application. The Private statement uses the same syntax as Public, although its sole difference is that it stipulates that all variables it declares have a scope restricted to their native module and that they are not visible to other modules.
2	(space)	
3	WithEvents	**Qualifier** In the context of a VBA class module (discussed in Chapter 9), WithEvents is used to state that the object reference declared with this statement may recognize its own events.
4	(space)	
5	*term*	**Variable** An arbitrarily (though sensibly) chosen name that is reserved by the VBA interpreter to exclusively refer to the allocated unit of memory, up until execution of the body of code containing the declaration statement is terminated.
6	! # $ % &	**Type-specifier character** (No default) Restricts the data type of the value returned by the function procedure to any of the following. ! Single precision floating point # Double precision floating point $ String % Short integer & Long integer **Rule:** This character takes the place of As *type* (parts **15** through **19**); both explicit type and type character may not be used within the same variable declaration.

	Part	Description
7	((left parenthesis)	
8	*lowerbound*	<u>Integer</u> When declaring arrays whose members will be referenced by number, *lowerbound* sets the index number of the first member of the array. If *lowerbound* is omitted (as is usually the case), the interpreter assumes this initial index to be 0 by default.
9	(space)	
10	To	Separates lower bounds of array range from upper bounds.
11	(space)	
12	*upperbound*	<u>Integer</u> When declaring arrays, *upperbound* sets the index number of the final member of the array. Members of the array are numbered consecutively from 0 or *lowerbound* to *upperbound*. If *upperbound* is omitted, the array is considered *dynamic*, and bounds must be specified later using a ReDim statement before it can be used.
13	, (comma)	When declaring arrays with more than one dimension (for instance, a table as opposed to a set or sequence), a comma is used to separate the index subscripts for different axes of the array. VBA recognizes arrays with up to 60 dimensions.
14	(space)	
15	) (right parenthesis)	Closes the subscript.
16	(space)	
17	As	Begins the specification of the new variable's type.
18	(space)	

Continued

Part		Description *(continued)*
19	New	Qualifier
		If New is used when designating an object class as the type for the variable (part **21**), the variable refers to a newly-formed object entirely independent of any existent object.
20	(space)	
21	*type*	Type or class
	Variant	States the type and structure of the new variable, and may enroll
	Byte	that variable as a member of a recognized class.
	Boolean	
	Integer	
	Long	
	Currency	
	Single	
	Double	
	Date	
	String	
	Object	
22	, (comma)	Separates two variables being declared with the same scope.
23	(space)	
24		Closes the declaration statement.

The differences between Public and Private in variable declarations and the same two terms used in restricting the scope of procedures are worth noting. A Private Sub or Private Function procedure may declare and utilize its own variables. The term used to declare those variables may be either Dim (introduced in Chapter 2) or Private — either one fulfills the same purpose, although Private is a bit more explicit to the human reader. A Public Sub or Public Function procedure is "visible" to all modules in an active VBA project, which means a procedure belonging to one module may place a call to a Public procedure in another. But a Public variable is declared at the top of a module, in what VBA calls either the Declarations section or the General Declarations section. It is "visible" to all procedures in that module, without having to be passed as an argument between them. However, you could use Dim instead of Public to declare variables in exactly the same section of the module; again, Public is simply the more explicit term.

On Point

If a procedure is declared `Static`, then all of its variables' values or settings are maintained by the interpreter after it processes the `End Sub` or `End Function` instruction for that procedure. Alternately, certain variables whose data needs to be maintained by the interpreter may be declared `Static` within the procedure. Otherwise, the interpreter discards references to all variables declared within a procedure, once the procedure's execution is terminated.

Variables declared within the body of a procedure are said to have local scope and are not addressable outside of that procedure. Variables with the same name as those declared within a procedure may be addressed, though they will not refer to the same data. Variables with modular scope may be declared in the Declarations section of a module using either the `Dim` or `Private` statement; these variables may be addressed by any instruction in any procedure within the module. To expand the scope of a variable to all modules within a given project, that variable may be declared in the Declarations section of any of that project's modules, using the `Public` statement.

Earlier, we looked at an example that involved a Word VBA program that, in the course of its main job, recorded several textual passages being referred to by a bibliography. If these arrays were to be utilized throughout the entire VBA module, then it would make sense for you to declare them within the Declarations section as `Public` variables. On the other hand, if the arrays were to be used exclusively by the collection procedure `Private Sub CatalogPassage()` and no other, then the arrays could easily be declared *within* the procedure using the `Static` statement. This way, the arrays remain local to the procedure, but still retain their values even when the procedure is not currently being executed. Is there an efficiency reason for declaring these array variables as local static instead of public? There is if you take into account the possible portability of the text collection procedure. If you ever intend for the procedure to be utilizable in more than one VBA program, if your arrays are to be `Public`, their declaration needs to be imported into the module separately, because each VBA module only has one Declarations section. Because a `Static` declaration would be part of the procedure, it would get imported along with the rest of the instructions.

Binding and Type Checking

Table 3-1 listed how much memory the standard VBA variable consumes. The state of the world economy has had a direct effect on how programmers devise their databases; today, as memory prices go through the floor, there is a proportional decrease in the efficiency of databases and data structures in modern applications.

The pervasive attitude is that because memory is cheap, consumption is not an issue. A victim of a similar selective blindness on the part of world markets is the petroleum industry. When crude oil is cheap – as it most undoubtedly was at the time of this writing – it seems to be a far less limited resource than it was ten years earlier. Journeymen economists accredit the low price of oil to its apparent abundance; the fact is, any glut is an illusion caused by a brief period of overproduction.

Another digression? Not really. With ever increasing demand exceeding the capability of producers to keep up, you would think that the price of computing parts and all other forms of integrated circuits would be climbing through the roof. The truth is that another economic force has drawn a "line in the sand" of sorts – a price boundary above which consumers and businesses historically have been unwilling to pay. What does this have to do with binding and type checking in Office 2000 VBA? I promise you'll see my connection in a moment: The ever-increasing speed of CPUs has presented us with the illusion that computers are, on the whole, becoming faster. In fact, the ever increasing stress on these processors, imposed by multiple simultaneous processes – most of which belong to the operating system and not the applications – has made the bandwidth for processing user applications proportionally narrower. The result is that Office 2000 is, in fact, slower than ever before in terms of the work it's capable of performing within the limited processor cycles it's given – not necessarily through any fault of its own.

Where do you, as a programmer, draw your line in the sand? Impose some strict conservationist methodologies of your own in your VBA programming. Explicit declaration of variables is one such methodology, because it forces VBA to reduce the memory it must use to handle data, thus not only reducing the processor time needed to manage that data in memory, but also reducing the time required for the processor to manage other data in its vicinity.

Why are there variants?

The original purpose for type checking in interpreters and compilers was to help enforce conservation of memory in data structures. You don't need 64 bits reserved for a data value that will only equal 1, 2, or 3 during its entire existence. If you declare a variable for that purpose As Integer or As Byte, you not only reduce the memory consumption for that variable up to one-eighth the number of bits, but you also cut the time consumed by the interpreter in retrieving this value from memory.

When you declare a variable without a type, or when you simply do not declare it at all before you use it, VBA allocates memory for that variable – whatever it may be – as a variant. This results in the automatic consumption of at least 16 bytes (128 bits) regardless of what the variable actually represents. Because a variable whose unsigned value will only range from 0 to 3 needs just two bits to symbolize itself, the other 126 bits would be wasted. They're not blank; they're actually filled with information that helps the interpreter to determine *dynamically* (on the fly) where the significant two bits are and what they mean. But all that technology would not be necessary if the declared variable were given the correct type to start with; this dynamic determination is more for the convenience of the programmer than the program.

Whenever you use a variable that is explicitly a variant, the VBA interpreter disengages type checking for that variable. This means that you could accidentally assign a string of characters to a variable that already had a numeral value in it; the string would replace the numeral, the numeral would cease to exist, and there would be no error message generated to inform you of your loss. You could, however, use a VBA instruction to determine the type of a variable in the course of a procedure's execution. VBA includes an intrinsic function `TypeName()` that registers the *true* data type of whatever is currently stored in a variable, even if that variable was a variant to begin with. So if you write `y = 16` and have never declared `y` formally, then `TypeName(y)` would return the word `Integer`. Variable `y` still consumes the 16 bytes-plus of memory, but at least you have a way of knowing what the contained variable really is before you accidentally overwrite it.

Still, the question raised by this segment remains: Why are there variants? Is there a situation in which you would ever explicitly require a variant? It's rare, but it's possible. A simple example involves a `Function` procedure, which is itself declared `As Variant`. Its return value, therefore, could be anything. You might expect the return value to be a `Double`, which would be a very precise number. But should the procedure encounter an error, the procedure could return a string – for instance, "Distance parameter too large." Your function call, upon seeing a string rather than a number, would not only know that an error occurred, but could pass the message on to the user in a dialog box without modification. The trick here is this: Because the `Function` procedure is capable of generating any kind of result, the receiving variable should be capable of expecting any kind of result. In other words, if the function call looks like this:

```
DSMax = DopplerShift(x, y, z, d, q)
```

and if `DSMax` had been declared earlier `As Double`, it could not receive the string error message without an error being generated. You see, type checking was turned off for the `Function` procedure's return value, but not for the receiving variable `DSMax`. So you would need to declare `DSMax` somewhere `As Variant` so that it too could receive either a number or a string.

Another reasonable use of an explicitly declared variant is in evaluating the integrity of a stored database table, such as one belonging to Access 2000. A procedure may study one field at a time extracted from the various records in the table in sequence. The contents of each field could be passed as an argument to the procedure. Fields in a database table may be of any general type, some of which don't actually correspond to VBA's own standard types. So it is important that the field-studying procedure *not* know what type the field is when it's trying to accept that field as an argument; otherwise, VBA's own type checking might result in the field not being able to get in the front door, as it were. In this case, the receiving argument might be written like this:

```
Private Function FieldExamine(vWhatever As Variant) As Boolean
```

The `Function` procedure itself might yield a `True/False` value indicating whether the field is valid; however, declaring the incoming argument `As Variant` gives it a wide berth.

Variant arrays may contain members with varying types

Because a single variant refers to contents of any type or object class at any time, the members of an *array* of such variants may refer to contents whose types or classes differ from one another's. So if you declare an array like this:

```
Dim vEntries(16) As Variant
```

then the contents of `vEntries(1)` may be a string, while `vEntries(2)` may have a currency value. At first it might seem that this is contrary to the behavior of arrays with other explicit types, such as one declared `As Integer` or `As String`. If the first member of a string array is found to be a string, it's a safe bet that the second member is a string as well. But this variation of content in a variant array is in keeping with the rule that arrays declared as one type all have members of the same *declared* type. Logically, if everything is anything, then any subset of everything must also be anything. Likewise, any portion of a variant array may have contents that are of a different type than any other portion.

Why would you ever need an array whose contents are explicitly declared to be of any type? This situation actually comes about fairly often in Excel 2000. In Excel, the contents of the data in a worksheet and the contents of data maintained by a VBA program – even if that program "belongs" to a worksheet – are kept separate from each other. Your VBA procedures have reference Excel's object library before it can poll the contents of cells in a worksheet and assign those contents to VBA variables. In other words, there is no automatic association between the key containers of data in Excel and VBA – respectively, the cell and the variable. So when you declare a VBA array whose members are to contain the contents of any number of cells in a worksheet whose structure and content have yet to be determined, specifying the type for each of the variables in the array may be premature.

The solution here is to declare the VBA array `As Variant`. That way, if cell A1 contains what VBA considers a `String`, and cell A2 contains something of VBA type `Currency`, then when you need an array to reflect the contents of A1, A2, and other cells, the array will be just as flexible in supporting the various types as is the worksheet itself. As we cover Excel in greater depth in future chapters, we'll return to this rather esoteric and complex methodology to see precisely how it works in a real-world situation.

Object declaration and binding are separate processes

Toward the end of the Chapter 2, I introduced you to the Set statement. There, you saw that variables may be declared so that they are capable of referring to certain object classes, but then the Set statement is used later to point those variables toward specific instances of objects. Now that you know more about memory allocation, you may have a greater appreciation of the process of instantiating objects in VBA.

Think of an object class as a mold for the casting of an indeterminate number of replicas. The term *instance* in VBA refers to a copy based on a model. When you declare a new variable As Integer, VBA sets aside 16 bits for future use. But the variable isn't really an integer until it is assigned a whole-number value. The declaration merely carves an integer-shaped chunk out of memory and reserves it for when the integer finally takes shape and fits itself into the slot. Similarly, when you declare a new variable as an object class, VBA sets aside as much memory as that class requires — it carves out an object-shaped niche in memory. The instance of the declared class — which often comes later, but sometimes immediately — then comes in and fits into the slot.

The act of generating an instance of a class is called — for want of more five-syllable words in our computing vernacular — *instantiation*. When a variable is instantiated as a member of a class, it acquires all of the properties associated with that class. So for example, a VBA variable may represent an entire Excel worksheet. The characteristics of that worksheet may be polled through properties of that variable. Thus, instantiation is VBA's way of casting a block of data in the mold provided by a class' definition. This definition may be provided by one of O2K's multiple object libraries, or it may be written as VBA source code, as you'll see in Chapter 9.

When you declare a new variable As Worksheet in Excel VBA, the interpreter sets aside as much memory as is required to store the properties and methods pertaining to an Excel worksheet, whether or not that worksheet is in existence. The Worksheet class object is instantiated when the Set statement is points the new variable to an existing worksheet in the Worksheets collection. It's important to note that the Worksheet class object and the worksheet itself are separate items. The object is used to describe and represent the data — the worksheet itself is maintained by Excel elsewhere in memory.

The process of making an object variable refer to a live data item like a worksheet or a document is called *binding*. When a variable is bound to a live O2K object, when the user changes the O2K application's document, the object representing that document is changed, and the variable bound to that object is changed in turn. Likewise, when the VBA application changes some aspect of the variable, the document to which that variable is bound (by way of the object) is changed as a result. For example, once you've instantiated a `Document` class object in Word 2000, and you invoke the `.InsertAfter` method on the `Range` constituent of that instance, the argument that passes to that method gets typed into the document, just as though the user typed it. The method works because the object variable that acts as the antecedent for the method – for instance, `docThis` in `docThis.Range.InsertAfter` – is bound to the data being changed by that method.

As was discussed in Chapter 2, certain objects in the Office 2000 Object Model are presumed to always exist, such as `ActiveDocument` and the `Documents` collection. When you set a variable to refer to one of these objects, you are binding that variable to the data element to which the object already refers. This isn't easy to understand, so let's look at a few examples. This instruction:

```
Set docThis = ActiveDocument
```

makes variable `docThis` refer to whichever document is currently active in Word. When the user switches to a new document window, `docThis` continues to refer to the same document – it doesn't switch to the new active document. Similarly, this instruction:

```
Set docThis = Documents(2)
```

makes `docThis` refer to whichever is the second document in the collection. Because documents in Word are often opened and closed, `docThis` may not always refer to the second document. The index 2 is only pertinent here in the binding process; after that, you shouldn't think of `docThis` as pointing to "the second document." **Once an object variable is bound to data, it stays bound to that data unless otherwise instructed, or until the data ceases to exist in memory.**

If the documents in our last two examples were preexisting, then exactly when is this instantiation supposed to take place? Here is where things get a bit confusing. From Windows' perspective, documents are objects. When the user selects File→New, she is instantiating a new document object. That's what Windows sees. From VBA's perspective, `docThis`, in the recent examples, is an object variable. It gets instantiated when the program declares that variable to be of a specific object class. Documents such as the kind that the user generates with all those File→New selections, are preexisting data that become bound to these object variables through the use of the `Set` statement.

So if variable `docThis` refers to `Documents(2)`, and the user happens to close "the second document," the variable does not adjust itself to whatever Word document becomes "the second one" after the closed document has exited memory.

Instead, docThis becomes *unbound*, reverting to the state it assumed immediately following the point at which it was declared. Remember, the act of declaration reserves memory for a variable and doesn't necessarily bind that variable to any active object — unless New is written as part of the declaration. So for most object variables, there's a span of time between the point at which they start to exist and the point in which they mean something. When the user removes the object from the scene — an act that is likely to occur at any time — the variable that referred to that object becomes unbound, though it does not cease to exist.

The New keyword invokes fresh instances of objects

When you use Dim or Public or Private to declare an object variable As New Document or As New Worksheet, you are not only calling a new instance of the class into existence (as you would be if you declared it As Document or As Worksheet), but also having the application whose object library you're utilizing generate a new document or new worksheet, thereby bringing it into the collection. For example:

```
Public docThis As New Document
```

In this case, the invocation of the new document, the instantiation of the document variable, and the binding of the variable to the data can take place in the declaration phase. However, suppose docThis has already been declared As Document. In this circumstance, the Set statement may take care of the remaining two jobs of invoking the document and binding it to the object variable, like so:

```
Set docThis = New Document
```

There are only certain object classes in O2KOM that allow you to use the New attribute to invoke them dynamically through VBA. Microsoft calls these special classes *automation objects*. (Less dynamic-sounding terms were available to Microsoft, but why miss out on the opportunity to sound like a comic book dooms-day weapon?) In Microsoft's Component Object Model, these classes of component objects are capable of instantiating themselves. There are separate programs — dynamic link libraries (DLLs) — that are called upon to generate these objects on behalf of so-called *container applications* such as Word. One catch here is that **the lifetime of an automation object instantiated with New is limited to the scope of the variable bound to that object.** So if your declaration instruction Dim docThis As New Document is local to a procedure, then the document itself will cease to exist once the interpreter executes End Sub or End Function.

In Theory: Pascal Lives

The Pascal programming language was named for Blaise Pascal, the gifted and celebrated French mathematician. Pascal's trade, if you will, was geometry. He became known for a technique called the *descriptive theorem*, which he used to explain mathematical principles in a more procedural manner. He needed this method to demonstrate that properties of a geometric shape are proportionally translated to any projection or shadow of that shape on a plane. Metaphysically speaking, the shadow of the truth contains all elements of the truth. But Pascal could not, and certainly would not, introduce metaphysics into his theorems; instead, he found himself drifting outside of mathematical language and relying more upon the French language to impose his principles upon his students, and anyone else with a shred of interest in shadows cast by hexagons inscribed in conics. Pascal's methods, thus, were more *procedural* than empirical.

For his reliance upon procedural methods, Blaise Pascal became immortalized, if you will, by the programming language that bears his name. The Pascal language's creator, the Swiss software engineer Prof. Niklaus Wirth, was more instrumental than perhaps any one person in history for moving the computer program out of its pedantic, single-scroll model into a modular, object-oriented model. It is perhaps because of Pascal and Wirth that C and C++ are the way they are, and Visual Basic and VBA are the way they are.

In an interview published in *Software Development* magazine, Prof. Wirth explained to correspondent Carlo Pescio that object-orientation was basically nothing new, but instead an extrapolation of practical procedure-based programming put to good use. What makes object-orientation seem new, said Wirth, is the language that surrounds it, which has, as he put it, "the purpose of mystifying the roots of object-oriented programming." Wirth went on to imply that perhaps it was the newness of the language itself that attracted newcomers to programming, and thus had the beneficial side-effect of teaching these people how to produce real-world processes, whatever you call them.

Reporter Pescio then put Prof. Wirth on the spot. Quoting from the box containing the latest version of Pascal, now called Delphi 2.0, he read, "Delphi 2.0 gives developers a language almost as readable as BASIC." Pescio was evidently trying to raise Wirth's blood temperature just a bit; Wirth and BASIC have always been at odds with one another. What Pescio received from Wirth was a comment that is testament to his brilliance. Quoting from the article, which appears in the June 1997 issue of *Software Development*:

> We must be careful with terms like readable, user-friendly, and so forth. They are vague at best, and often refer to taste and established habits. But what is conventional need not also be convenient. In the context of programming languages, perhaps "readable" should be replaced by "amenable to formal reasoning." For example, mathematical formulas are hardly what we might praise as easily readable, but they allow the formal derivation of properties that could not be obtained from a vague, fuzzy, informal, user-friendly circumscription.

> The construct `WHILE B DO S END` has the remarkable property that you may rely on B being false after the statement's execution, independent of S. And if you find a property P that is left invariant by S, you may assume that P also holds upon termination. It is this kind of reasoning that helps in the reliable derivation of programs and dramatically reduces the time wasted on testing and debugging. Good languages not only rest on mathematical concepts that make logical reasoning about programs possible, but also on a small number of concepts and rules that can be freely combined. If the definition of a language requires fat manuals of 100 pages and more, and if the definition refers to a mechanical model of execution (for example, to a computer), this must be taken as a sure symptom of inadequacy.

As you might imagine, I tremble upon reading that last sentence. However, Prof. Wirth's underlying point must be taken to heart. Blaise Pascal learned that some simple rules necessary for mathematics and geometry to grow and flourish are found in everyday, simple language. Niklaus Wirth has extended this discovery to the field of programming. For programming to flourish, people should not have to become "computer-literate." Instead, it is the computer that should become "human-literate."

In Brief

- ◆ An array is a set of variables of the same type or class, addressable as a sequence.

- ◆ A string variable represents an element of data made up of collected textual characters in memory.

- ◆ An expression combines values, symbolic variables, and mathematical operators into a logical process that yields a discrete result.

♦ A procedure is a grouping of instructions designed to be representative of at least one function within the VBA program. Its name becomes symbolic of that function, and the procedure is free to use its own symbology and restrictions regarding how it chooses to define that function.

♦ A call to a procedure uses the name explicitly given to that procedure in its declaration. In the case of a Function procedure, that name is representative of the function performed by that procedure, especially when it is invoked as part of an expression.

Chapter 4

The Contributions of the BASIC Language

IN THIS CHAPTER

- ◆ A better comprehension of computing symbology
- ◆ How conditional clauses work
- ◆ Building a stack system
- ◆ Dynamic arrays and how to manage them
- ◆ Multiple conditions in one clause
- ◆ An introduction to some intrinsic VBA functions
- ◆ Loop clauses and why they aren't exactly repetitious after all

BUILDING THE DATA elements that your program will use and performing logical operations on that data forms the foundation of your program. What you need now is to build on that foundation with the following advancements:

- ◆ You'll need to test the state or current value of your data to determine what course of action your VBA module will take or to set multiple possible courses of action.
- ◆ You'll need to engineer your data analysis processes within repeating loops, in order that they may work with lists, sequences, arrays, collections, or documents with multiple parts.
- ◆ You'll need to make use of many of VBA's *intrinsic functions,* that perform operations upon variables, values, or other data.

The Virtue of the Conversational Model

In Chapter 3, you saw how to construct a procedure, how to declare variables for that procedure, and how to manipulate the values in those variables. More thrilling endeavors have been undertaken since the dawn of the computer age, but you may be surprised to learn that few such endeavors having to do with software have failed to involve to some extent the construction of expressions with variables and operators.

It may seem a bit weird that a fully functional program somehow emerges from persistent and repeated tinkering with variables, values, and references. This weirdness fades completely away when you come to a fundamental realization: **All computing is symbolism.** Every word you type, file you save, field you fill in, form you submit, hyperlink you click on, sound you hear, and crash that Windows tries to hide is registered in memory as a symbol. The subjects of all programs you use, as well as all that you will program yourself or extend through VBA, are symbols that represent information that you understand. The computer doesn't understand it the same way you do, but it really wouldn't matter if it did; all that matters is whether you, or any other user, can make sense of the symbolism.

Manipulating symbols in turn manipulates data, which develops into information. This may sound esoteric, especially because the marketing divisions of computer companies commonly use the terms "data" and "information" interchangeably, and "symbol" hardly at all. Data and information in programming really are not interchangeable; one is the product of the other. When you build a computer program, you're devising a way for people to put information into a computer. When it gets there, it's not information any more – it's data. What changed the information into data? Symbology. How the programmer chooses to represent information as data is the governing symbology of the program. It directly affects the quality and quantity of the information that the user receives when the computer uses its symbology to manipulate the input data and output new information for the user.

Case in point: the spelling checker. It is a separate program that gets its input from a channel of sorts that's linked to whatever program is in charge of keyboard input – generally the word processor, but in Office 2000, the Proof spelling checker works with all of the other components. How does a spelling checker know when you've misspelled a word? Common sense might tell you that it checks *the word* once you've typed it, but that's not what happens. Modern spelling checkers are examining character sequences as you type them. By the time you get to the space character signaling the end of the word – and probably before then – the spelling checker already knows if you've misspelled the word. This is because it was performing the lookup process while you were typing the word, and already signaled the "miss."

Isn't this lookup process too complex; wouldn't it have been simpler if the spelling checker simply waited until it saw a space character? Actually, no. It was much simpler for the spelling checker to look up the word as you were typing it. Why? Because the way a word is stored in the spelling checker's lookup table, each new key pressed acts as an index, that "hops" its internal cursor over to the first word that matches all the previously keyed indexes (all the letters you've typed thus far). The moment it can't find a word is when it discovers there's no place in the database to "hop," and it knows it has reached that point several microseconds before your thumb has had a chance to reach for the space bar.

Single-key sequential indexing. . . that is the symbology you've just seen described. The information provided by that symbology is direct and succinct. The symbology was essential to how the original information was input, and equally essential to how the fact of correctness/incorrectness was presented to the user.

In Chapters 2 and 3, we dealt with the construction of symbols (declaration of variables, setting of object references) and how to use mathematical expressions to derive new information from the input data. Yet in Chapter 3, it probably didn't seem like you were doing anything as lofty and high-minded as "deriving new information from the input data." After all, we just added some numbers together and demonstrated why multiplication takes precedence over division, which couldn't possibly be any more exciting than operating the common pocket calculator. But many of the more complex programs you will write will do basically nothing other than those same mundane calculations — only significantly more of them.

Back to the spelling checker for a moment. It is only capable of reading in one input character, adding it to the list of ongoing indexes, and determining whether that index has a match in the database. That's all it does. What makes it work so well is that it does this *repeatedly*. The spelling checker knows just how much to repeat by continually testing the state of the incoming data. So *condition* and *repetition* are two of the foundations of this and all programs; and these very topics with respect to VBA are the focus of this chapter.

Implementing Conditions

A conditional clause is a mechanism used by a program for determining its current course of action. We call it a clause (Microsoft doesn't, but other programmers and I do) because it is an enclosure of instructions. Each clause begins with a lead statement, such as `If...Then` or `Select Case`, and then ends with a corresponding terminating statement, such as `End If` or `End Select`. Each of the instructions enclosed within the clause is dependent upon the results of executing the expression of comparison to which the clause is bound — this is the *binding expression*.

Many If...Then clauses handle either/or conditions

In Listing 2-1 of Chapter 2, for the procedure that replaces two-space sequences between sentences with one space and vice versa, one of the conditional clauses used was this one:

```
If iCount = iCmp Then
    .Text = ".  (<[A-Z])"
    .Replacement.Text = ". \1"
Else
    .Text = ". (<[A-Z])"
    .Replacement.Text = ".  \1"
End If
```

The expression of comparison for this If...Then clause is iCount = iCmp. Symbolically, what these two variables stand for are how many two-space sequences are being searched for, and how many were actually found, respectively. But nothing about this specific clause cares one iota about this representation; all it "knows" is that it compares the value of one variable to the value of another.

As you saw in Chapter 3, all expressions of comparison evaluate to True/False values. So iCount = iCmp has a value, as does any other comparison such as x < 40 or strIndex = "FINAL". Once an expression of comparison is evaluated, it is essentially replaced with True or False. The If...Then statement looks for True in order that it may run the instruction set immediately following. But if the conditional clause contains an Else grouping, as the one above does (it's an optional provision), the instructions in that grouping will be executed if the comparison evaluates to False.

Here is how an If...Then conditional clause is constructed:

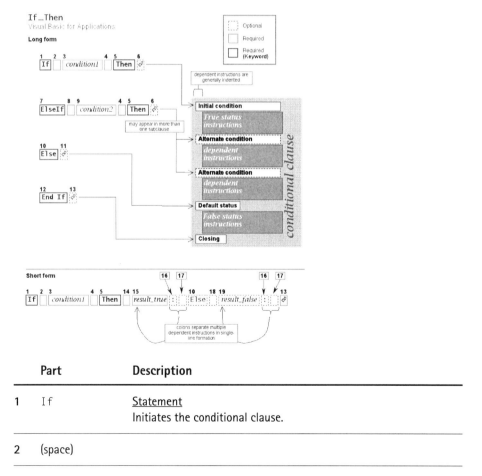

	Part	Description
1	If	**Statement** Initiates the conditional clause.
2	(space)	

3	*condition1*	Expression Any expression that evaluates to a True/False value. Generally, this is an expression of comparison, in which a variable's value or data is compared to another expression.
4	(space)	
5	Then	Statement Separates *condition1* (part 3) from the True instruction block. This block may contain one or more regular VBA instructions of any type, including other conditional clauses. Conditionals that appear within conditionals are considered *nested*, and are generally offset with an extra tab character at the beginning. Once execution of this main True block ends, the interpreter proceeds directly to End If (part 12), skipping any other conditions and instructions that may lay in between, even if those conditions may also have evaluated True.
6	(Enter)	For the **Long form syntax** (shown at the top of the syntax table diagram), the instructions in the True block (part **8**) are on lines by themselves, so the carriage return is necessary to isolate the first instruction in the block.
7	ElseIf	Statement Denotes an alternate expression of comparison that is evaluated *if and only if* the first condition (part **3**) evaluated False, and no other prior instruction blocks were executed as a result. This optional portion of the If...Then statement can trigger an alternate course of action depending entirely upon whether the previous condition was False. Rule: Use of ElseIf is restricted to long form syntax.
8	(space)	
9	*condition2*	Expression A mathematical expression whose *verity* (read: truth) is tested *if and only if* the initial condition (part **3**) evaluated False. If this expression evaluates True, then the instructions in its dependent block are executed.

Continued

	Part	Description
10	Else	Statement Indicates that the instruction block that follows is to be executed only if the initial condition (part **3**) evaluated False, and any conditions stated thereafter (part **9**) also evaluated False. Think of this as the "otherwise" or "if all else fails" segment of the statement.
11	(Enter)	
12	End If	Statement Terminates the conditional clause.
13	(Enter)	
14	(space)	For short-form syntax, this separates the Then portion of the statement (part **5**) from the first instruction (part **15**) in the True chain.
15	*result_true*	Instruction A valid VBA instruction, which will be executed if *condition1* (part **3**) is evaluated True. Short-form syntax follows the old rules for Microsoft BASIC conditional statements, prior to the advent of formal clauses. Following these old rules, a colon and a space separate pairs of dependent instructions from one another. **Rule:** In **Short form syntax** (shown at the bottom of the syntax table diagram), the *result_true* instruction is contiguous, and contains no carriage returns except at the end (part **13**). Although embedded If...Then short-form statements are permitted, they are generally unwieldy, especially with comparison to long-form syntax which is much easier to compose and read. Embedded Select Case clauses, and other clauses that require multiple lines, are not allowed in short-form syntax.
16	:(colon)	Separates all valid single-line instructions in this form of the If...Then statement from one another.
17	(space)	
18	(space)	Separates the optional Else portion of the statement from the first embedded result instruction in the False chain (part **19**).
19	*result_false*	Instruction A valid VBA instruction, which is executed if *condition1* (part **3**) evaluates False.

In Depth: How binding expressions are evaluated

In forming expressions of comparison for the If...Then clause, a comparison operator, such as =, <, >, <=, >=, or <>, is generally used. The most common type of self-explanatory clause might look like this:

```
If iStatesCounted = 50 Then
    Exit Sub
End If
```

However, any other type of expression that evaluates to a *nonzero* value is treated in this situation as though it evaluates to True. So a single variable name may be used as the binding condition for the clause, in order that the variable may be tested for a non-zero value. The following example uses the short form syntax of the If...Then instruction:

```
If iOverFlow Then Exit Sub
```

This situation would only be useful if 0 were a meaningless value to the variable; in other words, if the variable represents a temperature in mercury degrees, 0 would be a meaningful value, and thus would not signify the presence or absence of something, or any other type of dual state. Any type of expression you use for If...Then in place of an expression of comparison must be capable of a meaningful evaluation to 0, which is interpreted by VBA as False.

The If...Then conditional clause is an ordinary, everyday part of VBA programming. It crops up in the most common of situations, because it is one of a very few VBA instructions that actually *evaluate* the state of the symbols in your program. Because If...Then is so versatile, there doesn't need to be many more statements.

IF...THEN EXAMPLE

Here's a fairly ordinary example of If...Then in action, using Excel 2000: More than once when working on a worksheet, I've found myself having to leave a region where I'm entering figures, and move the cell pointer to some other location in order to look over the included formulas. Doing this means that my nicely selected range, where figures are being entered, disappears. I'd like to be able to move my indicator to wherever it needs to be to evaluate its cell formulas, and then be able to move back to that range and cell position when I'm done, using a single keystroke.

But what if I'm in the middle of evaluating cells, I've indicated *another* range, and I need to move the cell indicator elsewhere *again*. I would want Excel to be capable of remembering the previous cell range from a moment ago, and then still remember the *first* cell range so I could still return to it. What needs to be set up is a set of *stacks*, full of data recording cell indicator positions at different periods of time, plus a recall system where the last position recorded is the first one recalled. This is what we call in computing a *last-in-first-out* stack system, or LIFO. When I'm ready to move the cell indicator out of the range to go exploring, I can use a keystroke which triggers a process that makes Excel remember the currently indicated range, like a snapshot. Whenever I use that same keystroke later, the most recently recorded cell range will be *pushed* on top of the stack, lowering the others down one notch. I'll then use another keystroke to *pop* the most recently recorded range off the top of the stack, and have Excel automatically re-indicate that range and put the cell indicator back where it was.

Since the interpreter must keep track of these recorded ranges while the module itself is dormant (while none of its procedures are being executed), the variables that represent the stacks must be declared Public, using a declaration process outlined in Chapter 3. Here are the declarations for this example, from the module's Declarations section:

```
Public strStackCell() As String, strStackRange() As String, _
  strStackSheet() As String, strStackBook() As String
Public iShadows As Integer
```

Variables that are declared with public scope are retained by the VBA interpreter, even while procedures in the modules where those variables are declared are not running. The very moment the document containing a VBA module is opened, the VBA interpreter executes that module's Declarations section. At that time, a Public statement can call variables into existence, long before any of the procedures in that module are ever run. These public scope variables will continue to exist until that document is closed. This is different from the way other language interpreters work. Generally, when the program stops running, its variables are automatically unloaded; but in VBA, the program and its variables are dependent upon the active document. So the program – or rather, the module – isn't free to shut down operations until the user says, "I'm done with the *document.*"

We can take advantage of this persistence of variables by declaring all of our necessary stacks Public. This way, they're available whenever a user keystroke triggers one of the procedures. Notice, though, that while our string variables are all arrays, we've omitted their upper and lower bounds from the declarations. This is because our stacks should be *dynamic* so that they can grow indefinitely, and not have some arbitrarily imposed bounds. Later in this chapter, you'll see the ReDim statement used to extend or reduce the stacks' bounds, so that for any one point in time, exactly as much memory is used as is required. I'll explain ReDim in more detail later.

Listing 4-1 shows the procedure that will be triggered when the user tells Excel, through a Ctrl keystroke, to remember the currently indicated range.

Listing 4-1: Pushing the current range location onto the stacks.

```
Public Sub CollectShadow()
    iShadows = iShadows + 1
    ReDim Preserve strStackCell(iShadows), _
     strStackRange(iShadows), strStackSheet(iShadows), _
     strStackBook(iShadows)
    If TypeOf Selection Is Range Then
        strStackBook(iShadows) = ActiveWorkbook.Name
        strStackSheet(iShadows) = _
         ActiveWorkbook.ActiveSheet.Name
        strStackRange(iShadows) = Selection.Address
        strStackCell(iShadows) = ActiveCell.Address
    Else
        Beep
    End If
End Sub
```

Public variable iShadows is an integer that keeps a persistent count of how many remembered ranges, or "shadows," are on these stacks. Each time we add a range to the stacks, iShadows is incremented (iShadows = iShadows + 1).

In Excel, the *cell pointer* is that black rectangle that indicates the cells that are the focus of the next user command; in Excel 2000, the cell pointer has been given 1960s yellow-tinted shades. In Listing 4-1, the current location of the cell pointer is ascertained from four references: the workbook, the worksheet contained in the workbook, the indicated cell range in the worksheet, and the cell address itself. Excel needs all four references in order to uniquely identify any one cell or cell range, because more than one workbook (collection of worksheets) may be open at any one time. In Listing 4-1, the four stack arrays are dynamically redeclared.

Here's where the first If...Then statement comes into play (so *that's* what this example is supposed to be about!). This particular conditional clause utilizes an unusual, but relatively legible, comparison expression: TypeOf Selection Is Range. You don't need any parentheses or extra punctuation for the TypeOf function, which is rare but, in this case, welcome. As long as you know to what the object terms refer, the meaning of this statement is self-evident. The clause checks to see if whatever the cell pointer is currently indicating (and there's always something, by default) is a cell range, and not something else such as an embedded chart or an ActiveX control. The Selection object refers to the currently indicated area, and Range is an object class that affiliates all the valid methods for addressing *cells*, and nothing else, in Excel.

Our four stack arrays are string variables because character strings are the most conservative vehicles for remembering the recorded cell ranges. I could have used objects instead; rather than strStackBook(iShadows) = ActiveWorkbook.Name, I could have had Set rngStackBook(iShadows) = ActiveWorkbook. But all this module needs to know to get back to a recorded range is the object's name, not the entire object. A workbook in Excel has the default name of Book*n*, and a worksheet (spreadsheet) has the default name of Sheet*n*. The user may change these names at any time, but even so, they do uniquely reference their associated objects. `ActiveWorkbook` represents the worksheet collection that the user is currently viewing, and `ActiveSheet` represents the worksheet that's on the screen. Both `.Name` properties contain the given names of these objects. These names are simple strings, not objects in themselves, so you don't need the `Set` statement to assign their contents to string variables.

The `Address` properties both contain cell addresses. For `Selection`, such an address might be `$A$1:$R$15`. A range address like this denotes generally one, sometimes more, rectangular regions of cells. Remember that these addresses follow Excel's rules, not VBA's. Capital letters in the cell addresses denote columns in the worksheet, numerals denote rows, and the letters go first. The `$` character designates an *absolute* reference, which in Excel means "precisely this row" or "precisely this column," so that Excel won't adjust the reference if the formula making that reference is moved to a new cell. Although that fact isn't too important in this context, the `.Address` properties always include absolute references. When you see the colon in the address, read "to," so `$A$1:$R$15` reads "A-one *to* R-fifteen."

In Excel, there is always a currently indicated cell in the visible worksheet. If the user starts typing text or a formula, it will appear in the indicated cell. The user can click and drag on a worksheet, and in so doing, indicate or "select" a cell *range*. The reason a user would wish to do so is to define the bounds for a table full of values to be typed in manually, or to designate an area of existing values that will act as references for a new chart. The first cell the user clicked on will contain the cell indicator, and will continue to contain it as the drag proceeds. There are really two "selections" here: that of the active cell and that of the active range. If the user starts typing values or formulas into this range, then pressing Enter causes the cell indicator to proceed down to the next cell in the column. But when the indicator reaches the bottom cell in the active *range*, then pressing Enter sends it back to the top cell in the column to the right. So the cell indicator always floats within the indicated active range.

With all our terms defined, we can adequately describe the `If...Then` clause here: It checks to see if the currently indicated cell or range of cells qualifies as a `Range`, which can be addressed like `$A$1:$R$15`. If it is, then all four *textual* references are assigned to the string arrays. Otherwise, the `Else` portion of the clause kicks in, which merely signals a `Beep` to the user; no need to *punish* the user with some vindictive dialog box for indicating something that isn't a range. The `Beep` statement is just enough to tell the user, "No."

When it's time to recall the most recently pushed range, a separate keystroke will bring up the procedure in Listing 4-2.

Listing 4-2: Popping the most recently recorded range from the stacks.

```
Public Sub GoBackToShadow()
    Dim objBook As Workbook, objSheet As Worksheet
    Dim bDone As Boolean

    If iShadows > 0 Then
        For Each objBook In Workbooks
            If objBook.Name = strStackBook(iShadows) Then
                For Each objSheet In Worksheets
                    If objSheet.Name = _
                     strStackSheet(iShadows) _
                    Then
                        Workbooks(strStackBook(iShadows)) _
                        .Worksheets(strStackSheet(iShadows)) _
                         .Activate
                        Range(strStackRange(iShadows)).Select
                        Range(strStackCell(iShadows)).Activate
                        bDone = True
                    End If
                Next objSheet
            End If
        Next objBook
        iShadows = iShadows - 1
        ReDim Preserve strStackCell(iShadows), _
         strStackRange(iShadows), strStackSheet(iShadows), _
         strStackBook(iShadows)
    End If
    If Not bDone Then Beep
End Sub
```

There are three If...Then clauses here, and the one that starts furthest to the *left* (i.e., the one with the least indentation) is the one that the interpreter will see first. We'll call this the *primary* clause; the other two are *dependents*.

The purpose of the primary If...Then conditional clause in Listing 4-2 is to restrict execution of the most important instructions in this procedure to cases where there is a positive number of recorded "shadow" ranges on the stacks. If there's nothing for the main body of the procedure to recall, there's no point in executing it. The condition upon which this clause is *dependent* is a conventional expression of comparison iShadows > 0. Like most expressions used for If...Then, this one employs a variable, a comparison operator, and a value. You can read this particular statement as, "If the number of recorded shadow ranges is greater than 0, then...."

Validating object references, the only way you can

The next step for this procedure is to determine whether the recorded workbook and worksheet still exist in the workspace. It's no use trying to recall a cell position that is no longer valid. If the user deleted the worksheet, or otherwise removed it from the Excel workspace, the VBA interpreter wouldn't find out until it tried to reactivate a recorded cell range on the removed sheet.

Here is where we encounter one of the great "Catch-22" scenarios that surround Windows' design of object models: When using the Office 2000 Object Model (O2KOM), there's no way for you to directly test whether an object reference, such as a reference to a range of cells, is valid. The reason is because in order that the reference may be tested, it must be written explicitly, whether or not it is valid. And if the reference is invalid, then it can't be tested. Now, it would be valuable to us if a reference could be flagged or signaled as invalid. For it to be invalid, the reference would have to be . . . well, *invalid*. And if that's so, the reference is not an object, so it has no properties, and therefore no way to signal its own invalidity. You could write an instruction that tries the object reference, and then write a routine that traps the resultant error when the reference does turn up invalid. But for the error-trap routine to know what about the reference was necessarily invalid, it would have to know what precisely would make that reference *valid*; and for that, the routine would need to be *clairvoyant*.

But wait, you might be thinking, the online help for Excel 2000 VBA clearly refers to a function named `IsObject()`, whose purpose is to return a True/False value designating whether a given object is real or unreal. The sad truth about the `IsObject()` function is that it works exclusively with VBA object references. Its purpose is to determine whether an object reference variable – one that you would declare with a `Dim` or `Public` or `Private` statement – is valid. But `IsObject()` cannot determine whether the object to which the variable refers is valid, because then it would have to deliver a complex database query to the Excel object library . . . and VBA simply isn't that complex in the database department.

So for Listing 4-2, what we do instead is use `For Each...Next` loop clauses to cycle through all the names of open workbooks (.XLS files), then all the names of included worksheets, until a matching name is found. To do this, two local object reference variables `objBook` and `objSheet` were declared. These variables refer to each object in their respective collections in sequence – `objBook` to the members of `Workbooks` and `objSheet` to the members of `Worksheets`.

How members of Excel collections may be reliably identified

For the instructions that the "pop" the recorded range to ever be reached by the interpreter, three tests must be passed: First, there must be more than one recorded shadow range, indicated by a positive value in the public integer `iShadows`. Second, a matching workbook name must be found. Third, a matching worksheet name must be found. All three of these tests are accomplished with If...Then statements that employ conventional expressions of comparison. For the latter two tests, the recorded names strStackBook() and strStackSheet() are compared to the .Name properties of the local object references, which are cycling through all the open objects in the Excel workspace. The = operator is used to compare one character string to another, the same way the operator is used to compare an expression's evaluated result to a variable.

Variable iShadows represents the number of shadows pushed onto the stacks, which is also – not coincidentally – the index number of the first shadow to be popped off of the stack. The instruction that pops the references off the list is written as a chain, where the recorded worksheet is connected to the recorded workbook, and the recorded range is connected to that worksheet. Here we see the Excel object hierarchy in play, and how in VBA you can not only refer to a specific object in terms of what other object it belongs to, but also to the constituents of that specific object in the same instruction.

Again, character strings represented in the strStackBook(), strStackRange(), and strStackSheet() arrays uniquely identify the recorded .Name and .Address properties. There are a handful of ways to identify specific members of an Excel collection such as Workbooks, but not all of these ways can be relied upon over long periods of time. For instance, a workbook may be identified by its location in the Windows collection (one of Excel's globals). But if the user calls up another workbook whose title just happens to fall alphabetically *before* the title of this window, its location will be bumped further down the chain. So "Window #1" – or rather, Windows(1) – cannot be counted on to remain "Window #1" for the duration of the Excel session. Suppose instead that we had declared object references and set them early on to point to ActiveWorkbook or ActiveSheet using the Set statement. When the user opened a new workbook or added another worksheet, the references would change as well, and the point of *recording* names and addresses would be lost. In other words, when you declare a variable wbkThis and make it refer to the active workbook like so:

```
Set wbkThis = ActiveWorkbook
```

then variable wbkThis really does refer to the active workbook . . . whatever that may be at any time. You're not setting it to refer to the specific workbook that was active at the time that this instruction was executed. Instead, you're making wbkThis a mirror of ActiveWorkbook. What would be the point of this? Frankly, there truly is no good reason to do such a thing.

This is why Listing 4-1 records the *name* of the workbook and worksheet – things that are unlikely to change over time. Listing 4-2 recalls these names through string variables, and uses them to identify the recorded range locations. This is a more reliable way of going about this . . . but still, it is not the most reliable way. As you can imagine, the names of workbooks and worksheets are subject to change. More reliable ways to exclusively identify Excel collection members over time is one of the subjects we'll cover in Chapter 17. I trust you have a lot of patience.

"Activating" and/or "selecting" Excel objects

In the middle of Listing 4-2 you'll find two methods whose purpose is to substitute for the mouse in the act of reindicating the recorded range: .Activate and .Select. These are two methods whose distinction from one another is extremely esoteric and difficult to catch. One reason is that the following two instructions perform exactly the same task:

```
Range("A7:D14").Activate
Range("A7:D14").Select
```

One clear distinction between .Activate and .Select is this: In O2KOM, you can *activate* a workbook or a worksheet, though you cannot *select* either one. As the above pair demonstrates, you can activate or select a range of cells; there's no functional difference here. But notice in Listing 4-2 how the .Select method is applied to the recorded range of cells, and then the .Activate method is applied to a single recorded cell. Why? Because in Excel you have a cell pointer within the cell range indicator. Ever highlight a column of cells and then use the numeric keypad to enter values into those cells? Notice how the cell pointer (the white cell within the yellow block in Excel 2000) moves down the column, while the highlighting on the range stays right where it is? Placing the cell pointer in a specific location within the highlighted range is a job performed exclusively by the .Activate method. There's no simple way to remember this fact; it's simply the way things are in Excel.

After Sub GoBackToShadow() in Listing 4-2 sends the user back to where she was before, a local Boolean variable bDone is set to True. The purpose of this variable is to clear the interpreter from an alarm trap, which is found at the end of the procedure. It is an If...Then statement written using short-form syntax. It's not a clause here because there are no dependent instructions and no End If. But the interpreter allows that, as long as everything that it is supposed to execute if the test passes is written on one line to the right of Then. Here, the test is Not bDone. This is a *logical expression*, because it uses the Boolean operator Not. We want this test to pass if bDone fails. To accommodate this flip-flop, the Not operator is put before the Boolean-type variable bDone, so that the evaluated result of the logical expression is the *reverse* of bDone.

For these two previous listings, I used the ReDim statement to a significant extent, so the bounds of the stack arrays could be stretched and shrunk to fit. Here is how the ReDim statement is constructed:

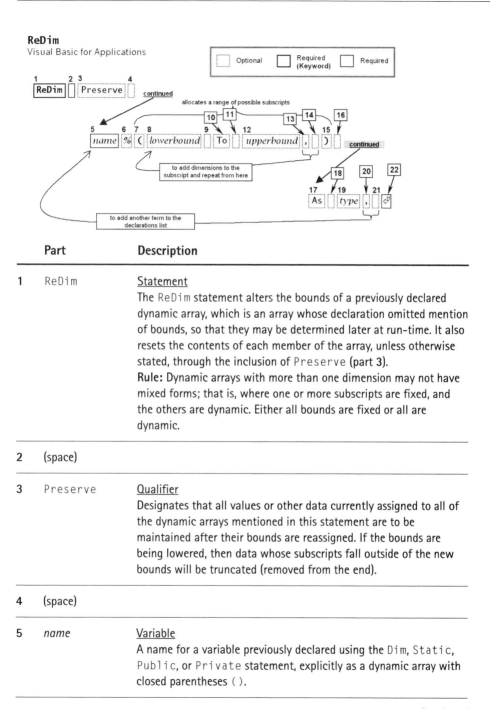

Part		Description
1	ReDim	**Statement** The ReDim statement alters the bounds of a previously declared dynamic array, which is an array whose declaration omitted mention of bounds, so that they may be determined later at run-time. It also resets the contents of each member of the array, unless otherwise stated, through the inclusion of Preserve (part 3). **Rule:** Dynamic arrays with more than one dimension may not have mixed forms; that is, where one or more subscripts are fixed, and the others are dynamic. Either all bounds are fixed or all are dynamic.
2	(space)	
3	Preserve	**Qualifier** Designates that all values or other data currently assigned to all of the dynamic arrays mentioned in this statement are to be maintained after their bounds are reassigned. If the bounds are being lowered, then data whose subscripts fall outside of the new bounds will be truncated (removed from the end).
4	(space)	
5	name	**Variable** A name for a variable previously declared using the Dim, Static, Public, or Private statement, explicitly as a dynamic array with closed parentheses ( ).

Continued

	Part	Description
6	!#$%&	<u>Type specifier character</u> (No default) Restricts the data type of the declared value to any of the following: ! Single precision floating point # Double precision floating point $ String % Short integer & Long integer
7	((left parenthesis)	
8	*lowerbound*	<u>Integer</u> When declaring arrays whose members are to be referenced by number, *lowerbound* sets the index number of the first member of the array. If *lowerbound* is omitted (as is usually the case), the interpreter assumes this initial index to be 0 by default.
9	(space)	
10	To	Separates the index for the lower boundary (part **8**) from the upper boundary (part **12**), when the lower boundary is included.
11	(space)	
12	*upperbound*	<u>Integer</u> Sets the index number of the final member of the array. Members of the array are numbered consecutively from 0 or *lowerbound* to *upperbound*. Unlike the case with a conventional declarative statement, **this value, as well as lowerbound (part 8), may be a variable.** This way, the size of the dynamic array can be determined at run-time, by storing that size in an integer variable and supplying that variable as the argument to ReDim.
13	,(comma)	Separates the index subscripts for different axes of the array. VBA recognizes arrays with up to 60 dimensions.
14	(space)	
15	)(right parenthesis)	Closes the subscript.
16	(space)	

17	As	If the dynamic array variable (part **5**) was previously declared As Variant, As written here begins the specification for the variant's type. This type may be changed for the variant with another ReDim statement later in the module, although if the type is being changed, Preserve (part **3**) must be omitted.
18	(space)	
19	*type*	<u>Type or class</u> States the type and structure of the variant. This must be a recognized object-type term that belongs to one of the object libraries currently referenced by the interpreter. **Rule:** The New qualifier may not be used in redeclaring a dynamic array.
20	, (comma)	Separates pairs of redeclared variables from one another.
21	(space)	
22	(Enter)	Closes the statement.

REDIM EXAMPLE

In Listing 4-2, the following instructions were used to reduce the size of the stack and to trim the stack arrays:

```
iShadows = iShadows - 1
ReDim Preserve strStackCell(iShadows), _
  strStackRange(iShadows), strStackSheet(iShadows), _
  strStackBook(iShadows)
```

By decrementing (lowering by 1) the value of iShadows, and then assigning that integer as the upper bounds of the stack, we lop off the last subscript in each of these arrays. But by including the Preserve part of the ReDim statement, we ensure that the remaining array contents are not cleared. If we had omitted Preserve, then the arrays would still be trimmed to the right size, but all of their contents would have been nullified.

Handling multiple permutations of conditions

The If...Then statement is well suited to handling as many as two or three dependent conditions. The problem with If...Then in a multiple-condition scenario, where only one or at least one condition is the "correct" one out of a set, is that the clause must list the entire expression of comparison for each condition in that set. It isn't as much a problem for the interpreter as it is for the programmer. Having seven or eight (or more) ElseIf extensions to an If...Then clause looks a little clumsy.

The cleaner alternative to multiple ElseIf extensions is the Select Case clause. Here, the dependent condition is broken into two pieces, which we'll call the *subject expression* and the *test expression*. Normally, the subject expression contains the part of the condition that would have gone in the If...Then statement to the *left* of the = equality operator. The test expression is the part that would have been written to the right of the = operator. There are other ways to phrase Select Case, but this is the most common way to go about it.

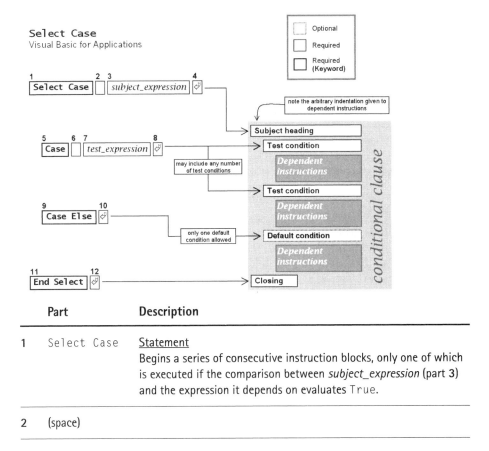

Part		Description
1	Select Case	**Statement**
		Begins a series of consecutive instruction blocks, only one of which is executed if the comparison between *subject_expression* (part **3**) and the expression it depends on evaluates True.
2	(space)	

3	*subject_ expression*	<u>Expression</u> An expression that evaluates to any discrete value or data. The test expressions which follow (part **8**) will be compared against this expression for equality — meaning that whatever the test expression evaluates to must equal (or match, in the case of text) whatever this subject expression evaluates to, in order for the subject's dependent instruction block to be executed.
4	(Enter)	
5	`Case`	Denotes the location of the test expression (part **7**).
6	(space)	
7	*test_expression*	<u>Expression</u> Compared to the subject expression (part **3**) for equality. In such case, the dependent instruction block is executed. **Rule:** In previous permutations of the `Select Case` clause, you could write several `Case` *test_expression* statements in succession, and have them all point to one instruction block below. This phraseology is no longer supported.
8	(Enter)	
9	`Case Else`	<u>Statement</u> Indicates a block of instructions that will be executed *if and only if* all other test expressions fail to evaluate equally to the subject expression. Consider this the "otherwise" or "if all else fails" portion of the `Select Case` clause.
10	(Enter)	
11	`End Select`	<u>Statement</u> Marks the end of the clause.
12	(Enter)	Closes the `Select Case` clause.

A Select Case clause tests for multiple conditions

In the `Select Case` clause, there are two important types of expressions at play. The first, of which there's only one, is what we call the *subject expression*. All of the other expressions, which we call *test expressions,* are compared against the subject expression. The VBA interpreter is testing for equality – whether whatever the test evaluates to is equal or equivalent to what the subject evaluates to. There are several different ways in which the subject and test expressions may be phrased. Most commonly, the two expression are phrased as flat values without any operators, like this:

```
Select Case iType
    Case 1
        'response to iType = 1
    Case 2
        'response to iType = 2
    Case Else
        'response to all other possible values
End Select
```

Here, iType is an integer variable. No logical operators are required within the test expressions for the interpreter to recognize that it is supposed to compare iType with 1 or 2 for *equality*. (By the way, the instruction lines above that begin with ' apostrophes are *remarks*, which are ignored by the interpreter. I added them above as placeholders to illustrate where certain types or categories of instructions go.)

For ranges of values, particularly fractional or floating-point, mathematical operators become necessary. For example:

```
Select Case sTemp
    Case < 0
        'less than zero
    Case = 0
        'equals zero
    Case > 0
        'greater than zero
    Case Else
        'never gets to this point
End Select
```

It isn't so obvious here, but the interpreter is still testing the subject expression against the test expression for equality. However, the rules change as to what the interpreter considers to be *the expression*. For this construction, the test expressions become sTemp < 0, sTemp = 0, and sTemp > 0, respectively. The interpreter uses the variable in the subject expression to fill in the missing gaps in the test expressions, prior to the mathematical operators. So what's the subject expression in this clause? Just True. You don't write that into the clause, but that is what the subject expression becomes when you write a Select Case clause this way. By the way, because the first three Case expressions cover all possible values, the instructions dependent on `Case Else` will never be executed. But it won't be "illegal" for you to write `Case Else` instructions; the interpreter won't try to stop you from doing so, even though it's futile in this case.

Back in Chapter 3 we discussed the concepts of binding and type checking. When you declare a variable `As Object`, you're telling the VBA interpreter that the new variable will indeed be an object reference, though exactly what *class* of object is not yet known or will be determined at run time. This object class deference is called *late binding.* When you finally do assign a real object from O2KOM to this object variable, you may use VBA functions to determine the object's type. On the surface, it would appear that the most convenient such function available for this job is the irregular `TypeOf`, which doesn't require parentheses and whose construction reads like a sentence. Here's an example of `TypeOf` in an everyday Excel situation, where the type of object currently indicated in a worksheet is being polled:

```
If TypeOf Selection Is Range Then
    'instructions which address the Range class
ElseIf TypeOf Selection Is ChartArea Then
    'instructions which address the ChartObject class
ElseIf TypeOf Selection Is Picture Then
    'instructions which address the Picture class
End If
```

Here, you would have to write out `TypeOf Selection Is` in its entirety for each condition. The convenience in using `Select Case` is that it has you write only the data to which the subject variable is being compared for each condition. But the `TypeOf` function only works in an `If...Then` clause, for some strange reason unbeknownst to me. The way to use `Select Case` for this purpose is to abandon `TypeOf` and instead utilize a lesser known VBA function, use `TypeName()`, which actually performs the same task. Here's how:

```
Select Case TypeName(Selection)
    Case "Range"
        'instructions which address the Range class
    Case "ChartArea"
        'instructions which address the ChartObject class
    Case "Picture"
        'instructions which address the Picture class
End Select
```

SELECT CASE EXAMPLE

To better illustrate how `Select Case` works in a real-world setting, here's a demonstration of a second *build,* if you will, of the procedures presented in Listings 4-1 and 4-2. In Excel 2000, there are many other types of objects that you can "select," or indicate with the mouse, other than just cell ranges. In the previous build of this module, the stack variables recorded just cell ranges; so if any other type of embedded object happened to be indicated at the time the user hit the "Record" keystroke, the module would simply beep and exit. We want procedures that can handle multiple selection *types*. Multiple types means multiple conditions, which present a perfect opportunity for a `Select Case` clause.

First, the public-scope variable declarations should be changed to reflect the fact that there's one more stack variable for which the module keeps track: the type – or, more accurately, the class – of the indicated object:

```
Option Explicit

Public strSelection() As String, strStackCell() As String, _
  strStackRange() As String, strStackSheet() As String, _
  strStackBook() As String
Public iShadows As Integer
```

Listing 4-3 shows a vastly revised recording procedure. The `Select Case` clause is used to determine the type of the indicated object, and to implement the recording process that best suits the ascertained type.

Listing 4-3: The indicated object recorder, build #2.

```
Public Sub CollectShadow()
    Dim objShape As Shape
    Dim bDone As Boolean
    iShadows = iShadows + 1
    ReDim Preserve strSelection(iShadows), _
      strStackCell(iShadows), strStackRange(iShadows), _
      strStackSheet(iShadows), strStackBook(iShadows)
    strSelection(iShadows) = TypeName(Selection)
    Select Case TypeName(Selection)
        Case "Range"
            strStackBook(iShadows) = ActiveWorkbook.Name
            strStackSheet(iShadows) = _
             ActiveWorkbook.ActiveSheet.Name
            strStackRange(iShadows) = Selection.Address
            strStackCell(iShadows) = ActiveCell.Address
        Case "ChartArea"
            strStackBook(iShadows) = ActiveWorkbook.Name
            strStackSheet(iShadows) = _
             ActiveWorkbook.ActiveSheet.Name
            strStackRange(iShadows) = Right$ _
             (ActiveChart.Name, Len(ActiveChart.Name) - _
             Len(ActiveSheet.Name) - 1)
```

```
        Case "OLEObject"
            strStackBook(iShadows) = ActiveWorkbook.Name
            strStackSheet(iShadows) = _
             ActiveWorkbook.ActiveSheet.Name
            strStackRange(iShadows) = Selection.Name
        Case Else
            For Each objShape In ActiveSheet.Shapes
                If objShape.Name = Selection.Name Then
                    strStackBook(iShadows) = _
                     ActiveWorkbook.Name
                    strStackSheet(iShadows) = _
                     ActiveWorkbook.ActiveSheet.Name
                    strStackRange(iShadows) = Selection.Name
                    bDone = True
                    Exit For
                End If
            Next objShape
            If Not bDone Then Beep
    End Select
End Sub
```

Notice first that one more variable has been added to the ReDim statement, accounting for the fifth stack. Immediately afterward, that new stack variable is assigned the results of the VBA intrinsic function TypeName(Selection). This is a quirky function, because not all objects, when they're indicated on the worksheet, attribute their indicated state to their own identities. Case in point: the embedded chart, whose class is ChartObject. When the user indicates an embedded chart with the mouse, the Selection object for Excel registers ChartArea, which is a constituent of ChartObject but not the same as ChartObject. Apparently, ChartObject is the class of object responsible for *creating* the chart, while ChartArea is responsible for *displaying* it. It doesn't mean there's more than one chart, but it does mean that someplace there's more than one object.

In Excel, the Selection object does not necessarily refer to whatever is under the cell pointer. When there are other classes of OLE objects embedded in the worksheet, then when the user clicks on one of these, the cell pointer goes away and the object is indicated by eight little square nodes along the object's perimeter. At that time, the embedded object is considered "selected," and the class of Excel's Selection object becomes that of the object, rather than its usual Range.

So in the Select Case clause in Listing 4-3, TypeName(Selection) becomes the subject expression, and "ChartArea" becomes its second test expression. When this class turns up, it's a signal that the user has indicated an embedded chart. Why the quotation marks? Because the TypeName() function returns a *string*, not a class; and when a string is written as a *literal*, you must surround it with quotation marks.

The `Select Case` clause evaluates the current setting for `TypeName` (`Selection`). If it matches any of the literal strings written beside `Case` as test expressions, the interpreter executes the instruction block below that `Case` statement. Notice there doesn't have to be some "End Case" instruction to close out the block; the next `Case` statement is enough to close the previous block.

Notice also that the functionality from the first build, dealing with cell ranges, was moved to the `Case "Range"` block. For the other supported types, the `strStackRange()` variable pulls double duty, recording whatever name is used to refer exclusively to the indicated object, so that it can be activated later.

While we're on the subject, let's clear up a potential point of discrepancy: What is the difference between *class* and *type*? A variable in VBA has a standard *type*, such as `Double` or `Integer` or `String`, unless it is being used as an object reference. In that case, the variable is best described by the object's class. **"Type" refers to ordinary units of data, whereas "class" refers to a structure that includes both data and functionality.** So why isn't there a "ClassType()" function to handle classes? Because `TypeName()` is all-inclusive. It registers the variable's type when it happens to be one of VBA's standard types, and then it registers its class name when it's an object reference.

Reconciling different object libraries

When we get to the point in O2K programming where we begin working with Forms 2.0 objects, such as labels, checkboxes, and drop-down combo boxes, we enter into yet another peculiarity regarding how Excel classifies objects from the two most often used libraries. The Forms objects all have their own class names, such as `Label`, `CheckBox`, and `DropDown`; and when the Excel user right-clicks on one of these objects floating on the worksheet, thereby "selecting" it, the `Selection` registers its class name. But when it comes time to address these objects later, because they are embedded within an Excel worksheet, they will need to be addressed in the context of Excel and not Forms 2.0.

So beneath `Case Else` in Listing 4-3, the `For Each...Next` loop cycles through each of the objects in the `Shapes` collection, where Excel lumps together many of the embedded objects it doesn't recognize and doesn't handle directly. Not every conceivable embedded object ends up being categorized as a `Shape`, so we'll permit those to be the miscellaneous unsupported objects that qualify for a curious `Beep` from the interpreter. The embedded `If...Then` clause checks the `.Name` property of the object currently being counted by the `For Each...Next` loop to see if it matches `Selection.Name`. This is perhaps the only way to determine whether the indicated object is also a registered Excel `Shape` class object. When a match does come up, then its vital data is recorded in the stack variables, and the beep-trigger variable `bDone` is "disarmed," if you will.

Listing 4-4 shows the new build of the procedure from Listing 4-2 that reactivates a recorded object:

Listing 4-4: Build #2 of the shadow object recall procedure.

```
Public Sub GoBackToShadow()
  Dim objBook As Workbook, objSheet As Worksheet, _
   objShape As Shape
  Dim bDone As Boolean
  If iShadows > 0 Then
    For Each objBook In Workbooks
      If objBook.Name = strStackBook(iShadows) Then
        For Each objSheet In Worksheets
          If objSheet.Name = strStackSheet(iShadows) Then
            Workbooks(strStackBook(iShadows)) _
             .Worksheets(strStackSheet(iShadows)) _
             .Activate
            Select Case strSelection(iShadows)
              Case "Range"
                Range(strStackRange(iShadows)).Select
                Range(strStackCell(iShadows)).Activate
              Case "ChartArea"
                Worksheets(strStackSheet(iShadows)) _
                 .ChartObjects(strStackRange(iShadows)) _
                 .Activate
              Case "OLEObject"
                Worksheets(strStackSheet(iShadows)) _
                 .OLEObjects(strStackRange(iShadows)) _
                 .Activate
              Case Else
                For Each objShape In ActiveSheet.Shapes
                  If objShape.Name = _
                   strStackRange(iShadows) Then
                    objShape.Select
                  End If
                Next objShape
            End Select
            bDone = True
          End If
        Next objSheet
      End If
    Next objBook
    iShadows = iShadows - 1
    ReDim Preserve strSelection(iShadows), _
     strStackCell(iShadows), strStackRange(iShadows), _
     strStackSheet(iShadows), strStackBook(iShadows)
  End If
  If Not bDone Then Beep
End Sub
```

All the nesting and dependency in this procedure has turned it into something of a lump. In its current incarnation, it relies on `For Each...Next` loop clauses for verification mechanisms. All of these clauses in Listing 4-4 cycle through collections of objects that are currently open in Excel, in search of objects whose names or addresses match those that the procedure in Listing 4-3 previously recorded.

Here in Listing 4-4, you may recognize a near mirror image of the `Select Case` clause in the previous procedure. All three object classes directly supported by Excel are presented here in the same order, with `Case Else` handling the possible members of Excel's `Shapes` collection. The `For Each...Next` clause within `Case Else` cycles through the members of `Shapes`, looking for objects that match the recorded name of the indicated `Shape` class object. Where there's a match, the `.Select` method is used to give that object back the focus. Again, Excel's object model uses the `.Select` method to give the focus to objects that may represent pluralities (a Forms 2.0 list box may contain multiple entries) and the `.Activate` method to give the focus to certain singularities, such as individual cells.

On Point

Conditional clauses are used to determine a program's course of action based on the results obtained by evaluating expressions of comparison. Each conditional clause is bound to at least one such expression. The `If...Then` statement binds a conditional clause that utilizes at least one expression of comparison, while the `Select Case` statement is bound by multiple permutations of one expression. `Select Case` can test for many possible variable values or property settings.

A dynamic array is one whose upper and lower bounds can be reset frequently over the course of the program. This flexibility allows you to build structures such as stacks, whose values are designed to be "pushed" on and "popped" off. The `ReDim` statement is used to reset the bounds of a dynamic array previously declared with `Dim`, `Public`, `Private`, or `Static`.

Utilizing Intrinsic Functions

The name *intrinsic function* is used in VBA to distinguish function terms that are reserved VBA keywords from the names you give to `Function` procedures. A VBA intrinsic function is a mathematical or otherwise logical operation, generally performed on one or more elements of data supplied as arguments, and which yields a discrete result to the expression in which the function appears.

Applying true meaning to "logic"

Now, what do I mean by "logical?" Anyone who has watched five minutes of *Star Trek* knows that the term is used there rather loosely, as though it were a philosophy or way of life. Mr. Spock would have appreciated Bertrand Russell, a man who did – at least at one time in his life – accept logic as a philosophy, but whose comprehension of the subject became so vast that he managed, in the study of it, to surpass it altogether. Russell's 1900 *Principia Mathematica* attempts to define the root principles of logic. But if you search there for a simple "sound bite" definition of logic, you won't find one; in fact, in the Introduction to the Second Edition (wherein he apologizes for parts of the First Edition), Russell tries to explain why he cannot define the term with mere words. The closest he comes is this: "To define logic, or mathematics, is therefore by no means easy except in relation to some given set of premises. A logical premise must have *certain* characteristics which can be defined: it must have complete generality, in the sense that it mentions no particular thing or quality; and it must be true in virtue of its form. Given a definite set of logical premises, we can define logic, *in relation to them* [italics his], as whatever they enable us to demonstrate." I have taken this to mean the following: Once a premise is cleansed and absolved of all exclusivity and specialty, to the point where only truth remains, then that premise is logical.

Logic in computing is, thankfully, easier to grasp, though it does not stray from this principal definition as Russell "defined" it. **A logical function in computing derives discretely valued information through purely objective and generalized analysis.** Any intrinsic function whose purpose isn't obviously mathematical achieves its purpose through logic. Even finding the third character in a given string – Mid$(a$, 3) – is a logical pattern matching operation. Rendering the current time is a logical operation. Database functions are accomplished through associative, procedural, or relational logic. *Boolean logic* (based on the principles of mathematician George Boole) provides the fundamental mechanics of all computing, and is concerned exclusively with True/False values. ("True" and "False" are almost always capitalized as references to Boolean values.)

So when I say a VBA intrinsic function is "logical," I'm not making a qualitative judgment or simply stating that it "makes sense." I am referring to a *generalized* analytical process – meaning that it applies to any given data of the proper type or class. We call it an *intrinsic* function to distinguish it from a Function procedure, whose function call syntax (profiled in Chapter 3) is roughly identical.

A function's syntax is based on calculus

If you're familiar with calculus, you'll recall how mathematical functions are given names – generally single letters, often italicized, and sporting a prominent pair of parentheses. The syntax style of a VBA intrinsic function is similar in the respect that it, too, has the parentheses, and no space between the function name and the left parenthesis. The function name, however, is generally a keyword of a handful of characters in length, and is often an abbreviation of an English language word. The following syntax table demonstrates the formation of all VBA intrinsic functions.

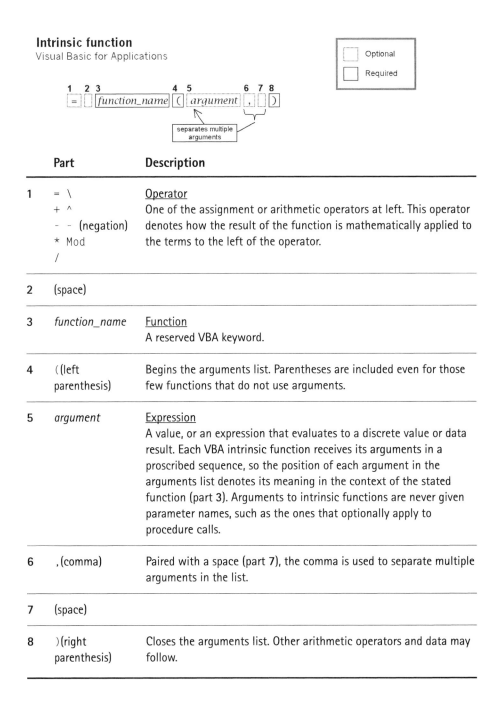

	Part	Description
1	= \ + ^ – – (negation) * Mod /	Operator One of the assignment or arithmetic operators at left. This operator denotes how the result of the function is mathematically applied to the terms to the left of the operator.
2	(space)	
3	*function_name*	Function A reserved VBA keyword.
4	((left parenthesis)	Begins the arguments list. Parentheses are included even for those few functions that do not use arguments.
5	*argument*	Expression A value, or an expression that evaluates to a discrete value or data result. Each VBA intrinsic function receives its arguments in a proscribed sequence, so the position of each argument in the arguments list denotes its meaning in the context of the stated function (part **3**). Arguments to intrinsic functions are never given parameter names, such as the ones that optionally apply to procedure calls.
6	, (comma)	Paired with a space (part **7**), the comma is used to separate multiple arguments in the list.
7	(space)	
8	) (right parenthesis)	Closes the arguments list. Other arithmetic operators and data may follow.

Intrinsic functions make up for Excel's unusual naming

Back in Listing 4-3, we used the following instruction to record the name of an indicated chart:

```
strStackRange(iShadows) = Right$(ActiveChart.Name, _
 Len(ActiveChart.Name) - Len(ActiveSheet.Name) - 1)
```

We had to put some muscle into this particular instruction because the way Excel handles embedded charts is a bit unusual. For any chart the user may indicate, the property `Selection.Name` is `Chart`. Not "Chart 2" or some useful, unique name, just `Chart`. So if a worksheet has more than one chart, and the procedure needs to reactivate just one of them, it can't ascertain which chart from just `Selection.Name`. On the other hand, `ActiveChart.Name` (representing the name of the chart with the focus, not just the *object* with the focus that `Selection.Name` represents), while it should point to the same object, actually records it differently. It does return a unique string, such as `Sheet1 Chart 3`. But when addressing the chart as a member of the `ChartObjects` collection, the entire name `Sheet1 Chart 3` isn't recognized. (Why? Well. . . I don't claim to know *everything*.) The collection does recognize the latter part, `Chart 3`, after the worksheet name is subtracted. So that's what the complex function accomplishes here.

The instruction is complex, because the expression to the right of the equality operator = utilizes two intrinsic functions within an intrinsic function. Here are the two functions that comprise this expression:

TABLE **4-1 INTRINSIC FUNCTIONS**

Term	Description
Right$()	Returns the rightmost characters from a given string expression or string literal.
	Arguments (in order):
	String — A character string, represented by a string expression (such as A$ or strOne & strTwo) a string literal (such as "Washington"), or a String type property (such as Selection.Name).
	Integer — An integer variable or a numeral relating the number of characters to return from the right side of *String*.
	Usage notes: The $ portion of the function name is optional.

Continued

TABLE **4-1** INTRINSIC FUNCTIONS *(Continued)*

Term	Description
	Note: The Right$( ) function has a counterpart Left$( ), which returns the leftmost characters from a given string; and a relative Mid$( ), which returns characters from the middle of a given string.
Len( )	Returns the length of the given string.
	Argument:
	String — Generally a variable or expression that evaluates to a string, or a property term that represents a string.

The string we start out with looks like Sheet1 Chart 3, but what we want is just the Chart 3 part. We have no way of knowing exactly how many characters are in the Sheet part (here it's obviously six, but we won't know for certain whether that part will be Sheet1 or Sheet43). The length of the right part doesn't matter, because we only need to precisely chop off the *left* part.

So the expression as written here tells the VBA interpreter to chop ActiveChart.Name into two parts, leave the Right part and drop the left part. The number of characters that *remain* is equal to the length of the original string ActiveChart.Name, minus the length of the smaller ActiveSheet.Name, which always makes up the left part of ActiveChart.Name, minus one extra character accounting for the space separating the sheet part from the chart part.

Utilizing Loop Clauses

Nearly every recently published text I've read on BASIC language programming that mentions loop clauses, has failed to make clear the key reason for writing them into your programs in the first place. The text will state that you write a loop clause at points where you want an instruction or set of instructions to be repeated. This isn't exactly correct. Very rarely in VBA will you ever require the interpreter to execute exactly the same instruction in exactly the same way more than once.

An iteration is a cycle of repeated instructions

The key to comprehending the loop clause lies in recognizing that a loop clause may repeat its instructions, though each time it changes the characteristics of those instructions. In its conventional construction, the For...Next statement, which binds a loop clause, keeps a running count using a variable bound to the statement. For example:

```
For x = 1 To 12
```

When the instructions within the loop clause's dependent block are executed for the first time, x will equal 1. After the interpreter reaches the statement Next x, these instructions are executed again. Each "round" or "cycle" between the top and bottom statements of the clause is what we call an *iteration*. At the second iteration of the loop clause, x will equal 2 (by default, the interpreter adds 1 each iteration). There's a reason for this; variable x should be important to the instructions in the dependent block. To make good use of a loop clause, the dependent instructions should take advantage of the change to the binding variable with each iteration.

Here's a short example of a loop clause that loads the contents of a Forms 2.0 list box with entries from a string array:

```
For x = 1 To 12
    lstDozen.AddItem strName(x)
Next x
```

Since you can only add one item to a list box at a time, the items from the array strName() have to be streamed in, in succession. The x used as the subscript for strName() is the same x used by the For line to keep count. The single dependent instruction here takes advantage of the fact that x changes with each iteration. To be more truthful about it, the reason why this loop clause was constructed the way it was, is because the strName() array contains precisely 12 elements, the first being numbered 1. So certainly the dependent instruction takes advantage of how the loop clause keeps count, but that's actually because that's what this clause was designed exclusively for.

For...Next is the most common loop clause binder

The For...Next statement binds the most common loop clauses in VBA and all BASIC languages. Here, in explicit detail, is how such a clause is put together:

For...Next
Visual Basic for Applications

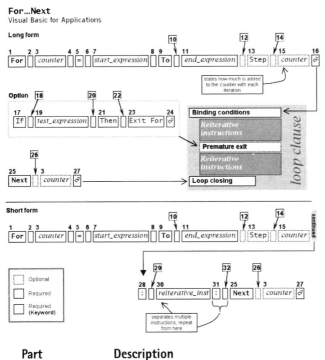

	Part	Description
1	For	**Statement** Begins a sequence of instructions designed to be executed repetitively. With each iteration (full cycle of execution), the value of a counter variable (part **3**) is changed.
2	(space)	
3	*counter*	**Variable** A valid variable term; that is, not a VBA keyword. This variable represents a value, not a character string or object. Generally, this variable is declared beforehand, though if this statement marks the first instance in which the variable appears, the interpreter dynamically declares it as a variant.
4	(space)	
5	=	**Operator** Denotes that a range of values between *start_expression* (part **7**) and *end_expression* (part **9**) will be assigned to *counter* (part **3**); the equality sign acts as assignment operator.

	Part	Description
6	(space)	
7	*start_expression*	Expression A literal value, or an expression that evaluates to a numeral value, that serves as the initial value of *counter* (part **3**) within instructions in the clause.
8	(space)	
9	To	Specifier Separates the range of values between *start_val* (part **7**) and *end_val* (part **9**).
10	(space)	
11	*end_expression*	Expression A literal value, or an expression that evaluates to a numeral value, that serves as the terminal value of *counter* (part **3**) within instructions in this clause. When the interpreter reaches Next (part **25**) and determines that the value of *counter* is at or beyond that of *end_expression*, the loop clause will be exited and execution will proceed to the instruction immediately following Next. Depending on the amount repeatedly being added to *counter* with each iteration, the value that actually results in termination of the loop may be *greater than* that of *end_expression*. Think of the end value as a checkpoint of sorts; if the interpreter determines that the counter variable is either at this checkpoint or has proceeded past it already, then it is time to exit the loop clause.
12	(space)	
13	Step	Specifier Denotes that the value to be added to *counter* (part **3**) each time the interpreter reaches Next (part **25**) is other than the default value of 1.
14	(space)	

Continued

Part		Description
15	*counter*	<u>Expression</u> A literal value, or an expression that evaluates to a value, that may be added to *counter* (part **3**) in place of the default of 1, each time the interpreter encounters `Next` (part **25**).
16	(Enter)	Divides the main body of the statement from the dependent instructions. Generally, these instructions involve the counter variable (part **3**) in some way, and take advantage of its progressively increasing value.
17	`If`	<u>Statement</u> Begins a conditional subclause that determines whether the loop clause should be exited prior to formal completion. The "premature" exit instruction is `Exit For` (part **23**), which instruction will be executed only if the *test_expression* (part **19**) evaluates `True`.
18	(space)	
19	*test_expression*	<u>Expression</u> An expression of comparison, which, if it evaluates `True`, will execute the premature loop termination (part **23**).
20	(space)	
21	`Then`	<u>Statement</u> Separates the termination condition (part **19**) from `Exit For` (part **23**).
22	(space)	
23	`Exit For`	<u>Statement</u> Terminates the loop clause. Execution then proceeds to the instruction immediately following the line containing `Next` (part **25**). Generally, `Exit For` is reached after the interpreter evaluates a conditional expression (part **21**) to be `True`. However, the conditional statement is not necessary to `Exit For` as long as you understand that once the interpreter reaches this statement, the loop clause will end. A conditional "roadblock" of some sort is probably may be necessary in order to avoid a situation in which the `Next` instruction is never reached.

24	(Enter)	

25	Next	Statement
		Denotes the bottom of the loop clause. At this point, the interpreter will check the value of the counter variable (part **3**) to determine whether it equals or surpasses the stated end value (part **11**). If it has not, the loop clause prepares to execute another cycle. The value of *counter* is adjusted by the set amount, and execution proceeds to the first instruction in the top dependent instruction block. If the variable equals or exceeds the end value, execution drops out of the loop clause to the instruction just below the Next line.

26	(space)	Normally, to help the human reader make sense of which Next line goes with which For line, the name of the *counter* variable (part **3**) is repeated following Next. For example, for a loop clause that increments a variable iCount with each iteration, the line Next iCount helps the reader distinguish that this is the termination of the clause that began with For iCount. However, repeating the counter variable is not required, even if other loop clause are nested within this one; the interpreter will distinguish which Next lines go with which For lines.

27	(Enter)	Closes the loop clause.

28	:(colon)	Separates the binding portion of the For instruction from its dependent instructions (part **30**). This is for the "old-style" form of the For...Next loop, which is still supported by VBA, although it is generally considered archaic.

29	(space)	

30	*reiterative_inst*	Instruction
		A single VBA instruction. For **Short form** syntax, this instruction must not include any multiple-line clauses; any dependent clauses must follow its own "old style" syntax.

31	:(colon)	With the space (part **32**), separates multiple instructions in a chain.

32	(space)	

In Depth: Changing how loops increment their counters

Normally, the interpreter *increments* the counter variable with each iteration of the loop clause, which means that it counts by one until it reaches (or surpasses) the stated end value. Using Step, you can have the interpreter change the progression of the counter variable to some other value. This is especially important in situations such as counting *down*, in which you could specify a negative integer as the Step value, like this:

```
For iCount = 10 To 0 Step -1
```

In cases where the counter variable represents a fractional value, the Step value could represent a fractional interval; for example:

```
For sRate = 0 To 100 Step .1
```

When the progression you intend to model is *parabolic*, or formulaic in some other respect, but in any event *non-linear*, you could use an expression as your Step value; for example:

```
For dCurve = dStart To dEnd Step dNtrvl * dNtnst
```

FOR...NEXT EXAMPLE

In Chapter 3, you saw an interpretation of a common short list sorting procedure using the BubbleSort algorithm. Here's that procedure again:

```
Private Sub BubbleSort(strArray() As String)
    Dim j As Integer, k As Integer, l As Integer, n As Integer, t$

    n = UBound(strArray)
    For l = 1 To n
        j = l
        For k = j + 1 To n
            If strArray(k) <= strArray(j) Then
                j = k
            End If
        Next k
        If l <> j Then
            t$ = strArray(j)
            strArray(j) = strArray(l)
            strArray(l) = t$
        End If
    Next l
End Sub
```

Now that you know something more about loop clauses, let's examine this procedure a little more closely: This procedure uses simple variable names. Here, variable n represents the index of the last entry of the array being sorted. So the meaning of For l = 1 to n suddenly becomes clear (or at least, as clear as these juxtapositions of letters and numbers can get). Variable l is a counter that proceeds from 1 up until the final entry n. There are two more pointers that come into play: Variable j picks up l's position and variable k starts at one entry past j and moves on. The secondary loop clause for k will move j up to k's position when it finds an entry that's out of place. Variable j acts as an "out-of-place" marker at this point. The secondary clause will keep moving j up until k finds the most out of place entry in the array, and makes j point to that. At that point, j's out-of-place entry is swapped for l's entry at the beginning, with the understanding that the most out-of-place entry must be the *latest* entry that the algorithm can find that belongs at the *earliest* position in the array. Variable l already marks that earliest position – or at least the earliest unsorted position – so when j's and l's entries are swapped with one another, the new l entry will be at the correct location. Then the main loop clause moves l up one notch.

Loop clauses geared for collections

All four of our long listings in this chapter have made use of the For Each...Next loop clause, which is Microsoft's permutation of the classic BASIC loop, especially for addressing members of collection objects successively. Before the advent of this type of clause, programmers relied upon a common property of collection objects, the .Count property, for clauses that looked like this:

```
For x = 1 To Documents.Count
    Set objDoc = Document(x)
    ' other instructions which refer to objDoc
Next x
```

The Set instruction would have been used to create an object reference that would cycle through each of the objects in the collection. The new For Each...Next clause takes care of that assignment automatically, and also eliminates the need for you to address the .Count property. Here's how the clause is constructed:

For Each...Next
Visual Basic for Applications

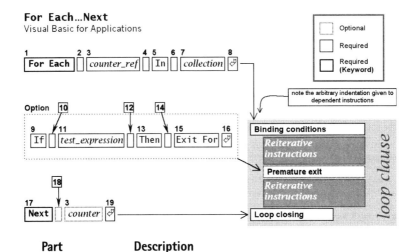

	Part	Description
1	For Each	<u>Statement</u> Begins a sequence of instructions designed to be executed repetitively. With each iteration a reference variable (part **3**) that points to an element of a collection (part **7**) is shifted to point to the next object in that collection.
2	(space)	
3	*counter_ref*	<u>Variable</u> An object reference variable previously declared to be of the same class as that of *Collection* (part **7**). This reference will point to each of the objects in the collection in succession.
4	(space)	
5	In	<u>Specifier</u> Separates the reference variable (part **3** from the collection name (part **7**).
6	(space)	
7	*collection*	<u>Object</u> The name of a collection object. This can be a recognized global collection in the Office 2000 object model or a collection variable previously declared As Collection.
8	(Enter)	Divides the main body of the statement from its dependent instructions.

	Part	Description
9	If	Statement Begins a conditional subclause that determines whether the loop clause should be exited prior to formal completion. The "premature" exit instruction is Exit For (part **15**), and that instruction will be executed only if the condition (part **11**) evaluates True.
10	(space)	
11	*test_expression*	An expression of comparison, which, if it evaluates True, executes the premature loop termination (part **15**).
12	(space)	
13	Then	Statement Separates the termination condition (part **11**) from Exit For (part **15**).
14	(space)	
15	Exit For	Statement Terminates the loop clause. Execution then proceeds to the instruction immediately following Next (part **17**).
16	(Enter)	
17	Next	Statement Denotes the bottom of the loop clause. At this point, the interpreter will shift the object reference to point to the next object in the collection. As long as there continues to be objects in the collection, execution will proceed from here to the instruction immediately following For Each (part **1**). When there are no later objects in the collection, the interpreter drops out of the loop clause, and execution proceeds to the instruction following Next (part **17**).
18	(space)	If the name of the *counter_ref* variable (part **3**) is to be repeated following Next (an option that may make the loop clause more legible to the human reader), this space is necessary to separate Next (part **17**) from the repeated variable.
19	(Enter)	Closes the loop clause.

VBA does provide for some other, less common loop clause statements, which will be examined in other chapters.

On Point

A loop clause repeats a set of instructions that are said to be bound to that clause. With each repetition, or iteration, some condition is changed; generally the value of a variable keeping count for the loop. The instructions within the clause utilize the changed count variable, taking advantage of its predictable incrementation or other value fluctuation. The most common loop clause formation is the classic For...Next loop, which keeps a running count within a single numeral-value variable. With each iteration the interpreter adds 1, or some other value stated beside the optional Step term, to the running count. A step value of 1 is convenient when cycling through the entries in an array, whereas a fractional value may be useful when graphing an algebraic function. VBA provides the For Each...Next loop clause exclusively for stepping through the contents of a collection object.

In Theory: HELLO Again

At the time of this writing, the BASIC programming language was 35 years old. Computers at the time of BASIC's creation were as different from computers today as the public transportation system of ancient Rome is from that of modern-day Singapore.

BASIC's inventors, Dartmouth College Professors John G. Kemeny and Thomas Kurtz, foresaw the development of computers just a bit differently than history had in store for them. Although few people had direct access to computers in 1964, Kemeny and Kurtz did project an era where individuals had direct, personal access to computers. However, they foresaw this access would take place at terminal stations, accessible from public institutions such as universities (this should give you a clue as to their inspiration), looking something like a row of oversized telephone booths supplied with typewriters the size of small refrigerators. Users would check in at the front desk to be assigned the next open terminal station – not unlike the way copier centers are run. These users would log on, type in their program, debug it, then run it. There were no screens and no mice, just a keyboard and a long spool of paper on which the user's commands, and the interpreter's responses, were typed, in a process sounding like the firing of semiautomatic weaponry.

With this usage model in mind, Kemeny and Kurtz designed their original BASIC to be *conversational*, imagining that people who used these computers on a time-sharing basis would want or expect them to be friendlier, like store clerks. So one of BASIC's first statements was HELLO, the user's way of signaling to the interpreter that a session was about to begin. The interpreter would respond with READY. Next, the user would type in the text of the program; the interpreter could distinguish program instructions from direct instructions like HELLO by the distinctive line numbers that appeared before program instructions. At that time, the interpreter sorted instructions by their line numbers, which designated where they belonged in the program. The user would then run the program by typing the RUN statement, the program printed its results, and the user tore those results off the spool, told the interpreter BYE, paid his fee to the front desk clerk, and took his hard copy home.

Of course, the idea that the output device could conceivably be used as an *input* device never entered into anyone's mind, because in the 1960s, it was physically impossible. The output device then was *paper*, which even today fails the interactivity test. Exactly how would one type a working dialog box onto a piece of paper?

The BASIC language's PRINT statement, once its cornerstone, has long since faded into antiquity, along with the likes of MAT, LINE INPUT, HELLO, and BYE. For me, they're like retired hall-of-fame ball players – revered, much missed, but obviously outmoded by their successors. What remains of the early BASIC language since Microsoft rose to the rank of its caretaker are a few noble relics of its once simplistic construction and versatility. They are not completely buried in new developments, although they have been adapted at times to suit new purposes. The If...Then and For...Next statements, and a faint whisper of the GoTo statement, have survived the decades – bruised, repaired, but intact.

In Brief

- A conditional clause evaluates an expression for logical verity (its True/False value), and is capable of undertaking separate courses of action based on the result of that evaluation.

- The If...Then statement is engineered to provide two possible courses of action for a program – one if a test expression evaluates True, another if it evaluates False.

- An array whose length at run-time is unknown at design time, can be declared as a dynamic array for now using the Dim statement or its equivalents, with no subscript between its parentheses. The number of elements in the array can be determined later at runtime by supplying that number as an argument variable to the ReDim statement.

- The Select Case statement evaluates a variable or other expression for multiple possible values, and provides a course of action for each possible result.

◆ A loop clause such as For...Next executes a set of instructions repetitively for a set number of cycles, or iterations. Between iterations, a variable's value is changed – generally by adding 1 to it – so that instructions within the loop clause that utilize that variable will perceive it differently, and thus perform different – not replicated – operations.

Chapter 5

Utilizing Forms Controls as Display Devices

IN THIS CHAPTER

◆ What a control is, in Windows' terms

◆ Where you build form modules in the VBA environment

◆ The UserForm object as a container of controls

◆ Programming VBA code for the form module

◆ How the environment helps build event procedures

◆ Planning how the user operates form modules

◆ Building, then rebuilding, the code for a form module

THE HALLMARK OF Microsoft's Visual Basic family of programming languages has always been that it enables programmers to build on-screen interactive panels and windows by simply stretching their platforms into the shape and size they want, then dragging their controls where they need to be. These controls can be named, set, and programmed later; for now, you can at least build a reliable facsimile of how you want your running program to appear.

For long-time professional programmers, this system of operation is somewhat peculiar, even foreign. For a programmer not to have the source code manage 100 percent of whatever is seen, done, and transacted within the program can give that programmer an awkward feeling — a bit like driving a car that is accustomed to accelerating itself. This is especially true for a programmer whose every program could be transcribed in its entirety onto lined printer paper. Yet if statistics are any indicator, this awkwardness doesn't linger for very long, and soon a sense of self-spoiling indulgence takes over.

Actually programming, byte by byte, the graphical resources used by a Windows application in the construction of the parts of a dialog panel or a window, is extremely difficult work. You won't have to do any of this work with VBA; because with the way Windows is built, these same resources are supplied by little component programs that take care of the difficult assembly of controls on a dialog panel or window on your behalf. Each text field, drop-down list box, and scroll bar is its own little program, communicating its status continually to Windows. Windows then makes that data available to the VBA interpreter, so that VBA can manage the behavior of those controls.

With VBA you assemble a dialog panel not with VBA instructions, but with your mouse and an ounce or two of manual dexterity. Using the mouse, you assemble the controls *onscreen* where you want them to be, then set them up to behave the way you need them to behave when the VBA module first starts up. Since controls are represented in VBA by objects, you set their initial appearance and behavior by means of these objects' properties. This isn't a difficult matter; you simply enter this data into the Properties window of the VBA workspace. While this does involve typing, it's more on the order of filling in a form than writing a procedure. **To set the initial appearance and default behavior of controls, in most cases, you need not write any VBA instructions.** There are exceptions (as a Windows programmer, you learn soon enough that there are always exceptions) but you won't encounter them until you begin building complex control mechanisms. Simple dialog boxes require zero instructions just for the setup.

What Are Controls?

For most Windows programs, the most common gadgets that are found on dialog panels and toolbars, such as checkboxes and fields where you type in text, are actually provided by small, independent programs. The gadgets themselves are called *controls*, and the programs that manage them are called *components*. For example, when you look at a dialog panel or a form that contains several fields where you type in text or numbers, you're most likely looking at several distinct *instances* of one running component, namely the text box or text field component.

A library is a file containing many small programs

You do not write the code for the component within VBA; this is a job that is already done for you. In Windows, a *library* is a single file that contains the machine code (the compiled program) for one or more components. This is preexisting code that VBA already knows how to contact and to manage. To write a VBA module using drop-in controls, you do not need to know the identity or whereabouts of this library file. However, if you intend to distribute your VBA module to others, you may need to make certain that your recipients have the same library file that you used for your controls. If your module only uses Forms 2.0 controls, you're safe, because if your recipients have Office 2000 (and they must in order to run your VBA module), then they do have the Forms 2.0 control library.

In the 1980s, Microsoft concocted the term *dynamic link library* (DLL) to refer to the type of file I call "library" in this text. Perhaps by itself, "library" wouldn't have had the raw sex appeal necessary for Microsoft to sell new gizmos like Windows

386 (remember that old blue box?). Today, the larger term has become something of a vestigial remnant, because there really isn't any other way for one program to link with another except dynamically, and there isn't any other type of program that performs this type of linking except a library. So, while these files maintain their old .DLL filename extensions, today they're basically referred to as "libraries."

A lexicon is an object's own vocabulary

Prior to 1996, the single library program that provided the functionality for the most common Windows gadgets and controls was the behemoth Microsoft Foundation Class (MFC) library. Today, MFC is at version 4.2, which spans more than 3.6 megabytes of the \WINDOWS\SYSTEM subdirectory. When Microsoft began its much-touted ActiveX campaign in 1996, marking the Corporation's move toward more component-based Windows programs, it began distributing a more compact (just under 1MB) library for the presentation of controls to Windows, called the Forms library. What distinguishes today's Forms 2.0 from MFC 4.2 is the fact that Forms controls have their own vocabulary – their own sets of properties, methods, and recognized events that make them addressable as objects through programming languages such as VBA. This text calls this vocabulary the *lexicon* of the objects that comprise the library. Meanwhile, the MFC library is designed for access from C++. So it does have an object-oriented "front end" of sorts, in the form of an object library that accompanies the dynamic link library, when MFC is being used within an environment such as Visual C++. However, the methodology by which the MFC library is contacted *by a Windows program* (as opposed to a programmer through his source code) is based on the older, more conventional mechanism of Remote Procedure Calls (RPC). Such procedure calls are very common to Windows programming, and resemble to some extent the VBA Function procedure calls we studied in earlier chapters.

Form Modules and the VBA Workspace

Before we begin, let's clear up some terminological points: A *form* in VBA programming is a panel to which OLE/COM controls are generally attached. So a *form module* is the VBA source code that produces and maintains a form as it is used in a VBA program. The product of a form is generally a *dialog box* whose purpose is to elicit certain information from the user. Sometimes in this text we'll shorten this term to just "dialog" the way we often shorten "menu bar" to just "menu," mainly because Windows has such an abundance of boxes and bars that it's a wonder all our programs don't end up looking like a Paul Klée exhibition.

A form module contains code that produces dialog boxes

The Forms 2.0 library is shipped as part of Office 2000. With VBA, you can use this library to build a dialog panel based on the Forms library's UserForm class. To build the form the way you want it to appear when the VBA module is run, you drag the most common Windows controls (supplied by Forms 2.0) from the VBA toolbox onto an *instance* of UserForm, where they snap into place and are instantly usable. From VBA's Properties window, you enter the initial, or default, property settings for all of the controls in the form, plus the form itself. Since each of the Forms controls, including UserForm, recognizes its own events — being clicked on, being double-clicked, being given the focus, losing the focus, having an item chosen from its menu — it's easy to define that control's behavior in response to those events by writing *event procedures*.

Figure 5-1 shows a typical view of the VBA programming environment, which is used for Word, Excel, and PowerPoint (Access programming takes place from within its own workspace).

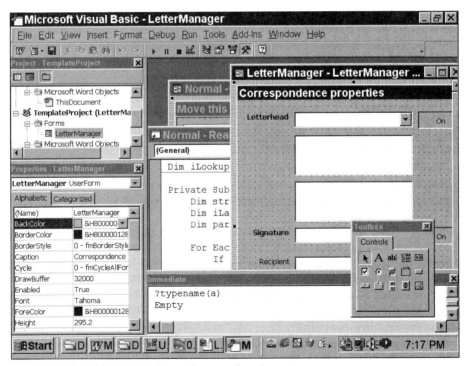

Figure 5-1: The VBA programming environment's main parts.

The various windows that make up the VBA environment can be placed anywhere within the workspace, without changing their function or purpose. The Project window presents a list, in a Windows Explorer-like "tree" format, of all the currently active projects. As you may recall, a "project" as VBA perceives it is any programmable component that's currently open in the workspace of the VBA environment's native application. So for Word 2000, `Normal` is always one of the active projects, because `Normal` is the name of its persistent template. Additionally, each open document has its own project in the list, and each open template upon which open documents are based has its own project. The project names in this window are all **boldfaced.**

The ThisDocument object manages key document events

For Word VBA's Projects window, if you click on the "+" button to the left of the word Normal, you'll find at least one subordinate listing for Microsoft Word Objects. Next, if you click on that listing's "+" button the listing for `ThisDocument` will be revealed. The `ThisDocument` code module is the container for all VBA code that pertains to the Word document as an object, especially procedures that respond to that document's own events. In the Word 2000 object library, the `Document` class recognizes a few key events. As an object, `ThisDocument` is a member of the `Document` class, so it recognizes three events:

_**New** is recognized whenever the document represented by `ThisDocument` is being initialized for the very first time – as when the user selects New from Word's File menu.

_**Open** is recognized whenever the document that `ThisDocument` represents already exists and is reopened in Word.

_**Close** is recognized just before the document is removed from the Windows Desktop.

Because of a peculiar rule having to do with how procedures address their own event procedures (explained, as best I can, in the next few pages), the names for the event procedures for these events always use the name of `ThisDocument`'s object *class*, not its own name. Thus `Private Sub Document_Open()` is executed whenever an existing document is loaded, not "Private Sub ThisDocument_Open()."

Each open document and template upon which an open document is based has its own listing in the Project window of the VBA editor workspace. Figure 5-2 demonstrates a typical Project window, where Word is the controlling application. Every project has one component part in particular, shown here as **Microsoft Word**

Objects. Listed below that are all the objects that play a direct role in the construction of the document. For Word 2000, a standard document or template is comprised of one main object, ThisDocument. Even embedded objects, such as graphics from outside sources, don't count here.

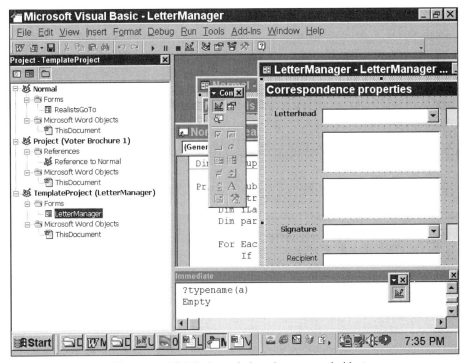

Figure 5-2: A typical Word 2000 VBA Project window shows several objects.

An Excel 2000 VBA project has a similar code module reserved for procedures pertaining to the workbook. It's called the ThisWorkbook object — naturally — and it is considered a member of Excel's Workbook class. But unlike Word, Excel maintains an object hierarchy here; by default, a new Excel workbook contains three worksheets. So while the ThisWorkbook object handles the critical procedure for opening the Excel file — Private Sub Workbook_Open() — the Project window of Excel VBA reveals separate code modules for each worksheet in the workbook, listed *beside* ThisWorkbook (in fact, above it) rather than *beneath* it as Excel's object hierarchy would have you assume. The worksheet-related modules contain code that pertains to the operation of the specific worksheet, including event procedures that respond to how the user utilizes the mouse while the worksheet is active.

In Depth: Embedding controls in Word 2000 documents

It isn't obvious from a simple scan of the VBA editor window, but Forms 2.0 controls and other ActiveX controls may be contained by document objects such as Word's `ThisDocument` and Excel's `ThisWorkbook`. A user or programmer may drop a control in a document, worksheet, presentation, or database form. Microsoft calls this type of functionality "active content." What that term implies, of course, is that some part of the document is meaningless when it's printed on paper, and thus is only useful in the context of the Office 2000 application that generated it.

You may be thinking, when would a control be placed in a *document*? In Word 2000, by using the Control Toolbox palette, a user can drag a series of controls to a page, making that document's page into an interactive form. If the author of a page doesn't mind sacrificing some of the printability of the document, the user can convert that document into a platform for a small program. A command button, for instance, embedded in a document, can be used to invoke a macro when the reader clicks it. The figure below shows a Word document on screen with several embedded Forms controls that make that document into an interactive form.

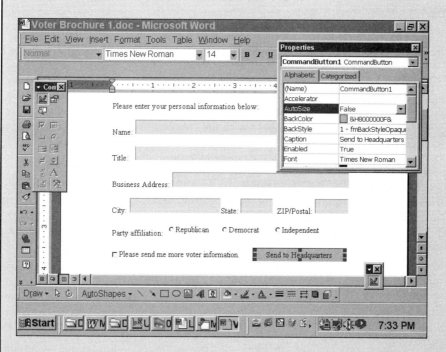

Continued

In Depth: Embedding controls in Word 2000 documents
(Continued)

Because UserForm is now available, however, much of this embedding of controls within documents — which made sense for the Office 95 edition of Word — is outmoded. Of course, it only makes sense to have a control in a document when the user of that document is looking at it onscreen rather than on paper. It is possible to embed a Forms control in a document which, when clicked on, activates instructions that change the contents of the document. So in a detached sense, embedded controls can have an effect on the printed state of the Word document.

The types of code modules supported by VBA

When you right-click one of the boldfaced project names in the Project window, and select Insert from the popup menu, VBA shows you the four types of modules that VBA supports:

♦ **UserForm** refers to the Forms 2.0 term for a platform upon which a *form module* is built. This chapter is mainly about form modules. With one of these, you build a dialog panel out of Windows components.

♦ **Module** refers, quite generically, to a standard or general module of VBA source code, which is independent of any forms. To this point, our examples have dealt entirely with the "Module" module type. To avoid sounding like Max Headroom, this text uses the term *general module* to refer to non-form, non-object code modules.

♦ **Class Module** refers to a body of VBA code in which a registered class of object is programmed from the ground up and imported into VBA projects. Class modules aren't crucial to VBA programming, though they can be of major help in complex projects, as you'll discover in Chapter 9.

♦ **DHTML Page** refers to a Dynamic HTML document that contains programmable data and controls, such as a form or a report, and whose functionality is provided by Office 2000, but which is actually run from the user's Web browser. (This feature requires Internet Explorer 5.0 to be installed. At the time of this writing, Microsoft had been developing its own DHTML format which, in places, diverged from proposed standards; some DHTML pages written for IE 5.0 may therefore not be displayable in Netscape Navigator 4.5.)

The UserForm object is a container for controls

In the Visual Basic vocabulary, a *form* is the platform that houses the other controls that comprise a dialog panel or a window. The Forms library was not designed exclusively for Visual Basic or VBA; nonetheless, among its controls is a platform control that it calls UserForm. Like the other controls, UserForm recognizes its own events, the most important of which is _Activate. This event is always recognized once, when the form first enters the screen and all its constituent controls "go live."

The UserForm object is designed to act as a *container* for other controls. It frankly has little or no other purpose; although it recognizes its own _Click event, few dialog panels ever designed have ever bestowed any meaning or function to the user clicking or double-clicking on the grey part of the panel itself. In the Forms library, UserForm is not the only control that can act as a container. The frame control, which acts as a rectangular boundary around groups of other controls, is a container for those controls as well, though it is also contained within UserForm. MultiPage, which serves as a platform for multiple tabbed settings pages within a dialog panel, is also a container that is itself contained.

There is a symbiotic relationship between a form and the controls it contains, as well as between a document and the controls contained within it. At design time, when you drop a control into a UserForm, in effect you assign that control to the form. As a result, most of the new constituent control's properties are now given pertinence. In other words, without the control being contained, these properties on their own would be null since they are measurements or characteristics that relate to how the control is contained. For example, the .Left and .Top properties, which represent the coordinate position of the upper left corner of the new control, now have positive settings assigned to it by the UserForm object. The control cannot have position at all unless UserForm, or some other container object, can give it position. By comparison, the .Width and .Height properties have meaning for a control, whether or not it's contained. It always knows its own size, and it doesn't need a container component to tell it what that size is.

A container also rounds out a control's overall sense of identity. For instance, a control's .Enabled property — which governs whether it's "turned on" and ready to receive user events — is also rendered unto it by UserForm. The control relies on its container to enable and disable it; on its own, the control is always enabled. Why is this? Because it takes a program running under the context of a dialog box to determine whether or not a control should be enabled. For example, an Undo button might start out life in a dialog box *disabled*. It would need to be re-enabled once the user has entered anything into that dialog box that could be undone. It takes the dialog box's own procedures to determine when re-enabling should occur. Besides, in VBA, single controls don't have their own code modules.

How the form module works

A *form module* is a collection of controls and procedures that pertain to a `UserForm` class object. The main body of VBA instructions that comprise a form module are event procedures, which are elements of code to which the VBA interpreter places automatic calls in response to something that the user, or Windows, has done. If you were to liken a VBA form to the console of a computer, then a form module would be its plug-in card. It provides an independent dialog panel or a window with the instructions necessary to give it usefulness and functionality.

A VBA module does not contain any form modules by default, and therefore the Project window doesn't naturally divulge where such modules would go. Dialog boxes are something that you add to a module, and thus something with which they are not equipped by default. Common sense might tell you that form modules, once created, would be listed in the Project window under **Modules**; once again, common sense would be wrong. Form modules, general code modules, and class modules are all listed separately in the Project window, each in its own tier of the tree.

Peculiarities when naming event procedures

The Visual Basic languages follow a peculiar rule having to do with how procedures within a module address the objects that are directly associated with that module. It's peculiar because it's esoteric, but moreover because if you don't know the rule exists, you'll be even more confused.

Suppose one of your VBA projects contains a form module. Even if you've named this form something else, the name of the event procedure that is executed when the form "goes live" *will always be* `Private Sub UserForm_Activate()`. Meanwhile, the event procedures for all the constituent controls borrow their names from the `.Name` properties you give to these controls. So for a button named `btnOK`, the `_Click` event procedure will be named `Private Sub btnOK_Click()`. The rule to remember is this: **Any event procedure pertaining to an object, belonging to a module that is associated with that same object, uses that object's class name rather than its `.Name` property setting as a reference to that object within the procedure's declaration statement.** So a form module's event procedure declarations use the class name `UserForm` to refer to its own form, and an event procedure for `ThisDocument` uses the class name `Document` in its event procedure declarations. It's a cruel rule to have to remember, and there seems to be no compelling reason for its existence, but nonetheless there it is.

The Toolbox represents multiple classes

The Toolbox window has become a visually mixed metaphor. Here, Microsoft has added a folder-tab element to the traditional Visual Basic toolbox (Visual Basic 5.0 uses a set of buttons where VBA uses folder tab controls), so you'll just have to imagine that you keep your tools in folders. When you start VBA for the first time through any program (including Access), the Toolbox contains icons that represent the classes of Forms 2.0 controls that can be contained in a UserForm object.

ACTIVEX CONTROLS IN THE FORMS 2.0 SUITE

Following are all the standard Forms 2.0 control classes, along with the icons that represent them in the Toolbox:

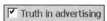

Figure 5-3: Check box. A control that represents a single choice, generally among a group, but not exclusive (as is multiple-choice).

Figure 5-4: Combo box. A list box whose choice may be edited by the user along the top line.

Figure 5-5: Command button. The common pushbutton that signals a command to the script; does not stay pressed and does not have a status.

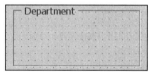

Figure 5-6: Frame. A border that also serves as a container control, that may be used to group other controls (no longer required to distinguish option and check groups from one another on a form).

Figure 5-7: Image. A graphics image frame, set to the URL (uniform resource locator) of a GIF or JPEG file.

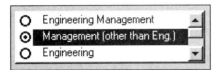

Figure 5-8: Label. A line of straight text that may be written using any font from the client system's font list, and at any angle with respect to the page, thus permitting sideways text.

Figure 5-9: List box. A list, which is comprised of string literals, that allows the user to choose one or more items. The list may contain any number of items, and yet all these items share a list window whose height never exceeds a set amount.

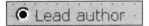

Figure 5-10: MultiPage. A container control that simulates the multiple tabs along the top edge of the newer Windows dialog boxes, while also supporting its own embedded optional page turner.

Figure 5-11: Option. A control that represents a selection from a list; when grouped together, choosing one option resets the selections of other controls in the group.

Figure 5-12: Scroll bar. The common device for scrolling windows.

Figure 5-13: Spin button. Generally used as an input device for fields that have numerical bounds in a form, such as record number selectors or volume knobs.

Figure 5-14: TabStrip. A version of MultiPage that does not act as a container for the controls in the region of the form that it surrounds.

Figure 5-15: Text box. The common form field where a user may enter text.

Figure 5-16: Toggle button. A button that represents an on/off state; it stays depressed when "on," and is released when "off."

In the often esoteric terminology of object-oriented programming, a *class* defines the functionality and operation of an object. A program may utilize more than one object at the same time belonging to the same class; a relatively easy example of this is how a dialog panel built with UserForm may contain more than one text field or more than one label. The Windows code that uses the same functionality in more than one place at the same time, is the code for that object's class. Each individual example of that class is an *instance* of that class. So each text field is an instance of the TextBox class as defined by Forms 2.0.

When you design a VBA program, it is crucial that all the esotericism necessary for you as programmer to be able to logically comprehend what you're doing, doesn't bleed through the screen and interrupt the user's train of thought. The most important feature of Windows program architecture has to do with how an application is perceived by its end user. The user's self-perception should not be as the operator of a bunch of simultaneously operational component programs, collectively producing a series of objects. Instead, the user's self-perception should be as running a single application that produces a document. As programmer, you will need to maintain the distinctions between the *alter ego* concepts of document and object, application and source code. Besides, if your VBA modules work seamlessly together, what should these distinctions matter to anyone, besides yourself? The user need only think about the document being built with Office VBA.

"Functionality" is not a term that's specific to Windows, so what is its meaning in this context? I like to define the term by means of a semantic tool called a Miller analogy: *Function* is to *functionality* as *person* is to *personality*. *Personality* is often what defines a person to an observer. *Functionality* is what defines the function of a program to its user. Users don't see the function, nor should they. That's private stuff — or, to use another psychological term, "latent." But it is important that the user should perceive some process in progress when using an application; so functionality becomes the face of the function.

Back to esoterics: Each icon in the Toolbox represents a class of control. When you click on a Toolbox icon, you're choosing the class for the new control that you are about to build on the form. Each time you drag the outline of a new control from that class on the form, you *instantiate* a new member of the class you've chosen from the Toolbox. Each instance has its own VBA procedures that govern how it, specifically, is to be operated *independently of the class*. So the library defines the operation of the class in general, and that definition is already programmed for you, while the VBA procedures you write within the form module define the operation of each specific instance of that class, over and above its default behavior.

Why is this important? Because you do not need to program how a drop-down combo box, for instance, responds each time the user clicks on its down arrow button. The fact that a menu drops down is part of its standard operation that the control already knows how to execute on your behalf. All you need to be concerned about is where the control is located, what's contained within it, what input if any the user has given to it, and what happens to that input data. In other words, your concern is that of the user of the VBA module within the Office 2000 application, not that of the programmer of Windows 98 or NT.

VBA builds event procedure frameworks for you

The control informs your program of everything that the user is doing with it, or any significant changes that your program is making to its behavior; that is the purpose of its events. So your program is told precisely when it is time to respond with instructions. These responses are the event procedures.

In Chapter 3, you saw how the `Sub...End Sub` and `Function...End Function` statement pairings serve as borders around procedures. (Property procedures for class modules are handled with different statements, as you'll see demonstrated in Chapter 9.) Whether VBA writes an event procedure declaration instruction for you or you write it yourself — as you'll see in a moment — notice that it includes a `Sub` statement with a `Private` qualifier. You do have to write the body of the event procedure yourself, of course, though the interpreter can at least write the declaration instruction for the event procedure, along with the `End Sub` or `End Function` statement at the end of the procedure.

You still have to know by name which particular events will trigger your procedures. However, you may have noticed the two drop-down list boxes, shown in Figure 5-3, which crown each code window in the VBA workspace. When you place the cursor in a procedure listed in a VBA code window, the list on the left shows the name (specifically, the `.Name` property) of the control to which that procedure is bound. A non-event procedure is bound to nothing; in such cases, the left list reads **(General)**. When the left list does read **(General)**, the right list shows the name of the procedure bearing the cursor (minus the declaration statement and the parentheses). However, when it's an event procedure that bears the cursor, the name of the event appears in the right list.

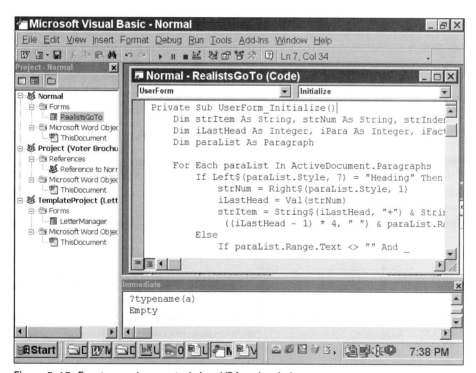

Figure 5-17: Event procedure controls in a VBA code window.

In the drop-down portion of the left list at the top of the code window are the names (.Name property settings) of all of the controls currently in the active VBA form, plus UserForm itself. So to start a new event procedure, you'd first dial up the name of the control receiving the event from the left list. VBA actually starts an event procedure at this point; if you look in the code window, and the event it's using is the one you need anyway, then you can go ahead and place the cursor between the Private Sub and End Sub statements and start writing. If this isn't the right event. . . well, *oops!* You might need to go back later and erase these statements if you're not going to use them, or just ignore them and let the interpreter deal with the excess code baggage it made for itself. When you do need another event, you dial it up from the right list.

Let's take a moment and examine how the ordinary event procedure declaration statement is phrased. Here's an example:

```
Private Sub GoThere_DblClick(ByVal Cancel As _
   MSForms.ReturnBoolean)
```

It's a Sub procedure, not a Function, so it doesn't return a value to any instruction that may call it. After all, the event procedure is designed not for other instructions to call it, but for the VBA interpreter to trigger it automatically. It's declared Private, so it isn't made visible in the "Macros" list of an Office 2000 application, and it is not accessible by way of code in some other module – especially some other form that might contain a control with the same .Name property. The event procedure name itself is constructed by piecing together the .Name property of the control, plus the name of the recognized event, and an _ underscore to separate the two. If the procedure doesn't receive any arguments from the interpreter, the event name is immediately followed by () empty parentheses; otherwise, the interpreter automatically writes the declarations for variables receiving the arguments. You can change the names of these variables if you feel you need to, but you shouldn't change the declared *types* because the interpreter will only pass arguments of these declared types anyway.

Just out of curiosity, what kind of type is MSForms.ReturnBoolean? First of all, the period is there for a reason: It divides the name of the library file MSForms (which, by the way, is the real subject of this chapter) from the type name ReturnBoolean that is defined by that library. And what type is that? Well . . . basically, it's Boolean, by another name. You could, conceivably, violate the rule stated in the last paragraph, change the declared variable type to just Boolean, and get away with it. So why the long version? This is one of those wonderful unanswerable questions, ranking right up there with, "Where do you want to go today?" You're safe just leaving it alone.

Constructing Form Module Prototypes

Our first example of a form module involves Word 2000. The way VBA works, you decide how a form and its controls will look *first*, then you write the functionality into those controls next. The official programming term for this process is *backwards*. Prior to the advent of Visual Basic, a programmer generally prototyped the program's functional schematics before she dared tinker with such frills as graphics. But in VBA, it's actually necessary for controls, such as text boxes and command buttons, to exist before the instructions that manage those controls are capable of knowing know what controls they're supposed to manage. This is why we build a form prototype first, and the functional portion later.

Conceiving a Word 2000 paragraph browser

The new version of Word already has a system in place for "browsing" an open document by flipping through its open pages, or headings, or sections, or footnotes, or any of several other divisions of the page. When you drag and drop the "thumb" portion of a scroll bar, Word displays a "ToolTip," which tells you the page you would see if you dropped the thumb at that point, along with the first few words of the heading (the paragraph formatted with a "Heading *x*" style) nearest the drop point. But paragraphs are not among Word's browseable divisions; in other words, Word has no graphical tools for browsing through paragraphs based on their first few words. This isn't really a design omission on Microsoft's part. You'd only really need such a tool if you were writing a document with the general format of this chapter you're reading now, and not all documents are formatted like this chapter. Yet as an entity, this chapter is fairly conventional as documents go, in that it contains sets of paragraphs, set off with headings and subheadings, with the occasional table or program fragment. When a document constructed like this one is in the Word workspace, it might be convenient to have a paragraph browser that lists the first portions of each paragraph in the active document, while leaving that document's main scroll bar where it is.

We'll build a simple example of a dialog box that acts as a paragraph browser, leaving out many of the frills that might make such a device especially interesting until later in the project's development. For now, we just want a list box that displays the first few words of a paragraph, indented slightly to indicate that paragraph's place in the heading hierarchy. All sequences of text ending with carriage returns will be included as paragraphs, including headings themselves. We just need a few options at the bottom of the dialog box, plus the usual OK and Cancel buttons. Figure 5-18 shows the goal we're working toward:

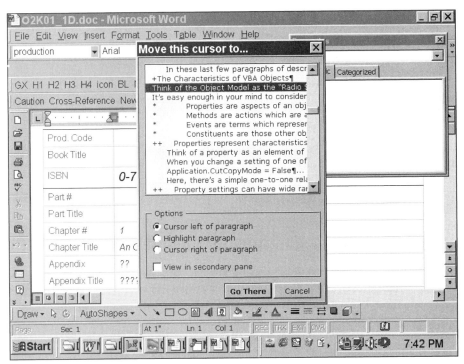

Figure 5-18: The paragraph browser dialog box in its completed form.

At Present: Word 2000's Document Map displays only existing headings

A more limited feature that is similar to what we're programming for this example already exists as part of Word 2000 . The Document Map, which follows, brings up a pane along the left side of the active document window. Within this pane is a separate outline view of the current document in the right pane. The Document Map by default displays the first three heading levels; like Outline view, it can display up to eight levels. For this feature to work — just like for our example form module — the headings within the document have to be formatted using the available heading styles: Heading 1, Heading 2, and so forth. But text that falls between the headings, and that has been given a non-heading style, is not shown in whole or in part within the Document Map. Granted, such a feature would not just make the map cluttered, it may also be redundant; why give the user a large windowpane full of *all* the text to help her navigate through another windowpane full of the same text? Our example form module, however, is capable of excerpting the first few words from each non-heading paragraph, which may prove useful in navigating long essays (examples of which appear here at the end of each chapter) in which headings are few and far-between.

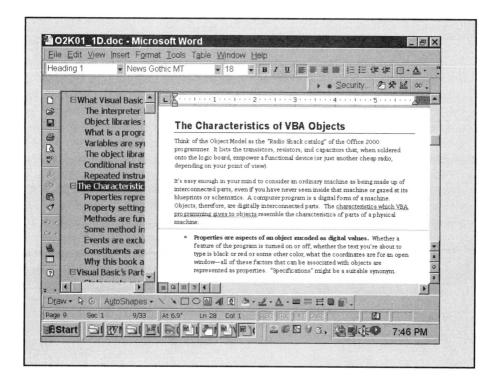

Templates and form modules must be initialized separately

The first question you must answer when starting to build a form module is this: To which project should the form truly belong? As we've already concluded, a device such as this one is probably unnecessary for every type of document you'll ever construct with Word. So the form module should belong to a template that contains the styles and layouts associated with the type of document that really would use this type of device.

You cannot create a template in the VBA environment. The Project window lists the templates and documents open within the Office application at any one time, and it is that very same Office application which is required to create or open those elements. So if the template you need for building a document appropriate to our example project does not yet exist, you need to create it in the Word environment, not in the VBA environment of Word.

Here is how you start a new form module belonging to a *template*:

1. Open or create your new template in Word, and save that template to disk. It doesn't need to be a *complete* template yet; that is, it doesn't have to have all the styles and layout elements necessary to be fully functional yet. It merely needs to exist for now.

2. If VBA isn't already open, then from Word's Tools menu, select **Macros**, followed by **Visual Basic Editor**. The VBA editor will soon appear.

3. In the Project window, right click on the **TemplateProject** heading beside the name of your saved template (listed to the right, in parentheses); and from the context menu, select **Insert**, followed by **UserForm**. VBA will bring up a new window, which itself contains a prototype window for the new form. The Toolbox window should also appear (as per VBA's default behavior). Your window may appear similar to the one depicted in Figure 5-5.

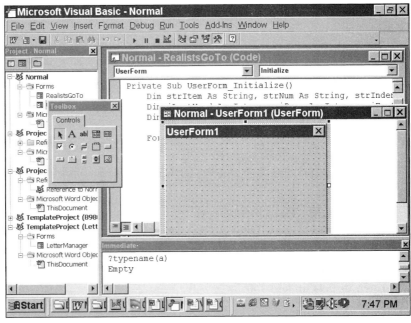

Figure 5-19: A new form module enters the VBA workspace.

It's important to remember that, since the functionality you're building with VBA is to be a part of the template, you should not close the template you've just initialized and open a document based on that template. If you're a veteran user of Word, you may be accustomed to devising a *style* template where you import all your necessary styles, boilerplate text, and page layout, then close that template before opening a document based on that template. When you're devising VBA-based functionality, you need to break that habit. Leave the template file open. When you're testing the template's functionality, it's more convenient for you to have the template on-hand, so you can break and make changes to source code without having to terminate your program, close the document file, reload your template, and find your place again.

On Point

A form is VBA's term for a window that contains common controls and that generally acts as a dialog box for your VBA project. A form module is made up of a `UserForm` object that is filled with controls from Windows' Forms 2.0 object library, and which is programmed using VBA instructions.

The `UserForm` object serves as the background platform for a dialog box. Using the VBA environment, you drag controls from the Toolbox window onto the prototype form. From that point on, the controls are said to be "contained" by the form. Both the form and the controls within it recognize their own events. Events may be generated by the user (such as `_Click` and `_DblClick`), by the VBA interpreter (such as `_Activate` and `_Deactivate`), or by either one (such as `_Change`). In any case, you program the form module to respond to these events by writing event procedures. These are `Private Sub` procedures whose names are concatenations of the `.Name` property of the object receiving the event, plus the underscore `_` character, plus the name of the event.

A form's initial properties should be set right away

At this point, the new form is probably not the size you require, and has none of the characteristics of the final product aside from being a familiar shade of gray. But little square nodes along the perimeter indicate the new form, as you can see in Figure 5-5. These square nodes are commonly called *handles*; but in the programmers' lexicon, something else is also called "handles" — certain pointers to regions of data in memory — so it's important that we maintain distinctions between our handles in our minds. (Sounds like lyrics for an old Fifth Dimension song, doesn't it?) For most graphic objects so indicated, these handles will be white, in which case you may click and drag them to reshape the object. Forms 2.0 controls are generally resizable, as well as forms themselves. When an object cannot be resized in a particular direction, the handle along the perimeter facing that direction will be black. You may still use a black handle to move the control to a new position. Or, more reasonably, you may ignore the black handles altogether and click and drag the body of the control itself to move it. (Next time there's a conference on "Fundamentals of User Interface Design," I'm going to bring up the issue of displaying graphical elements so that they can be ignored.)

You can also go over to the Properties window while the form is indicated, and change its own listed properties, such as its `.Height` and `.Width`, to nice, round numbers. You can also set the `.Name` property for the form, which is listed at the top of the list in the Properties window. All the other so-called *design-time properties* that can be set while you're designing the form, are listed below `.Name` in alphabetical order. A design-time property determines the default behavior or appearance of UserForm or one of its controls, once the form module is actually run.

A new form or control already has its own default behavior the moment you generate it from the toolbox; you could conceivably run a new object just as it is, without changing any properties. In other words, nothing is missing. But nothing at that point has much of a purpose, either, so you do need to set a new object's design-time properties, probably before you begin programming VBA instructions for that object. To change a property of an indicated object, double-click the property's line in the window, then either type a replacement setting, or use whatever tool that pops up instead (often a drop-down list box, sometimes an entire dialog box) to choose an available setting with the mouse.

For our example project, we set the specific UserForm properties listed in Table 5-1, and left the others as they were.

TABLE 5-1 UNIQUE SETTINGS TO OUR EXAMPLE USERFORM PROPERTIES

Property	Setting
.Name	frmRealistsGoTo
.Caption	Move this cursor to...
.Font	Verdana Regular, 8 pt.
.Height	286
.Width	200

How a form is officially designated

The form's .Name property serves as its official designation, especially for the benefit of code in other modules that may need to refer to a setting in one of the form's controls. The .Caption property contains the text that appears in the form's title bar. That text is often used to identify the window in printed documentation, but it does not serve that same purpose for VBA; the .Name property is the form's name for VBA's purposes. I arrived at the .Height and .Width properties by dragging the form to what I believed was an appropriate size, and then using the Properties window to trim the results.

A form's .Font property establishes the default font for its controls. Although there's no text that will be written into the form itself, setting the .Font property for the form establishes the default .Font property settings for all constituent controls that will be added to the form later. So setting the form's .Font property now will save you several steps later.

You may be wondering why I picked Verdana as the default font, when it looks so much like Tahoma — which is VBA's default font anyway? There's only one aesthetic reason: The spacing between letters is greater for the Verdana font than it is for the similarly styled Tahoma font. This makes Verdana a bit easier to read, especially at higher resolutions. Unlike the case with Word's own paragraph styles, the gaps between characters in a Forms 2.0 label cannot be changed. As a result, Windows applies the maximum amount of kerning it can for Tahoma — and for 8 point text on a screen of 1024 × 768 or higher, squinting has been known to result. Verdana and Tahoma are both installed automatically by Windows 98 as well as by Office 2000.

A form's .StartUpPosition **property denotes where it will be positioned at startup.** This is a flag property that represents the relative position of the form when its module first starts up. By default, the property is set to (1) Center Owner, which means that the newly loaded form will appear in the center of the active document window (the "owner"). I could have had the form centered in the middle of the screen (2), positioned manually by means of VBA instructions (0), or handled entirely at Windows' discretion (3). Generally, 1 works just fine. But this serves to demonstrate that you should review the Properties window in its entirety for each new form or control you add to a form. Even the default property settings should be intentional on your part.

How to attach a new control to the form

The next step in the construction of the form module is the attachment of new controls. A control such as a text box or an option button is supervised, if you will, by its own independent program in Windows. Several controls of the same type are run from one program that is responsible for that type. Still, each instance of a type of control is represented in Windows by an exclusive set of data. So while one program — namely, Forms 2.0 — runs every operative text box and option button, Windows is capable of perceiving each control as an independent entity, or an *instance*. It therefore follows that bringing in a new instance, is officially another kind of "instantiation," in that VBA is generating a new member of a formal class, from the "mold" defined by that class.

The first, and most important, control in the frmRealistsGoTo form for our example, is the control that will list the first few words in each paragraph in the document, in sequence. Here is how you add a new Forms 2.0:

1. Make the form window active in the VBA workspace. (If you're adding a new control to another container control, such as a frame, click on that container so that VBA knows what the container will be.)

2. Click on the icon in the Toolbox that represents the class of control you're adding to the form.

3. Click and hold the left mouse button over one corner of the form where you want the control to appear.

4. Drag the pointer to the opposite corner so that the shadow rectangle is the size you want the control to be, and release the button.

How to set a property for a control

When a new control first appears on your form, it may be close to or at the position you want, and it might have something approximating the shape you want. You then use the Properties window to give the new control the precise properties you require for it, such as absolute coordinate position, width, height, color, and textual contents. This too is a simple process:

1. Indicate the control whose properties you intend to change, either by clicking on that control in the prototype form (so that its handles surround it), or by choosing the name of that control from the list box at the top of the Properties window.

2. Choose the property you wish to change by clicking once on the line in the Properties window that contains the name of that property.

3. If the property setting is entirely alphanumeric (for instance, `.Caption`, which is all text, or `.Height`, which requires all numerals), type the replacement property setting and press Enter to finalize it. The new setting will appear in the line you just clicked on. If a graphical control is available for choosing the new property setting from a menu or other element, a grey button appears at the right portion of the chosen line. Click on this button to bring up the control and choose the new setting from there.

If you particularly enjoy the Properties window, or if you find yourself using it anyway whenever you attach a new Forms 2.0 control to a form, there is another way to attach a control to a form: First click on the control's icon in the Toolbox, then click *once* (not twice) anywhere on the form. The control will appear on the form at approximately the area you clicked on, with its default shape and size – which cannot possibly be what you want or where you want it. So you use the handles or the Properties window to make adjustments. For me personally, this is the "long route." I have watched other programmers in VBA and Visual Basic for several years now, and for them, this is the "short route."

For our paragraph browser, I attached a list box control using the first process above, and gave it the exclusive property settings listed in Table 5-2 using the second process above.

TABLE **5-2** PROPERTY SETTINGS FOR THE LIST BOX CONTROL IN OUR FORM

Property	Setting
.Name	lstLocator
.BackColor	&H00C0FFFF& (manila yellow)
.Height	142
.Left	6
.SpecialEffect	**6** – fmSpecialEffectBump
.Top	6
.Width	186

The .BackColor property setting gives this particular list box control a manila yellow appearance, while the .SpecialEffect setting gives it a little ridge along its edges.

A frame helps departmentalize controls

You might not have thought much about the presence of *frames* in dialog boxes, but they serve a very useful purpose: They corral groups of related controls and separate these groups from one another. They also help the user more readily identify the purpose of a group of controls with respect to one another, as well as to the other controls in the form. A standard Windows frame control contains a brief label, which is situated just to the right of the frame's upper left corner. The label serves to categorize the contents of the frame.

For our example, the frame is being used more cosmetically; there's only one group to worry about. Table 5-3 shows the special properties we gave to our frame.

TABLE **5-3** PROPERTY SETTINGS FOR THE FRAME CONTROL IN FRMREALISTSGOTO

Property	Setting
.Name	Options
.Height	76

Continued

TABLE **5-3** PROPERTY SETTINGS FOR THE FRAME CONTROL IN FRMREALISTSGOTO
       (Continued)

Property	Setting
.Left	6
.SpecialEffect	3 – fmSpecialEffectEtched
.Top	156
.Width	186

Naming the frame formally was inconsequential in this context; we were fine with leaving the .Name property set to the default of Frame1 since we have no plans to refer to the frame in our source code. When a new control is first attached, VBA sets that control's default .Name property to a concatenation of its class name, plus one more than the highest-numbered default name in the control's class. If we were to add a second frame to this form now, VBA would give it the default name Frame2.

The way to make new controls – such as the option button set and check box – belong to the frame is to attach them inside the frame. In other words, if you drag the pointer from one corner *inside* the frame perimeter to an opposite corner either in or out of that perimeter, then the new control will "belong" to the frame. The upshot of this is that, when you move the frame, you move all of the controls within it, just like moving a dinner plate on a dining room table. This belonging doesn't affect how you refer to the controls contained within the frame within VBA instructions.

Perhaps you're wondering, what happens if you drag the size of the new control so that some of its boundaries are outside of the frame? VBA accepts your choice of boundaries, even if you can't see the new control in its entirety. Why? Because you can then set the .ScrollBars property of the frame to 3 – fmScrollBarsBoth, so that at run time, the user can use the frame like a scrollable window, peering at the contents "beneath" the frame. This multi-planar form construction is perhaps inadvisable from an ease-of-use standpoint, but at least it's available should you ever feel the need to be inventive.

How option buttons are made to work with one another

In our example paragraph browser, the three option buttons in Frame1 are marked, "Cursor left of paragraph," "Highlight paragraph," and "Cursor right of paragraph."

These labels are reflected in the `.Caption` property settings for those controls. The purpose of this set of options is to let the user tell the VBA program where to place the Word cursor after it brings up the chosen paragraph – should it go at the beginning of the paragraph or at the end? Or should the paragraph be highlighted as though it were about to be cut to the Clipboard? These three controls were given `.Name` properties of `optCursor1`, `optCursor2`, and `optCursor3`. But the fact that these three properties have the same prefixes does not give VBA enough reason to logically group them together. Remember, when the user makes a choice from one option in the set, the previously chosen option is reset. But because a form may contain more than one option set, the form has to know which currently set option to reset; in other words, it has to know which black dot to turn white again. Forms 2.0 maintains a property called `.GroupName` specifically designed to give all the choices that make up a set something in common with one another. So the three option buttons here are all given the `.GroupName` setting `CursorPoint`. As long as you give these buttons the same `.GroupName` property setting, VBA will group them together as one set.

The `.Value` property of an option button control represents whether that button is set or reset. After the button was attached, I used the Copy and Paste menu commands to make two copies of this control. As long as the frame control remains indicated, then when Paste is selected, the newly cloned control will also belong to the frame, just like the model on which it is based. But the new control will have all the property settings of its predecessor, including its `.Caption` and `.Value` properties.

This can result in a number of problems unless you correct them before you run the form for the first time: First of all, two or more option buttons with the same `.Caption` property are obviously susceptible to confusion. Secondly, **the default option button in a set is not determined until the run time for the form that contains them.** In other words, if you copy and paste an option button whose `.Value` property has already been set to `True`, then the copy will be `True` as well, and two (or more) true options in a set will result in what folk singer Arlo Guthrie might call "a whole lot of no fun." Now, VBA is smart enough to set an option to `False` when another button in the same set has been set to `True` through the Properties window. But if you copy an option button whose `.Value` property is already `True`, then the pasted buttons will all be `True` as well. Likewise (and just as confusing), a copy of a `False` option button will result in multiple `False` buttons. The best way around this problem is to go ahead and make copies of `False` option buttons, then set the default option button to `True` once all the buttons in the set are in position.

By the way, the VBA interpreter will not clone the `.Name` property of a control during a copy and paste maneuver. Instead, VBA will give that control the name it would have had, had it been dragged in from the Toolbox.

Table 5-4 shows the exclusive property settings for the three option buttons in our example.

TABLE 5-4 PROPERTY SETTINGS FOR THE OPTION BUTTONS IN FRMREALISTSGOTO

Property	Option button 1	Option button 2	Option button 3
.Name	optCursor1	optCursor2	optCursor3
.Caption	Cursor left of paragraph	Highlight paragraph	Cursor right of paragraph
.GroupName	CursorPoint	CursorPoint	CursorPoint
.Height	15	15	15
.Left	6	6	6
.Top	6	19	32
.Value	True	False	False
.Width	160	160	160

The settings for the upper left corners of these option buttons are worth noting because they are relative to the coordinate system of the frame control, not the form. When a control is contained within another control, the container lends its coordinate system to the contained control. This way, if you were to change the position of the frame, nothing about the positioning of the contained controls would have to change.

The Forms 2.0 check box control is constructed almost exactly the same way as an option button. I placed this check box in the same frame as the option buttons; but note that a check box represents a yes/no choice unto itself, so it has no reason to share the same .GroupName property setting as the option buttons. (In fact, it has no reason to support a .GroupName property in the first place, since check boxes cannot be grouped either with option buttons or other check boxes.) Table 5-5 shows the check box's exclusive property settings for the example:

TABLE 5-5 PROPERTY SETTINGS FOR THE CHECK BOX IN OUR FORM

Property	Setting
.Name	chkPane
.Caption	View in secondary pane

Property	Setting
.Height	15
.Left	6
.Top	51
.Width	160

Reconciling the default command button with the Enter key

You use the Forms 2.0 command buttons to serve as the dialog box form's main switches, letting the user either sign off on his form and submit it, or dismiss it without proceeding with the command. A command button is a very simple push button, sensitive to being clicked on as well as being "grazed," if you will, by the mouse pointer.

For our example, "Go There" is caption for the OK button of our form. We want this to be the control that reacts to the user pressing Enter – in other words, the default command button. So we set its .Default property to True, which results in VBA giving that button the familiar thick border that users expect for the dialog box button that means "do this and get out of here." Since pressing Enter is the functional equivalent of clicking on the form's default button, pressing Enter also triggers the _Click event procedure for that button, even though the mouse isn't involved. The true purpose of that procedure, after all, would be to initiate the processing of the command; so it would be redundant to have two event procedures – one for the mouse, the other for the keyboard – that perform mainly the same processes.

You must be careful here, because it's entirely possible for the .Default property of more than one button to be set to True. If you set any command button's .Default property to True, then the True .Default property setting of any other command button will immediately become False. The same behavior holds true for the .Cancel property. These are good things. But if you were to copy the default button to the Clipboard and paste it into the same form, the clone would also have a .Default property of True. The result at run time would be confusion on the part of the VBA interpreter. When initializing the form, the interpreter would probably treat the first such button it encounters as the default – although surprisingly, this won't always be the case. It's up to you to ensure that a form has no more than one default command button.

Table 5-6 shows the property settings for the two command buttons in our example.

TABLE 5-6 PROPERTY SETTINGS FOR THE COMMAND BUTTONS IN OUR FORM

Property	Default button	Cancel button
.Name	btnGoThere	btnCancel
.Cancel	False	True
.Caption	Go There	Cancel
.Default	True	False
.Font	Verdana 8 pt. Bold	Verdana 8 pt. Normal
.Height	18	18
.Left	90	142
.Top	238	238
.Width	54	54

No two Windows are alike

Due to the extraordinary abundance of graphics card brands and display formats, it has become an everyday fact of programming that a dialog box on one screen is likely not to be identical to the same dialog box from the same program on another screen. The example programs in this and other IDG books are reviewed for technical accuracy by experienced technical editors, some of whom are authors themselves. The paragraph browser has appeared in an earlier book, and as a result has been reviewed by more than one technical editor. The first such editor complained that the controls inside the frame were too large – that they spilled over the edge of the form. So I shortened them by one point. The most recent technical editor has complained that the same controls are too small.

The fact that the size, shape, and spacing of the controls you attach to your forms appears correct to you at design time on your own development system, provides no assurance that those same controls will appear correctly on another system. One way you can avoid some potential future problems is to avoid packing your controls too tightly, and give your controls perhaps more height and width than they appear to require. However, it is possible that some may think your controls are too big, though this is less of a possibility than your controls appearing too small if you've given them plenty of space and a wide enough berth on the form.

A common cause of size discrepancies is the fact that Windows may be operated not only with different resolutions, but also different *font size ratios* (the so-called "Large Fonts" mode in the control panel multiplies font sizes by 125%). The settings for the .Width and .Height properties of Forms 2.0 controls are supposed to correspond to *points* ($^1/_{72}$ inch), but few Windows screen drivers seem to be capable of approximating that unit of measurement with any degree of success. If settings were to be reduced, low-resolution users would be happy, but high-resolution users would be squinting. So sometimes proper form design involves the search for a happy medium.

Notice elsewhere in Table 5-6, that the counterpart of the .Default property is the .Cancel property. The command button whose .Cancel property is set to True should be the single button on the form that forces the menu command to be canceled. Cancellation in this case is not synonymous with ending the module's run. In some cases, it's really the beginning of a shutdown process, which itself must be programmed using VBA instructions. Like the default button, the cancel button of a dialog box has an associated keystroke, the Esc key. When the user presses Esc, the VBA interpreter treats that keystroke exactly as if the user had clicked on the des-

On Point

Here again are some of the facts we have discovered so far, after plowing headlong into this form module project: The official designation for a graphic object such as a form or control is known in code as its .Name property. Once an object has this property set, event procedures may borrow its name as part of their own, and VBA will know which control is to be monitored for those events automatically.

Although one program is responsible for the maintenance of a given class of control, each instance of a control in a form is treated by VBA as a separate component with a separate .Name property. So controls that have to operate in tandem with one another, such as option buttons, have to be given some property setting in common — in the case of the option button, it's the .GroupName property.

A command button in a dialog box often has a major job: either to accept the user's choices and proceed, or to cancel the operation. Windows allows the user to make these major directives either with a mouse click or a keyboard press, both of which are arguably separate events. By setting the .Default property of an OK button to True, you can have the _Click event procedure for the OK button respond to both a mouse click and the user pressing Enter. Similarly, setting .Cancel property of a Cancel button to True makes it sensitive to both a mouse click and the user pressing Esc.

ignated cancel button. So the _Click event procedure, if there is one, will be executed for that cancel button in both circumstances.

Adding Functionality to the Prototype

For many professional programmers, building the shell of a program and then stuffing it with functionality seems a bit backwards – a bit like building a cheese log from the outside in. Yet this is the way the Visual Basic genre is designed to work, especially for a program such as the Word 2000 paragraph browser example. Such an event-driven program needs objects in order for the interpreter to be capable of determining just what all the events concern.

The _Initialize event sets up a form before it's seen

Visual Basic for Applications modules will tend to be primarily, if not entirely, event driven. Even the instructions that initialize the modules are executed in response to a formal event – specifically, UserForm_Initialize. Because this module does not need to be made unnecessarily complex, we used the Private Sub UserForm_Initialize() procedure – which runs just after the form module is started, but *before* the form actually enters the screen – to load the list box with entries from which the user makes a choice. In fact, that's really the entire purpose of this procedure. Listing 5-1 lists the first build of the procedure:

Listing 5-1: Initializing the list box control before it's seen.

```
Private Sub UserForm_Initialize()
    Dim strItem As String, strNum As String, strIndent As String
    Dim iLastHead As Integer
    Dim paraList As Paragraph

    For Each paraList In ActiveDocument.Paragraphs
        If Left$(paraList.Style, 7) = "Heading" Then
            strNum = Right$(paraList.Style, 1)
            iLastHead = Val(strNum)
            strItem = String$(iLastHead, "+") & String$ _
            ((iLastHead - 1) * 4, " ") & paraList.Range.Text
        Else
            If paraList.Range.Text <> "" And _
            Asc(Right$(paraList.Range.Text, 1)) <> 7 Then
                If iLastHead Then
                    strIndent = String$((iLastHead - 1) * 5, " ")
                Else
```

```
                        strIndent = ""
                End If
                strItem = strIndent & _
                  Left$(paraList.Range.Text, 50) & "..."
            End If
        End If
        If strItem <> "" Then
            lstLocator.AddItem strItem
            strItem = ""
        End If
    Next paraList
End Sub
```

The Forms 2.0 text box control is a simple character-based control; the only data you can assign to it are straight letters and numbers, without formatting. The effect we want is to have the text from paragraphs written beneath a heading with a numbered style, such as "Heading 2," to be indented just slightly. With a text-only control such as this, the only way we can accomplish this is to add spaces prior to the paragraph excerpt. With the rule established that one paragraph excerpt is given no more than one line, we can program the procedure to add five extra preceding spaces for each *subheading* level. So the procedure should count the current heading level, subtract one, and multiply the result by five to attain the actual number of spaces to add in front of *each* line. If the heading level is 1, then 1 − 1 = 0, and 0 × 5 = 0; so we can rely on math rather than explicit instructions to restrict heading level 1 lines from receiving any leading spaces.

The procedure uses three local variables of class `String`. Variable `strItem` holds the text line while it is being assembled, before its contents are assigned to the list box control. Variable `strNum` is used to extract a heading number from the paragraph style, while `strIndent` is used to assemble the proper number of spaces to be added to the front of each line, even if it's zero. Integer variable `iLastHead` is used to remember the heading level of the previous paragraph; this is how the procedure knows to indent successive paragraphs after a numbered heading. Finally, `paraList` is used as an object reference that cycles through all of the paragraphs in the document, represented by `ActiveDocument.Paragraphs`.

EXAMPLE OF A FOR EACH...NEXT LOOP CLAUSE

As the variable `paraList` cycles through each paragraph in the currently open Word document, the main conditional clause inside the `For Each...Next` loop clause first checks to see if `Heading` constitutes the first seven letters in that paragraph's assigned style. If it does, then the line in the list box where the heading will be duplicated is marked with as many plus signs as the indicated heading level. This is accomplished by borrowing some more of VBA's intrinsic functions, as shown in Table 5-7.

TABLE **5-7** INTRINSIC FUNCTIONS

Term	Description
`Val()`	Returns a value equivalent to the amount stated by the given string expression or string literal. **Argument:** *String* – A character string, in the form of an expression, a literal, or a `String` type property.
`Asc()`	Returns an integer from a lookup table that represents the ASCII (actually the ANSI) code number for the given character. **Argument:** *Character* – A single character, represented by a character string of length 1 or a literal.
`Left$()`	Returns the leftmost characters from a given string expression or string literal. **Arguments (in order):** *String* – A character string, in the form of an expression, a literal, or a `String` type property. *Integer* – An integer variable or a numeral relating the number of characters to return from the left side of *String*. **Usage notes:** The $ portion of the function name is optional.
`String$()`	Returns a string consisting of the character in the second argument, repeated as many times as the integer in the first argument. **Arguments (in order):** *Integer* – An integer variable, numeral, or expression relating the number of times to repeat the character in *String*. *String* – A string variable or literal whose initial character is the one that is to be repeated. Any other characters in the string are ignored. **Usage notes:** The $ portion of the function name is optional.

The main `If...Then...Else` conditional clause is entirely dependent on VBA intrinsic functions. The `Left$()` function (which was profiled in Chapter 4) removes the first seven characters from the current paragraph's assigned style. If the expression turns up `Heading`, then the `Right$()` function is used to extract the final numeral from the heading style name (assuming that the enumeration stops no later than at 9). For instance, if the style name is `Heading 2`, then the `Heading` part will trip the first portion of the conditional clause, and then the 2 part will be extracted. The `Val()` function is used next to turn that numeral into a value that we can actually work with, because you cannot multiply a number by a string. The value is assigned to the integer variable `iLastHead`. Then the `String$()` function is used twice in the next instruction, first to render as many plus signs as indicated by `iLastHead`, and second to indent all those paragraphs beneath headings greater than 1, with four spaces per heading level, as stated by (`iLastHead - 1) * 4`.

The excerpt from the paragraph that will appear in the list box is represented by `strItem`. It's assembled as a concatenation of the plus signs, plus the spaces, plus the *entire* text of the paragraph. Because the paragraph is just a heading, it can be presumed to be no more than one sentence long. The text may run over the right side of the list box, but it won't wrap to another line, which is fine.

Word's multi-faceted Range object

The paragraph's text is represented in the Word 2000 object library by the `.Text` property of the `Range` constituent of the `Paragraph` class object being examined — thus `paraList.Range.Text`. The `Range` term has a multiplicity of meanings in Word depending on how and where it is invoked. Here, as a property of a `Paragraph` class object `paraList`, `Range` refers to the region of the document that's consumed by the paragraph. The `.Text` property, then, is the actual text within that range. Why the three-step maneuver? Why isn't `.Text` a property of the `Paragraph` class? Chapter 10 will present this design philosophy in detail; for now, suffice it to say that Word distinguishes between *format* and *content*. A `Paragraph` class object is defined by its placement, layout, and format; content is an extension of that object, and `Range` is the object responsible for that extension.

The second part of the main conditional clause in `Private Sub UserForm_ Initialize()` is executed when the assessed paragraph style is *not* a heading. For the nonheading paragraph to qualify for being excerpted it must meet two conditions: First, it must have some real content. Thus the first conditional expression, `paraList.Range.Text <> ""`, checks to see if the range is *not empty* — or literally, if you'll excuse the double negative, not equal to nothing.

The second condition is one that we encountered in testing and debugging this module. It so happens that *tables* within a Word document are separated by rows and, at the end of each row, the word processor inserts a line feed character, ANSI code 7. For the character not to be mistaken for a table cell, Word places the character between rows, but *outside* of the table. Unfortunately, this means that Word counts this character as an entire paragraph, which is therefore counted as a member of the `Paragraphs` collection. Because character code 7 is, arguably, *something*, it is therefore *not nothing*, and therefore passes the first condition. This means that, not only a non-paragraph paragraph, but a non-character character could be entered as one of the entries in the list box. So I added the second condition, which tests for the presence of character code 7, and ignores the paragraph if that is all it is.

If the paragraph passes both conditions, then variable iLastHead — which would not have been cleared since the loop clause's last iteration — still contains the heading number of the previous paragraph. By allowing it not to be cleared, the integer can be used here to refer to the active heading level. The String$() function is used again to assemble five spaces per each heading level above 1, but only if iLastHead has any value whatsoever. This is why the third-tier conditional clause If iLastHead Then... is phrased like it is, without any conditional operator or comparison value. Variable iLastHead will pass this conditional test as long as it is not False (0); thus, any non-zero value passes the test.

The second part of the main If...Then...Else clause — the Else portion — concludes by assembling strItem for the list box in a different manner. It begins with the indentation spaces strIndent, and adds to the end of that the first 50 characters of the paragraph, excerpted using the Left$() function. The excerpt will probably spill over the side of the line anyway, but that's okay. In case it doesn't, I've added an ellipsis at the end.

After the main conditional clause is exited, strItem should contain something that the list box can use. If it doesn't, then the current paragraph pointed to by paraList doesn't qualify, so we shouldn't add a "non-choice" line to the list box. The final test checks whether strItem does not, as it were, equal nothing. If it doesn't, then the entry is added to the list box. Inserting a new item into a list box is exceptionally simple: We use the .AddItem method, which is recognized as part of the lexicon of the Forms 2.0 list box control. The instruction Locator.AddItem strItem addresses the list box by its .Name property setting, Locator. Variable strItem acts as the argument to the .AddItem method; a second integer argument after strItem could have been specified to specify the position in the list where we wanted strItem to be added. Without that argument, however, Forms 2.0 knows to put the item at the end of the list.

Directing the cursor across document boundaries

At this point in the program's run, the list box is full of excerpts from the entire active document, and we can assume that the form is awaiting a response from the user. We don't need instructions to inform the form of what it needs to do while it's waiting. Windows will handle that job for us; during the waiting period, the form is actually out of VBA's purview and into Windows'. What we need next is a general procedure that performs the actual job of moving the cursor to the designated paragraph. We need this to be a general procedure, not an event procedure, because in designing the form, we ascertained that the act of dismissing the form and executing the command can take place as a result of more than one event. The user can either click once on the excerpt in the list box and then click on the Go There button, or just double-click on the excerpt. In short, this same process may respond to more than one event. We need the event procedures for both events to point to a single external procedure containing the routine that handles the cursor relocation.

Listing 5-2 shows the general procedure I devised. It is not the most efficient procedure that I could have come up with, but it is the most direct and easy to produce.

Listing 5-2: Moving the cursor to the chosen position.

```
Private Sub MoveCursor()
    Dim iPara As Integer, iFact As Integer
    Dim paraList As Paragraph

    If chkPane Then
        ActiveWindow.SplitVertical = 50
    End If
    If lstLocator.ListIndex = -1 Then Exit Sub
    Selection.HomeKey Unit:=wdStory, Extend:=wdMove
    Do Until iPara = lstLocator.ListIndex + 1
        iFact = iFact + 1
        Set paraList = ActiveDocument.Paragraphs(iFact)
        If paraList.Range.Text <> "" And _
          Asc(Right$(paraList.Range.Text, 1)) <> 7 Then
            iPara = iPara + 1
        End If
    Loop
    ActiveDocument.Paragraphs(iFact).Range.Select
    If optCursor1.Value = True Then
        Selection.Collapse wdCollapseStart
    ElseIf optCursor3.Value = True Then
        Selection.Collapse wdCollapseEnd
        Selection.MoveLeft Unit:=wdCharacter, Count:=1
    End If

    Unload frmRealistsGoTo
End Sub
```

The problem with this procedure is that, as far as Word is concerned, the first line of a paragraph is no indicator of the identity of that paragraph. Word identifies Paragraph class objects by their accession number, which is an index that represents the order of each paragraph's appearance in the document. So this procedure has to run the qualification test on each paragraph for each entry in the list box. The theory is this: The list box enumerates each item in its own list, and knows what item the user chose by its own index number. If the procedure can simply count the paragraphs from the document that qualified for the list until it reaches that same index number, it will have arrived at the chosen paragraph.

So two integers are needed for two separate counts. Variable iFact counts the number of paragraphs searched in the document, while iPara records the number of qualifying paragraphs found. The object reference `paraList` makes a cameo appearance here, once again representing the currently counted paragraph.

The first order of business for `Private Sub MoveCursor()` is to look at the check box named `chkPane` to see if the user has directed that the chosen paragraph be brought up in a separate pane. With Word, the document window may be subdivided into two so-called *panes*. Both panes provide views of the same document, though at independent positions. If the user checks the box, its `.Value` property is set to `True`. But there is no mention of `.Value` in the conditional statement `If chkPane Then...` There doesn't have to be, since `.Value` is the *default property* of the check box control, and just stating `chkPane` by itself implies `chkPane.Value`. In this case, if the box registers `True`, then the `.SplitVertical` property of Word's `ActiveWindow` object is employed to bring up the pane, and place the horizontal border between them positioned `50` percent of the way down the page (if the pane already exists, then the property setting merely resets its position).

List box controls enumerate their contents beginning with 0

The next conditional test, `If Locator.ListIndex = -1 Then Exit Sub`, is a little trapdoor that drops execution out of the procedure if the list box registers that no item was chosen whatsoever. I don't want to punish the user; I just want to end the program. The Forms 2.0 list box control is a bit awkward, in that it registers the *first* entry at the top as number 0, the *second* as number 1, and so on. So "no entry chosen," which is the default state of the control, is registered as number –1.

Following the single-line condition, the next instruction looks like it was written in an altogether different language. `Selection.HomeKey    Unit:=wdStory, Extend:=wdMove` is a directive to the Word's cursor, which is addressed as an active element with a direct handle on how the document is edited and formatted. (Even though this isn't really the case as far as the application's own architecture is concerned, `Selection` does tend to represent the active edit in progress.) In the often confusing language of the Word 2000 object library, the term *story* refers to the *content* of a document as a whole (whereas *text* refers to the characters that make up the content of a document, without regard to their formatting). The `.HomeKey` method of the `Selection` object directs Word to move the cursor as though the user had pressed the Home key on the keyboard. But in what context would it have been pressed? This is answered by the `Unit` argument, which is set to `wdStory`, a constant that represents the active story (the content of the entire document). The other argument, set to the constant `wdMove`, tells Word not to extend the text indicator as though the user were dragging the mouse pointer, or holding down the Shift key. Instead, just lift the cursor and move it elsewhere.

The type of loop clause I chose for `Private Sub MoveCursor()` is a Do...Loop clause. The reason for this choice is because we require an exclusive condition, not just a counter being ticked off with each iteration like a For...Next loop. In effect, we already have a counter variable in the form of iPara, but we don't need iPara to be "ticked" unless the paragraph to which it points is a "qualifying" paragraph. Do...Loop gives us the flexibility to state the condition being testing for, and to either *continue* the loop clause or *exit* the clause. In this case, with the Until specifier, once the condition evaluates True, the loop clause is exited. Although we're free to manage iPara, the subject of the condition, however we choose, although we do need to explicitly state the "ticking" part, iPara + iPara + 1, otherwise we'll be in this loop forever.

Within this loop clause, a secondary counter iFact ticks off each paragraph in the Paragraphs collection. The Set statement makes paraList point to each successive paragraph, using iFact as a subscript. Then the If...Then clause checks whether paraList points to a qualifying paragraph and, if it does, iPara is incremented manually. The Loop part of the clause takes execution back to the top, where the condition is then re-evaluated. Remember that the list box control counts the first item 0, the second 1, and so on. The .ListIndex property represents the index number of the chosen entry, and 1 is added to it to put it in sync with the Paragraphs collection. When the integer and the property match, the loop drops out, and iFact registers the *real* index number of the chosen paragraph.

Changing a document's text by altering

In Listing 5-2, the next instruction after the loop clause, ActiveDocument. Paragraphs(iFact).Range.Select, moves the cursor to the correct chosen paragraph and indicates ("selects") that paragraph in reverse text, white on black. If the second option button on the form – the one marked "Highlight paragraph" – is chosen, things could be left as they are. There is no need to check whether the *second* option button is set, though there is a need to check whether the first or the third option button has been set. These choices would move the cursor to the beginning or the end of the chosen paragraph, respectively. (Why have the program select the paragraph and then un-select it if the user so chooses? It requires fewer instructions.) When the Selection object represents an expanse of text rather than just the position of the cursor, the method used to unselect the text is .Collapse. The two constants recognized here have obvious meanings. If the first option is set, the .Collapse method places the cursor at the beginning of the text it had previously indicated; if the third is set, the cursor is placed at the beginning of the line *following* the text it had previously indicated. This is important, because the .MoveLeft method is then required to scoot the cursor up one character to the *real* end of the paragraph, following the final period.

The final duty for this procedure is to remove the form from the screen and from memory. The Unload statement here does both, referring to the form frmRealistsGoTo by its .Name property (not by its class name).

A form is made usable through event procedures

Next, we finalize the program by completing the crucial user events. Two of these events must be linked to `Private Sub MoveCursor()`:

```
Private Sub btnGoThere_Click()
    MoveCursor
End Sub


Private Sub lstLocator_DblClick(ByVal Cancel As _
MSForms.ReturnBoolean)
    MoveCursor
End Sub
```

These two procedures handle clicking on the **Go There** button, and double-clicking the list box, respectively. They pass execution to the same general procedure so that both actions can have the same effect. For event procedures that take arguments, the VBA interpreter inserts the declaration for those arguments automatically. So `ByVal Cancel As MSForms.ReturnBoolean` is written into the declaration, even though variable `Cancel` isn't used anywhere in this terribly brief procedure. You shouldn't remove this declaration yourself, however, because something needs to be present to receive the incoming argument in order for the event procedure to even run.

There's one more event procedure to take into account: What if the user presses Cancel?

```
Private Sub btnCancel_Click()
    Unload frmRealistsGoTo
End Sub
```

There's no logic to be utilized here; all that is needed is for the procedure to shut down the form. Other form modules may not have as simple a procedure for their cancel buttons, especially in situations where the form can make changes to the active document or some feature of the application while the user is making choices. Such a form is recognizable by its prominent "Apply" button, alongside "OK" and "Cancel" – such a button generally means, "Try this choice, but allow me to undo it if I don't like what I see."

A Public Sub procedure makes a form module a "macro"

In order for us to begin testing the form module in the real world, the module needs something to "expose" itself to the document template where it will be utilized. This template can be NORMAL.DOT, or whatever template you've created in Word to contain the form module. **A form module is, by design, cut off from the Word** workspace, even if it belongs to the template's own **VBA project.** It doesn't take much to connect the form module, but it does need to be done.

The startup procedure for a form module must reside outside of the form module, in a location where Word VBA looks for `Public Sub` procedures, which is either of two locations:

◆ **Within the** `ThisDocument` **code module,** located in the Projects window, under the folder marked **Microsoft Word Objects.** Normally this is the module that contains procedures that address the document as an object, or an instance of the `Document` class. Event procedures such as `Private Sub Document_Open()` are to be found here. But for the sake of your own convenience, you may place all public procedures whose job is to initiate form modules, in the `ThisDocument` code module.

◆ **Within a general code module,** located in the Projects window, under the **Modules** folder. You may find it preferable to create one general module exclusively for form startup procedures, and name that module `FormStartups`, or some similar name.

For our example, here is our entire startup procedure:

```
Public Sub RealistsGoToMain()
    frmRealistsGoTo.Show
End Sub
```

Here, `frmRealistsGoTo` is the name of the form. VBA recognizes this as a form as long as the form module exists (in the Project list under the **Forms** folder). The `.Show` method brings the form into the Word workspace and activates it — which is a longer story than perhaps it deserves to be, although it will be discussed in detail in Chapter 6.

Rethinking the efficiency question

After you've been programming for awhile (about fifteen minutes), one of the things you learn is that the most efficient way to undertake a task doesn't really present itself until after you've already designed another way to do it. With the paragraph browser example, the methodology that was used was sufficient and simple, but not *efficient.* It suffered from a common deficiency of event-oriented programming: It compels us to take inventory of the user events and write the core functionality to fit with them, rather than build the core functionality first and design the form to fit the function.

If you've tried out the `frmRealistsGoTo` form module, you might have noticed that, for a moderately long document, it takes the module much longer to move the cursor toward the *end* of the document than it does to move it toward the *beginning.* My technical editor clocked a long jump at 46 seconds, which is a lot of hang time by anyone's standards. This is because `Private Sub MoveCursor()`, the procedure which handles the relocation of the cursor to the chosen paragraph, starts out with no information to go on other than the `Paragraphs` collection itself—which is a global—and the index number of the list entry that the user clicked on. It has to find everything else out on its own, re-evaluating each paragraph in the collection, starting at the beginning. The further the procedure has to go to find the chosen paragraph, the more time that is consumed.

The solution to the problem works like this: We need a way for the data already ascertained by the `_Initialize` event procedure to be made available to `Private Sub MoveCursor()`. We can't pass the data as an argument to the procedure without passing execution to it as well—which would be wrong, since execution of the procedure should be initiated by a user event. There's time in-between `Private Sub UserForm_Initialize()` and `Private Sub MoveCursor()`, which is filled by the form awaiting response from the user.

The solution (at least in the near-term) is to build a module-level dynamic array that stores the paragraph data from `Private Sub UserForm_Initialize()`, and maintains that data for whenever `Private Sub MoveCursor()` is executed. For the first step in the second build of the paragraph browser, this instruction is added to the Declarations section of the form module:

```
Dim iLookup() As Integer
```

In Chapter 4, I told you that a dynamic array has an indeterminate length when it's declared with `Dim`, although its length is set later using the `ReDim` statement. We can't use `Public` to declare this array because a form module is considered by VBA an "object module," and objects aren't allowed by protocol to "export" their elements without using object-oriented terminology. In other words, any data *exposed*, to use Microsoft's term, by an object has to be a property of that object, not just a variable. So `Public` is right out, and we're stuck with `Dim`.

Listing 5-3 shows how `Private Sub UserForm_Initialize()` was rewritten for the second build, to take the opportunity to store the paragraph data into the dynamic array:

Listing 5-3: The second build, which stores the data it ascertains for later.

```
Private Sub UserForm_Initialize()
    Dim strItem As String, strNum As String, strIndent As String
    Dim iLastHead As Integer, iPara As Integer, iFact As Integer
    Dim paraList As Paragraph

    For Each paraList In ActiveDocument.Paragraphs
        If Left$(paraList.Style, 7) = "Heading" Then
            strNum = Right$(paraList.Style, 1)
            iLastHead = Val(strNum)
            strItem = String$(iLastHead, "+") & String$ _
```

```
                ((iLastHead - 1) * 4, " ") & paraList.Range.Text
        Else
            If paraList.Range.Text <> "" And _
             Asc(Right$(paraList.Range.Text, 1)) <> 7 Then
                If iLastHead Then
                    strIndent = String$((iLastHead - 1) * 5, " ")
                Else
                    strIndent = ""
                End If
                strItem = strIndent & Left$(paraList.Range.Text, _
                50) & "..."
            End If
        End If
        If strItem <> "" Then
            ReDim Preserve iLookup(iFact)
            iLookup(iPara) = iFact
            iPara = iPara + 1
            lstLocator.AddItem strItem
            strItem = ""
        End If
        iFact = iFact + 1
    Next paraList
End Sub
```

Here, we've added the integer variables iPara and iFact, which should be familiar from Listing 5-2. The purpose of the iLookup() array is to record the index number of the qualifying paragraphs from the Paragraph array. If a paragraph doesn't qualify for the list box, it won't get recorded in the array. As a result, the entries in the array match up with the arrays in the list box. When the user chooses an entry from the list box, Private Sub MoveCursor() will use the .ListIndex property returned from the list box as an index for pulling up the Paragraphs collection index number.

Near the bottom of Listing 5-3, the ReDim Preserve statement is used to add one unit to the end of the iLookup() array whenever there's a new list box entry to be accounted for, while maintaining whatever contents may already be in the array. Variable iPara is incremented only when strItem <> ""—when the entry made ready for the list box does not equal nothing. But iFact is incremented for each iteration, keeping count of the paragraph currently being examined. It is the value of iFact that is stored within the array, using the instruction iLookup(iPara) = iFact.

With that data stored, we can greatly streamline Private Sub MoveCursor(), as demonstrated in Listing 5-4:

Listing 5-4: The programming equivalent of liposuction.

```
Private Sub MoveCursor()
    If chkPane Then
        ActiveWindow.SplitVertical = 50
    End If
    If lstLocator.ListIndex = -1 Then Exit Sub
    ActiveDocument.Paragraphs(iLookup(lstLocator.ListIndex + _
     1)).Range.Select
    If optCursor1.Value = True Then
        Selection.Collapse wdCollapseStart
    ElseIf optCursor3.Value = True Then
        Selection.Collapse wdCollapseEnd
        Selection.MoveLeft Unit:=wdCharacter, Count:=1
    End If

    Unload frmRealistsGoTo
End Sub
```

It's a significantly shorter procedure now, with the re-evaluation instructions having been entirely removed. What has also changed is the `.Select` method instruction. There, `iLookup(Locator.ListIndex + 1)` represents the index number of the paragraph being chosen. First, the `.ListIndex` property is ascertained, and 1 is added to make it correspond with reality. The result is used as a subscript of `iLookup()`, rather than the integer used in the previous build that was discovered only through reassessing the document from the top.

In praise of renovation

Hopefully the two builds of the paragraph browser have served as an example of how and why certain programming decisions are made. There is a tendency when we write and publish books on programming to make it seem to the reader like perfect code flows through our fingertips on first attempt. The truth is, much of the time, efficiency only reveals itself once inefficiency stares us in the face. Furthermore, it might be more obvious to you now why the design of *data* is as important as the design of your program. The second build of the paragraph browser form module was more efficient than the first because we redesigned the data that the program uses, which is the foundation of any program. It was the redesign of the data that made this program more efficient, and eliminated its former lag time problem.

Of course, the work done in the second build was mainly a correction of a problem built into the first build. In hindsight, it could be stated that better insight into the design of data could make us all more efficient programmers, call that the moral of the story, and be done with it. The truth of the matter, however, is that the job of programming is mostly one of rebuilding. Even the masters of the art (a title which I do not dare claim) are adept rebuilders of their code. Learning how to truly program is partly a process of understanding when and how to rebuild, and do so effectively.

On Point

Since the `_Initialize` event is the first one recognized for a form, and actually takes place before it's brought onto the screen, you can make use of the `Private Sub UserForm_Initialize()` event procedure to set up the contents of controls while the form is still "behind the curtain." The contents of list boxes, for instance, cannot be set at design time; how could the Properties window know how many entries there may be in a list box at startup? Instructions have to be written to accomplish this task; and if they're running while the user can not only see but *operate* the form, undesired activity may occur as a result.

There is nothing about a form module in and of itself that makes it accessible from within an Office 2000 application. At least one procedure outside of the form module, in a general area belonging to the active document or template, must jump-start the form manually by means of its `.Show` property. This `Sub` procedure should be declared `Public` so that it becomes accessible to the Macros list, as well as to a template's menu bar or toolbars. A custom toolbar button can be made to activate this `Public` `Sub` procedure, which then starts the form by invoking its `.Show` property. It does not formally pass control to the form, however, although it does suspend its own operation while the form is running. So any instructions that fall after the `.Show` instruction in the `Public` procedure must wait until after the form has exited the workspace. Meanwhile, execution of instructions within the form module can be triggered by setting up a startup routine inside the `_Initialize` event procedure for the form.

In Theory: In English, Please

In every technical industry, there are numerous standards committees and consortia dedicated to the mission of finding the right names for things. The perennial problem of what to call a gadget — or, most recently, what to call an *object* — has often proven itself at least as difficult, if not more so, than how to build the thing in the first place.

The English language is a curious and unique machine. I consider it the tool of my trade. Its usefulness has historically been a product of widespread implementation and adaptation by a few billion of its practitioners. Even if you're reading a translation of this work in another language, I hope you can appreciate the feeling of being able to use a tool that works its way *through* you — that is, on some higher level, a living thing. English, like all other common languages, is the product of thousands of years of contributions, both purposeful and accidental. By contrast, mathematics is considered a universal, logical language that is less an amalgamation of contributions than a systematic process of discoveries. By no means dead, math is said to be a language unto itself, waiting to be uncovered in bits and pieces;

it is a whole entity, and our relationship with it puts us more in the role of expeditioners than conquerors.

Along these planes of conceptual existence, terminology exists in a sort of intermediate netherworld. The people whose job it is to determine what to call a new gadget or object do not have the luxury of relying on the people at large to point them toward a more common or more adaptable term. The best that "terminologists," if I may call them, can hope for is to be able to uncover the *metaphor* that satisfactorily depicts, however symbolically or analogously, the principle that the gadget embodies. "Mouse" was a lucky find. "User interface" is a sad, though passable, substitute for a good term for the graphical computing model. "Universal Resource Locator" has the ring of someone whose mind is at the meeting but whose heart is wrapped in a comic book. "Dynaset" is. . . unfortunate.

When metaphors from two realms – or two committees – collide, they often become grafted together. "Throwing an exception" is a term C++ programmers use to describe a more purposeful methodology for handling a problem situation. The first part, "throwing," is the product of a beautiful baseball analogy engineered by C++ creator Bjarne Stroustrup. This analogy helps a programmer get past the mental roadblock of attempting a method that hasn't been 100% perfected. When a program tests positive for unwarranted conditions, the programmer gathers those conditions into a little wad – namely, an exception object – and then passes that wad by means of a call named throw. Inside a sort of programmatic bullpen is a block of instructions labeled try. Here, a set of functions that look for the specific contents of several classes of wads each receive their respective classes by means of catch instructions. The classification for these wads is "exception," a term whose heritage dates back to the progenitor of C++, the C language. There, the gifted programmer and writer P. J. Plauger was responsible for proffering a more politically correct term for "error." Plauger has the clarity of vision and strength of character to have been able to ask the following of what was then a small, elite, self-styled group of self-proclaimed perfectionists: If a program that does the wrong thing is doing exactly what it was programmed to do, just whose error is it? Certainly not that of the program. But rather than punish the programmer, let's apply a term from mathematics: Let's just say that an unexpected result may be following its own set of rules. No one gets punished, and no one's feelings or circuits are hurt. The handler for that set of rules becomes the "exception handler." Now, Stroustrup and Plauger both know each other, so it isn't that they live in separate worlds. But their two flavors of genius here conspired to produce the type of mixed metaphor that could only have come from computing, where analogies and metaphors abound.

During the last ten years, the direction of computing development has become more driven by market forces than by pure, unadulterated engineering. As a result, the various committees, working groups, consortia, and task forces that build or derive standards for software, have had less of a say regarding the terminology used to describe their creations than they had previously enjoyed. Most recently, those whose job it is to package and market software have had a greater say in this endeavor. Since software is part physical matter and part conceptual understanding, terminology becomes a key constituent in the product, unlike with railroad trestles, laundry detergent, or frozen cannelloni. In the conventional consumer goods market, the mutation of common language is a frequently used tool for positioning an item squarely within the center of our brains. Marketing masters long ago learned that people will tune out a dull, dreary, grammatically correct speech; but they will take note of, and even record in their own memory, a phrase out of the blue that doesn't sound quite right. Someplace in our minds is a gadget responsible for catching the thrown exceptions of everyday language.

When a spoken sentence or printed paragraph uses common language incorrectly, it triggers our awareness of it on a subconscious level. I myself rely on this reflex action in my own work as an editor. But I also have to rely on my own concept of what is "correct" and what is "incorrect" – a concept that is indisputably unique. The rules of common language often dictate that what constitutes correct usage is what also constitutes the most *accepted* usage, at least within the boundaries of a given dialect. But the terminology of software – as opposed to, say, English – becomes disseminated long before it ever becomes accepted. So my own criteria for what is correct terminology with regard to a technology must often be based less upon what I hear or read and more upon what I know to be true, or at least to be reasonable.

Because the BASIC programming language has had such a multifarious history, its terminology at any one time looks less like a quilt, and more like the contents of the dumpsters at the Central Intelligence Agency. At present, there is no absolute standard for what certain programming elements of BASIC are called. . . beyond the covers of this book. I have programmed in BASIC for longer than there has been a Visual Basic. Since that time, I've watched the amount of documentation from Microsoft diminish to a mere electronic wisp of the massive volumes the company once produced. The fact that the VBA Help system has become just another new application for Internet Explorer (part of the seemingly interminable, often unfathomable, perhaps illegal grafting of operating system, application, and browser) has made the constitution of the VBA Help system a matter more for the marketing division than programming. As a result, the terminology presented therein shows signs of selective reformation. Today, its terms and mine tend not to equate.

So why don't I change with the times? After all, Microsoft is the manufacturer of VBA; don't they have first say about what to call their own concepts? In a sense, no. VBA still has a prominent "B" in the middle that stands for "BASIC," and Microsoft is not the inventor of that. BASIC is a technology that Microsoft chose to adopt. In so doing, Microsoft has a certain responsibility to its heritage – for which Microsoft itself has played a major role. Maybe Microsoft doesn't need to go through the motions of assembling a standards committee just to set in stone whether a line of code should be called a statement or an instruction. But before the company takes further measures to make its concepts more saleable, palatable, and marketable, it should humbly consider that part of what it states – even if only in electronic form – survives through several generations of programmers, and outlives countless versions. When Microsoft consciously breaks with the past, the inconsistencies it generates lead to confusion, especially when those with closer ties to the past choose to follow the conceptual course that the languages founders, Profs. Kemeny and Kurtz, originally set for it.

In Brief

♦ The `UserForm` object in VBA represents a container program for multiple ActiveX controls.

♦ Each class of control in a VBA form module is maintained by a component program registered by OLE to handle that class.

♦ An instance of a control — even when there is more than one instance of the same control on a form — is a separate data product of one component program.

♦ Processes that respond to events in a form's "lifetime" may be written within event procedures belonging to the `UserForm` class.

♦ Code within a form module must be made available to an Office 2000 application by at least one `Public` procedure declared and written outside of the form module, generally as part of the active document or template.

Chapter 6

The Common Terminology of Controls

IN THIS CHAPTER

◆ The object-oriented terms – properties, events, and methods – common to all Forms 2.0 controls

◆ The entire vernacular of the UserForm object examined and explained

◆ How a dialog box can be made to cancel an operation in progress

CHAPTER 5 INTRODUCED you to the concept of the form module and gave you some idea of how a simple one is designed and executed within the VBA environment. In this chapter, and continuing on into Chapter 7, I get down to brass tacks (or whatever substitutes for brass in Windows) and show you the individual parts of UserForm – its properties, events, and methods. Along the way, I'll demonstrate why all these parts work the way they do. But there are quite a few of them, and it's difficult at times to make any sense of them unless we look at all of them in the same spotlight.

Common Event Terms for Forms 2.0 Controls

Once you've assembled the controls belonging to a form module, you can rely on them and the UserForm container to keep your program informed of all the important actions taken by the user. Now, the purpose of most form modules is to carry out a *command*; so it only seems sensible that the way the module goes about this process is by responding to the user action that's already indicated by the VBA interpreter.

A form module program is made up of two main divisions; the relationships between their components are depicted in Figure 6-1. Here, the "engine" processes the directive of the user, and the event procedures nail down the specifics of that directive. When the user operates one of the controls, a process is triggered, *whether or not* you've written any VBA code that responds to that process. You ascertain what it is the user wants the form module to do by carefully scripting your module's responses to this and other events.

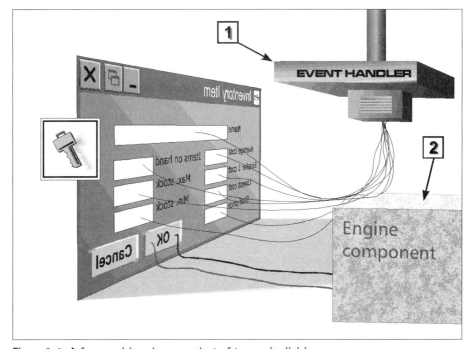

Figure 6-1: A form envisioned as a product of two main divisions.

This segment lists the event terms common to most or all of the Forms 2.0 controls that can be instantiated within UserForm, including some that are actually recognized by UserForm. Each control does recognize its own unique events, which you'll see in detail in Chapter 7.

_AfterUpdate

WHEN IT OCCURS
The _AfterUpdate event occurs immediately after the interpreter has formally recognized the changes made to the contents of a control by the user. The "update" refers to the change in the underlying data that supports the control, not the graphical contents of the control. Thus _Change is recognized for a text box each time the user types a character into it, yet _AfterUpdate (and _BeforeUpdate) are recognized once only, when the focus moves out of the control and the changes are to be finalized.

HOW TO USE IT

If you've set up your control's events properly, then if the _AfterUpdate event even occurs, you can assume that the data that the user entered into the control is valid. The key to making this assumption comfortably is in how you handle the _BeforeUpdate event procedure. Especially in the case of a text box, the procedure for _BeforeUpdate can be programmed to validate the incoming data, and perhaps make corrections to it before the code in the _AfterUpdate procedure acts on that data.

EXAMPLE

Suppose an Excel worksheet contains a cell whose value represents a temperature in degrees Celsius. The value entered into this cell comes from a text box control contained by a Forms 2.0 form. The value is immediately programmed for echoing into the currently indicated cell of the active worksheet. But, also, the background color of the cell is automatically colored to reflect the temperature entry. Here is the _AfterUpdate event procedure for the form:

```
Private Sub Temperature_AfterUpdate()
    ActiveSheet.Range(ActiveCell.Address).Interior.Color _
    = RGB(155 + sTemp, 192, 255 - sTemp)
    ActiveCell.Value = Str$(sTemp)
    sCurTemp = sTemp
End Sub
```

The first instruction in the procedure colors the background of the cell, based on the input temperature value sTemp. The VBA intrinsic function RGB() is used to calculate a color value, ranging from pastel blue (cold) to pastel red (hot). The next instruction copies the temperature value itself into the cell. Notice two very important things: First, this procedure already knows the temperature value, sTemp. Obviously, it was ascertained elsewhere – namely, from the _BeforeUpdate event procedure. This also means that sTemp must be a module-level variable, along with sCurTemp, which holds the "undo" value in case of erroneous input. Secondly, the procedure doesn't have to correct sTemp. This has already been done. If this procedure is even executed, sTemp must be a valid value. This is because the _BeforeUpdate event procedure has the power to prevent _AfterUpdate from being recognized, by setting its own Cancel variable to True. . . as you'll see momentarily.

Essentially, _AfterUpdate works like the _Change event, except that it is limited to content updates that take place as a result of user input. So if you write an instruction that changes the contents of a text field control, that control's _AfterUpdate event will not be triggered. For instance, an expression such as LastName.Text = "" will not result in an _AfterUpdate event, but it will result in a _Change event.

When you're programming with Excel VBA, you might have an idea sometime to program a *custom function* (one that works alongside regular instructions in your Excel formulas) that changes the style or appearance of the cell in which a formula utilizing that function may appear. You'll be surprised to learn, as I was, that *this cannot be done.* Unlike any other VBA environment, Excel VBA is exclusively geared to prevent direct changes to both the content and appearance of a cell or any part of an open worksheet or workbook, while a custom function triggered by a formula is being executed. In other words, the Excel workbook is locked down during a custom function's run time. So the only way you can have an Excel VBA program adjust the appearance of any part of the worksheet, as a result of what you or another user may enter into a formula, is through the use of event procedures. The reason for this is that event procedures kick in *after* the custom function is completed, and the lockdown has been lifted. My thanks to my IDG colleague, John Walkenbach, for educating me on this odd fact of Excel programming.

_BeforeUpdate

WHEN IT OCCURS
The _BeforeUpdate event occurs when the user has changed the textual contents of a control, immediately after the cursor has been moved outside the control, just prior to the formal recognition of those changes by the interpreter.

HOW TO USE IT
The execution of the _BeforeUpdate event procedure is your first opportunity to examine the completed edit made by the user to a control — especially a text box control — to determine whether what the user entered is valid. The _Change event is recognized with each individual change; so for a text box, _Change would occur with each typed character. It's logical to expect that when the cursor or focus *leaves* a control, editing for that control is complete. _BeforeUpdate is the first event that "fires" after the focus leaves the control; _Exit comes later.

ARGUMENT

Cancel   May be set within the _BeforeUpdate event procedure at any time to
          True, in order to prevent the interpreter from recognizing the
          _DblClick, _AfterUpdate, and _Exit events. Any of the procedures
          for these events may include instructions that commit the user's data
          to record; setting Cancel to True here may prevent that from
          happening

EXAMPLE

Here, in a continuation of our Excel temperature cell example, the _BeforeUpdate
event procedure evaluates the freshly entered data. It does this in a rather trusting
manner, as the code below demonstrates:

```
Private Sub Temperature_BeforeUpdate(ByVal Cancel As _
  MSForms.ReturnBoolean)
    sTemp = Val(Temperature.Text)
    If sTemp <> 0 And Temperature.Text <> "0" Then
        If Abs(sTemp) > 100 Then
            sTemp = 100 * Sgn(sTemp)
        End If
    Else
        sTemp = sCurTemp
        Cancel = True
    End If
End Sub
```

First, this procedure assigns the converted value of the .Text property of the
text box, whatever that may be, to the module-level variable sTemp. The VBA
intrinsic function used for this is Val(), which returns a value equivalent to what
the text apparently represents. The conditional clause checks for two conditions,
which is the only way we can determine for certain that the entry is indeed
numeric. If the text is *non-numeric* (that is, erroneous), then
Val(Temperature.Text) yields 0. But since sTemp represents a temperature, 0 may
very well be a valid entry; so the second condition in the clause is required to check
whether the user really did explicitly enter a 0.

This secondary conditional clause uses a trick of math to check two conditions
at once: The Abs() intrinsic function returns the absolute value of a numeric argument: Abs(100) = 100 and Abs(-100) = 100. This function is used here so that
we're assured the temperature value will not exceed 100 in either direction on the
number scale. If it were to do so, the conditional clause could not know implicitly
which side of the scale the value transgressed. So the instruction sTemp = 100 *
Sgn(sTemp) trims the excessive value to 100, multiplied by 1 with the sign of the

original sTemp value. The intrinsic function Sgn() returns either 1 or -1 depending on the sign of the argument.

The Else portion of the main conditional clause, which takes place if the entry is invalid, recalls the "undo" value sCurTemp — prepared earlier by the _AfterUpdate event procedure — and, perhaps more importantly, sets the Cancel variable to True. This results in a squelching of all future event procedures related to this particular edit to this control.

_Change

WHEN IT OCCURS

The _Change event occurs when either the user or the interpreter has changed data maintained by the control. For a control such as a text box that contains characters entered directly by the user, the _Change event is recognized whenever a single character is typed into the field, or whenever any amount of characters are removed from the field. If another procedure resets the state of a control, its _Change event will be recognized.

HOW TO USE IT

If there is anything you need for your form module to do each time the state of a control is changed by something or someone, then the _Change event procedure is where you would place your instructions.

EXAMPLE

Suppose you have an Excel worksheet that contains an embedded text box control. Once the user enters something into that control, its contents are to be automatically echoed into a cell in an Excel worksheet. The procedure below accomplishes this:

```
Private Sub Quantity_Change()
    Range(strQty).Value = Quantity.Text
End Sub
```

The .Name property for the text box control is Quantity, and that is reflected in the name for this event procedure. String variable strQty contains a cell address, which is used in association with the Range object like a subscript. The single instruction echoes the textual contents of Quantity to whatever cell in the worksheet is pointed to by strQty.

_Click

WHEN IT OCCURS
The _Click event occurs when the user clicks once on the control, just after the mouse button is released. The purpose of this event is to account for the user's activation of the command or choice represented by this control, rather than to track the behavior of the mouse. The _MouseDown and _MouseUp events handle the transition in the mouse button's state, and are provided mainly as vehicles for you to provide some cosmetic effects to the form or the control.

HOW TO USE IT
You should treat a control's _Click event as a signal to you (or, more accurately, to your VBA module) to "do *this*," referring to whatever is implied by the caption on the control.

EXAMPLE
Here is exactly how most event procedures that respond to a click on a dialog box's Cancel button, actually appear:

```
Private Sub btnCancel_Click()
    Unload frmSubEdits
End Sub
```

   In this procedure, frmSubEdits is a form whose "cancel" button is called btnCancel. The single instruction merely dismisses the form, without committing any changes the user may have selected.

_DblClick

WHEN IT OCCURS
The _DblClick event occurs when the user double-clicks on the control.

HOW TO USE IT
Generally, a double-click on a common control in a form or dialog box is designed to mean, "Do *this*, or do something with *this*, and just get on with it." It chooses the item or the command, and then dismisses the control.

ARGUMENTS

Index_   (MultiPage, TabStrip controls only) An integer that is set to the index
             of the item in the control's collection that was double-clicked on

Cancel   A Boolean variable which, when set to `True`, prevents the _Click event from being recognized a second time. Because a double-click is, naturally, two clicks, Windows will "fire" the _Click event during the first click of a two-click sequence, prior to "firing" _DblClick. Normally, Windows would "fire" a second _Click event following the _DblClick event; setting `Cancel` to `True` prevents this from happening

EXAMPLE

Suppose in Word 2000, you have a dialog box which contains a list box showing open documents. When the user double-clicks on one of the titles in this list, the document is made visible. Here's a procedure which accomplishes this:

```
Private Sub lstTitleList_DblClick(ByVal Cancel As _
 MSForms.ReturnBoolean)
    Dim docThisDoc As Document
    For Each docThisDoc In Documents
        If lstTitleList.List(lstTitleList.ListIndex) = _
        docThisDoc.Name Then
            docThisDoc.Activate
        End If
    Next
    Unload UserForm1
End Sub
```

For simplicity's sake, our dialog box is provided by a form given the default name `UserForm1`. This procedure begins by declaring an object reference `docThisDoc` of type `Document`. This reference is then made the subject of a `For Each...Next` loop which cycles through each document in Word's `Documents` collection. The embedded `If...Then` clause checks to see if the text of the list box item the user double-clicked on (the text being the `.List` property, whose subscript is given its own `.ListIndex` property) is equivalent to the name of the document currently being perused by the loop clause. There's no fancy algorithm to this process; since `Documents` is unsorted, it can only look through each document name in the collection, starting at the top. When a match is found, then the `.Activate` method for the found document brings it to the fore, and the form is unloaded from memory.

Unlike the MultiPage and TabStrip controls, the list box control doesn't receive the index of a clicked on entry as a parameter of one of its exclusive event procedures. Instead, it supports a `.ListIndex` property which is set to the index of the chosen item, and that can be retrieved manually – as it is here – within a standard _DblClick event procedure.

In Depth: How to execute a cancellation

The purpose of the `Cancel` argument for the `_DblClick` event procedure, as well as for others, is to give you a mechanism for squelching the regularly scheduled events that would otherwise subsequently happen. This, in turn, can give the user a way to easily cancel changes that would normally be made as a result of his input.

Events that pertain to controls or to the `UserForm` object often follow a domino-like sequence, one leading to the next. The Forms 2.0 library treats these sequences like a chain, and for the first time gives you a means for breaking this chain should a procedure determine that continuing the current course of events would be wrong. This is an esoteric concept, so let me give you a slow example:

When the user types text into a text box control and moves on to another control, the form assumes the totality of the text in that control to be a complete entry by the user. But does that text constitute a valid request? In other words, is it reasonable for the user to be asking the form module to perform its task using the contents the user just typed into the text box as a parameter? If for some reason the text the user entered is wrong, the form needs an effective, though gentle, means to correct the entry, and keep that entry from becoming an argument to the form module's final processed command.

The means which Forms 2.0 has chosen is very un-BASIC-like, and is also in most of Microsoft's documentation very ambiguous. It is this peculiar `Cancel` argument that shows up in event procedures, which isn't really an incoming argument (despite the fact that it's declared `ByVal`) as much as it is a pair of wire clippers that lets you snip the event chain whenever you need to simply by setting it to the Boolean value `True`. The current event procedure plays itself out, but successive events in the chain are squelched.

For a text box control, the `_BeforeUpdate` event procedure can be used to determine if the text of the control constitutes a valid directive — some parameter that the form module is capable of working with. In your conditional clause, you would set `Cancel` to `True` if it's not valid. The automatic result would be that the text box would return to its former state, before the user added characters to it. The cursor would remain in the text box, and the `_AfterUpdate` and `_Exit` events that normally follow the text box losing the cursor and the focus would not be recognized. So, you can use the `_AfterUpdate` event procedure safely to process the data in the text box, assured that it has already been passed by the `_BeforeUpdate` event procedure.

Continued

> ## In Depth: How to execute a cancellation *(Continued)*
>
> There are two other crucial event chains for which a `Cancel` system also exists. When the user double-clicks on some controls, Forms 2.0 has the controls register the `_Click` event, followed by `_DblClick`, then `_Click` a second time, in that order. This could result in the `_Click` event procedure for that control being executed twice, unless you have the `_DblClick` event procedure set its `Cancel` variable to `True`. Also, you can cancel a drag-and-drop event in progress, or just prior to the drop, if you've determined that the incoming data is somehow invalid or incorrect. Setting the `Cancel` variable to `True` in the `_BeforeDragOver` event procedure will stop the drag operation once the pointer arrives in the region of the target control. Setting `Cancel` to `True` in the `_BeforeDropOrPaste` event procedure will stop a drop from taking place when the user releases the mouse button over the target control.

_Enter

WHEN IT OCCURS
The `_Enter` event occurs when the control receives the focus, which generally follows either the user pressing Tab — which results in the highlight being moved over the control — or the user clicking on the control.

HOW TO USE IT
If there is any preparation, graphical or otherwise, that needs to take place when the control receives the focus, prior to it receiving data from the user, the `_Enter` event procedure is where you would place the instructions that prepare the control. The instructions there *are* executed prior to any user input being recognized by the control; there's no chance that the user will be too fast on the draw and beat the `_Enter` event procedure.

EXAMPLE
Here is a simple procedure that makes a text box control named `txtImportant` turn yellow and clear itself whenever it receives the focus:

```
Private Sub txtImportant_Enter()
    txtImportant.BackColor = "FFFF00"
    txtImportant.Text = ""
End Sub
```

The _Enter and _Exit events for Forms 2.0 ActiveX controls are the counterparts of the _GotFocus and _LostFocus events, respectively, of Visual
Basic 6.0 controls.

_Error

WHEN IT OCCURS
The _Error event occurs when the control detects an error caused by something
within its own purview: for instance, its own program, or by the COM/OLE components currently running within Windows. Errors in the VBA module, or error conditions caused by the VBA interpreter itself, do not count here.

HOW TO USE IT
In the Windows COM component hierarchy, the VBA interpreter is in a position
where it can *recognize* an error condition, although it is in no real position to take
any remedial measures. About all you can do with the _Error event procedure is to
facilitate a graceful shutdown of your form module. It isn't mandatory for you to
even use the _Error event in any of your form modules; when COM/OLE does
make an error, graceful exit or no, it can still be ugly.

ARGUMENTS

Number	Set to an integer representing the error number designated by the control that is handling the error.
Description	Set to a string literal containing a brief textual description of the error (in cases where the component generating the error processes such textual messages; otherwise, this string may often be blank).
SCode	Set to a bitwise value representing the status code recognized by OLE. Here, the error number Number is reflected in the least significant 16 bits, whereas the most significant are reserved for other flags. Programs that micro-manage OLE may be able to use this bitwise value in debugging.
Source	Set to a string literal naming the name of the internal OLE component responsible for the error.
HelpFile	Set to a string literal reflecting the local client path to a Windows help file, wherein a page may describe the error.

HelpContext   Set to a long integer value representing the context-ID number for the page in the help file that describes the error. This way, a dialog box that describes the error may contain a "Help" button that takes the user to the specific file HelpFile, and to its specific page HelpContext.

CancelDisplay   Set to a Boolean value representing whether the application should display a message or dialog box describing this error — in other words, whether OLE has ascertained this error is not important for the user to know about. (Generally this value is set to False.)

All of the above arguments are incoming, which means that they are set outside of the procedure and received by it. OLE is responsible for setting these arguments' values automatically as it initiates the _Error event. All you have to do as programmer is determine how to process the incoming data. Don't confuse an _Error event for a Forms control with an error condition generated by VBA with regard to its own instructions. If something erroneous happens from the Forms library's point of view, it will not necessarily trigger an error condition within VBA.

EXAMPLE

Only a serious internal OLE error would cause the following event procedure to be executed:

```
Private Sub lstTitleList_Error(ByVal Number As Integer, _
 ByVal Description As MSForms.ReturnString, ByVal SCode As _
 Long, ByVal Source As String, ByVal HelpFile As String, _
 ByVal HelpContext As Long, ByVal CancelDisplay As _
 MSForms.ReturnBoolean)
    If CancelDisplay Then Exit Sub
    Dim strErrTitle, strErrDesc
    strErrTitle = "Internal COM/OLE Error #" & Str(Number)
    strErrDesc = Source & " reports:" & Chr$(13) & Description _
     & Chr$(13) & "(Press F1 for help)"
    MsgBox strErrDesc, 1, strErrNum, HelpFile, HelpContext
End Sub
```

Here, the parameters passed to the procedure by OLE itself are partly reformatted, so that they can themselves be sent as parameters by the MsgBox statement. For MsgBox, the fourth and fifth parameters are optional, but when present they enable the user to press the F1 key to pull up the designated help file HelpFile at page HelpContext. The Chr$() intrinsic function, by the way, places a character in the string that otherwise can't be typed. Code 13 is the ANSI code for a carriage return, which you can't type directly into a VBA instruction unless you actually mean to terminate it.

_Exit

WHEN IT OCCURS

The _Exit event occurs just prior to the control losing the focus — in other words, before the highlight or the cursor moves away from the control to another control in the UserForm.

HOW TO USE IT

The _Exit event is the proverbial "last chance." In a complex situation where all the control's "shutdown" events are put to use, the _Exit event procedure could be used to remove any graphical flourishes added to the control. However, in simpler circumstances, _Exit can be used to evaluate the entry in the control, and hold the focus on the control if the entry is somehow invalid. All controls are exited, even by virtue of the form that contains them being dismissed. What makes _Exit different from _AfterUpdate and _BeforeUpdate is that _Exit is recognized whether or not the user made any changes to the control's value, whereas the others are recognized only if changes were made.

ARGUMENT

Cancel   A Boolean variable, which, when set, prevents the cursor or focus from leaving the current control.

EXAMPLE

Suppose you have a small dialog box that prominently features a text box, which awaits the user entering her password. Here's the _Exit event procedure for when the user has just completed this entry:

```
Private Sub txtPassword_Exit(ByVal Cancel As _
 MSForms.ReturnBoolean)
    If txtPassword.Text = "" Then
        Cancel = True
        MsgBox "Please enter a password."
    End If
End Sub
```

Here `txtPassword` is a text box that requires some input from the user for authorization to proceed. The conditional clause here is simple enough; it sets `Cancel` to `True`, thereby leaving the focus on `txtPassword` if there's nothing in the control.

NOTE The following events are recognized by the VBA interpreter in the sequence listed: `_Enter`, `_BeforeUpdate`, `_AfterUpdate`, `_Exit`.

_KeyDown

WHEN IT OCCURS
The `_KeyDown` event occurs for a control when a key on the keyboard is pressed while that control has the focus.

HOW TO USE IT
The VBA interpreter assumes that while a control has the focus, any keys being pressed are intended to send data to that control. A text box control is already engineered to receive data input from the keyboard; but a customized control, especially one created using the Forms 2.0 image control as a model, might be engineered to utilize keypresses differently. The `_KeyDown` and `_KeyUp` events can be used to engineer exclusive keyboard behavior for a control.

ARGUMENTS

KeyCode   An integer value representing the key that was pressed (*not* the ASCII or ANSI value for the character). The VBA function `Chr$(KeyCode)` may be used to interpret which key was pressed, although the return value of the function will not directly correspond to the key's label. For instance, the "x" key is treated not as letter "x" or capital letter "X", but the physical key on the keyboard between Z and C. KeyCode represents the number that signals to the computer that this key was pressed, not that any particular letter was typed.

Shift   A bitwise value indicating which keyboard control keys may have been pressed concurrent with the mouse button (bit 0 – Shift, bit 1 – Ctrl, bit 2 – Alt). Bitwise values are binary (base 2) numerals that translate into base 10 integral numerals. For a return value whose bit 0 is set, add 1; if bit 1 is set, add 2; and if bit 2 is set, add 4. The sum will register which combination of the three keys was pressed.

EXAMPLE

Suppose `frmPicScan` is a form whose only purpose is to display a picture. You want the user to be able to press the left and right arrows to zoom this picture out and in, respectively. Assume the `.PictureAlignment` property of the form is set to 0 – fmPictureAlignmentTopLeft. (You'll have to forgive Microsoft for getting its Hungarian notations mixed up with "form" and "frame.") Here's the event procedure that handles these two keys:

```
Private Sub UserForm_KeyDown(ByVal KeyCode As _
 MSForms.ReturnInteger, ByVal Shift As Integer)
    Dim iInc As Integer

    Select Case KeyCode
        Case 39     'right arrow
            iInc = 10
        Case 37     'left arrow
            iInc = -10
    End Select
    If frmPicScan.Zoom > 0 And frmPicScan.Zoom < 500 Then
        frmPicScan.Zoom = frmPicScan.Zoom + iInc
    End If
End Sub
```

Each key on the keyboard has a corresponding key code in Windows, which is not the ASCII/ANSI code for the letter which that key represents. The right and left arrow keys have no ANSI equivalent anyway, since they are not officially characters (although they do generate signals which some terminal emulators treat as "back-one" and "forward-one" characters). The _KeyDown event procedure is the only reliable way for testing for these keys, whose key codes are 39 for the right arrow and 37 for the left. A press of either of these keys sets the incrementer variable `iInc` to a value which is later added to the .Zoom property of the form, as long as that property's current setting is between 0 and 500.

Neither the _KeyDown nor _KeyUp events are recognized for a control with respect to the Esc key if the form contains a "Cancel" button (one whose .Cancel property has been set to True), or to the Enter key if the form contains an "OK" button (one whose .Default property has been set to True).

_KEYPRESS

WHEN IT OCCURS

The _KeyPress event occurs for a control when a key on the keyboard representing a typeable character is pressed while that control has the focus. In this case, a "typeable character" is one which has an ANSI code number, and may be represented as a character in a file. So "x" and "X" (Shift+X) are treated separately. However, this event does not account for the Ctrl and Alt keys, either used in conjunction with other keys or on their own, nor does it account for the Shift key on its own.

HOW TO USE IT

Both the _KeyPress and the _KeyDown events are concerned with individual keys as they are being pressed. But when your control is more concerned with the character that the pressed key represents (was it an A or a B, for instance) than the location of the pressed key (e.g., left arrow, right arrow) then you should use the _KeyPress event procedure for the control to assess the keypress.

ARGUMENT

KeyAscii   The ASCII (actually ANSI) numeral code for the specific character that was pressed.

EXAMPLE

Here's a _KeyPress event procedure for a check box control that changes the way it is made operable through the keyboard:

```
Private Sub Check3_KeyPress(ByVal KeyAscii As _
 MSForms.ReturnInteger)
    Select Case Chr$(KeyAscii)
        Case "x"
            Check3.Value = True
        Case "n"
            Check3.Value = False
    End Select
End Sub
```

Here Check3 is a check box control. If the incoming character is a lower-case "x" (not shifted) then the check box is checked; if it's an "n," the box is unchecked. If the instruction Case "X" were to appear here, the control would be checking whether the user had pressed Shift+X, . The resulting instructions would be exclusive to Shift+X, and would not be executed if the user had just pressed "x" by itself.

The typeable characters represented in Windows' version of the ANSI code (which is slightly different from the real ANSI code itself) cannot generally be reproduced by holding down Ctrl or Alt instead of Shift. The _KeyPress event concerns itself only with characters that may be represented through this code. For this reason, if you're concerned with the state of Ctrl or Alt during the key press, you'll want to use the _KeyDown event instead. That event's procedure receives two parameters, the second of which is a bitwise value representing the simultaneous up/down state of all of the so-called *extender* keys – Shift, Ctrl, and Alt.

In Depth: The trouble with trapping keypresses

Suppose you are building a form where the keyboard has been enlisted as an alternative method for operating the controls on the form. Although UserForm can receive the _KeyPress event, it can only act on that event when it has the focus. A *form* can't have the focus unless either all of its controls are disabled – which is a practical unlikelihood – or one of the event procedures set the Cancel variable to True. The latter should only happen when the form is about to "escape;" in other words, if it's about to shut itself down without processing the user command. So the UserForm object should not be entrusted with the responsibility for keypress events.

However, you might have a form that contains a series of command buttons that collectively work like a numeric keypad. In such a situation, the user may expect to be able to press *one* key on the keyboard to operate the corresponding key on the onscreen keypad, not some Alt or Shift keystroke. But in VBA, each individual control in a form can't handle its own _KeyPress event unless, by coincidence, that control has the focus. The only way a control could be given the focus is (1) if the user clicked on it once anyway, or (2) if the user pressed Tab until the highlighter passed over the control's caption. Both of these actions are entirely unreasonable.

In such a situation, I've found myself working this way:

1. I choose one of the controls on the form, and use its .SetFocus method to give it the focus at all times.

2. I then make this control the "Enter" button, which would make it reasonable for it to have the focus all the time; if the user presses the *real* Enter key on the keyboard, it would naturally activate this onscreen "Enter" button.

3. Next, I use the _KeyPress event procedure for this "Enter" button to ascertain which keyboard key the user has pressed.

Continued

In Depth: The trouble with trapping keypresses
(Continued)

4. Using a `Select Case` clause, I then redirect execution to the on-screen buttons' own `_Click` event procedures — which is something most Visual Basic programmers don't know you can do. It works something like this:

```
Private Sub btnEnter_KeyPress(ByVal KeyAscii As _
MSForms.ReturnInteger)
    Select Case Chr$(KeyAscii)
        Case "1"
            btn1_Click
        Case "2"
            btn2_Click
        Case "3"
            btn3_Click
        ' more cases here as necessary
    End Select
End Sub
```

The `btnx_Click` instructions place calls to the `_Click` event procedures of the command buttons, and the interpreter will run those procedures just as though the `_Click` event for the command buttons were actually recognized. Finally, at the end of each of these `_Click` event procedures, I include the instruction `btnEnter.SetFocus` to put the focus back on the "Enter" button so that it can process the `btnEnter_KeyPress` event again.

_KeyUp

WHEN IT OCCURS

The `_KeyUp` event occurs when a key on the keyboard is released while the control receiving the event has the focus.

HOW TO USE IT

If one of the controls in your form is to be operated like, a mechanical device, where pressing and holding down a key performs some action, and releasing the key stops the action, then `_KeyUp` is the event that tells you when the user means to "stop." Take note: The `_KeyDown` event is not repetitive. It only happens once. There is no continuous signal in the Forms 2.0 library that tells you, "The user is still holding down this key." So you need the `_KeyUp` event to tell you not only that a key has been released, but also which one – especially in circumstances when two or more keys may be used simultaneously for different purposes.

ARGUMENTS
Same as for the _KeyDown event.

EXAMPLE
Suppose you have a large form that represents items that a user may choose, and that also includes a sort of "corral" along the left side where chosen items are automatically moved. Each item is represented by a command button control. The user receives information on the item represented by each button by clicking on it, though he "chooses" that button by pressing the "K" key on the keyboard. The choice is to be registered at the time the "K" key is *released*. A form-level variable iLocale is initialized in the Declarations section, like so:

```
Dim iLocale As Integer
```

This variable will hold the vertical coordinates of the upper left corner where the chosen control will be moved. Here is the procedure that handles what one of the chosen buttons does when it has the focus, and when the user releases the "K" key:

```
Private Sub CommandButton1_KeyUp(ByVal KeyCode As _
  MSForms.ReturnInteger, ByVal Shift As Integer)
    If Chr$(KeyCode) = "K" Then
        ActiveControl.Move 10, iLocale
        iLocale = iLocale + ActiveControl.Height + 5
    End If
End Sub
```

Because of the nature of the _KeyUp event, this procedure will not be executed unless CommandButton1 has the focus at the time of the keypress. When the user clicks on this button, Windows gives it the focus. The .Move method relocates the button to a spot whose upper left corner is 10 points from the left of the form, and iLocale points from the top of the form. After the move, the height of the command button (the .Height property) plus 5 points of margin, are added to iLocale to produce the upper left corner for the next move.

The term ActiveControl is maintained by the Forms 2.0 library, and is a constituent of the UserForm class. It refers to whatever control currently has the focus – which, in the case of the event procedure above, is CommandButton1. Documentation will tell you that CommandButton1 is the "default object" in an event procedure that bears its name, so methods such as .Move and properties such as .Height should not have to write out the default object name outright. Try this principle yourself and you'll discover it doesn't work. You might be tempted to use the reflexive reference Me; but in a form module, Me refers to the main *container* object at work here – which, in this case, is the form. We could, of course, have simply written `CommandButton1.Move` and `CommandButton1.Height`, and achieved the same results as our example above. But in a form which would contain multiple command buttons, it would be easier for us if we could copy the source code from one `_KeyUp` event procedure to another with as minimal editing as possible. In this case, no editing is required at all to move the body of this procedure to `Private Sub CommandButton2_KeyUp()` and `Private Sub CommandButton3_KeyUp()`.

_MouseDown

WHEN IT OCCURS
The `_MouseDown` event occurs immediately following the user pressing down a mouse button while the mouse pointer is over the control.

HOW TO USE IT
The `_MouseDown` and `_MouseUp` event procedures let you know not only *when* the mouse button is pressed and released, but *where* (with respect to the control's own coordinate system), using what button, and in conjunction with what extender key (Shift, Ctrl, Alt) on the keyboard.

ARGUMENTS

`Index`   (TabStrip control only) Indicates the page in the control that received the mouse pointer. This parameter is omitted with regard to all other controls in the Forms 2.0 suite besides TabStrip.

`Button`   A bitwise value that indicates which mouse button was pressed (bit 0 – left, bit 1 – right, bit 2 – middle).

`Shift`   A bitwise value that indicates which keyboard control keys may have been pressed concurrently with the mouse button (bit 0 – Shift, bit 1 – Ctrl, bit 2 – Alt).

`X, Y`   Integer values that indicate the horizontal and vertical distances, respectively, from the mouse pointer "hot spot" to the left and upper edges, respectively, of the control.

EXAMPLE
For our example of the mouse-oriented events, we present a form that converts an ordinary command button control into a replacement for both horizontal and vertical scroll bars. This example will demonstrate two of the least appreciated features of the command button: its capability to display images, and the fact that its `_MouseMove` event procedures can register the location of the pointer at the time the button was clicked. In the midst of the demonstration, you'll also see how the Forms

2.0 Frame control acts as a more versatile image display device than the Image control in the same library. Figure 6-2 shows this deceptive form in action; note the square control at lower left.

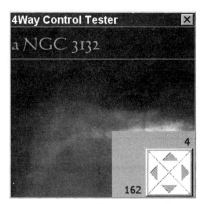

Figure 6-2: An ordinary picture display form bearing an unordinary scroll control.

This form will contain two frames: one for displaying the image, and another which will contain the controls you use to scroll the image about back and forth, up and down. The scrolling control is an ordinary command button. The way we will set up its _MouseDown event procedure, this square button will have four sensitive areas, whose boundaries can be imagined if you draw a big "X" through the button in your mind. Setting up the form and its controls is a tricky matter; you won't be able to just scan the photograph included here and craft a form that looks like it. The two frames, you see, are invisible. When this form runs, the user won't notice or recognize the frame controls, because their conventional boundaries and demarcations will be missing.

Table 6-1 starts things off by presenting the changes made to the form's default properties:

TABLE **6-1 PROPERTY SETTINGS FOR FRM4WAY**

Property	Setting
.Name	frm4Way
.Caption	4Way Control Tester

Continued

TABLE **6-1** **PROPERTY SETTINGS FOR FRM4WAY** *(Continued)*

Property	Setting
.Height	200
.Width	200

Table 6-2 shows the vital settings for the five controls inside this form:

TABLE **6-2** **INTERIOR CONTROLS' PROPERTY SETTINGS**

Control	Property	Setting
Frame	.Name	fmDisplay
	.BorderStyle	**0** – fmBorderStyleNone
	.Caption	*(empty string)*
	.Height	200
	.KeepScrollBarsVisible	**0** – fmScrollBarsNone
	.Left	0
	.PictureAlignment	**0** – fmPictureAlignmentTopLeft
	.ScrollBars	**0** – fmScrollBarsNone
	.SpecialEffect	**0** – fmSpecialEffectFlat
	.Top	0
	.Width	200
Frame	.Name	fmControls
	.BorderStyle	**0** – fmBorderStyleNone
	.Caption	*(empty string)*
	.Height	78
	.KeepScrollBarsVisible	**0** – fmScrollBarsNone

Continued

TABLE 6-2 INTERIOR CONTROLS' PROPERTY SETTINGS *(continued)*

Control	Property	Setting
	`.ScrollBars`	0 – fmScrollBarsNone
	`.SpecialEffect`	0 – fmSpecialEffectFlat
	`.Top`	108
	`.Width`	104
Command button	**located inside** *fmControls*	
	`.Name`	btn4Way
	`.Caption`	*(empty string)*
	.LEFT	**108**
	`.Height`	50
	`.Left`	36
	`.MousePointer`	2 – fmMousePointerCross
	`.Picture`	**4WAY.BMP**
	`.PicturePosition`	12 – fmPicturePositionCenter
	`.Top`	18
	`.Width`	50
Label	**located inside** *fmControls*	
	`.Name`	lblX
	`.Font`	Tahoma 11 pt. Regular
	`.Height`	12
	`.Left`	2
	`.TextAlign`	3 – fmTextAlignRight
	`.Top`	54
	`.Width`	30

Continued

TABLE **6-2** INTERIOR CONTROLS' PROPERTY SETTINGS *(continued)*

Control	Property	Setting
Label	located inside `fmControls`	
	`.Name`	`lblY`
	`.Font`	Tahoma 11 pt. Regular
	`.Height`	12
	`.Left`	48
	`.TextAlign`	3 – fmTextAlignRight
	`.Top`	4
	`.Width`	30

The purpose of the label controls is for us to verify that the frame contents are indeed scrolling, and by how much. The secret to making the scrolling technique work is to set up a region for the picture content that is broader than the area of the frame itself — indeed, genuine windowing. The way we do this is by setting the `.ScrollHeight` and `.ScrollWidth` properties of the frame control `fmDisplay` to values larger than the frame's `.Height` and `.Width` settings, and twice as large as the height and width of the picture that the frame is to contain. We could do this at design time, but it's a cumbersome process. You see, **the scale that VBA uses to determine the size of an included picture is different from the scale used to determine the size of the control that is including the picture.** There is a simple conversion factor: The picture size setting, which is registered in a unit of measurement Microsoft unfortunately dubbed "twips" (1/1440 inch), may be divided by 20 to arrive at the scale used to size the frame (points, or 1/72 inch). But the reason why computers were invented was so it could perform calculations for us, not the other way around; so we'll set up our procedure to calculate the proper proportions at run time.

We want the picture inside the `fmDisplay` frame to be scrollable in two ways: either by the user clicking on the `btn4Way` button, or clicking and dragging the frame itself. In trying to develop this form module smoothly, we have to overcome 1) a key deficiency of the frame control's design, and 2) an outright Microsoft bug. We'll show both to you as we come to them. For now, let's start by declaring the form-level variables that the entire form module will use:

```
Dim sX As Single, sY As Single
Dim sOldX As Single, sOldY As Single
```

```
Dim sLastX As Single, sLastY As Single
Dim bytDirection As Byte, bPlunk as Boolean

Const LEFT As Integer = 1
Const RIGHT As Integer = 2
Const UP As Integer = 4
Const DOWN As Integer = 8
Const CLEAR As Integer = 0
```

Variables sX and sY will contain amounts that instruct one of the event procedures as to how much to scroll the image in the frame, based on *how* the user operates the command button (remember, there's more to it than just clicking on it).
Two pairs of variables, sOldX and sOldY, sLastX and sLastY, will record previous
positions so that procedures will be able to calculate how much to scroll the image
in the frame. Variable bytDirection will contain an integer constant designating
which direction the image is being scrolled, so that a procedure will know which
direction to *continue* scrolling. The whole purpose of this variable is to overcome
both the deficiency and the bug. Meanwhile, bPlunk will register an on/off state
denoting whether a click-and-drag operation on fmDisplay is in progress. The five
constants will be used later in recording which general direction the pointer is
moving. The fact that our choice of values for these constants are all powers of 2
will play an important role later in flagging which way the mouse pointer appears
to be moving.

The customary initialization procedure in a form module is Private Sub
UserForm_Initialize(). All such procedures have this exact name, regardless of
whatever the form's .Name property may be. Here you see where we calculate the
size for the "interior" of the frame, which contains the image in its entirety plus
elbow room for scrolling it:

```
Private Sub UserForm_Initialize()
    frm4Way.fmDisplay.ZOrder 1
    fmDisplay.Picture = LoadPicture("C:\Hubble_9839a.JPG")

    fmDisplay.ScrollWidth = (fmDisplay.Picture.Width / 20) * 2
    fmDisplay.ScrollHeight = (fmDisplay.Picture.Height / 20) * 2
    fmDisplay.ScrollLeft = (fmDisplay.ScrollWidth / 2) - _
     (fmDisplay.Picture.Width / 20)
    fmDisplay.ScrollTop = (fmDisplay.ScrollHeight / 2) - _
     (fmDisplay.Picture.Height / 20)

    sX = fmDisplay.ScrollLeft
    sY = fmDisplay.ScrollTop
    sOldX = sX
    sOldY = sY
```

```
        lblX.Caption = Str$(Int(sX))
        lblY.Caption = Str$(Int(sY))
End Sub
```

The .ZOrder method instruction at the top of this procedure ensures that the fmDisplay frame is placed *beneath* the other four controls, at the bottom of the order. This is important because, if the frame were to slip on top of the other controls — such as the scrolling button — the user wouldn't be able to access them. How could this ever happen? It simply can, as my tests proved, so this instruction is a preventive measure.

The next instruction loads a test image into fmDisplay. In this case, the image is a Hubble telescope photo of a planetary nebula, which we conveniently located in the root directory of drive C:. The loading of this image has to happen before the instructions that follow can ascertain how big to make the "interior" scrollable area of the frame. Here you see the conversion factor at work, as the .Width and .Height properties of the Picture constituent are converted into the scale used by the frame control. The .ScrollWidth and .ScrollHeight properties represent the width and height of the scrollable area. Here, they're set to two times the width and height, respectively, of the contained image. The .ScrollLeft and .ScrollTop properties represent the position of the upper left corner of the *visible* area of the frame relative to the upper left corner of its *scrollable* area. Since the .PictureAlignment property of fmDisplay was set earlier at design time to 0 – **fmPictureAlignmentTopLeft**, the formulas used here will set the upper left corner of the image to correlate with the upper left corner of the frame.

Next, the sX and sY variables are initialized, so that they register the current scroll position of the image. Variables sOldX and sOldY are set to the same values, in order to register *no change* between the old values and the current ones — meaning, there's no motion at present. Finally, the two label controls are given the current .ScrollLeft and .ScrollTop property settings, so we can verify that the scroll button does indeed work, and our eyes are not being deceived.

Now the fun begins. When the mouse pointer goes down over the button, its _MouseDown event is triggered. Here's the procedure for that event:

```
Private Sub btn4Way_MouseDown(ByVal Button As Integer, _
  ByVal Shift As Integer, ByVal X As Single, ByVal Y As Single)
    Dim L As Integer, iInc As Integer

    Select Case Shift
        Case 1
            iInc = 5
        Case 3
            iInc = 10
        Case Else
```

```
            iInc = 1
    End Select

    L = btn4Way.Width
    If Y < X Then    'upper right
        If Y > (L - X) Then      'right
            sX = sX + iInc
            btn4Way.Picture = LoadPicture("C:\4WayRight.bmp")
        ElseIf Y < (L - X) Then     'up
            sY = sY - iInc
            btn4Way.Picture = LoadPicture("C:\4WayUp.bmp")
        End If
    ElseIf Y > X Then 'lower left, equal ruled out
        If Y > (L - X) Then      'down
            sY = sY + iInc
            btn4Way.Picture = LoadPicture("C:\4WayDown.bmp")
        ElseIf Y < (L - X) Then     'left
            sX = sX - iInc
            btn4Way.Picture = LoadPicture("C:\4WayLeft.bmp")
        End If
    End If
End Sub
```

This is the procedure that geometrically divides the button control into four segments, and programs a different response for each one. First, however, the procedure adjusts the amount of the response based upon whether the user has the Shift or Ctrl+Shift keys pressed. Variable iInc will contain the number of points to move the image in any direction. The way this procedure's Shift argument works, the Shift key counts as 1, the Ctrl key as 2, and the Alt key as 4 — not 3. This is so any combination of the three keys may be tested for by simply adding their values together. So to test for Ctrl+Shift, you add their respective values together (2 and 1), and test for the sum (3).

Microsoft calls the arguments for the location of the mouse pointer X and Y. I didn't name these variables; Microsoft did. So in keeping with the more conventional naming scheme here, I declared a variable L to account for the width of the command button. Since the button is a perfect square (otherwise the geometry would fail), L may also be considered the length of any one side.

The first test determines whether the pointer is in the upper right or lower left halves of the button. It accomplishes this by comparing X to Y. In the geometry of a Windows control, borrowing Euclidean (x, y) notation for a moment, (0, 0) is not the *center* of the control as convention would dictate, but instead the upper left corner. So the values of X and Y will always be positive. If the value of X were equal to that of Y, then the pointer must be along the line extending from the upper left to lower right corner — say, at (15, 15) or (31, 31). This entire borderline is counted out—if our procedure obtains a reading like this, it's ignored. Thus, if Y happens to be less than X, the pointer must be *above* this borderline. This first test establishes the first division of the nested If...Then clause. If the test yields True, then execution proceeds inside the first subclause; if False, execution jumps to the ElseIf instruction where the opposite test is given. Why can't we just write Else without a second test, and proceed from there? Because we intend to throw out any reading where X = Y; and since Else means "otherwise," any case where Y < X = False would include X = Y.

The inner, or *nested*, If...Then clauses in Private Sub btn4Way_MouseDown() test for the second division of the button, from the upper right to lower left corner. Here, any case where Y = L - X (the length of the button minus X) reveals that the pointer is on this second borderline. So think of these two tests as though we were slicing a square pepperoni pizza across its corners, and any pepperoni that's in the way gets cut.

Subtracting an amount from an X coordinate moves it to the left; likewise, subtracting from a Y moves it up. The converse of both cases are true. So iInc is made negative whenever the image in the frame is to move left or up, and positive whenever it's to move right or down. Notice in all four cases, the Picture constituent of the command button is replaced with a new image. Each of these bitmaps paints a black arrow blue in the direction of motion, adding to the illusion that these are four buttons instead of one. (Why not have just programmed four buttons in the first place? Because Forms 2.0 command buttons are always rectangular, and cannot be made triangular.)

This _MouseDown event procedure sets up sX and sY (the new scroll coordinates) so that the image may be shifted. It does not, however, actually shift the image. This process is accomplished with the _Click event procedure for the button, which is always executed next:

```
Private Sub btn4Way_Click()
    If sX <> sOldX Then
        lblX.Caption = Str$(Int(sX))
        sOldX = sX
        fmDisplay.ScrollLeft = sX
    End If
    If sY <> sOldY Then
        lblY.Caption = Str$(Int(sY))
        sOldY = sY
        fmDisplay.ScrollTop = sY
    End If
End Sub
```

Whenever sX and sY are changed, they will cease to equal their counterparts sOldX and sOldY. As a result, they will pass the conditional tests here, and the appropriate properties of the frame will be changed. Then sOldX and sOldY are set to equal sX and sY so that these same tests may be accurate next time.

Why did we separate the process that plots the amount of the scroll and that executes the scroll, into two procedures? Because customarily, the _Click event procedure is used to interpret the user input as a command. If we wanted to use this test module in a more comprehensive program, it would be convenient to have fresh values for sX and sY so that we can apply them to future features like undo buffers. A more comprehensive program might also be making adjustments to sX and sY before the scrolling of the image is finally executed. The _Click event procedure is generally used to process the command represented by the control, while _MouseDown and _MouseUp deal more with the management of the control itself.

We're not done with this example; we have two more events to cover.

When the user's mouse driver is set up to treat the middle mouse button as a "drag-lock" — in which simply pressing the middle button performs the same function as clicking and holding the left button — both the left and middle buttons may be perceived by VBA as "button 1." In such cases, the value of the Button argument for the _MouseDown, _MouseMove, and _MouseUp events will be 1 whether the user pressed the left or middle mouse button. There is no VBA-specific solution to this dilemma. Unless you are absolutely certain that your users will have middle mouse buttons that are set up for fully independent behavior — for instance, Logitech's "HyperJump" functionality — regrettably, you should ignore the middle button as an input device. (Now that Microsoft has embraced the third button in its own designs, perhaps this state of affairs will change.)

_MouseMove

WHEN IT OCCURS
The _MouseMove event occurs after the mouse pointer has traversed any distance while its "hot spot" (for example, the tip of the arrow) is sighted over the control.

HOW TO USE IT
The _MouseMove event is merely a signal that the mouse pointer is within the boundaries of the control. It might not necessarily be indicative of user input; sometimes the pointer has to cross over a control on its way somewhere else. The event could be used as an opportunity to give the control some graphical flourish – perhaps enhancing its icon with a spotlight or some other glow that implies, "If you click on me, this will happen." However, _MouseMove is the only event that gives

you a way to manage a click-and-drag operation in progress, by tracking the direction of the pointer.

ARGUMENTS
Same as for the _MouseDown and _MouseUp events.

EXAMPLE
For our scrolling image example, one other way we developed for moving the image within the frame is by clicking and dragging the image directly. The Forms 2.0 controls are a bit more limited than the MFC objects available to a C++ programmer. As a result, scooting the image around the frame *in any random direction* is not as smooth a process as one might wish. This is because the frame control's .ScrollLeft and .ScrollTop properties handle the horizontal and vertical axes separately. When you make changes to one axis by adjusting one of these properties, the change is automatically reflected in the state of the control. So a diagonal scroll tends to look a bit jerky.

Here is where the bug we mentioned earlier comes in: When .ScrollLeft and .ScrollTop are adjusted, the coordinate system that determines the current location of the mouse pointer (which affect the values of the X and Y arguments to the _MouseMove event procedures) is very briefly shifted in the same direction. The result is the illusion that the mouse is being violently jerked back and forth instead of being smoothly dragged. So we have to impose a "locking" mechanism of sorts that estimates which way the pointer appears to be moved, so that any appearance of a violent jerk in the opposite direction is ignored. Here's the _MouseMove event procedure for the fmDisplay form in our example:

```
Private Sub fmDisplay_MouseMove(ByVal Button As Integer, ByVal _
  Shift As Integer, ByVal X As Single, ByVal Y As Single)
    If Button = 1 Then
        If bytDirection = CLEAR Then    'sample mouse movement
            If bPlunk = False Then
                bPlunk = True
                sLastX = X
                sLastY = Y
                Exit Sub
        Else
            If sLastY < Y Then
                bytDirection = bytDirection Or DOWN
            ElseIf sLastY > Y Then
                bytDirection = bytDirection Or UP
            End If
            fmDisplay.ScrollTop = fmDisplay.ScrollTop + _
             (sLastY - Y)
            sLastY = Y
```

```
        lblY.Caption = Str$(Int(fmDisplay.ScrollTop))

        If sLastX < X Then
            bytDirection = bytDirection Or RIGHT
        ElseIf sLastX > X Then
            bytDirection = bytDirection Or LEFT
        End If
        fmDisplay.ScrollLeft = fmDisplay.ScrollLeft + _
         (sLastX - X)
        sLastX = X
        lblX.Caption = Str$(Int(fmDisplay.ScrollLeft))
    End If
Else
    If bytDirection And UP Then
        If Y < sLastY Then
            fmDisplay.ScrollTop = fmDisplay.ScrollTop _
             + (sLastY - Y)
        End If
    ElseIf bytDirection And DOWN Then
        If Y > sLastY Then
            fmDisplay.ScrollTop = fmDisplay.ScrollTop _
             + (sLastY - Y)
        End If
    End If
    lblY.Caption = Str$(Int(fmDisplay.ScrollTop))
    sLastY = Y

    If bytDirection And LEFT Then
        If X < sLastX Then
            fmDisplay.ScrollLeft = fmDisplay.ScrollLeft _
             + (sLastX - X)
        End If
    ElseIf bytDirection And RIGHT Then
        If X > sLastX Then
            fmDisplay.ScrollLeft = fmDisplay.ScrollLeft _
             + (sLastX - X)
        End If
    End If
    lblX.Caption = Str$(Int(fmDisplay.ScrollLeft))
    sLastX = X
End If
    End If
End Sub
```

The bug is this: After the _MouseMove event procedure has detected a mouse movement, the way it executes the scroll is by setting the .ScrollLeft and .ScrollTop properties of the frame. But after this happens, the mouse pointer appears to the interpreter to have moved back in the opposite direction, when what has truly happened is that the pointer – whose new position has yet to be resampled – has stayed in the same place. The _MouseMove event is fired once more, with the direction of movement appearing to have been reversed. It isn't exactly an equal and opposite reaction – if it were, we could simply calculate what it was going to be beforehand and discard it when it happened.

This procedure doesn't apply the ideal solution to the bug, but it does apply a workable one. (For the ideal version, we'd need another chapter.) In general terms, the procedure samples the direction that the pointer is moving at first. Any detected movement that appears to be in the opposite general direction is counted out. The downside of this methodology is that the scrolling action doesn't precisely follow the mouse movement; instead, it starts in one compass direction and continues in that direction until the mouse button is released.

Perhaps you've noticed this event procedure is one big conditional clause, that is only executed If Button = 1 – in other words, if the left mouse button is being held down. Variable bytDirection holds a series of four bits representing the four compass directions. If one such bit in the variable is set, the scroll must be heading straight in that direction; if two bits are set, the direction must be diagonal. The way you set a bit in a byte is with the Boolean Or operator. With DOWN being a constant previously declared with the value 8, and 8 being 2^3 (two raised to the power of three), the operation bytDirection Or DOWN sets bit #3, which is the *fourth* bit from the right (since $1 = 2^0$).

Variable bPlunk is set when the mouse button is first detected down. The first readings for sLastX and sLastY are taken then. On the very next iteration of the procedure, X and Y are compared to sLastX and sLastY to arrive at a general direction. Notice how the conditional clauses for X and Y are separate from one another, and do not intrude into each other's territory. Once bytDirection has a positive value at the third iteration of the procedure and thereafter, the Else portion of the main conditional clause subtracts X and Y from their previously recorded values sLastX and sLastY, to obtain the vector of change. Only when the general direction is in keeping with the first sampled compass direction as recorded in bytDirection, do properties .ScrollLeft and .ScrollTop get amended.

As you'll see momentarily, there are two _MouseUp event procedures that play critical roles in our example.

The _MouseMove event is not a trustworthy indicator of the specific movement that the user is making with the mouse. Since the event occurs "every so often," for lack of a better scale of measurement, the event will happen less often for a pointer traveling quickly over a control than it will if it travels in the same path but more slowly. For slower computers, if the pointer moves too fast, Windows may simply count it as having jumped over the control, and the event may not be recognized at all.

_MouseUp

WHEN IT OCCURS
The _MouseUp event occurs immediately after the user has released a mouse button while the mouse pointer is over the control.

HOW TO USE IT
VBA has no recurring or repetitive event that occurs as long as the mouse button is being held down. The _MouseMove event generally occurs several times, but only when the mouse is actually moving, not when it's holding still. Add to that the fact that _MouseMove occurs more times for any direction of movement while the mouse is moving *slowly* than for when it is moving *fast*, and you'll understand the need for a separate event that basically says, "Drag-and-drop is over; time to wrap things up." This is the purpose of the _MouseUp event. It does not preclude any future _MouseMove or _MouseDown events from happening. It merely gives you the opportunity to detect when any click operation designed to have *length* has been completed.

ARGUMENTS
The same arguments apply here as for _MouseDown.

EXAMPLE
In our scrolling image example, the _MouseUp event procedure for the four-part command button has the simplest of purposes, as shown below:

```
Private Sub btn4Way_MouseUp(ByVal Button As Integer, ByVal _
  Shift As Integer, ByVal X As Single, ByVal Y As Single)
    btn4Way.Picture = LoadPicture("C:\4Way.bmp")
End Sub
```

Here, the procedure restores the button's original appearance, since it's designed to show which of its four parts was clicked on by way of replacing its default image with another bitmap.

The _MouseUp event procedure for the scrolling image frame fmDisplay is a bit more complex:

```
Private Sub fmDisplay_MouseUp(ByVal Button As Integer, ByVal _
  Shift As Integer, ByVal X As Single, ByVal Y As Single)
    If bytDirection And UP Then
        sY = fmDisplay.ScrollTop
    ElseIf bytDirection And DOWN Then
        sY = fmDisplay.ScrollTop
    End If
    sOldY = sY

    If bytDirection And LEFT Then
        sX = fmDisplay.ScrollLeft
    ElseIf bytDirection And RIGHT Then
        sX = fmDisplay.ScrollLeft
    End If
    sOldX = sX

    bytDirection = CLEAR
    bPlunk = False
End Sub
```

Once the user lifts her finger off of the mouse button, it's possible that she may move the pointer to the command button and operate that control. So the variables intrinsic to the command button – namely sX and sY, sOldX and sOldY – will need to know where the frame control left off, so the button will know where to pick up again. Finally, bytDirection and bPlunk are cleared, so that if the user uses the frame control again and not the button, it can start off in a fresh direction.

While this has been an example of VBA's mouse-related events in action, it has also served to demonstrate the nature of programming when two controls are set to operate one device. It's necessary for both controls to have their own independent variables – in this case, sOldX and sOldY were kept separate from sLastX and sLastY. But here in this last _MouseUp event procedure, you see a potential hand-off taking place – one control getting things prepared for another. When your controls are to be more than text input lines and push buttons, this is how you will start to program, and a taste of how you may begin to think.

The order of execution for mouse-related events is as follows: _MouseDown, _MouseUp,_Click,_DblClick.

Intrinsic functions used in the examples

Throughout the event procedure examples, I utilized some VBA intrinsic functions that I have not previously discussed. I've listed them in Table 6-3.

TABLE **6-3** INTRINSIC FUNCTIONS

Term	Description
Str$()	Returns an alphanumeric string containing the digits that form the numeral passed to the function as an argument.
Argument:	*Value* – Any numeral value, integer or decimal
Abs()	Returns the absolute value of the numeral, which is the numeral value without a positive or negative sign.
Argument:	*Value* – Any numeral value, integer, or decimal
Sgn()	Returns the value 1 multiplied by the sign of the value argument; thus, Sgn() would return 1 if the argument is positive, –1 if it is negative.
Argument:	*Value* – Any numeral value, integer, or decimal
Chr$()	Returns the single alphanumeric character whose ASCII (ANSI) table number was passed as the argument.
Argument:	*Code* – A valid ANSI character code, ranging from 0 to 255
LoadPicture()	Returns a bitmapped image to a control that supports the .Picture or .Image property. The image is loaded into the control.
Argument:	*Filename* – A valid local filename (not a network name or Internet address) that points to an image file in the noncompressed Windows bitmap (.BMP) format

Common Forms 2.0 Control Properties

This section lists the property terms that are common among Forms 2.0 controls. All of the controls in the suite utilize these properties, some perhaps differently from others – those differences are noted here. In Chapter 7, you'll see some of the properties that are peculiar to specific Forms 2.0 controls.

.Accelerator

Set to a single-character string representing the Alt keystroke that enables keyboard access of a control. Keyboard access results in recognition of the _Click event for the control.

   Default setting: (null)

EXAMPLE

```
Cancel1.Accelerator = "c"
```

   Here, Cancel1 is the name of a command button used to cancel an operation, the .Caption property of which is likely "Cancel". The Alt+C keystroke will now activate the _Click event for Cancel1.

By convention, the choice of character to be assigned as a control's .Accelerator property is one of the characters in that control's .Caption property — generally the first one, but usually the leftmost unique character in the caption. After assignment, the leftmost character of the caption equivalent to the property setting will automatically appear underscored. The .Accelerator property setting is case sensitive; so if a caption reads "Cancel," and the property is set to "c", the lowercase "c" in the caption will appear underscored.

.AutoSize

Set to a Boolean value (True or False) that represents whether the .Height and .Width properties of a control may be automatically sized by Windows' Graphics Device Interface (GDI) to fit its contents snugly without excess margin.

   Default setting: False

.BackColor

Set to a code that represents the color that the interpreter will assign to the background of the control (not the text in the foreground).

 At design time, you may take advantage of the Properties window to set the initial .BackColor of a control to a special code that represents a color from the Windows Control Panel color table. This way, a control's color will follow the user preferences set on the client system.

Otherwise, in VBA you may set .BackColor to the result of the RGB() function. This function takes three parameters ranging from 0 through 255, representing amounts of red, green, and blue, respectively. This function relieves you from having to look up the rather odd native color coding for the control.

.BackStyle

Set to a Boolean value that represents whether the background of a control is opaque or of solid color (False represents transparency).
   Default setting: True

.BorderColor

Set to a code that represents the color that the interpreter will assign to the perimeter of the control, assuming the .BorderStyle property is set to 1.

.BorderStyle

Set to an integer flag that represents whether the control is given a single-pixel-width, solid line of the given .BorderColor property.

POSSIBLE SETTINGS

0   **(Default)** The control is given its standard border, which may be no border at all in the case of the frame control.

1   The control is given a single border line, whose color is defined by the current .BorderColor property setting.

.CAPTION

For a control with non-editable textual contents, `.Caption` is set to the textual contents of the control.

EXAMPLE

```
Cancel1.Caption = "Close"
```

Here, `Cancel1` is a command button, the textual contents of which may be set to `"Close"` when, for instance, the user has made changes to settings in a dialog box and clicked the Apply button to make those changes permanent.

 The `.Caption` property is the default property for many Forms 2.0 controls, especially the label. In other words, in assigning text to this property, you may omit reference to it altogether. The following example accomplishes the same assignment as the example above:

```
Cancel1 = "Close"
```

.ControlTipText

Set at design time to an alphanumeric string containing the text that the user will see when the mouse pointer hovers over the control for a short interval, without the mouse button being pressed.

.Enabled

A Boolean value representing whether the control is active and receiving user events. A `False` setting generally results in the control being *grayed* or otherwise made obviously unresponsive.

Default setting: `True`

EXAMPLE

```
SubmitButton.Enabled = False
```

Here `SubmitButton` is a command button reserved for completing a data input form and submitting it for processing. The `.Enabled` property for this button may be set to `False` until certain necessary text has been entered by the user, such as a username or password. In such a case, the event procedure `Sub Password_Change` may contain the instruction `SubmitButton.Enabled = True`.

.Font

Set to an object that represents the properties of the Windows font used in the rendering of all text associated with the control.

SUBORDINATE PROPERTIES

.Name	**(Default)** The name used by Windows to identify the font, generally comprised of the typeface name followed by any effects, such as "Book" or "Condensed."
.Bold	Set to a Boolean value representing whether the font is boldfaced. **Default setting:** False
.Italic	Set to a Boolean value representing whether the font is italicized. **Default setting:** False
.Size	Set to the relative size of the font, expressed in "points." Generally, a point is 1/72 inch; but Windows typefaces have been known to treat this setting rather loosely.
.StrikeThrough	Set to a Boolean value that represents whether text is displayed with a single horizontal line drawn through the *middle.* **Default setting:** False
.Underline	Set to a Boolean value that represents whether text is to be displayed with a single horizontal line drawn along its baseline. **Default setting:** False
.Weight	For TrueType fonts that support this setting (few do), .Weight is set to an integer value representing the relative width of the "pen" used to render the strokes for the characters in the font.

.ForeColor

Set to a code representing the foreground color for the control. Foreground color is generally applied to text and certain graphic embellishments, such as rules and frames. See .BackColor for rules that apply.

.Height

Set to the distance between the upper and lower edges of the control (or of the rectangular area surrounding the control), expressed in *points* 1/72 inch). As a rule, measurements concerning the form and its contents are expressed in points, while measurements concerning the *screen* or the contents of a bitmap in memory (such as a contained picture, represented by the `Picture` object) are expressed in what Microsoft calls *twips* $^1/1440$ inch).

.HelpContextID

Set to a long integer that represents the exclusive ID number used by the Windows Help file associated with the VBA form module, to document the use of the control.

.LayoutEffect

An integer flag set at run time that indicates whether the coordinates of the control with respect to its container, were changed within the `_Layout` event procedure for that container.

.Left

The horizontal distance between the upper left corner of the control and the left edge of the object that contains it. This containing object is generally `UserForm`, though it can also be a frame control, MultiPage, or TabStrip. The `.Left` property of a control is expressed in points ($^1/72$ inch), while the `.Left` property of `UserForm` is expressed in *twips* ($^1/1440$ inch). The space spanned by one so-called "inch" on different client screens may be variable depending on their graphics drivers.

.Locked

For a control with textual contents that can be edited by the user, `.Locked` is set to a Boolean value representing whether the user is prevented from placing the cursor in the control.

Default setting: `False`

EXAMPLE

```
CreditCardNo.Locked = True
```

Here, `CreditCardNo` is a text field that may be locked from user access while a procedure checks whether the number entered into the field is valid.

.MouseIcon

At design time, when the `.MousePointer` property for a control is set to `99`, `.MouseIcon` is set to the filename of an image. This image is displayed in place of the mouse pointer image while the pointer is over the control.

.MousePointer

Set to an integer code that represents an image to be displayed whenever the mouse pointer passes over the control.

 It's easy to mistake this property as a setting for the mouse pointer itself. Setting this property does not change the appearance of the mouse pointer directly at the time the property is being set. Instead, the property merely changes the default state of the pointer only while it is passing over the control.

POSSIBLE SETTINGS

0   (Default) Does not affect the standard or expected behavior of the mouse pointer over the control

1   White arrow pointing NW (standard Windows pointer)

2   Crosshairs

3   I-beam (generally used for text fields)

6   Two-headed arrow pointing NE, SW

7   Two-headed arrow pointing N, S

8   Two-headed arrow pointing NW, SE

9   Two-headed arrow pointing W, E

10   Arrow pointing up

11   Hourglass

12   Circle with slash (meaning, "Not here")

13   Arrow pointing NW with hourglass

14   Arrow with question mark (meaning, "Help for this item?")

15   Four-headed arrow pointing N, S, E, W

.Name

Set at design time only to the term that will be used to identify the control within the source code of the program. This name is used by other VBA instructions to refer specifically to the control when addressing its properties, events, or methods.

.OldHeight

Used within the `Private Sub UserForm_Layout()` event procedure to refer to the previous height of the control prior to being changed. This property, along with its companions `.OldLeft`, `.OldTop`, and `.OldWidth`, have no function in or bearing upon any other body of code in a VBA project other than the `_Layout` event procedure for the form. The `_Layout` event is recognized as a form when its size is changed at run time.

.OldLeft

Used within the `Private Sub UserForm_Layout()` event procedure to refer to the previous horizontal coordinates of the upper- left corner of the control prior to their being changed.

.OldTop

Used within the `Private Sub UserForm_Layout()` event procedure to refer to the previous vertical coordinates of the upper- left corner of the control prior to their being changed.

.OldWidth

Used within the `Private Sub UserForm_Layout()` event procedure to refer to the previous width of the control prior to being changed.

.Parent

An object reference to the container of the control. The `Parent` term in this capacity substitutes fully for the container's own term; if the control is contained by an instance of `UserForm` whose `.Name` property is `Form2`, then `Parent` will have all of the property terms and settings, as well as methods, associated with `Form2`.

.Picture

Set at design time to the filename of a bitmap image that will be displayed as part of the background content of the control.

.TabIndex

Set to the ordinal position of the control in the tab-stop sequence maintained by the form. The tab-stop sequence specifies the route taken by the focus as the user repeatedly presses the Tab key. A control belongs to the tab-stop sequence if its `.TabStop` property is set to `True`.

.TabStop

Set to a Boolean value that represents whether a control belongs to the tab-stop sequence maintained by the form.

Default setting: `True`

.Tag

Set to an alphanumeric string whose meaning and purpose are left entirely to you to define. You can use the `.Tag` property to store any supplemental data associated with a control that can be described as a string, or converted to one.

.Text

For a control with textual contents that are editable by the user, `.Text` represents the textual contents of the control.

Default setting: (null)

EXAMPLE

```
UserName.Text = strUserName
```

Here, `UserName` is a text field in a sign-up form, and `strUserName` is a string variable containing the name entered by the user when the user accessed the sign-up form. This expression places the contents of the string variable into the text field, making those contents editable by the user.

.Top

Set to the vertical distance in points (@@bf1/72 inch) between the upper-left corner of the control and the upper edge of the object that contains it (generally `UserForm`).

.Value

At any one time, `.Value` represents the state or contents of the control. Depending on the nature of the control, `.Value` may be expressed as a Boolean `True`/`False` value, as a numeral, or as a string literal.

On Point

The Forms 2.0 library considers an "update" of a control a complete data entry into that control, as opposed to a "change," which is defined as any change of contents. So typing text into a text box or combo box will result in one update once the focus leaves that control, but any number of change events in the interim. Also, only the control in the form that has the focus can receive the _KeyPress event. The _Click event for a control can be activated from the keyboard if you've set in advance the .Accelerator property for that control to a letter key, and if the user presses that key in conjunction with Alt while the form is active. But a _KeyPress event looks for just one character key; so to have the entire form process single-key alternate keystrokes for many or all of the controls in a form, a single control must be designated the handler of the _KeyPress event. That control must continually be given the focus using the .SetFocus method, rendering the focus useless for its usual purpose as the indicator of the current stop in the form's tab-stop sequence.

.Visible

Set to a Boolean value representing whether the control may be seen by the user.
Default setting: True

EXAMPLE

```
Undo.Visible = True
```

Here Undo is a command button that is visible to the user only after the interpreter has recorded an action that can be undone.

.Width

Set to the distance between the left and right edges of the control, expressed in points ($^1/_{72}$ inch).

Common Forms 2.0 Control Methods

You'll recall that a *method* in VBA is like a verb that describes an action that an object may perform, or a command to which an object may respond. There are few methods common to all of the Forms 2.0 controls – precisely, there are *three*, which are listed below:

.Move

Moves the control to a new location relative to the upper left corner of the form. When the optional third and fourth parameters are included, the `.Move` method also resizes the control to new dimensions.

ARGUMENTS

`Left:`, `Top:`	An integer pair representing the coordinates of the Layout form where the upper-left corner of the control will be moved.
`Width:`	(Optional) An integer representing the new width for the moved control, expressed in points ($1/72$ inch).
`Height:`	(Optional) An integer representing the new height for the moved control.
`Layout:`	\(Optional) A Boolean value indicating whether the `_Layout` event for the moved object (when supported, which signals to the interpreter that the object should be redrawn) should be recognized. `UserForm`, the frame control, and MultiPage support the `_Layout` event. **Default:** `False`

EXAMPLE

```
Private Sub Item12_Click()
    Item12.Move iCollect.Left, iCollect.Right, 72, 72
End Sub
```

Here, `Item12` is an image control acting as an icon. When the user clicks on this icon, it is added to a collection of similarly chosen icons. The current open location in this location is represented by the coordinates `iCollect.Left`, `iCollect.Right`. The control is then resized to a $1/2$-inch by $1/2$-inch square.

.SetFocus

Places the focus on the control, so that it is visibly highlighted. This makes the control open to receiving keyboard events.

EXAMPLE

```
Private Sub lblReOrder_KeyPress(ByVal KeyAscii As _
 MSForms.ReturnInteger)
    If Chr$(KeyAscii) = "l" Then
        lstInventory.Enabled = True
        lstInventory.SetFocus
    End If
End Sub
```

Here, lblReOrder is a label control whose purpose is to "unlock" a list box control that contains an inventory of items. Its .TabStop property is set to True at design time to better enable the label to act as a real control. **A label has all the mechanics of a command button, just without the animation.** While lblReOrder has the focus, if the user simply presses the "l" key (no Shift or Alt required) then the list control lstInventory is "unlocked" and re-enabled, turning its contents from gray to black. Then the .SetFocus method for the list box moves the focus from the label control to the first entry in the list.

.ZOrder

In a situation where controls in a form may overlap one another, the .ZOrder method is used to place the control at the top or bottom of the stack. Placing the control at the top of the stack makes it overlap all controls that intersect its region.

ARGUMENT

zPosition: An unsigned flag that represents whether the control is placed at the top of the stack (0) or the bottom (1).

EXAMPLE

```
Private Sub Card28_Click()
  Card28.ZOrder zPosition:=0
End Sub
```

Here, Card28 is one in a long series of image controls arranged in a cascade fashion or like a spread deck of cards. A piece of each card is visible, and that piece is sensitive to user events. By clicking the twenty-eighth card in this stack, the .ZOrder method moves it to the top of the stack, making the whole image visible and sensitive to events.

The Mechanism of a Form

What makes an event-driven program like a form module work is an almost complete reliance upon the user, not the programmer, to direct the program's course of action. Most of the effort expended by the VBA instructions in a form is for the sole purpose of ascertaining what it is that the user wants it to do. Keep this in mind as you study the following text, which lists in quite a bit of detail *all* of the object-oriented terms associated with the `UserForm` object.

Characteristics

Purpose: General control containment
Default source name: `UserForm.x`
ProgID: `Forms.Form.1`
Description: The `UserForm` object serves as a platform for ActiveX controls that constitute the operable elements of a form or dialog box.

Forms 2.0 UserForm properties

.ACTIVECONTROL

An object reference to the control contained by the form that currently has the focus.

.BACKCOLOR

A code that represents the color that the interpreter will assign to the background of the form (not the text in the foreground). This color does *not* translate to the `.BackColor` properties of newly instantiated controls on the form.

.BORDERCOLOR

A code that represents the color that the interpreter assigns to the perimeter of the *operable* area of the form (not counting the title bar). This setting is meaningful to the user only if the `.BorderStyle` property is set to 1 (single line).

.BORDERSTYLE

An integer flag that denotes whether a separate border is to be given to the client region of the form.

0	**(Default)** The form is given the standard border treatment defined by Windows.
1	The form is given a single border line, whose color is defined by the current `.BorderColor` property setting. The upper portion of this border extends *beneath* the title bar, when present.

.CANPASTE

Set *at run time* to a Boolean value that denotes whether the form may receive the data that currently resides on the Windows system Clipboard. For UserForm, this is a rare occurrence.

.CANREDO

Set *at run time* to a Boolean value that denotes, as long as the UserForm object is recording user actions (i.e., if its .CanUndo property is set to True), whether the form can also record *undone* user actions so that they may be *redone* at the user's request. For a redo to take place, a VBA instruction must be implemented using the .RedoAction method for the form.

.CANUNDO

Set *at run time* to a Boolean value that represents whether the UserForm object is to record user actions, so that they may be undone at the user's request. For an undo to take place, a VBA instruction must be implemented using the .UndoAction method for the form.

.CAPTION

Set to the textual contents of the form's title bar.

.CYCLE

A flag value that denotes the behavior of the Tab key with regard to moving the focus along the objects in the form's tab-stop sequence.

POSSIBLE SETTINGS

0	**(Default)** Designates that the focus should move to the first control in the *next* form's tab-stop sequence, after it has reached the final control in this form's sequence and the user presses Tab again. The "next" form in this case is whichever form has been invoked by a VBA instruction *after* the form that has the focus was invoked. If there is only one form active, the focus cycles back to the first control in that form's sequence.
2	Designates that the focus should always move to the first control in the current form's tab-stop sequence, whether or not there is more than one form active.

.DRAWBUFFER

Set to the number of bytes reserved by the VBA interpreter for rendering the form's contents *off-screen* before making those contents visible. A larger number of bytes (larger than the default, at least) may increase the form's overall graphical speed, since it is quicker for the interpreter to render graphical contents off-screen than on-screen. For a form without major graphical embellishments, this property can be safely left alone.

Default setting: `32000`

.ENABLED

A Boolean value representing whether the form, and all controls belonging to that form, are active and receiving user events. The form remains visible and all contained controls appear as they would if the form were enabled.

Default setting: `True`

 A disabled form (whose `.Enabled` property has been set to `False`) may not be dismissed by the user with the close box, nor may it be moved or even minimized. But if the form's `.ShowModal` property is set to `True` (which is the default), the form will not turn over control to any other window while it remains on the screen. So the form will be disabled and so will everything else. There is, therefore, no point to disabling a modal form at run time other than to frustrate the user.

.FONT

A constituent object that represents the Windows font used to render the text belonging to the form. This object, when set at design time, is then transferred automatically to all controls instantiated for that form. See the Common Forms 2.0 Control Properties section earlier in this chapter for subordinate properties of the `Font` object.

.FORECOLOR

A code representing the foreground color for the form. Foreground color is generally applied to text and certain graphic embellishments, such as rules and frames. This property is *not* translated to any controls instantiated later on the form.

.HEIGHT

The distance in points between the upper and lower edges of the form, *including* the title bar and space given by Windows to the form's exterior border.

.HELPCONTEXTID

A long integer that represents the exclusive ID number used by the Windows Help file associated with the VBA form module to document the use of the form.

.INSIDEHEIGHT

Set *at run time* to the distance, in twips, between the upper and lower edges of the so-called *client region* of the form. This is the area that is capable of containing controls, not counting the title bar or border area of the form's window.

.INSIDEWIDTH

Set *at run time* to the distance, in twips, between the left and right edges of the client region of the form, not counting the border area of the form's window.

.KEEPSCROLLBARSVISIBLE

When the form is designed to behave like an ordinary window, `.KeepScrollBarsVisible` is set to an integer value that represents whether the form continues to display scroll bars, even when the visible area of the window mandates that either or both scroll bars are unnecessary. For this property to be meaningful, the `.ScrollBars` property must be set so that the corresponding scroll bars *can* be visible; with `.ScrollBars` set to 0, no scroll bars will be visible anyway.

POSSIBLE SETTINGS

0   Allows both scroll bars to be made invisible if the contents of the form fit within its borders

1   Maintains the horizontal scroll bar for the form at all times

2   Maintains the vertical scroll bar for the form at all times

3   **(Default)** Maintains both scroll bars for the form at all times

.LEFT

The horizontal distance in twips between the upper-left corner of the form and the upper left corner of the screen. This property is only recognized if the form's `.StartUpPosition` property is set to 0, allowing `.Left` and `.Top` to specify where the form is to appear on screen. The value of this property, as well as `.Top`, is expressed in twips (1/1440 inch). The space spanned by one so-called "inch" on client screens may be variable depending on the graphics drivers used.

.MOUSEICON

At design time, when the `.MousePointer` property for the form is set to 99, `.MouseIcon` is set to the filename of an image. This image is displayed in place of the mouse pointer image while the pointer is over the form. This image becomes the default mouse pointer image for all controls in the form as well. These controls may still override this default setting with `.MouseIcon` property settings of their own.

.MOUSEPOINTER

An integer code that represents an image to be displayed whenever the mouse pointer passes over the form. See the Common Forms 2.0 Control Properties section earlier in this chapter for possible settings.

.NAME

Set at design time only to the name which will serve to identify the form as an object term throughout the VBA source code. This name is used by other VBA instructions to refer specifically to the form when addressing its properties, events, or methods.

.PICTURE

Set at design time to the filename of a bitmap image that is displayed as part of the background content of the control.

.PICTUREALIGNMENT

Set at design time to an integer that represents how the interior image stated by the .Picture property setting, is to be positioned with respect to the border of the form.

POSSIBLE SETTINGS

0   Picture is aligned against the upper left corner of the form

1   Picture is aligned against the upper right corner of the form

2   (Default) Picture is centered with respect to the form

3   Picture is aligned against the lower left corner of the form

4   Picture is aligned against the lower right corner of the form

.PICTURESIZEMODE

An integer value that denotes how the form is to treat the sizing of the interior picture referred to by the .Picture property. By default, the picture is rendered in its native size, though this property permits you to refer to the form's own size in designating the size of the picture.

POSSIBLE SETTINGS

0   (Default) Does not change the pixel mapping of the interior picture with respect to the form. Any overhang by the picture is cropped.

1   Stretches or shrinks the picture to fit the edges of the form, however much the picture might have to be distorted.

3   Enlarges or reduces the size of the picture so that it consumes as much of
       the form's client region as possible *without* distorting the image.

.PICTURETILING

A Boolean value representing whether the form is permitted to repeat the contained
image, pointed to by the form's .Picture property setting. When this property is
set to True, the entire client area will be filled with one or more instances of the
image, repeated horizontally and vertically like floor tile.

   Default setting: False

 If the .PictureSizeMode property is set to 1, the .PictureTiling
property will have no obvious effect on the form.

.SCROLLBARS

An integer value denoting which scroll bars the form will be capable of displaying,
when its contents exceed the form's borders.

POSSIBLE SETTINGS

0   **(Default)** Scroll bars will never be displayed

1   Horizontal scroll bar will be displayed if text exceeds the right boundary

2   Vertical scroll bar will be displayed if text exceeds the lower boundary

3   Either or both scroll bars will be displayed when necessary

.SCROLLHEIGHT

When set to a nonzero value, .ScrollHeight specifies in points the vertical distance between the upper and lower edges of the total contents of the form displayable within the client region. When this value exceeds the .InsideHeight
property setting, the vertical scroll bar may be used to scroll through the contents
of the form. When set to 0, the .ScrollHeight property designates that the form is
not designed to be scrolled vertically.

   Default setting: 0

.SCROLLLEFT

The horizontal distance in points between the upper left corner of the *visible* portion of the form's client region and the actual upper left corner of the client region.

This setting only makes sense when the .ScrollWidth property is set to a value that is greater than that of the .InsideWidth property setting, and the horizontal scroll bar is visible.

Default setting: 0

.SCROLLTOP

The vertical distance in points between the upper left corner of the *visible* portion of the form's client region and the actual upper left corner of the client region. This setting only makes sense when the .ScrollHeight property is set to a value that is greater than that of the .InsideHeight property setting, and the vertical scroll bar is visible.

.SCROLLWIDTH

When set to a nonzero value, .ScrollWidth specifies, in twips (not points), the horizontal distance between the left and right edges of the total contents of the form displayable within the client region. When this value exceeds the .InsideWidth property setting, the horizontal scroll bar may be used to scroll through the contents of the form. When set to 0, the .ScrollWidth property designates that the form is not designed to be scrolled horizontally.

Default setting: 0

.SPECIALEFFECT

An integer value that represents the style of frame given to the client region of the form.

POSSIBLE SETTINGS

0   Flat; no special treatment is given to the border, besides what settings may have been made to the .BorderStyle and .BorderColor properties

1   Raised; the client region appears to stand out from the form

2   (Default) Sunken; the client region appears to be recessed into the form

3   Etched; a thin line appears to be etched into the perimeter of the client region

6   "Bump;" a thin line appears to have been etched from the inside-out along the perimeter of the client region

The .BorderStyle and .SpecialEffect properties are incompatible with one another. At design time, if you set one, you've undone the effect of another. Setting the .BorderStyle property in turn sets .SpecialEffect to 0.

.STARTUPPOSITION

An integer flag denoting the position of the form relative to the screen at startup.

POSSIBLE SETTINGS

0   Allows the form's `.Left` and `.Top` property settings to specify where the form is to appear relative to the coordinate system of the screen

1   Centers the form relative to the active application's window

2   Centers the form relative to the screen

3   Allows Windows to determine where the new form should appear. Generally, Windows wimps out and places the form along the upper left corner of the *screen*, instead of the active application workspace

The `Private Sub UserForm_Activate()` procedure is executed in response to the `_Activate` event, which occurs before the form is made visible to the user. You can take advantage of this procedure to set at run time the `.Left` and `.Top` properties of a form whose `.StartUpPosition` property is set to `0`. This way, the procedure can ascertain the position of other screen elements first, and then determine based on that data the most appropriate place for the form to be displayed.

.TOP

The vertical distance in twips between the upper left corner of the form and the upper left corner of the screen. This property is only recognized if the form's `.StartUpPosition` property is set to 0, allowing `.Left` and `.Top` to specify where the form is to appear onscreen.

.VERTICALSCROLLBARSIDE

An integer flag representing whether the vertical scroll bar is displayed on the right (0, **Default**) or left (1) side of the form.

.WHATSTHISBUTTON

An unsigned Boolean value indicating whether the title bar of the form is to display the question mark button at run-time. This button, when clicked on by the user, allows the user to click next on one of the controls in the form, and have the interpreter start the Help engine for the module, pulling up the page indicated by the `.HelpContextID` property of that control. The `.WhatsThisHelp` property must be set to `True` as well, and `.HelpContextID` must point to a legitimate Help file page index in order for the setting for `.WhatsThisButton` to be meaningful.

Default setting: `False`

.WHATSTHISHELP

A Boolean value indicating whether the user can invoke a specific page from a Help file for this form and the controls within it. The user can generally invoke Help for a control by giving it the focus and pressing the F1 key. Alternately, if the `.WhatsThisButton` property is set to `True`, the user may click on the question mark button in the title bar, then click on the control in question to invoke the Help file page for that control.

.WIDTH

The distance in points between the left and right edges of the form, including any space given by Windows to the form's exterior border.

.ZOOM

An integer value that represents a percentage of normal magnification to be given the client region of the form and all of its contents. A percentage greater than 100 usually triggers display of scroll bars, if the `.ScrollBars` property is set to a value other than 0.

Default setting: `100`

The full effect of the `.Zoom` property on a form is best felt when its `.Font` property and the `.Font` property of all of its controls are set to a TrueType font. Unlike a Windows bitmap font, a TrueType font can be resized to 0.1 point.

Forms 2.0 UserForm methods

.HIDE

Renders the form invisible without unloading it from memory or de-activating the form module. The form can be made visible again using the `.Show` method.

.MOVE

Relocates the form to the specified coordinates relative to the screen. Optionally, the `.Move` method may be used to change the size of the form.

ARGUMENTS

Left: (Optional) The screen coordinate for the form's new horizontal position, in twips

Top: (Optional) The screen coordinate for the form's new vertical position, in twips

Width: (Optional) A new .Width property setting for the form, in points

Height: (Optional) A new .Height property setting for the form, in points

.PRINTFORM

Sends a bitmapped image of the form to the printer and ejects the printer's page when done.

.REDOACTION

For a form whose .CanRedo property is set to True, the .RedoAction method forces a redo of the previously undone action by the user.

.REPAINT

Signals to Windows a request to redraw the contents of the form, plus all of its contained controls. Windows generally responds affirmatively (often depending on its mood at the time).

.SCROLL

For a form whose .InsideHeight or .InsideWidth properties are set above the form's own .Height or .Width settings, the .Scroll method forces the client region of the form to be scrolled, as though a scroll bar for that region (visible or not) were present. The method's arguments are integer flags that specify what parts of the "virtual scroll bars" are to be activated.

ARGUMENTS

ActionX: Portion of the horizontal "scroll bar" to be activated

ActionY: Portion of the vertical "scroll bar" to be activated

SETTINGS FOR ARGUMENTS

0   No action

1   The equivalent of clicking on the scroll bar's up or left arrow button

2   The equivalent of clicking on the scroll bar's down or right arrow button.

3	The equivalent of clicking on the region between the thumb and the up or left arrow button
4	The equivalent of clicking on the region between the thumb and the down or right arrow button
5	The equivalent of moving the thumb to the beginning of the scroll bar
6	The equivalent of moving the thumb to the of the scroll bar

.SETDEFAULTTABORDER

Allows the form to reassess automatically a tab-stop sequence for its controls, utilizing a top-to-bottom, left-to-right algorithm.

.SHOW

Causes the designated form's _Activate event to be recognized and brings the form to the screen. If the form is not in memory yet (that is, if it has not been *loaded* yet using the Load statement), then the .Show method loads the form prior to its being shown.

.UNDOACTION

For a form whose .CanUndo property is set to True, the .UndoAction method forces the previous action made by the user on the form to be rescinded. If the .CanRedo property is set to True, the undone action is recorded, and can be reexecuted using the .RedoAction method.

.UNLOAD

Removes the form from the screen, forces its _Deactivate event to be recognized, and then removes the form from memory. It and its controls are no longer addressable until the form is loaded into memory again using the Load statement.

.WHATSTHISMODE

Forces the module into a Help mode, where the next control the user clicks on invokes the Help page for that control. This page is designated by the control's .HelpContextID property setting. While in this mode, the mouse pointer changes so that the arrow is supplemented by a question mark.

Forms 2.0 UserForm events

_ACTIVATE

Occurs just after the form has been loaded into mcmory, and just prior to it being displayed on screen. The _Activate event procedure for a form may be used to prepare its contents for viewing.

_ADDCONTROL

Occurs whenever a control has been instantiated on a form at run time. Dynamic instantiation of a control can take place as a result of executing the `CreateObject()` function for that control. The `_AddControl` event procedure can be used to validate, and otherwise prepare, the control's contents and appearance prior to its being shown.

_BEFOREDRAGOVER

Recognized when an drag-and-drop operation is in progress and the mouse pointer has been moved over the form. The data being moved is referred to as the *source*, and the form receiving the data is called the *target*. This event may be recognized more than once as the mouse pointer proceeds.

ARGUMENTS

`Cancel`:	A Boolean variable which, when set to `True`, cancels the drag in progress and prevents the `_BeforeDropOrPaste` event from occurring, leaving the data contents of the target control as they were.
`Control`:	An object reference to the control currently being dragged over the form, or to the control responsible for the object or other item that is being dragged over the form.
`Data`:	Refers to the object-addressable form of the data that is currently being dragged over the form. Microsoft calls this the "data object," which is not really the same as an object. This object has its own methods that are used to actually access the raw text or contents of the data object. For instance, the method `Data.GetText` returns the text of the data being dragged between two controls.
`X`:	A single-precision value representing the mouse pointer's current *x*-axis coordinate.
`Y`:	A single-precision value representing the mouse pointer's current *y*-axis coordinate.
`DragState`:	An integer representing the mouse pointer location relative to its last known source. Possible values: 0 – has just moved within range; 1 – is moving out of range; 2 – remains within range.
`Effect`:	An integer that represents the OLE event that the user has apparently commanded should take place. Possible values: 0 – no response necessary; 1 – copy source to target; 2 – move source to target; 3 – either copy or move source to target (program's discretion; registered when OLE is unsure of source application's representation of the directive).

Shift: A bitwise value that represents the keyboard keys that were depressed at the time of the event. **Possible values:** 0 – no key pressed; 1 – Shift; 2 – Ctrl; 4 – Alt.

_BEFOREDROPORPASTE
Recognized when an OLE drag-and-drop operation is being concluded while the mouse pointer is over the form.

ARGUMENTS

Cancel: An integer variable that, when set to True, prevents the paste from occurring and leaves the contents of the control as they were.

Control: An object reference to the control currently being dragged over the form, or to the control responsible for the object or other item that is being dragged over the form.

Action: An integer value that represents the user directive. **Possible values:** 2 – Paste command; 3 – Drag-and-drop has concluded.

Data: Refers to the source object as OLE type DataObject. Methods may be invoked on this object to retrieve its contents.

X: A single-precision value representing the mouse pointer's current *x*-axis coordinate.

Y: A single-precision value representing the mouse pointer's current *y*-axis coordinate.

Effect: An integer that represents the OLE event that the user has apparently commanded should take place. **Possible values:** 0 – no response necessary; 1 – copy source to target; 2 – move source to target; 3 – either copy or move source to target (program's discretion; registered when OLE is unsure of source application's representation of the directive).

Shift: A bitwise value that represents the keyboard keys that were depressed at the time of the event. **Possible values:** 0 – no key pressed; 1 – Shift; 2 – Ctrl; 4 – Alt.

_CLICK
Occurs when the user clicks once on the form, just after the mouse button is released.

_DBLCLICK

Occurs when the user double-clicks on the form, just after the mouse button is released for the second click.

ARGUMENT

Cancel   A Boolean variable that, when set to True, prevents the _Click event (already recognized once prior to _DblClick) from being recognized a second time. You should perhaps set this to True in any event.

_DEACTIVATE

Occurs whenever the form loses the focus to another window, either in the VBA project or elsewhere in Windows.

_ERROR

Occurs when the control detects an error caused by something within its own purview, such as its own program, or by the OLE components currently running within Windows. Errors in the VBA module, or error conditions caused by the VBA interpreter itself, do not count here.

_KEYDOWN

Occurs when a key on the keyboard is pressed while the form has the focus.

ARGUMENTS

KeyCode   An integer value that represents the key that was pressed (*not* the ASCII or ANSI value for the character).

Shift   A bitwise value that indicates the keyboard control keys that may have been pressed concurrently with the mouse button (bit 0 – Shift; bit 1 – Ctrl; bit 2 – Alt).

_KEYPRESS

Occurs when a key on the keyboard representing a typeable character is pressed while the control has the focus.

ARGUMENT

KeyAscii   The ASCII (actually ANSI) numeral code for the specific character that was pressed.

_KEYUP

Occurs when a key on the keyboard is released while the control has the focus. Arguments here are the same as for the _KeyDown event.

_LAYOUT

Occurs whenever the form changes size. Since a Forms 2.0 UserForm object cannot be stretched by the user (unlike a Visual Basic 5.0 form), this can only happen as a result of an invocation of the form's .Move method, using the third and fourth arguments of that method.

_MOUSEDOWN

Occurs immediately following the user pressing down a mouse button while the mouse pointer is over the form.

ARGUMENTS

Button	A bitwise value that indicates which mouse button was pressed (bit 0 – left; bit 1 – right; bit 2 – middle).
Shift	A bitwise value that indicates the keyboard control keys that may have been pressed concurrently with the mouse button (bit 0 – Shift; bit 1 – Ctrl; bit 2 – Alt).
X, Y	Integer values indicating the horizontal and vertical distances, respectively, from the mouse pointer "hot spot" to the left and upper edges, respectively, of the form.

_MOUSEMOVE

Occurs after the mouse pointer has traversed any distance while its "hot spot" (for example, the tip of the arrow) is sighted over the control. Arguments are the same as for _MouseDown and _MouseUp.

_MOUSEUP

Occurs immediately after the user has released a mouse button while the mouse pointer is over the control. The same arguments apply here as for _MouseDown.

_QUERYCLOSE

Occurs just prior to the shutdown process for a form. This gives the form module the opportunity to inform the user that the form is about to shut down so that the user may cancel that process.

ARGUMENTS

Cancel   A Boolean variable that, if set to True, cancels the shutdown process for the form. The _Terminate event is not recognized if Cancel is set to True.

CloseMode An integer flag that represents who or whatever is initiating the shutdown process.

Possible CloseMode settings

0   Indicates that the user has clicked on the close box (the big "X") on the title bar.

1   The Unload statement has been executed.

2   Windows is being shut down.

3   The program is being shut down by the "Task Manager," which in Windows 95 or NT is really the Close Task dialog box that shows up when you press Ctrl+Alt+Delete.

_REMOVECONTROL
Recognized at run-time whenever a control has been removed from the form as, for example, by using the .Remove method of the Controls collection. This collection is used by the MultiPage control, among others, to refer to controls spread out among multiple pages indirectly.

_SCROLL
Occurs whenever one of the form's scroll bars has been operated. This event is also recognized after the .Scroll method is invoked.

_TERMINATE
Recognized just *after* the form has left the screen, but just *prior* to its being unloaded from memory. The form *will* be unloaded once the Private Sub UserForm_Terminate() event procedure reaches End Sub.

_ZOOM
Occurs whenever the .Zoom property for the form has changed. This gives your form module the opportunity to alter the contents of the form prior to the magnification being made visible to the user.

ARGUMENT

Percent   Registers the new magnification percentage for the form.

> **On Point**
>
> Many sequences of events that happen in a cascading order can be canceled in progress if it's determined that the data input in that control is somehow invalid. These cancelable sequences are: `_BeforeUpdate`, `_AfterUpdate`, `_Exit`; and `_Click`, `_DblClick`, `_Click`; and `_BeforeDropOrPaste` or `_BeforeDragOver` followed by a conclusion of the drag-and-drop process. The cascading sequence can be canceled by setting the `Cancel` variable to `True` for those event procedures in which `Cancel` masquerades as an incoming argument.

In Theory: Buy This! Yes / No / Cancel

A truly interactive form is one that begins by eliciting information of a specific type from the user. It provokes this information by the manner of its presentation. It then uses this same information as data presented to the user with which she may craft a body of information that is both satisfactory to her and crucial to the operation of the database maintained by the form's program. The final saved or submitted product represents the product of an "agreement" of sorts between the program and the user; the program presents the user with what is feasible, and the user provides the program with what is practical and desirable.

Now, all of this may sound to you like psychology rather than programming, so let's examine a real-world example: When database managers became formalized applications in the early 1970s, once users stopped feeding punch cards into a chute, they began typing in data from a keyboard, and what they typed appeared on a screen. There was nothing on the screen but the data; so these old neon-tube screens served as nothing more than electronic sheets of paper. Errors were frequent, and punch cards as a result were considered to be more reliable, even if they were more expensive to maintain.

The first word processor ever produced for the mass market was a quite capable 1978 product from Bröderbund called Electric Pencil, first written for the Apple II. What made this product so magnificent was the fact that some of the words on screen were symbols for some of the functions of the program – the first example of a menu bar in practice. At last, here was something presented to the user from moment one that elicited a response. Once that response came and was presented on screen, tools were offered to the user (through keyboard commands) that made the on screen representation of that data response more satisfactory. The data was amended and perfected before it was officially submitted; the *rendering* and the *saving* of the data were made separate acts. The space between these acts gave the user an opportunity to perfect the product of her work.

There is no entirely automatic way to accomplish interactivity for something other than a human being. Many Web sites established in the interest of self-promotion provide what are often called "interactive versions" of what are undoubtedly just their sales brochures. What makes these sites interactive in the minds of their developers is that they have a lot of buttons on them. The other day, I encountered a so-called "interactive book." Not an electronic book or a Web site, mind you, but a printed volume. Its purpose was to teach young adults how to perform everyday tasks, such as the laundry, ironing, or taking the cat to the vet. What made the book interactive from the publisher's point of view was the use of visual elements on each and every (full-color) page that pointed the reader to some other possibly related task on some other (full-color) page: "Cool beans! Want to know more? Making waffles is on page 58!"

Interactivity and jumping around data back and forth are entirely separate concepts. Electric Pencil jump-started the development of truly interactive software because it

♦ responded to the user in a reasonable, comprehensible fashion

♦ elicited a response from the user in a reasonable, sensible manner

By this definition, no application developed since that time has ever been any *more* interactive than Electric Pencil. No single implement developed by humankind better embodies the marketing concept of "interactive" than the microwave oven.

In Brief

♦ The most common event for Forms 2.0 controls is `_Click`, which occurs when the user clicks once on the control. When utilized by a command button, the `_Click` event procedure may be utilized for processing the main job of the form module — especially if it's the OK button for the form.

♦ Many controls recognize `_BeforeUpdate` and `_AfterUpdate` events for making certain that the user's data entry or other interaction is valid, and for making certain that the right actions are taken as a result. The `_BeforeUpdate` event is recognized prior to any change made by the user to the control being considered "official;" this way, the input can be evaluated and thrown out if it's invalid. After the evaluation, the `_AfterUpdate` event procedure for a control can be used to process the valid data — which you can be certain is valid here, because if the `_BeforeUpdate` procedure threw out the data, `_AfterUpdate` would not even occur.

◆ Event procedures that are specifically concerned with *where* the mouse
  pointer is when the user clicks on a control, and what buttons the user
  used to do so, are bound to the _MouseUp and _MouseDown events.

◆ Controls that display text that the user can change have .Text properties;
  controls that display text that the user *cannot* change have .Caption
  properties.

◆ The .Enabled property for a control determines whether it is sensitive to
  user events (True if it is, which is the default); the .Visible property
  determines whether the user can actually see the control.

Chapter 7

Extending Office 2000 with ActiveX Controls

IN THIS CHAPTER

◆ The properties, methods, and events that are specific to each control in the Forms 2.0 ensemble

◆ An extended examination of the TabStrip and MultiPage controls

◆ The good and bad side of dynamic control instantiation

THIS CHAPTER PEERS into the *unique* characteristics of the Forms 2.0 controls. In Chapter 6, we looked at the *common* characteristics of those controls, and examined how the UserForm object works in conjunction with them. Here you'll see those individual features, along with some familiar features that the Forms controls use in unique ways.

A few things to know when reading the tables that follow: At the top of each table, we mention something called a *ProgID* (pronounced *prawg·eye·dee*). What in the world is this contraption? In Chapter 9, you'll be introduced to an interesting VBA function called CreateObject(), and you'll see how controls and other COM/OLE/ActiveX components can be called into existence during the course of the VBA program. Object Linking and Embedding (OLE), one of the "engines" running within Windows, recognizes certain *monikers* that uniquely identify components in the Windows System Registry. For executable code, these monikers are called "program identifiers" or "ProgIDs" for short. The ProgID terms I list in each of these tables are the arguments to use for the CreateObject() function to dynamically instantiate (that is, call into existence a new instance of) one of these components.

The Forms 2.0 controls whose graphical portions are supplied by outside graphics files, support these standardized formats:

.BMP   Windows bitmap

.ICO   Windows icon

.CUR   Windows mouse pointer image

.WMF   Windows metafile

.GIF   GIF89a

.JPG   JPEG

Also, for many of these controls, you'll notice we've exclusively pointed out their *value properties*. Such a term could also be called a "default property," or the property term to which your instruction would be referring if you did not write a property term out explicitly. For example: The textual contents of a Forms 2.0 text box control named txtLastName would be addressed normally with the term txtLastName.Text. But since .Text is the value property of the text box control, you could also refer to the contents of the text box with just txtLastName alone. So if you have a string variable strSearch, and you write an instruction strSearch = txtLastName *without* the trailing property term, you are still writing a valid instruction that assigns the setting of the value property — in this case, the .Text property — to the string variable. **The value property, where there is such a thing, is the property that may be referenced either by default or by omitting the property term.**

The Command Button

We begin with the command button, which is, from a mechanical standpoint, the simplest of the Forms controls. The command button is a standard push button. Its purpose is to send a directive to the form module. The event that generally means, "Do *this*," where "*this*" is a command, is the _Click event. "*This*" is generally represented on the button face by a simple term (represented by the text of the .Caption property setting) or an icon (represented by the .Picture property setting).

Characteristics

Purpose: User directive signaling
Default source name: CommandButton*x*
ProgID: Forms.CommandButton.1
Description: The command button is a standard push button. The function of the command is generally represented on the button face by a simple term or an icon.

Value property

.CAPTION
Represents the textual contents of the command button.

Special properties

.PICTURE
A constituent object of class `StdPicture` representing the image file assigned to the command button.

EXAMPLE   The default property (or more accurately, the *value property*) of this constituent is `.Name`, so you may set the picture property to a filename, like this:

```
Command1.Picture = "C:\4way.bmp"
```
The value property term may be omitted in references to that term, as long as you specify the proper object that uses that term. So the above instruction does the same job as the one below:

```
Command1.Picture.Name = "C:\4way.bmp"
```

The `Picture` object does have other important properties, especially its own `.Height` and `.Width`. You may poll these properties' settings with the instructions below:

```
sPicWidth = Command1.Picture.Width
sPicHeight = Command1.Picture.Height
```

The `Picture` object's value property is set to a filename, which refers to a file that exists on the programmer's system. This, of course, implies that the image file must also exist on any other system in which the VBA module is installed.

.PICTUREPOSITION
Set to an integer representing the relative locations of the command button's image (when present) and its caption.

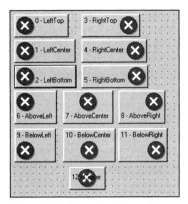

Figure 7-1: Examples of possible
.PicturePosition property settings.

POSSIBLE SETTINGS

0   Image at left, caption aligned along image's top edge

1   Image at left, caption aligned to vertical center of image

2   Image at left, caption aligned along image's bottom edge

3   Image at right, caption aligned along image's top edge

4   Image at right, caption aligned to vertical center of image

5   Image at right, caption aligned along image's bottom edge

6   Caption at bottom, image aligned along caption's left edge

7   Caption at bottom, image aligned to horizontal center of caption

8   Caption at bottom, image aligned along caption's right edge

9   Caption at top, image aligned along caption's left edge

10   Caption at top, image aligned to horizontal center of caption

11   Caption at top, image aligned along caption's right edge

12   Image in middle, caption atop image in absolute center

A command button's image and caption will appear simultaneously only when its .AutoSize property has been set to True. The button will resize itself at design time to accommodate both.

.TAKEFOCUSONCLICK

Set to a Boolean value that represents whether the button is to assume the focus when the user clicks on it.

Default setting: True

.WORDWRAP

Set to a Boolean value indicating whether words in the button's caption may be allowed to wrap down to new lines (True) or text must stream to the right (False).

With both the .WordWrap and .AutoSize properties of a relatively thin command button set to False, it might not have enough pixel width to hold a long caption. In case of overlap, since captions are generally centered, the user may only see the *middle* of the caption.

The Label Control

What isn't obvious on the surface is that the Forms 2.0 label control has very much the same mechanical characteristics as the command button, just without the animation. Generally, the label is just a line or two of text that rests beside an operable or *active* control, indicating to the user the meaning or purpose of the control to which it points. So the label usually ends up as a passive control – in fact, it might seem out of place to call it a "control." But the truth is that the Forms 2.0 label control does receive _Click and _DblClick events just like a command button; it just doesn't respond to those events as long as you have not written event procedures for them. However, unlike the command button, the label control was not designed to receive the focus – which is that highlight device that roams the form when you press Tab and Ctrl+Tab. If you give the label control a .Picture property (an *icon*) to go along with its .Caption property, and then find an appropriate .SpecialEffect setting for the label, the user may be able to recognize the label as an *active* control.

Characteristics

Purpose: Text display
Default source name: Label*x*
ProgID: Forms.Label.1
Description: The label acts as a region in which fixed text of a set size, font, and color may be displayed, sometimes accompanied by icon.

Value property

.CAPTION
Represents the textual contents of the label.

Special properties

.BACKSTYLE
Set to an integer value representing whether the background of the label (behind the text) is solid (1) or transparent (2).

.CONTROLSOURCE
For Excel VBA, this property is set to a string containing the address of the cell in a worksheet from which the setting for this control's value property (.Caption) is to be acquired. If no worksheet is specified within the cell address, then the interpreter assumes the active worksheet; likewise, if no workbook is specified, the interpreter assumes the active workbook. Examples of valid cell addresses appear below:

G15	Cell G15 of the active worksheet
$G$15	Cell G15 of the active worksheet, stated as an absolute address
Totals!G15	Cell G15 of the worksheet named Totals in the active workbook
[Sales.xls]Totals!G15	Cell G15 of the worksheet named Totals in the workbook whose filename is Sales.xls.

.PICTURE
A constituent object of class StdPicture representing the picture contained by the label control. Image formats supported are .BMP (Windows bitmap); .ICO (Windows icon); .CUR (Windows mouse pointer image); .WMF (Windows metafile); .GIF (GIF89a); and .JPG or .JPEG (JPEG). (See command button for notes regarding the .Picture property.)

.PICTUREPOSITION

Set to an integer representing the relative locations of the command button's image (when present) and caption. (See command button for settings.)

.SPECIALEFFECT

Set to an integer value representing the style of frame given to the label.

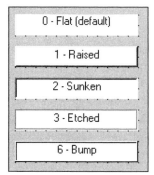

Figure 7-2: Examples of `.SpecialEffect`
property settings given to a label control.

POSSIBLE SETTINGS

0   **(Default)** Flat; no frame

1   Raised; the label appears to stand out from the form (like a command button)

2   Sunken; the label appears to be recessed into the form

3   Etched; a thin line appears to be etched into the perimeter of the label area

4   "Bump;" a thin line appears to have been etched from the inside out, surrounding the label area

When the `.BorderStyle` property of a label is set to 1, it creates a thin, dark line around the control area, and the `.SpecialEffect` property is automatically set to 0.

.TEXTALIGN
Set to an integer value specifying toward what part of the control textual contents are oriented.

POSSIBLE SETTINGS

1   **(Default)** Left margin

2   Center

3   Right margin

.WORDWRAP
Set to a Boolean value indicating whether words in the button's caption may be allowed to wrap down to new lines (`True`), or text must stream to the right (`False`).

The Text Box Control

The text box (also known as the "text field") is a rectangular container for text to be entered by the user. It isn't a full-fledged character input device such as something you would find in a word processor, particularly because it only displays text in one typeface and one font at any one time. However, it is a surprisingly sophisticated OLE drag-and-drop device. For a form that contains multiple text boxes, you can highlight a passage of text first with the mouse, then drag from one text box to another, or cut or copy it to the Windows System Clipboard.

Characteristics

Purpose: Textual input plus editing
Default source name: `TextBox`*x*
ProgID: `Forms.TextBox.1`
Description: The text box is a rectangular container for text to be input by the user.

Value property

.TEXT
Represents the full textual contents of the text box.

Special properties

.AUTOTAB

Set to a Boolean value representing whether the focus will automatically proceed to the next control in the form's tab-stop sequence, once the user has typed the maximum allowable number of characters for the text box (as set by the .MaxLength property).

    Default setting: False

 When set to True, .AutoTab is only functional when the .MaxLength property is set to a non-zero value.

.AUTOWORDSELECT

Set to a Boolean value that represents a cursor behavior for the text box. Suppose .AutoWordSelect is set to True for a control that contains more than one word. The user places the cursor *inside* one of the words, and then drags the pointer to a point beyond the space character at either end of that word. In this case, the highlighter will automatically extend itself to encompass the entire text of the word.

.CONTROLSOURCE

For Excel VBA, this property is set to a string containing the address of the cell in a worksheet from which the setting for this control's value property (.Text) is to be acquired. If no worksheet is specified within the cell address, then the interpreter assumes the active worksheet; likewise, if no workbook is specified, the interpreter assumes the active workbook. Any changes made to the text box's contents are immediately reflected in the designated worksheet cell.

.CURLINE

Set at run time to the index of the line where the cursor of the text box is currently positioned, where 0 is the first line. This property always returns 0 for a text box whose .MultiLine property is set to False.

.CURX

Set to the distance in *himetrics* (approximately 1/1000 meter, assuming the form is running at 640 x 480 resolution on a 15" diagonal monitor) between the current cursor location in the text box, and the left edge of the control.

While the value of the `.CurX` property may be set at run time to some other value, the results of such settings are dubious. At the time of this writing, I noticed the following behavior:

* For a text box whose `.MultiLine` property is set to `False`, any setting made to the `.CurX` property, regardless of its value, will reset the cursor to the beginning of the line.

* If the .MultiLine property is set to True and the cursor resides on the first text line in the control (.CurLine = 0), then any setting made to .CurX will reset the cursor to the beginning of that line.

* If .MultiLine is True and the cursor resides on any line below the first line, and .CurX is set to a value less than the length of the line in himetrics (my sincere apologies for having to introduce you to yet another convoluted unit of measurement), then the first setting made to .CurX indeed places the cursor at the break between characters that is nearest to that setting. This is indeed the intended behavior for the property. However...

* Any subsequent setting to the .CurX property places the cursor at the beginning of the entire text, at the top line.

In short, the usefulness of this property at present is questionable.

.CURTARGETX
Set at run time to the distance in *himetrics* (approximately 1/1000 meter, if you happen to be using a computer in which 1/1000 meter equals 1 himetric) between the point where a drag-and-drop operation would place text being dragged into the text box control, and the left edge of that control.

.DRAGBEHAVIOR
Set to a Boolean value representing whether the client may make use of drag-and-drop to move blocks out of this text box and into another control containing text.
   Default setting: `False`

.ENTERFIELDBEHAVIOR
Set to a Boolean value representing whether the textual contents of the field are automatically highlighted when the focus enters the text box.
   Default setting: `True` (text is highlighted)

.ENTERKEYBEHAVIOR

Set to a Boolean value that specifies how pressing Enter affects the focus behavior for the control.

POSSIBLE SETTINGS

False   (Default) Pressing Enter while the cursor is in the text box moves the focus to the next control in the form's tab stop sequence.

True   Pressing Enter while the cursor is in the text box moves the cursor to the next line in the box, leaving the focus on the control.

.HIDESELECTION

Set to a Boolean value that represents whether highlighted text is to remain high-lighted when the focus leaves the control.

Default setting: False

.INTEGRALHEIGHT

Set to a Boolean value that denotes whether the height of the control is to be auto-matically resized to fit the *exact* height of text lines in their entirety.

POSSIBLE SETTINGS

False   A line of text at the bottom of the control may be partly obscured by the lower edge of the control.

True   (Default) A line of text that would otherwise be partly obscured by the bottom edge of the control, is totally hidden by that edge, which is resized upward to fit only whole lines.

.LINECOUNT

Set at runtime to the number of lines of text in the control. For a text box whose .MultiLine property is set to False, this property always returns 1.

.MAXLENGTH

When set to a nonzero value, .MaxLength represents the maximum number of characters allowed to be typed into the text box.

.MULTILINE

Set to a Boolean value that denotes whether the text box allows text to wrap to a new line below when text exceeds the right margin.

With both .AutoSize and .MultiLine properties for a text box set to True, the control will start out at run time as a small box (regardless of its initial .Width setting), whose height will be expanded by one text line for nearly each character the user types — which can't possibly be what anyone would want. With .AutoSize set to True and .MultiLine to False, if the user types beyond the right margin, the text box is automatically stretched to fit. With .AutoSize set to False and .MultiLine to True, if the user types beyond the bottom margin, existing text will automatically scroll up, and the right scroll bar will appear if .ScrollBars is set to True. If both .AutoSize and .MultiLine are False, and the user proceeds to type beyond the right margin, text automatically scrolls to the *left*, leaving the cursor visible at all times, but rendering the first characters typed invisible and out of range.

.PASSWORDCHAR

Set to a single character that the text box will display when the user types a character, instead of the character that the user typed. This is so a text box being used as a password entry field may mask text with a character such as an asterisk, to prevent onlookers from detecting what is being typed.

   Default setting: *(empty)* – Displayed text echoes typed characters

.SCROLLBARS

Set to an integer value that denotes which scroll bars the text box is capable of displaying when text exceeds its margins.

POSSIBLE SETTINGS

0   (**Default**) Scroll bars are never displayed.

1   Horizontal scroll bar is displayed if text exceeds the right boundary.

2   Vertical scroll bar is displayed if text exceeds the lower boundary.

3   Either or both scroll bars are displayed when necessary.

When .AutoSize is set to True, scroll bars for a text box are never displayed, regardless of the .ScrollBars property setting.

.SELECTIONMARGIN

Set to a Boolean value that indicates whether a mouse click just to the left of text in the text box will result in the entire text being highlighted.

Default setting: `True`

.SELLENGTH

Set at run time to the number of characters currently highlighted within the text box.

.SELSTART

Set at run time to the index position of the first character of text currently highlighted within the text box, where 0 refers to the first character.

.SELTEXT

Set at run time to the text currently highlighted within the text box.

.SPECIALEFFECT

Set to an integer value that represents the style of frame given to the text box.

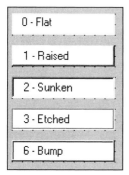

Figure 7-3: Examples of possible settings for a text box's `.SpecialEffect` property.

POSSIBLE SETTINGS

0   Flat; no special treatment is given to the surrounding frame

1   Raised; the control appears to stand out from the form

2   **(Default)** Sunken; the control appears to be recessed into the form

3   Etched; a thin line appears to be etched into the perimeter of the control

4   "Bump;" a thin line appears to have been etched from the inside out along the perimeter of the control

.TABKEYBEHAVIOR

Set to a Boolean value that represents whether pressing the Tab key while typing in the text box results in a tab being entered (True), or whether it moves the focus to the next control in the tab stop sequence (False, **Default**).

.TEXTALIGN

Set to an integer value that specifies toward what part of the control textual contents are oriented.

POSSIBLE SETTINGS

1   **(Default)** Left margin

2   Center

3   Right margin

.TEXTLENGTH

Set at run time to the total number of characters currently being displayed by the text box.

Microsoft documentation indicates that the .TextLength property for a text box whose .MultiLine property is set to True will account for carriage return and line feed characters along with other characters. However, you cannot type a carriage return into a multi-line text box; and a line feed (Shift+Enter) is treated as two characters.

.WORDWRAP

Set to a Boolean value that indicates whether words in the text box are allowed to wrap down to new lines (True) or text must stream to the right (False). This property is ignored if the .MultiLine property for the text box is set to False.

Unlike the text entry field for a word processor, the text box control wraps space characters separating words to the next line. The result is that if a word spilling over the right margin is wrapped to the next line, the space before it is wrapped also, creating a leading space in that new line.

Associated methods

.COPY
Copies the highlighted text, if any, to the Windows System Clipboard.

.CUT
Cuts the highlighted text, if any, from the control and stores it in the Windows System Clipboard.

.PASTE
Recalls text stored to the Windows System Clipboard, and places it within the text box at the current cursor position, replacing any highlighted text.

Recognized events

_BEFOREDRAGOVER
Recognized when a drag-and-drop is in progress and the mouse pointer has been moved over the control. The data being moved is referred to as the *source*, and the control receiving the data is called the *target*. This event may be recognized more than once as the mouse pointer proceeds.

ARGUMENTS

Cancel:	A Boolean variable that, when set to True, forces future drag events to be recognized by the containing object (generally UserForm) rather than by the control.
Data:	Set to refer to the object-addressable form of the data that is currently being dragged over the control. Microsoft calls this the "data object," which is not really the same as an object. This object has its own methods that access the raw text or contents of the data object. For instance, the method Data.GetText returns the text of the data being dragged between two controls.
X:	Set to a single-precision value that represents the mouse pointer's current *x*-axis coordinate.
Y:	Set to a single-precision value that represents the mouse pointer's current *y*-axis coordinate.
DragState:	Set to an integer that represents the mouse pointer location relative to its last known source. **Possible values:** 0 – has just moved within range; 1 – is moving out of range; 2 – remains within range.

Effect: Set to an integer that represents the OLE event that the user has apparently commanded should take place. **Possible values:** 0 – no response necessary; 1 – copy source to target; 2 – move source to target; 3 – either copy or move source to target (program's discretion, registered when OLE is unsure of source application's representation of the directive).

Shift: Set to a bitwise value that represents the keyboard keys that were depressed at the time of the event. **Possible values:** 0 – no key pressed; 1 – Shift; 2 – Ctrl; 4 – Alt.

_BEFOREDROPORPASTE

Recognized in either of two conditions:

1. When a drag-and-drop operation is concluded while the mouse pointer is over the control

2. When the control currently has the focus and Windows has processed a Paste command from the user

ARGUMENTS

Cancel: A Boolean variable that, when set to True, forces future drag-related events to be recognized by the containing object (generally UserForm) rather than by the control.

Action: Set to an integer value that represents the user directive. **Possible values:** 2 – Paste command; 3 – Drag-and-drop has concluded.

Data: Set to refer to the source object as an object of class DataObject. Methods may be invoked on this object to retrieve its contents.

X: Set to a single-precision value that represents the mouse pointer's current *x*-axis coordinate.

Y: Set to a single-precision value that represents the mouse pointer's current *y*-axis coordinate.

Effect: Set to an integer that represents the OLE event that the user indicated has apparently commanded to take place. **Possible values:** 0 – no response necessary; 1 – copy source to target; 2 – move source to target; 3 – either copy or move source to target (program's discretion, registered when OLE is unsure of source application's representation of the directive).

Shift: Set to a bitwise value that represents the keyboard keys that were
                      depressed at the time of the event. **Possible values:** 0 – no key
                      pressed; 1 – Shift; 2 – Ctrl; 4 – Alt.

In Depth: Drag–and–drop operations for text boxes

The idea of executing OLE drag-and-drop operations for controls as simple as Forms
2.0 text boxes was perhaps more ambitious than it was successful. Still, you can set
up multiple text boxes in a form so that text may be dragged, in whole or in part,
from one control to another and pasted in place.

Making a text box in a form capable of exporting its text via drag-and-drop is as
simple as setting its .DragBehavior property to **1 – fmDragBehaviorEnabled**. Even
if a text box has a .DragBehavior setting of 0, it may receive text being dragged
into it from another text box whose .DragBehavior property is set to 1.

Just before the dragged text enters the area of the text box, its _BeforeDragOver
event is recognized. Similarly, just before the user releases the mouse button to
effectuate a drop, its _BeforeDropOrPaste event is recognized. The event
procedures for both events receive an argument variable curiously called Data (whose
name is actually a reserved word in BASIC, and should not have been used for this
purpose). Its type, as stated in the automatic event procedure declaration, is
MSForms.DataObject. This is an object class supported by the Forms 2.0 library,
and is reserved exclusively for text that can be transported between controls by way
of the Clipboard or via drag-and-drop.

An instance of the DataObject class has no properties, just methods. (The difference
may be slight, and merely semantic in nature.) The .GetText method is used to
obtain the textual contents of a DataObject class object; so for the two "Before"
events, you may assign this text to a string variable with an instruction such as this:

```
strDragText = Data.GetText
```

One reason you might want to poll the text represented by the DataObject class
object prior to its being dropped inside a text box, is that you can make adjustments
to the text prior to the drop. Here's an instruction that limits the drop to the first 100
characters of text:

```
Data.SetText Left$(Data.GetText, 100)
```

A drag-and-drop operation may also be canceled outright by setting Cancel –
another argument of the "Before" events – to True. The dropped text will disappear
into the digital abyss.

Continued

In Depth: Drag-and-drop operations for text boxes (Continued)

One more note on this subject: If you set the `.ShowModal` property for your form to `False`, making it a modeless dialog box at run time, then any text box or other control whose `.DragBehavior` property is set to 1 may have any part or all of its text dragged into a control *outside of the form* — say, onto a Word document or Excel worksheet.

The Option Button Control

The option button (also known as the *radio button*) is a dot with a caption that represents a choice that a user may make from a set. In most cases, a set of option buttons appears in a vertical stack, contained by a frame control. The `.Caption` property of the frame control relates to the user the purpose of the option set. But the option buttons do not have to be contained within a frame in order for the VBA interpreter to group them, as had been required for option controls in Visual Basic's past. Now, the `.GroupName` property for each control in a set designates that set for the interpreter. You give all of the options in the set identical `.GroupName` settings. You can then have more than one set of options within the same container (frame, form, or MultiPage tab), and allow the `.GroupName` property to differentiate between those sets.

Characteristics

Purpose: Choice presentation from multiple set
Default source name: OptionButton*x*
ProgID: Forms.OptionButton.1
Description: The option button is a dot with a caption that represents a choice that a user may make from a set.

Value property

.VALUE
Represents whether the item has been chosen by the user.

Special properties

.ALIGNMENT
Set to an integer that represents the position of the control's caption relative to its graphic element, where 0 = (Default) left justification; 1 = right.

.CONTROLSOURCE
For Excel VBA, this property is set to a string containing the address of the cell in a worksheet from which the setting for this control's .Value property is to be acquired. If no worksheet is specified within the cell address, then the interpreter assumes the active worksheet; likewise, if no workbook is specified, the interpreter assumes the active workbook. The contents of the designated cell are read in as a Boolean value. The display format of that cell is then automatically changed to Boolean, so that the cell registers **TRUE** or **FALSE**. Any changes made to the value of the option button are immediately reflected in the contents of this cell.

.GROUPNAME
Set at design time to the name of the collection of option buttons to which this control belongs. Setting this option button to True at run-time automatically sets other option buttons that have the same .GroupName property to False.

.PICTURE
A constituent object that represents a valid image file. See example at Command Button for details.

Both picture and caption are only visible when the .AutoSize property for the control is set to True.

.PICTUREPOSITION
Set to an integer code that represents the relationship between the portion of the control where graphics are rendered (the location of the dot) and the portion of the control where text appears.

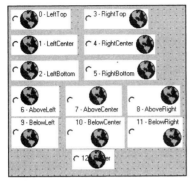

Figure 7-4: Examples of .PicturePosition property settings for an option button.

POSSIBLE SETTINGS

0	Image at left, caption aligned along image's top edge
1	Image at left, caption aligned to vertical center of image
2	Image at left, caption aligned along image's bottom edge
3	Image at right, caption aligned along image's top edge
4	Image at right, caption aligned to vertical center of image
5	Image at right, caption aligned along image's bottom edge
6	Caption at bottom, image aligned along caption's left edge
7	**(Default)** Caption at bottom, image aligned to horizontal center of caption
8	Caption at bottom, image aligned along caption's right edge
9	Caption at top, image aligned along caption's left edge
10	Caption at top, image aligned to horizontal center of caption
11	Caption at top, image aligned along caption's right edge
12	Image in middle, caption atop image in absolute center

.SPECIALEFFECT

Figure 7-5: Examples of .SpecialEffect
property settings for an option button.

Set to an integer code that represents an optional 3D effect for the dot portion, where 0 = flat; 2 (**Default**) = sunken.

.TRIPLESTATE

Figure 7-6: Examples of .TripleState
property settings for an option button.

Set to a Boolean value that represents whether the option button may be set by the user to any of three states, rather than the default (either of two states). The third state, a grayed box referred to as "null," is often used to represent a partial choice rather than a full one, or a state that is only partly in effect (such as text which is underlined only in parts), or a "maybe" choice.

Default setting: False

.WORDWRAP

Set to a Boolean value representing whether words within the control's caption may be allowed to wrap to multiple lines (True setting), or whether text should be forced to stream to the right on one line (False).

Default setting: True

The .WordWrap property setting is best experienced when the .AutoSize property for the option button is also set to True.

The Check Box Control

The check box control is, mechanically speaking, an option button that's been "unplugged." Clicking on an active checkbox does not change the state or contents of any other checkbox or option button anywhere else on the form.

What might not be obvious to the programmer is that the entire control is sensitive to user events; this is true for the option button as well. When the user clicks the caption portion of the control, the control responds as if the user had clicked on the graphical portion. Furthermore, it is the .Width property of the checkbox and the option button that determines the active area of the control, not the length of the text in its caption. Even if the .Width property is set much longer than the textual caption, there is still a transparent area of the control that can be clicked on, and that will trigger the control's _Click event.

Both the option button and the check box maintain _BeforeDragOver and _BeforeDropOrPaste events. It's difficult to imagine dragging text into a check box. If you try it yourself, you'll find you can't get it there no matter how hard you try, nor can you drag text into an option button. However, the _BeforeDragOver events for both controls are functional. If you ever find a reason for doing so (and if you do, please write me, and I'll try to work it into the next edition), you can have your check box or option button respond to text being dragged over it, perhaps by changing its own .Caption setting to reflect the results of the Data.GetText method.

Characteristics

Purpose: Single choice representation
Default source name: Check boxx
ProgID: Forms.Check box.1
Description: The check box control is comprised of a square plus an optional textual label or optional picture. The entire control is sensitive to user events.

Value property

.VALUE
Normally set to a Boolean value that represents whether the box is checked (True) or empty (False). When the .TripleState property of the check box is set to True, a third setting (Null) becomes available, representing a partial choice or "maybe" state.

Special properties

.ALIGNMENT
Set to an integer that represents the position of the control's caption relative to its graphic element, where 0 = (Default) left justification; 1 = right.

.CONTROLSOURCE
For Excel VBA, this property is set to a string containing the address of the cell in a worksheet from which the setting for this control's .Value property is to be acquired. If no worksheet is specified within the cell address, then the interpreter assumes the active worksheet; likewise, if no workbook is specified, the interpreter assumes the active workbook. The contents of the designated cell are read in as a Boolean value. The display format of that cell is then automatically changed to Boolean, so that the cell registers **TRUE** or **FALSE**. Any changes made to the value of the check box are immediately reflected in the contents of this cell.

.GROUPNAME
Set at design time to the name of the collection of check boxes to which this control belongs. Grouping check boxes together doesn't actually affect the operation of any of the boxes individually, since each check box represents an exclusive choice rather than a multiple choice. However, a check box may not belong to the same group as an option button, since the type of choice an option button represents (one of many) is inherently incompatible with the type of choice represented by a check box (either/or).

.PICTURE
A constituent object of class StdPicture that represents a valid image file being maintained and displayed by the control. See Command Button for details.

.PICTUREPOSITION

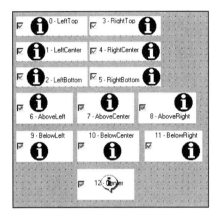

Figure 7-7: Examples of valid `.PicturePosition`
property settings for a check box.

Set to an integer code that represents the relationship between the graphic image for the control (not the box itself, and when present) and its caption. Valid codes are depicted by the sample controls in the accompanying figure, and are identical to the codes listed for the `.PicturePosition` property for the option button.

Default setting: 7 (above horizontal center)

.SPECIALEFFECT

Figure 7-8: Examples of valid `.SpecialEffect`
property settings for a check box.

Set to an integer code that represents an optional 3D effect for the box portion, where 0 = flat; 2 (**Default**) = sunken.

.TRIPLESTATE

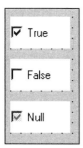

Figure 7-9: Examples of valid .TripleState
property settings for a check box.

Set to a Boolean value that represents whether the check box may be set by the user to any of three states, rather than the default (either of two states). The third state, a grayed box referred to as "null," is often used to represent a partial choice rather than a full one, or a state that is only partly in effect (such as text which is underlined only in parts), or a "maybe" choice. Often this third setting is used to denote a True/False setting for *some*, not all, of a chosen set of elements. Suppose, for example, that a form contains a list of items in inventory. A check box control whose .Caption property is "Available" could be set to Null to indicate that only some of these items are on hand.

Default setting: False

.WORDWRAP

Set to a Boolean value that represents whether words within the checkbox's caption may be allowed to wrap to multiple lines (True setting), or whether text should be forced to stream to the right on one line (False).

Default setting: True

The Scroll Bar Control

The everyday Windows user expects to see a scroll bar control along the right or bottom edge of a window, or along the right (sometimes left) edge of a list box. Indeed, the Forms 2.0 list box and text box controls have the capacity to display their own scroll bars for themselves. But the scroll bar control that is part of the Forms 2.0 ensemble is a stand-alone device whose purpose is entirely up to you to define. It represents a value *state* with respect to a range of possible values.

Characteristics

Purpose: Value selection from set range
Default source name: ScrollBar*x*
ProgID: Forms.ScrollBar.1
Description: The scroll bar represents a range of integer values, where the position of the slider or "thumb" along the bar stands for the value held by the control within that range. Traditionally, the scroll bar is used to position the contents of data within a window; but among Forms 2.0 controls, there exists no such window. In this context, the scroll bar should be used as a range selector.

 For those of you keeping score at home, both the scroll bar control and the spin button maintain their own _BeforeDragOver and _BeforeDrop OrPaste events. Just ignore them. As Roger Miller might have sung, you can't drop text into a scroll bar control.

Value property

.VALUE
Set to an integer that represents the user's choice of values within the set range.

Special properties

.DELAY
Set to an integer that specifies, in milliseconds, a delay interval governing when the scroll bar's _Change event is processed, as the user makes a continuous action with the scroll bar. A continuous action is a click-and-hold over the up or down (or left or right) arrows, or in one of the page change regions between the slider and the arrows. During such behavior, the following behavior is indicated:

- ◆ The first _Change event is always processed immediately.

- ◆ As the user holds down the mouse button, the second _Change event is delayed until five times the specified .Delay interval between the first and second events.

- ◆ The third and all subsequent _Change events are delayed until one .Delay interval has passed.

.LARGECHANGE

Set to an integer value that specifies the amount of change in the scroll bar's .Value that takes place when the user clicks on one of the "page change" regions between the slider bar and the up or down arrow.

Default setting: 1

.ORIENTATION

Set to a value that represents how the scroll bar is to be rendered on screen.

POSSIBLE SETTINGS

-1   **(Default)** Windows determines the best rendering for the scroll bar automatically, depending on its shape

0   Vertical

1   Horizontal

.PROPORTIONALTHUMB

Set to a Boolean value that represents whether the size of the slider box (or "thumb") is to be continually resized at run time to represent (very roughly) the .Value property's share of the entire range. For instance, a scroll bar for a range of 10,000 units contains a slider that is smaller than for a scroll bar for a range of six units. Figure 7-10 depicts a proportionally sized slider, whose slider box represents approximately one-third of the total or amount represented by the slide area between the arrows.

Default setting: True

Figure 7-10: Here, the "thumb" represents "one-third," relative to the scroll bar's height.

Conventionally, the proportional slider is used to represent the ratio of a window's length or width to that of the document the window is displaying. Because we are not using scroll bars in this context, the .Proportional Thumb property has a slightly different purpose: to represent the size of $1/n$, where *n* is the range of the scroll bar.

.SMALLCHANGE

Set to an integer value that specifies the amount of change in the scroll bar's .Value that takes place when the user clicks on the up or down arrow. Usually, this is a smaller value than that set for the "page change" regions of the scroll bar.

Default setting: 1

Unique event

_SCROLL

Occurs whenever the slider is moved within the scroll bar either directly by the user or indirectly through another region of the scroll bar. The scroll bar's .Value property is updated when _Scroll is recognized.

When a scroll takes place, the change of value for the scroll bar — and thus the _Change event — takes place only once, whereas the _Scroll event takes place while the scroll bar is being repositioned. More accurately, it takes place whenever the graphics system re-renders the control. Thus a faster system may recognize the _Scroll event more times than a slower system for the same scroll action.

The Spin Button Control

The spin button is essentially a small, slimmed down version of a scroll bar. Its purpose is to act as a two-part button, one part up, one part down. It's designed to give the user a means to increment (add 1 to) or decrement (take 1 away from) a value, which is maintained by some other independent variable. Generally, the value of this variable is depicted elsewhere onscreen by a label or text box control. The text box would give the user an alternative way to enter the value, and the _Before Update event procedure for the text box could be used to validate the data in the text box. But the `_SpinUp` and `_SpinDown` events of the spin button would also be used to replace the text box contents with updated, valid data.

Characteristics

Purpose: Value incrementation/decrementation
Default source name: `SpinButton`*x*
ProgID: `Forms.SpinButton.1`
Description: The spin button gives the user a means to increment or decrement a value. This value is maintained by the control internally, though not displayed by it; usually another control echoes its value.

Value property

.VALUE
Represents the value being maintained by the control.

Special properties

.CONTROLSOURCE
For Excel VBA, this property is set to a string containing the address of the cell in a worksheet from which the setting for this control's `.Value` property is to be acquired. If no worksheet is specified within the cell address, then the interpreter assumes the active worksheet; likewise, if no workbook is specified, the interpreter assumes the active workbook. The contents of the designated cell must be numeric for the cell to be accepted as the spin button's control source. Any changes made to the value of the spin button are immediately reflected in the contents of this cell.

.DELAY
Set to an integer that specifies, in milliseconds, a delay interval governing when the spin button's `_Change` event is processed, as the user holds down its down or up arrow (or right or left arrow). See the `.Delay` property of the scroll bar control for details.

.MAX
Set to a long integer representing the maximum `.Value` property to be maintained by the spin button.

.MIN
Set to a long integer representing the minimum `.Value` property to be maintained by the spin button.

.ORIENTATION
Set to a value that represents how the spin button is to be rendered on screen.
Possible settings

-1   **(Default)** Windows determines the best rendering for the spin button automatically, depending on its shape

0   Vertical

1   Horizontal

.SMALLCHANGE
Set to an integer value that specifies the amount of change in the spin button's .Value setting that takes place when the user clicks on the up or down arrow.
   Default setting: 1

Unique events

_SPINDOWN
Occurs when the user clicks on the down (or left) arrow of the spin button. This results in a subtraction, in the amount of .SmallChange, to the control's .Value property.

_SPINUP
Occurs when the user clicks on the up (or right) arrow of the spin button. This results in an addition, in the amount of .SmallChange, to the control's .Value property.

The Toggle Button Control

The toggle button is the key element in the construction of a makeshift toolbar. It looks, and to some degree behaves, like a standard command button, except that it maintains a *state*. In programming terms, it's a Boolean state, which is a "true/false" or "on/off" condition. Generally a row of these toggle buttons are used to symbolize a single "on" selection from a choice or range, not unlike the option button control (discussed earlier in this chapter). The toggle button's Boolean state is maintained by its .Value property and is an indicator of whether the button is pushed in or out. Although it resembles an ordinary command button, the toggle button also serves as an indicator of some *bit*, literally, of data.

Characteristics

Purpose: Boolean state representation
Default source name: ToggleButton*x*
ProgID: Forms.ToggleButton.1
Description: The toggle button appears like a command button, but rather than represent a command to the program, it represents a Boolean state to the user (and the program in turn). A Boolean state is a "true/false" or "on/off" condition. The button represents this by appearing graphically to have an "in" or "out" position.

Value property

.VALUE
Set to a Boolean value that represents the state of the button.

Special properties

.CONTROLSOURCE
For Excel VBA, this property is set to a string containing the address of the cell in a worksheet from which the setting for this control's .Value property is to be acquired. If no worksheet is specified within the cell address, then the interpreter assumes the active worksheet; likewise, if no workbook is specified, the interpreter assumes the active workbook. The contents of the designated cell are read in as a Boolean value. The display format of that cell is then automatically changed to Boolean, so that the cell registers **TRUE** or **FALSE**. Any changes made to the value of the toggle button are immediately reflected in the contents of this cell.

.PICTURE
A constituent object of class StdPicture that represents a valid image file being maintained by the toggle button. See Command Button for details.

.PICTUREPOSITION
Set to an integer code that represents the relationship between the graphic image for the control (not the box itself, and when present) and its caption. (See Command Button for valid settings and examples.)
   Default setting: 7 (above center)

.TRIPLESTATE
Set to a Boolean value that represents whether the toggle button can be set by the user to any of three states, rather than the default (either of two states). The third state (Null) is often used to represent a partial choice rather than a full one, or a state that is only partly in effect (such as text that is underlined only in parts), or a

"maybe" choice. For the toggle button, a null state is represented by the button being "out," but its text being grayed.

Figure 7-11: Examples of valid `.TripleState` property settings for a toggle button.

Default setting: `False`

.WORDWRAP
Set to a Boolean value that represents whether words within the toggle button's caption may be allowed to wrap to multiple lines (`True` setting), or whether text should be forced to stream to the right on one line (`False`).
Default setting: `True`

The Image Control

The Forms 2.0 image control is not to be confused with the Picture box control in Visual Basic Standard Edition. The picture box is like a little graphics terminal, and recognizes methods that can draw graphics directly to the control like a little plotting pen with ink. The image control, though it has the same icon in the VBA Toolbox window as the Picture box has in the Visual Basic window, is not nearly as richly endowed. It is basically a vehicle for displaying graphics files.

In addition to the usual .BMP format, the image control can show .GIF and .JPG images, which are the two most common formats today. In addition, the image control supports some of Windows' other formats: .WMF, .CUR, and .ICO. Yet the command button, label, option button, checkbox, and toggle button can all also display these formats; so what is the true purpose of the image control? It has a lower overhead than the other controls for displaying an image as a backdrop or a decoration, if that is all you require. The image control does, however, support `_Click` and `_DblClick` events, if you ever feel an urge to do something with them.

If you need for your displayed image to be scrollable or "zoomable" in or out, you should use the frame control instead. The frame is somewhat more versatile than the image control (as our example in Chapter 6 demonstrated), but has a greater overhead. But since the frame control's main purpose in life is to draw a box around other controls, and overhead doesn't seem to be much of a factor there, issues of conservation can probably go out the window with your 386 computer as you're deciding whether to use a frame. Use an image control when you need your image to remain right where it is, and look exactly as it does at startup throughout the form module's run time.

Characteristics

Purpose: Display of stored, bitmapped image
ProgID: Forms.Image.1
Default source name: Imagex
Description: The Image control acts as a frame for the display of a graphic image from a file, and is not sensitive to user input.

Value property

The image control does not support a value property.

Special properties

.PICTURE
A constituent object of class StdPicture representing the picture contained by the label control. Image formats supported are .BMP (Windows bitmap); .ICO (Windows icon); .CUR (Windows mouse pointer image); .WMF (Windows metafile); .GIF (GIF89a); and .JPG or .JPEG (JPEG).Constituent properties

.Height   The height in twips (1/1440 inch) of the contained image.

.Width   The width in twips of the contained image.

 An image file may be assigned to the .Picture property at run time using the LoadPicture() function, whose single argument is the path of an image file, and whose return value is a StdPicture class object.

.PICTUREALIGNMENT
Set at design time to an integer that represents how the interior image stated by the .Picture property setting is to be positioned with respect to the border of the control.

POSSIBLE SETTINGS

0   Picture is aligned against the upper left corner of the control

1   Picture is aligned against the upper right corner of the control

2   (Default) Picture is centered with respect to the control

3   Picture is aligned against the lower left corner of the control

4   Picture is aligned against the lower right corner of the control

.PICTURESIZEMODE

An integer value that denotes how the image control is to treat the sizing of its interior picture, referred to by its .Picture property. By default, the graphics file is rendered in its native size; though this property permits you to use the image control's own size to designate the size of the interior picture.

POSSIBLE SETTINGS

0   (Default) Does not change the pixel mapping of the interior picture with respect to the control. Any overhang by the picture is cropped.

1   Stretches or shrinks the picture to fit the edges of the control, however much the picture might have to be distorted.

3   Enlarges or reduces the size of the picture, proportionately, so that it consumes as much of the control as possible *without* distorting the picture.

.PICTURETILING

A Boolean value that represents whether the image control is permitted to repeat the contained picture, pointed to by its .Picture property setting. When .PictureTiling is set to True, the entire image control is filled with one or more instances of the picture, repeated horizontally and vertically like floor tile.

   Default setting: False

 If the .PictureSizeMode property is set to 1, the .PictureTiling property will have no obvious effect on the control.

The List Box Control

The list box is a scrollable sequence of entries that allows the user to choose usually one item. Generally the list box is tall enough to show multiple entries; but in some cases, to save space, the list box is only one entry tall. In such a case, a little scroll bar pops up along the right side, letting the user move the list up and down, one entry at a time. The entry that remains showing is then treated as the user's chosen entry.

Characteristics

Purpose: List presentation with single or multiple choice
ProgID: `Forms.ListBox.1`
Default source name: `ListBoxx`
Description: The list box is a scrollable sequence of entries, which allows the user to choose usually one item, sometimes multiple items.

Value property

.TEXT
Represents the text of the current, or most recent, choice in the list, or `Null` if no entry is chosen.

Special properties

.BORDERSTYLE
Set to a Boolean value representing whether a single-pixel-width line is placed around the control.

.BORDERCOLOR
When `.BorderStyle` is `True`, `.BorderColor` is set to a code representing the color given to the control's border. A code beginning with 8 represents a lookup from the client's current Control Panel settings.

.BOUNDCOLUMN
Indicates the column from which the current value (`.Text` property) of a multi-column list box is located, where 0 is the index for the first column. In other words, when a row represents one choice, and that row contains multiple columns, this property represents what part of the row constitutes "the chosen item."

.COLUMN

Used by an expression in the script to assign text to a multi-column list box (whose .ColumnCount property is set to greater than 1). As an array, .Column() can be assigned the contents of a two-dimensional string array by way of an expression.

ARGUMENTS

Column:, Row: Coordinates for the cell in the list box where .Column(0, 0) refers to the cell in the upper left corner, and .Column(0, 1) refers to the cell to its immediate *right*.

.COLUMNCOUNT

Figure 7-12: A list box showing multiple columns —
so many that the horizontal scroll bar is on.

Set to the number of columns in the list box. A multiple column list box might appear like the one shown in Figure 7-12.

Default setting: 1

.COLUMNHEADS

For Excel VBA, this property is set to a Boolean value representing whether a multi-column list box is to display headings over all columns. For column headings to work properly, the .RowSource property for the list box must be set to a valid range. This is because the list box will acquire its column headings from the contents of the corresponding cells in the row just above the range pointed to by .RowSource.

Default setting: False

.COLUMNWIDTHS

Set to a string which specifies the width of each column in the list box. For a multi-column list box, this string may consist of the width amounts for each column, represented as single-precision numbers, separated from one another by semicolons (;). As an example, 72;36;36;72 would set a four-column list box so that its columns are 1 inch, 1/2 inch, 1/2 inch, and 1 inch wide, respectively. For a three-column list box given this same setting, the fourth part would be ignored; for a five-column list box or greater, those columns following the fourth would be given the default width of 72 points (1 inch).

For each column specified in this property setting, the unit of measurement is presumed to be points (1/72 inch) unless another unit of measurement is specified. Valid abbreviations for units of measurement are as follows:

pt   Points (1/72 inch)

cm   Centimeters (1 cm = 28.35 pt)

in   Inches

So for a three-column list box, a `.ColumnWidths` setting of `36 pt;2 cm;1 in` would set the columns to 36 points, 56.7 points, and 72 points, respectively. Settings made to this property at design time are all converted to points automatically.

.CONTROLSOURCE

For Excel VBA, this property is set to a string containing the address of the cell in a worksheet from which the setting for this control's value property (`.Text`) is to be acquired. If no worksheet is specified within the cell address, then the interpreter assumes the active worksheet; likewise, if no workbook is specified, the interpreter assumes the active workbook. The interpreter will search down the list until it locates an entry that matches the text of this cell. The first matching entry located will be automatically chosen when the form starts up; otherwise, its `.Text` property will be set to `Null`. Any choice made from this list will immediately be reflected in the contents of the designated cell.

.INTEGRALHEIGHT

Set to a Boolean value that denotes whether the height of the control is automatically resized to fit the *exact* height of text lines in their entirety.
Possible settings

0   A line of text at the bottom of the control may be partly obscured by the lower edge of the control.

1   A line of text that would otherwise be partly obscured by the bottom edge of the control, is totally hidden by that edge, which is resized upward to fit only whole lines.

.LIST

Used by an expression in the script to assign text to a list in a list box. As an array, `.List()` can be assigned the contents of a string array by way of an expression.

ARGUMENTS

Row: Index of the row of the list box being addressed, where 0 is the top row.

Column: (Optional) Index of the column of the list box being addressed, if the combo is multi-column. `.List(0, 0)` refers to the cell in the upper-left corner, and `.List(1, 0)` refers to the cell to its immediate right.

For a two-dimensional array and multicolumn list box, `.List` works similarly to `.Column`, although the order of the coordinate pair is reversed.

.LISTINDEX

Used at run time to reference the index of the currently chosen entry in the combo box list, where 0 is the first entry in the list.

.LISTSTYLE

Figure 7-13: A list box featuring the optional option dots, where `.ListStyle = True`.

Set to a Boolean value that represents whether each row contains an option dot along the left side, like the example in Figure 7-13.

.MATCHENTRY

Set to an integer value that specifies which entry in the list is highlighted as the user types characters while the list box has the focus.

POSSIBLE SETTINGS

0   **(Default)** When the user types the first character of the text field, the control searches from the top down for the first entry it sees that begins with the typed character. When this entry is found, the control highlights that field.

1   Same initial behavior as for 0, though the control continues to fetch the first item from the list that matches what is being typed, and highlights that field as typing proceeds.

2   Control does not react to typing.

.MULTISELECT

Set to an integer value that represents whether the user may choose one or more than one item in the list box.

POSSIBLE SETTINGS

0   (**Default**) Only one entry from the list may be chosen.

1   More than one entry may be chosen from the list, by clicking on that entry once, or by using the arrow keys to move the focus around that entry, then pressing the space bar.

2   More than one entry may be chosen from the list, using the mouse, using the arrow keys and space bar, by holding down the Ctrl key while clicking to choose individual items, or by holding down Shift while clicking to choose all entries between the location of the focus (the dotted marquis that surrounds a list entry) and the entry that was clicked on.

.ROWSOURCE

For Excel VBA, this property is set at design time to a string containing a valid Excel range address. This address points to the rows where data filling the list box will be acquired. As an example, for a five-column list box, a setting of $B$4:$F$16 will set the list box so that, at startup, it automatically contains a copy of the data in that range of the worksheet that is active at the time the form module commenced. By comparison, a .RowSource setting of $4:$16 will set the list box to acquire its data from rows 4 through 16 of the active Excel worksheet. Data acquisition will begin with column A, and will proceed for as many worksheet columns as there are columns in the list box.

.SELECTED

Addressed as an array, .Selected is set at run time to a Boolean value that indicates whether a specified item in the list has been chosen by the user.

ARGUMENT

integer   An index that corresponds to the .ListIndex setting for the list entry, where 0 is the first entry in the list. This index acts as a subscript for .Selected, as though it were an array. When the user chooses an item from the list, its corresponding index in the .Selected array will be set to True. This is the case for multiple selections from a list box whose .MultiSelect property has been set to True. (Not a named argument.)

EXAMPLE

```
If lstJobs.Selected(i) Then
  strJ = lstJobs.List(i)
End If
```

Here, `lstJobs` is a list box, `strJ` is a string variable that will receive the text of the chosen item from the list box, and `i` is a counter variable in a loop.

.SPECIALEFFECT

Set to an integer value representing the style of frame given to the list box.

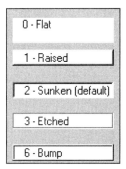

Figure 7-14: Examples of valid `.SpecialEffect` property settings for a list box.

POSSIBLE SETTINGS

0   Flat; no special treatment is given to the surrounding frame

1   Raised; the control appears to stand out from the form

2   **(Default)** Sunken; the control appears to be recessed into the form

3   Etched; a thin line appears to be etched into the perimeter of the control

6   "Bump;" a thin line appears to have been etched from the inside out, surrounding the control

.TEXTCOLUMN

For a multi-column list box, `.TextColumn` may be set to the number of the column from which text is to be returned to the list box's `.Text` property when an entry is chosen by the user. For this property, the first column is column 1, not column 0 (like it is everywhere else). When `.TextColumn` is set to -1 **(Default)**, the list box will not search particular columns for a .Text property – essentially the same as a setting of 1.

Associated methods

.ADDITEM

Assigns the string contents to a new entry at the bottom of the list maintained by the list box or, when specified, at a particular list index, moving the entries that follow it down one position.

ARGUMENTS

Item: Text of the entry being added to the list

VarIndex: **(Optional)** Location where the entry is to be added, where 0 is the first entry in the list.

The .AddItem and .RemoveItem methods are intended for use exclusively with single-column list boxes.

.CLEAR

Removes all entries from the list box.

.REMOVEITEM

Removes the entry with the specified index from the list box; all entries that follow it are moved up one position.

The Combo Box Control

The combo box is a fairly sophisticated control. Functionally, it allows the user to choose an item from the list or to type an entry manually into the text field. Mechanically, however, the combo box is like a miniature client-side database manager. It has all the elements of a flat-form DBMS: a records format (multiple columns with heads), database filling using an internal cursor (the .AddItem method), random access (through the .List() or .Column() array), direct reference access (through the .ListIndex property), and a key field (.BoundColumn). It's missing internal sorting – a feature that the combo boxes in the Visual Basic

Standard Edition have, but which for some reason was dropped in Forms 2.0. Yet all in all, it qualifies as a flat-form database, plus it adds the benefits of ease of use — that is, if your definition of "ease-of-use" was conceived by Rube Goldberg.

Characteristics

Purpose: List choice with editable entry
ProgID: `Forms.ComboBox.1`
Default source name: `ComboBox.r`
Description: The combo box is a drop-down list combined with an editable text field. It allows the user to choose an item from the list or to type an entry manually into the text field.

Value property

.TEXT
Represents the current selection, which may or may not mirror one of the entries in the list.

Special properties

.AUTOTAB
Set to a Boolean value that specifies whether the focus will proceed to the next control in the tab stop sequence of the form, when the user has entered more than the maximum number of characters (as set by the `.MaxLength` property) into the combo box's text field.

.AUTOWORDSELECT
Set to a Boolean value that represents a cursor behavior for the text field portion of the combo box. When `.AutoWordSelect` is set to `True`, if the text field contains more than one word, and the user places the cursor *inside* one of the words, and then drags the pointer to beyond the space at either end of that word, the highlighter will automatically extend itself to encompass the entire text.

.BORDERSTYLE
Set to a Boolean value that represents whether a single-pixel-width line is placed around the control.

.BORDERCOLOR
When `.BorderStyle` is set to `True`, `.BorderColor` is set to a code representing the color given to the control's border. A code beginning with 8 represents a lookup from the client's current Control Panel settings.

.BOUNDCOLUMN

Indicates the column in which the current value (.Text property) of a multicolumn combo box is located, where 0 is the index for the first column.

.COLUMN

Used by an expression in the script to assign text to a multi-column combo box (whose .ColumnCount property is set to greater than 1). As an array, .Column() can be assigned the contents of a two-dimensional string array by way of an expression.

ARGUMENTS

Column:, Row:	Coordinates for the cell in the combo box, where .Column(0, 0) refers to the cell in the upper left corner and .Column(0, 1) refers to the cell to its immediate right.

.COLUMNCOUNT

Set to the number of columns in the combo box.
   Default setting: 1

.COLUMNHEADS

For Excel VBA, this property is set to a Boolean value representing whether a multi-column combo box is to display headings over all columns in the drop-down portion. For column headings to work properly, the .RowSource property for the combo box must be set to a valid range. This is because the combo box will acquire its column headings from the contents of the corresponding cells in the row just above the range pointed to by .RowSource.**Default setting:** False

.COLUMNWIDTHS

Set to a string that specifies the width of each column in the drop-down portion of the combo box. See List Box for details.

.CONTROLSOURCE

For Excel VBA, this property is set to a string containing the address of the cell in a worksheet from which this control's value property setting (.Text) is to be acquired. If no worksheet is specified within the cell address, then the interpreter assumes the active worksheet; likewise, if no workbook is specified, the interpreter assumes the active workbook. The interpreter will search down the entries in the list until it locates one that matches the text of the designated cell. The first matching entry located will be automatically chosen in the list when the form starts up. Whether or not a matching entry is located, the combo box's .Text property will be set to the contents of the cell. Any choice made from the drop-down list portion or typed into the text field portion will immediately be reflected in the contents of the designated cell.

If the .MatchRequired property for a combo box is set to True, the combo box will acquire its startup data from the cell designated by the .ControlSource property setting, even if that data does not match any entry in the drop-down list portion.

.DRAGBEHAVIOR

Set to a Boolean value that represents whether the client may make use of drag-and-drop to move blocks of text within the text field portion of the combo box.

Default setting: False

.DROPBUTTONSTYLE

Set to an integer value that represents the contents of the drop-down button.

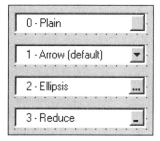

Figure 7-15: Examples of valid .DropButtonStyle settings for a combo box.

POSSIBLE SETTINGS

0   Plain

1   (**Default**) Down-arrow

2   Ellipsis

3   "Minimize" box

.ENTERFIELDBEHAVIOR

Set to a Boolean value that represents whether the textual contents of the field are automatically highlighted when the focus enters the text field portion of the combo box.

Default setting: True (text is highlighted)

.HIDESELECTION
Set to a Boolean value that represents whether highlighted text is to remain high-lighted when the focus leaves the control.
   Default setting: False

.LIST
Used by an expression in the script to assign text to a combo box. As an array, .List() can be assigned the contents of a string array by way of an expression.

ARGUMENTS

row   Index of the row of the combo box being addressed; 0 is the top row. (Not a named argument.)

column   **(Optional)** Index of the column of the combo box being addressed, if the combo is multicolumn..List(0, 0) refers to the cell in the upper-left corner and .List(1, 0) refers to the cell to its immediate right. (Not a named argument.)

> For a two-dimensional array and multicolumn combo box, .List works similarly to .Column, although the order of the coordinate pair is reversed. Also, because this term is a property and not a procedure call, you cannot *name* the arguments using the Name:=value syntax. Since there are only two arguments anyway, this shouldn't be a problem.

.LISTCOUNT
Set at run time to the number of entries in the combo box list; or more accurately, to the number of rows in the list, counting column heads. .ListCount is not reliable in multi-column lists.

.LISTINDEX
Used at run time to reference the index of the currently selected entry in the combo box list.

.LISTROWS
Set to the maximum number of rows the combo box will display before placing a vertical scroll bar along the right of the list.
   Default setting: 8

.LISTSTYLE

Set to a Boolean value that represents whether each row contains an option dot along the left side, as depicted in Figure 7-16.

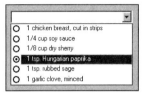

Figure 7-16: A combo box whose choices
feature the optional option dots.

.LISTWIDTH

When set to a nonzero value, .ListWidth represents the maximum width of the drop-down list portion of the combo box in linear points. Be careful to leave enough room for the text of your longest list entry so as to avoid a situation such as that shown in Figure 7-17.

Figure 7-17: A combo box whose
.ListWidth is less than its .Width.

.MATCHENTRY

Set to an integer value that specifies the behavior of the text field portion of the combo box as the user types characters.

POSSIBLE SETTINGS

0   When the user types the first character of the text field, the combo box searches from the top down for the first entry it sees that begins with the typed character. Upon finding this entry, the combo writes the entire entry to the text field.

1   (**Default**) Same initial behavior as for 0, though the combo box will continue to fetch items from the list and write them to the text field as typing proceeds.

2   Combo box will not react to typing in the text field.

.MATCHFOUND

(Read-only) Set at run time by the interpreter to a Boolean value that represents whether the contents of the text field of the combo box matches one of the items in its list.

.MATCHREQUIRED

Set to a Boolean value that represents whether the contents of the combo box's text field must correspond to the text of one of the entries in the list.

 In essence, a combo box that requires such a match is an overgrown standard list box. When the text field doesn't match one of the entries, the combo box brings up an error dialog "Invalid property value," which is not only annoying and condescending, but potentially meaningless to a user more likely to associate "property value" with real estate.

.MAXLENGTH

When set to a non-zero value, .MaxLength represents the maximum number of characters allowed to be typed into the combo box's text field.

.ROWSOURCE

For Excel VBA, this property is set at design time to a string containing a valid Excel range address. This address points to the rows where data filling the list box will be acquired. As an example, for a five-column list box, a setting of $B$4:$F$16 will set the list box so that, at startup, it automatically contains a copy of the data in that range of the worksheet that is active at the time the form module commenced. By comparison, a .RowSource setting of $4:$16 will set the list box to acquire its data from rows 4 through 16 of the active Excel worksheet. Data acquisition will begin with column A, and will proceed for as many worksheet columns as there are columns in the list box.

.SELECTIONMARGIN

Set to a Boolean value that indicates whether a mouse click just to the left of text in the text field will result in the entire text field being highlighted.
   Default setting: True

.SELLENGTH

Set at run time to the number of characters currently highlighted within the text field portion of the combo box.

.SELSTART

Set at run time to the index position of the first character of text currently high-lighted within the text field portion of the combo box, where 0 refers to the first character.

.SELTEXT

Set at run time to the text currently highlighted within the text field portion of the combo box.

.SHOWDROPBUTTONWHEN

Set to an integer value that represents the circumstances under which the down-arrow button is displayed.

POSSIBLE SETTINGS

0   Down button is *never* shown

1   Down button is only shown when the combo box has the focus

2   (Default) Down button is always shown

    With setting 0, the list itself never actually drops down. Instead, the user flips through entries in the list using the up and down arrow keys.

.SPECIALEFFECT

Set to an integer value that represents the style of frame given to the combo box.

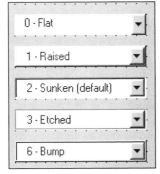

Figure 7-18: Examples of valid `.SpecialEffect` property settings for a combo box.

POSSIBLE SETTINGS

0   Flat; no special treatment is given to the surrounding frame

1   Raised; the combo control appears to stand out from the form

2   **(Default)** Sunken; the control appears to be recessed into the form

3   Etched; a thin line appears to be etched into the perimeter of the control

6   "Bump;" a thin line appears to have been etched from the inside out

 The effects of being "raised" or "sunken" are achieved by a consistent play of light throughout the Windows front end; controls appear to be lighted from the upper left, and cast shadows to the lower right.

.STYLE
Set to an integer value that represents the behavior of the combo box.

POSSIBLE SETTINGS

0   **(Default)** The choice line at the top of the combo box is editable to any value by the user.

2   The choice line is not editable; and besides the presence of a choice line, the combo acts as a standard list box.

.TEXTCOLUMN
For a multi-column combo box, `.TextColumn` is set to the number of the column from which text is to be returned to the combo box's `.Text` property when a row is chosen by the user.

Unique event

_DROPBUTTONCLICK
Occurs when the user clicks on the combo box's drop-down button, as well as when the user chooses an item from the list.

Associated methods

.ADDITEM
Assigns the string contents to a new entry at the bottom of the combo box's list or, when specified, at a particular list index, moving the entries that follow it down one position.

ARGUMENTS

Item: Text of the entry being added to the list.

VarIndex: (Optional) Location where the entry is to be added, where 0 is the first entry in the list.

 The .AddItem and .RemoveItem methods are intended for use exclusively with single-column combo boxes.

.CLEAR
Removes all entries from the combo box list.

.COPY
Copies the highlighted text, if any, to the Windows System Clipboard.

.CUT
Cuts the highlighted text, if any, from the control and stores it in the Windows System Clipboard.

.DROPDOWN
Forces the combo box's drop-down list to display; or, if it's already visible, dismisses the list.

.PASTE
Recalls text stored on the Windows System Clipboard and places it in the text field portion of the combo box at the current cursor position, replacing any highlighted text.

.REMOVEITEM
Removes the entry with the specified index from the combo box's list; all entries that follow it are moved up one position.

In Depth: Binding Forms 2.0 controls to Excel worksheet cells

If you were to use VBA instructions to load a Forms 2.0 list box or combo box with contents from an Excel 2000 worksheet, you could generate quite a bit of source code. One of the least appreciated features of Forms 2.0 controls is their inherent capability to borrow their own contents from devices from worksheets without the need for explicit VBA instructions. (This feature is perhaps unappreciated because it hasn't entirely worked until just recently.)

A simple link may be established between one of many Forms 2.0 controls and a worksheet cell by setting the .ControlSource property of the control to the address of the cell. The cell in question cannot just be any cell. It is either a cell in the active worksheet (if a worksheet isn't explicitly specified by name), or a cell in the worksheet named in the cell address. Here, you are providing *Excel* with the name of the cell, not VBA; so you can't rely upon O2K collection objects such as the Workbooks, Worksheets, or Windows collection to give you access to "the fifth worksheet" or "the worksheet in the fourth open window."

Leaving the name of the worksheet out of the cell address for the .ControlSource property setting is dangerous, because a form module is associated with the whole workbook, not just one worksheet. The only way to ensure the identity of the active worksheet when a form module starts up is to write an instruction like Sheet1.Activate in the Private Sub UserForm_Initialize() event procedure. But even then, it will be too late for the form module whose .ControlSource property was set at design time, because the source's contents will already have been read by the time the _Initialize event procedure begins execution. The VBA interpreter will allow an instruction within the _Initialize event procedure that sets the .ControlSource property to a string containing the cell address, at the form's run time subsequent to activating the named worksheet. It will allow the instruction, but it will be meaningless—it won't work, and it won't generate an error condition stating that it didn't work. The .ControlSource property should only be set at design time, because although runtime settings are allowed, they are also ignored. So whichever cell you choose for the .ControlSource setting, make certain that it can be addressed using Excel's cell reference format.

The .RowSource property was built into the list box and combo box controls explicitly for use with Excel. At design time, it is set to an (explicit) address of the worksheet range whose contents are to be copied into the control at startup. This process is far preferable to setting up a .List() array. The same cautions apply to

Continued

> ## In Depth: Binding Forms 2.0 controls to Excel worksheet cells *(Continued)*
>
> `.RowSource` as for `.ControlSource`; the workbook and worksheet should be named in the address whenever possible, and the setting should be made at the form's design time. Be advised, though, that the relationship between `.RowSource` and the worksheet is, unlike `.ControlSource`, one-way; no changes can be made to the list contents of a list box or combo box that affect the contents of the worksheet. More accurately, no changes can be made to the list contents at all as long as `.RowSource` is valid; settings to the `.List()` array for the control are disallowed in this case.

The Frame Control

The frame control is primarily a transparent container of other controls, almost like a miniature form. It consists of a thin border supplemented by a caption along its upper edge. When you drag a new control onto a frame at design time, it "sticks" to that frame because it truly is contained by the frame. The new control's `.Left` and `.Top` properties contain coordinates that are stated with respect to the *frame*, not the form. When you cut a control from a form and paste it onto the frame, the pasted control also sticks to the frame.

By virtue of the `.ScrollHeight` and `.ScrollWidth` properties — which are also supported by `UserForm`, as you saw demonstrated in Chapter 6 — a frame on a form can now act as its own miniature window, complete with horizontal and vertical scroll bars. You can attach a control to a frame that is actually far larger than the frame itself, and then let the user scroll through the contents of the frame using its built-in scroll bars. Then, you could build another control that changes the magnification factor of the frame — perhaps a spin button with a text box. The magnification is easily maintained by means of the frame control's `.Zoom` property.

Characteristics

Purpose: Control compartmentalization
ProgID: `Forms.Frame.1`
Default source name: `Framex`
Description: The frame acts as a labeled lasso around a set of controls within a dialog box. It also serves as a container for those controls in such a way that Windows registers those controls as "belonging" to the frame rather than to the `UserForm` object containing the frame.

Special properties

.ACTIVECONTROL
An object reference to the control contained by the frame that currently has the focus.

.BORDERCOLOR
A code that represents the color that the interpreter assigns to the perimeter of the frame. This setting is meaningful to the user only if the `.BorderStyle` property is set to 1 (single line).

.BORDERSTYLE
An integer flag that denotes whether a separate border is to be given to the frame.

POSSIBLE SETTINGS

0   No border is drawn for the frame.

1   **(Default)** The frame is given a single border line, whose color is defined by the current `.BorderColor` property setting.

.CANPASTE
Set at run time to a Boolean value that denotes whether the controls in the frame may receive the data that currently resides on the Windows System Clipboard.

.CANREDO
Set at run time to a Boolean value that denotes, as long as the frame's `.CanUndo` property is set to `True`, whether the frame may record *undone* user actions so that they may be *redone* at the user's request. For a redo to take place, a VBA instruction must be implemented using the `.RedoAction` method for the frame.

.CANUNDO
Set at run time to a Boolean value that represents whether the frame is to record user actions so that they may be undone at the user's request. For an undo to take place, a VBA instruction must be implemented using the `.UndoAction` method for the frame.

.CYCLE
A flag value that denotes the behavior of the Tab key with regard to moving the focus along the objects in the frame's own independent tab-stop sequence.

POSSIBLE SETTINGS

0   (**Default**) Designates that the focus should move to the next control following the frame in the *form's* tab-stop sequence after it has reached the final control in the *frame's* sequence and the user has pressed Tab again.

2   Designates that the focus should always move to the first control in the frame's tab-stop sequence when the focus has reached the final control in that sequence and the user has pressed Tab again. The user would need to use the mouse to move the focus *out* of the frame.

.INSIDEHEIGHT
(**Read-only**) Set at run-time to the distance in points (1 point = $^1/_{72}$ inch), between the upper and lower edges of the frame, without taking the frame border into account.

.INSIDEWIDTH
(**Read-only**) Set at run time to the distance in points between the left and right edges of the frame, without taking the frame border into account.

.KEEPSCROLLBARSVISIBLE
An integer value that represents whether the frame continues to display scroll bars, even when the visible area of the frame mandates that either or both scroll bars are unnecessary. For this property to be meaningful, the .ScrollBars property must be set so that the corresponding scroll bars *can* be visible; with .ScrollBars set to 0, no scroll bars may be made visible.

POSSIBLE SETTINGS

0   Allows both scroll bars to be made invisible if the contents of the frame fit within its borders

1   Maintains the horizontal scroll bar for the frame at all times

2   Maintains the vertical scroll bar for the frame at all times

3   (**Default**) Maintains both scroll bars for the frame at all times

.PICTURE
A constituent object that represents a valid image file. See example at Command Button for details..PictureAlignment

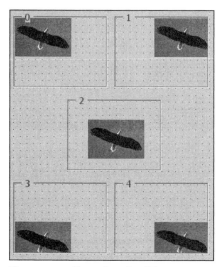

Figure 7-19: Examples of valid .PictureAlignment
property settings for frame controls.

Set at design time to an integer that represents how the interior image stated by
the .Picture property setting is to be positioned with respect to the border of the
frame.

POSSIBLE SETTINGS

0   Picture is aligned against the upper left corner of the frame

1   Picture is aligned against the upper right corner of the frame

2   (Default) Picture is centered with respect to the frame

3   Picture is aligned against the lower left corner of the frame

4   Picture is aligned against the lower right corner of the frame

.PICTURESIZEMODE
An integer value that denotes how the frame is to treat the sizing of the interior
picture referred to by the .Picture property. By default, the picture is rendered in
its native size, though this property permits you to use the frame's own size to designate the size of the picture.

POSSIBLE SETTINGS

0   (Default) Does not change the pixel mapping of the interior picture with respect to the frame. Any overhang by the picture is cropped.

1   Stretches or shrinks the picture to fit the edges of the frame, however much the picture might have to be distorted.

3   Enlarges or reduces the size of the picture, proportionately, so that it consumes as much of the frame as possible *without* distorting the image.

.PICTURETILING

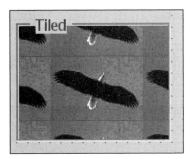

Figure 7-20: This frame's .PictureTiling setting is True while .PictureAlignment is centered.

A Boolean value that represents whether the frame is permitted to repeat the contained image pointed to by its .Picture property setting. When set to True, the entire frame is filled with one or more instances of the image, repeated horizontally and vertically like floor tile.
Default setting: False

If the .PictureSizeMode property is set to 1, the .PictureTiling property will have no obvious effect on the frame.

.SCROLLBARS

An integer value that denotes which scroll bars the frame is capable of displaying when its contents exceed the frame's boundaries.

POSSIBLE SETTINGS

0   (**Default**) Scroll bars are never displayed

1   Horizontal scroll bar is displayed if text exceeds the right boundary

2   Vertical scroll bar is displayed if text exceeds the lower boundary

3   Either or both scroll bars are displayed when necessary

.SCROLLHEIGHT

When set to a non-zero value, .ScrollHeight specifies, in twips (not points), the vertical distance between the upper and lower borders of the frame. When this value exceeds the .InsideHeight property setting converted to twips (multiplied by 20), the vertical scroll bar may be used to scroll through the contents of the frame.

Default setting: 0

.SCROLLWIDTH

When set to a non-zero value, .ScrollWidth specifies, in twips (not points), the horizontal distance between the left and right edges of the frame. When this value exceeds the .InsideWidth property setting converted to twips (multiplied by 20), the horizontal scroll bar may be used to scroll through the contents of the frame.

Default setting: 0

.SCROLLLEFT

The horizontal distance in twips (not points) between the upper left corner of the *visible* portion of the frame and its actual upper left corner. This setting only makes sense when the .ScrollWidth property is set to a value that is greater than that of the .InsideWidth property setting converted to twips, and the horizontal scroll bar is visible.

.SCROLLTOP

The vertical distance in twips (not points) between the upper-left corner of the *frame* and its actual upper left corner. This setting only makes sense when the .ScrollHeight property is set to a value that is greater than that of the .InsideHeight property setting converted to twips, and the vertical scroll bar is visible.

.SPECIALEFFECT

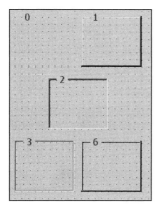

Figure 7-21: Examples of valid `.SpecialEffect`
property settings for frame controls.

An integer value that represents the artistic effect given to the border of the frame.

POSSIBLE SETTINGS

0   Flat; no special treatment is given to the border, besides what settings may have been made to the `.BorderStyle` and `.BorderColor` properties

1   Raised; the frame's interior appears to stand out on a platform

2   Sunken; the frame's interior appears to be recessed into the containing form

3   **(Default)** Etched; a thin line appears to be etched into the perimeter of the frame

6   "Bump;" a thin line appears to have been etched from the inside out along the perimeter of the frame

The `.BorderStyle` and `.SpecialEffect` properties are incompatible with one another. At design time, if you set one, you've undone the effect of the other. Setting the `.BorderStyle` property in turn sets `.Special Effect` to 0.

.VERTICALSCROLLBARSIDE

An integer flag that represents whether the vertical scroll bar is displayed on the right (0, **Default**) or left (1) side of the frame.

.ZOOM

An integer that represents the percentage of magnification that the interpreter applies to the contents of the frame; 100 implies a 1:1 ratio of visible size to actual size.

Default setting: 100

Associated methods

.REDOACTION

For a frame whose `.CanRedo` property is set to `True`, the `.RedoAction` method forces a redo of the previously undone action by the user.

.REPAINT

Signals to Windows a request to redraw the contents of the frame plus all of its contained controls.

.SCROLL

For a frame whose `.InsideHeight` or `.InsideWidth` properties are set above the frame's own `.Height` or `.Width` settings, the `.Scroll` method forces the interior region of the frame to be scrolled as though a scroll bar for that region (visible or not) were present. The method's arguments are integer flags that specify which parts of the "virtual scroll bars" are to be activated.

ARGUMENTS

`ActionX:`   Portion of the horizontal "scroll bar" to be activated

`ActionY:`   Portion of the vertical "scroll bar" to be activated

SETTINGS FOR ARGUMENTS

0   No action

1   The equivalent of clicking on the scroll bar's up or left arrow button

2   The equivalent of clicking on the scroll bar's down or right arrow button

3   The equivalent of clicking on the region between the thumb and the up or left arrow button

4   The equivalent of clicking on the region between the thumb and the
        down or right arrow button

5   The equivalent of moving the thumb to the beginning of the scroll bar

6   The equivalent of moving the thumb to the end of the scroll bar

.SETDEFAULTATBORDER

Allows the frame to reassess automatically a tab-stop sequence for its contained
controls, utilizing a top-to-bottom, left-to-right algorithm.

.UNDOACTION

For a frame whose `.CanUndo` property is set to `True`, the `.UndoAction` method
forces the previous action made by the user on the form to be rescinded. If the
`.CanRedo` property is set to `True`, the undone action is recorded and can be re-
executed using the `.RedoAction` method.

Unique events

_ADDCONTROL

Occurs whenever a control has been instantiated as a member of the frame at run-
time. Dynamic instantiation of a control can take place as a result of executing the
`CreateObject()` function for that control, or by utilizing the `.Add` method of the
frame's `Controls` constituent collection.

_REMOVECONTROL

Recognized at run time whenever a control has been removed from the frame; for
instance, using the `.Remove` method of the `Controls` collection. This collection is
used by the MultiPage control, among others, to refer to controls spread out among
multiple pages, indirectly. (See Chapter 9 for details on dynamic instantiation of
COM/OLE/ActiveX controls.)

The TabStrip Control

Unlike the other controls in the Forms 2.0 suite, TabStrip and MultiPage are
capitalized, almost like brand names. The capitalization is but one indicator of their
unique functionality. The TabStrip control is a mechanism for partitioning parts
of a control into pages, which may appear to collect related controls or related
content.

MultiPage is a container, but TabStrip is not

To better understand how the TabStrip control works, it's best to first examine it in the context of a visual enclosure around other objects. A text field on screen may contain text, but that text is not an object. Moreover, that text is a property of the text box control, which is addressed in the script as an object. TabStrip is a component that *appears* to contain other components, although those components continue to maintain their own properties as though TabStrip were never present.

Other controls may be placed inside a MultiPage control, and as a result the MultiPage *component* acts as a *container* for these controls – in much the same way that the UserForm object acts as a container for its controls. More accurately, in the sense that a container of a control is sometimes called its "parent," MultiPage is actually more of a "grandparent." MultiPage is the container of separate objects, called *pages* or Page objects. They are not Forms 2.0 controls *per se*, though mechanically they are basically frame controls without the little border or caption. Some properties of those contained controls, such as those involving coordinates, are rendered with respect to the Page object rather than the window at large.

By comparison, the TabStrip *object* is the container of other objects, but not so much in the visual sense. The "tab" referred to in "TabStrip" is not the same tab implied by such properties as .TabStop and .TabIndex. Instead, the Tab object contained by TabStrip is like the tab that sticks up from the top of a manila folder. TabStrip surrounds a set of controls in the way that a frame control *appears* to do, but TabStrip does not contain these controls in any way. Rather, by virtue of being drawn first, and the interior controls later, the TabStrip *appears* to contain these other controls. The "active page" in the TabStrip control appears to rest on top of the others. The user brings an "inactive page" to the front by clicking on its tab.

While the TabStrip control has properties of its own, it is also designed to contain a Tab object, which represents one of these pages. As a plurality, all of the Tab objects may be addressed as one unit, Tabs, if only to obtain its current .Count property. But a Tab object does not have its own .Name property, so it has to be addressed as a member of the Tabs collection, using the following syntax:

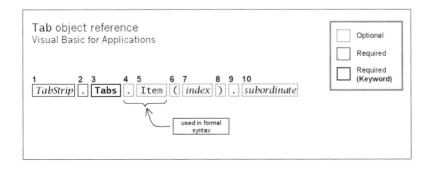

	Part	Description
1	*TabStrip*	.Name property The name of an instance of the TabStrip control, as specified by its .Name property setting. The term can be omitted from the instruction if the instruction appears within a With block, and if the root term of that With block is *TabStrip*.
2	. (period)	Separates the name of the TabStrip control (part **1**) from the reference to the Tabs collection (part **3**). If the instruction appears within a With block, the period must still remain.
3	Tabs	Collection Represents all of the Tab objects currently being maintained by the referenced TabStrip control (part **1**).
4	. (period)	Separates the reference to a member of the Tabs collection (part **3**) from the constituent term (part **5**) in the formal construction of this reference.
5	Item	Constituent Used in a more formal construction of the reference, where Item is addressed as a member of the Tabs collection, and the index denotes "which item" as opposed to "which tab." The result is exactly the same.
6	((left parenthesis)	Used to set off the subscript index (part **7**).
7	*index*	Integer A numeral or an integer variable used to reference the specific member of the Tabs collection.
8	) (right parenthesis)	Used to set off the subscript index (part **7**).
9	. (period)	Separates the Tabs collection reference from its property or method term (part **10**).
10	*subordinate*	Property or method A valid property or method term recognized by the Tabs collection. The Tab object has no default or value property.

    With that background taken care of, we can examine the terminology of
TabStrip in detail and know what's going on. The following segment shows the
unique terms used by TabStrip.

TabStrip characteristics

Purpose: Form partitioning without added container
ProgID: `Forms.TabStrip.1`
Default source name: `TabStrip`*x*
Description: The TabStrip control is a mechanism for partitioning parts of a control
into pages, which may appear to collect related controls or related content.

Value property

.SELECTEDITEM
Represents the index of the currently active TabStrip page. This property is addressable as a `Tab` object and is given those properties associated with a `Tab` object.

Special properties

.MULTIROW
Set to an integer value that represents whether tabs may be allowed to occupy more
than one row of the TabStrip control.

    Default setting: `False`

.STYLE

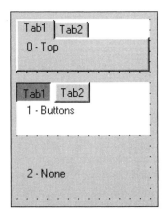

Figure 7-22: Examples of three valid `.Style`
property settings for the TabStrip control.

Set to an integer value that represents the appearance of the TabStrip control.

POSSIBLE SETTINGS

0   **(Default)** The control is set up as a frame, with tabs that, when pressed, pull up the page beneath that tab.

1   The control is set up as a row of toggle buttons. One button, when pressed, stays "in," resetting the button in the row that was previously set "in."

2   No tabs or buttons (or anything) are made available by the control, effectively hiding the control from sight or use by the user. (In other words, this is a pointless setting.)

.TABFIXEDHEIGHT

When set to a nonzero value, .TabFixedHeight represents the height, in points (1 point = $^1/72$ inch), of all tabs in the control. When this property is set to 0, Windows will size the height of tabs according to the height of the typeface presently assigned to the control's Font.Name property.

Regardless of how low the .TabFixedHeight property may be set, the height of tabs is always enough to accommodate the current font plus a couple of points margin.

.TABFIXEDWIDTH

When set to a nonzero value, .TabFixedWidth represents the width, in points, of all tabs in the control. When this property is set to 0, Windows sizes each tab to fit the text of its individual .Caption property.

.TABORIENTATION

Set to an integer value that indicates which edge of the control contains the tabs.

POSSIBLE SETTINGS

0   **(Default)** Top

1   Bottom

2   Left

3   Right

TabStrip collective object

TAB

Representative of all the characteristics of a specific page within the TabStrip instance, as opposed to the control as a whole. (The collection of these pages is referred to as `Tabs`.)

Tab object properties

.CAPTION

Set to the text that appears within the tab onscreen.

.ENABLED

Set to a Boolean value that represents whether the tab receives `_Click` events. When set to `False`, the text inside the tab appears grayed, indicating its inactive state to the user.

.HIDDEN

Set to a Boolean value that represents whether the tab can be seen by the user. When set to `True`, the tab continues to exist, but is not seen; other tabs fill in its gap.

.INDEX

Represents the ordinal position of the tab in the set.

Tabs collection properties

.COUNT

Set at runtime to the number of tabs located in the TabStrip set.

.ITEM

Addressed as an array, `.Item` represents the sequence of tabs belonging to the TabStrip collection. Here, `.Item(0)` represents the first tab in the collection. This property is assigned to an indirect object reference for the `Tab` object.

Example

```
Dim tObject As Object
Set tObject = TabStrip1.Tabs.Item(3)
```

In this example, tObject is an indirect object reference, `TabStrip1` is a TabStrip control, and `Tabs` is the collection of tabs associated with the control. The `Set` statement here assigns the *fourth* item in the collection (since the first is #0) to reference tObject.

Tabs collection methods

.ADD
Places a new tab in the TabStrip. Unless specified, this tab is placed at the end of the sequence.

 The Tabs.Add method actually *creates* a Tab object. It can go so far as to give this object an indirect reference and assign to it its initial .Caption property. The Tab object need not be declared beforehand; it is created here.

ARGUMENTS

Index:	(Optional) Specifies the ordinal position of the new tab in the sequence, where 0 specifies the first tab.
Key:	(Optional) An arbitrary string or literal used in later instructions to refer to the specific member of the Tabs collection maintained by the TabStrip control.
Caption:	(Optional) Textual contents of the tab onscreen, and the .Caption property setting for the Tab object. If omitted, Windows will generate a "Tab*x*" caption.

.CLEAR
Removes all items from the Tabs collection, thus "blanking" the control.

.REMOVE
Removes a specific indexed item from the Tabs collection.

ARGUMENT

Index: Ordinal number of the item to remove; 0 is the first item in the collection.

Example

TabStrip1.Tabs.Remove Tab3.Index

In this example, `TabStrip1` is a TabStrip control and `Tab3` is an object reference to a member of the `Tabs` collection.

The MultiPage Control

As a control, MultiPage has much of the same functionality and appearance of TabStrip, except that MultiPage may act as a full-fledged container of other controls rather than something that *appears* to contain those controls. One of the chief mechanical differences between the two is that TabStrip acts as the keeper of a `Tabs` collection, while MultiPage acts as a keeper of a `Pages` collection. MultiPage is a wonderful container, letting the user click on tabs or buttons and have controls disappear and others appear just as though the user were flipping pages of a book. It positions several containers, called pages or `Page` objects, on top of one another in a stack, with the topmost page visible to and operable by the user. A `Page` object has roughly the same characteristics of a frame control, except that it isn't truly a control *per se*, and it can be made a member of a VBA collection object.

In a manner similar to how the TabStrip control contains `Tab` objects, MultiPage contains `Page` objects belonging to the `Pages` collection. Addressing the controls contained by MultiPage is a three-stage process that leads from the `.Name` property of the MultiPage control to the `Pages` collection to the `.Name` property of the constituent object. The syntax table below demonstrates:

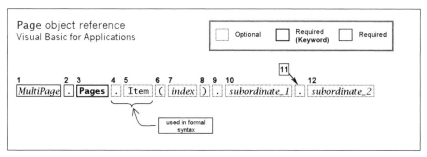

Part		Description
1	*MultiPage*	`.Name` property The name of an instance of the MultiPage control, as specified by its `.Name` property setting. The term can be omitted from the instruction if the instruction appears in a `With` block and the root term of that `With` block is *MultiPage*.

Continued

	Part	Description
2	. (period)	Separates the name of the MultiPage control (part **1**) from the reference to the Pages collection (part **3**). If the instruction appears within a With block, the period must still remain.
3	Pages	Collection Represents all of the Page objects currently being maintained by the referenced MultiPage control (part **1**).
4	. (period)	Separates the reference to a member of the Pages collection (part **3**) from the constituent term (part **5**) in the formal construction of this reference.
5	Item	Constituent Used in a more formal construction of the reference, where Item is addressed as a member of the Pages collection and the index denotes "which item" as opposed to "which tab." The result is exactly the same.
6	((left parenthesis)	Sets off the subscript index (part **7**).
7	*index*	A numeral or an integer variable used to reference the specific member of the Pages collection.
8	) (right parenthesis)	Sets off the subscript index (part **7**).
9	. (period)	Separates the Pages collection reference from its property or method term (part **10**).
10	*subordinate_1*	Object
(a)		A valid property or method term recognized by the Pages collection. The Page object has no default or value property.
(b)		The .Name property of a control contained within the designated Tab object.

Part		Description
11	. (period) _ (underscore)	When part **10** is a constituent object of the `Page` class (described by (a) in part **10** above), the punctuation is necessary here to separate that term from its own subordinate property or method (part **12**). When part **10** is the name of a contained control (described by (b) above), this punctuation is necessary to separate that name from its subordinate property, method, or event (part **12**).
12	*subordinate_2*	<u>Constituent</u> A valid property, method, event, or constituent object recognized as part of the lexicon of the object named in part **10**.

Here are the key terms specific to the MultiPage control:

MultiPage characteristics

Purpose: Form partitioning through interior divided container
ProgID: `Forms.MultiPage.1`
Default source name: `MultiPage`*x*
Description: The MultiPage control is a formal container for other controls that is divided into separate pages (`Page` objects) whose contents may be covered up by other pages when necessary. Unlike TabStrip, MultiPage is responsible for maintaining the illusion of multiple pages.

Value property

.SELECTEDITEM
Represents the index of the currently active page. This property is addressable as a `Page` object, and is given those properties associated with a `Page` object.

Special properties

.MULTIROW
Set to an integer value that represents whether pages are allowed to occupy more than one row of the MultiPage control.
Default setting: `False`

.TABFIXEDHEIGHT
When set to a nonzero value, `.TabFixedHeight` represents the height in points of all tabs in the control. When this property is set to `0`, Windows sizes the height of tabs according to the height of the typeface presently assigned to the control's `Font.Name` property.

.TABFIXEDWIDTH

When set to a nonzero value, .TabFixedWidth represents the width, in points, of all tabs in the control. When this property is set to 0, Windows sizes each tab to fit the text of its individual .Caption property.

.TABORIENTATION

Set to an integer value that indicates which edge of the control contains the tabs.

POSSIBLE SETTINGS

0   **(Default)** Top

1   Bottom

2   Left

3   Right

MultiPage collective object

PAGE

Representative of all the characteristics of a specific page within the MultiPage instance, as opposed to the control as a whole. (The collection of these pages is referred to as the Pages collection.)

Page object properties

.ACTIVECONTROL

An object reference to the control contained by the page that currently has the focus.

.CANPASTE

Set at run time to a Boolean value that denotes whether the controls in the page may receive the data that currently resides on the Windows system Clipboard.

.CANREDO

Set at run time to a Boolean value that denotes, as long as the frame's .CanUndo property is set to True, whether the page may record *undone* user actions so that they may be *redone* at the user's request. For a redo to take place, a VBA instruction must be implemented using the .RedoAction method for the page.

.CANUNDO

Set at run time to a Boolean value that represents whether the page is to record user actions so that they may be undone at the user's request. For an undo to take place, a VBA instruction must be implemented using the `.UndoAction` method for the page.

.CYCLE

A flag value that denotes the behavior of the Tab key with regard to moving the focus along the objects in the page's own independent tab-stop sequence.

POSSIBLE SETTINGS

0   **(Default)** Designates that the focus should move to the next control in the *form's* tab-stop sequence after it has reached the final control in the *page's* sequence and the user has pressed Tab again.

2   Designates that the focus should always move to the first control in the page's tab-stop sequence when the focus has reached the final control in that sequence and the user has pressed Tab again. The user would need to use the mouse to move the focus *out* of the page.

.INDEX

Represents the ordinal position of the page in the set, where 0 is the index of the first page.

.INSIDEHEIGHT

Set at run time to the distance in points (1/72 inch) between the upper and lower edges of the page.

.INSIDEWIDTH

Set at run time to the distance in points between the left and right edges of the page.

.KEEPSCROLLBARSVISIBLE

An integer value that represents whether the page continues to display scroll bars, even when the visible area of the page mandates that either or both scroll bars are unnecessary. For this property to be meaningful, the `.ScrollBars` property must be set so that the corresponding scroll bars *can* be visible; with `.ScrollBars` set to 0, no scroll bars are visible anyway.

POSSIBLE SETTINGS

0   Allows both scroll bars to be made invisible if the contents of the page fit within its borders

1   Maintains the horizontal scroll bar for the page at all times

2   Maintains the vertical scroll bar for the page at all times

3   **(Default)** Maintains both scroll bars for the page at all times

.PICTURE

A constituent object which represents a valid image file. See example at Command Button for details.

.PICTUREALIGNMENT

Set at design time to an integer that represents how the interior image stated by the `.Picture` property setting is to be positioned with respect to the border of the page.

POSSIBLE SETTINGS

0   Picture is aligned against the upper left corner of the page

1   Picture is aligned against the upper right corner of the page

2   **(Default)** Picture is centered with respect to the page

3   Picture is aligned against the lower left corner of the page

4   Picture is aligned against the lower right corner of the page

.PICTURESIZEMODE

An integer value that denotes how the page is to treat the sizing of the interior picture referred to by the `.Picture` property. By default, the picture is rendered in its native size, though this property permits you to use the page's own size to designate the size of the picture.

POSSIBLE SETTINGS

0   **(Default)** Does not change the pixel mapping of the interior picture with respect to the page. Any overhang by the picture is cropped.

1   Stretches or shrinks the picture to fit the edges of the page, however much the picture might have to be distorted.

3   Enlarges or reduces the size of the picture, proportionately, so that it consumes as much of the page as possible *without* distorting the image.

.PICTURETILING

A Boolean value that represents whether the page is permitted to repeat the contained image pointed to by its .Picture property setting. When set to True, the entire page is filled with one or more instances of the image, repeated horizontally and vertically like floor tile.

Default setting: False

If the .PictureSizeMode property is set to 1, the .PictureTiling property has no obvious effect on the page.

.SCROLLBARS

An integer value that denotes which scroll bars the page is capable of displaying when its contents exceed the page's boundaries.

POSSIBLE SETTINGS

0   **(Default)** Scroll bars are never displayed

1   Horizontal scroll bar is displayed if text exceeds the right boundary

2   Vertical scroll bar is displayed if text exceeds the lower boundary

3   Either or both scroll bars are displayed when necessary

.SCROLLHEIGHT

When set to a non-zero value, .ScrollHeight specifies, in twips (not points), the vertical distance between the upper and lower borders of the page. When this value exceeds the .InsideHeight property setting converted to twips (multiplied by 20), the vertical scroll bar may be used to scroll through the contents of the page.

Default setting: 0

.SCROLLWIDTH

When set to a nonzero value, .ScrollWidth specifies, in twips (not points), the horizontal distance between the left and right edges of the page. When this value exceeds the .InsideWidth property setting converted to twips (multiplied by 20), the horizontal scroll bar may be used to scroll through the contents of the page.

Default setting: 0

.SCROLLLEFT

The horizontal distance in twips (not points) between the upper left corner of the *visible* portion of the page and its actual upper left corner. This setting only makes sense when the .ScrollWidth property is set to a value that is greater than that of the .InsideWidth property setting converted to twips (multiplied by 20), and the horizontal scroll bar is visible.

.SCROLLTOP

The vertical distance in twips (not points) between the upper left corner of the page and its actual upper left corner. This setting only makes sense when the .ScrollHeight property is set to a value that is greater than that of the .InsideHeight property setting converted to twips (multiplied by 20), and the vertical scroll bar is visible.

.TRANSITIONEFFECT

An integer flag that denotes which, if any, animation is applied when the user clicks on a MultiPage tab and one page is substituted for another.

POSSIBLE SETTINGS

0   **(Default)** No animation

1   A "wipe" effect, in which the contents of the new page gradually replace those of the old page, proceeding from the bottom edge to the top

2   Wipe, bottom left to top right

3   Wipe, left to right

4   Wipe, top left to bottom right

5   Wipe, top to bottom

6   Wipe, top right to bottom left

7   Wipe, right to left

8   Wipe, bottom right to top left

9   A "push" effect, in which the new page pushes the old page off the edge, proceeding from the bottom edge to the top

10   Push, left to right

11   Push, top to bottom

12   Push, right to left

.TRANSITIONPERIOD

An integer specifying in microseconds the duration of the page-changing effect specified by the .TransitionEffect property.

    Default setting: 10000

.VERTICALSCROLLBARSIDE

An integer flag that denotes whether the vertical scroll bar is to be displayed on the right (0, **Default**) or left (1) side of the page.

.ZOOM

An integer that represents the percentage of magnification that the interpreter is to apply to the contents of the page, where 100 implies a 1:1 ratio of visible size to actual size.

    Default setting: 100

Page object methods

.REDOACTION

For a frame whose .CanRedo property is set to True, the .RedoAction method forces a redo of the previously undone action by the user.

.REPAINT

Signals to Windows a request to redraw the contents of the frame plus all of its contained controls.

.SCROLL

For a frame whose .ScrollHeight or .ScrollWidth properties are set above the frame's own interior .Height or .Width settings (converted to points), the .Scroll method forces the interior region of the frame to be scrolled, as though a scroll bar for that region (visible or not) were present. The method's arguments are integer flags that specify what parts of the "virtual scroll bars" are to be activated.

ARGUMENTS

ActionX: Portion of the horizontal "scroll bar" to be activated

ActionY: Portion of the vertical "scroll bar" to be activated

SETTINGS FOR ARGUMENTS

0   No action

1   The equivalent of clicking on the scroll bar's up or left arrow button

2   The equivalent of clicking on the scroll bar's down or right arrow button

3   The equivalent of clicking on the region between the thumb and the up or left arrow button

4   The equivalent of clicking on the region between the thumb and the down or right arrow button

5   The equivalent of moving the thumb to the beginning of the scroll bar

6   The equivalent of moving the thumb to the end of the scroll bar

.SETDEFAULTATBORDER
Allows the frame to reassess automatically a tab-stop sequence for its contained controls, utilizing a top-to-bottom, left-to-right algorithm.

.UNDOACTION
For a frame whose `.CanUndo` property is set to `True`, the `.UndoAction` method forces the previous action made by the user on the form to be rescinded. If the `.CanRedo` property is set to `True`, the undone action is recorded and can be re-executed using the `.RedoAction` method.

Pages collection properties

.COUNT
Set at run time to the number of tabs located in the MultiPage set.

.ITEM
Addressed as an array, `.Item` represents the sequence of tabs belonging to the MultiPage `Pages` collection. Here, `.Item(0)` represents the first page in the collection. This property is assigned to an indirect object reference for the `Page` object.

Pages collection methods

.ADD
Places a new tab in the MultiPage. Unless specified, this page is placed at the end of the sequence.

On Point

This chapter has presented the unique features of the Forms 2.0 control suite, which is used in building form modules for VBA. During the course of the chapter, we touched on some key mechanical similarities and differences between the controls. For instance, the toggle button is mechanically the same as the command button although it maintains a Boolean state. The spin button is really a stripped down scroll bar. The image control is really the same as a label control, though without some of the overhead and without the textual caption; and the label control is surprisingly very much the same as the command button, though without the animation. Meanwhile, TabStrip and MultiPage appear to have very similar purposes, although TabStrip is a container of mere *names,* whereas MultiPage is a container for whole *panels* — entire containers of controls. These containers, called pages, are very similar to frame controls, just without the thin border and upper caption.

ARGUMENTS

Index:
(**Optional**) Specifies the ordinal position of the new page in the sequence, where 0 represents the first page.

Key:
(**Optional**) An arbitrary string or literal used in later instructions to refer to the specific member of the Pages collection maintained by the MultiPage control.

Caption:
(**Optional**) Textual contents of the tab at the top of the page on screen and the .Caption property setting for the Page object. If omitted, Windows will generate a "Page*x*" caption.

.CLEAR

Removes all items from the Pages collection, thus "blanking" the control.

.REMOVE

Removes a specific indexed item from the Pages collection.

ARGUMENT

Index:
Ordinal number of the item to remove, where 0 is the first item in the collection

In Theory: Speak now or forever hold your peace

I have in mind the ultimate custom control. With this control, you can sit down at your computer and tell it what to do.

Apparently I'm not alone with these dreams; I've been told some chap named Asimov had a similar perspective on computing. The stumbling block to making voice recognition work, it has been said up to now, has been the science of the voice. Individual people have individual voices; and it is not yet entirely known what there is about one person saying, "Computer!" that is physically equivalent or similar to another person saying, "Computer!" In other words, our minds know the answer, but our brains don't. We look at two voice patterns and, well, we might find *some* correlation between them. But those same correlations are unlikely to apply to a third voice pattern, and less likely to a fourth.

An editor of mine shared with me an incident involving a colleague of hers who works in the field of digital voice recognition. The goal of his project was to record a spoken English-language sentence, and produce an audible Russian translation. When the engineer spoke into the microphone, "The spirit is willing, but the flesh is weak," the translation came through, for any Russian listeners who might find meaning in it: "The wine is good, but the meat is rotten." Sure, the meaning is good, but the *context. . .*

IBM has developed perhaps the best voice recognition to date. In a publicly televised demonstration in 1996, IBM engineers invited audience participants to come up to the stage, talk to the machine, and tell it what to do. You can literally, said the engineer, tell the computer what to do. Literally.

Too literally. "Mouse up," said the engineer to the machine. "Mouse stop. Mouse click." There were some metacommands in the system, to be fair. "Drag worksheet to trash. Load worksheet S-E-C-dot-W-K-S-Enter. Type, 'Dear Sir, It was a weak week for woks. Sid said this side was sad with sod.'" Then the audience participant sat down at the microphone and was told to ask away. "Hi there," said the eager voice to the computer. "No, no, no!" the engineer admonished him, trying to train his focus on what he believed to be the job at hand. "All right then," said the voice, "I want to type a letter." "Okay," said the engineer, eager to prove once again the density of the randomly picked individual's mind, "so what do you want the mouse to do?" "*Mouse*?" said the participant. "I want to type a letter." "Okay, you want it to go up then?"

As this experience with coaching the obviously non-clairvoyant participant went on for some minutes, sadly, the truth became clear to me. IBM saw sound as a way to communicate graphics. In other words, audio was becoming just another graphics driver. Computing was being redeveloped for computing's sake, using the limited scope of vocabulary and technology developed in just the past few weeks, rather than the scope of knowledge amassed through the decades. Forgotten were people and their everyday needs, none of which have much to do with spelling out DOS-style eight-dot-three filenames.

At the dawn of the graphical era of computing in the early 1980s, it seemed as though engineers such as Butler Lampson and Alan Kay had hit upon the ideal that would define the operation of the computer for the next hundred years. Seeing what you wanted and pointing to it made so much sense at the time. Since Microsoft first embraced this concept after having shunned it for so long, it has developed all of the essential elements of the modern Windows operating system — drag-and-drop, embedded objects, extendable menu bars, the "Active Desktop," "View as Web Page," the Blue Screen of Death — under the premise of an environment defined by what the user *sees*. The application model in Windows, as well as in MacOS and graphical UNIX, is predicated upon the graphical position of the data being operated on by the applications, which is managed by what Windows calls "device contexts." A device context is, in many ways, a virtual rendering machine — a screen, a printer, or a plotter — even if it isn't being used in that manner by the application that calls upon it.

The modern computing model is indeed Visual. (If the name "Microsoft" had not already been an established trademark by 1990, the company would probably be called "Visual" today.) So when Bill Gates reveals that his company is moving toward a *voice*-driven model and that voice is the key to the future, many of us look at such statements in the context of handles to device contexts, window drivers, and drag-and-drop, and wonder, how can this be?

The vision of computing projected to the world in the 1950s by brilliant people, such as Isaac Asimov, would not have been so well embraced by engineers were it presented as a self-supporting structure rather than a server for people's needs. Even when computers in science fiction were made villainous, they presented the world with an eerie, terrifying model of efficiency. The vision of computing initiated in the 1980s by Lampson, Kay, and their colleagues at Xerox PARC would not have been so well embraced by engineers were it presented as a self-supporting *browser*, rather than a more simplistic, reasonable way to approach the job of managing information. Now that processors are orders of magnitude more efficient than they were ten years ago, capable of performing what not long ago was considered supercomputing, the ideal of being able to speak commands to your computer, and have it speak volumes in return, seems a bit more clouded. It hasn't vanished; it's merely obscured. This obscurity has to do with the ill-researched belief that what people want to do with computers, and what they can do with computers today are the same thing.

What people want is simplicity. How people define "simplicity" has to do with everyday life, where there are no mouse pointers floating in space, where today's tasks and today's news aren't being marshaled by device contexts, and where "virtual reality" is a brand name. In everyday life, simplicity is achieved through communication. Communication is facilitated by the receiver's being able to comprehend, to interpret, what it is you've said.

There, at last, is the true stumbling block – not the voice recognition patterns, but the communicated message. The computer, at present, does not understand us. If it is ever to understand us, then computing engineers need to be made aware that it is not the people who need to be re-educated.

In Brief

♦ ActiveX controls including the Forms 2.0 controls generally have a value property of some sort. Often that property is explicitly called .Value; at times, both a separate property term such as .Text and .Value may refer to the same property. In any event, this property is often considered the default property for an object; if an expression contains an object reference without a property attached, this default property is assumed.

♦ While the list box and text box control may at times sport their own scroll bars (when their contents become too large for their own surface area), Forms 2.0 does offer a scroll bar control that may be used independently for other purposes.

♦ In a list box or combo box control, the .Text property at any one time contains the text of the most recently chosen item in the list. For a multicolumn control, this .Text property is acquired from the column whose number is represented by the .BoundColumn property setting. The row number of this choice is represented by the .ListIndex property.

♦ The frame control is a container in itself. Controls instantiated here have .Left and .Top properties whose coordinates are relative to the frame, not to the form. Option button sets not given .GroupName settings are automatically grouped by frames.

♦ The TabStrip control is not a container, though the MultiPage control is. They both look very much the same, but MultiPage maintains a set of containers within its Pages collection that are unique frames unto themselves. Clicking on a tab in a MultiPage control causes MultiPage to switch to that page automatically; for a similar effect to happen for TabStrip, you would have to program it yourself. However, TabStrip has a significantly less memory overhead than MultiPage, unless your procedure for managing the TabStrip effect is not as efficient as it could be.

Chapter 8

Why the Component Object Model Matters

IN THIS CHAPTER

♦ The origins of the underlying COM system of Windows

♦ How applications behave in a component-based operating system

♦ The communications system employed for objects to contact one another

♦ How OLE and Office 2000 coalesce to produce compound documents

♦ Why OLE runs Windows' System Registry

♦ How VBA binds components that need to contact one another

♦ Early and late binding and their purposes

♦ DCOM and the three-tier communications model

THE COMPONENT OBJECT MODEL (COM) is perhaps the best idea ever to have been implemented in Windows. Its premise is a great deal simpler than its implementation: As long as every modern computer program is to be made up of multiple modules, only those modules needed by the computer's processor at any particular time are loaded into memory and running.

Some will say that's too simple a description, so for them I'll reiterate in a slightly more complex fashion: Historically, the binary code of a computer program has either been fully compiled into executable code by a compiler (like C++), or interpreted on the fly as the source code is examined (like VBA). Single-task operating systems such as MS-DOS (without Windows) were only capable of loading into memory the binary code of a compiled program in its entirety, or the binary code of the interpreter and the source code of the program it was interpreting in its entirety. Some applications such as dBASE managed to fool DOS into thinking it was seeing a program in its entirety, when in fact they contained so-called *overlay linkers* that generated linked code on the fly. The use of .OVL files marked the beginning of the trend towards compartmentalization and components in computing applications. But at that time, the operating system in place did not directly support the technology – more accurately, it was blissfully unaware of its existence.

The idea of the Component Object Model is not exactly to break up each single program into parts or bits,; but instead to remodel the applications that we write so that they're not responsible for everything the computer is capable of doing at any one time. Thus, a spelling checker need not *belong* to an application in order for that application to contact it and make use of it. Furthermore, the text renderer or typeface engine need not belong to that application.

The basic principle alluded to here is *dynamic linking.* Assume that every portion of executable code that a processor will run during a session is "the program." Historically, all of those parts or modules have had to be *linked* together into a single cohesive unit. DOS could not run this program unless it was in addressable memory in its entirety, or at least appeared to be. (DOS veterans will remember hard disk caches, which "paged" unused regions of memory onto the hard disk drive. Actually, Windows still does this today. But even the old DOS-based caches simply increased the area of addressable memory in its map, and tacked the hard disk's free space onto that map.) In Windows, a word processor and the program for the Open dialog box are stored in two separate files, and they are indeed two separate programs. But when the word processor needs the Open dialog box, it knows how to contact its program, and Windows knows how to cohesively connect that program to the word processor's running code while that program is running – thus, dynamic linking. No C++ compiler was necessary to compile the source code for the word processor and the source code for the dialog box into one binary stream.

To be accurate, Windows performed dynamic linking prior to the complete adoption of COM. Yet it does provide the foundation for the complete COM system. In a full-fledged COM environment, an application may be responsible for directly managing one type of practical data – such as a spreadsheet, word processor document, or presentation. But that application is capable of utilizing the services of other programs to produce or provide other types of data than that for which it is directly responsible. So an application that utilizes COM fully is not only capable of providing its own native data, but it can provide all of the other formally registered classes of data on your computer as well. To be thoroughly accurate, an application that uses COM correctly will only be *perceived* as having its own native data; it actually utilizes its own class of data in the same way it utilizes any other class. For native data, an application may be quicker or more direct about the job; for remote data, there may be a few extra steps involved. But behind the scenes of the window that the user is operating, a COM application makes contact with remote data in much the same way as with native data.

So ends the simple part of this chapter. In the same way that reading the Constitution of the United States won't prepare you for a conversation with a political consultant, reading the principles that inspired COM won't prepare you for the quagmire that is the Model in practice at Microsoft. Thankfully, this chapter is not about the inter-corporate and intra-corporate melee brought about in the name of COM. What has happened in the courtrooms is a topic for another book. And there are other books that take this subject into account, as though it were a grand, evil conspiracy worthy of the attention of Agents Mulder and Scully. Feel free to indulge yourself in these books, but have plenty of salt on hand, because you will need several grains.

But this chapter does get into some strange and difficult areas, albeit entirely about programming, and certainly fit for family reading. The purpose of my presenting it is to give you a clear picture of why there are objects in Windows and VBA, and what you can truly do with them if you knew how. If you understand COM, you can utilize it to take control of several applications at once through VBA – even applications outside of Office 2000.

Windows' Perception of Objects

The COM project began at Microsoft in 1987 as Object Linking and Embedding (OLE), an acronym that is still used today to identify the program responsible for facilitating the exchange of data across multiple applications. OLE grew out of an earlier project that came into fruition in Windows 3.0, called Dynamic Data Exchange (DDE). Although DDE did an adequate job of shuttling data back and forth between two applications without that data having to be duplicated, it relied on the user to load both of those applications. With OLE, the idea was introduced that an application could be split into two primary components: loosely put, the engine and its container. The engine would be responsible for maintaining the data, but the container could make contact with other engines than its own.

The origin of the document-centric model

When OLE technology officially became a part of Windows in version 3.1, it was billed as the first step toward the deployment of a new type of computer program called a *meta-application.* The idea was that several programs could eventually, under OLE or a successor system, work together as tools or components in the production of a single data document. This document would not be a "word processor document" or a "spreadsheet document," but just a "document," such as something an office would have ordinarily produced prior to the advent of computers. Each document, from the computer's point of view, would be internally organized according to a set of rules stating what the individual things are that comprise the document, what operates these *things,* and how they are supposed to work together. (Think about it: Is a document truly composed of sentences and paragraphs, or fonts and device contexts?)

Many companies took it upon themselves to write such rules for these things, which were inevitably called *objects* for lack of a more concrete term. One group of such companies, steered primarily by Microsoft, came up with a set of rules – a sort-of English-language "constitution" – that they hoped would apply to objects in general. This document became the 1.0 specification for the Component Object

Model. Like the U.S. Constitution, the COM document is periodically revised; but unlike the Constitution, it is nearly impossible for the untrained eye to tell where the original document stops and the revisions begin.

Microsoft's COM is not a data format

The original intention of Microsoft in its stewardship of the COM model was profound and, arguably, quite noble. Microsoft knew that if any operating system were to allow multiple applications from multiple manufacturers to operate on the same data, all of these manufacturers would have to agree on some common ground as to how the data works.

However, it would be foolish for anyone to believe these manufacturers could all come to some mutual agreement over the actual *format* of the data that would last into the next millennium. So COM specifies a system whereby the defining aspect of an object is how it communicates with other objects – in a sense, the "face" it puts on for the rest of the world. A manufacturer could go on producing whatever format it comes up with for its data; but if that manufacturer wants its product to be a part of the broader architecture, its programs must *relate* that data to other programs using the format in the COM specification. The manufacturer could then change its data format when it needs to, as long as it leaves the communications model the same; then other programs in a multitasking system would not need to know or care about that manufacturer's data format, how old it is, or what version it is. A word processor from one company should be able to read the data from the database of another company, with neither program being concerned about how the other is internally structured.

OLE is Microsoft's implementation of the COM model for Windows. While Microsoft has played such a large part in the ongoing creation of COM, it actually does not own the model, nor has it ever owned the model. COM is a concept in the public domain; theoretically, some other company could develop an object protocol that follows the COM model – which is about as likely as Mercury developing a car for someone other than Ford. Still, it leaves the possibility open for companies other than Microsoft to make COM-adherent object facilities for processors other than Intel and DEC – say, Motorola PowerPCs (the engines of Power Macintosh), or the SPARC processors abounding in the UNIX realm of Sun Microsystems and SCO. This possibility may have to be helped along if Microsoft's plans are ever to gain wide acceptance in the broader world of the Internet, where Intel processors are a substantial plurality rather than the majority.

In Depth: The executable DLL

The dynamic link library (DLL) is the original reusable code component of Microsoft Windows, dating back to its first edition. A DLL is, from the C/C++ programmer's standpoint, a set of functions without a comprehensive sequence of program execution to link them all together. Instead, the DLL contains disjoined functions designed to be called by other programs, and return values or perform processes for those programs. The name "dynamic link" dates back to an early Microsoft process model where programs within Windows would contact each other formally but asynchronously, like passing maritime vessels that happen to notice one another on their scopes. But the type of *link* that takes place when Windows initiates a function from a DLL is not the same "middle-L" as in OLE, where a document makes reference to an included object by passing partial control over to its originating application.

What kind of object model is COM?

The strange truth is, the COM model that is the foundation for OLE and ActiveX is a simple model as object models go. C++ objects and the mechanisms that support them are far more structurally complex than OLE objects. Yet C++ is made to seem simpler to novices because its semantic foundation – the part of the C++ product used by people to describe C++ to other people – is far more comprehensible. To its credit, OLE's semantic foundation is presented quite logically. Yet logic, while establishing the basis of reason, is not always the mortar that holds it together. One can no more easily build a semantic foundation with associative logic alone than one can build a barricade with loose sand. Consider the following: *X* is defined as that which does *Y* to *Z*. *Y* is the thing that *X* does to *Z*. *Z* is that which has *Y* done to it by *X*. You see the relations and, well, they do make sense. They just don't *mean* anything.

So allow me a few paragraphs, if you will, to explain the basic foundational principles of COM – the concepts one would naturally discover from working with it. If you take these principles to heart and actually use them to build an OLE application that follows these principles to the letter, please write Microsoft and tell them how you did it.

The keystone of COM architecture is the *object,* which, to reiterate, is a body of data combined with instructional code that gives that data some purpose and meaning. There are a handful of categories of OLE programs, which are called *components.* No, I won't use these two terms interchangeably. (You're welcome.) This book defines *component* as the program that produces the data, and *object* as the form of that data. The job of an OLE component is to produce objects of a particular type, called a *class,* the structure of which is strictly defined within the context of the component, but loosely defined within the context of OLE. In other words,

OLE does not prescribe the object's format or composition, but instead presents rules as to how that object communicates with other objects.

How we (currently) distinguish the trademarks

From time to time, Microsoft has used its various component technology trademarks to mean different things – sometimes two or more things at once. This book will try to hold consistently to these associations:

COM   Microsoft's foundation technology and conceptual model for interprocess communication, whose underlying principle is that any properly constructed component object should be able to contact and exchange data with any other properly constructed component object.

OLE   The program responsible for handling component-based communication in Windows, based on the principle that compound documents can be created by chaining together data elements maintained simultaneously by multiple programs.

ActiveX   A trademark applied by Microsoft to three supplemental technologies in COM: (1) in-process graphical controls that may be instantiated within forms and Web pages; (2) the use of elements of HTML to distribute and certify binary components of Web pages; and (3) the program (ActiveX Data Objects) used to facilitate exchanges between a database server such as SQL Server, and a data client such as Jet.

In Depth: ActiveX, the miracle ingredient

One of Office 97's major selling points after its release in the first quarter of 1997, was that it included the dazzling new technology known as ActiveX. What makes the form modules in VBA work are ActiveX controls. Indeed, the UserForm object itself is one such control, even though it was designed to contain other controls. The ActiveX trademark has lost and regained favor with Microsoft more than once during its brief history. Today, the term generally stands for that part of OLE that manages *controls* – those portable elements of programs that get instantiated into dialog boxes, which was the topic of Chapters 5 through 7. As a VBA programmer, you won't be able to escape the new, component-driven nature of the modern Windows application, whatever Microsoft chooses to call it this week.

From a practical standpoint, ActiveX is a registered trademark of Microsoft Corporation. Therefore, the equally practical answer to the question, "What is ActiveX?" is, "ActiveX is whatever Microsoft defines it to be at the time." In late 1996, Microsoft redefined it entirely, to mean the entire object-oriented technology of Windows — a *replacement* for the term OLE. Microsoft then actually ceded "stewardship" of ActiveX to a group of developers, software manufacturers, department stores, and oil companies — no kidding — whose job ended up being to reiterate that ActiveX is whatever Microsoft defines it to be — which is what everybody already knew. Then in late 1997, the stewardship group unofficially collapsed, and ActiveX became *acronym non grata* (mixing Greek and Latin there) until mid-1998, when it re-emerged as the mysterious driving force behind ActiveX Data Objects (ADO), the replacement for Data Access Objects (DAO) made popular by Access.

What Component Objects Do

The process model for Object Linking and Embedding is based around one computer (as opposed to a network). This means the communications processes OLE establishes between program components are, at least for now, presumed to exist on the same computer. So the OLE client (called the *object*) and the OLE server (called the *server*) are part of the same Windows computer.

For each computer, OLE manages a communications network of its own that connects many categories of components. The most important of these components are the objects. The many OLE manuals disagree about the definition of this term, so permit me to give you the correct definition: An *object* in computing is a body of data that is paired with encoded instructions giving that object a measure of functionality, and giving other programs properly restricted access to that data. A COM component object (or just "COM object") contains a program that represents the functionality of a unit of data that belongs to a particular class, for the sake of other programs. Together, the program and the data are considered the object. Unlike the average data file, an object isn't restricted to symbolic numbers and characters arranged in a specified format, but also includes something which describes in code, for the purpose of some other program, the data's purpose and function.

Think of *object* more in its grammatical, rather than material, sense, as in the *object* of a sentence. An object term gives the program — and thus, the programmer — some way to address bodies of program and bodies of data as whole entities, rather than as address points or blocks of memory.

Many elements of the realm of computing subscribe to the general definition of *object* to varying degrees. In C++, for example, an object is an abstract class of internal data, of which the more specific classes are derivatives, inheriting functionality from the parent classes. In Visual Basic, historically, an object has been one of those little things you drag from the Toolbox window onto a form. The COM object is actually somewhere in between – not as specific as C++, while not as rudimentary as Visual Basic, which assumes the omnipresence of every important binary object within the locality of the active project. While OLE is not a programming language, it does have a lexicon of sorts, and languages that reference the OLE system borrow from it. This communications lexicon constitutes the OLE set of interfaces. COM component objects do not share C++ objects' characteristics of polymorphism and inheritance; veteran programmers would argue that this makes the OLE object model violate three of Bertrand Meyer's fabled "Seven Steps Towards Object-Based Happiness." But if we agree to define *objects* as necessarily abstract entities, we should permit some degree of abstraction in their implementation as well. Thus we should permit Microsoft's objects to be treated abstractly in their own context, and feel reasonably happy about doing so.

The main categories of component objects

The true objective of OLE is for its user to be able to construct a *compound* data document that, unto itself and without all the import/export nonsense, may contain any and all types of data and functionality the user's entire library of software may produce. This would make a spreadsheet document from the user's point of view no different from a word processor document from the computer's point of view. In working toward this goal, OLE manages two types of applications, called the *container application* (or simply *container*) and the *object application*. The latter produces one type – or rather, one *class* – of data. The container is capable of combining data of all classes, without restriction or exception, into a single view of the document that eliminates all confusion for the user.

Figure 8-1 depicts the interrelationship between the main categories of OLE components, assuming you could turn your computer to one side a bit and peek behind the window. For this figure, I've connected the parts of OLE as though they were tangibly interlinked machines. The container application provides a façade, if you will, of a massive all-in-one application for the sake of the user. That façade hides the fact that all the functionality is being provided by COM objects that are managed by the OLE facilities of the operating system.

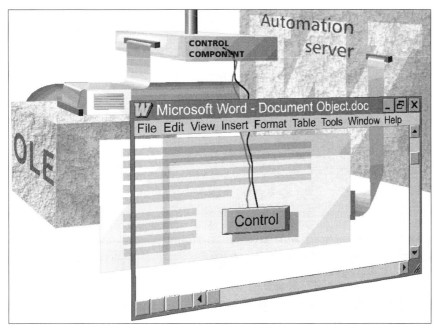

Figure 8-1: An exploded view of OLE in a client computer.

Besides the container and the control, there is a third crucial OLE component category. In the conventional (i.e., non-COM) model of the application, its functionality is defined entirely by it and is contained within it; how that application communicates with programs in the outside world, if it does so at all, is a matter solely for it to decide for itself. But in OLE, this communication is governed – in other words, regulated rather than being strictly defined – by the main OLE server program (OLE32.DLL) on each Windows user's local system. (Here you have to become accustomed rather quickly to talking about a "server" as a piece of software.) Because applications built around OLE need to be available to be addressed by one another, those addressable portions of these applications are often separated (especially within the Office 2000 suite) into separate DLL programs called *automation servers*.

What makes an automation server unique is that another Windows program can literally strike up a conversation with it, unbeknownst to the user. Each Office 2000 application contains one such OLE automation server, which provides that application with the capability to process its registered class of document. The "front end" of the application – the part that loads itself into the Windows workspace when you double-click on its icon – does none of this processing on its own. Instead, the front-end launcher contacts its automation server, which does this part on the launcher's behalf.

An automation server has its own *interface*, which consists of terms that at least partly resemble spoken language, which the server recognizes as requests or procedure calls. (Technically, the automation server has several official interfaces, or sets of remote procedure calls that it uses or recognizes; but the sum of these interface terms are also collectively referred to as the component's interface.) For another program to contact Excel 2000, all it needs to do is *instantiate* an Excel object, name the instance internally, and place procedure calls to the object using the vocabulary of that object's interface. Excel is then awakened, and handles the interface call directly. Again, the user never sees any of this taking place, just the results – which are hopefully reflected in the quality of the data.

In VBA, as you'll see in the examples to come, the function used to instantiate an instance of an automation server is `CreateObject()`. A PowerPoint VBA module could use this function to contact Excel and give instructions to it directly. The `CreateObject()` function names the application using the name that is registered in the System Registry for that application. So PowerPoint can contact Excel and have it perform instructions using the syntax that the Excel VBA interpreter recognizes. The two interpreters – the one for PowerPoint and the one for Excel – handle the job of converting the instructions written in each other's native *lexicon*, into interface calls that their own automation servers recognize. So you as a VBA programmer don't actually have to write the interface calls verbatim, although you do have to be aware of their existence.

In Depth: Correcting misuse of "interface" at last

In this context, the term *interface* means what it used to mean prior to the discovery of new metaphors: It is a specification for how one mechanical item connects to another mechanical item. Programs qualify as mechanical items in this context. People do not. For instance, the Small Computer Systems Interface (SCSI, now on revision 3) specifies how any computer or peripheral may make contact with, and exchange data with, another computer or peripheral. The interface standard is specific. The terms and phraseology used by an OLE component in addressing another one, or being addressed by another one, constitute that component's interface. Again, the standard is specific to the precise bitwise digit. Now, consider how a specification might be written for a mechanical device or a program to exchange data with a device that is entirely under its own control – say, *you*. Whenever you or any other human entity becomes involved, the variable of absolute choice comes into play, and a discrete specification becomes impossible. In the language of such governing bodies as the Institute of Electrical and Electronics Engineers (IEEE), therefore, an interface also becomes impossible. The term "user interface," therefore, is a misnomer.

Office 2000 as an automation server suite

The type of work an Office 2000 application can perform as an automation server on an OLE object is limited to the capabilities and specifications of that object. But an object in this sense is only an object while it is in memory; when its data is stored on disk, there's no built-in program functionality there — it's just a *file*. So sometimes OLE has to cheat a bit and defer to an OLE server program, such as Excel or Word, to fill in the functionality part of the object when all there is to show for the object is its data file. This is why we consider an OLE data object as data paired with the program or functionality that gives it meaning. Stored as a file, at least to human eyes, the data may have no spontaneous meaning whatsoever. This need for OLE components to contact other OLE components directly has spawned a need among programmers to separate the part of the application *displaying* the data from the part *processing* it.

In fact, the .EXE file that users double-click on to launch an O2K application doesn't process any document or object data at all. That job is delegated to another type of component called the *engine*. This is an OLE component that processes non-OLE data, giving that data functionality it does not possess by itself.

The reason for interprocess communication

To the programming newcomer, it may not be obvious just why data has to communicate with other data. In the early days of programming, prior to the advent of multitasking and graphical user models, programs performed explicit procedures, maintained tight-knit databases, and produced conservative but reliable data. That data didn't have the need then to get up and say, "Hi!" to some other data; so why is there a sudden trend toward extroversion now?

The reason has to do with what history has taught us: The nature of *work* in any business environment is not strictly defined by any *single* specification or standard or process model — to the dismay of the International Organization for Standardization (ISO). Self-contained applications of the 1970s and 1980s, such as Valdocs and dBASE, dealt with strictly defined work processes. The results of these processes were massive databases whose formats were fixed in stone, and which were resistant to change when the nature of the business or the needs of any one office changed. Since these applications ran their own program scripts, they seemed on the surface — as well as to the new and fledgling computer press — to be flexible and adaptable. These program scripts themselves were of no special value to businesses; it was the databases that those scripts operated and maintained that were perceived as having value. Yet while the sizes of these databases were free to grow into infinity, their "shapes" — their format and schematics — were generally fixed in stone at the moment of their creation. So while these self-contained applications were groundbreaking and revolutionary in their time, their users spent more time adapting to them than they did to their users.

In OLE, the term *process* takes on the same broader concept that the term *job* has in UNIX and in hardware engineering. If you hail from either of these fields, then to help comprehend OLE, reverse the meanings of those two words. Otherwise, depict *process* in your mind as a *loop*.

In the late 1980s, office computing with single-processor systems began its path toward obsolescence, with the rapid infusion of network environments into the office. But the operating systems technology had changed faster than did the applications technology. As a result, businesses were faced with investing tens of thousands of dollars into software-based file server and security systems, the purpose of which was basically to maintain the illusion – for the sake of the old applications, not for anyone else – that one database was being accessed by one user. The need to remodel the old applications only became obvious when continuing to use them in their newer environments had long since become ridiculous.

The goal of the 1990s application has been to be adaptable to the work processes of whatever organization in which that application is put to use. Today, this is accomplished through the inclusion of two key elements of modern programming: *delegation* and *abstraction*. Let's address delegation first: Today, one program alone never performs the entire database processing job. Aspects of that job are delegated to separate processes, and some of these processes are designated as receivers of explicit commands from the user – not just macros, but complex scripts that seem to be capable of making a lot of judgment calls. These scripts are – at least in theory – as flexible and adaptable to the job at hand, as the job itself is to the needs of employees and of their company. The components which respond to and execute these scripts are called *automation servers* in Windows. Multiple components are more easily adaptable to unique and unpredictable work processes. But it does take *one* process to determine which others are necessary to undertake the job at hand; thus we have delegation, a distribution of work processes.

Next, abstraction: How does a programmer determine how to divide an application into separate process components and delegate work among them? The answer can be found by analyzing the nature of the final product documents that modern businesses utilize and require. Business data is part linguistic, part tabular, and part graphical. Yet these parts are rarely separated from one another; indeed, in order that the collective whole of this data can make sense to people, the parts are collected into *compound documents*. It was the need for compound documents, wherein many categories of data share the same space and purpose, that instigated the development of the Component Object Model in the first place.

But just what is a *category* of data? Is a data category necessarily definable by the application that produces it – for instance, "Excel data" categorized as contrary to "WordPerfect data" or "CorelDRAW data?" This type of categorization is, in an everyday work environment, impractical. This was readily discovered after half-a-decade of individuals "importing" and "exporting" files among countless name-brand data formats – a process that, in a magazine series I wrote back in 1986, I called "cloneverting." A class of data should have neither a brand name nor some exclusive format. Yet at the same time, a class of data should not be defined so specifically as to preclude it from assuming new and dynamic forms that can be put to use for new purposes as they arise. Thus in OLE, as in other object models, classes of data are defined *abstractly*, in terms that are broad and, at times, fuzzy. *Fewer*, though still multiple, components may therefore be used to handle these broader categories, and to ascertain how they can best be utilized within a compound document.

How, then, does this ascertainment take place? Through a system of symbols and signals that components can send to one another, as well as recognize once they're received; **for this reason a communications system between processes becomes necessary.** But once the facilities for interprocess communication are put in place, just what can one process say that another would be able to interpret? In any conversation between two *people*, whatever information traded between them that is not implied must be explicitly specified in order to be understood. Both implication and specificity require definition, and definition requires an underlying framework of conceptual understanding – a single mutual context. This underlying concept of just what things are is precisely what a computer does not have. So instead, to make processes understand each other, we use *abstract* mathematical logic. For example: Let's define X as that which does Y to Z. Then Y is the thing that X does to Z, and Z is that which has Y done to it by X. The closest thing to enlightenment a computer process may ever attain is the recognition of the logic behind these abstract symbols. For a program, this has meaning.

Shielding the user from abstract logic

When you design an application that utilizes OLE to any degree, the innermost conversations between the components you utilize are not anything that needs to be shared with the user. A computer application should not be a transparent thing on its face. The user at large is generally disinterested – to the dismay of authors everywhere such as myself – with the inner mechanisms of computing. It isn't because the topic is necessarily uninteresting, but instead because the work that the user is doing is far more pressing than the need to understand how component A says hi to component B. What compels people such as myself to remain programmers is the fact that we maintain a keen interest in the symbology and methodology of computing. But we cannot mislead ourselves into believing that the people who will use the tools we create will share our interest in these matters.

Furthermore, we must not forget that, although it makes sense during the construction phase for us programmers to build features into our applications that tell us what is going on and what is going wrong, when it comes time to distribute these applications – even if they are extensions of O2K applications – we must reprogram our components to shut up. If our application does not work properly, that fact will be obvious enough to the user, and the reasons why will only make sense to us programmers.

What makes the concepts of component objects and linking and embedding so compelling as marketing tools is not the fact that great bodies of symbolic logic may be inferred from them, but instead the fact that they are brand names that imply the presence of some deep, inner mechanism that you really don't want to know about. Pay no attention, in other words, to that man behind the curtain. This is why these terms are now used almost interchangeably – why "ActiveX" refers to one methodology one month and another category of methodologies the next. What is more important than the Component Object Model is the concept of programming with component objects. While the former appears to be the receptacle for the latter, the concept is, in itself, broader than the Model makes it out to be. The same principles of component object programming are inherent in both COM and its rival model, Common Object Request Broker Architecture (CORBA). To subscribe to the concept is not to sign on to one brand name or the other. But to sign onto a brand name is not necessarily to embrace the principles that name implies.

However high-minded or pragmatic you choose to be as a programmer, there is one principle that you must adopt if you are to stay a programmer: Your users must perceive the work they do with a computer as the same work they would have done without the computer, only substantially easier and more productive. The product of a component application, in COM or any other model, is the document. As programmers, we apply deep philosophical meanings to the concept of document production. But users should not have to be any more philosophical about that concept than they would be about the quite similar concept that the product of a typewriter is the document.

There is one merging of the two concepts of document and object that you, and only you, need to consider, and that is the *compound document.* In OLE, this is manifest as a precise ordering of OLE objects that come together through either linking or embedding (processes described later in this chapter) to produce the document the user perceives. Each object in the compound document is managed by a program which COM calls the *object handler component,* or just *handler.* The purpose of the handler is to produce and manage objects of the same type and purpose – which is to say, objects of the same class. Should several objects of the same class inhabit the same memory, then the same handler will manage all of them.

Distinguishing the control from the container

The user builds a compound document by means of a *container application,* which, to the user, is just an application. In a sense, a container application rents out its space to OLE components in exchange for access to their functionality. This functionality makes it possible for a user to create data belonging to particular COM classes. The tools that initiate this functionality, such as menu commands and toolbar buttons, are provided by means of a type of component called the *control,* which in COM is considered part of the handler. When I refer to ActiveX controls, this is the component I mean. The control is the part of the handler that the user can get a hold of, by way of a button, or command, or some visible screen element.

While the control's main job is to provide the user with access to OLE functionality, it can also be the provider of that functionality. This is the case with all ActiveX controls implemented in form modules and embedded in O2K documents. All the gadgets that comprise the Forms 2.0 suite (FM20.DLL) are fully self-contained components. Self-contained components provide functionality to the user, access to that functionality through the container, and direct process control over that functionality to the programmer.

Analyzing OLE's "personality"

OLE component objects present different functionality – different "faces" – to different users. To the end user of an application, the functionality of OLE is largely defined by the capability of data to be functional by means other than the application program that first generated that data. To the high-level language programmer – the user of Visual Basic for Applications – the functionality of OLE is found in *libraries*, which could more accurately be described as "dictionaries." A library presents the high-level programmer with the properties, methods, and events (such as those introduced in the previous chapters) with which the programmer directly addresses the functions of the component. To the low-level language programmer – the user of C++ – the functionality of OLE is specified by *interfaces*, which are bound by a moderately regulated scheme for handling ordinary C++ procedure calls. (A "middle-level" of sorts is enabled by the advent of Visual Basic Standard Edition, which uses high-level tools to model low-level functionality.)

The way in which the user of an OLE application makes contact with and interacts with that application's data is defined by the control. Although not all OLE components are considered controls by name, they each contain a control as part of their construction – a way for the container application to make contact with the component's data. ActiveX controls are those self-contained, so-called *in-process*, components that provide such features to applications as scroll bars and animated buttons. Yet the automation server is a separate, *out-of-process* component that provides data to a container, even if that container doesn't "belong" to the application or other package that installed that server program on the user's computer. The server component makes itself available to the container by way of the control portion of that component's own handler. This type of control is, admittedly, not nearly as much fun to talk about as the in-process control, though it merits mention here because without it, the document engine could not make contact with Word 2000, nor could the worksheet engine make contact with Excel 2000. You see, the parser runs *out-of-process* with respect to the container; as far as the client computer is concerned, the parser and the container with the menu and all the buttons on top are not the same program.

Figure 8-2 depicts the relationship between the components of a self-contained (*in-process*) ActiveX control and those of the container application. The relationship is shown from the user's point of view, though it does give you a peek at what goes on behind the scenes. Any gadgets such as toolbar buttons or *handles* placed around the object in the container window are devices provided and maintained by the ActiveX control. If the function of the control isn't truly interactive – for instance, if it's just a display device like the image control in Forms 2.0 – then the manner of display is defined by the control. The container application is a passive participant in all of this.

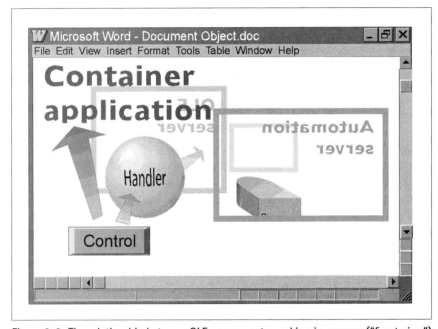

Figure 8-2: The relationship between OLE components working in-process ("front view").

An OLE container application provides the user with the face of the compound document. An ActiveX control provides the user with the face of the function of a class of data. This defines the perception of OLE/ActiveX from the user's perspective. Take this model in your mind now, rotate it 180 degrees, and let's examine the other side – from the perspective of the operating system, as depicted in Figure 8-3. The handler for an object (something the user never sees) manages that object's creation and its content. It also manages both temporary and permanent storage for that object, in memory and on permanent media. OLE maintains its own independent storage system for objects, which "maps" or corresponds to the Windows filing system but is, nonetheless, removed from it. So OLE/ActiveX objects have *monikers* that the user never sees nor has to be concerned with, and which we will concern ourselves with later once we're rested and ready for that topic.

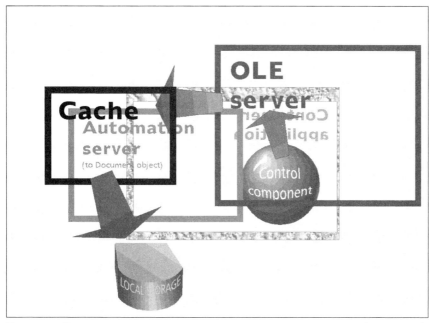

Figure 8-3: The relationship between OLE components working in-process ("back view").

The control is part of the handler for a class of objects. To make the functionality of a component accessible to the programmer, the handler establishes a working vocabulary for the objects it maintains. At last, COM has been given a name for this vocabulary. Unfortunately, that name — the component's *methods* — clashes with the name used in VBA for a procedure of an instantiated object. Furthermore, some methods in COM are methods in VBA, and other methods in COM are *properties* in VBA (here we go again!). So this chapter uses its own term to refer to the vocabulary of a component: *lexicon*. Why would Microsoft use one term to mean two different things? Because the division of Microsoft responsible for COM, and the division responsible for VBA, are disparate arms of the company that may be on opposite sides of the office complex, but are actually as far apart as Redmond is from Cairo.

 By the way, if you've ever wondered why the long-promised merger of Windows 98 with Windows NT has been nicknamed "Cairo," take this simple test: On any globe, put your left index finger on Redmond, and your right on Cairo. Notice where they are with respect to each other and you'll realize the inside joke.

On Point

The cornerstone of the Component Object Model is the *object*, whose precise definition is often obscure. The most reasonable way to think of the object is as data combined with instructional code of some form which gives that data meaning to some program, or even to some person. The programs in COM that make use of objects are *components*. These components manifest themselves as objects within the source code of applications and programs such as the type you write with VBA.

An ActiveX control is a COM component. It is designed to be run by a *container application* that makes contact with that component directly, as though it were part of the container's own process. For this reason, this pairing of container and control results in what OLE calls an *in-process server*, or a single process that provides the user with access to OLE objects. Internet Explorer is a container application capable of functioning, along with ActiveX controls, as an in-process server. It also manages some OLE components that are *out-of-process*, such as its scripting engines and automation servers. This last part handles the precise interpretation and display of the application document (in this case, the HTML page).

A true story

This business of handlers, interfaces, controls, and lexicons may seem to be a wild and rather long digression, since the cornerstone of OLE technology is supposed to be the "L" and "E" part. Yet, as you'll see demonstrated shortly, these other topics all come together to produce the linking and embedding functionality that application users expect. First, a little digression of my own:

OLE made its formal premiere in Windows technology with the introduction of Microsoft Office, the first bundling of applications that actually initiated and utilized the OLE.DLL portion of Windows 3.1. Office as a formal product was "rolled out," to use the marketing term, in 1989, and I covered the rollout party thrown by Microsoft's Dallas division. There, one of the authors of Excel 3.0 demonstrated to an audience how a spreadsheet could be dragged from its home in the Excel workspace, and dropped into a Word document without any of the import/export fuss to which users had then become accustomed. There were gasps of excitement as many correspondents, for the first time, saw OLE actually work. Curiously, though, I noticed that this programmer had not been referring to OLE specifically by name during any part of his demonstration. When he opened the floor for questions, in keeping with a dangerous personal trait I had developed, I was the first with my hand up. I introduced myself, stated the name of my magazine, and asked, "Sir, how much of the functionality that you've demonstrated here is a native part of the Excel program, and how much is part of Windows' object *binking and enledding*?"

About ten seconds later I realized what I had said, though there were no smirks from anyone in the audience, and the gentleman at the podium proceeded to point out that OLE, the portion of Windows that had been present though not actually utilized by any applications at that time, was indeed being initialized by Excel. He went on to give credit to another division of Microsoft for making this drag-and-drop concept possible, and I started to breathe a bit easier, and even began thinking of the greater Dallas area as a community of decent, forgiving souls who really do work together for a brighter tomorrow, and so all would be well. "So what this all comes down to," the gentleman concluded his remarks, gazing decisively in my direction, "is that you can now bink and enled things faster and better than you could ever bink and enled them before." "I appreciate that, sir," I responded above the roar of the crowd, "and now I wish to go back to my office and bink and enled myself to my desk." "Well, now you can," the gentleman shot back, "thanks to Microsoft."

OLE is the binder of the compound document

Anyway, back to programming and the important roles that bink. . . that *linking and embedding* play: A compound document is a chain of objects strung together in a particular sequence. This chain is held together not by any one OLE-compliant application, but by OLE itself – part of the Windows operating system. Linking and embedding are the two methodologies that are used to chain objects together; either or both may be in play for any one document.

Earlier, I distinguished *components* (programs that represent data) from *objects* (data that represents programs); here, the importance of this distinction is under-scored. An object is made up of data, and a component is the program that operates upon that object's class of data. A compound document may chain together many objects of the same class; in such a case, one single version of the component would act as the handler for each instance of that class. (That is to say, if the component was programmed correctly; there should not have to be six or seven programs simultaneously running for six or seven option buttons in a `UserForm` object.) But a document, whether it chains together a series of other objects or contains no other class of object whatsoever, is itself recognized as a single object. In the Word 2000 object library, the term `Document` refers to the characteristics of its native document, while Excel uses the term `Workbook` to refer to its native document. For each open document in an application, there is one corresponding document object, whatever the application's object library chooses to call it.

In the standard OLE system (this is your warning that there are exceptions to the rule that follows), when a container application encounters an object of a particular class, the container has the responsibility of invoking the component that handles that class. For instance, if a control on a toolbar is provided by an ActiveX component, then it's up to the container application to launch that component; it can't launch itself. If a document contains an instance of something as simple as a control – for instance, an ordinary command button, stuck in the middle of a page – then the container application invokes that control's component, connecting it to the container and running it in-process with the container.

A document object is not a control. By itself, that sentence may seem a bit eso-teric, but it makes more sense if you consider it like this: A spreadsheet is not a but-ton. A user may embed an Excel worksheet within a Word document. That worksheet has its own document object, while the contents of Word's document object make reference to the Excel document. Yet it's the job of Word's container application to notice this reference and load the handler for Excel at the appropri-ate time. In the case of Microsoft Office applications, these handler components are automation servers, which lend their lexicons to VBA. The handler takes over, and manages and executes the interpretation and display of all instances of its docu-ment object class within the container's document. So it is Excel that is displaying the embedded worksheet, not Word. But Excel's handler can't know to display that worksheet unless Word's container application tells it to.

Linking and embedding, compared and contrasted

What distinguishes linking from embedding is the manner in which document objects are referenced within a compound document. Figure 8-4 depicts the diver-gent principles of linking and embedding. A single linked document object may appear to the user to be a native part of several compound documents; yet on the same workstation, the object in reality only exists once. It is a native part of only one document object, referred to as the *source*. Contained within the other docu-ments are links that make reference to the source object, and which result in iden-tical copies of that source object being *displayed* seamlessly within those link documents. Notice I said "displayed," not "contained." **The linked object appears to be part of the main document, when it is in fact part of its own.** It is the *user* who creates these links, generally by way of an editing process involving the Windows System Clipboard and a menu command, which shows up in Office 2000 as **Paste Special**. So OLE protocol expects the user to keep track of which document is the source of the link, even though Windows provides no directory scheme to the user for keeping track of such links.

By contrast, an embedded object, while it too has a single source, is actually copied to the physically stored version of the compound document, even if the application responsible for saving it is other than that responsible for actually building the embedded object. So the object data may exist more than once; and what's more, edits made to that object in one compound document *are not auto-matically reflected* in the same object within another compound document. An instance of an embedded object, therefore, is not merely an echo of one file's con-tents, but moreover it is an exclusively *edited* copy of an original source object. The edits made by the user are saved, along with the copy, within the compound docu-ment that invokes the document object. The handler for the source of the original edition of that object is still responsible for managing and displaying that object within the container application, but the data that is being displayed comes from the file generated by the document object of the container application, not the source application.

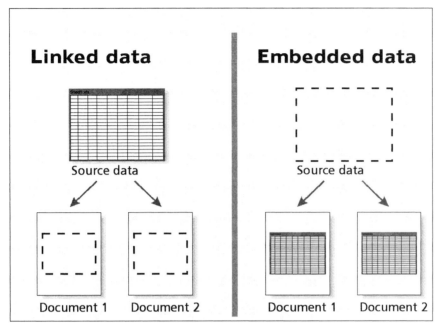

Figure 8-4: Object linking or embedding: the contrasting document object relationships.

The true difference between linking and embedding is that a linked object is a replica of the source for display only that *is not stored* with the compound document, whereas the embedded object is a snapshot of the source as it appeared at one time plus any newer edits that may have been made to it, all of which *is stored* with the compound document. Why is this distinction even important? Because for some documents, it is important that all linked documents be given one view of the one true version of the data, whereas for others it is important that the document be linked to the version of that data that existed at a particular time, or to a version that is somehow modified for the exclusive purposes of the containing document.

Conceivably, the end result of the linking and embedding schemes should be that all data produced by Windows OLE applications are not "Excel documents" or "PowerPoint documents," but just "documents." The document objects produced by the various applications would all be linked or embedded together in a chain to produce an OLE file whose purpose can be designated solely by its users, not by any one application that played a role in producing it. That, plus Republicans and Democrats would without hesitation set aside their differences, postpone their fundraising stops, and negotiate harmonious agreements toward bipartisan campaign finance reform. Despite all the promises that get Office 2000 installed on our systems just as easily as we're compelled to vote for more Republicans and Democrats, pure document centricity is not the basis for how Windows currently operates. A document still has its own exclusive source application, which specifies the format of its native data. OLE data is comprised of document objects that are either referenced by or included with the source file. In short, OLE objects are *sub-ordinate*. They are not the root document objects of Windows. . . at least not yet.

Is a control an "L" or an "E"?

So far, both linked and embedded objects appear to be *document objects*, produced and maintained by an automation server or some controlling container application. If that's the case, where do *controls* fit in this scheme of things? Are controls linked or are they embedded? Microsoft's documentation describes ActiveX controls as being embedded within an OLE document. But is this technically correct? Following the definition for embedding that I just gave you, no. An embedded object by the long-standing OLE definition is an object copied from an original source; ActiveX controls have no original source. So evidently we have reached the terminological border where OLE ends and ActiveX begins. An ActiveX control is a running instance of a program; thus, it is *instantiated* within a document. The reference to the control placed within the document directly accesses the control's type library, which, once it's installed within a client, is listed in the System Registry file. We can state that linked and embedded document objects are instantiated as well; though we have no other exclusive term available to us that describes the relationship between a control and the document or other object that instantiates it.

The parts of a component's lexicon

The lexicon of a COM component object is comprised, for the most part, of active English-language words. Those words that represent tasks that can be performed by the component are called *methods*. The purpose of these methods is to symbolize, in a definitive though abstract manner, the nature of the operations that a component performs. "Open" is the most common method among components; and its general meaning can be interpreted by human beings as, "Bring a file associated with an application from storage into memory." Other similarly broad-ranging methods within a component's lexicon include "Add," "Insert," and "Print."

The relationship between a method term and its associated component object, to borrow some terms from English grammar, can be *transitive* or *intransitive* depending on the situation. In English, a transitive verb is one that describes the action performed by the subject of the sentence on the object of the sentence – "Mr. Gates eats his competition for lunch," for instance. Whereas an intransitive verb has no direct object other than the subject itself – "Mr. Gates eats." In Word 2000, `Documents.Open` is a method that acts as a command instructing the `Documents` collection to open another document by name, and to add that document to the collection. This would be a "transitive" method. However, if `paraThis` is an object reference to a member of the `Paragraphs` collection, then `paraThis.OpenUp` is an instruction that tells the referenced paragraph to give 12 points of leading between itself and the paragraph above it. This would be an "intransitive" method. There is no "hard-and-fast" rule governing the varying transitivity of any method. Suffice it to say, however confusing this may appear in print, that some method terms use their object as their "subject," whereas others use them as their "object."

The other parts of speech common to components – though not necessary for their existence – are *properties* and *events*. As you've seen, properties are very much like variables in that they symbolize values or memory contents – they represent the *state* of something. Events, by contrast, are signals of the *incidence* of something; they have no value unto themselves other then their own binary "happening/not happening" state.

The Component Communication Process

The basic method of communication between COM components is, simply put, *binary*. All components end up signaling one another and trading parameters using the same C++ remote procedure calls (RPCs) to which programming veterans are accustomed. But the communications process is modeled such that you as programmer need not utilize these elaborate C++ function libraries in order to facilitate their own OLE processes. That's what all this lexicon stuff was about earlier – terms which symbolize in a broader and more tangible form, the more complex processes that are actually accomplished by the C++ functions.

The first tier: the binary interface

The set of binary functions necessary for a COM component to communicate with another is called the *interface* for that component. Every component has an interface with which other components can address it. The object terms you use in VBA as directives to other components are *not* interface calls; instead, they are terms from the calling component's lexicon that get translated into interface calls. The majority of interface terms, such as `IPersistStorage` and `IOleCache`, are presented for the sake of making and breaking the communications connections between components. As long as components have a way of "seeing" each other, and basically telling one another to start or stop doing whatever it is that they are programmed to do, the remainder of the construction of an ActiveX component can concentrate on being an ordinary program. OLE's role in Windows is to facilitate component communication. It *marshals* data, to use the COM term for overseeing something as it marches from place to place, but OLE does not manage nor does it create data outside of what it must use for its own purposes.

The second tier: the type library and the lexicon

The lexicons for such components as automation servers and controls are written into separate files called *type libraries*, for reasons unbeknownst to anyone today, since "type" is not a term defined elsewhere in the OLE or COM specifications. (To companies such as Adobe and CG, "type library" means something else entirely: a collection of binary fonts belonging to typefaces.) The name of the type library for a component is listed in the System Registry file of each client in which that component is installed. When a script, macro, or other program seeks to initiate contact with a component, the name of that component class is checked against the System Registry in order to ascertain the location of the type library.

The second tier of the communications process is through the lexicon itself, and the parties in this communication are generally the OLE automation servers of two applications. Assume, for example, that a document object component originated by Excel is embedded within a Word document. Remember, the container application for the worksheet is one component, but the worksheet itself is another. For Word to "call" the worksheet object, it requires a "directory assistance operator" of sorts to help it find the "number" for the component that manages the worksheet class. The directory assistance in this case is provided by the System Registry, which is installed on every OLE client's local system. Word has the "operator" (OLE itself) look up the worksheet class' number (its class identifier, or CLSID) by giving OLE the name of the class' component: `Excel.Sheet`. OLE looks in the System Registry under the main heading `HKEY_CLASSES_ROOT` for a key named `Excel.Sheet`. If that component is installed, OLE responds with the magic number `{00020820-0000-0000-C000-000000000046}`.

Next, OLE looks up this CLSID number elsewhere in the System Registry, under the subheading of `CLSID` under `HKEY_CLASSES_ROOT`. If OLE has gotten this far in the lookup process, then *it will find the CLSID number* (if the number weren't there, OLE wouldn't be looking for it). In that number's listing, under the subheading `LocalServer32`, is `C:\Program Files\Microsoft Office\Office\excel.exe`, the installed path of the main Excel application. This is the program that is launched to fulfill the request for `Excel.Sheet`. Yes, it's the same file as the one the user double-clicks on to launch Excel; but Excel knows when it's being invoked by an OLE component and when it's being invoked by a user.

Once Excel is launched, how does Word talk to it? (Remember that no two OLE components necessarily have the same lexicon.) The answer comes by way of another lookup process: Under the subheading of `TypeLib` for the CLSID number, OLE finds yet another magic number, `{00020813-0000-0000-C000-000000000046}`. So OLE next takes this number and looks under the separate `TypeLib` subheading of `HKEY_CLASSES_ROOT`. Again, if OLE has come this far in the lookup process, it will find the number. Once that listing is obtained, then under its subheading `1.3` (the latest edition of the type library), under sub-subheading `0` (first component interface number for that edition, where "0" is always the first), under sub-sub-subheading `Win32` (cross-platform implementation type for the given interface), OLE will find the local path of the file `excel9.olb`. This is the dynamic link library that provides Word with the type library for the Excel worksheet class.

So now Word has the lexicon for an Excel worksheet and knows how to pass directives to the component using its own specific terminology. What happens when Word receives a call back from the Excel component? The registered in-process handler for Excel – in this case, OLE32.DLL – processes these directives by translating them back into OLE interface calls from the first tier of communications, mentioned a few paragraphs back.

The first tier redux

This takes us right back to the first tier of communications between components. How, then, does Word actually retrieve the binary functions implicitly referred to by the second-tier directive from Excel? Within each component's type library is a list of the *binary interfaces* that the component utilizes. Binary interfaces are the true interfaces of COM; there are a few other ways in which the term "interface" is used, though for the most part, the term implies "binary." An interface in this sense is simply a named list of remote procedure calls that the component might use during its instantiation. The average OLE component utilizes dozens if not hundreds of such interfaces, including those it must support in order to qualify as OLE components.

One component's interfaces can find another component's interfaces because, in the end, every COM interface is built on the foundation of the same root, called IUnknown. This interface contains only three remote procedure calls, but they're the most important three: QueryInterface helps a component ascertain whether another component supports a certain interface that is passed to the function by name. AddRef tells the contacted component to give the caller a duplicate pointer to its interface functions; this way the owner of the interface can keep track of which other components are in contact with it. Release tells the referenced component that it's done with the reference. In short, the three calls mean, "Can you do this?" "Plug me in," and "I'm done now." Every interface, no matter how complex, contains these three calls because they are principal to every single connection between COM components. More complex interfaces issue the type of function calls you'd expect to see in an ordinary application – and you'd probably need to be the programmer of that ordinary application to know exactly what they mean. But COM needs these principal three RPCs to get to the point where components can "talk shop."

You won't be writing any of these RPC calls into your VBA program. But whenever you declare a new VBA object reference variable As New Worksheet or As Document, you know these RPC calls are being made.

Binary interfaces are also OLE components, listed in the System Registry below the HKEY_CLASSES_ROOT heading under the Interface subheading. An interface referred to in a component's type library is checked against this Registry listing, to see whether the OLE globally-unique ID number (GUID) for the type library is the same as the GUID listed for the given interface under the sub-subheading TypeLib. That having been verified, the interface is loaded into memory (assuming it's not there already). When I say an interface is a *list* of remote procedure calls, I mean that literally – the calls themselves aren't there. The calls are referred to indirectly, by means of what Microsoft calls a *virtual table* (abbreviated "vtbl," for reasons unbeknownst to modern science).

Now that OLE knows what the function names for one component are, how does it link those functions to another component at run time? Again the System

Registry comes into play. When the calling program (in our example, Word) makes reference to an Excel worksheet object through one of its elements referenced by an interface such as `IHyperlink`, the CLSID for `IHyperlink`'s interface component is found in the type library. OLE looks up this CLSID under `HKEY_CLASSES_ROOT`. When it finds the component's CLSID key, OLE looks through its subheading `Interface`, sub-subheading `ProxyStubClsid32`. Here, OLE finds the CLSID number for the *handler* of the component that utilizes this interface. For our example, OLE finds `{00020420-0000-0000-C000-000000000046}`. Cross-referencing this number against the `CLSID` section of the Registry, OLE finds a component named `PSDispatch`, whose registered in-process server name (located in the `InprocServer32` key) is `OLEAUT32.DLL`, the library for the OLE 2.2 extension to Windows. This program is responsible for fetching the interface. This tells you something quite important about the way Office 2000 applications work; some of their functionality is actually provided by components of Windows.

The proxy and the stub

The two important parts of a component's handler for communications purposes are, as the subheading implies, the *proxy* and the *stub*. In Figure 8-5, I've imagined the proxy and stub, and the components they serve, as floating Aristotelian objects in space so that you can better envision the relationships between them.

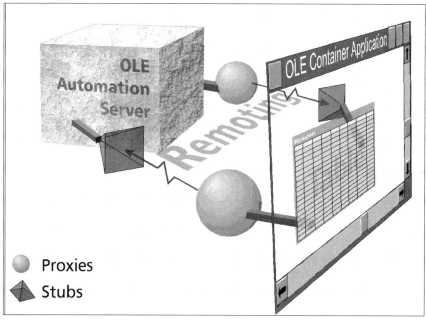

Figure 8-5: A model of the relationships between container, proxy, stub, and an object instance of a component.

The proxy's job is to act on behalf of its associated OLE component (say, Word 2000 from our example) to send the remote procedure calls to the recipient component (Excel). The stub, in turn, is the part of the recipient's handler that receives the call and coordinates its execution. The handoff of the OLE message takes place between proxy and stub – which, for any one OLE application or control component, are provided as part of the same handler. The message being sent is the remote procedure call mentioned in the interface of the sending component. The origin of this message is the virtual table, which belongs to one of the interfaces employed by the receiving component. The calling component knows *what* this function is; it isn't unaware of the receiving component's vocabulary, and it doesn't rely on the receiver to teach it what the receiver's functions are. What the receiving component doesn't know – what it *cannot* know on its own – is *where* this function is. The receiver doesn't have an interpreter that recognizes function calls by name; if it did, then every receiver would need one, and every component in COM would be at least two megabytes large. So the virtual table – supplied by the receiver's requested interface – supplies the location to the sender's *local server* or *in-process server* (two different types of COM servers, depending on the task at hand). The dynamic link takes place here.

Which program is the in-process server? It's an executable file, whose local path can be found in the System Registry under the `CLSID` subheading, using the same CLSID number taken from `ProxyStubClsid32`. From there, look for the subheading `InProcServer32`, and you'll find the name of the executable file that acts as the in-process server component for the OLE application. Generally it's a .DLL file; by contrast, a `LocalServer32` component often uses a more conventional .EXE file.

At last, through a very complex process of lookup and translation, simple directives are translated into complex operating system processes. When COM works, and works *well*, this is how it happens.

In Depth: Does COM really make room for platforms other than Windows?

Is it feasible to make COM a *cross-platform* system capable of running on Macintosh or UNIX? You've just been given a peek into one of the "degrees of separation" that Microsoft might exploit to this end. In order for OLE to retrieve a type library for a component, it looks in the System Registry under the current platform – in the example case, under `Win32`. Only after this point, when OLE retrieves the .DLL file with the type library, does the system need to be concerned with executing *binary code* – which is the part of OLE that must be different for each platform with which it will be concerned. A PowerMac version of the type library for the same OLE component, for example, with the same CLSID and type library ID, could then be listed and treated separately from the `Win32` version. So there does appear to be a mechanism in place for traversing the boundary between uniform access and binary compatibility.

In-process and out-of-process components

In the relationship between container application, ActiveX control, and automation server, the container and the ActiveX control communicate using the handler's lexicon *(in-process)*. These two have bonded with one another and have established a closely knit rapport. This particular control now belongs to the container and to no one else; for another application to access the same functionality, it has to get its own instance of the same ActiveX control.

In-process component relationships, such as the one between a container application and an ActiveX control, are the exceptions to the rules of component relationships outlined a few paragraphs ago. Container and control do not have to break down their lexicons into procedure calls in so many steps; or, as Microsoft's terminology puts it, in-process applications don't perform *remoting* (all those steps in the two-tier process are referred to as remoting). Instead, a container can address an ActiveX control using its own lexicon, and the control's handler breaks those terms down directly from object-oriented syntax to C/C++ syntax. The control can do this because once it has been instantiated by the container, as far as the operating system can tell, that control is the same program as the container. The control's library of RPCs appears to belong exclusively to the container application.

On the other hand, a control has to communicate with an automation server by means of remoting *(out-of-process)*. In this relationship, each component has its own lexicon which it expects the other to use in addressing it. Through the remoting process outlined earlier, a lexicon-based instruction from the control is translated into a remote procedure call to the automation server. The server may respond in the usual way — with a result value passed back to the calling function — or with a callback function placed by the automation server to the control. No "bonding" takes place between control and automation server, because this server is an independent entity and does not belong to anything but itself.

There may be special circumstances where ActiveX controls may rely upon automation servers for their own functionality (case in point: IWebBrowserApp, the interface for Internet Explorer presented in the guise of an ActiveX control). In these situations, several container applications may use their own control instances to independently access the same automation server, using terms from those controls' lexicons. In-process communication takes place between all the containers and their control instances, yet each control utilizes remoting to initiate out-of-process communication between itself and the automation server.

How OLE facilitates the document object

As I mentioned earlier, a document object serves as an instance of a component's data. This is important from the perspective of a container application that is attempting to manage, print, or display this data, because it requires the program that originated the data to provide instructions to the container as to how to go about that process.

Each document object in OLE is managed by a handler component, which is provided by the application that originated the document object. For example, if you construct a table in Excel and later build a Web page that contains this table, then it is Excel's handler that displays the table within the page. This is achieved as a result of a three-way, or perhaps four-way, communications process within the client system. The component assigned responsibility for the object is generally called the *default handler*; in special cases, a *custom handler* may be assigned instead. For this discussion, we'll assume one handler is in play, whether it be the default or the custom handler. The communications scheme for an embedded OLE/ActiveX document object is depicted in Figure 8-6.

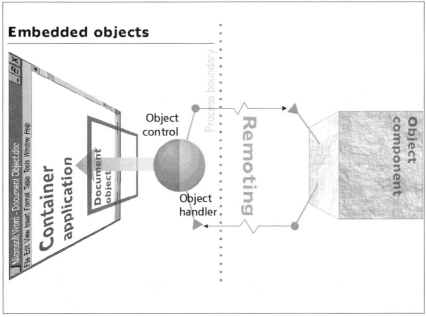

Figure 8-6: Communications, or "data flow," between container, embedded document object, and automation server.

Here, the handler for the document object contains the control facilities, which interface the control with the container, and the remoting facilities that initiate communication between the document object and the automation server of its original application. Notice this crucial feature of OLE architecture: The relationship between document object and container application is *in-process*, while the relationship between document object and the application that originally generated it – the one you would think the object "belongs" to – is *out-of-process*. Remoting, therefore, takes place between the originating application and its own product. For an embedded document object – whose container application is responsible for maintaining any exclusive edits that are made to the object – the relationship starts to make sense. After all, the stored file that contains the embedded object is a file exclusively maintained by the container.

For a *linked* document object, on the other hand – where the object is independent of the stored file that "contains" it, or rather makes reference to it – the relationship has to be made a bit more complex. Here is where the *four*-way process takes place, as depicted in Figure 8-7.

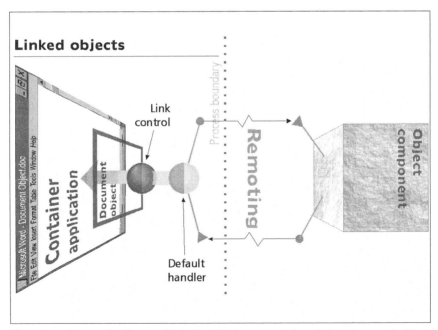

Figure 8-7: Communications, or "data flow," between container, linked document object, and automation server.

In the linked object situation, what is generally perceived as the document object is represented by *two* components. The link itself has a component, which includes the control portion necessary for it to link seamlessly with the container for in-process communication. Independently, the handler for the automation server of the originating object includes its own control, which enables it to communicate with the linked document object in-process. The result of the in-process communication between link component and handler component is the appearance of a single, seamlessly composed document object for the sake of the container. This architecture makes sense because a linked document object is designed only to be referred to by container documents, not contained by them. Any edits made to the linked object by any application (or more accurately, by means of any application contacting the originator's automation server) are reflected immediately in all the other container documents that refer to it. The link object is also stored independently, which means that all that the containers have to be concerned with storing are the references to the link.

On Point

Communication between components is a two-tiered process. Components are capable of sending directives to one another by way of sensibly named terms. These terms belong to the exclusive *type libraries* of their components and comprise those components' *lexicons*. Each lexicon contains the properties, events, and methods applicable to that control. The precise usage and phraseology of these terms within a script or high-level program points the way to the C/C++-style remote procedure calls that components need to run in order to process OLE directives. These RPC calls are listed within *interfaces*, which are virtual tables of OLE binary function calls. All communication between COM controls is maintained by the *handlers* for those controls, which consist of *proxies* that send the RPCs and *stubs* that receive them.

Instantiation for Fun and Profit

In the chapters to follow, we'll occasionally use VBA instructions to call forth an object that belongs to an application *other* than the one presently responsible for the VBA interpreter. By now, you should be familiar with the Set statement, which assigns an object reference to point to a particular object. Using the Set statement, you can generate under the VBA environment successful instances of the following two types of ActiveX components:

◆ **The automation server** for an application, which is represented in O2KOM by the Application object for each of its libraries;

◆ A **document object** produced by an application, such as a Word 2000 Document, Excel Worksheet, or PowerPoint Presentation object.

So why "create" either of these two types of objects? As you'll see throughout the remainder of the book, if a document object already exists in one of the other O2K applications, you may need an object reference that points to it within VBA's native application. This way you can assess data under development within the other application. Also, you may actually need to build that other class of object, or at least initiate the process of building that object. You'd use the New qualifier with the Set statement to call forth a new instance of the listed class of object.

The process of linking Windows components through VBA so that they can establish contact with one another and share data, is called *binding*. With VBA, binding takes place when a variable that has been declared to refer to some type of object, or to an Object in general, becomes associated with a real object someplace in the system. The relationship between a freshly declared object reference and a *bound* reference is analogous to that between a coffee cup and a cup of coffee. As you'll see, there are a number of ways in which binding may take place, and which method you choose depends on the circumstances of your program.

Office 2000 applications as automation servers

In the various libraries that make up the Office 2000 Object Model, the Application object represents the main automation server of an application — from the component programmer's standpoint, its engine. The term itself is generally omitted from references to an automation server's own subordinate terms and constituents within that server's own copy of the VBA interpreter. But when more than one O2K application server is required for a particular task, the Application term is used as a tie-in for one automation server's VBA interpreter to contact another application server. For example, Access/VBA would refer to the document currently open in Word as Word.Application.ActiveDocument. The library name is mentioned first in order to distinguish this particular instance of Application from the default instance, which for Access is, naturally, its own.

Bringing an entirely new instance of any automation server into the current Windows session is accomplished not with an ordinary statement or a method, but a declaration. To declare an object reference within one O2K application's VBA to refer to another application's automation server, you add one word — New — to the standard declaration:

```
Dim appWord As New Word.Application
```

Assume we're working from Access/VBA. This instruction will *prepare* a variable to refer to an instance of the Word automation server. But it doesn't need to be set using the Set statement to refer to any specific object; the New part of the instruction handles this part. Once any other instruction refers to any subordinate term of appWord, Windows will invoke the entire application. The Access/VBA module can then open some Word document, ascertain its contents, and then close the application using this instruction:

```
Set appWord = Nothing
```

This releases the object reference from Access/VBA memory and closes Word. What is the benefit of necessarily opening a new instance of Word – or some other application – rather than searching for an existing instance and starting a conversation with it? For one thing, your VBA module could operate without disturbing whatever the user may be doing with that other open application.

The older method for invoking another application's server involves the use of either the `CreateObject()` or `GetObject()` function. In the Declarations section of the VBA module, you build the reference to the Word automation server, but you don't use `New`, so it isn't instantiated yet:

```
Dim appWord As Word.Application
```

At this point, `appWord` is not yet ready to handle direct references to Word. Imagine, if you will, that the `Dim` instruction here cast variable `appWord` in the "shape" of `Word.Application`, but not quite yet in the "form" of that application – a bit like gelatin having been poured into a mould though not yet cooled. To chill things into shape, you need to invoke the `Set` statement before you invoke any other instructions that use `appWord`. To start a new instance of Word, you would use this instruction:

```
Set appWord = CreateObject("Word.Application.9")
```

The single argument of this particular `CreateObject()` function is the program identifier (ProgID) of Word 2000 as it appears in the OLE System Registry, complete with version number `.9` tacked to the end. This is where the ProgID finally comes into play. Using `New`, VBA would have to look up in the System Registry the ProgID referred to by `Word.Application` (the fact that the term's associated ProgID without the version number is `Word.Application` is coincidence). By comparison, using the `CreateObject()` function, you've looked up the ProgID on VBA's behalf.

Immediately after you declare an object reference variable `As Application`, whatever that application might be, the terms from that application's object library – in other words, its *lexicon* – are made available to that variable. If your declaration is `As New Application`, then those terms may actually be invoked in an instruction right away. Otherwise, there may be some steps you have to take in-between. **Even though an object library's lexicon may have been made available to a VBA term, the use of those terms in an instruction in the current context may not be applicable.**

Building objects listed in the System Registry

By means of the `CreateObject()` and `GetObject()` functions, OLE gives you the capability from any VBA interpreter within any application to construct and deploy any of the objects whose ProgID names are listed in the `HKEY_CLASSES_ROOT` tier of the System Registry, provided these conditions are in place:

♦ An object library must be attainable for the instantiable object. This may be an interface attached to the front of the object's DLL, or, in the case of many automation servers including O2K applications, a separate .OLB file entirely.

♦ The lexicon presented by this object library must be rich enough to permit instantiation entirely independently of the library's native application.

The version-specific ProgID for an Excel 2000 workbook is `Excel.Sheet.8`. If you're wondering why an application's document – arguably its product rather than its own component – has a *program* identifier. . . then you're learning how to be confused along with the rest of us. Equally confusing may be the fact that this ProgID refers to a *workbook*, which in practice is a *series* of worksheets rather than just one.

You could conceivably create, populate, save, and release an entire working Excel workbook from within the VBA interpreter of some application other than Excel. If that doesn't surprise you, then perhaps this will: **Instantiating a document product of an application using `CreateObject()` will in turn invoke that application's automation server, but will refrain from bringing up its container application.** Thus a VBA module from Word, Access, or PowerPoint could generate an Excel document without the user ever seeing Excel materialize on her Windows Desktop.

The rule we've uncovered is this: When you instantiate the automation server, you get its container application. But when you instantiate the document product of an automation server, pre-existing or not, you do get that document's automation server, but not its container application. In short, to have VBA use Excel without the user seeing Excel, instantiate the document `Excel.Sheet.8`, not the automation server `Excel.Application.9`.

Here is how you can have VBA build a foreign application's document without even having to check that application's object library in the References dialog: First, declare an object reference to *nothing in particular*, like this:

```
Dim objXLBook As Object
```

By declaring the reference `As Object`, you're telling VBA that this won't be an ordinary variable, and that you're precluding it from immediately contacting the object library. At this point, you have two options: You could generate an entirely new Excel workbook using this instruction:

```
Set objXLBook = CreateObject("Excel.Sheet.8")
```

or you could access an already existing Excel workbook from a stored file, and instantiate that file as an object, like this:

```
Set objXLBook = GetObject("C:\My Documents\Gorgonzola.XLS", _
 "Excel.Sheet.8")
```

With the `GetObject()` function, you direct the interpreter to the file stored on disk. VBA (actually OLE) should be able to detect what class of object this is based on the file's own header, but we supplied the optional parameter `"Excel.Sheet.8"` to serve as the "class" – in a looser sense – of this document.

Most of the component communication process discussed earlier in this chapter is kept hidden from you, the VBA programmer. The primary purpose of `CreateObject()` is to instantiate an object recognized in the OLE System Registry; but what the function also does is initiate the entire handshaking and interfacing process between the VBA interpreter, the automation server of the application running the interpreter, the automation server responsible for the object, and the library for that object. If you look in the System Registry, you'll find `Excel.Sheet.8` is associated with CLSID number `{00020820-0000-0000-C000-000000000046}`. Under the subheading with that number of the `CLSID` tier of `HKEY_CLASSES_ROOT`, you'll find that the component entitled "Microsoft Excel Worksheet" (again, actually the *workbook*) is attributed to `excel.exe`, the executable file for Excel's automation server. Its type library is listed in the `Type Library` subheading, as GUID `{00020813-0000-0000-C000-000000000046}`. If you move from the `CLSID` tier to the `TypeLib` tier and look for this latest number, you'll find the `Win32` version of the Excel 9.0 type library listed as file `excel9.olb`. This is the necessary lexicon for VBA to be able to contact the Excel automation server.

Once the System Registry has located these components, it is up to the components to introduce themselves to each other using the standard OLE remote procedure calls that comprise their interfaces. Obviously, this process will leave quite a few programs running in Windows. But what about the end result: Can you generate an object and then effectively link or embed it into a foreign application's open document? Indeed you can, but it's a tricky maneuver.

We learned that, under the present VBA system, you cannot use `CreateObject()` or `GetObject()` to generate an instance of an object that you can embed within a document or paste as a link. You can use either function to generate an original Excel worksheet that Word will copy in textual form, and insert it into a document as a textual table in Word's own format – in a sense, an automatic form of "cloneversion" as I defined it earlier, regenerating the same data into another application's format. Listing 8-1 shows a simple test of such a process:

Listing 8-1: Generating an original object that gets "cloneverted" into Word.

```
Public Sub MakeAnExcelSheet()
    Dim objXLSheet As Object

    Set objXLSheet = CreateObject("Excel.Sheet.8")
    objXLSheet.ActiveSheet.Range("A1").Value = "Test string"
    objXLSheet.ActiveSheet.Range("A1:C5").Copy
    Word.ActiveDocument.Content.PasteSpecial

    Set objXLSheet = Nothing
End Sub
```

Assume a textual message of some sort exists in cell A1 of the active Excel worksheet. This example copies a three-by-five-cell area from the top of an Excel worksheet, and pastes that segment into the active Word document. Variable `objXLSheet` is declared `As Object`, although it could just as easily have been declared `As Excel.Workbook` with the same results having been achieved from the user's standpoint, as long as the Excel 9.0 Object Library was made one of VBA's active references in advance. It is the `CreateObject()` function that gives `objXLSheet` its true type: class `Excel.Sheet.8` taken from the System Registry. The `.PasteSpecial` method retrieves the segment that was copied to the Clipboard using the `.Copy` method. What gets pasted ends up as a Word 2000 table rather than an Excel worksheet segment. It's fully capable of being formatted using Word's table-oriented commands, but it can't be double-clicked on and edited like a worksheet. And no links exist, so changes in the original are not reflected in the copy; for that matter, there isn't any *real* original to begin with.

Why can't there be a link between this object that is represented by `objXLSheet` and Word 2000? Because the object we instantiated is a data document, and not the automation server responsible for that document. True, the data document does end up loading the automation server in order for it to manage the document. But VBA does not know this. Why? Because the automation server wasn't mentioned in the procedure. **For a link to work, communication must be established between an explicitly identified automation server and the VBA interpreter.** The identified automation server then maintains the link.

Listing 8-2 shows a `CreateObject()` operation that *does* generate a working linked Excel worksheet segment. The secret here is to instantiate the automation server and tell it to generate the worksheet using its own lexicon of commands.

Listing 8-2: A working paste link trial using the CreateObject() function.

```
Public Sub MakeAnExcelSheet2()
    Dim appExcel As Object

    Set appExcel = CreateObject("Excel.Application.9")
    appExcel.Workbooks.Add
    appExcel.ActiveSheet.Range("A1").Value = "Test string"
    appExcel.ActiveWorkbook.SaveAs "test5.xls"
    appExcel.ActiveWorkbook.ActiveSheet.Range("A1:C5").Select
    appExcel.Selection.Copy
    Word.Selection.Collapse wdCollapseStart
    Word.ActiveWindow.View.Type = wdPageView
    Word.ActiveDocument.Content.PasteSpecial Link:=True, _
     DataType:=wdPasteOLEObject

    Set appExcel = Nothing
End Sub
```

The ProgID used here is `Excel.Application.9`, which brings the automation server into existence. The `Set` statement assigns variable `appExcel` to refer to the server – again, not the document. Through `appExcel`, Excel is told to generate a new workbook using the `.Add` method. Since the container application is not responsible for loading the Excel automation server, when it starts up, it has no open workbooks, and thus no open worksheets. So we have Excel create a blank workbook, knowing that once we do, its first of three worksheets will immediately become active.

The next step in Listing 8-2 is to save the workbook. **A clandestine link operation will not work unless the workbook being linked is saved to disk first.** This process apparently validates the object in memory as a legitimate object. What you call the saved workbook file is immaterial as long as you call it something.

Excel is then told to clip the three-by-five area. Word is made ready by collapsing the selection area (the necessity for which is explained in Chapter 13), and then changing the active view to Page Layout. The user cannot see the pasted worksheet segment unless the view is first changed to Page Layout. Next, the `.PasteSpecial` method is invoked, with two arguments added. `Link:=True` tells the interpreter that this is to be a paste link rather than an ordinary paste, while `DataType:=wdPasteOLEObject` classifies the data on the Clipboard as an OLE registered object rather than an ordinary bitmap, metafile, or text. This ensures that Windows will not apply a Clipboard data type classifier to identify what's going into the Word document, and will instead try to find the object's OLE ProgID.

There is one more way to accomplish this same feat, this time without using `CreateObject()`. It involves referencing Excel's type library and instantiating Excel's automation server using the `New` portion of the object declaration, as demonstrated in Listing 8-3:

Listing 8-3: A working paste link trial using the New qualifier.

```
Public Sub MakeAnExcelSheet3()
    Dim appExcel As New Excel.Application

    Set appExcel = Excel.Application
    appExcel.Workbooks.Add
    appExcel.ActiveSheet.Range("A1").Value = "Hi ho!"
    appExcel.ActiveWorkbook.SaveAs "test4.xls"
    appExcel.ActiveWorkbook.ActiveSheet.Range("A1:C5").Select
    appExcel.Selection.Copy
    Word.Selection.Collapse wdCollapseStart
    Word.ActiveWindow.View.Type = wdPageView
    Word.ActiveDocument.Content.PasteSpecial Link:=True, _
     DataType:=wdPasteOLEObject

    Set appExcel = Nothing
End Sub
```

The major differences between Listings 8-2 and 8-3 are the explicit declaration of `appExcel As New Excel.Application` at the top (early binding), and the rewriting of the `Set` statement. In Listing 8-3, the statement points `appExcel` toward a term from the Excel object library, `Excel.Application`. If you read VBA's own documentation, you'll get the impression that you don't need the `Set` statement in this context. Ignore that and forgive the authors; you need it or the process won't work.

In Depth: Dynamically adding controls to containers . . . or not

In Chapters 6 and 7, I noted that the `UserForm` object and the Forms 2.0 Frame control recognized two event terms: `_AddControl` and `_RemoveControl`. They take place for a `UserForm` class object whenever any ActiveX control, whether or not it belongs to the Forms 2.0 library, is added to that container *during run time*. When you're building your program, you add controls to forms all the time *at design time*, and each time you do, these two events do not take place. So how does a control become contained at run time in the first place?

Both the Forms 2.0 frame control and `UserForm` maintain constituent collections called `Controls`. These collections represent all of the controls within these containers, each of which is addressable through an index number. The number itself is determined by the order in which each control was originally created, which *usually* means the order in which *you* entered the controls into the container at design time. But during the course of programming, you'll rarely find yourself referring to individual controls by their index number in the `Controls` collection — that's why there are such things as `.Name` properties.

However, the `Controls` collection does give you a vehicle for having your VBA form module place a new control within a container during run time: the `Controls.Add` method. Nonetheless, none of the controls that you dynamically insert using the `.Add` method can trigger event procedures, even if the name you give the `.Add` method as an argument for the new control's name matches the name you've given an event procedure in your form. You see, **the VBA interpreter binds an event procedure to a control in your form at design time.** If you wrote an event procedure first, and then created the control for that procedure in the VBA workspace later, the event procedure would work because it would still have officially been design time, when the interpreter can effectively bind the control to the event procedure. But at run time, the interpreter does not have this capability; all binding stops when you press the F5 key to run your form module. This means that, in most cases, adding controls dynamically is rather pointless. Submitted for your collection, another pointless pastime.

You could conceivably create an instance of an ActiveX control, such as a command button or list box, with a pair of instructions like this:

```
Dim btnDynamic As CommandButton

Set btnDynamic = CreateObject("Forms.CommandButton.1")
```

However, there's no way within VBA to assign a parent object to this new control `btnDynamic`. So even if an instance of the control is made to run in memory through dynamic instantiation with the `Set` statement, there's no way to bring that control into a form and make it functional. You cannot use the `Controls.Add` method of the `UserForm` object to give this newly instantiated object life in the world where the rest of us live and work, because the `.Add` method newly instantiates a class rather than invokes an existing instance.

You might be wondering (unless you've completely given up) how an instance of a control can run in memory without ever being able to be seen by the user. It is the component for a control that gives it its running instance, but it is the *container* of the control that makes it visible and functional. Without the form, or `UserForm` object, the control isn't "plugged in."

The Three-tier Distributed Component Model

What the originators of the Component Object Model did not anticipate over a decade ago was the rapid proliferation of the network, and the disintegration of most of the boundaries that separate any two processors anywhere in the world. OLE – which was COM's original incarnation – was and is structured around a single-processor model, where every addressable component is local, and all memory is mapped and unified into one contiguous space. OLE was designed to facilitate components on a computer – literally, *one* computer.

DCOM works because it goes behind OLE's back

Microsoft's Distributed Component Object Model (DCOM) tries to resolve this dilemma by deploying OLE in a networked system wherein it doesn't really know that anything's changed at all. DCOM attempts to bring about a computing environment wherein every object type in existence on a network does not have to be "installed" on every client in the network. So a component could be provided to an application from within the processor space (conventional COM/OLE) or outside of the processor space (DCOM). The trick is to not inform OLE of this little change in plan.

DCOM is not ActiveX; in many ways, it is a (potential) solution to the problems that ActiveX shed so much light on when it was Microsoft's candidate for its distributed data model in early 1997. ActiveX's way of "distributing" component objects was to embed references to them in the documents that utilized them, and then have those references trigger a download process. In this way, the remote component became the local component anyway; ActiveX would actually have the component transferred from a named source (not necessarily the network server) to the client and be installed there. DCOM, by contrast, truly distributed what needed to be distributed – not the component itself, but the product of its work. **A DCOM component can run on a remote processor or network server, and its data products may be transmitted to your client processor.** The client will never know the difference.

To draw an analogy: If COM components were, say, *the news*, then ActiveX's way of distributing those components would be to install presses and a team of reporters in every home. DCOM, by contrast, settles for distributing just the news, not the mechanism for printing it.

DCOM doesn't actually change the Component Object Model at all; more accurately, it facilitates COM over a network by extending one of its services to a separate tier of communication. This network layer involves a component on a network server called Microsoft Transaction Server (MTS). At one time, this product was sold separately; now it's fully integrated into Microsoft Internet Information Server (IIS), which is shipped with Windows NT. (Familiar pattern, isn't it?) A DCOM component on the client system simply performs the remoting process outlined earlier with MTS, using a network communications protocol such as TCP/IP or NetBEUI in-between. What in our diagram constituted the process boundary becomes the *processor* boundary in DCOM; not much changes except the addition of a suffix and perhaps several hundred miles of intervening cable.

But there is a split in communication caused by DCOM, an important second tier that is handled by MTS. Think of the DCOM client as a "regional airport" and MTS as a hub. The job of MTS is to handle "connecting flights." But it doesn't interfere with the job of the local airports. OLE's communications take place between such local COM components as automation servers, document objects, and ActiveX controls. To that mix, DCOM adds a DCOM client that, to OLE, looks like just another valid Windows system service. But the DCOM client is handling connecting flights to the hub: MTS on the network server. Keep this in mind as we appear to switch topics.

Introducing the heart of a distributed application

Today's most important network applications are handled by database servers. Access is a decent database manager, but it not a robust database server; FoxPro is more robust, but it was not at all designed with networks in mind. Microsoft SQL Server, Oracle 8.0, and Informix are robust and efficient database servers in their own way. These are interpreters that manage all the requests, additions, updates, and deletions from dozens, perhaps hundreds, sometimes thousands of database clients. The client applications are not written in the languages of these database servers, because they reside. . . well, on the *server*, naturally, of the network. Access makes an adequate platform for a client application driven by an outside database server, although a local server such as Jet (a relatively shy component of Office 2000, as you'll see in Chapter 17) often performs convenient intermediate tasks.

The jobs performed by database servers involve accounting for and managing perhaps several million individual transactions during the course of a business day. Wait a moment...Didn't we just see the term "transaction" a few paragraphs back? Indeed, by no coincidence, Microsoft Transaction Server is the facilitator for database transactions in a Windows network. While MTS is handling OLE-style remoting processes, it is also handling database queries. These are separate things entirely, but both are critical to the smooth operation of truly distributed database applications.

If you look closely at a database query and the constitution of a database transaction, you'll find nothing that relates to anyone their processor of origin, or to what memory address space they exclusively belong. A database transaction – once you've stripped off the added data that helps it to pass through a network – is exactly the same in its syntax and constitution over a network as it would be if the server and client of a database application were on the same computer. Sound like a familiar circumstance? OLE believes the world is flat, too. So MTS performs the same type of job for the database server on the network server as it performs for

OLE on the client system: It opens a separate tier of communication with remote components so that the local components don't have to be concerned with anything that happens outside their own local realm.

Connecting the proverbial dots

For modern database managers, all data is made up of objects. In COM, objects are represented by components. We can now make the conceptual leap between ordinary data (names, addresses, amounts owed), the objects that represent them in a language such as VBA (classes, constituents, collections), and the components which represent and locally manage that data (Access, Jet, and other automation servers). It's as though object orientation were a wrapper that can enclose – or rather, *encapsulate* – the data, and the components were wrappers that can encapsulate objects. Components become, if you will, transactional outerwear and objects become (forgive me) transactional underwear.

So the tier of communication that DCOM opens beneath OLE at the client and the tier of communication that DCOM opens beneath the database server at the network server, *are the same tier.* Thus the three-tier application model that you might have read about, but have never seen defined, takes shape:

1. **Client-level application management.** Here, Office 2000 applications play a decisive role, and Visual Basic Standard or Enterprise Edition may be used to quickly and effectively craft a completely customized front end for a distributed, networked application.

2. **Middle-level transaction management.** Here, Microsoft Transaction Server is squarely in command.

3. **Server-level database management.** Any true database server that utilizes Structured Query Language (SQL) qualifies here.

Why is all of this important? Because as a VBA programmer, the types of objects you instantiate for an application running on a network client may be local to a processor, or they may be remote with respect to that processor. With DCOM in place (and with your network properly administrated by adequately intelligent human beings), **the identity of the source computer for any given component or type library will be immaterial to the how the user operates the application.** So if it's immaterial, why bring it up here? Because **anything that must be made immaterial to the proper and efficient use of the application must in turn be material to you** – after all, who else is going to know? To recall a point that I made earlier: The user of an application must be presumed to have no interest in the inner workings of the application. For you to adequately shield the user from those inner workings, you as programmer must know both explicitly and implicitly just what it is you are shielding the user from. In short, you must shield the user from practically everything that this chapter was about.

On Point

The process of binding determines when contact is made between two components in OLE. So-called "early binding" takes place at design time, while the VBA program is actually being written. When you write an explicit declaration of an object reference invoking a class name as in `As Document` or `As Worksheet`, the VBA interpreter instantly makes use of the referenced type library to ensure that references to constituents, properties, or methods of the declared object are in order. "Late binding" takes place during the program's run time. When you declare an object reference `As Object`, then assign it to point to a particular type of object with the `CreateObject()` or `GetObject()` function, using the ProgID for that object from the System Registry, you can invoke the automation server responsible for that object without loading the container application for that object into memory. This is useful for having one O2K application generate for itself an object that is native to another O2K application without the user seeing that other application.

The Distributed Component Object Model extends COM by creating back channels of communication for both the server application and the client application. DCOM employs Microsoft Transaction Server — now part of Windows NT — to handle remoting for OLE across processor boundaries. A DCOM client on the client computer routes transactions through to MTS on the network server. MTS also handles database transactions on their way to the database server, and can consolidate and route their queries in a more efficient manner than shuttling them straight through. MTS creates a second tier of communication beneath OLE, and a second tier beneath the database server. These tiers are, in fact, one and the same; so client application, transaction layer, and database server are bridged together by way of the three-tier service model.

In Theory: Public volume

The proper construction of a distributed database application has only recently become recognized by the programming elite. And yet distributed computing is a concept that has existed for more than 30 years — far longer than the existence of the microprocessor.

The first networked personal computers were run by *disk servers*. Under this system, one hard disk drive on the disk server revealed portions of its contents to its individual clients, which were really terminals in the true sense of the word. Each terminal had its own exclusive share of the network disk drive, and all terminals had equal share of one so-called "public volume." But because no protocols existed for determining which terminal would get permission to overwrite what file at what time, the public volume was made read-only. A terminal had read/write permissions for its own exclusive volume, but that's all. The convenience of a disk server system was that. . . .Heck, who am I kidding? There was no convenience. Since hard disks at that time averaged about 20 MB, a public volume was generally no larger than two or three high-density floppy diskettes. And since applications loaded from the public volume had to run entirely on the terminal, and every extension file for an application (the embryonic form of the DLL) had to be within the same directory as its main executable in order for DOS to make sense of things, every application's features and services had to be entirely self-contained inside one .EXE file. This way, it could be transmitted in one lump sum from the disk server to the terminal. Otherwise, the application might not work.

The first networked applications (if you consider a network to be as complex as, say, a slipknot) ran on disk server-based networks. To use one was scary. Each terminal contained a local replicated copy of that *morning's* edition of the main database. The terminal read and wrote to that local file. At the end of the business day, all the local files were transmitted back to the disk server, where a utility (generally one that was bootstrapped by something called a terminate-and-stay-resident program) loaded itself into memory and reconciled all the changes into one amalgamate file for the next morning. One glitch destroyed everything.

I forgot to mention how long ago this was. Actually, it was last week, at a place where I rent videos. A national chain. Every one of its outlets in the U.S. continues to use this system, copyright 1982. Next time you rent a video, ask the manager to show you the store's disk server.

This chapter examined how computing can work when both program components and hardware components are networked. Our examination took place on a very low level, technologically speaking. ("Low level" is an oft-used computing term for "fine-grained" or "fundamental.") Translating this concept of efficiency into real-world applications is an extraordinarily difficult task. For some companies, it's an impossible one. Many firms cannot be coerced into recognizing the cost savings to be gained by investing in an efficient system *now*, rather than paying for extended maintenance down the road.

But those who deploy networks in their businesses cannot be held entirely to blame for this slowness to adopt. Much of the software upon which businesses rely (Office 2000 being the exception here) is far older than the machines that run it. Some of my own company's consulting clients are looking for ways to run Windows 3.1, or even MS-DOS 6.22, on their new Pentium II machines simply because they're dependent on their software, and that software has not changed with the times.

The Component Object Model does not describe the ideal computing environment – at least not yet. But both COM and CORBA are closer to a true model of efficiency than computing has ever come before. In a truly efficient system, a client would make a request and the server would logically deduce the best way to fulfill that request. At present, neither DCOM nor CORBA have facilities for this "logical deduction," although CORBA does appear to have space allocated for such a facility should it ever come about – giving it the conceptual jump on DCOM by about a week or two. For now, distributed computing relies on such tools as registries

(DCOM) and object brokers (CORBA) to look up and retrieve the component that the programmer of the calling component knew it was going to retrieve anyway. At least these models are predictable.

For most established companies – both manufacturers and users of software – adopting either or both of these methodologies requires a rethinking of the entire concept of what applications are and how work is performed by processors. This rethinking requires humanpower, and humanpower costs money. For some companies, this is the stumbling block.

You and I are limited as to what we can do about "some companies" or "most established companies." But we have a lot to say about what happens within our own. Let neither of us go down in defeat because we were too afraid to take the initiative.

In Brief

♦ Dynamic linking is the process of connecting two disparate processes together and having them exchange data with one another, while either or both processes are fully compiled and running.

♦ The Component Object Model specifies how one program can place a remote procedure call to a separate program by means of an interface that describes the procedure calls that the separate program may recognize.

♦ An in-process server component (generally a control) makes contact with its container application as though it were an integral part of that application. By contrast, an out-of-process server component (such as an automation server or a document object) utilizes OLE to shuttle messages back and forth between itself and its container or containers, in a process called remoting.

♦ A linked document object is a single object that may appear in multiple containers, whereas an embedded document object is a copy of a source document component, each copy of which may include changes.

♦ All COM objects communicate with one another on a binary level using remote procedure calls dictated from within their respective interfaces. Many COM objects communicate on a second tier using a lexicon of terms described within their type libraries. Automation servers, document objects, and ActiveX controls are among these components. VBA is specially designed to be able to incorporate the terms from their type libraries' lexicons into its source code.

Chapter 9

Devising Runtime Objects

IN THIS CHAPTER

◆ How to build a class module that defines a class at run-time

◆ Establishing a class' own method terms

◆ Constructing property procedures that validate assignments

◆ Establishing a "wrapper" class around an existing O2KOM object class

◆ Building a runtime collection for a runtime class

THE REAL REASON FOR THE advent of object-oriented software engineering is more selfish than the literature on the subject would have you believe. Most of the time, professional programmers find themselves engineering an application that, almost without exception, contains at least one-third the same code as the application they developed just prior. By the early 1980s, reprogramming applications for different platforms became three-fourths of the work that programmers did. After a year or so of tenure, programmers became capable of predicting their own *déjà vu*. What the best of these programmers realized they needed was a simple way of transporting the source code for one application into another without having to spend so much time investigating how little work was necessary to re-engineer that code. Objects provided them with a mechanism for interchangeability.

Up to this point, you've seen and done some programming involving other people's objects – namely, the Office 2000 Object Model. The nature of VBA programming, as you've probably deduced, is re-engineering. You're devising functionality that one or more of the Office 2000 applications do not have, and you're accomplishing this on a platform that someone else constructed. With that in mind, how does the fact that VBA is based on a language for *building* objects come into play?

Programming in Advance

When you work in any office in which two or more people are responsible for specifying information policy (which is, by definition, any office with two or more people), no single process or way of working will ever be entirely satisfactory for everyone. This is partly why O2K applications support more than one way for the user to access basic functions and commands, and why customization has become as popular a feature as standardization. VBA has filled the shoes (all of them) of a handful of so-called "macro languages," whose express purpose originally was to record and play back a sequence of those basic functions and commands. But a recorded sequence was exactly that — *one* sequence. As a result, a macro — especially one written for Lotus 1-2-3 — was generally capable of satisfying only its programmer. Using such a macro meant having to re-adapt one's habits to support someone else's methodology. Since each "power user" in an office will inevitably develop his own personal templates, workspaces, and desktops, you could use VBA to construct and maintain personalized functionality for each of those people . . . individually. You'll soon experience that certain feeling that only the French can describe accurately, as you learn that each person's individual tastes and methodologies are but twists or angles applied to basic operating premises.

A language that uses (or in the case of VBA, borrows) object-oriented terminology gives you the means to easily divide basic operating premises from personal operating preferences, so that you don't find yourself engineering both at once, each time you work on one person's project. VBA gives you the means to construct objects that can be utilized in much the same way as the O2K Object Model. These objects have their own properties, their own methods, and to a limited extent, their own constituent objects. The purpose for this mechanism is sincerely not to give you something new to fool around with. What it does give you is a convenient way to produce reusable functionality for one project, and introduce it easily into others later.

A class module provides a mechanism for reusable code

VBA calls its object mechanism *class modules*. The purpose of class modules in VBA is not self-evident, even in projects that do utilize them. Here, we'll discuss and demonstrate class modules in the manner in which they lend the greatest efficiency to VBA. The best way to begin to understand class modules is by contrasting them with the general module with which you're already partly familiar.

A general module (represented on VBA's menus by just "module") contains `Sub` procedures which are called by name, which perform tasks represented by their names, and which do not give any value or data back directly to the instructions that call them. In other words, these procedures do what they're told, quit, and pass execution back to the caller. `Function` procedures are also contained in a general module. They, too, are called by name, but when they've finished, they pass values or strings or some other data back to the instructions that call them. So the name of a `Function` procedure is as good as its return value, especially in the context of a mathematical expression. The name doesn't just mean "go do something;" it means, "Solve this data and show me the result."

The general module concept in Visual Basic was originally intended to serve as a program unto itself that could be brought into a larger project and utilized in a broader context. To accomplish this, beginning with Visual Basic 3.0, certain procedures in a general module could be declared `Public` in order to register them as capable of being contacted by procedures in other modules in a project. This way, other procedures which happen to be declared `Private` in a general module would not have to interfere with, or be interfered with on account of, other procedures in other modules. To use Microsoft's term, certain procedures were *exposed* to the outside world. Also, a general module could maintain its own variables by means of `Private` declarations, and only "expose" those variables that the programmer felt might be useful to the outside world through `Public` declarations. This way, general modules could have "front doors" of sorts, while at the same time maintaining "off limits" areas and restricting access to certain of its valuables. When a programmer lent his general modules to others, he could at least be certain that they would make use of his functionality in exactly the way he intended, and not try to make changes through some "back door."

This is the beginning of object-like functionality in Visual Basic. The class module concept in VBA (which also resides in today's Visual Basic Standard and Enterprise editions) takes this concept a few steps further. A class module is explicitly represented in another module through the declaration of an object variable at the head of that module – in the Declarations section, with a `Dim` or `Private` statement. This explicit declaration creates a visible binding between the outside module and the class module. For an ordinary general module loaded into a project, its `Public` procedures are contacted simply by name, as though those procedures belonged to the outside module. At times, the name of the module may be tacked onto the name of a contacted procedure just to resolve ambiguities; otherwise, there is no visible association within the source code between the contacting module and the contacted one.

Public procedures in a class module become methods

A class module's methods are made up of its own `Public` procedures. These procedures can either return a value (`Public Function`) or not return a value (`Public Sub`). A method call to one of these procedures involves the name of the procedure attached to the class module's object variable. So a procedure named `Sort` attached to a class module named `OverMail` instantiated as `clsMail` would first be instantiated with an instruction in the Declarations section like this:

```
Dim clsMail As New OverMail
```

The `Sort` procedure would then be addressed as the `.Sort` method, like this:

```
clsMail.Sort
```

The *performance* gains attainable from accessing outside procedures in the manner of methods are not obvious. For the programmer, there are some improvements in technique that can be exploited. Unlike a general module, a class module can be instantiated more than once. This way, two objects may refer to two separate sets of data, and since each set has its own separate identity, any method instruction refers to each object directly. For instance, if a module invokes two instances of class `OverMail`, and the class module for `OverMail` maintains its own private variable `MailCount`, then there will be two such variables in existence – one for each instantiation of `OverMail`.

From the perspective of phraseology, a reference to an object doesn't have to be passed to a method as a parameter. This is the difference between `Sort clsMail` and `clsMail.Sort` – merely a matter of grammar. But even though the code within the class module may be the same for any two or more instances of the same object, the *instances* of that code running on the system are separate, just as any two object references `As Document` or `As Database` are separate. So if a class may be made to represent a "thing," there can be some purpose for the simultaneous existence of two or more "things."

An event is a signal sent by a class module

This book has already familiarized you with the concept of *events*. Controls in a form (dialog box) recognize certain events, which generally take place as a result of user interaction. The form itself triggers an `_Initialize` event when its code module is first accessed, an `_Activate` event when it first becomes visible, and a `_Terminate` event when it starts to wrap up its own execution. A private event procedure can be written for automatic execution whenever one of these events happens; so `Private Sub UserForm_Terminate` begins the form's wrap-up process.

Beginning with Office 2000, a class module can set up its own runtime events. (Actually, the keywords for an event mechanism existed in Office 97, but they simply didn't work.) The purpose for events in this context is to give the programmer utilizing your class module several opportunities to write code *outside* the class module that responds to activities that take place *inside* the class module. The details of how this happens are discussed later in this chapter, although you may be surprised to find that implementing events is one of the simpler features of the class module. At the header of the class module, you declare each event term using the `Event` statement. Then at each place in the source code of the class module where it would be logical for the event to occur, you write the name of the declared event within a `RaiseEvent` statement. It is basically that simple; and again, you'll see the details later.

A class module's property is a unit of regulated data

The true performance gains in utilizing a class module are to be found in how it implements properties. While a class module's methods are analogous to a general module's `Public` procedures, a class module's properties are *not* analogous to a general module's `Public` variables. Instead, a class module handles properties in a very sophisticated manner.

Referencing one of the properties for an instance of a class triggers the execution of a procedure within its class module. This procedure is solely responsible for ascertaining whether the reference is valid and, in the case of a value or data assignment to the property, whether the assigned data is acceptable. So unlike any other programming element of VBA, a class module's property procedure is responsible for defining, in terms of VBA instructions, the rules that another part of VBA – the instructions referencing an instance of the class – must follow.

This is a difficult concept to grasp, so we'll stay on it for awhile. Suppose a VBA class module named `Diagram` is instantiated by a variable named `diaThis`. A `Set` statement points `diaThis` toward a specific instance – toward the data generated by the `Diagram` class that the variable will represent. Suppose one element of this data is a property named `.FileName`. On paper, this property could be defined as the file location of the image represented in the diagram. Whenever one of your procedures in an outside module (a general or form module) makes reference to `diaThis.FileName`, a procedure within the class module is immediately triggered. It is not a `Sub` or a `Function` procedure – which makes this all the more unconventional for Visual Basic. Instead, the procedure is headed by an instruction such as this:

```
Public Property Get FileName() As String
```

As you might have guessed, we'll explore such statements with the appropriate boxes and arrows throughout this chapter. For now, here's a brief description of the above instruction: The statement keyword here is actually two words, `Property Get`. It alerts VBA that this procedure is about one element of data, similar to the way a `Function` procedure is about one element of data. What's different here is that this particular procedure is triggered whenever an instruction is trying to *retrieve* that element of data – that's what the `Get` part is about. So the first restriction on how that data can be retrieved is encoded right here, at the heading of the procedure: The `As String` qualifier tells VBA that the only type of outside variable allowed to receive this property must be a `String` or something that functions as a string, such as a `Variant`. For example, in this outside instruction:

```
strThisFile = diaThis.FileName
```

the variable strThisFile must be a string or a variant, otherwise the expression will generate an error. The error will arise because the expression broke a rule that you, the programmer, yourself devised. Why would you want to knowingly *create* situations for errors to occur? Because **an error is a tool for steering the flow of a program back in the proper direction.** As the programmer of a class module, you're developing functionality that not only you, but others as well, may use. So here – unlike anywhere else in VBA programming – it is up to you to decide what "the proper direction" is. You set the boundaries for the programmer utilizing your class module, whether that programmer is yourself or someone else. The quality of your programming may be determined by how well you enforce the boundaries you set. Declaring a Property Get procedure As String is just one such boundary. What's worse than not having the boundary is having someone else attempt to assign a string property to an integer variable.

On the flip side, an outside expression that assigns data to a property triggers a procedure within the class module with a header like this:

```
Public Property Let FileName(strIncoming As String)
```

This time, the keyword (pair) is Property Let, which distinguishes itself – albeit through the exchange of one letter – from Property Get. The Let procedure will only be triggered when an instruction like this is attempted:

```
diaThis.FileName = strChosen
```

VBA cannot rely on the Hungarian notation applied to variable strChosen; such notation is an option of the programmer, not of the VBA environment. The type checking that takes place here is to make certain that strChosen truly is a string, before its value is assigned to the .FileName property. Notice in the header for the Property Let procedure, how the As String qualifier appears *inside* the parentheses. For the Property Get procedure, the qualifier is outside the parentheses. There's a clear reason. With the Property Let procedure, strIncoming does not represent an argument like one you would use for a Function procedure. Instead, it represents the data at the other side of the equal sign in the expression. So the type checking happens to the received data, not the outgoing data – therefore, the qualifier appears inside the parentheses along with the received data.

Even the simplest Property Let procedure can perform the most important job: filter incoming data. A class module maintains its own set of private variables, and those variables are the final representatives of the data that the class module is designed to operate. Each property that a class module manages has its own private "shadow variable," if you will. The key point here is that the shadow variables are private and unseen by outside modules; the property acts as a public portal – albeit well guarded – that leads to the private stash. For the .FileName property, the portal can be as simple as the following:

```
Public Property Let FileName(strIncoming As String)
    If FileSystem.Dir(strIncoming) <> "" Then
        strFilename = strIncoming
    End If
End Property
```

Here, strIncoming represents the local incoming argument – the assignment made by an expression such as diaThis.FileName = "C:\WINDOWS\" – while strFileName is the module-level private mirror variable responsible for maintaining the property contents. This particular procedure makes use of a utility object installed by Office 2000 called FileSystem. Methods sent to this object mimic commands that you would write for MS-DOS. Here, strIncoming should contain a legal filename. If it is legal, then the method FileSystem.Dir(strIncoming) will return exactly the contents of strIncoming – which, for the purposes of this If...Then conditional test is *something* rather than nothing. So the condition tests to make certain the method does not return nothing (<> ""). If it passes the test, then and only then are the contents of strIncoming assigned to the shadow variable strFilename. Notice there are no other instructions here; if the argument fails the test, nothing happens. This purposeful omission constitutes one of those self-imposed rules mentioned earlier. This procedure defines a property that can only be set if the filename it represents is legal; otherwise the property stays as it is.

The counterpart of this procedure returns the value of the property's shadow variable to the expression that references that property:

```
Public Property Get FileName() As String
    FileName = strFilename
End Property
```

The Property Get procedure concludes here like a Function procedure, assigning the final result to the name of the procedure itself.

In a few pages, we'll explore some further examples of class modules that utilize property procedures. First, as promised, here are the details of how the instructions that bind property procedures are constructed.

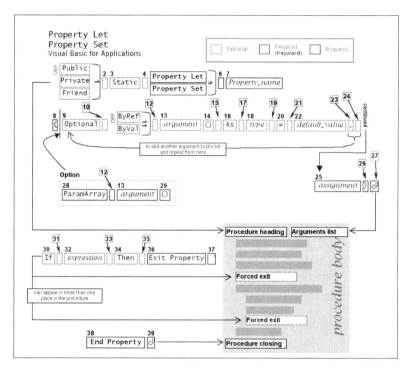

Part		Description
1	Public. Private Friend	**Attribute** Specifies whether the property procedure may be called by procedures in other modules. By default, a property procedure is public, which in this case means that the *property* is public, not the *procedure*. If you write Private instead, the property may be utilized by instructions within the class module, but not outside it. The Friend term declares a procedure that may be called by a procedure in any module within the module that instantiates the class instance (like a Public procedure) but that may not be called by any other module even if the class instance is visible to that module (*unlike* a Public procedure). This results in an "in-between" level of privacy, which allows the class module programmer to distinguish between self-serving properties and others that are more practical to the job at hand.
2	(space)	

	Part	Description
3	Static	**Attribute** Directs the interpreter to maintain the values of all local variables declared within the property procedure after it is exited for use later when the procedure is reentered. If you don't write `Static`, the interpreter discards the procedure's local variables upon reaching `End Property` (part **37**).
4	(space)	
5	Property Let Property Set	**Statement** Denotes the beginning of a property procedure. The `Property` term is used both as a procedure declaration, and as a declaration of the presence of a property *Property_name* (part **7**) belonging to the class module for the property's instantiated object class. A property procedure is invoked in the source code when an instruction makes reference to a property term associated with the class. There are three types of property procedures — one for retrieving property settings and two for actually making the setting. The term `Property Let` denotes that this procedure is to receive assignments of a standard VBA type; in other words, not an object. `Property Set`, by contrast, specifies that the procedure handles assignments to properties that are themselves members of object classes. For example, a picture being assigned to a `.Picture` property may be of the recognized type `Image`, in which case a `Property Set` procedure is required.
6	(space)	
7	*Property_name*	**Literal** A name that identifies the property of the class. This name must be unique among all properties belonging to the class. It need not be unique among all properties belonging to *all* classes in the current project; in other words, two or more class modules may contain properties with the same name. **Rule:** The name of a property must begin with an alphabetical character, although it may be followed by up to 254 characters, including alphanumerics and the _ underscore character.

Continued

Part		Description *(Continued)*
8	((left parenthesis)	Begins the property procedure's grouping of arguments. Unlike a `Sub` or `Function` procedure, a `Property Let` or `Property Set` procedure must have a minimum of one argument, representing the value, data, or object to be assigned to the property. This argument must fall at the end of the arguments list, if there is more than one argument in that list.
9	`Optional`	<u>Attribute</u> Used before an argument that the interpreter is to treat as optional. With this attribute in place, an expression outside this procedure that makes an assignment to the named property (part 7) may either include or omit the optional argument. **Rule:** After the first argument variable you declare `Optional`, all other successive arguments between the parentheses will also be treated by the interpreter as optional, *up until the final argument,* which for `Property Let` and `Property Set` is always included, which is not optional and which represents the assignment being made to the property. **Rule:** `Optional` cannot be used within the same arguments list as `ParamArray`.
10	(space)	
11	`ByRef.` `ByVal`	<u>Attribute</u> States the relationship between a variable passed as an argument to the property procedure and the variable declared within the property procedure that receives the argument. When the VBA interpreter makes changes to the value or contents of an argument variable, by default those changes are reflected in the variable outside of the procedure that passed the argument (unless the argument was passed as a literal). You can write `ByRef` in order to make this default state clearer. If you instead write `ByVal` before an argument, the procedure receives a *copy* of the value or contents of the variable passing the argument, and the passing variable will be unaffected.
12	(space)	

	Part	Description

13	*argument*	<u>Variable</u>
		An arbitrary name that represents the argument being received from the calling body of the program. All rules for variable names apply here. This variable will be local in scope, and will be dropped from memory at `End Property` (part **38**) unless `Static` (part **3**) is written earlier.
		Rule: The name you choose for a variable will also be used outside of the procedure as the *parameter name* for the argument passed to this procedure. So for a procedure declared thus:
		`Property Let SortOrder(iColumn As Integer, iWhich _ As Integer)`
		the following property assignment for an object called `blocNames` is legal:
		`blocNames.SortOrder(1) = 2`
		Here `iColumn` receives the value 1, while `iWhich` — the final argument in the list — receives the assigned value 2.

14	( )	Denotes that the argument is an array, containing any number of elements. An array may be declared at any position in the arguments list. The VBA interpreter performs type checking to ensure that the passed argument is indeed an array.
15	(space)	
16	`As`	Denotes that the incoming argument should be of the type or class stated in part **18**.
17	(space)	

Continued

	Part	**Description** *(Continued)*
18	*type* Variant. Byte Boolean Integer Long Currency Single Double Date String Object	<u>Type or class</u> States the data type of the variable that receives the incoming argument. The interpreter will check the data type of the incoming argument against that of the variable declared here and, if they are not compatible, it may generate an error. Commonly recognized object types are listed at left, though the name of an Office 2000 class or one defined by a VBA class module may be used instead. A composite variable type (declared with the Type statement) is not allowed.
19	(space)	
20	=	<u>Operator</u> Assigns the named argument a default value (part 22).
21	(space)	
22	*default_value*	<u>Literal or constant</u> Sets the default value of *argument* (part 13) to *default_value*, in cases where Optional (part 9) is also stated. This way, if the function call omits this argument, the interpreter can assign *default_value* to the argument's corresponding variable, rather than initialize that argument to Nothing or 0. This only works if *argument* is a standard VBA type, not a class. The standard type of *default_value* must match the stated *type* (part 18). **Rule:** Since the final argument in the list must not be optional (it represents the property assignment), its default value may not be assigned by an expression here. However, a default property setting may be made explicitly by an instruction within the procedure.
23	, (comma)	Separates two arguments in a group.
24	(space)	When the property procedure contains multiple arguments, a comma and space are used to separate them.

	Part	Description
25	*assignment*	<u>Variable</u> An arbitrary name that represents the value or data to be assigned to the property. The key purpose of the property procedure is to evaluate this *assignment* to certify that it is valid in the context you've defined for the class, and to take appropriate measures if it is not valid. **Rule:** This argument is required. For a procedure with multiple arguments, this one must fall at the end of the list.
26	) (right parenthesis)	Closes the arguments list.
27	(Enter)	Terminates the header and formally begins the procedure.
28	ParamArray	As an option, ParamArray *argument( )* may be written as the next-to-last argument for the procedure header statement. ParamArray directs the interpreter to accept an indefinite number of incoming arguments from this point in the sequence forward, from the list of arguments passed by the calling body of the program. In such a case, *argument* should be followed by empty parentheses (part **29**). The contents of the array are of the type Variant; the type specifier (part **17**) is omitted here. **Rule:** ParamArray cannot be included in an arguments list that contains Optional (part **9**).
29	( )	When ParamArray (part **28**) is included, then the empty parentheses ( ) are included here to underscore that this receiving variable is an array whose purpose is to collect all the incoming arguments, however many there may be, in order of their appearance in the procedure call. In this case, the interpreter performs type checking to ensure that all of the incoming parameters are *not* arrays in themselves, but unit values.

Continued

	Part	Description *(Continued)*
30	If	<u>Statement</u> Used in a situation where execution of the property procedure may need to be exited prior to reaching `End Property` (part **39**).
31	(space)	
32	*expression*	A mathematical test that returns a Boolean True/False value. If the test returns True, then the statement following `Then` is executed — in this case, `Exit Property` (part **36**).
33	(space)	
34	Then	Separates the expression (part **32**) from the directive (part **36**).
35	(space)	
36	Exit Property	<u>Statement</u> Forces execution of the property procedure to be terminated immediately. Execution proceeds to the instruction immediately following the property assignment expression.
37	(Enter)	
38	End Property	<u>Statement</u> Denotes the formal end of the property procedure. Upon reaching this line, execution proceeds to the instruction immediately following the property assignment expression outside the procedure.
39	(Enter)	End of the procedure.

In Depth: Nuances of Property Let and Property Set

A Property Let procedure within a class module is invoked from a module that has instantiated that class by an instruction that sets that property to a common value type (that is, not an object reference), such as a numeral or string. The assignment expression is basically no different than the type with which you're already familiar. It bears this syntax:

```
instance.property_name = expression
```

where *instance* is the .Name property for the member of the class, and *expression* evaluates to a standard designated type. When the Property Let procedure is called, type checking is performed by the interpreter to ensure that *expression* evaluates to the type designated for the final argument in the arguments list (part 25 in the syntax table above); a type mismatch error will be raised if it is not.

The Property Let procedure receives the evaluated value of *expression* as its parameter. After type checking has matched the value of *expression* with the argument's declared type, the procedure may then assess whether this argument is a logical and appropriate setting for the property. If your instructions determine that the value is inappropriate, then you may generate your own exception routines for handling the class' response to this improper assignment.

A Property Set procedure within a class module is invoked from a module that has instantiated that class by an instruction that sets that property to an object reference, which, by definition, is not a common value type. The assignment expression again has a familiar syntax:

```
Set instance.property_name = reference
```

where *instance* is the .Name property for the class, and *reference* evaluates to a designated object type. This type must be stated in the declaration for the final argument in the list. When the Property Set procedure is called, type checking is performed to ensure that *reference* is of the same object class as in part 25 above; a type mismatch error will be raised if it is not.

The purpose of the Property Set procedure is to assign an object *reference* to the property term denoted in the assignment instruction. The Property Set procedure receives *reference* as its argument. After type checking, the procedure may then evaluate the object and its contents to determine whether it represents a logical assignment for the property, as you have defined that property for your class. If your instructions determine that the value is inappropriate, then you may generate your own exception routines for handling the class' response to this improper assignment.

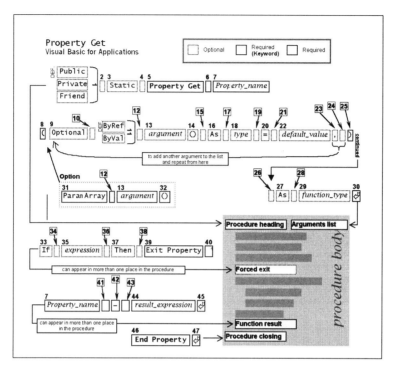

Part		Description
1	Public. Private Friend	<u>Attribute</u> Specifies whether the Property Get procedure may be called by procedures in other modules. By default, a Property Get procedure is public. If part **1** is omitted, the interpreter assumes a public scope, making the procedure callable from all modules in all currently loaded projects within the Office 2000 application. If you write Private instead, the procedure may only be called from other procedures sharing the class module. For Property Get procedures within a class module, declaring the procedure as a Friend makes it visible to other procedures within its native project, but shields it from code that may instantiate that class.
2	(space)	
3	Static	<u>Attribute</u> Tells the interpreter to maintain the values of local variables within the Property Get procedure after it is exited for use later when the procedure is reentered. If part **3** is omitted, the interpreter discards the procedure's local variables upon reaching End Property (part **46**).

	Part	Description
4	(space)	
5	Property Get	**Statement** Tells the interpreter that the procedure enclosed by this statement is meant to return a value, or another datum such as a string or object, to the instruction or expression that calls it.
6	(space)	
7	*Property_name*	**Literal** A name that identifies the property being polled.
8	((left parenthesis)	Begins the Function procedure's grouping of parameters.
9	Optional	**Attribute** Tells the interpreter to treat the next argument (part **14**) as optional. If the call to the Function procedure omits this argument, the interpreter will not generate a fault. **Rule:** After the first parameter variable you declare Optional, all other successive parameters between the parentheses will also betreated by the interpreter as optional, and will also require the Optional attribute. **Rule:** Optional may not be used within the same parameters list as ParamArray.
10	(space)	
11	ByRef. ByVal	**Attribute** States the relationship between a variable passed as an argument to the Function procedure and the variable declared within the Function procedure that receives the argument. If ByRef (default when omitted), argument passing is assumed to be *by reference*, so any changes made by the Function procedure to the receiving variable will automatically be reflected in the passing variable (assuming the argument has not been passed by a literal). If ByVal, argument passing is assumed to be *by value*, so changes to this variable will not be reflected in the passing variable.
12	(space)	

Continued

	Part	Description *(Continued)*
13	*argument*	<u>Symbol</u> An arbitrary name that represents the argument being received from the calling body of the program at this position in the sequence of the arguments list. All rules for variable names apply here. This variable is local in scope and is dropped from memory at End Function unless Static is specified (part **3**).
14	( )	Denotes that the argument is an array and may contain any number of elements. The interpreter will performs type checking here to ensure that the incoming argument at this position is indeed an array. A fixed or dynamic array may be used in the instruction that passes this argument.
15	(space)	
16	As	Denotes that the incoming argument should be of the type stated in part **19**.
17	(space)	
18	*type* Variant. Byte Boolean Integer Long Currency Single Double Date String Object	<u>Type or class</u> States the class of the object reference that receives the incoming argument. The interpreter will check the class of the incoming against that of the variable declared here and if they are not compatible, it may generate an error. The class name used here may be a class recognized by the Office 2000 object library, or any other active object library that the VBA interpreter may currently reference; or it may be the name of a class defined by an active VBA class module.
19	(space)	
20	=	<u>Operator</u> In circumstances where a given argument (part **14**) has been declared Optional (part **10**), the equal sign here attributes a default value (part **23**) to the argument.

	Part	Description
21	(space)	
22	*default_value*	<u>Expression</u> Sets the default value of the argument (part **13**), in cases where it has been declared `Optional` (part **9**). This way, if the procedure call omits this argument, the VBA interpreter will assign *default_value* to that argument, rather than initialize it to `Nothing` or `0`. If a type is specified for the argument (part **18**), then the interpreter will employ type checking to ensure that the type for *default_value* matches the argument's type.
23	, (comma)	Separates arguments in a grouping.
24	(space)	When more than one argument is being declared, the comma and space are used to separate them.
25	) (right parenthesis)	Closes the arguments list.
26	(space)	
27	`As`	Denotes that the result value of the `Property Get` procedure should be of a given type (part **29**).
28	(space)	
29	*function_type*	<u>Type or class</u> Denotes the data type of the value or data returned by the `Function` procedure. A specific object class name may also be used in place of *type*, if that class belongs to one of the active Office 2000 object libraries or other such libraries, or if its class module belongs to the current VBA project. A composite variable type name may also be used, but only if its `Type` declaration appears within the current module, and if `Optional` (part **9**) is omitted.
30	(Enter)	

Continued

	Part	Description *(Continued)*
31	ParamArray	Indicates to the interpreter that the procedure is to accept any number of arguments from this point forward, and to assign those arguments in sequence to an array variable of type Variant to be named by part **13**. By protocol, a ParamArray argument is the last in the declared arguments list for a Function procedure. **Rule:** ParamArray cannot be included in an arguments list that contains Optional. **Rule:** All ParamArray arguments are considered to be of type Variant. The interpreter will perform type checking to ensure that all of the incoming parameters are *not* arrays in themselves, but unit values. However, this type checking does not extend to the specific type of the argument; as with all newly –declared variants, types will be assigned to them upon receiving initial values. So if ParamArray is stated, parts **15** through **18** must be omitted.
32	( )	Underscores the use of the argument (part **13**) as a parameter array.
33	If	<u>Statement</u> Used in a situation where execution of the Property Get procedure may need to be exited prior to reaching End Property (part **46**).
34	(space)	
35	*expression*	A mathematical test that returns a Boolean True/False value. If the test returns True, then the statement following Then is executed — in this case, Exit Property (part **39**).
36	(space)	
37	Then	Separates the expression (part **35**) from the directive (part **39**).
38	(space)	
39	Exit Property	<u>Statement</u> Forces execution of the Property Get procedure to be terminated immediately. Execution proceeds to the instruction immediately back to the instruction line where the Function procedure was called and may complete the expression that contains the call.
40	(Enter)	
41	(space)	

Part		Description
42	=	Operator Separates the result of the Property Get procedure (part **44**) from the name that represents that result (part **7**).
43	(space)	
44	*result_expression*	Expression Specifies a return value for the Property Get procedure by assigning a final value, or an expression that evaluates to a final value, to the *Property_name* (part **7**), repeated here from the Property Get procedure's declaration line.
45	(Enter)	
46	End Property	Statement Denotes the formal end of the Property Get procedure. Upon reaching this line, execution proceeds back to the expression that polled the property.
47	(Enter)	Ends the Property Get procedure.

In Depth: How Property Get works

A Property Get procedure is invoked within a class module whenever an instruction in a module that has instantiated the class polls the current setting for that property using the syntax:

```
variable = instance.property_name
```

where *instance* is the .Name property for the class module, and *variable* has been declared with the designated type or class of the property. When the Property Get procedure is called, type checking is performed to ensure that *variable* is of the same type as that declared for the procedure; a type mismatch error will be raised if it is not.

The purpose of the Property Get procedure is to logically render a property setting for *variable*. The invocation of this procedure is automatic, so the setting for *property_name* is updated immediately after *property_name* is invoked. Like a Function procedure, once the final property setting has been assessed, it is assigned to the name of the procedure itself, using the syntax *property_name = setting*. The procedure officially ends when End Property or Exit Property is reached.

Putting the Class Module to Work

There is no simple example of property procedures or even of class modules in general. There are many examples with varying degrees of complexity. The example presented here is a noble attempt to make matters as simple as they can possibly be, at least for the time being. Understanding the *real* purpose of the class module can only come after having thoroughly investigated and examined one in its entirety, at work performing *more than one* real-world job. Once you see a class module perform in *two* settings, you at last encounter the threshold of clarity. You might actually hear something go "Ding!" in the vicinity of your head.

Our example involves Word 2000, and how it handles a type of object that Word so unromantically calls *inline shapes*. A document such as the one you're reading now may include *figures*, which are pictures that are numbered for your reference and catalogued for the publisher's. There's quite a bit of housekeeping work that takes place when numbered figures or diagrams are included in a document submitted for formal publication. (Oftentimes, authors don't actually drop figures into their documents,but rather submit them in separate files.) Formal figures or diagrams are collected together by Word along with ordinary graphical embellishments, into a single group of so-called inline shapes. But formal figures should be associated with data that would be pointless for ordinary clip art, such as captions, associated documents, and perhaps a connection to any callouts (circles and arrows) that may apply.

The goal of our example is to create a special class for diagrams that may be individually numbered or labeled, perhaps given their own captions, and later singled out for special treatment — for instance, a "thumbnail sheet." For the sake of both convenience and consistency, it would be preferable for diagrams to be given the same type of treatment as Word's object library already gives documents: simultaneous addressability as individual units and as a plurality. In other words, optimally, `Diagram` and `Diagrams` would both be recognizable in VBA. But the special treatment given to diagrams must remain transparent; in the end, the images to which objects of these classes point must remain inline shapes so that Word will continue to handle them in the same way as before.

My example for this chapter is a stripped-down prototype of the final class module structure. Throughout this book, I come back to this example to polish it and make it more functional. For now, you need to see the chassis of runtime classes.

Overcoming the limitations of scope and lifetime

In an absolutely perfect world, you could instantiate new object references `As Diagram` or `As New Diagram`, and then make use of a collection object `Diagrams` to check how many diagrams you're working with — as opposed to all other types of inserted images in a document — and call up a particular diagram by its index number. You could bring a new object into the collection with an instruction such as `Diagrams.Add`; and this instruction could instantiate the new diagram as well. This is similar to how O2KOM presents such objects as Word's `Document` class; you normally build a new document with a general instantiation such as `As New Document`, but you could also use `Documents.Add`. VBA is not a product of an absolutely perfect world. We can work to build functionality that is as similar as possible to the way O2KOM works. But we cannot escape the fact that VBA **builds the constitution of a class defined by a class module at run time.** The result is that any new VBA project cannot know what a class is or does until it encounters your instructions. Because these instructions can only be encountered in sequence, you must always concern yourself with *when* an instance comes into being, and when its properties are set properly and in order. For a different type of object such as a component of a Forms 2.0 form and its component objects, you have the luxury of defining each object's startup property settings at design time; with the VBA class module, everything is constructed on the fly.

The first and foremost problem that must be tackled in any implementation of online classes in VBA is *object lifetime.* Every instance of a class has a limited lifespan; generally it ends when the module responsible for it ends. This is a trickier business than it truly ought to be. There are three types of code modules in a Word 2000 project besides the class module itself: the general module, the form module, and the code that applies to the active document or active template called `ThisDocument`. (You'll find this last module listed in the **Microsoft Word Objects** tier of the Projects window in the VBA workspace.) Any one project may use any or all of these module types. But each of these types has its own limited lifetime; and when a code module is terminated, the variables that were declared by that module – private *or* public – cease to exist. When you take into account that an instance of a class, such as `Diagram`, is represented by a variable, you see the problem. A project such as our Diagrams example should maintain *persistent data* that lasts for the entire Word session, or at least for as long as the user works with a document based on the Diagrams template.

The form module is an unreliable instantiator

The way to begin solving the problem of object lifetime is to determine which module will be responsible for the instantiation of your run-time objects. Most VBA projects that you will write that gather data from the user will make use of at least one dialog box – thus you will have at least one form module. Since what the user does with the dialog box is likely to trigger the creation of a new class instance, it's tempting to have the form module be responsible for the instantiation – for executing a statement such as `Set diaThis As New Diagram`. But two factors stand in the way:

◆ First, your document template's capability to instantiate an object must exist *prior* to the invocation of the dialog box. The reason: Suppose the user loads into Word a document that already contains several instances of your runtime object. Word, the word processor, doesn't know these objects are special instances of a class; only VBA knows this. If your form module were responsible for instantiating your class instances, then the user would not be able to utilize the functionality you created for those objects until he brought up the dialog box. The user should only bring up the dialog box when he wants to, not because he has to for the sake of your VBA project. It is the document template that must inevitably be responsible for what that template is capable of doing; the form module must play an ancillary role.

◆ Secondly, objects that are declared and instantiated by your form module are local to that module and cease to exist once the form module is terminated. Once the user clicks on OK or Cancel those objects are gone. There are ways around this problem, but they're not pretty. One way is to have an outside module *declare* the object reference as public (`Public diaMain As Diagram`) and then allow the form module to instantiate a new instance and set the reference to point to that instance (`Set diaMain As New Diagram`). Another way is to have an outside module declare a collection as public (`Public Diagrams As Collection`) and then allow the form module to instantiate the object and add it to the collection (`Diagrams.Add diaMain`). Both workarounds cede some responsibility for the class instances to another module.

In the case of the Diagrams example, if the instances of the `Diagram` class were suddenly to go away, the user wouldn't know it at first because all the imported images would still be there in his document. Our class module is a sort of *wrapper*, if you will, around these inline shapes, giving them functionality they didn't have before; but as far as the constitution of the Word 2000 document is concerned, it's the same as it was before the class module was ever devised. In one way, that's a blessing; in another, it's a problem. Whatever functionality you build into Word, the application, cannot and does not alter Word, the document format. So it's up to you to make it look like it does.

In Depth: Declaring objects, instantiating objects, and referring to objects

We've covered these three elements in previous chapters, but since they're esoteric and difficult for sensible people to comprehend, I thought you would appreciate a review: VBA uses arbitrarily named *variables* to represent objects. A new variable is introduced to your source code by means of a *declaration* such as `Public diaThis As Diagram`. Such a declaration tells VBA to expect `diaThis` to be used as an exclusive term later on, and to reserve enough memory for that variable commensurate with an object of the size of any member of the `Diagram` class. But at this point, `diaThis` still means nothing.

Before VBA can make use of the new term to refer to data, an object of the stated class must be *instantiated* — which means that a new set of data is generated to fit the die-cut mold established by the class. One way to instantiate a class member is with the `Set` statement, as in `Set diaThis = New Diagram`. This tells VBA to call forth a new member of the `Diagram` class, and to make the term `diaThis` point to that member from now on — at least until VBA executes a statement such as `Set diaThis = Nothing`, or until the object with which the code module is associated goes "out of scope" or is terminated. If it's convenient to do so, both declaration and instantiation may take place with the same statement: `Public diaThis As New Diagram`. Joining these two jobs assumes that the module responsible for declaration, and the module responsible for instantiation, is the same; and as you'll see in a few pages, that cannot always be the case.

After a variable has been declared, it is called an *object reference*. After instantiation, we can say that reference points to a *class instance* (or "instance of a class"). The variable thus becomes representative of the instance.

ThisDocument cannot handle public objects

Although the code module for `ThisDocument` is often used to handle general code, it is officially an *object module* along with the form module. It seems we're running out of English-language words for these things, so I'll try to draw a clearer distinction: **An object module is a body of code best suited to manage an object that the user can see and manipulate directly.** Such a "graphic object" might be a form module, a Word 2000 document (`ThisDocument`), or an Excel 2000 workbook (`ThisWorkbook`). Even if the Word user operates one document for the duration of a session, the capability for the user to close that document — thereby terminating the existence of any instantiated objects associated with that document — still exists, and therefore must be taken into account.

The `ThisDocument` module for a template may contain event procedures for any document constructed with that template. In the headings for these event procedures, `Document` represents the sensitive object; so the events handled by `ThisDocument` are `Document_New`, `Document_Open`, and `Document_Close`. In case you're wondering, `Private Sub Document_New()` is the "AUTOEXEC" procedure that is automatically executed for a newly created document; `Private Sub Document_Open()` is the "AUTOEXEC" procedure that is automatically executed for a reopened document. Besides these event procedures, this module is open for such types of procedures as `Public Sub` and `Private Function`.

Not only does every open document have a `ThisDocument` code module automatically associated with it, but every active template also has its own `ThisDocument` module. (Notice that it is not a "ThisTemplate" module.) Nonetheless, these modules have separate identities. When you open a document constructed with a template other than Normal, VBA maintains no less than three ThisDocument modules for it: one for the Normal template, one for the document's native template, and one for the instance of the document itself. It's quite rare that you would ever need to write special code exclusively for one document, but if the need does arise, here is where you would do it.

Because ThisDocument represents a graphic object, and the lifetime of a graphic object is considered finite, the module cannot be used to declare public references to a runtime class. In other words, neither a graphic object module such as ThisDocument nor a form module can export object references that it creates for itself. It can use other modules' public object references, but it cannot create any for other modules to use. If the graphic object ceases to exist, it takes its own variables and private data with it into the great beyond; thus, if it could declare any type of data as public, there would be no way for other modules that borrow those public references to know when those references have ceased to exist until it's already too late.

Any references to class modules that you intend to be persistent throughout a session, must be declared public by a module whose lifetime is also persistent. This leaves one remaining candidate: the general code module, which is listed under **Modules** in the Projects window of VBA. A general module by definition contains no event procedures, and is not associated with any one object. But VBA knows to read and execute its module-level declarations (at the head of the module) first, before it even executes Private Sub Document_Open().

As you'll soon see, solving this problem may actually create a new one: **Because a general module may not include event procedures, it also may not be used to declare a public class that defines its own events.** Normally, declaring a class that has its own events is accomplished with a term such as Private WithEvents mailCon as Mailsort. Here the WithEvents qualifier tells VBA to expect and utilize the class instance's own defined events. But Public and WithEvents are not allowed together. If a class such as Diagram defines its own events, such as _Insertion and _Deletion, and you want instances of the class to at least be potentially persistent, how can you accommodate the class – is there, in the end, no room in the inn? There is if you kick the door down; and with VBA, every once in a while, that's what you have to do.

The only place for event procedures pertaining to a class' *defined* events is the ThisDocument module. But even if you declare a persistent instance as public within the general code module (sounds like "general court martial" if you're not paying close attention, doesn't it?), the ThisDocument module cannot make use of its events right away. The solution – which is, again, not pretty – is to go ahead and let the general code module declare a persistent object reference like this:

```
Public diaMain As New Diagram
```

This statement both declares and instantiates the object, so the class instance now officially exists. Next, within the header of the ThisDocument module, declare a second variable using its own standard rules:

```
Private WithEvents diaCom As Diagram
```

If you're not careful here, you'll create two separate instances of the `Diagram` class when you only want one. The trick is to make `diaCom` and `diaMain` be the same instance, which is absolutely permissible by VBA. In fact, you can declare any number of variables to refer to the same object. So within both the `Private Sub Document_New()` and `Private Sub Document_Open()` procedures, you would include this instruction:

```
Set diaCom = diaMain
```

You're not using `Set` here to instantiate any new class instance; presumably, one is already in existence and `diaMain` already points to it. You're just telling VBA to make `diaCom` point to the same object that `diaMain` points to. At this point, although your event procedures must refer to `diaCom` instead of `diaMain` — as in `Private Sub diaCom_Deletion()` — they will continue to be events that pertain to the same persistent instance of the class that was brought forth by the general code module.

How a runtime collection works

The next problem faced in conceiving our example — for which there is only one (painful) solution — concerns the problem of giving each diagram its own identity while at the same time giving the template a way to address all of the diagrams as a collection. O2KOM recognizes many of its automation objects and other OLE objects as both individual entities (`Workbook`) and members of a collection (`Workbooks`). Although this is a technical issue, it ends up looking as simple as a singular noun and a plural noun. Add `s` and you have a collection.

Runtime class modules devised with VBA are not automatically members of collections. On the surface, it would appear that building a collection is a simple matter. In the Declarations section (the header) of a general module, a collection is declared like this:

```
Public Diagrams As Collection
```

A collection does not have to be declared with any specific class. (In fact, there's nothing preventing a collection from containing objects of more than one class, although in practice this proves not only inconvenient but inefficient.) Officially, `Collection` is not a class. VBA only keeps track of the new collection's name and its scope. A runtime collection automatically supports four and only four member terms, listed in Table 9-1. Here, the collection term is the antecedent, as in `Diagrams.Add`.

TABLE 9-1 MEMBER TERMS OF AN OBJECT DECLARED AS COLLECTION

.Add	(Method) Attaches an object to a collection. **Arguments:** Item: – A reference to the object being attached. Key: – (Integer, **optional**) An index that denotes the position in the sequence that the attached object is to assume. An error will be generated if this number exceeds the total number of objects in the collection plus one. Before: – (Integer, **optional**) An index that denotes the position in the sequence before which the attached object is to fall. After: – (Integer, **optional**) An index that denotes the position in the sequence after which the attached object is to fall. Since collections declared at run time do not permit members to be addressed by name, the use of these last two arguments to designate "before #5" or "after #12" proves less practical than simply designating the location by name.
.Count	(Property, integer) The number of items currently in the collection.
.Item	(Constituent) Provides a more formal mechanism for referring to a member of a collection. **Example:** Diagrams.Item(iThis) refers to the same member as Diagrams(iThis). This constituent is provided mainly for compatibility with older versions of Visual Basic, even though at the time those older versions were available, VBA did not exist.
.Remove	(Method) Takes the stated member out of the collection. The object itself is not deleted. **Argument:** Index: – The position in the sequence of the member to be removed.

Reconciling individual identity with collective identity

As was mentioned earlier, runtime classes defined by class modules do not automatically support collections. So just because you have a class Diagram does not mean that you automatically have a collection Diagrams. The collection has to be declared, and the process of doing so, as you've seen, is relatively easy. The first problem you'll face is in granting a code module responsibility for declaring the collection.

An object module cannot be trusted to declare public object references. Instead, an object module should limit itself as much as possible to declaring object references privately for its own use, and only borrowing those public objects that an outside general module has declared. There is a very good reason for this: Each time you instantiate a member of a class module, the new instance declares those terms that it will need for its own use. If the new instance declared a Public variable, perceptible to all other modules in the project, then the next new instance to come into being could declare the same Public variable, resulting in ambiguity. Furthermore, since a declaration statement is not considered a "procedural" instruction, it cannot be executed conditionally. This means you can't have a clause that says, "*If* the collection does not exist yet, go ahead and declare it."

In using terms such as "cannot be trusted" and "*should* limit itself as much as possible," I seem to be implying that an object module *can* declare public references. This is quite correct – although Public WithEvents is not permitted in an object code module. What I am saying is that it is generally bad practice for the object module to declare public objects, except in rare circumstances (you just knew there would be exceptions). One such exception is illustrated in exactly two paragraphs.

Could one Private term be declared As Collection, so that any other terms with the same name declared by successive instances are set to point to the first one – a collection of collections, if you will? This is not possible, because "the first one" in this case would have to be Diagrams(1). To check whether this term exists, it would have to be invoked in an instruction – which means that the term would have to exist. If it hasn't been declared, it doesn't exist, and the program you're writing will not compile.

This is where we learn one of the sad truths about VBA architecture: **A separate class module must be responsible for a collection object designed to contain instances defined by another class module.** This does not mean the second class module must be called Diagrams; remember, you are not instantiating a Diagrams class, because Diagrams is a collection, not a class. Rather, the second class module must be responsible for declaring the public Collection. Now, didn't I just get through saying that an object module should not declare public object references? Indeed I did, but first, it is worth noting that a collection is not a class. But that's not enough of an excuse. An architectural counterargument comes into play here: **The functionality for any particular class module should be entirely and completely defined within that class module.** With respect to our diagrams example: The class responsible for maintaining the Diagrams collection needs to reference the term Diagrams for its own purposes – not just to declare the collection, but also to use it. It would be counterproductive to require another programmer who makes use of this class module to write a separate declaration instruction for Diagrams. To do so would force that programmer to complete the unfinished job of the collection maintenance class.

So, in the course of just four paragraphs, a rule is discovered, established, and effectively broken. This happens quite often in the course of VBA programming.

Defining a multiple instance class

For there to be a collection, there must be something for VBA to collect. The following code listings present a prototype of the Diagram class module system, which will be expanded significantly in future chapters. For now, we want the Diagram class to represent all of the *extra* functionality that should be attached to an inline shape to make it operate and behave like a formal, numbered figure.

SHADOW VARIABLES REPRESENT PROPERTIES' TRUE SETTINGS

The header of the Diagram class module declares the "shadow variables," as I call them, which will hold and maintain the values and data that appear to be assigned to the property terms. An assignment to a Diagram instance's property outside the class module will flow through to one of these shadow variables inside the class module. Listing 9-1 shows those declarations we used for the first prototype:

Listing 9-1: Diagram class shadow variable declarations.

```
Private strFilename As String
Private iThisIndex As Integer
Private markWhere As Word.Bookmark
Private docWhere As Word.Document
```

Variable strFilename will maintain the name of the image file being used as the diagram. The integer iThisIndex is a private accession number given to the newly instantiated Diagram class object, so that it can distinguish itself from other like objects. Word 2000 utilizes a device called a *bookmark* to record a position or range of characters in a document; markWhere will point to the bookmark used to record the spot just in front of the diagram. Finally, since a template can be used to generate more than one document at one time, docWhere is necessary to point to the document in which the diagram appears. All of these variables have private scope; none of the other modules in a project may see these variables. Properties act as guarded gateways to these private variables; data assignments can only reach these variables once they have passed the tests posed to them by the property procedures.

On Point

A property is made available to a class module through the implementation of property procedures. This way, any assignment of a property to a variable, or a value or data to a property, triggers the execution of a property procedure within the class module. An assignment of a standard type value to a property is handled by a Property Let procedure, whereas the assignment of an object reference to a property of object type is handled by a Property Set procedure. An assignment of an existing property setting to a variable outside the class module is handled by a Property Get procedure.

The examples that follow examine these procedures at work. Much of the bulk of a class module is made up of property procedures, mainly because the validation of an incoming property can often require several instructions, and often necessitates the use of error handler routines. This is not because these procedures are by their nature accident prone; indeed in some cases, the actual generation of an error (and the trapping of it so that it doesn't halt the program) is the only way to determine whether an object reference may be erroneous.

THE SIMPLEST PROPERTY PROCEDURES SIMPLY ADMIT ASSIGNMENTS

Our first edition of the `Diagram` class module is made up mainly of property procedures. Although there is no formal rule for this, I've made it my own protocol to pair together the property procedures for retrieval and assignment. For instance, Listing 9-2 shows the simplest procedure pair in the class, which declares and handles the `.DocOfOrigin` property. This points to the Word 2000 document to which the antecedent diagram belongs.

Listing 9-2: Diagram class procedure pair for the .DocOfOrigin property.

```
Public Property Get DocOfOrigin() As Word.Document
    Set DocOfOrigin = docWhere
End Property

Public Property Set DocOfOrigin(docThis As Word.Document)
    Set docWhere = docThis
End Property
```

Many property procedure pairs you will write in the course of your work will need to perform intensive validation to certify that the receiving variable in a procedure is of the right type or class, and that the data being assigned to a property is of the right type and follows the rules of the job at hand. But in the case of the `.DocOfOrigin` property, whose declared class here is `Word.Document`, there isn't much you need to do. For the `Property Get` procedure, if the receiving object reference is of class `Word.Document` (or just `Document`), then that's the entire test this particular property needs. Likewise, with the `Property Set` procedure, if the incoming assignment is of class `Word.Document`, then the main test is passed.

APPLYING ANALYSIS TO AN INCOMING PROPERTY SETTING IN PROPERTY LET

Listing 9-3 turns up the heat on the incoming and outgoing properties ever so slightly. This pair deals with the `.Index` property, which is an internal accession number.

Listing 9-3: Diagram class procedure pair for the .Index property.

```
Friend Property Get Index() As Integer
    Index = iThisIndex
End Property

Friend Property Let Index(iThis As Integer)
    If iThisIndex = 0 Then
        iThisIndex = iThis
    End If
End Property
```

This is the first opportunity we've had to show procedures declared with the `Friend` scope. The module that contains the procedure that instantiates a `Diagram` class object has access to this `.Index` property. It's a public property as far as that particular module is concerned. But even if that module declares the `Diagram` class instance public, any other module with access to the instance will *not* have access to the `.Index` property. So you should consider this term, therefore, to mean that the property is only visible to the "friend" that instantiated the object — or perhaps a more politically correct term for "Eyes Only.".

The extra degree of analysis comes when the incoming `.Index` property setting, represented by `iThis`, is being examined. Index numbers for this system will always start at 1. So the `Property Let` procedure makes the assignment to the shadow variable `iThisIndex` only if the variable is set to its default value of 0, which means that no index has previously been assigned to it. This way, an existing index value cannot be overwritten. Notice there is no `Else` division to the `If...Then` clause. If the incoming assignment doesn't qualify, the procedure simply leaves it alone. No error is generated. (It is possible to force an error to be generated manually, as you'll see in a later build of the `Diagram` class.)

Listing 9-4 turns up the heat quite a bit. The `.FileName` property is of the standard type `String`, but the `Property Let` procedure here makes certain that the contents of the property at all times point to a valid file. This is a variant of the procedure introduced to you earlier in the chapter.

Listing 9-4: Diagram class procedure pair for the .FileName property.

```
Public Property Get FileName() As String
    FileName = strFilename
End Property

Public Property Let FileName(strIncoming As String)
    If FileSystem.Dir(strIncoming) <> "" Then
        strFilename = strIncoming
        PlaceImage
    End If
End Property
```

The variation comes in the form of the instruction `PlaceImage`, which is a call to `Private Sub PlaceImage()` inside the class module. This procedure is responsible for placing the inline image in the document. It's a separate procedure because more than one property procedure may need to place images. The reason `Public Property Let FileName()` needs to place an image has to do with facilitating instantaneous response. The `.FileName` property represents the location of the file containing the image in the document. If any change you made to the `.FileName` property setting were passed without incident, it would fail to correspond to the image in the document. So `PlaceImage` is called here so that the class module may respond to a change in filename with a corresponding change in the diagram. This enables a programmer to change the diagram by changing its `.FileName` property, in the same way changing the `.Picture` property of a Forms 2.0 image control loads a new image into that control. The `PlaceImage` procedure is discussed shortly.

AN ERROR HANDLER ROUTINE IS NECESSARY IN CASE OF AN INVALID REFERENCE

In Listing 9-5, you see for the first time in this book an error handler routine. Thus far, we haven't examined *routines* at all; for Visual Basic and VBA, they rarely come up, thanks in large part to the neat and tidy way procedures are structured. In VBA, a routine is generated through a forced branch using a `GoTo` statement or some derivative, from one part of a procedure to another.

Listing 9-5: Diagram class procedure pair for the .Location property.

```
Public Property Get Location() As Word.Bookmark
    Set Location = markWhere
End Property

Public Property Set Location(markThis As Word.Bookmark)
    On Error GoTo Invalid1

    If docWhere.Name = "" Then Exit Property
    If docWhere.Bookmarks.Exists(markThis.Name) Then
        Set markWhere = markThis
        If strFilename <> "" And _
        markWhere.Range.InlineShapes.Count = 0 Then
            PlaceImage
        End If
    End If
    Exit Property
Invalid1:
    On Error GoTo 0
End Property
```

At the top of the `Property Set` procedure for the `.Location` property, the statement `On Error GoTo Invalid1` sets up a situation where in the event of an error, the VBA interpreter, instead of generating an ordinary error message and shutting down, *branches* or jumps execution to the instruction that follows the label `Invalid1:`. You can tell `Invalid1:` is a *label* and not an ordinary instruction by the inclusion of the colon (:) at the end. Under normal circumstances, the error handler routine would start here at `Invalid1:`, but in this situation, the procedure merely shuts off the forced branch with an `On Error GoTo 0` statement, and drops out of the procedure. (The shutoff is necessary so that *future* errors don't cause the interpreter to branch to this point — yes, it can happen.) So the error handler responds to an error situation by simply leaving the property alone.

Why have an error handler routine here in the first place? This property involves an object class in the Word 2000 object library — namely, the `Bookmark` class. The `Property Set` procedure certifies that any bookmark assigned to this property exists within the document pointed to by variable `docWhere`, the shadow variable for the `.DocOfOrigin` property. At this point, it's entirely possible that the `.DocOfOrigin` property has not been set, so there's no way to certify that a bookmark exists if its document of origin is unknown, or if it doesn't even exist itself. This is one of the countless quirks in O2KOM: Although the `Bookmarks` collection supports an `.Exists` property that returns True if a given bookmark exists and False if it does not, the `Documents` collection supports no such property. To see if the `.DocOfOrigin` property is set, the procedure polls its shadow variable, which is itself a `Document` object. Without a handy ".Exists" property, the procedure tests for nonexistence by checking whether the shadow variable's `.Name` property is blank (`If docWhere.Name = ""`). If it is, the procedure makes a forced exit with `Exit Property`. If the `Property Set` procedure for the `.DocOfOrigin` property has yet to be executed, then the `docWhere` variable has yet to be instantiated. In that case, the reference to `docWhere.Name` would generate an error — which is, at long last, why there is an error handler routine here. Because that erroneous possibility is, in fact, a likelihood, we need a routine that, insofar as VBA is capable of doing so, says to the interpreter, "Relax, forget it, go on to something else."

A second conditional clause checks whether the assigned bookmark exists. If it does, it assigns that bookmark to shadow variable `markWhere`. Then an embedded conditional clause evaluates two conditions: whether a filename has *not* been assigned to the image (`strFilename <> ""`) and whether there are *not* any placed figures in the vicinity of the bookmark (`markWhere.Range.InlineShapes.Count = 0`). If both conditions are true, there's no diagram yet near the existing bookmark, so a call is placed to the `PlaceImage` procedure.

Before we go on, notice the `Exit Property` statement. It has no conditions attached to it, so normal execution will reach this point and force execution to jump out of the property procedure. This statement is, unfortunately, necessary to guard the interpreter from accidentally executing the error handler routine (marked with `Invalid1:`) below it. So wherever you place an error handler routine in a procedure, you have to use execution control statements such as `Exit Property`, or even a few loose GoTo statements, to make certain that error handling instructions are not executed accidentally.

A READ-ONLY PROPERTY IS ESTABLISHED BY OMITTING PROPERTY LET

Our prototype for the Diagram class does support one read-only property, .ImageType. This is a derivative property that returns a string that denotes the format of the diagram in question. The reason this is a read-only property is simple – perhaps the simplest part of this whole chapter: **Omitting a** Property Let **or** Property Set **procedure for a property makes that property read-only.** You don't have to write any code barring the admission of a setting from a property; the VBA interpreter handles this by assuming that your omission of an incoming handler was intentional. The body of the Property Get procedure for this property, shown in Listing 9-6, works for the most part like a Public Function procedure.

Listing 9-6: Diagram class procedure for the read-only .ImageType property.

```
Public Property Get ImageType() As String
    Dim strEndTag As String

    strEndTag = Right$(strFilename, Len(strFilename - _
    InStr(strFilename, ".")))
    Select Case strEndTag
        Case "JPG"
            ImageType = "JPEG"
        Case "JPEG"
            ImageType = "JPEG"
        Case "TIF"
            ImageType = "TIFF"
        Case "TIFF"
            ImageType = "TIFF"
        Case "BMP"
            ImageType = "Windows Bitmap"
        Case "GIF"
            ImageType = "GIF"
        Case "WMF"
            ImageType = "Windows Metafile"
        Case Else
            ImageType = "Unknown"
    End Select
End Property
```

This procedure ascertains the image type at the time the property is polled outside the class module. No shadow variables are involved here. It relies on the premise that the extender for the filename of the image will denote the format of that image. Since extenders in Windows don't have to be three letters long anymore, an elaborate instruction uses the `InStr()` function to locate the position of the period in the filename, counting from the left; and then uses the `Len()` function to count the number of characters in the filename so that the result of `InStr()` can be subtracted from it (resulting in the number of characters after the period), and then uses `Right$()` to strip off that number of characters from that point to the end — the right side — of the filename. The `InStr()` function is embedded within the parentheses of two other functions; so although it appears last in the instruction, it gets executed first. `Len()` is executed next, because it's only embedded in one set of parentheses; and `Right$()` is executed last, because it's not embedded at all.

AN ORDINARY PRIVATE SUB PROCEDURE CAN BE WRITTEN FOR A CLASS MODULE

The procedure that takes care of the business of placing the diagram into the document is `Private Sub PlaceImage()`, which is presented in Listing 9-7.

Listing 9-7: Diagram class private function for placing a new diagram.

```
Private Sub PlaceImage()
    Dim strPlaceholder As String

    On Error GoTo Invalid3

    If strFilename = "" Or docWhere.Name = "" Then Exit Sub

    docWhere.Activate
    strPlaceholder = "DiagramMaticPlaceholder" & _
     Format$(iThisIndex, "0000")
    docWhere.Bookmarks.Add strPlaceholder, Selection
    markWhere.Select
    With Selection
        .MoveRight Unit:=wdCharacter, Count:=1, Extend:=wdExtend
        If .InlineShapes.Count = 1 Then
            .InlineShapes(1).Delete
        End If
        .InlineShapes.AddPicture FileName:=strFilename, _
         LinkToFile:=True, SaveWithDocument:=True, _
         Range:=markWhere.Range
        .Collapse wdRight
    End With
    docWhere.Bookmarks(strPlaceholder).Select
    docWhere.Bookmarks(strPlaceholder).Delete
    Exit Sub
```

```
Invalid3:
    On Error GoTo 0
End Sub
```

This is one of the more involved procedures we've dealt with thus far. Many of the details here have to do with the inner workings of the Word 2000 Object Library, which are discussed extensively in Chapter 13. For now, here's a quick run-through of what this procedure does: After setting up the now-familiar error trap, the procedure terminates itself if there's either no filename for the figure or no bookmark for its location. Next, the document of origin is brought forth (docWhere.Activate). A placeholder bookmark is added at the current cursor location in the event that the diagram will be placed at a location other than where the cursor is. In Word, the Selection object represents the cursor location.

Next, the cursor is moved to the bookmark where the diagram is to be added (markWhere.Select). Because the next several instructions have to do with the Selection object, a With clause is added so that Selection becomes the default object of the included instructions. Thus, the exposed points shown on the left side of those instructions signals the implied presence of Selection in those instructions.

The cursor is made to move one character to the right, just as though the user were clicking and dragging the mouse pointer over that character. If along the way the cursor "runs over" an existing diagram (If .InlineShapes.Count = 1), that diagram is deleted to make room for a new one. The next very long instruction utilizes the .AddPicture method to place the new diagram into the document. Then the cursor area is "collapsed" so that it doesn't appear to be "running over" the new diagram. Finally, the cursor is returned to the placeholder position where it was before, and then deleted so it doesn't get in the way.

Implementing the collection maintenance class

Earlier, I stated that a separate class module was necessary for declaring and implementing a collection to be made up of instances of a class defined by another module. For the Diagrams example, I devised the DiagramConsole class to act as the collection handler, as well as the overall manager and instantiator of Diagram class objects. Listing 9-8 shows the declarations for the initial build of the DiagramConsole class module:

Listing 9-8: DiagramConsole variable declarations.

```
Public Diagrams As New Collection
Private diaThis As Diagram
Public iIndexCount As Integer

Public Event Deletion(ByVal iIndex As Integer)
Public Event Insertion(ByVal strThisFile As String)
```

AN INTRODUCTION TO HOW EVENTS ARE DECLARED IN A CLASS MODULE

There are no shadow variables here because this class module won't need any properties – at least for now. Only methods are necessary. But notice our first declarations of runtime events. These declarations, using the `Event` statement, look somewhat like procedure headers; indeed, they do contain argument declarations. But these arguments are *outgoing*, to be received by the event procedures in the module responsible for handling `Diagram` class events – for our example, the `ThisDocument` module. This way, when you go into the code window for `ThisDocument` and dial up the `Diagram` class object and the `_Deletion` event, VBA will generate the following code automatically:

```
Private Sub diaCom_Deletion(ByVal iIndex As Integer)


End Sub
```

The cursor will be placed in the space between these instructions. Here `diaCom` is the variable declared within the `ThisDocument` module by the statement `Private WithEvents diaCom As DiagramConsole`.

Listing 9-9 shows the procedure that is the reason for the presence of the separate class module.

Listing 9-9: DiagramConsole class' critical method.

```
Public Sub InsertDiagram(strThisFile As String, _
  iWidth As Integer, iHeight As Integer)
    Dim strThisMark As String

    If FileSystem.Dir(strThisFile) = "" Then Exit Sub

    iIndexCount = iIndexCount + 1
    strThisMark = "DiagramMark" & Format$(iIndexCount, "0000")
    ActiveDocument.Bookmarks.Add strThisMark, Selection
    Set diaThis = New Diagram
    diaThis.Index = iIndexCount
    Set diaThis.DocOfOrigin = ActiveDocument
    Set diaThis.Location = ActiveDocument.Bookmarks(strThisMark)
    diaThis.FileName = strThisFile
    Diagrams.Add diaThis
    Set diaThis = Nothing
End Sub
```

The `.InsertDiagram` method is designed to be activated by a form module after the user has brought up the proper document and has chosen a new diagram from a dialog box. We've made it a rule here for a form module never to try to instantiate a public instance of a class, because it will go away when the dialog box is dismissed and unloaded. But for this method to be contacted, the form module has to have a "live" instance of the DiagramConsole class, and it needs for that instance to be recognized outside of the form module's scope. A bit more about how this is achieved shortly.

The procedure for this method receives three arguments: the filename where the image is contained, and integer values that represent the width and height of the image to be placed into the document. This way, the user can choose how big or small to make the diagram from the main dialog box. Using the technique you saw earlier, the procedure for this method begins by making certain the filename for the image exists. Once that's cleared, the next instruction increments the official index ticker iIndexCount, whose main purpose for this prototype is to make sure no two bookmarks are given exactly the same name. This is accomplished by using the intrinsic function Format$() to turn iIndexCount into a four-digit number (so that 1, for instance, shows up as 0001). The digits are then attached to the right side of the literal DiagramMark, resulting in a bookmark name that the user is unlikely to type for himself. Next, a bookmark with the newly generated name is attached to the current Word document ActiveDocument so that it points to the current cursor location Selection.

Now the process of bringing the new Diagram class object into fruition begins. Unlike bringing up a new form module whose dialog box contents are prepared in advance to its being seen by the user, a newly instantiated object is made real first with an instruction such as Set diaThis = New Diagram, and then its property contents are loaded into it. But it must first exist, which means that, even for a brief time, it spends part of its existence blank. This is why the object's properties must be set *now*, before anything else happens.

The new instance is represented here by the reference diaThis. This is not the instance's name for the duration of the project — only a pointer to it for the next few instructions. Later on in the program's run, diaThis will point to some other Diagram class instance. The first order of business after instantiation is to give the instance its official index number. Because the Property Let procedure for the .Index property was declared Friend, only this module — the one that instantiated diaThis — is capable of setting this property.

Next, the .DocOfOrigin, .Location, and .FileName properties are set, in that order. The order here is important. Recall that, the way the Property Set procedure for .Location was constructed, the bookmark doesn't get cleared unless its document of origin is ascertained. This requires that .DocOfOrigin be set first — an inconvenient rule for now, but a necessary one.

Next, Diagrams.Add diaThis makes the new instance a member of the Diagrams collection — one of the primary jobs of the DiagramConsole class. Finally, the reference diaThis is removed altogether with Set diaThis = Nothing.

Normally, when a reference to an instance is removed by setting it to Nothing, and no other reference to that instance remains, the instance itself is terminated. But here diaThis was made a member of the Diagrams collection just prior to the release of diaThis from memory. So all that happens is that diaThis no longer refers to the instance, but the instance still exists as a member of the collection.

ONE LONE DECLARATION MAKES THE ENTIRE CLASS/COLLECTION SYSTEM POSSIBLE

In the next chapter, we'll build upon this prototype by giving it a form module for a dialog box, by setting up custom events for the Diagram class, and by borrowing a few functions that Windows uses but VBA officially does not. To make the entire class system that we've established thus far work, we need to build a general (that is, nonobject) module and give it this one declaration, if no other instruction at all:

```
Public diaMain As New DiagramConsole
```

No declaration is necessary for the Diagram class because the public, persistent instance of DiagramConsole takes care of that for us. As you'll see in the next chapter, any object module, such as a form module or ThisDocument, may draw on this public instance diaMain while still maintaining the "private instance only" protocol I established earlier. The way to do this is by declaring that private reference, and using the Set statement to tie it to diaMain. For instance, ThisDocument may legally declare Private WithEvents diaCom As DiagramConsole. We want no more than one instance of the DiagramConsole class at any one time, so as early as possible, this reference is set to refer to the same instance as diaMain, using the instruction Set diaCom = diaMain. Now the ThisDocument module has a way to handle the DiagramConsole instance's events, while still allowing that instance to remain public in scope.

To close, here are some of the new intrinsic functions introduced in the examples in this chapter:

TABLE 9-2 *VISUAL BASIC FOR APPLICATIONS*
          INTRINSIC FUNCTIONS

Format$() Format()	Generates a textual string consisting of digits and special characters based upon a given value and a symbolic template that is applied against that value. This template uses characters to represent the placement of digits and characters such as decimal points, currency marks, and placeholders. **Arguments:** *Value* – A numeral value to be reformatted into a string.

String - The pattern that the function will use in generating the string form of the value. Characters included in this pattern string perform these roles:

0   Places a digit at this place in the string, relative to the location of the decimal point, regardless of whether the value contains a digit for that place.

Places a digit at this place in the string if and only if the value contains a digit for that place. Also places digits to the left of this place in the string if the value contains digits to the left.

.   Represents the decimal location of the point in the string.

$ (*or any other nondigit character*) Places that character in its corresponding position in the string.

Examples:

```
Format$(12.9, "#.00")
        returns the string 12.90
Format$(.125, "0.00")
        returns the string 0.13
Format$(149.95, "$#.00")
        returns the string $149.95
```

Note: The role of the `Format$()` function in reformatting dates, times, and other nondigit strings is discussed later in the book.

Instr()

Returns an integer that denotes the first location, counting from the left of a string being examined, of a given character. The first character in the string is numbered 1, not 0.

Arguments (in order):

Integer – (**optional**) The location in the string, counting from the left, where the search is to begin.

String – A variable or literal referring to the string to be examined.

Character – A single character to be located within the string. If this argument contains more than one character, only the first character of the argument applies.

Constant – (**optional**) Determines whether the interpreter is to compare the character against the string in a case-sensitive (1) or non-case-sensitive (0 – **default**) manner.

Examples:

```
Instr("WIN.INI", ".")
        returns 4
Instr("helLo", "L")
        returns 4
Instr("helLo", "L", 1)
        returns 3
```

On Point

One purpose for a pair of procedures that manage a property is to ensure that the hand-off between the variable outside the class module, the property term, and the shadow variable inside the class module is both smooth and valid. Another purpose is to instigate such actions that may be warranted or expected when a property is accessed or, especially, changed.

For a `Property Let` or `Property Set` procedure to guard against the occurrence of an improper reference to an undeclared or uninstantiated object reference, it may have to attempt that reference and trap the resulting error if it happens to be improper. The trap is set using the `On Error GoTo` statement, which forces a branch to the instruction following the stated labeled line. In some circumstances, the entire purpose of the trap is to nullify the error and drop out of the property procedure, leaving the property setting untouched. Generally, this is so the end user does not have to be bothered with some cryptic error message that actually pertains to another programmer's misuse of a class module that you've devised.

In Theory: Basic in What Way?

The "B" in "BASIC" stands for "Beginners," or at least stood for it at one time. The concept of *beginning* is informative in that it implies a progression to some other state at some later time. Today, a person can have a very comfortable career in Visual Basic programming; there's a high demand for VB skills, and VB's efficiency in getting desperate jobs accomplished quickly has given it a level of respect once reserved for the lower-level, fully compiled languages. So one may certainly begin his career today as a VB programmer, and may possibly stay one for the remainder of that career.

Is BASIC still a beginners' language conceptually? In the sense that swimming the English Channel prepares one for the deep end of the pool, perhaps. I've leveled with you thus far in admitting that modern programming, especially with a derivative of BASIC, is a difficult topic; and that what I will attempt to do here is make that topic more reasonable. But could the so-called "advanced" languages perhaps be any less conducive to reason?

C++ is an intricate, well structured system of surprisingly few terms that are carefully applied. In the act of developing any process with VBA, it's difficult for me not to run across some matter of everyday methodology — how to get a form module to recognize the same object instantiated by the module responsible for perpetuating the data, for instance — that wouldn't be solved quite simply by C++ on a conceptual level. C++ does not utilize class modules *per se*, but instead utilizes code modules that happen to define any number of classes. A C++ object has its own member functions, as well as its own public and private member variables (here, "friendship" means something else entirely). One of C++'s most clever devices is something it calls a *pointer* (denoted by the * character, and which is actually a modified holdover from the C language). When a variable, data structure, object, or even a function has been declared (and it makes so much sense in C++ to declare functions the way you declare variables), a pointer declared with the same type or class ends up being the same "size." Think of data stacked like rasters in memory, and a C++ pointer drawing a same-size frame around a particular region of memory organized in the same way as the pointer's declared type or class. Whereas a variable represents data directly, a pointer represents memory, and can be shifted around memory to reveal a portion that is the same "size and shape" of a variable.

C++ would solve the problem of the collection outlined in this chapter by storing the pointers to each instance of a class in a simple array. This array would contain the *locations* of each instance in memory, and those locations could be appended or trimmed as necessary. To locate a pointer to a particular instance, you'd simply declare another pointer, this time to the array – a pointer to a pointer (denoted by **). If you wanted to cycle through each instance, you'd simply use a for loop to increment the pointer each iteration, with an instruction as simple as **p++.

It is a simple and enviable elegance to anyone caught in the mire associated with making converging and conflicting technologies work together – which is what VBA is all about. And yet, after thinking about it for just a short while, you realize a far more *basic* truth that comes from observing things more pragmatically and not always so conceptually: Working with smaller tools results in greater work. Although it would be much easier to solve the communication problem *conceptually* with C++, it is actually easier to solve that same problem *practically* with Visual Basic or VBA, not because VBA is directly linked to Office 2000 (that's an obvious convenience), but because it gives the programmer enough tools with enough dangerous potency to be able to bend the rules until they break, if that solves the problem at hand. As an artist, I'm aware that, although it may be more aesthetically pleasing to carve marble with a hammer and chisel, it's fundamentally more practical to chunk the big pieces off with a power saw. VBA has enough brute-force keywords and techniques for you to be able to craft a workable, if not always efficient and certainly not always pretty, solution to the problem at hand, with far fewer instructions and in much less time.

The BASIC language has always been the programmer's equivalent of modeling clay. It's always pliable, sometimes even malleable, and rarely, if ever, fixed or unyielding. It is that characteristic of BASIC that has made it so maligned among the programming elite throughout history, the holders of chisels. It has led all too often to the mistaken belief that BASIC is unstructured, undisciplined, and unprincipled. The truth is, programming principle, as we know it today, was born in BASIC. The BASIC language is the proving ground of principle in programming. For that reason, a thorough explanation of those principles it continues to maintain will always seem a little grandiloquent, a little exhausting, but in the end, never always quite enough.

In Brief

♦ A class module provides the VBA programmer with a mechanism for devising reusable code that can be inserted into multiple projects, with clearly defined principles and guidelines for its own use and reuse.

♦ A method is a `Public Sub` or `Public Function` procedure belonging to a class module. The name of this procedure is "exposed" to the instantiator of a class instance as a method term, which may take arguments.

♦ A property is declared within a class module by means of a special procedure or pair of procedures. The `Property Get` procedure is declared with the name of the property as its own name, and establishes the process by which a value or data is assigned to a property reference outside of the class module. The `Property Let` (for standard types) and `Property Set` (for object classes) procedures establish the processes by which data is assigned to a property term by an expression outside of the class module.

♦ When a project contains more than one module, some of those modules may need to declare objects only `As Private`, so that the project doesn't export any volatile references to modules in the "outside world." When an object module (such as a form module or `ThisDocument`) needs to utilize this public instance in a manner reserved for private references, it may go ahead and declare that private reference, and then set as early as possible using the `Set` statement to refer to the public instance.

♦ A class module should not be responsible for maintaining a collection of itself. It is technically possible for it to do so, though it is an extremely messy and treacherous matter that is susceptible to programmer error. Although it is not always the most desirable solution, by far the easier one is to devise a second class module that is responsible for declaring and maintaining a collection for the first class.

Chapter 10

What Windows Knows That VBA Doesn't

IN THIS CHAPTER

◆ How to make a VBA program call a Windows API function

◆ Acquiring vital data about your computer at run-time

◆ Wrapping difficult API functions in an easier-to-use class module

◆ Using API functions to read from and write to Windows initialization (.INI) files

◆ Instantiating a class module from a form module

◆ Programming and utilizing Windows' familiar common dialog boxes

◆ Learning and utilizing Boolean arithmetic

◆ Making VBA make some noise other than `Beep`

SINCE VERSION 2.0, the design of Microsoft Windows has been centered around a few basic dynamic link libraries (DLLs) that handle many of the system's most common tasks. The functions that handle these tasks were originally written in the C language; today they retain the C-style headings that make them callable with the conventional function syntax — function name first, followed by arguments in parentheses. Collectively, Microsoft refers to these functions as the Windows Applications Program Interface (API).

While comprehensive knowledge of the Windows API is no longer critical for programmers to be able to develop most modern applications (Microsoft Foundation Class now handles that feat), it still provides the infrastructure for those applications — Microsoft Foundation Class (MFC) provides an+1 object-oriented wrapper for API functions. But because Visual Basic and VBA development does not involve MFC, they still borrow functions from the API, especially when they need to get a handle on what's happening in Windows when native keywords will not suffice.

There are several thousand functions in the current Windows 32-bit API (Windows 98, NT 4.0). This chapter could provide you with the obligatory smattering of formless functions, and then leave you to your own devices in finding out whether they benefit your program or crash your system. But then, it will not have been worth your while or my effort. Instead, this chapter will explain in detail how

VBA makes contact with the API, and implement some of the most useful of the API functions in a real-world situation involving class modules. The class module example introduced in Chapter 9 is expanded upon here. You'll see how the API may be used to generate and maintain initialization files to make permanent your program's critical parameters between sessions; and I'll compare this methodology to using the Windows System Registry for the same purpose. You'll also see how the same process used to contact the API can be applied to other Windows DLLs to add common functionality to your VBA programs – such as the regular Windows Open and Save dialog boxes.

On Point

The road ahead for this chapter is wild and bountiful. It draws substantially on information set forth in Chapter 9, where you learned about the major components of a VBA class module, including its exclusive `Property Get` and `Property Let/Set` procedures. A `Property Let` procedure is a mechanism for screening an incoming value that is being assigned to a term outside of the class module. Inside the class module is a private variable that is used to support the value of the property. The procedures set the rules for what values or data can be assigned to these private variables, how, and when. The `Property Get` procedure certifies that the data being requested from a property makes sense in the context of the process requesting it.

In Chapter 9, we began to build the DiagramMatic class module set for Word 2000. This example continues here. In Chapter 9, you saw that two class modules were required to maintain a collection of objects that represent data in Word. The main class module `DiagramConsole` creates and manages the `Diagrams` collection, while the document template – the source of Word's functionality – instantiates `DiagramConsole`. This weird-sounding term means to make a separate and distinct copy of the data required for the class to function, and then call that functionality into existence for that data.

This chapter builds on that foundation of knowledge in the following ways: First, after we examine how Windows API functions are declared and utilized in the normal course of a VBA program, you'll see a class module that acts as a "wrapper" around several of these functions, making them not only easier but safer to use in everyday Office 2000 programming. Then this class module will be attached to `DiagramConsole`, giving it capabilities that VBA alone cannot grant it. The Windows API is an open library (the degree of its openness is disputed in court from time to time) into the basic functionality of Windows. Because that functionality is so raw, and because it is expressed in C – which is as different from VBA as the rules to Monopoly are from the US Tax Code – invoking API functions reminds one of having to speak a foreign language using just a dictionary. The class module will serve as a translator, so that you and other VBA programmers can invoke API functionality in a VBA fashion.

Declaring External Functions

The collective Windows API is like a dictionary without an index. When VBA establishes contact with an API function, it relies on a statement in one of the modules' General Declarations section. While it's structured like the heading of a VBA procedure, the `Declare` statement doesn't introduce an enclosure of VBA instructions, as would a `Sub` or `Function` statement. It simply makes the name of the API function visible to the VBA program.

Argument passing is unorthodox by VBA standards

To begin, here's a simple example, after which we'll examine the `Declare` statement in more detail: One common API function reveals the name of the directory on the local processor where Windows is installed. You may be thinking, "That's no big deal; it's C:\WINDOWS." Maybe for most people, but not for everyone. For most everyone, Windows is installed on drive C: (yes, it can be installed elsewhere). And many NT servers and workstations use directory `C:\WINNT`. So the directory where Windows files are installed is not written in stone; for this reason, the API provides the function `GetWindowsDirectory`.

Each Windows API function must be declared separately and independently. There is no class or interface that contains API functions, because the API is not object-oriented, and is not comprised of COM objects. So for `GetWindowsDirectory()`, you add this statement to a module that has public scope to make this function available to all modules in the program:

```
Declare Function GetWindowsDirectory Lib "kernel32" _
  Alias "GetWindowsDirectoryA" (ByVal lpBuffer As String, _
  ByVal nSize As Long) As Long
```

The good news about this monster of an instruction is that **you do not have to write each API function declaration yourself.** Since each API function requires a specific `Declare` statement, you can simply copy the declaration in its entirety from the WINAPI.TXT file located on the CD-ROM included with this book – which includes all the `Declare` statements you could ever want or need – and paste it into General Declarations.

Still, it's important that you know some crucial concepts about how this statement and all `Declare` statements are constructed:

◆ From a C programmer's perspective, all of the components of the Windows API are considered functions. Yet VBA applies the same rule to these components as it applies to its own procedures: The `Declare` statement calls an API function `Function` if and only if it returns some value or data – even if it's just a True/False Boolean indicator. `Declare` calls the function `Sub` if it does not return a value – if it's what C considers a "void function."

◆ Historically, Windows has called its three main DLL components **KERNEL**, **USER**, and **GDI**. The modern 32-bit versions of Windows have added a –**32** suffix to these names. So Lib "kernel32" in the example above refers to the operating system's core library, which is the source of the API function GetWindowsDirectoryA().

◆ Because API function names are subject to change (with notice), it sometimes becomes necessary for the newer main DLLs to support an older and newer version of a function simultaneously, at least until it no longer remains feasible to support the older version. In the above example, GetWindowsDirectoryA() is a newer version of an API function originally entitled GetWindowsDirectory(). But older Visual Basic and VBA programs may contain calls to GetWindowsDirectory() that it would be inconvenient for their programmers to have to update. So in the example above, the name of the API function that is actually called is marked with the qualifier Alias, while the name by which the function will be known in the VBA program is written beside Function without the –A suffix.

◆ The names used for the arguments passed to the API function are almost entirely unimportant. They are here as placeholders, and are not the names of variables used within the API function. (Remember, the function is already compiled, and does not retain symbolic variables *per se*.) These names will show up in a ToolTip when you are typing calls to the function in your source code in order to remind you of the order of the arguments you're typing. Otherwise, they fulfill no other purpose in VBA.

◆ With only two exceptions in the entire Windows API – which covers some tens of thousands of passed arguments – all arguments to API functions are passed ByVal (by value). Yet API functions are often capable of changing the contents of the variables used in the function call (not the variables used as placeholders in the declaration – remember, they don't matter much). So the arguments responsible for the call are susceptible to change just as if the declaration were a conventional VBA procedure declaration receiving those arguments ByRef (by reference). GetWindowsDirectoryA() is one example, which you'll see in detail in a few pages. Why actually write ByVal, then; why not write ByRef instead? **Because the API function does not receive the VBA variable.** It wouldn't know what one was if it had one. Like all C functions, they receive data, not variables, as arguments by default. But a C function is capable of *dereferencing* the memory location of any argument it receives, and changing the data contents of memory at that location as part of the job it's programmed to perform. If a C function were to receive an argument "by reference," as C defines that phrase, it would receive the memory address of the data where the argument is contained – which is not exactly the same as receiving a VBA variable ByRef. In VBA, the received reference *includes* the memory address, as well as its type or class information and a few other elements.

Because `GetWindowsDirectoryA()` is really a C function, it must be contacted like one — a process which is quite different than calling a VBA procedure. This function has been programmed to send its results — the central directory for Windows — into a specific buffer location in memory. VBA can translate this location to the function by showing the function a string whose size is the same as that of the buffer. More accurately, you declare the string and fill it up with blank space, and then use the string as an argument. VBA sends the API function just the contents of that string `ByVal`. The C-language API function sees this buffer space as a blank slate of sorts and writes its results to that buffer. The second argument to `GetWindowsDirectoryA()` is simply the length of that buffer, so that the API function can stop itself from writing off the edge and onto other memory that may belong to something else.

API function results are often returned in buffers

Here's the process in practice: First, you declare the string that will represent the buffer. Then you fill the buffer with blank space, using an instruction like this:

```
strWinDir = String$(255, 0)
```

The `String$()` function here produces a chain of 255 characters, all of them being ANSI character code 0. For API functions, "blank space" consists not of space characters (ANSI 32), but code-zeroes (ANSI 0). A *code-zero* is not printable. The way C examines memory contents, a code-zero generally means "nothing here," and a string of characters formally ends with a code-zero.

Next, the call to the API function is placed; pay close attention to the syntax here:

```
GetWindowsDirectory strWinDir, 255&
```

Why is there an ampersand following the 255, which is a numeral and not a variable? Because the argument receiving this numeral was declared `As Long`; and VBA by default interprets a number as low as 255 using as an `Integer`, whose positive value falls between 0 and 32,767. (Why not the `Byte` type, which is narrower and consumes less memory? Because `Byte` is a relatively new type, and the interface between VBA and other components must adhere to the older standard in which `Byte` was not recognized — in keeping with one of the dictums of the Component Object Model.) So the type identification character & is used so that VBA will phrase 255 with the memory space generally afforded a long integer; the C function will accept nothing less.

Also, this API function was declared as a VBA `Function`, returning a value `As Long`, so why doesn't this call instruction return a value to a variable? Indeed, you could write the call like this instead:

```
lReturn& = GetWindowsDirectory(strWinDir, 255&)
```

In Depth: The numerology behind 255

When declaring the optimum length for a character buffer being used by a Windows API function, why use two hundred and fifty-five characters instead of, say, eleven? Enough, say, to handle C:\WINDOWS, which is the customary Windows directory, and slightly larger than the alternate C:\WINNT? After all, isn't memory consumption important in *all* programming? The reason for 255 has to do with the way Windows works. The Windows API expects any character buffer that may contain a directory path to be as long as the maximum allowable DOS directory. That's right, I said, "DOS." (And you thought it was dead.) In C and C++ programming, this number is represented by the constant MAX_PATH, which is a constant you never have to worry about unless you declare it yourself in VBA. In any event, the value of MAX_PATH is 255.

So why 255, and not 254 or 256? Because 255 is equal to 2^8 (two to the eighth power) minus one, or the binary value 11111111. In other words, 255 is the highest *decimal* (base 10) value a byte may represent, because in binary (base 2), it's the value of a byte when all of its bits are set to 1. The value 256 would be represented in binary as 100000000, and in the computer as 0000000100000000, because once a value exceeds 255, it requires two 8-bit bytes to represent it. So 256 becomes a 16-bit value, while 255 is merely an 8-bit one. The value 255 becomes the highest number you may address with a single 8-bit byte.

The results would be the same, except for the extra baggage of variable lReturn& holding some positive numeral value. This value is entirely meaningless to VBA; there's nothing you can do with it. So it's just as well that the return value is thrown out and that the API function is addressed as though it were declared Sub.

In either case, once execution resumes in VBA, variable strWinDir contains the path where Windows is installed. It also contains a lot of useless code-zeroes at the end – the remnants of having been a 255-character buffer.

VBA's intrinsic function RTrim$() removes the trailing *spaces* from a string, but not the trailing *code-zeroes*. So it takes an embedded VBA intrinsic function similar to the one you saw in Chapter 9 to hack the zeroes off the end and leave a usable string behind:

```
strWinDir = Left$(strWinDir, InStr(strWinDir, Chr$(0)) - 1)
```

On Point

For those of you keeping score at home, there are three terms "function" in play simultaneously here in this chapter. No, there's no alternative term for any of them, otherwise I would be happy to use it in this book. But I do owe you at least some reminder of the distinctions between them:

API function – A compiled body of binary code which is generally part of a DLL, and which is called in VBA using its name and any arguments (parameters) it may require, in a format similar to a standard procedure call.

Function procedure – A body of VBA source code that generally receives a series of arguments, performs logical and mathematical processes on those arguments or other data, and returns a discrete value to the instruction which called it. This return data may be received or ignored.

intrinsic function – A keyword in the VBA vernacular which is definable, in terms of types of BASIC-language instructions, as a "function" as opposed to a "statement." In this sense, a VBA intrinsic function may be written as being representative of a value — namely, the value which the VBA interpreter returns after executing its pre-programmed processes on the given data.

The embedded `InStr()` function locates the position of the first code-zero (represented by `Chr$(0)`), which is one ahead of the last usable character in the return value. So after `InStr()` returns its value, one is subtracted from it, backing us up one character. Everything from the beginning up to that point is extracted using `Left$()`, and then reassigned to `strWinDir` — the trailing code-zeros are now effectively lopped off. I could have written the two intrinsic functions here as `Left()` and `Chr()`, leaving off the trailing $. They're here mainly because these functions have been a part of BASIC since the beginning, and I've been programming with them now for over two decades. I'm in the habit of including them, and I can't seem to break it. But how come `InStr()` doesn't have a trailing dollar sign? Because it never did have one; this intrinsic function is a latecomer to BASIC.

Here now, step by step, is how a `Declare` statement is constructed:

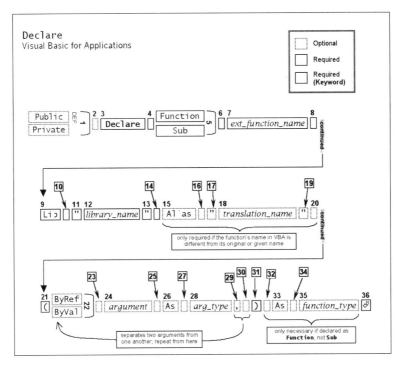

Part		Description
1	Public Private	**Qualifier** Denotes the accessibility of the declared external function to procedures in other modules. Because an external function such as an API function is, for all intents and purposes, the same for one module as it is for any other, and because the rules regarding VBA variables do not apply to C-language functions, the function may safely be declared Public (or left public in scope by default). The exception is for a class module, which should declare its external functions Private. Any other object module that requires an external function may either declare it Private for itself, or rely upon another general module's Public declaration, with no practical difference.
2	(space)	
3	Declare	**Statement** Denotes that the function being declared here is external to the VBA project and is being supplied by a dynamic link library (DLL). This library may be part of the Windows API, or one of the Windows common libraries such as Common Dialog (COMDLG32.DLL).

	Part	Description
4	(space)	
5	Function Sub	**Identifier** States whether the external function is to return a value to the VBA instruction. An external function that does return a value is considered a `Function` by the VBA definition; a nonreturning function — or what C calls a `void` function — is considered by VBA a `Sub`.
6	(space)	
7	*ext_function_ name*	**Literal** The name of the external function as it will appear in function call instructions within VBA. This may be identical to the name of the function as stated within its native DLL; in which case, the `Alias` portion of the `Declare` statement (parts **15** through **20**) are not required. This name should be unique among all declared external functions as well as all internal VBA procedure names. As a matter of habit, you should not give a VBA procedure a name identical to that of a known external function. In situations where two or more libraries contain two or more external functions to be declared here, all having the same name, you should give those functions unique names here and resolve the ambiguity by stating an alias for all but one, if not all, of the like-named functions.
8	(space)	
9	Lib	**Qualifier** States that the name which follows (part **12**) refers to the dynamic link library to which the external function belongs.
10	(space)	
11	" (quotation mark)	**Delimiter** Sets off the name of the library (part **12**) from the rest of the `Declare` statement.

Continued

	Part	Description *(continued)*
12	*library_name*	<u>Literal</u> The filename of the DLL housing the compiled external function, minus the period and extender. For API functions in 32-bit Windows 95, 98, and NT 4.0, this library may be any of thee following:
	Kernel32	Provides the operating system's core functionality and self-sustaining features
	User32	Deals with how the user operates Windows, through controls, physical devices, and onscreen devices
	GDI32	The graphical rendering subsystem of Windows, responsible for plotting graphics onscreen and for the printer
13	" (quotation mark)	<u>Delimiter</u>
14	(space)	
15	Alias	<u>Qualifier</u> Denotes that the name of the external function being called is different from the name that will be used to contact the function within the VBA program. Stating an alias has become necessary in situations where the Windows API has been revised, so as to support both a newer function and an older function for the same purpose. Microsoft's protocol has been to attach an A to the end of the newer version of an API function. To adapt an older Visual Basic or VBA program to support the newer function, only the Declare statement need be changed by adding the Alias phrase. The function calls elsewhere in the program may remain as they were.
16	(space)	
17	" (quotation mark)	<u>Delimiter</u> Offsets the external function's given name (part **18**) from the rest of the statement.
18	*translation_ name*	<u>Literal</u> The given name of the external function, as written and compiled into its native DLL.
19	" (quotation mark)	<u>Delimiter</u>

Part		Description
20	(space)	
21	((left parenthesis)	Begins the argument list. If there are no arguments in the list, both parentheses (parts **21** and **31**) remain, and are left empty ( ).
22	ByRef ByVal	<u>Qualifier</u> States how the argument (part **24**) is to be passed to the external function. Usually this argument is passed by value rather than by reference. By default, VBA passes arguments by reference, so ByVal is absolutely necessary here. Exceptions include situations in which the type of the argument is to be determined by the task performed by another argument, in which case you admit outright you don't know the argument type using a declaration such as ByRef lvParam As Any. Here Any means "not known at the moment." It's necessary in this situation to write ByRef (or leave the qualifier off) so that the external function has some data available to it to determine the argument type at run-time. (VBA procedures are not so capable.) One and only one other exception involves a relatively new API function InsertMenuItemA to pass a structure containing the contents of a new menu selection. Otherwise, since a C function cannot make use of a VBA variable, it should not be passed by reference.
23	(space)	
24	*argument*	<u>Variable</u> A term that represents the value, string, or data structure to be sent to the external function. This term need not represent any specific VBA variable, nor need it represent the name of the received argument in the external function (such names were part of the function's symbol table prior to compilation, and no longer exist anyway). The term need only represent the spot where the argument appears in the declaration.
25	(space)	
26	As	Denotes that the term which follows will specify the argument's type.
27	(space)	

Continued

	Part	Description *(continued)*
28	*arg_type* Variant Byte Boolean Integer Long Currency Single Double Date String Object Any	<u>Standard or composite type</u> States the argument's type. This portion is required for all arguments wherever they appear in the Declare statement's arguments list (unlike declarations for VBA procedures). **Rules:** ◆ The declared type of an external argument may not be a class — either an OLE component class or a VBA run-time class. External functions are not object-oriented, and do not interpret classes. ◆ An external argument's declared type may not be Variant. Variants are specific to the Visual Basic family of languages. ◆ Any standard VBA variable type may be written here. The type you specify delegates how much memory is used to store the argument — which is the most important information the DLL function needs. ◆ The declared type may be the name you've given to a composite Type structure earlier in the Declarations section (Type structures are discussed later in this chapter). A Type structure is a composite which collects together several variables of either standard type or themselves composite type, in a defined order like a record. The members of this structure may then be addressed like properties of a class, although this structure is not a class. An example structure is the left, right, top, and bottom coordinates of a rectangle that is to be called Type RECT, and which is often used for window manipulation functions in the GDI32 library. ◆ With this VBA statement only, an argument may be declared As Any when its type as regarded by the API function is unspecific, or possibly what is considered in the C language a union (a region of memory that may contain data of one or more types at the same time, depending on how the variable receiving the argument is "cast.") An argument declared using both ByVal and As Any results in the allocation of a block of memory with zero-length, whose length may be expanded later by the API function. This is VBA's (and Visual Basic's) way of saying to the API function, "I know something goes here, but I'm not equipped to handle it, so you take care of it."
29	, (comma)	Separates multiple arguments from one another in the arguments list.
30	(space)	
31	) (right parenthesis)	Closes the arguments list.

	Part	Description
32	(space)	
33	As	Denotes that the term that follows this one states the type of the declared external function. This is only necessary if the function was declared as a VBA `Function`.
34	(space)	
35	*function_type*	Standard type One of VBA's standard variable types, *not* a class of any kind and *not* a composite type. Most often, Windows API functions return values of either of two standard types: `Long` and `Boolean`. A long integer is generally a result code, which would be informative if you were programming in C or C++, but is useless in the context of VBA. Nevertheless, the long type must still be listed here, because the act of returning a value is necessary for the external function to work. A Boolean return value is generally a True/False result code, which is helpful here since it indicates a "worked/did not work" condition.
36	(Enter)	Closes the external function declaration.

In Depth: When an API function is not a function

As you may have gathered by now, the term "API function" is semantically independent from the term `Function` as VBA defines it. By the VBA definition, a `Function` procedure returns a discrete value to the body of code that calls it. An API function is *une affaire du C* ("a thing of C"), which means we must switch mindsets, put aside Microsoft's for a moment, and pick up the mindset of UNIX the way we'd put on a different hat — or, in this case, a beret. A function in C is a body of code, simply put. It might return a value or, in the case of a `void` function, it might not.

When an API function has *not* been designed to return a value, the statement we use to declare it in VBA begins with `Declare Sub`. Otherwise, if the API function does return a value, the declaration statement begins with `Declare Function`. Later in the code when the API function is called, you may still call a `Function` function like a `Sub`, without assigning the return value to a variable (sometimes the return value is pointless to VBA anyway). But it is important that you distinguish between an API function that's a `Sub`, and an API function that's a `Function`, for this small reason alone.

The API can register the type of processor being used

Here's one more simple example before we tackle the more difficult ones: Suppose you want to determine what type of processor VBA is currently running on. Perhaps you don't want to engage a particular time-intensive algorithm if the user is on an old 486DX. The API function you need to invoke is GetSystemInfo().

Before you declare this API function, however, you must define the Type structure for its single argument. This structure represents all of the data that GetSystemInfo() returns; so rather than supporting nine very long arguments, GetSystemInfo() uses just one argument that supports all nine members. The following code must be entered *before* the Declare statement for GetSystemInfo(), or the declaration itself will fail to work:

```
Type SYSTEM_INFO
    dwOemID As Long
    dwPageSize As Long
    lpMinimumApplicationAddress As Long
    lpMaximumApplicationAddress As Long
    dwActiveProcessorMask As Long
    dwNumberOrfProcessors As Long
    dwProcessorType As Long
    dwAllocationGranularity As Long
    dwReserved As Long
End Type
```

This is code that you'll find conveniently located in the WIN32API.TXT file on the CD-ROM accompanying this book; a simple cut and paste operation is all that's necessary. If your VBA program only needs to refer to one member of this structure, you still need to provide the entire Type structure declaration as it appears here. Unlike a C++ compiler, VBA will not fault you for declaring a variable or member that you never use.

Next, the Declare statement is entered *after* the Type structure declaration:

```
Declare Sub GetSystemInfo Lib "kernel32" (lpSystemInfo As _
  SYSTEM_INFO)
```

Notice here how VBA recognizes SYSTEM_INFO as though it were a standard type or class, although it's neither. Instead, it represents a pattern for assembling a contiguous section of memory where all the declared members of the structure are lined up together. Since all members of the type SYSTEM_INFO have specific sizes in memory, the structure itself has its own defined size. This is what makes the structure convenient for the C language function to use; if it were not so defined, the function would be unable to determine where one data value ends and another begins.

The `GetSystemInfo()` API function does not return a value by way of an expression — it was declared using `Declare Sub`, not `Declare Function`. So the instruction `x = GetSystemInfo(typeLocal)` would be erroneous. Instead, the function returns its data into the argument you supplied. First, you declare the argument, like this:

```
Dim typeLocal As SYSTEM_INFO
```

Then within a procedure, you make the call to the API function *without* using an expression, like this:

```
GetSystemInfo typeLocal
```

When that's done, you can poll `typeLocal.dwProcessorType` for the number that refers to the type of CPU (unfortunately without a brand name; you can't tell whether it's an Intel or an AMD processor from here). The return code is immediately recognizable: A Pentium-class CPU shows up as 586, and a Pentium II-class registers a 686.

The `Type` declaration is necessary for both the `Declare` statement and `Dim` to know what a type `SYSTEM_INFO` actually is. Here is how this declaration is constructed:

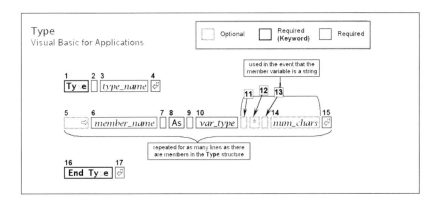

	Part	Description
1	Type	**Statement** Begins a clause that declares a structure that consists of a specific sequence of variable types. A variable that is later declared with this type will be a composite variable, consisting of members whose respective types are as declared within the Type clause. The Type clause always appears in the General Declarations section of a module, and its scope is always limited to that module. Another module in the project that needs to make use of the same type, may declare its Type clause separately.

Continued

	Part	Description *(continued)*
2	(space)	
3	*type_name*	Literal A unique name which will identify the composite variable type in later instructions that declare variables. This name should be different from any other composite type name or class name used by your VBA project. Microsoft protocol has been to distinguish composite types from standard types, such as Integer, by capitalizing the name; for example, LOGFONT.
4	(Enter)	
5	(Tab)	To help the human reader isolate individual Type clauses from one another, especially in a program where several may appear, it is common to indent the declared members of the structure.
6	*member_name*	Variable A name that identifies one member of the Type structure. This name must be unique among other such variable names *within the same structure*. The member name should not be the same as a VBA reserved keyword. However, the name does not have to be unique among all member names in all Type structures used by the VBA program, or even among all variables used by the program. The member name may even be the same as the name of a property or other term used by an active object library, such as O2KOM. This is because the name of the structure itself will be invoked in all later references to the member, thus ensuring its uniqueness even when the member name seems rather general. For instance, in the reference EmployeeRecord.Name, the Type structure EmployeeRecord helps identify the member Name.
7	(space)	
8	As	Prepares the interpreter for the name of the declared member's type (part **10**).
9	(space)	

Part		Description
10	*var_type* Variant Byte Boolean Integer Long Currency Single Double Date String Object	Type, class, or structure Denotes the recognized type of this member of the Type structure. This may be a VBA standard variable type, or a name given to another Type structure encountered earlier in the module. It may also be the name of a class, either from a recognized object library or a VBA class module loaded into the current project. The variable type may also be Object, allowing for late binding at a future time — although this formation is generally impractical.
11	(space)	
12	* (asterisk)	Prepares the interpreter to accept the following numeral (part **14**) as the number of characters in the String member.
13	(space)	
14	*num_chars*	Integer The total number of characters in the member string, for situations where *var_type* (part **10**) is declared String. This number fixes the length of the string. Any assignment made to the string that is greater in length than this number is truncated, and any assignment that is lesser is padded with enough space characters (not code-zeroes) to make it the designated length. This designation is most often used when a Declare statement requires the Type structure for a Windows DLL function — especially an API function. Many such C-language functions view strings as a fixed-length block of characters, rather than a variable-length sequence terminated by a code-zero. Using part **14** helps the C-language function to recognize the string.
15	(Enter)	
16	End Type	Closes the Type structure.
17	(Enter)	

In Depth: Composite variables versus classes

You may have noticed that the member of a `Type` structure is referenced like the property of a class. For instance, if a variable `Arena` is declared `As RECT`, and a `Type RECT` clause defines the composite type as having four coordinate members, `Arena.Left` designates the coordinate position for the left edge. A `Type` structure is helpful in situations where an item being represented by the program is best described by more than one variable.

In earlier versions of Visual Basic, the `Type` structure was used to group together related variables, especially data belonging to a record. Originally, Microsoft pointed to this compositing of variables as its answer to the container/member relationship embodied in C++. The concept of the class module was introduced later, in Visual Basic 4.0. But compositing still has its purposes in VB and VBA. **Declaring a Type structure makes sense when the name of the structure is not representative of anything pertinent that is independent of its member variables.** For instance, for the `Diagram` class used in our examples, each individual `Diagram` class object is an entity unto itself. Its various properties describe aspects of it; but you can presume there's something there independent of those properties. That particular "something" may need to be managed through event procedures such as `Class_Initialize` and `Class_Terminate`. But the member variables of a `Type` structure define the data in that structure in its entirety; without the members, the structure is just a template. A `Type` structure is leaner, with significantly lesser overhead than a class module. A variable declared with this structure lacks the capability of a class instance to be told what to do by means of a method instruction; but since a `Type` structure isn't supposed to be representative of a *thing* like an object anyway, a method would be out of context.

Implementing API Functions in a Class Module

This next stage of the "DiagramMatic" example program for Word 2000, begun in Chapter 9, demonstrates how the Windows API can be put to very good use in building your very own .INI initialization file. Veterans of Microsoft Word will recall that the application allows the user to store so-called "custom properties" along with the user's document or template. But such properties generally have to do with the textual content of the document, or other information that defines the document's or template's role in the business at hand – say, the client code of the recipient, or the department codes for all the research heads responsible for reviewing the document. Information dealing with the operation of a VBA program would be inappropriate in this context; why bother the user with data about which she does not have direct involvement?

Resurrecting the .INI file

The initialization file (or "inny" file, if you're desperate for a nickname) is a throwback to the days of 16-bit Windows, whose operating characteristics were at all times specified by two files, WIN.INI and SYSTEM.INI. It's a simple ASCII (ANSI) text file that can be loaded into Notepad (or WordPad, when its size balloons past 64K in Windows 98). Applications for Windows 3.1 either utilized their own .INI files or borrowed some real estate from the main WIN.INI file. Today, although Microsoft recommends that programmers write their applications' settings and parameters to the gargantuan OLE System Registry, the .INI file system is still available. It's a leaner system, it takes a little less run time, and the individual files are easier to manage. (The latter fact may actually be detrimental if security is an issue.)

Every .INI file has a simple structure. Single parameters are given single names. Every parameter is either a string or an integer. Its value is assigned to it with a simple expression that always uses this syntax: parameter name, equal sign, setting. It's up to the application to parse its own string; so for multiple-number settings, it's the responsibility of the application to detect where the separating commas are. Each setting resides on its own line. Groups of like parameters may be grouped together in a cluster. A string set off by [square brackets] identifies the category for that cluster. Surprisingly, PowerPoint still uses an .INI file, albeit a tiny one. Here is one category from POWERPNT.INI on my system as an example:

```
[OLE Play Options]
AVIFile=Movie,1,1
MIDFile=Sound,1,2
```

Note the name of the category set off in square brackets, the names of the parameters to the left of the equal sign, and the setting to the right. Here, PowerPoint must parse the three-part setting; in other words, `Movie,1,1` is one entire string, whose commas will be recognized not by Windows but by PowerPoint.

The Windows API functions that manage .INI files do some very simple things: They create and locate parameters within designated categories. That's their job, as simply as it can be put. When a parameter doesn't exist yet, and data is assigned to it, the parameter is created automatically. When the category doesn't exist yet, it is created automatically. When the designated .INI file doesn't exist yet, it gets created automatically. Once you clear the hurdle of declaring the API functions, the rest of the matter is surprisingly straightforward.

For DiagramMatic, we will create a new class module called `INIControl`, whose job will be to "expose" this API functionality to the rest of the VBA project in a safe, controlled, and object-oriented manner. One of the jobs of DiagramMatic's own .INI file will be to retain the location of the directory where diagram image files are generally located. This way, whenever the user goes searching for another diagram — whether it be a minute from now or sometime next week — the user won't have to make the "Open File" selector box plow through the same directories each time.

(Later in this chapter, you'll see how the standard "Open File" box can be put to use in DiagramMatic by means of a `Declare` statement and an external function.)

The beauty of the `INIControl` class module – if I may be allowed such a grandiose adjective – is that there is nothing about it that is specific to any one O2K application. The module can be exported from Word to any project in Excel, Access, or PowerPoint. (Excel actually has a more replete set of functionality for its `Application` object than the other O2K applications, going so far as to include methods for writing .INI file parameters and System Registry keys. But for consistency's sake, `INIControl` can be used in Excel as well.)

The API functions for .INI files handle "profiles"

The first order of business is to endow `INIControl` with declarations for the API functions it will be using. These are `Declare` statements that are placed in the class module's General Declarations section, along with its own module-level variables. Listing 10-1 shows the declarations used:

Listing 10-1: General Declarations section for the INIControl class module.

```
Private Declare Function GetPrivateProfileInt Lib "kernel32" _
 Alias "GetPrivateProfileIntA" (ByVal lpApplicationName _
 As String, ByVal lpKeyName As String, ByVal nDefault As Long, _
 ByVal lpFileName As String) As Long
Private Declare Function GetPrivateProfileString Lib "kernel32" _
 Alias "GetPrivateProfileStringA" _
 (ByVal lpApplicationName As String, ByVal lpKeyName As Any, _
 ByVal lpDefault As String, ByVal lpReturnedString As String, _
 ByVal nSize As Long, ByVal lpFileName As String) As Long
Private Declare Function WritePrivateProfileString Lib _
 "kernel32" Alias "WritePrivateProfileStringA" (ByVal _
 lpApplicationName As String, ByVal lpKeyName As Any, _
 ByVal lpString As Any, ByVal lpFileName As String) As Long
Private Declare Function GetPrivateProfileSection Lib "kernel32" _
 Alias "GetPrivateProfileSectionA" (ByVal lpAppName As String, _
 ByVal lpReturnedString As String, ByVal nSize As Long, _
 ByVal lpFileName As String) As Long
Private Declare Function WritePrivateProfileSection _
 Lib "kernel32" Alias "WritePrivateProfileSectionA" _
 (ByVal lpAppName As String, ByVal lpString As String, _
 ByVal lpFileName As String) As Long

Private Declare Function GetWindowsDirectory Lib "kernel32" _
 Alias "GetWindowsDirectoryA" (ByVal lpBuffer As String, _
 ByVal nSize As Long) As Long
Private Declare Function GetSystemDirectory Lib "kernel32" Alias _
 "GetSystemDirectoryA" (ByVal lpBuffer As String, ByVal nSize _
```

```
As Long) As Long

Private strWinDir As String, strSysDir As String, strINI As String
Private strThisModule As String
Private bFileExists As Boolean, bOK2Overwrite As Boolean, _
bOK2Create As Boolean
```

The `Declare` statements look more cumbersome than they truly are, mainly because I have the luxury of being able to copy them from the WIN32API.TXT file directly. (A rare case of condoned plagiarism.) The seven API functions declared here perform the following tasks:

`GetPrivateProfileInt()`	Reads a parameter setting from the designated .INI file, and returns an integer value (actually a `Long` integer, because the API functions have all been converted to 32-bit).
`GetPrivateProfileString()`	Reads a parameter setting from the designated .INI file, and returns a string. The only real difference between this and `GetPrivateProfileInt` is that this version does not *convert* the returned value into an integer.
`WritePrivateProfileString()`	Writes a parameter setting to the designated .INI file. This is the only write function there is; it assumes that the (VBA) program will handle the job of converting any values or integers into strings prior to performing the write operation.
`GetPrivateProfileSection()`	Returns the entire textual contents of all parameters belonging to an .INI file category, into an established string buffer.
`WritePrivateProfileSection()`	Flushes a buffer (hopefully) that contains the textual contents of all parameters belonging to an .INI file category, into the .INI file directly, replacing the entire category if it already exists.
`GetWindowsDirectory()`	Returns the main Windows directory (generally C:\WINDOWS, but perhaps elsewhere).
`GetSystemDirectory()`	Returns the system subdirectory where the core API libraries are located.

On Point

The `Declare` statement ties an external function compiled into a DLL, to a VBA module, making that function accessible from the module. The arguments in the `Declare` statement set up the interface, if you will, between the multifarious realm of VBA and the melodramatic realm of the C-language function. The Windows API is made up of three primary DLLs: KERNEL32, USER32, and GDI32. Some texts consider accessory DLLs, such as COMDLG32, part of the API, while other texts treat them as mere "accessory DLLs." How they're treated in this regard does not affect their functionality with regard to Office 2000.

Frequently, the true return value of an external function such as a Windows API function is not assigned to some receiving variable, nor can the function call represent its own return value in an expression like calls to `Function` procedures in VBA. Instead, the return data is sent to a preconfigured buffer of a given number of so-called *code-zeroes*. These are not zero characters such as 0 as in a string variable, but are truly the value of zero stored in memory — blank bytes. VBA can set a string variable to act as a reference to this return buffer area in memory by assigning it a given number of code-zeroes using VBA's `String$()` function.

The -`Private`- portion of the API function names indicates that the API functions are referring to .INI files that are separate from the formerly "main" WIN.INI file. Windows still supports the `GetProfileInt()`, `GetProfileString()`, and `WriteProfileString()` API functions, all of which deal exclusively with settings stored in WIN.INI. The versions declared here may still use WIN.INI (actually, that will be our default file), as long as that filename is supplied to to the API function explicitly.

At the end of Listing 10-1, three conventional `Private` instructions declare variables that will be used during the course of the listings to follow.

Is the class instance one unto itself or one of many?

Unlike a `Diagram` class object, the `INIControl` class will not represent a *thing* that you would want to make multiple instances of and group together in a collection. Instead, it's more of a *device* (like `DiagramConsole`) that represents the capability to utilize .INI files. There's no logistical reason for that capability to be duplicated in the same project. So we can assume that the class will be instantiated once and once only.

This brings us to the matter of how a class instance sets itself up. A VBA class module recognizes two of its own events: `_Initialize` and `_Terminate`. (C++ programmers will recognize their event procedures as VBA's rough equivalents of class constructors and class destructors, respectively.) When a class instance comes into being, the interpreter executes any code that exists in the `Private   Sub Class_Initialize()` event procedure in that class' module. So if there were more than one instance of the class, its `_Initialize` event procedure would be executed more than once. This is important, because an `_Initialize` **event procedure needs to know whether it is setting up the functionality for the entire O2K application or just for one instance of the class among many.** The distinction here is more architectural than syntactic; there's nothing about VBA that explicitly defines a class instance as being "general" or "replicable."

So for `INIControl`, the `_Initialize` event procedure's job is to set up *everything* related to the task of utilizing .INI files. This includes setting up the initial or default settings of all the instance's private variables. Listing 10-2 shows the establishment of `INIControl`'s critical data.

Listing 10-2: The first nondeclarative instructions executed for INIControl.

```
Private Sub Class_Initialize()
    strThisModule = VBE.ActiveVBProject.Name & ".INIControl"
    strWinDir = String$(255, 0)
    GetWindowsDirectory strWinDir, 255&
    strWinDir = Left$(strWinDir, InStr(strWinDir, Chr$(0)) - 1)
    strSysDir = String$(255, 0)
    GetSystemDirectory strSysDir, 255&
    strSysDir = Left$(strSysDir, InStr(strSysDir, Chr$(0)) - 1)
    strINI = strWinDir & "\win.ini"
    bFileExists = True
    bOK2Overwrite = True
End Sub
```

Using the VBE object to make a module refer to itself

From the top: The `VBE` object refers to a class library set up by VBA itself. (VBE stands either for "Visual Basic Editor" or "Visual Basic Environment," depending on whom you ask.) Its constituent, `ActiveVBProject`, refers to the currently loaded and running modules in VBA. Note, not "ActiveVBAProject," for reasons probably dealing more with accident than design. For this project, `VBE.ActiveVBProject.Name` would return the string `DiagramMatic`, referring to the `.Name` property given to the template file responsible for all the modules. I could have written that filename out as a literal `"DiagramMatic"`, but I intend for `INIControl` to be portable into any project in any O2K application, which is why I have the instruction generate the name for us on the fly. The reason I'm doing this is to build a string `strThisModule` (declared earlier at module-level) that identifies this module whenever it needs to generate an error message on its own behalf. The title bar for our error message windows will read `DiagramMatic.INIControl`.

You may recall that API functions often require preconstructed return strings of a specified length, all filled with code-zero characters (ANSI code 0). Here in `Private Sub Class_Initialize()`, the module-level variables `strWinDir` and `strSysDir` are being preloaded with 255-character strings padded with code-zeroes. The calls to API functions `GetWindowsDirectory()` and `GetSystemDirectory()` appear here, because these variables will be used to support read-only properties whose settings absolutely will not change for the duration of the instance's run time. Toward the end, we borrow `strWinDir` to establish the location of WIN.INI, which is the default file for our class module and the initial setting for variable `strINI` — the shadow variable for this class' `.FileName` property. Since the design of Windows assures us that this default file does indeed exist, variable `bFileExists` is set to `True`. Remember, the `WritePrivateProfileString` API function will create the .INI file if it doesn't exist yet; so `INIControl` will support a `.FileExists` property that can alert the instantiator (the controller of the class instance) as to whether the API function is about to create the file. The instantiator can respond to this by setting `INIControl`'s `.OK2Create` property to `False`, thereby stopping the instance from invoking the API function that creates the file.

Variable `bOK2Overwrite` supports a property that clears the `Property Let` procedure to write a setting for a parameter into an .INI file when that setting already exists. Since it makes sense to replace an existing setting unless otherwise noted, the default value of `bOK2Overwrite` is set to `True`. But what about variable `bOK2Create`; shouldn't it be set to `False` by default? Actually, it already is, because the default value of initialized value-bearing variables is 0, and `False` is 0.

The way our key API functions for `INIControl` are named, it's tempting to have written *methods* as wrapper functions, such as "GetString" or "WriteInt." But conceptually, since it makes more sense to think of .INI file parameters as static values, it should be easier for the programmer of the VBA application — the user of the `INIControl` class module — to make use of two properties that represent those values as though they were variables. So `.ProfileEntryString` and `.ProfileEntryInt` are written as properties, each of which has its own `Property Get` and `Property Let` procedures. Listing 10-3 shows the `Property Get` procedure for `.ProfileEntryString`, which were written first:

Listing 10-3: Property Get procedure for .ProfileEntryString.

```
Public Property Get ProfileEntryString(strCategory As String, _
  strItem As String, Optional vDefault As Variant) As String
    Dim strReturn As String, strDefault As String

    If IsMissing(vDefault) Then
        If Me.ParameterExists(strCategory, strItem) = False Then
            Exit Property
        Else
            strDefault = ""
        End If
```

```
    Else
        strDefault = CStr(vDefault)
    End If
    strReturn = String$(128, 0)
    If GetPrivateProfileString(strCategory, strItem, strDefault, _
      strReturn, CInt(Len(strReturn)), strINI) Then
        ProfileEntryString = Left$(strReturn, InStr(strReturn, _
          Chr$(0)) - 1)
    Else
        ProfileEntryString = strDefault
    End If
End Property
```

Optional variants may be declared Missing

The most unusual part of this procedure is in the header, with regard to the third argument, vDefault As Variant, which was declared Optional. The API function that this procedure will use — GetPrivateProfileString() — requires a default string for a return value. But this argument is a variant, not a string. The single reason for this is that **VBA can only test for the absence of an optional argument if that argument is a variant.** If the argument is of any other standard type, the IsMissing() intrinsic function will always return False, because VBA will have generated a default value for that argument automatically.

In everyday use, the vDefault argument will most likely be absent. This Property Get procedure needs to generate some default return string strDefault, either based on the contents of vDefault or set to an empty string "". Without a default return string, if the requested parameter does not exist in the .INI file, there's nothing for the API function to get. But since the API function returns *something* — either the contents of the .INI file or a copy of the default string — there's almost no way to know absolutely for certain, just from examining the results of the API function, whether it returned the default string or real contents. So this property procedure actually relies on the .ParameterExists **property,** which is another property in the same class module, to determine whether there's a parameter by the given name strItem whose setting can be "gotten." If there isn't, then Exit Property sends us out of here.

The default return string is actually a required argument to the Windows API function GetPrivateProfileString(); note that strDefault is the third argument there. But it isn't always reasonable in every real-world situation for there to be such a thing as a default return value; sometimes, if something wasn't meant to be found, the most meaningful return value is truly *nothing*. But Windows will not take nothing for an answer. So variable vDefault is declared as an Optional argument for the sake of the programmer who may not care to use it for anything. VBA's intrinsic IsMissing() function determines whether the argument is indeed supplied; and if it is not, then if the requested parameter truly does exist, the procedure generates an empty string "" for the default argument. Remember, even a null string could be meaningful information; it could mean "blank" or "not set yet." If the optional argument *is* supplied, then the procedure uses the CStr() type conversion function to render a string strDefault based on the contents of the variant vDefault. When calling a normal VBA procedure, an argument that happens to be a variant will pass as any standard declared VBA type — in other words, under normal circumstances, you would not need this conversion function. But these are not normal circumstances; a C-language function recognizes a string in memory differently than a variant in memory. So the conversion must take place to be safe.

Continuing with Public Property Get ProfileEntryString(): As you've seen before, strReturn pads the return string with code-zeroes before making the API function call. It's not obvious, but GetPrivateProfileString() does return a value to an expression that calls it — in this case, a 1 if successful, a 0 if not. This isn't exactly the VBA equivalent of Boolean, where True is the same as -1. Still, it yields a nonzero result for success, which is enough to qualify it for use as the test expression in an If...Then clause. If and only if the call is successful, the return value string has its code-zeroes trimmed from the end. There isn't much to prevent the API function from being "successful" by Windows standards. If the API function finds nothing in the .INI file, then it returns the default argument instead — which also means the call was "successful." You cannot use a 0 return value as an indicator that an item was not located. Still, on the off chance that low system resources or a natural disaster makes the Windows API misbehave, the Else side of the conditional clause manually assigns the default value to the property, in case of lack of success.

Arguments in property procedure pairs must match

Because the Property Get procedure for .ProfileEntryString was declared with an Optional argument, that same argument must appear in the Property Let procedure shown in Listing 10-4.

Listing 10-4: Property Let procedure for .ProfileEntryString.

```
Public Property Let ProfileEntryString(strCategory As String, _
 strItem As String, Optional vDefault As Variant, strSetting _
As String)
    If strItem <> "" And strCategory <> "" Then
        If Me.ParameterExists(strCategory, strItem) Then
            If Not bOK2Overwrite Then
                Exit Property
            End If
        Else
            If Not bOK2Create Then
                Exit Property
            End If
```

```
        End If

        If WritePrivateProfileString(strCategory, strItem, _
          strSetting, strINI) Then
            bFileExists = True
        Else
            Err.Raise vbObjectError + 513, strThisModule, _
              "Cannot write to " & strFilename & "."
        End If
    End If
    bOK2Create = False
    bOK2Overwrite = True
End Property
```

As a rule, the arguments for a Property Let procedure must have arguments of the same type and in the same position as the arguments in its associated Property Get procedure, plus one extra argument at the end that represents the incoming setting to the property. The type or class of that final argument must be the same as the declared return type for the Property Get procedure. Thus, this particular header breaks a rule of VBA, and does so successfully: The *next-to-last* argument is declared Optional, but the final argument is mandatory – a situation that would not be permitted elsewhere.

But what role does vDefault play in the Property Let procedure? Honestly, none whatsoever. The WritePrivateProfileString() API function doesn't actually need it. But if we get rid of that argument, the VBA interpreter won't precompile the procedure because the argument must reside at that same position in the Property Get procedure.

Let's walk through this Property Let procedure: The incoming parameter name and category, represented by strItem and strCategory, respectively, are both checked for non-null contents; if either is null, there's no reason to go on. Next, the process used in the Property Get is mirrored to determine whether the parameter already exists. If it does, then we need to check whether we're *not* clear to overwrite an existing parameter setting (If bOK2Overwrite = False). By default, we should be clear to do so, thanks to an initial setting made to bOK2Overwrite in the Class_Initialize() procedure. But if someone purposefully set the .OK2Overwrite property to False, thereby rendering the support variable False as well, then we should be prevented from overwriting the existing parameter setting. On the other side of the equation, suppose the requested parameter does not exist. In the Else side of the conditional clause, we check to see if we're *not* clear to create the nonexistent parameter. (The Windows API function does so automatically without prompting.) By default, we *cannot* create this parameter; someone has to set the .OK2Create property to True prior to making this attempt.

If all of those hurdles have been cleared, then the WritePrivateProfileString() API function is invoked. Again, it's written here in the function format so that its return value is its success code. If that code is True, then we can definitely confirm that the .INI file exists — we've just written a parameter to it.

If we can't write to the .INI file, having cleared all the hurdles we've cleared, then something's definitely wrong. So our procedure actually *creates a new error*. It uses the .Raise method of VBA's Err object to generate the error signal and begin the termination of the program. The instruction even creates its own error code, at the beginning of the "user-defined" region, which is 513 positions past the one referred to by constant vbObjectError. The only reason for this arbitrary code number is so that instantiating modules can test for this error after trapping it, and perhaps apply remedial measures (whatever they may be). Assuming the error does not get trapped and remedied, the VBA error message window will be labeled with the name of the class module (remember strThisModule from earlier?), and will contain an error message displaying the name of the .INI file that VBA can't seem to write to.

The procedure closes by returning the bOK2Create and bOK2Overwrite to their default values of False and True. This ensures that no new parameter is created by accident, though an existing parameter can be overwritten. The bOK2Create flag is important here, because **there is no Windows API function for removing a parameter from an .INI file.** You can create one and you can overwrite one, and you can even assign it a null string, but you cannot delete it once it's there. (Later in this chapter, you'll see how to fix that little omission.) So the bOK2Create flag — which supports the .OK2Create property — acts as a self-locking mechanism. You can assign a True value to the .OK2Create property prior to writing a parameter that you believe may be new, and rest assured that the setting will be tripped back to its default False value after the write has occurred (or after it has failed).

The property procedure pair for .ProfileEntryInt is based in large part on those for .ProfileEntryString, with some slight adjustments to account for the use of a numeral rather than a string. Listing 10-5 shows both.

Listing 10-5: Property procedure pair for .ProfileEntryInt.

```
Public Property Get ProfileEntryInt(strCategory As String, _
  strItem As String, Optional vDefault As Variant) As Long
    Dim lDefault As Long

    If IsMissing(vDefault) Then
        If Me.ParameterExists(strCategory, strItem) = False Then
            Exit Property
        Else
            lDefault = 0&
        End If
    Else
        lDefault = CLng(vDefault)
    End If
    ProfileEntryInt = GetPrivateProfileInt(strCategory, strItem, _
```

```
        lDefault, strINI)
End Property


Public Property Let ProfileEntryInt(strCategory As String, _
 strItem As String, Optional vDefault As Variant, lSetting As Long)
    If strCategory <> "" And strItem <> "" Then
        If Me.ParameterExists(strCategory, strItem) Then
            If bOK2Overwrite = False Then
                Exit Property
            End If
        Else
            If bOK2Create = False Then
                Exit Property
            End If
        End If

        If WritePrivateProfileString(strCategory, strItem, _
         Trim$(CStr(lSetting)), strINI) Then
            bFileExists = True
        Else
            Err.Raise vbObjectError + 513, strThisModule, _
             "Cannot write to " & strFilename & "."
        End If
    End If
    bOK2Create = False
    bOK2Overwrite = True
End Property
```

Although the API function handled by `Private Property Get ProfileEntryInt()` itself contains the telltale letters `Int`, in the modern Windows 98/NT 4.0 incarnation of the function, its type has actually become `Long`. For the `Property Get` procedure, the default value has become `lDefault`, and its own default value is zero (`0&`, or the `Long` form of 0), not a null string. The `Property Let` procedure, however, has the job of hiding the fact that the Windows API does not have a "WritePrivateProfileInt()" function. So the procedure creates a string whose characters are based on the incoming value `lSetting`, using the `CStr()` function to convert the value. (`CStr()` is essentially identical to `Str$()`, and is offered as an optional intrinsic function to coincide with `CInt()` and `CDbl()`.)

For these previous property procedures to work properly (Dr. Seuss would have loved that preposterous prepositional phrase), they need to be capable of testing for the existence of an API file parameter. All four property procedures we've seen thus far poll a method — actually, a `Public Function` procedure — named `ParameterExists()`, and shown in Listing 10-6.

Listing 10-6: Should this be a method or a property? You decide.

```
Public Function ParameterExists(strCategory As String, strKey _
  As String) As Boolean
    Dim strBuffer As String, iPosition As Integer

    If strCategory <> "" And strKey <> "" Then
        strBuffer = String$(8192, 0)
        If GetPrivateProfileSection(strCategory, strBuffer, _
         Len(strBuffer), strINI) Then
            iPosition = InStr(strBuffer, strKey)
            If iPosition > 0 Then
                If Mid$(strBuffer, iPosition + Len(strKey), 1) _
                 = "=" Then
                    ParameterExists = True
                End If
            End If
        End If
    End If
End Function
```

We'll get into matters of grammar shortly. For now, notice that this `Function` procedure declares an 8K buffer—plenty large for your average textual category. The `GetPrivateProfileSection()` API function brings in the text of all the parameter settings in the category, including the category name itself, into this buffer. Next, the procedure launches a search for the designated parameter name, using the `InStr()` function. If the return value is nonzero, then this may yet be a parameter. There's one more test, however: Is the parameter name immediately followed by an equal sign? Recall that parameter names are all to the left of their own lines, and are all separated from settings with an equal sign, without exception. If the `InStr()` function just happened to find the same text as a parameter name, but instead it was a parameter setting, then it wouldn't be followed with an = but instead with a code-zero. If the = is found, the parameter name is officially declared existent.

The grey area between functions and properties

In an earlier build of this project, I wrote this `Function` procedure as a read-only property instead, heading it with `Public Property Get ParameterExists (strCategory As String, strKey As String) As Boolean`. What's the difference? Surprisingly, not much. The VBA module that instantiates `INIControl` would call this property in exactly the same way it would call the `.ParameterExists` method and the return value would be of the same type. When the class module itself makes a call to `ParameterExists`, all it would need to add in order to address it as a property rather than as a function procedure, is a reference to the reflexive object `Me`, as in `If Me.ParameterExists("Media", "Path") Then`…. But if `ParameterExists` is written as a standard `Function` procedure instead, it qualifies as a method so the `Me` reference would not have to be removed. You could leave it in or take it out and VBA would not know the difference.

So from another programmer's perspective – the user of `INIControl` – should it matter whether we call this a property or a method? For the term's own sake, perhaps not. But for the sake of consistency, the choice of grammatical part needed some rethinking. **A property, by definition, should describe some state or condition of the object to which it is associated.** If `INILocal` is an instance of class `INIControl`, then the `INILocal.ParameterExists` property should describe something about `INILocal`. But it doesn't. Instead, it describes some state or condition of the supplied arguments. This makes the functionality more applicable to the arguments rather than to the antecedent object. In such a case, in order to maintain consistency with other procedures whose purpose is not so much in doubt, the procedure should remain a standard `Sub` or `Function`, making it a *method* in the context of a class module.

Removing an .INI file parameter by brute force

Earlier, I mentioned that there is no Windows API function for removing a parameter from an .INI file. There is a simple reason for this: **Parameter names for an .INI file category are intended to be permanent.** For an application I wrote some years back, I was tempted to manage an .INI file where the names of files that have been opened at least once are attributed to a string representing some facts about that file; for example, `INTRUTH.DOC=15,5,4`. This way, if the application or the computer crashed, the vital statistics about the file could be retrieved from the surviving .INI file. This would be convenient, except that the `INTRUTH.DOC` parameter would remain in the .INI file long after the file itself was disused.

Microsoft suggests that programmers no longer use .INI files, not for performance reasons, but mainly to promote its vision of a cohesive, single System Registry. Since Microsoft seems to no longer be concerned with what happens to the .INI file concept, I believe it therefore falls upon us to operate the things as we please. For `INIControl`, I wrote a method that, quite easily, removes a parameter from a designated .INI file, leaving the remainder intact – a feature the Windows API currently lacks. The API is actually invoked to make this procedure work – it just doesn't have a real clue as to what it's being asked to do. Listing 10-7 shows my little rule-breaker.

Listing 10-7: Proof that rules are literally made to be broken.

```
Public Function RemoveParameter(strCategory As String, strKey _
  As String)
    Dim strBuffer As String
    Dim iSnipLeft As Integer, iSnipRight As Integer

    If strCategory <> "" And strKey <> "" Then
        If Me.ParameterExists(strCategory, strKey) Then
            strBuffer = String$(8192, 0)
```

```
                If GetPrivateProfileSection(strCategory, strBuffer, _
                Len(strBuffer), strINI) Then
                    iSnipLeft = InStr(strBuffer, strKey)
                    iSnipRight = InStr(iSnipLeft, strBuffer, Chr$(0))
                    strBuffer = Left$(strBuffer, iSnipLeft - 1) & _
                    Right$(strBuffer, Len(strBuffer) - iSnipRight)
                    WritePrivateProfileSection strCategory, _
                    strBuffer, strINI
                End If
            End If
        End If
End Function
```

This procedure sets up an 8K buffer in memory and has `strBuffer` point to it. It then has the API function `GetPrivateProfileSection()` load the entire category contents into the buffer. There, we do a "parameter-ectomy" on the buffer contents, using the `InStr()` function twice to locate where the parameter name begins (the first letter in its name) and where the parameter setting ends (the code-zero at the end of the line). Whenever the `InStr()` function has three arguments (or more), the *first* argument refers to the position in the buffer where the search for the character begins. So `iSnipLeft` as the first parameter in the search for `iSnipRight` tells `InStr()` to begin the next search where the prior one left off.

Once the beginning and end of the ex-parameter are located, the `Left$()` and `Right$()` functions extract the portions of the buffer on both sides of the parameter, and then glue those portions together into the new `strBuffer`. The `WritePrivateProfileSection()` then replaces the existing category contents in the .INI file, with the newly sewn-together `strBuffer`.

The rest of the properties in `INIControl` are basically for housekeeping purposes. While they're not extravagant, they do serve as examples of the types of properties that a service-oriented class module should support for it to be full-featured. For instance, the `.FileName` property is necessary for the instantiator to designate the location of the .INI file to be used. Listing 10-8 shows the procedure pair for this property:

Listing 10–8: Procedure pair for the .FileName property of INIControl.

```
Public Property Get FileName() As String
    FileName = strINI
End Property

Public Property Let FileName(strSetting As String)
    If UCase(Right$(strSetting, 4)) <> ".INI" Then
        strSetting = strSetting & ".INI"
    End If
    strINI = strSetting
    If FileSystem.Dir(strWinDir & "\" & strSetting) <> "" Then
```

```
            bFileExists = True
    Else
            bFileExists = False
    End If
End Property
```

When an assignment is made to the `.FileName` property, the `Property Let` procedure checks whether the filename contains the telltale `.INI` file extender. If it doesn't, it goes ahead and adds the extender. Next, it uses the familiar `FileSystem.Dir` method to check the Windows directory `strWinDir` for the presence of the .INI file. If it doesn't exist, `bFileExists` is set to `False`. Variable `bFileExists` is a support variable for the read-only `.FileExists` property. Whenever this property is polled, as shown in Listing 10-9, the support variable is refreshed through the `FileSystem.Dir` method.

Listing 10-9: Property Get procedure for the .FileExists property.

```
Public Property Get FileExists() As Boolean
    If FileSystem.Dir(strWinDir & "\" & strINI) <> "" Then
            bFileExists = True
    Else
            bFileExists = False
    End If
    FileExists = bFileExists
End Property
```

Two read-only properties give the instantiator access to the location of the Windows and System directories, as shown in Listing 10-10.

Listing 10-10: Read-only properties for determining Windows installation location.

```
Public Property Get WindowsDirectory() As String
    WindowsDirectory = strWinDir
End Property

Public Property Get SystemDirectory() As String
    SystemDirectory = strSysDir
End Property
```

The two variables `strWinDir` and `strSysDir` were set by the `Class_Initialize()` procedure and, of course, do not change during the program's run time. These are virtually constants rather than variables; but only literal values may be assigned to true VBA constants, while it takes API functions to determine the values for `strWinDir` and `strSysDir`.

Finally, as Listing 10-11 shows, the simplest of property procedures is all that's necessary to support the two Boolean properties `.OK2Create` and `.OK2Overwrite`.

Listing 10-11: Boolean properties for setting permissions.

```
Public Property Get OK2Overwrite() As Boolean
    OK2Overwrite = bOK2Overwrite
End Property

Public Property Let OK2Overwrite(bSetting As Boolean)
    bOK2Overwrite = bSetting
End Property

Public Property Get OK2Create() As Boolean
    OK2Create = bOK2Create
End Property

Public Property Let OK2Create(bSetting As Boolean)
    bOK2Create = bSetting
End Property
```

At this point, the INIControl class module is in complete working order. This code didn't just manifest itself in the form in which you see it here; I experimented with a few other methodologies first. For instance, I considered making separate methods .GetProfileString and .SetProfileString. They might have made sense, but the matter of conceptual continuity would have cropped up.

On Point

Many external functions, such as Windows API functions, maintain a structure of values in memory. This structure is divided into segments, with each segment representing some aspect or characteristic of the work performed by the function. VBA can be used to set up this exclusive region of memory by declaring a Type structure. This sets up a composite variable type that can be used in declarations in place of a VBA standard type or a class. A Type structure is comprised of member variables, so that a variable declared with that structure may be used to refer to individual members in the same way that properties of an object are referenced.

The reference openParams.flags — which is shown in an example later in this chapter — refers to the flags member of variable openParams. In that example, variable openParams is declared As OPENFILENAME and the meaning of OPENFILENAME is established through the declaration of a Type OPENFILENAME clause that lists its members in sequence, along with their types. All Type structures used for API functions have fixed sizes in memory; so member strings must have a fixed number of characters, even if they're all zeroes. Variants are counted out because their shape and size are, by definition, uncertain until they are actually used.

Connecting Form Modules with Class Modules

The next step in the development of DiagramMatic is to bring in a form module so that the user may find diagrams to insert into her document. The `INIControl` class comes into play when the form module needs to know where to begin looking for image files to include as diagrams. The default directory for image files on the user's system will be stored as a parameter in the user's local DIAGRAM.INI file.

Distinguishing factors between service and data classes

Chapter 9 discussed the problems of an object module in a VBA project being capable of utilizing a class module. An *object module* in this instance is a form module, the `ThisDocument` or `ThisWorksheet` module for a document or template, or another class module. The main problem with object module *A* utilizing object module *B* is that both *A* and *B* are presumed to have limited "lifetimes" that may be shorter than that of the project. When the code for *A* is terminated, so is the code for its private instance of *B*. It makes sense, therefore, for *A* to instantiate *B* only when *B* truly "belongs" to *A*. If *A* instantiates *B* but *C* also makes use of *B*, then when *A* goes down, taking *B* with it, *C* doesn't know there is no longer a *B* until it tries to refer to *B*.

A class module like `DiagramConsole` (introduced in Chapter 9) – represents a service that a VBA program can perform rather than some element of data contained within a document. It doesn't make sense, conceptually, for this service to exist *twice* in the same document template, especially because `DiagramConsole` maintains the `Diagrams` collection for that template, and if there were two instances of `DiagramConsole`, there would be two simultaneous `Diagrams` collections. It seems sensible enough to restrict these *service classes*, if I may coin a phrase, to one instance per project. But as you'll see, simply because there's only one instance of a service class, it does not mean that all modules in a project use the same reference to that instance.

On Point

Although they were discussed in prior chapters, the concepts of class, instance, and reference are not self-evident. So let's take a few moments to review them and explain them as plainly as English can be written with regard to the art of programming.

◆ A *class* represents a *way* in which a process is done.

Continued

On Point *(Continued)*

◆ An *instance* represents one such process in progress — in the act of being done.

◆ A *reference* is a name given to that process in progress.

When you write a class module, you're explaining in code how something can happen. Within that code, you mention certain acts to which that something can respond (*methods*), certain conditions to be aware of (*properties*), and certain occurrences that should be broadcast to all concerned parties (*events*).

When you instantiate a class, you're making a separate code module responsible for making the process you described happen. Once that process is started, this separate code module must give it a name — that's its reference. There are many reasons to do this, the most important of which is to distinguish one of your processes from another simultaneous instance of the same process, should that ever come about.

In some circumstances, it's necessary for two modules in a project to refer to the same process — to the same instance of a class. For that reason, there are many ways in VBA to generate a new reference to a process that already has a reference in some other module. You've already seen how the Set statement can accomplish this. The next segment shows how a form module may receive a reference as an argument, and then make use of the instance to which the argument refers.

Before we see that demonstrated, let's address one important quandary: Of the class, the instance, and the reference, *which one is the object?* This is, after all, supposed to be "object-oriented programming." "Orientation" does imply the existence of some central concept around which all the others are based. Where is this central concept among these three terms? The answer is a bit geometric in nature, in that it implies a line of reasoning that bisects all three planes of comprehension: **The object is found in how the computer perceives your process.** When the VBA interpreter peers through the reference to your instance, and through that sees the original process that you described in your class module, therein lies the object.

The owner of an object reference handles its events

When a general module declares a public instance of a class using a statement such as Public WithEvents diaMain As DiagramConsole, then that module is responsible for handling the procedures that respond to those events. This is important, because it answers the question, "Where do the event procedures go?" They go in the same module where the reference was declared.

You would think this would solve a lot of problems, but it actually creates one: As you saw in Chapter 9, an object module such as a form or ThisDocument cannot "export" a public instance of any type of object that utilizes its own custom events. Furthermore, an object module should refrain from declaring its own class instances `Public`, unless you can reasonably guarantee that no other module whose lifetime may be longer than that object module will refer to those instances. Besides, **a general module cannot declare a reference to a class instance** `WithEvents`. That's an honor reserved for object modules, which are the only modules that know how to handle events.

Our plan is for the `DiagramConsole` class to utilize events that broadcast to the project when a diagram has been inserted, when one has been deleted, and when the list of diagrams within a document have been checked for accuracy – or "reconciled." Such events would be especially important to a dialog box which contains a list of active diagrams. Whenever the list of diagrams in a document is altered or augmented, it would be nice for a dialog box displaying a copy of that list to know that a new copy is available.

For that to happen, the form module handling the dialog box would need to be made privy to the events managed by `DiagramConsole`. Now, if the main instance of `DiagramConsole` is declared `Public` by a general module outside of the form module, then the form can see that instance, reference its properties and public variables, and invoke its methods. It cannot, however, see its events because it is not an object module by definition.

It would seem the whole purpose of events as they were originally conceived was to broadcast an important occurrence to all interested parties; what's the use of doing so if some of those parties are unable to respond? We have to go about this in a different way: A form module – which is an object module – can declare a reference to an instance of a class with an instruction like this:

```
Private WithEvents diaGrab As DiagramConsole
```

When a reference like `diaGrab` is declared without the `New` qualifier (and you can't use `New` in the same declaration with `WithEvents` anyway), it has yet to refer to anything specific. Because declarations in general modules are executed on startup, we can assume that the general module `DiagramMain` that contains the following declaration has already been executed:

```
Public diaMain As New DiagramConsole
```

This instruction not only declares a reference but instantiates the class as well. So we can assume `diaMain` is alive and well by the time the VBA interpreter ever sees the declaration for `diaGrab`.

We now have two separate references: one that belongs to everyone although it is incomplete, and one that belongs exclusively to the form module but that is full-featured. There's no rule against making both references refer to the same instance. **A declared reference is merely a tool for accessing an instance.** No one-to-one relationship is assumed. When the form module starts up, the first procedure it runs is `Private Sub UserForm_Initialize()`, which is presented in Listing 10-12.

Listing 10-12: The first procedure executed for the DiagramConsole form.

```
Private Sub UserForm_Initialize()
    Dim strLastFile As String

    Set diaGrab = diaMain
    strPath = diaGrab.MediaPath
    lblPath.Caption = strPath
    strLastFile = diaGrab.LastImage
    If strLastFile <> "" Then
        txtGraphic.Text = strLastFile
    End If
    comDlg.FilterTitle(1) = "Image files"
    comDlg.FilterExtenders(1) = _
      "*.BMP; *.WMF; *.JPG; *.JPEG; *.GIF; *.TIF; *.PCX"
End Sub
```

The key instruction here is Set diaGrab = diaMain. It effectively makes the private reference diaGrab refer to the same instance of DiagramConsole instantiated as diaMain. But the result is that the form module can now process the events generated by DiagramConsole. So if something the user does in this dialog box results in one of these events, the program can respond in a way that's unique to the dialog box — in a different way than the program may respond to the same event happening elsewhere, outside the dialog box.

Immediately after the Set instruction, the "media path" — the default location for diagram files — is retrieved from diaGrab and assigned to the private module-level variable strPath. Later, the .LastImage property is acquired from diaGrab and assigned to variable strLastFile. Both of these properties are acquired from parameters stored in DIAGRAM.INI, and retrieved from that file by INIControl. But notice there's no reference to INIControl or INI files in this procedure. This is the case for every procedure in the form module. The instantiator of DiagramConsole will never need to deal with INIControl — the handling of .INI files is a process kept completely hidden from the programmer using DiagramConsole. This is one more example of the "abstraction of underlying processes" that is one of the purposes for utilizing objects in programming in the first place.

When multiple modules refer to the same instance

You may be wondering, if the instantiator of diaMain has event procedures, and the instantiator of diaGrab has procedures for the same events, which ones are executed when both references point to the same instance? The answer is, surprisingly, *both*. For example, diaMain_Insertion and diaGrab_Insertion are both executed when the instance of DiagramConsole fires off the _Insertion event. Because diaMain was declared first, diaMain_Insertion is executed first, followed by diaGrab_Insertion.

Toward the end of `Private Sub UserForm_Initialize()` in Listing 10-12 above are three instructions that refer to an object `comDlg`. This term is a reference to an entirely different class module, which will be explored in a few pages. The `CommonDialogs` class "exposes" the functionality of one of the DLLs in Windows that handles the standard, familiar dialog boxes that are found in most Windows programs, including Windows itself. This class makes those dialog boxes available to your Office 2000 VBA programs. You'll see how it works after we build our custom dialog box for diagram insertion.

Setting up the form module with class instantiation

The first form that's critical to the DiagramMatic project allows the user to scan through directories for single image files to be inserted one-at-a-time as formal diagrams. Figure 10-1 shows how this form looks at this stage of the project's construction. It's assembled entirely using Forms 2.0 controls, with minimal property adjustments.

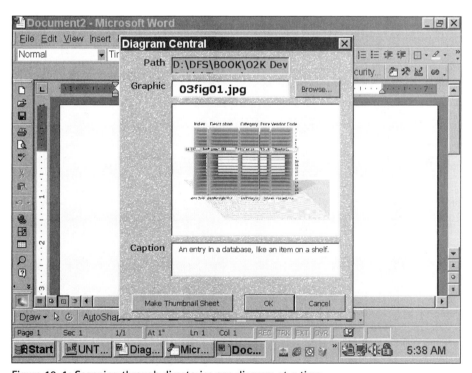

Figure 10-1: Scanning through directories one diagram at a time.

Table 10-1 shows the identities of and property *adjustments* to the various controls used in this form, as well as the form itself:

TABLE 10-1 INITIAL PROPERTY SETTINGS FOR DIAGRAMCENTRAL FORM

Object type	Properties	Settings
Form	.Name	DiagramCentral
	.Height	300
	.Picture	\Microsoft Office\Office\ Bitmaps\Styles\acsndstn.gif
	.PictureSizeMode	0 – fmPictureSizeModeClip
	.PictureTiling	True
	.ShowModal	False
	.SpecialEffect	1 – fmSpecialEffectRaised
	.Width	250
Label	.Name	LblPath
	.Caption	*(null string)*
	.Font	Verdana Regular 10 pt.
	.Height	18
	.Left	54
	.SpecialEffect	2 – fmSpecialEffectSunken
	.Top	6
	.Width	126
Label	.BackStyle	0 – fmBackStyleTransparent
	.Caption	Path
	.Left	12
	.TextAlign	3 – fmTextAlignRight
	.Top	6
	.Width	36
Text box	.Name	TxtGraphic
	.Font	Verdana Bold 10 pt.
	.Height	18
	.Left	54

Object type	Properties	Settings
	.TabIndex	1
	.Text	*(null string)*
	.Top	30
	.Width	126
Label	.BackStyle	0 – fmBackStyleTransparent
	.Caption	Graphic
	.Left	6
	.TextAlign	3 – fmTextAlignRight
	.Top	30
	.Width	42
Command button	.Name	BtnBrowse
	.Caption	Browse...
	.Height	18
	.Left	186
	.TabIndex	2
	.Top	30
	.Width	48
Image	.Name	ImgGraphic
	.Height	138
	.Left	54
	.PictureSizeMode	3 – fmPictureSizeModeZoom
	.SpecialEffect	2 – fmSpecialEffectSunken
	.Top	54
	.Width	180
Text box	.Name	TxtCaption
	.Font	Verdana Regular 9 pt.
	.Height	36

Continued

TABLE 10-1 INITIAL PROPERTY SETTINGS FOR DIAGRAMCENTRAL FORM *(continued)*

Object type	Properties	Settings
	.Left	54
	.MultiLine	True
	.ScrollBars	**2 – fmScrollBarsVertical**
	.TabIndex	3
	.Text	*(null string)*
	.Top	198
	.Width	180
Command button	.Name	BtnRenderTable
	.Caption	Make thumbnail sheet
	.Height	18
	.Left	12
	.TabIndex	4
	.Top	252
	.Width	108
Command button	.Name	BtnOK
	.Caption	OK
	.Default	True
	.Height	18
	.Left	132
	.TabIndex	5
	.Top	252
	.Width	54
Command button	.Name	BtnCancel
	.Cancel	True
	.Height	18
	.Left	186

Object type	Properties	Settings
	.TabIndex	6
	.Top	252
	.Width	54

The way this dialog box works (that is, its *usage model*) is fairly simple: The Word 2000 user places the cursor at the point where she wants the diagram to be inserted and then clicks on the custom toolbar button that brings up the DiagramCentral form. Here, the default storage path for image files is displayed in the uppermost label named lblPath. It's a label, not a text box, because it isn't necessary for the user to type anything into it. The label retains a grey background as a visual cue to the user that it's not an editable control. The cursor begins life in the text box marked **Graphic**. The moment the user types the filename of an existing image file, that file will appear in the preview window in the middle of the dialog box. But we can't expect the user to have memorized the filename she wants to use, so we supply her with a Browse button. Clicking on this button brings up the very familiar Open dialog box used by most Windows applications. When the user double-clicks on the name for an image file from this dialog box, it appears in the preview window.

Let's walk through this process as VBA interprets it: When the UserForm_Initialize() event procedure assigned strLastFile — the filename for the last file browsed — to the .Text property of the text box txtGraphic, that triggered the _Change property for that text box. The way this form module works, whenever the text inside this box changes, it's examined to see whether it's a valid filename. This takes place even if the user's in the middle of typing a filename, and hasn't entered all the characters yet. Once the filename is valid, the _Change event procedure loads the image in that file into the preview area — which is a Forms 2.0 image control. Listing 10-13 shows this procedure:

Listing 10-13: Triggering the loading of an image in the preview area.

```
Private Sub txtGraphic_Change()
    If FileSystem.Dir(strPath & txtGraphic.Text) <> "" Then
        imgGraphic.Picture = LoadPicture(strPath & txtGraphic.Text)
        btnCancel.Caption = "Cancel"
    End If
End Sub
```

The contents of txtGraphic show just the filename, without the path. So this text is tacked onto the end of strPath, which holds the default image file location. If the FileSystem.Dir method responds with a non-null string for the given file path and filename, then the file must exist. In that case, the LoadPicture() function brings the image into the imgGraphic control.

Clicking on the **Browse** button is an easier way for the user to locate a specific image. Listing 10-14 shows how the form module responds.

Listing 10-14: Bringing up the Open dialog box to search for a new image.

```
Private Sub btnBrowse_Click()
    With comDlg
        .ExplorerStyle = True
        .ReadOnlyBox = False
        .FileMustExist = True
        .ShowHelpButton = False
        .OpenMultipleChoice = False
        .ActiveDirectory = strPath
        .ActiveFile = strLastFile
        strReturn = .OpenDialog

        strPath = .ActiveDirectory
        lblPath.Caption = strPath
        txtGraphic.Text = .ActiveFile
    End With
End Sub
```

The return data from the .OpenDialog method would normally be the filename with path of the file to be opened. But this procedure has opted to obtain its return data another way: It polls the .ActiveDirectory and .ActiveFile property settings after the .OpenDialog method has been invoked and the Open File dialog has left the screen. Both lblPath and txtGraphic controls on the form are updated; and as you've seen, whenever the text in txtGraphic is changed, its _Change event procedure loads the chosen image into the preview area. So this _Click event procedure does not have to be responsible for handling the preview area; as long as any procedure can place a valid filename into txtGraphic.Text, the image loading is handled automatically. Now you see why event procedures are so valuable in VB and VBA programming.

The chosen diagram is added to the active Word document when the user clicks on the OK button. Listing 10-15 shows the procedure for that event:

Listing 10-15: Placing the chosen diagram into the Word document.

```
Private Sub btnOK_Click()
    If txtGraphic.Text <> "" Then
        diaGrab.InsertDiagram ActiveDocument, strPath & _
            txtGraphic.Text, imgGraphic.Picture.Width / 30, _
            imgGraphic.Picture.Height / 30, txtCaption.Text
```

```
      End If
      btnCancel.Caption = "Close"
End Sub
```

The .InsertDiagram method of the DiagramConsole class performs the work of both placing the diagram into the document and enrolling that diagram into the Diagrams collection. The method takes five arguments, the first being a reference to the active Word 2000 document. The second argument is the full filename of the image file being enrolled as a diagram. The next two arguments represent the width and height, respectively, of the *picture* contained within the imgGraphic control; these are not the height and width of the control. VBA maintains separate properties for the Picture object contained within a Forms 2.0 Image control. But the native system of measurement within the control is about 30 times more "granular," if you will, than that of the Word document itself; so in order that we don't insert a diagram 30 times larger than it needs to be, we divide both size properties by 30. Finally, the fifth argument, txtGraphic.Text, contains the caption that will appear below the diagram – which could be anything, or even left blank.

Closing down the form is a simple matter. After the diagram is inserted, the OK_Click() procedure leaves the form open so that the user may continue adding diagrams. The user clicks on **Cancel** (or **Close**, after a diagram has just been inserted) to dismiss the dialog box. The _Click event procedure for the Cancel button marks the beginning of the end:

```
Private Sub btnCancel_Click()
    Unload DiagramCentral
End Sub
```

When the unloading procedure is under way, VBA recognizes the _Terminate event for the form. Listing 10-16 shows how things are cleaned up.

Listing 10-16: The cleanup process for the DiagramCentral form.

```
Private Sub UserForm_Terminate()
    If strPath <> "" Then
        diaGrab.MediaPath = strPath
        If txtGraphic.Text <> "" Then
            diaGrab.LastImage = txtGraphic.Text
        End If
    End If
End Sub
```

If there's a valid path and a loaded image in the dialog box, their names are recorded for the next time by assigning them to their respective properties of diaGrab. There, those properties become parameters and are stored in the DIA-GRAM.INI file.

If you're a veteran Visual Basic programmer from way back, you may have grown accustomed to letting your Cancel button's _Click event procedure handle the shutdown process. It's **vitally important that you let the** _Terminate **event procedure handle the shutdown process for a form module.** This is because the user can easily click on the close box of the window to dismiss that dialog box, and there is no event procedure that responds to a click on the close box.

Utilizing Windows' Common Dialogs

In the course of using Windows, you've undoubtedly run across the Open and Save dialogs, the path search selector, the color and font chooser, and the Print Setup dialog. Regardless of what program you're using, or whether you're using part of Windows itself, these dialogs have a uniform appearance. They are provided to applications throughout the Windows environment as library functions in the \SYSTEM subdirectory of Windows. Whether they are officially part of the Windows API depends on whom you ask. The library that provides these dialogs for Windows 98 and NT 4.0 is COMDLG32.DLL, which is not KERNEL32, USER32, or GDI32. Over the years, Microsoft Office and other Microsoft applications have been known to substitute their own version of this library on top of the one already installed. These substitutes generally bear no striking or substantive visual difference from their forebears, although they often have several bugs corrected.

Engaging these dialogs is not the simplest of processes, especially from the perspective of a pure Visual Basic programmer. The library functions of COMDLG32.DLL have their roots in C. So rather than initial properties, all of the dialog functions in COMDLG32 utilize Type structures that have lists of member variables, some of which are quite long. These member variables are considered *flags* that represent the on/off state of some feature of their respective dialog. The external functions all return information into predefined string buffers, which must be trimmed for the excess code-zeroes that VBA does not know how to use – or more accurately, how to properly ignore. Retrofitting a VBA program with common dialogs can be a rigorous process (although a program for Excel is a curious exception, since Excel's Application object has its own common dialog functions built-in). What we have done to simplify this process is embed the functionality of these common dialogs in a VBA class module that can be utilized more readily and, hopefully, more sensibly.

Our VBA custom class module CommonDialogs performs the following services on behalf of your VBA program:

♦ It wraps the various member variables of the external functions' associated Type structures into VBA properties with explicit names.

♦ It wraps the various flags maintained by one member variable of each Type structure into VBA properties of type Boolean.

♦ It establishes the data and internal structures necessary for the C-language COMDLG32.DLL functions to mesh with VBA.

◆ It gives you a simple, on-demand mechanism for engaging a common dialog, whether or not you've set its properties explicitly beforehand.

Invoking the standard Open File dialog box

There isn't enough space in this chapter – or even in the two following chapters – to list and explain every setting this class module uses for all the common dialogs. So let's concentrate on the one common dialog that the `DiagramCentral` form uses, the Open File dialog. Figure 10-2 should refresh your memory as to how this dialog box appears, if you haven't seen it yourself during the last five minutes of using your computer.

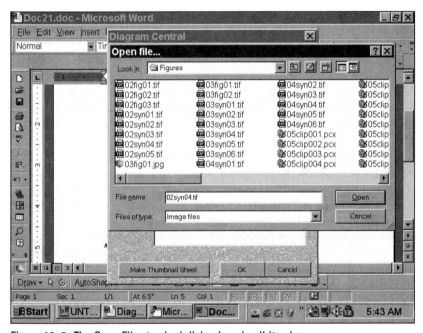

Figure 10-2: The Open File standard dialog box, in all its glory.

In the General Declarations section for the `CommonDialogs` class, six flags utilized by the Open File dialog are declared as constants. Here are some (not all) of the critical constants:

```
Private Const OFN_READONLY = &H1
Private Const OFN_ALLOWMULTISELECT = &H200
Private Const OFN_HIDEREADONLY = &H4
Private Const OFN_SHOWHELP = &H10
Private Const OFN_EXPLORER = &H80000
Private Const OFN_FILEMUSTEXIST = &H1000
```

Bitwise logic for storing multiple states in one variable

The values you see assigned to these constants are expressed in hexadecimal (base 16). You know they're base 16 from the &H prefixes. We could have employed the base 10 equivalents here without incident: 1, 512, 4, 16, 32768, and 4096, respectively. In either event, notice that each of these settings is equal to a power of 2; that is, 2^x power (where x is the exponent) equals one of these values. There's an important reason for that.

When you think of values as binary numbers (base 2), all of its digits are either 1 or 0. The placement of these digits in a base 2 numeral sequence is based on a power of two. Whereas the value 100 in base 10 represents "one times ten to the second power," the numeral 100 in base 2 represents "one times *two* to the second power," or 4 in base 10. Now, keep in mind that ones and zeroes may represent all True/False settings, and that 1 and 0 are the only two digits in the base 2 system.

A long integer may be employed to represent as many True/False values as the maximum number of digits for that long integer in the base 2 system. Because a long integer is a 32-bit value in Windows, it can represent up to 32 True/False settings simultaneously. So suppose a VBA variable were declared As Long. Each base 2 digit in this long integer variable could have its own particular meaning.

Which takes us back to the Private Const declarations above. Each of those constants utilizes a linguistic symbol such as OFN_HIDEREADONLY (the OFN here stands for "Open File Name") to represent a value that is describable by only one 1 digit in the binary numeral system. The six values declared here would, in the order of their declaration, look like this in binary: 1, 1000000000, 100, 10000, 10000000000000000, and 1000000000000. Because there's only one 1 digit in each of these values, they may be used to refer to the place in the long integer assigned to represent some true/false flag setting.

Standard dialogs have numerous characteristics

Keep all of this in mind for a moment as we move on to the Type structure required by the Open File dialog. Don't try to read the following too intently; it could drive you mad.

```
Private Type OPENFILENAME
        lStructSize As Long
        hwndOwner As Long
        hInstance As Long
        lpstrFilter As String
        lpstrCustomFilter As String
```

```
        nMaxCustFilter As Long
        nFilterIndex As Long
        lpstrFile As String
        nMaxFile As Long
        lpstrFileTitle As String
        nMaxFileTitle As Long
        lpstrDirectory As String
        lpstrTitle As String
        flags As Long
        nFileOffset As Integer
        nFileExtension As Integer
        lpstrDefExt As String
        lCustData As Long
        lpfnHook As Long
        lpTemplateName As String
End Type
```

The critical external function GetOpenFileName requires *all of this* in order to operate properly. These member variables are essentially properties, just not programmed as such. VBA can't even use some of these members anyway even if it tried; they're intended for Visual Basic, which has a much better handle (deep-inside pun intended) on how Windows manages the various windows. They must still be declared here, if only to reserve their place in memory so that the C function can locate the places of that data which VBA *can* use. Some of these member variables will be "wrapped," if you will, into CommonDialogs properties. But if you look closely, you'll find flags As Long. It doesn't matter to the external function that this variable is called flags; it won't see this name. What it will see is a long integer. It is here in the Type structure that the long integer maintaining the True/False values will be placed.

This brings us to the critical Declare statement that makes the external function visible to the VBA program:

```
Private Declare Function GetOpenFileName Lib "comdlg32.dll" _
  Alias "GetOpenFileNameA" (pOpenfilename As OPENFILENAME) As Long
```

The only argument passed to the external function GetOpenFileName is a reference to a variable with the Type structure you glanced at above. What our CommonDialogs class module does to make the management of this structure more sensible, is wrap these member variables inside properties whose settings are protected against invalidity. **You can crash Windows 98 by making an invalid call to one of the library functions in COMDLG32.DLL.** I know. I'm a survivor a hundred times over.

The constitution of Open File's filter mechanism

First, there is the matter of what this library calls the *filter*. This controls the contents of the drop-down list box marked **Files of type**. A filter for these purposes is a very long string separated into segments by code-zero characters. Each pair of segments in the sequence represents a category of file that the dialog box can show. These segments are arranged in the following order:

1. The title of the category to be chosen by the user; for example, **Word Document (*.DOC)**

2. A code-zero, or `Chr$(0)`

3. The actual filter, which may consist of any number of partial filenames with wildcards attached; e.g., `*.DOC`, or `*.JPG; *.JPEG; *.GIF`.

4. Another code-zero. This sequence repeats from part 1 until there are no more choices. Generally, the final choice is **All files (*.*)**, whose filter is `*.*`

The `CommonDialogs` class module makes it somewhat simpler, if perhaps not entirely easy, to plug these filters into the Open File dialog. Listing 10-17 shows a pair of properties that work like arrays:

Listing 10–17: Handling the programming of filters for the Open File dialog box.

```
Public Property Get FilterTitle(iWhichOne As Integer) As String
    If UBound(strFilterTitle) = 0 Or iWhichOne <= _
    UBound(strFilterTitle) Then
        FilterTitle = strFilterTitle(iWhichOne)
    End If
End Property


Public Property Let FilterTitle(iWhichOne As Integer, strEntry _
 As String)
    Dim iOverMax As Integer, iCtr As Integer

    iOverMax = UBound(strFilterTitle) + 1
    Select Case True
        Case iWhichOne > iOverMax
            iWhichOne = iOverMax
        Case iWhichOne = iOverMax
            ReDim Preserve strFilterTitle(iOverMax)
        Case iWhichOne < iOverMax
            ReDim Preserve strFilterTitle(iOverMax)
            For iCtr = iOverMax To iWhichOne + 1 Step -1
                strFilterTitle(iCtr) = strFilterTitle(iCtr - 1)
```

```
            Next iCtr
    End Select

    strFilterTitle(iWhichOne) = strEntry
End Property

Public Property Get FilterExtenders(iWhichOne As Integer) As String
    If UBound(strWildcardRack) = 0 Or iWhichOne <= _
     UBound(strWildcardRack) Then
        FilterExtenders = strWildcardRack(iWhichOne)
    End If
End Property

Public Property Let FilterExtenders(iWhichOne As Integer, _
 strEntry As String)
    Dim iOverMax As Integer, iCtr As Integer

    iOverMax = UBound(strWildcardRack) + 1
    Select Case True
        Case iWhichOne > iOverMax
            iWhichOne = iOverMax
        Case iWhichOne = iOverMax
            ReDim Preserve strWildcardRack(iOverMax)
        Case iWhichOne < iOverMax
            ReDim Preserve strWildcardRack(iOverMax)
            For iCtr = iOverMax To iWhichOne + 1 Step -1
                strWildcardRack(iCtr) = strWildcardRack(iCtr - 1)
            Next iCtr
    End Select

    strWildcardRack(iWhichOne) = strEntry
End Property
```

The display names shown to the user are handled by the .FilterTitle property, while the actual filters are handled by .FilterExtenders. The single argument iWhichOne used in the Property Get procedures for both properties acts like a subscript of an array — which is absolutely intentional, because the support variables are indeed arrays. There are two support arrays: one for the display title strFilterTitle(), and one for the filter contents strWildcardRack(). They are both dynamic arrays, which means that they can be expanded in size by one element using the ReDim Preserve statement.

When assigning a string to either of these properties, the instantiator of CommonDialogs must provide the ordinal position of the incoming entry in the array. For example, if the outside procedure knows that the new entry will appear in the second position from the top of the drop-down list, it must provide as an argument either a 2 or some variable that equals that amount. If the amount supplied is greater than the size of the array, neither Property Let procedure punishes you; it simply trims the incoming argument to one greater than the current number of entries. If the number supplied to Property Let is less than the total number of entries, all the entries from that position on are moved up one to make room. But since both arrays are independent of one another, it cannot be guaranteed that the Open File dialog box will not be opened prematurely while one array is longer than the other one. So a custom error is generated when an open attempt is generated and the arrays don't match in size; that error-generating instruction is discussed later.

The .ActiveDirectory property is simple enough in that it sets the dialog box to point to the given path at startup, but only if that path actually exists. Listing 10-18 shows a now familiar scheme:

Listing 10-18: Property procedure pair for the .ActiveDirectory property

```
Public Property Get ActiveDirectory() As String
    ActiveDirectory = strDirectory
End Property

Public Property Let ActiveDirectory(strSetting As String)
    If FileSystem.Dir(strSetting) <> "" Then
        strDirectory = strSetting
    End If
End Property
```

The .WindowTitle and .ActiveFile properties — which hold the contents of the dialog box's title bar, and the first file it pulls up from the list, respectively — are managed by the simplest of property procedures, shown here:

```
Public Property Get WindowTitle() As String
    WindowTitle = strWindowTitle
End Property

Public Property Let WindowTitle(strSetting As String)
    strWindowTitle = strSetting
End Property

Public Property Get ActiveFile() As String
    ActiveFile = strActiveFile
End Property

Public Property Let ActiveFile(strSetting As String)
    strActiveFile = strSetting
End Property
```

Here is where we come back to those multiple flags maintained by a single long integer. The `CommonDialogs` class module maintains a single support variable `lOpenFlags` for all of the flags that will be assigned later to the `flags` member of the `OPENFILENAME` structure. For the Open File dialog, each flag is represented by its own VBA property. The `Property Let` procedure for that property sets or resets the appropriate bit of the long integer, using the `Private Const` constant associated with that bit as a sort of template, telling it where the bit is located. Remember that each constant's value can be written in base 2 with only one 1 digit and the rest as 0 digits.

Using one support variable for six or more properties

The six key True/False properties whose settings are mapped into flags are these:

`.OpenMultipleChoice`	Represents whether the user may choose more than one file from the list.
`.ReadOnly`	Represents the state of the **Open as read-only** checkbox on the dialog (when visible), where 1 – Set; 2 – Reset. This property may be preinitialized before startup, as well as read after the dialog box is dismissed.
`.ReadOnlyBox`	Represents whether the **Open as read-only** checkbox is visible on the dialog.
`.ShowHelpButton`	Represents whether the question mark button appears next to the close box on the dialog's title bar.
`.ExplorerStyle`	Represents whether the dialog box has the new "Explorer" style or the old Windows 3.1 style.
`.FileMustExist`	Designates that when the user types in a filename that does not exist, the dialog box will generate a warning and will not close until the filename entered does exist.

To get an idea of how all of these flag-based properties are managed, let's examine the `Property Let` procedure for the `.FileMustExist` property, shown in Listing 10-19.

Listing 10-19: Property Let procedure for the .FileMustExist property.

```
Public Property Let FileMustExist(bSet As Boolean)
    If bSet Then
        lOpenFlags = lOpenFlags Or OFN_FILEMUSTEXIST
    Else
        lOpenFlags = lOpenFlags And Not OFN_FILEMUSTEXIST
    End If
End Property
```

Here, Boolean arithmetic is used to set the proper bit in the long integer. For `OFN_FILEMUSTEXIST`, this is the thirteenth bit from the right, representative of 2^{12}. The incoming variable `bSet` denotes whether the bit is to be set for `True` or `False`. The variable is its own conditional expression, because it naturally yields True or False anyway.

The way Boolean arithmetic works, one set of bits is compared against another set at the same position. The result is a third set of bits whose individual values denote something logical about the comparison. It's easier to comprehend what's going on here with an example in which the "sets of bits" are all one bit long. Consider each bit as representing True or False. The Boolean `Or` operator results in True whenever one or the other bit in the comparison is `True`. So if both bits are True, the `Or` operator results in `True`. Why is this important? Because when you set a bit to True, you want that final value to be True even if it was already True to begin with. The Boolean `Or` comparison accomplishes this result.

In Depth: Comparing the Boolean operators, literally and figuratively

The five Boolean comparison operators supported by VBA are:

`And`   Yields a True result if both compared bits are True

`Or`   Yields a True result if one or both compared bits are True

`Xor`   Yields a True result if *only* one compared bit is True

`Eqv`   Yields a True result if both compared bits are equal

`Imp`   Yields a True result when the second compared bit does not contradict the proposition of the first; that is, when the state of the first bit *implies* the state of the second bit. This is used when comparing the result of two comparisons; it logically asks, "Is it reasonable to presume the result of the second comparison is correct, given the outcome of the first comparison?" A False first comparison gives us nothing to go on when questioning the validity of the second, yet no reason to doubt it either — so the result is True regardless. But if the first comparison yields True, the result of the second "should therefore follow;" if it's False, it's considered a contradiction, and the operator yields False.

The grid below presents what we call a *truth table* for all of the Boolean operators recognized by VBA. A truth table is a list of the results for all four possible comparisons between a 1 bit and a 0 bit.

Truth table for Boolean VBA operators

Operator x	Bit A	Bit B	A x B	A x Not B
And	0	0	0	0
	0	1	0	0
	1	0	0	1
	1	1	1	0
Or	0	0	0	1
	0	1	1	0
	1	0	1	1
	1	1	1	1
Xor	0	0	0	1
	0	1	1	0
	1	0	1	0
	1	1	0	1
Eqv	0	0	1	0
	0	1	0	1
	1	0	0	1
	1	1	1	0
Imp	0	0	1	1
	0	1	1	1
	1	0	0	1
	1	1	1	0

In our `Property Let` procedure, the value of the constant `OFN_FILEMUSTEXIST` is analogous to "Bit B" in the truth table shown in the accompanying sidebar. The "tool" in this constant is the 1 bit; but with `Boolean` comparisons, 0 bits are meaningful as well. The constant is applied against the bitwise value of the current variable `lOpenFlags` — "Bit A." Remember, even though our primary job is to change the setting of one bit, there is the safety and well-being of all the other bits in `lOpenFlags` to take into account. So we cannot use a Boolean operator in which a 0 bit in our constant results in a change in the existing state — only a 1 bit is allowed to make a change.

When setting Bit A to True, you want to leave Bit A True if it is already that way, but make any False Bit A into True. The other bits in the long integer must remain as they are when they are compared to 0 bits. The truth table for the Or operator fits that pattern perfectly. Likewise, when setting Bit A to False, you want to leave any existing bits as they were after the comparison to 0 bits. You only want the 1 bit on the B side to change any 1 (True) on the B side to 0 (False). So, we insert the Boolean system's only *unary* operator to help us out (the rest are called *binary* operators because they deal with two terms). The Not operator is inserted before the second value, *reversing* that value prior to the comparison using And.

Boolean arithmetic is an interesting, but tricky, business. **All mathematical operations that take place in a computer are implemented at their lowest level in Boolean arithmetic.** Adding, multiplying, dividing, and finding the square root of a number are all processes that, at their lowest level, utilize the machine-language equivalent of the operators listed in the truth table.

For the complementary Property Get procedures for the flag-based properties, a VBA intrinsic function is used to shorten the property retrieval process to one instruction:

```
Public Property Get FileMustExist() As Boolean
    FileMustExist = CBool(lOpenFlags And OFN_FILEMUSTEXIST)
End Property
```

The body of this procedure could have been phrased like this instead:

```
If lOpenFlags And OFN_FILEMUSTEXIST Then
    FileMustExist = True
Else
    FileMustExist = False
End If
```

But Boolean arithmetic gives us a way to condense this process significantly. As you can see in the truth table, the And comparison is only concerned with those bits that are being compared with 1 — all others yield 0. If the bit in the same spot as the 1 bit in OFN_FILEMUSTEXIST equals 1, then the result will yield a 1 in that same location. That's a True result for that particular bit, but a positive integer from the point of view of VBA. So the CBool() function is used to convert the result of the comparison to the True or False result expected by a procedure whose declared type is Boolean.

Listing 10-20 shows the property procedure pair for another flag property, .ReadOnlyBox, which we implemented "in reverse:"

Listing 10-20: Procedure pair for the .ReadOnlyBox property.

```
Public Property Get ReadOnlyBox() As Boolean
    ReadOnlyBox = CBool(Not (lOpenFlags And OFN_HIDEREADONLY))
End Property
```

```
Public Property Let ReadOnlyBox(bSet As Boolean)
    If bSet Then
        lOpenFlags = lOpenFlags And Not OFN_HIDEREADONLY
    Else
        lOpenFlags = lOpenFlags Or OFN_HIDEREADONLY
    End If
End Property
```

We wanted the .ReadOnlyBox to represent the True/False state of the visibility of the **Open as read-only** checkbox in the Open File dialog. But in Microsoft's implementation, the associated flag OFN_HIDEREADONLY is set to 1 if the checkbox is *invisible*. To set things up so that this property could yield the reverse of its associated flag, I added a Not unary operator to the Property Get procedure, reversing the result of the And comparison. And in the Property Let procedure, the order of the instructions in the If...Then clause was simply reversed so that the And Not comparison – not the Or comparison – occurs when the incoming setting is True.

Another way of accomplishing this involves a VBA intrinsic function based on an old spreadsheet function, to reduce the body of this Property Let procedure, as well as the others based on flag settings, to one instruction:

```
lOpenFlags = IIf(bSet, lOpenFlags And Not OFN_HIDEREADONLY, _
 lOpenFlags Or OFN_HIDEREADONLY)
```

The IIf() function is like an If...Then clause in that it evaluates a comparison expression and takes action based on its true/false result. But in this case, instead of taking action, the function returns a designated result – one or the other – to the variable to the left of the equal sign. IIf() takes three arguments, the first being the comparison expression. The second is the result of the function if the comparison is True, the third the result if False. This function does save some space in the source code as well as some execution time, at the expense of legibility on the part of human beings.

The .ReadOnly property is not as powerful as it might appear. Nothing about setting its value to True makes the chosen file in the Open File dialog read-only. It merely denotes the current state of the **Open as read-only** choice. If .ReadOnlyBox is initialized to False so that the user doesn't see the checkbox, and .ReadOnly is set to True, then .ReadOnly will remain True after the dialog box is dismissed. Its sole purpose is as an indicator of whether the VBA program should employ its own measures to prevent the user from writing to or overwriting the chosen file or files.

When .OpenMultipleChoice is set to True, the string returned by the GetOpenFileName external function is assembled somewhat differently. It consists of multiple segments separated by spaces (" "), the first segment of which is the directory in which the chosen files appear. The remaining segments are the filenames of all of the chosen files. These filenames show up in the Open File dialog with quotation marks separating each one; those quotation marks are *absent* from the returned string.

The `Private Sub Class_Initialize()` procedure for `CommonDialogs` takes care of the default property settings for the Open File dialog, so it's actually ready to go even if the instantiator of `CommonDialogs` sets no properties in advance of calling up the dialog. The instructions that handle the setup are as follows:

```
ReDim strFilterTitle(1)
ReDim strWildcardRack(1)

strThisModule = VBE.ActiveVBProject.Name & ".CommonDialogs"
strWindowTitle = "Open file..."
strDirectory = "C:\"
lOpenFlags = 0& Or OFN_SHOWHELP Or OFN_EXPLORER
```

The two filter arrays are established with their first, blank elements. The `strThisModule` variable is loaded with the name of the class module, in case the `Err.Raise` method ever becomes necessary. Then the support variables for the `.WindowTitle` and `.ActiveDirectory` properties are set. We can leave the support variable for `.ActiveFile` alone, because its initial value may safely be a null string. The `lOpenFlags` long integer has two of its bits set to True by "Or-ing" them with `OFN_SHOWHELP` and `OFN_EXPLORER`. This effectively sets the `.ShowHelpButton` and `.ExplorerStyle` properties to `True`. If `.ExplorerStyle` is set to `False`, the Open File dialog that's brought up looks more like the old Windows 3.1 style.

Wrapping the API function call in a method procedure

Once all the initial properties are set, the instantiator of `CommonDialogs` places a call to the `.OpenDialog` method. No arguments are necessary here because the parameters for the dialog box have already been set up and are ready to load into a composite variable that the C-language function will use. Listing 10-21 lays out this critical method's procedure:

Listing 10-21: Bringing the Open File dialog box into view.

```
Public Function OpenDialog() As String
    On Error Resume Next

    Dim openParams As OPENFILENAME
    Dim lReturn As Long
    Dim iMaxTypes As Integer, iCtr As Integer
    Dim iPtrLeft As Integer, iPtrRight As Integer
    Dim strFilter As String, strExtractor As String

    If UBound(strWildcardRack) <> UBound(strFilterTitle) Then
        Err.Raise vbObjectError + 514, strThisModule, _
            "Filter property arrays are uneven."
```

```
     Exit Function
End If

With openParams
     .hwndOwner = GetActiveWindow
     .lStructSize = Len(openParams)
     iMaxTypes = UBound(strWildcardRack)
     For iCtr = 1 To iMaxTypes
          strFilter = strFilter & strFilterTitle(iCtr) & _
           Chr$(0) & strWildcardRack(iCtr) & Chr$(0)
     Next iCtr
     strFilter = strFilter & "All Files" & Chr$(0) & "*.*" _
      & Chr$(0)

     .lpstrFilter = strFilter
     .nFilterIndex = iMaxTypes
     .lpstrFile = strActiveFile & String(257 - _
       Len(strActiveFile), 0)
     .nMaxFile = Len(.lpstrFile) - 1
     .lpstrFileTitle = .lpstrFile
     .nMaxFileTitle = .nMaxFile
     .lpstrDirectory = strDirectory
     .lpstrTitle = strWindowTitle
     .flags = lOpenFlags

     lReturn = GetOpenFileName(openParams)
     lOpenFlags = .flags
     strDirectory = .lpstrDirectory
     OpenDialog = Left$(.lpstrFile, InStrRev(.lpstrFile, _
      Chr$(0)) - 1)
     If lOpenFlags And OFN_ALLOWMULTISELECT Then
          iPtrLeft = InStr(.lpstrFile, " ")
          strDirectory = Left$(.lpstrFile, iPtrLeft - 1) & "\"
          ReDim strChosenFiles(0)
          iCtr = 0
          Do
               iPtrRight = InStr(iPtrLeft + 1, .lpstrFile, " ")
               If iPtrRight = 0 Then Exit Do
               iCtr = iCtr + 1
               strExtractor = Mid$(.lpstrFile, iPtrLeft + 1, _
                iPtrRight - iPtrLeft - 1)
               ReDim Preserve strChosenFiles(iCtr)
               strChosenFiles(iCtr) = strExtractor
```

Continued

Listing 10-21: Bringing the Open File dialog box into view. *(Continued)*

```
                iPtrLeft = iPtrRight
          Loop
          iChosenFileCount = iCtr
      Else
          ReDim strChosenFiles(1)
          strExtractor = Left$(.lpstrFile, InStr(.lpstrFile, _
          Chr$(0)) - 1)
          strDirectory = Left$(strExtractor, _
          InStrRev(strExtractor, "\"))
          strChosenFiles(1) = Right$(strExtractor, _
          Len(strExtractor) - InStrRev(strExtractor, "\"))
          iChosenFileCount = 1
      End If
    strActiveFile = strChosenFiles(1)
    End With
End Function
```

First, the filter arrays are checked to make certain they are the same size. If they're not, the programmer needs to be informed and the function exited. If that hurdle is cleared, all of the vital property settings (and none of the ones VBA doesn't use or need) are loaded into the openParams structure.

Making use of Windows' handle for a window

The first setting in the With clause for openParams, .hwndOwner = GetActiveWindow, may look unfamiliar: GetActiveWindow() is actually a Windows API function that is declared earlier in the CommonDialogs class module using this instruction:

```
Private Declare Function GetActiveWindow Lib "user32" () As Long
```

We haven't discussed much about *handles* in the context of VBA programming, because they rarely play a role there. In lower-level programming, Windows gives every window that's either visible or lurking in the background, its own unique "license plate," if you will. It's a long integer that uniquely identifies the window, and that ceases to exist whenever the window is *destroyed* – to use Microsoft's dramatic term for removal from memory. The GetOpenFileName() function makes use of the handle for the active window as an identifier for the window to which the Open File dialog should be attached. "Attachment" in this context refers to the delegation of responsibility. If we set the .hwndOwner member to 0 (meaning, no window at all), the Open File dialog is completely independent of any other window. This means that if a form such as DiagramCentral brings up the Open File dialog, then the user clicks on the Cancel button on the *form,* the Open File dialog remains on the screen, to eventually return its chosen file or files to no one and nothing.

When `DiagramCentral` does bring up Open File, most likely it already is the active window. So the `GetActiveWindow()` API function retrieves its handle and the instruction assigns that handle to the `.hwndOwner` member. The result is that the `GetOpenFileName()` function can suspend the operation of that window so that the user can't operate any part of the calling form — especially the Cancel button — while the Open File dialog is showing.

After the window handle business is out of the way, in the `.OpenDialog` method procedure, inside the `With` clause, the remaining members of the `openParams` structure are loaded, especially the `lOpenFlags` long integer which is assigned to `.Flags`. Then the `GetOpenFileName()` API function is invoked. As a *modal* dialog, it suspends Windows operations until its work is done and the user has dismissed it. Immediately after that happens, the function updates some of the members of `openParams` to reflect the user's choices. Most important among these, of course, is the string that contains the chosen file or files.

Multiple choices change the returned data's syntax

The `OpenDialog()` procedure is responsible for parsing this string into values which may be polled by way of the `.ChosenFile`, `.ChosenFileCount`, `.ActiveFile`, and `.ActiveDirectory` properties. The `If...Then` clause checks `lOpenFlags` to see if its `OFN_ALLOWMULTISELECT` bit is set. If it is, the procedure retrieves the directory name from the first segment of the return string, and then extracts each returned filename. It does this first by locating the space characters on either side, and then using `Mid$()` (or `Mid()`, depending on your tastes) to lift out the characters in-between. Each time a new filename is found, one element is added to the end of the `strChosenFiles()` array with the `ReDim Preserve` statement.

Notice the `Do...Loop` clause construction here. The clause itself doesn't test for any condition; conceivably, this loop could be iterated forever. What causes execution to drop out of this loop is an `Exit Do` statement, which is encountered when the `InStr()` function cannot find another space character in the return string.

When the Open File dialog is set up for only one returned filename, its return string contains the full storage path for the file. So the `Left$()` and `Right$()` functions have to be used to divide the string into its path and filename components for assignment to `strDirectory` and `strChosenFiles(1)`.

The `.ChosenFile` and `.ChosenFileCount` properties are read-only. Their Property Get procedures appear in Listing 10-22.

Listing 10-22: Procedures that manage which file or files the user chose.

```
Public Property Get ChosenFileCount() As Integer
    ChosenFileCount = iChosenFileCount
End Property

Public Property Get ChosenFile(iWhichOne As Integer) As String
    iWhichOne = Abs(iWhichOne)
    If iWhichOne > iChosenFileCount Then
```

```
        iWhichOne = iChosenFileCount
    End If
    ChosenFile = strChosenFiles(iWhichOne)
End Property
```

To prevent the crazy occurrence of someone supplying a negative subscript as an argument for iWhichOne, the Property Get procedure utilizes VBA's Abs() intrinsic function, which returns the absolute value of its single argument. This is basically the same as the argument's value stripped of its sign – so a positive value appears positive, whereas a negative value is no longer negative.

Throughout the book you'll find other examples of the CommonDialogs class put to work in generating other, recognizable dialog boxes. Chapter 14 shows how a Word 2000 document can be put to work managing the diagrams generated using the DiagramConsole and Diagram class. But as a fitting *denouement* for this chapter, here's a bonus that anyone blessed with hearing will appreciate.

Sound, Courtesy of Windows

Visual Basic for Applications maintains one statement of its very own that makes use of the massive multimedia sound system for which you paid hundreds, if not dozens, of dollars. Here it is:

```
Beep
```

You're looking at its syntax. You can always, of course, beep twice:

```
Beep
Beep
```

While VBA is practically mute with regard to the subject of sound, the Windows API features the most important sound function that you can have – the one that plays a .WAV file. It takes a mere two arguments, one of which is the filename of the .WAV file. Its declaration statement is as follows:

```
Private Declare Function sndPlaySound Lib "winmm.dll" _
 Alias "sndPlaySoundA" (ByVal lpszSoundName As String, _
 ByVal uFlags As Long) As Long
```

There are a number of constants you can declare for function sndPlaySound() in advance; but for most VBA purposes, you will not need them all.

Wrapping sound in a sealed container, so to speak

To wrap this API function in a VBA class module, two goals come to mind: The filename for the .WAV file referred to must exist prior to the module trying to play the sound. It should also be possible for an instantiator of the sound class to refer to a sound by its "nickname," if you will, if it doesn't know the filename of the .WAV file.

Our sound class is called Victrola. It maintains only two module-level variables, declared thus:

```
Private INIJukebox As New INIControl
Private strMediaPath As String
```

The second declaration should look familiar to you; it's based on the strMediaPath variable that DiagramConsole uses to locate the default file directory. Listing 10-23 should look familiar to you as well; it retrieves the stored default path from the VICTROLA.INI file:

Listing 10-23: Class initialization event procedure for Victrola class.

```
Private Sub Class_Initialize()
    INIJukebox.FileName = "victrola.ini"
    strMediaPath = INIJukebox.ProfileEntryString("Media", "Path")
    If strMediaPath = "" Then
        strMediaPath = INIJukebox.WindowsDirectory
        If FileSystem.Dir(strMediaPath & "\MEDIA\") <> "" Then
            strMediaPath = strMediaPath & "\MEDIA\"
        Else
            strMediaPath = strMediaPath & "\"
        End If
    End If
End Sub
```

As before, if the default directory – or the .INI file itself – doesn't exist yet, the procedure asks for the Windows directory and attaches \MEDIA\ to that directory. If no such directory exists, the root directory of Windows is used instead. The key method exposed by class Victrola is .PlaySound, presented in Listing 10-24:

Listing 10-24: The procedure that plays the sound file. At last!

```
Public Function PlaySound(strSoundName As String) As Boolean
    Dim strSoundFile As String, strStoredSound As String

    strSoundFile = strMediaPath & strSoundName
    If FileSystem.Dir(strSoundFile) = "" Then
```

```
        strStoredSound = INIJukebox.ProfileEntryString("Sounds", _
        strSoundName)
        If strStoredSound <> "" Then
            strSoundFile = strMediaPath & strStoredSound
            If FileSystem.Dir(strSoundFile) = "" Then
                strSoundFile = ""
            End If
        End If
    End If
    If strSoundFile <> "" Then
        sndPlaySound strSoundFile, SND_ASYNC Or SND_FILENAME
    End If
End Function
```

The incoming string argument could either be a filename or a "nickname," which is a parameter in the [Sounds] category of the VICTROLA.INI file. If the assessed strSoundName argument is not a valid filename, then the procedure checks to see if the string equals a parameter supplied by the .INI file. If it does, then the setting for that parameter is retrieved, and that is used for the filename for the sound file. If the sound file is never found, then strSoundFile is made into a null string, which keeps the sndPlaySound() API function from processing it.

The constant SND_ASYNC tells Windows to play the sound *asynchronously*, so that other processes may proceed while the sound is going on – it doesn't stop everything just for a bit of noise. SND_FILENAME instructs Windows to look for a sound file rather than a corresponding sound entry in WIN.INI. The Or operator here does not mean "one or the other." It means that one set of bits is compared to another set of bits, with the result being a third set that has the 1 bits of both compared sets. These two 1 bits act as flags for the second argument of the sndPlaySound() API function.

Implementing sound responses through custom events

This class can be put to work through *other* class modules. When a class module declares a custom event, an instantiator can respond to that event by playing a sound. So within the instantiator module, you define the event and you define the response.

Here's an example involving the DiagramConsole class: In the General Declarations section are these three statements:

```
Public Event Deletion(ByVal iIndex As Integer)
Public Event Insertion(ByVal strThisFile As String)
Public Event Reconciliation()
```

These are neither procedure headers nor procedure calls. They are merely declarations, almost like those used by C++. They define custom events that a class module supports and that instantiators of that class can respond to. The variable names here are like the variable names in `Declare` statements for external functions in that they're placeholders for variables or values that will be passed later when the event itself is generated, or *raised*. What's important about these arguments, more than the names of the placeholder variables, is the types stated, as in `As Integer` or `As String`. They specify the types of arguments that VBA will pass to the event procedures in the instantiating module.

In the `DiagramConsole` class module, the `.InsertDiagram` method takes responsibility for placing the chosen diagram into the Word 2000 document. Once that's done, an instruction can be added that acts as a signal that the insertion is successfully completed. This signal is the `_Insertion` event declared above. The instruction that sends this signal is quite simple:

```
RaiseEvent Insertion(strThisFile)
```

The variable `strThisFile` contains the filename of the inserted diagram. Any valid string variable or literal could have been used here as long as there is one argument only, and it's a string as declared earlier.

The following instructions are located in the General Declarations section in the `ThisDocument` object module for the DiagramMatic template:

```
Private WithEvents diaCom As DiagramConsole
Private vicTory As New Victrola
```

The first instruction instantiates the `DiagramConsole` class and makes the module capable of recognizing the events that it generates: `_Insertion`, `_Deletion`, and `_Reconciliation`. The second instruction both instantiates a `Victrola` class object and declares a reference `vicTory` to that object. With both these references in play, the `ThisDocument` module can include this custom event procedure:

```
Private Sub diaCom_Insertion(ByVal strThisFile As String)
    vicTory.PlaySound "Musica Asterisk.WAV"
End Sub
```

The sound file chosen here is from one of the "themes" installable from the Windows 98 CD-ROM. Note that this is a filename, not a "nickname." But with this event procedure in place, whenever you insert a diagram into a document using the `DiagramCentral` form (or by any other means devised later), you'll hear a nice plucked violin.

The two VBA instructions to thank for this little musical interlude are `Event` and `RaiseEvent`. Here's how you construct a `RaiseEvent` declaration:

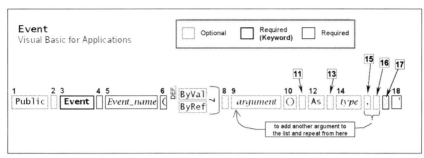

	Part	Description
1	Public	<u>Qualifier</u> Denotes the accessibility of the declared event to procedures in other modules. An event is, by definition, public anyway; the appearance of this term helps to underscore that fact.
2	(space)	Necessary only in the event that part **1** appears.
3	Event	<u>Statement</u> Declares that the class module in which this instruction appears is to utilize a unique term (part **5**) that is to represent an occurrence or kind of occurrence within the class module. The result is something like a procedure call, except that it is broadcast to all modules in the VBA project that have declared instances of the class module using the WithEvents qualifier.
4	(space)	
5	Event_name	<u>Literal</u> A unique name that represents the event within modules that instantiate this class module. This name should not be the same as any VBA keyword, or any variable that is to be used within a module. It can, however, "coincidentally" be the same as a property, method, or event term used by another library class or class module.
6	((left parenthesis)	Begins the arguments list.

	Part	Description
7	ByVal (DEFAULT) ByRef	Qualifier Denotes whether the argument to be received by the header of the event procedure is to refer simply to a value (ByVal) or if it is instead to be linked by reference to the variable that passed the argument in the RaiseEvent statement (ByRef). By default, arguments are passed to an event procedure by value — which means that the received values have no ties to variables in the class module. If a variable is used within RaiseEvent to pass an argument by reference, then whenever the event procedure changes the value of the argument that was declared in the same place within the Event statement as that passed argument in the RaiseEvent statement, those changes are reflected within the RaiseEvent argument in the class module.
8	(space)	
9	*argument*	Variable or literal Represents the value or data to be received by the event procedure. Whenever a programmer creates an event procedure using a VBA code window by choosing the event name (part 5) from the rightmost drop-down list, this argument with this name will appear in the event procedure header at this position.
10	( ) (closed parentheses)	Denotes that the argument to be passed will be an array. Upon receipt of this argument by the event procedure, the variable will set up as a fixed (not a dynamic) array whose length is equivalent to that of the array used here in passing the argument.
11	(space)	
12	As	Specifier Denotes that the following term (part 14) is to state the type or class of the argument (part 9).
13	(space)	

Continued

	Part	Description
14	*type*	<u>Type or class</u>
	Variant *	A valid name for a VBA standard type, or a recognized object type,
	Byte	either from an active object library or a VBA class module loaded
	Boolean	into the current project. Although the type of a passed argument in
	Integer	an event defaults to Variant, in practice, it is vitally important
	Long	that types be explicitly specified and that variants are used
	Currency	explicitly only when necessary.
	Single	
	Double	
	Date	
	String	
	Object	
15	, (comma)	Along with a space (part **16**), separates more than one argument in the list.
16	(space)	
17	) (right parenthesis)	Ends the arguments list.
18	(Enter)	Ends the Event statement.

* DEFAULT

If the Event statement is similar to a procedure *declaration*, then the RaiseEvent statement is similar to a procedure *call*. The difference here is that the call works in the reverse direction, like a "callback function" in C or C++. In other words, it sets up a situation in which *some other* procedure is to call the one named by RaiseEvent. Its syntax appears below:

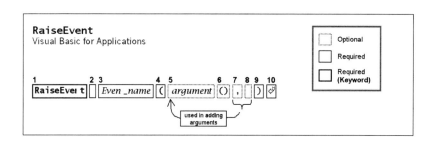

	Part	Description
1	RaiseEvent	**Statement** States that at this point in the program's run, the named event (part **3**) is to be recognized. In effect, this is a procedure call to any and all outside modules in the project that expect this event.
2	(space)	
3	*Event_name*	Literal The name of the event to be broadcast, as declared by the Event.
4	((left parenthesis)	Begins the arguments list.
5	*argument*	Variable or literal Representative of the value (or reference, if the receiver is declared ByRef) to be received by the event procedure. A variable used here is not a placeholder like in the Event procedure, but an actual variable, to be treated in the same vein as a variable used in a procedure call.
6	( ) (closed parentheses)	Denotes that the variable being passed is an array. A subscript is not included; if it were, the argument passed would be a unit variable.
7	, (comma)	Coupled with a space, separates multiple arguments from one another.
8	(space)	
9	) (right parenthesis)	Closes the arguments list.
10	(Enter)	Ends the RaiseEvent statement.

To start summing things up, let's take a look back at what we've accomplished: We've uncovered how to acquire certain information about Windows and the processor running it. Next, we set up a sophisticated system for utilizing old-style .INI files to handle persistent variables and parameters. Already, you have a data management system in place that transcends Office 2000. Then we connected this initialization file system to the DiagramConsole class and the DiagramCentral form module, so that certain values can be maintained long after the DiagramMatic template is shut down. Next, we learned about Boolean arithmetic, and how it can be used to help a long integer store as many states as it has bits. Then finally, we brought in yet another class module in order that we may install a long-awaited sound system in O2K. We have come a very long way in a mere mountain of pages.

We introduced quite a few intrinsic functions over the course of this chapter. Here they are again in Table 10-2 for your review.

TABLE 10-2 VISUAL BASIC FOR APPLICATIONS INTRINSIC FUNCTIONS

`IsMissing()`

Returns a Boolean (True/False) value that denotes whether the given argument, supplied by way of a procedure call and declared both `Optional` and `As Variant` in the procedure header, is present or absent. This function is used to determine whether processing should proceed with regard to this argument. Argument receivers declared as standard types other than `Variant` are automatically given their default values, and are therefore not considered "missing."

Argument:

variant – The name of the variable declared `Optional` and `As Variant` in the procedure header.

Note: The formation `If IsMissing(x)` is generally preferred over `If x = Missing` because the latter formation tends not to work.

`CBool()`
`CByte()`
`CCur()`
`CDate()`
`CDbl()`
`CDec()`
`CLng()`
`CSng()`
`CVar()`
`CStr()`

Converts the single argument expression into a form that may be assigned to a variable declared `As Integer`. Decimal values are truncated though are not rounded. Values exceeding the limitations of type `Integer` (less than –32,768, or greater than 32,767) will result in overflow errors. Strings are converted into values by translating their digits into numerals, so value is generally not lost in the conversion. Values converted into strings are rendered as digit characters, though strings cannot be used in arithmetic or logical operations.

Argument:

Numeral – Any numeral value which may be adapted to being represented as an `Integer` type.

Note: The `CInt()` function dates back to the earliest days of Microsoft BASIC. It is currently one of many similarly-named conversion functions which handle the following types:

Function	Converts to type
`CBool()`	Boolean
`CByte()`	Byte
`CInt()`	Integer
`CCur()`	Currency
`CDate()`	Date

Function	Converts to type
CDbl()	Double
CDec()	Decimal
CLng()	Long
CSng()	Single
CVar()	Variant
CStr()	String

From a logical standpoint, the CInt() function performs the same task as the Int() function, and CStr() performs the same task as Str$(). But this full set of type conversion functions was provided for the sake of making data fit somehow within differently-sized containers in memory. In C/C++ programming, this is called *type casting* (the UNIX guys just love puns). The CVar() function is probably provided just to be fair to the Variant type; recasting any data whose type is already known into a Variant would be odd, and is actually unnecessary for assigning any data to a Variant type variable anyway.

Trim$() Trim()	Returns a form of the string supplied as an argument with any leading or trailing spaces removed. **Argument:** *string* – The series of characters to have its spaces trimmed. **Note:** The LTrim$() and RTrim$() functions trim just the leading spaces and just the trailing spaces, respectively, from the supplied string argument.
Iif()	(Short for "inline IF") Evaluates the expression supplied as the first argument, and returns a copy of the second argument if the expression evaluates True, and a copy of the third argument if the expression evaluates False. **Arguments:** *expression* – The comparison expression to be evaluated. This takes the same form as an expression of comparison used in an If...Then clause. *true_value* – The result to be returned if *expression* evaluates True. *false_value* – The result to be returned if *expression* evaluates False. No type restrictions are applied to these return results.
Ubound() Lbound()	Returns the index number applicable to the first (UBound()) and last (LBound()) entry in one of the axes of the stated array. For a one-dimensional array, the axis number need not be stated. **Arguments:** *Array name* – **(string)** The variable name of the array in question, minus the parentheses

Continued

TABLE **10-2** VISUAL BASIC FOR APPLICATIONS INTRINSIC FUNCTIONS *(Continued)*

	Dimension – (integer, necessary for multi-dimensional arrays) The number of the subscript or axis whose bounds are being tested, where 1 refers to the first subscript. **Usage notes:** The UBound() function safely returns the number of subscripts for all arrays whose lower bound is known to be 0 or 1. If an array has been declared with a different lower bound value – for instance, Dim curValue(15 To 30) As Currency – the UBound() function will return the index number of the highest ordered subscript – for this example, 30 – and not the number of subscripts in the array. To return a guaranteed number of subscripts in the array, UBound() may be used in conjunction with its counterpart function, LBound(), as in this example: iSubscripts = UBound(curValue) - LBound(curValue)

InStrRev()	Returns an integer denoting the first location, beginning from the *right* of a string being examined, of a given character or sequence of characters. The result is the ordinal position of that character counting from the *left*; although for InStrRev(), the search begins at the right and counts *down* toward the left. This is the counterpart of the InStr() function, which both searches from the left and counts from the left.
	Arguments (in order):
	integer – (optional) The location in the string, counting from the right, where the search is to begin.
	string – A variable or literal representing the string to be examined.
	objective – The character or string being searched for.
	constant – (optional) Determines whether the interpreter is to compare the character against the string in a case-sensitive (1) or non-case-sensitive (0 – **default**) manner.
	Examples:
	InStrRev("WIN.INI", ".")
	      returns 4
	InStrRev("www.idgbooks.com", ".")
	      returns 13
	InStrRev("helLo", "L")
	      returns 4
	InStrRev("helLo", "lL")
	      returns 3

Abs()	Returns the absolute value of the supplied argument's value, or the value of the argument with its sign stripped.

Argument:
value – The amount to be evaluated.
Examples:
Abs(14)
> returns 14

Abs(-39.95)
> returns 39.95

On Point

Many external functions utilize arguments, or variables that are members of Type structures that are long integers whose bits are utilized individually. Along with the Type structures and Declare statement necessary for VBA to recognize and utilize an external function, a set of constant declarations using the Const statement is often added to the General Declarations section. These constants represent *bitwise* patterns — binary or base 2 digits translated into base 10 (decimal) or base 16 (hexadecimal) — where generally only one 1 bit appears. This single 1 bit is used in a Boolean process that sets a particular flag bit within a long integer member variable. The Or operator is used to compare the constant to the flag variable's existing value, and to set the bit corresponding with the 1 bit in the constant, to 1. Similarly, the And operator is joined with the Not operator to compare the member variable with the binary inverse of the constant, such that the resulting bit in question is always reset to 0.

The most commonly used dialog boxes for ordinary functions, such as choosing a file to open, are provided by a DLL in Windows called COMDLG32. One external function in this DLL, GetOpenFileName(), can be encapsulated by a method procedure in a class module. The members of the Type structure developed for use by the function, can all be utilized as support variables for properties in this class module. This enables property procedures to act as gateways into the private data of the API function, ensuring its safe use in the VBA program.

A class module can declare its own custom events or signals that indicate to the instantiator of that class that something of importance has occurred. Once an event is declared using the Event statement, the signal can be generated with RaiseEvent, and data from the class module can be sent along with the event as arguments. These arguments are received by the event procedure in the instantiator module. Declaring the reference to the class instance using the WithEvents qualifier makes these event procedures possible.

In Theory: Objective reality

More often than ever before, professional programmers find themselves on the hot seat when trying to sell their services, and in so doing, pass themselves off as knowledgeable, capable practitioners of the digital arts. In the interview process, the interviewer – whether or not a programmer himself – frequently has read some measure of literature on programming as an art, as a science, and, these days, as nearly a political party. This tends to make the interviewer more literate in the terminology with which a methodology is *marketed* than with the terms one uses in a practical setting.

In one such interview a few months back, I was asked how I would write a Visual Basic object that represents an invoice. I told him I wouldn't. An invoice, I said, is data, and data in a program, like blood through a living organism, is both liquid and flowing. An object, by contrast, is solid. It should represent the organisms and devices that are responsible for the healthy and managed flow of that data. My object would represent the devices, both virtual and physical, which process invoices.

I, too, have a lexicon I use to market my own methodologies.

This particular interviewer was an intelligent, experienced programmer himself with whom I would work if my services were employed. But he vehemently disagreed with my point of view; what's more, I felt he thought I was using poetic license to put on something of a front, to hide that I didn't really know what I would do. Never mind that my résumé explicitly shows my two decades' experience – let's just say I've answered his question in practice more than a few times already.

So he asked me if I had read what had been published on the philosophy of objects. I answered that not only had I read it, I'd written some of it. He quoted from a famous programmer: "There is beauty in objects because they model reality." The interviewer then looked me squarely in the eye – with some other witnesses watching carefully – and posed this question with all the fervor of David Boies finding a new glitch in Microsoft's videotape: *"Do you deny this?"*

"That depends on how you define re – "I began, but was cut off.

"Don't give me your dependencies, and don't shirk the question; yes or no, do you deny that objects model reality?"

"Yes." It was the only logical response open to me. In the reality I live in, governed by people, not processors, objects are tangible. In the conceptual reality of computers, by their very definition, objects are abstract. In fact, they are made more useful in computer programs by their own abstraction – if you read Dennis Ritchie, P. J. Plauger, Bertrand Meyer, and their colleagues, you understand this abstraction. This is what I would like to have said next, had I had the floor.

Instead, I heard: "Then you cast aside thirty years of history. You, from your vantage point, have the authority to turn your back on everything Microsoft stands for?"

"Microsoft?" was the word on the verge of escaping from my lips, as if to ask, "What have *they* to do with this?" But then I restrained myself, and said instead, "I'm not turning my back on anyone. My experience has simply placed me at a different vantage point, which works as well for me as for those who waste their time making objects out of invoices." (I had published a series of articles back in the 1980s called "Vantage Point," one of which presented a one-on-one interview with the man named Zack Urlocker who helped coin the term "instantiation," but this fellow wasn't aware of that.)

The truth of the matter is, I don't really disagree with the *heart* of the concept that objects model reality. In reality, processes take place all the time that are best described as mathematical, procedural phenomena. Computer programs do not invent some artificial reality wherein these processes have entirely different meaning – as much as some might like for them to, simply for the opportunity to exploit them for science fiction. All reality is based on perception; and the best programs ever written were conceived by those people who have the clearest, most precise perception of reality – albeit from their own vantage point of reality. Yet any program devised to be capable of handling and interpreting multiple future, unforeseen situations and circumstances must be capable of treating those circumstances with a modicum of what James Boren, the brother of the former US Senator from Oklahoma, called "fuzzification." Without it, too much mathematics would need to be applied to write the rules and exceptions that distinguish one set of circumstances from another.

But in the end, you may be wondering, after the fog from all the instantiation and fuzzification had cleared, was I hired? After all the methodological clamor, did we ever get down to the business of real-world work? Let's just say I've had more time to think about the answer to that question than I expected to have.

In Brief

◆ The `Declare` statement sets up the rules for data interchange between a VBA program and an external function belonging to a compiled dynamic link library (DLL). This interface allows the VBA program to make contact with the function at run time.

◆ The `Type` statement sets up a series of data elements in memory, and gathers them together using a collective variable. This composite variable is only similar to a class in that its members are addressed like properties of a class. Aside from that, `Type` is far less functional than a class module for the deployment of variables that describe characteristics of data. However, `Type` declarations are often necessary to establish data structures that are compatible with external functions.

◆ The initialization file in Windows was created in order for an application to be capable of maintaining a small number of permanent parameters, especially between sessions. Its role in Windows has largely been replaced by the System Registry, which, in effect, gives us an indirect sanction to utilize the private portion of the .INI system for our own purposes.

♦ When developing a VBA class module, your property terms should refer exclusively to aspects of the object to which they're attached in the reference. If a property term actually describes some aspect of its arguments (inside the parentheses), it should be rephrased as a method.

♦ A class module declares a custom event with the `Event` statement, and then signals that event to the class' instantiator with the `RaiseEvent` statement.

Chapter 11

Packaging and Distributing Office Functionality

IN THIS CHAPTER

◆ Constructing a viable add-in project

◆ Building new and permanent functionality into custom Excel toolbars

◆ Writing redistributable code for the different Office 2000 applications

◆ Importing VBA functionality into the user's own templates painlessly

◆ Using the Setup Wizard, featured with Office 2000 Developer

THIS CHAPTER FOCUSES ON VBA projects that are designed to be distributed and installed on multiple processors, and that augment or change the functionality of Office 2000 applications in a noticeable, and seemingly permanent, manner. This is about making a real improvement in how everyone uses an O2K application all the time – not just one type of document or one specific template, but the application as a whole.

Redefining the Office Application

As Excel 2000 evolves as an application, its classification as a spread-*sheet* program becomes something of a misnomer. Large sheets are being replaced in user's workspaces by smaller, multiple information nuclei that are bridged together by the common bond of the workbook. (It's really Borland's Quattro Pro that deserves credit for being the first application to use the concept of spreadsheet binding.) Excel has added some tools to help the links between data across worksheets make more sense to the human user. For instance, when the user places the cursor into the formula bar now, Excel color-codes the cell addresses in the formula, then draws temporary borders around those same ranges among the open worksheets using the same colors. This way, the user may more easily attribute a cell address in a formula to "this area here," rather than have to imagine the area in his mind.

With the trend toward multitudes of related worksheets, one may wonder whether it's time to add to Excel some of the functionality that a user depends on for his Web browser. Excel 2000 does provide something called a *hyperlink*, but it's really more of a control that shuttles the user to a designated document, which is generally *not* another worksheet but an HTML file. What if instead, Excel were to have "Back" and "Next" buttons like a Web browser, taking the user from one spot to another in a logical sequence?

HTML documents already have encoded locations, called "targets," which serve as the predefined destinations for hyperlink-initiated jumps from points in the text called "anchors." Excel worksheets have no such built-in connection points; but perhaps without too much difficulty or added esotericism, the user can be compelled to define these places on his own — to "record" the most important cells for later recall, not unlike hitting the "M+" key on the everyday pocket calculator.

Chapter 4 presented a "shadow cell recorder," for lack of a better term, that remembered certain locations the user had designated, and returned to them when the user pressed a certain keystroke. Borrowing the heart of that project, I developed a new project for this chapter that adds toolbar buttons to Excel. These buttons serve as hybrids between the "Previous" and "Next" buttons on a Web browser, and the "memory" buttons on a calculator. The objective with this new edition is to give the user the ability to record certain important locations, and browse through the workbook to locate them again later. Whatever recorded location this process pulls up is one that the user intended to recall later, not some insignificant location, thus making it somewhat easier for a user to find certain important data when he cannot recall any details about its location. Figure 11-1 shows the Excel window endowed with the finished product of this project.

What makes this project different from our Chapter 4 procedure is that, although the storage-and-retrieval mechanism is still last-in-first-out (LIFO), it now maintains an internal pointer to the spot in the stack arrays where recorded "shadow" regions will be stored — that is, the regions are moved toward the top of the stack as the user browses back, without the stored regions at the end of the array being deleted. This way, the user can "turn around" and browse forward, giving the user the sense of floating freely through the sequence...or at least, floating as freely as a spreadsheet application may compel one to float.

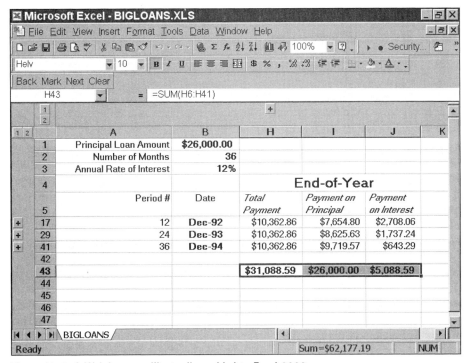

Figure 11-1: A Web browser-like toolbar added to Excel 2000.

Excel does not categorize template files separately

When you begin a new template project in Word 2000, you select New from the File menu, then in the dialog box that pops up, you click on the option marked **Template**. Excel 2000 has no such option, nor does it have any specific type of worksheet that you can designate as a template when you *begin* a project. **An Excel worksheet becomes a template when you first save it.** So your first step in programming a new template for Excel – before you do anything else – is to save your work. In the Save As dialog box, under the list box marked **Save as type**, is the entry **Template (.xlt)**.

Toolbar setup procedures must be in general modules

Before we begin, a disclaimer of sorts: The Windows component responsible for managing the toolbars for all the O2K applications is the same component. So the way toolbars work in this example is not specific to Excel.

In keeping with the trend to make things more modular, I was forced to place the major procedures for our Excel template project within an independent general module called BackNext, although it would have been more convenient for them to have appeared in the ThisWorkbook module. The reasons for this are numerous, inescapable, and esoteric: Toolbar controls as defined within Office 2000 applications are not ActiveX controls, as are the Forms 2.0 controls used in generating form modules. Instead, they are elements of MFC that are looking for "function pointers" – a type of tool that VBA does not provide. The only way that VBA can satisfy MFC's need for function pointers is for the interpreter to supply MFC with a table of addresses for its Excel "macros." We already know that Excel VBA procedures are not really macros by the standard definition; but when an Excel user tries to execute what Excel itself calls a "macro," he is presented with a list of public procedures located in general modules. The list provided to MFC contains these procedures. **Procedures in object modules, whether they are public or private, do not qualify as Excel "macros" in its Macros list.** So a Public Sub procedure inside the ThisWorkbook module is, by definition, invisible to a CommandBar object, whereas a Private Sub procedure inside a general module is, by definition, visible to that object. So much for clear-cut rules of scope.

The Office object library treats a toolbar button as a Control class object, which is a constituent of the CommandBar class. Every Control class object requires the name of the procedure to be executed whenever the user operates it. Not an event procedure *per se*, because Control objects don't recognize events the way we've come to understand them in Chapter 10. In fact, the name of the procedure is supplied as a *literal* that's assigned to a *property* of the object representing the Control object. For example, in ctrlThis.OnAction = "GoBack" the name of the procedure Public Sub GoBack() is supplied to the .OnAction property of the object ctrlThis. So when the user clicks on this Control object, GoBack() responds to it, rather than the "Private Sub ctrlThis_Click()" procedure we'd rather use.

The handler procedures for toolbar buttons must appear in general (i.e., non-object) modules. But the procedure needed for setting up the toolbar is Private Sub Workbook_Open(), which is an event procedure of the ThisWorkbook module – undeniably an object module. Even if the body of the setup procedure is set off in a separate procedure, it needs to at least be triggered by the Workbook_Open event. We're forced to divide the toolbar procedures among two modules: one general and one ThisWorkbook. This means that some variables necessary for managing a custom toolbar's contents must be declared Public; if they were declared Private, they would only be visible to about half the toolbar-oriented procedures.

Which module gets the responsibility for declaring the public and module-level variables? The custom toolbar will require *arrays* to maintain the contents of any number of buttons. Here we run into yet another barricade: VBA does not allow an object module to declare dynamic arrays as Public. This is because object modules are unofficially COM *components*, and the interface between those components must be explicitly specified. Shared data under COM follows specific rules, among them the one that prohibits two components from sharing structures of elements whose size and breadth cannot be explicitly defined at run time. So although a VBA object module or class module is a "pretend" component (it becomes a component at run time and ceases to be a component when execution ends), it follows this rule of COM like the cleverest of impostors.

This same set of COM rules hinders us on the opposite end of this project. Perhaps you'll recall this little gem from Chapter 10: **VBA does not allow a general module to declare object references or class instances** WithEvents. By definition, a general module does not know how to handle the mechanisms of an object. We need to declare a reference WithEvents to the most important object available, Excel itself. The reason is because we require the toolbar to be responsive to certain events generated by Excel.Application, the object that represents Excel's automation component. One of these events is _SheetSelectionChange, which occurs whenever the cell indicator is moved, either by the user or by Excel. So the event procedures must be located in the object module ThisWorkbook. But they will require access to some of the same data used by the procedures that set up the toolbar.

As a result of all of this, we have to make development decisions that are based more on methodological politics than program architecture. The Public declarations for arrays must be placed in the general module – which in this example is named Console, and which will also contain the handler procedures for the toolbar buttons. These declarations are as follows:

```
Public strSelection() As String, strStackCell() As String, _
-strStackRange() As String, strStackSheet() As String, _
-strStackBook() As String
Public iShadows As Integer, iWhereNow As Integer
Public bJustMark As Boolean
```

A reference to Excel.Application must be declared if only to enable the events recognized by that object, and even if the reference itself is never utilized in any other instruction besides the one that makes it point to Excel.Application. Hold on a moment – isn't that a bit redundant? You first declare the reference As Excel.Application, then you make it point to Excel.Application later? That's exactly right. The instruction you place in the Declarations section of ThisWorkbook is this:

```
Private WithEvents appThis As Excel.Application
```

Then in an early procedure, such as `Private Sub Workbook_Open()`, you invoke this instruction:

```
Set appThis = Excel.Application
```

The object module is now capable of handling event procedures such as `Private Sub appThis_SheetSelectionChange()`. Now you know several more reasons why, in Chapter 9, we established a protocol that an object module should refrain from declaring public variables.

Some more information about public variables before we continue: I dubbed each remembered worksheet range a "shadow." Our new "cursor," to borrow a term from database programming, is `iWhereNow`, which will hold the mutual index for the locations in all of the arrays where the next recorded shadow will be stored. As the user browses "Back" through the list, `iWhereNow` is decremented. When the user stores a new shadow region in the middle of the list, the tail end is cropped off, and `iWhereNow` points to the end of the list. This is similar to the way a Web browser stores and recalls HTTP addresses. When the user clicks on the Web browser's Back button several times, and then clicks on a hyperlink on the recalled page, the stored Web pages that the user passed over along the way back are discarded. Our system here will work in much the same way. Variable `iShadows` will hold the total number of shadows currently in memory, and `bJustMark` will act as a utility variable that makes this toolbar behave the way a user expects.

Setting up a toolbar through the CommandBars object

Listing 11-1 presents the procedure that gets our project off the ground. It involves setting up a new, exclusive toolbar with its own buttons that will run for the duration of this project in memory, and will terminate itself once Excel is exited.

Listing 11-1: Setting up the toolbar controls in the Console general module.

```
Public Sub SetupToolbar()
    Dim cmdBar As CommandBar, ctrlThis As CommandBarButton

    iWhereNow = 1
    Set cmdBar = Application.CommandBars.Add(Name:="BackNext")
    Set ctrlThis = Application.CommandBars("BackNext").Controls _
     .Add(Type:=msoControlButton, Temporary:=True)
    With ctrlThis
        .OnAction = "GoBack"
        .Style = msoButtonCaption
        .Caption = "Back"
        .Visible = True
        .Enabled = False
```

```
    End With
    Set ctrlThis = Application.CommandBars("BackNext").Controls _
     .Add(Type:=msoControlButton, Temporary:=True)
    With ctrlThis
        .OnAction = "MarkThis"
        .Style = msoButtonCaption
        .Caption = "Mark"
        .Visible = True
        .Enabled = True
    End With
    Set ctrlThis = Application.CommandBars("BackNext").Controls _
     .Add(Type:=msoControlButton, Temporary:=True)
    With ctrlThis
        .OnAction = "GoForth"
        .Style = msoButtonCaption
        .Caption = "Next"
        .Visible = True
        .Enabled = False
    End With
    Set ctrlThis = Application.CommandBars("BackNext").Controls _
     .Add(Type:=msoControlButton, Temporary:=True)
    With ctrlThis
        .OnAction = "ClearAll"
        .Style = msoButtonCaption
        .Caption = "Clear"
        .Visible = True
        .Enabled = False
    End With
    With cmdBar
        .Position = msoBarTop
        .Visible = True
    End With
End Sub
```

The toolbar must be set up immediately after the worksheet template is officially loaded. At that particular moment, Excel recognizes the _Open event for the Workbook object. We can use that event as a trigger for the toolbar setup procedure, with this event procedure:

```
Private Sub Workbook_Open()
    Set appThis = Excel.Application
    SetupToolbar
End Sub
```

You would think that, since a toolbar is really an object – a `CommandBar` class object that is a member of the `CommandBars` collection – its handler procedures would need to be located in an object module. Ironically, because the toolbar is the type of object that makes itself available to more than one O2K application, its handler procedures must be assembled in a *non*-object module.

How VBA addresses an application's toolbars

Excel, like the other O2K applications, maintains a collection object named `CommandBars` that represents the set of all toolbars used by the application. Its constituents are `CommandBar` class objects that contain, simply enough, `Command-BarButton` objects. Beginning to sound like Power Rangers? Just imagine all of Excel's toolbars addressed together as `CommandBars`, with each individual toolbar referenceable by a `CommandBar` class variable. The controls within a toolbar are numbered consecutively, and addressed collectively as `Controls`, and as the constituent of a `CommandBar`. That should be clear enough; all of the controls in a toolbar are collectively a constituent of that toolbar. Each individual control in the `Controls` set is a `CommandBarButton` class object (forgive the inconsistency, but that's the way it is).

As it stands now, `CommandBars` represents all of the toolbars that Excel came in with at startup. Each member of the collection can be indexed by its index number – which is impractical since ordinal position is generally unimportant – or by its `.Name` property, which is the same name for the toolbar that appears in the popup menu when you right-click on Excel's toolbar area. Thus `Command Bars("Standard")` refers to the Excel toolbar that has the New, Open, and Save icons. With VBA, you add a new toolbar to the collection by means of the `.Add` method. Here, `CommandBars.Add` is phrased like a function, the return value of which is a reference to the new `CommandBar` class object that's assigned to variable `cmdBar`. Its sole required argument is the `Name:` parameter that will be used to index the new toolbar in the `CommandBars` collection – in this case, `"BackNext"`. (When you work with `CommandBars` for any substantial length of time, you find yourself yearning for crunchy, peanutty nougat.)

Our new command bar – which was assembled in Listing 11-1 – will contain four controls, which are added one at a time. The process is pretty much the same with each of the four controls: An `.Add` method introduces a new control to the toolbar's collection. The `Type:` parameter setting `msoControlButton` distinguishes the control as a button, as opposed to a combo box, a drop-down list, a standard text entry field, or a popup menu. The method returns a reference to the new control, which is assigned to the variable `ctrlThis`. Leaving out the `Id:` parameter from this `.Add` method allows the new control to be "user-defined," which is a poor term for a control whose characteristics are not defined by the program.

Within a `With` block for `ctrlThis`, the essential properties are set. The `.Style` property setting of `msoButtonCaption` assigns the button as text only, no icons. If I had set `.Style` for `msoButtonIcon` instead, the `Id:` parameter from the `.Add` method would have been used to designate which icon in Excel's repertoire to use as the button face. Excel has a limited inventory of "button faces" – icons used for its own buttons – so unless you want your toolbar to look suspiciously similar to an existing one, you might want to stick with captions for now.

Toolbar buttons link to old-style handler procedures

What will be unusual to first-time VBA programmers, but perhaps familiar to long-time Excel programmers, is the way that modern toolbar buttons use the old-style *handler procedures* to respond to user actions. Handler procedures are a throwback to the time before event procedures. The names of the handler procedures were (and in this case, are) entirely arbitrary, but they are then assigned as string literals to certain properties of the `Control` class object, so that it knows the name of the procedure to execute when the user operates it. In the case of the four toolbar buttons, `GoBack`, `MarkThis`, `GoForth`, and `ClearAll` are names of procedures that are executed in response to the user clicking on their respective controls. These names are assigned to the `.OnAction` property for the controls.

The final `With  cmdBar` clause in `Public  Sub  SetupToolbar()` sets the `.Position` property for the new toolbar to the upper part of the workspace frame and then makes it visible. All new toolbars are invisible by default until their `.Visible` properties are set to `True`.

The crucial procedure for this project is still `Private  Sub  CollectShadow()`, revised but still resembling its prior logic, as Listing 11-2 shows.

Listing 11-2: Revising the LIFO structure for a floating pointer.

```
Public Sub CollectShadow()
    Dim objShape As Shape
    Dim bDone As Boolean

    If iWhereNow < iShadows Then
        iShadows = iWhereNow
    Else
        iShadows = iShadows + 1
    End If
    ReDim Preserve strSelection(iShadows), _
     strStackCell(iShadows), strStackRange(iShadows), _
     strStackSheet(iShadows), strStackBook(iShadows)
    strSelection(iWhereNow) = TypeName(Selection)
    Select Case TypeName(Selection)
        Case "Range"
            strStackBook(iWhereNow) = ActiveWorkbook.Name
            strStackSheet(iWhereNow) = _
```

Continued

Listing 11-2: Revising the LIFO structure for a floating pointer. *(Continued)*

```
            ActiveWorkbook.ActiveSheet.Name
        strStackRange(iWhereNow) = Selection.Address
        strStackCell(iWhereNow) = ActiveCell.Address
    Case "ChartArea"
        strStackBook(iWhereNow) = ActiveWorkbook.Name
        strStackSheet(iWhereNow) = _
        ActiveWorkbook.ActiveSheet.Name
        strStackRange(iWhereNow) = Right$(ActiveChart.Name, _
        Len(ActiveChart.Name) - Len(ActiveSheet.Name) - 1)
    Case "OLEObject"
        strStackBook(iWhereNow) = ActiveWorkbook.Name
        strStackSheet(iWhereNow) = _
        ActiveWorkbook.ActiveSheet.Name
        strStackRange(iWhereNow) = Selection.Name
    Case Else
        If ActiveSheet.Type = xlWorksheet Then
            For Each objShape In ActiveSheet.Shapes
                If objShape.Name = Selection.Name Then
                    strStackBook(iWhereNow) = _
                    ActiveWorkbook.Name
                    strStackSheet(iWhereNow) = _
                    ActiveWorkbook.ActiveSheet.Name
                    strStackRange(iWhereNow) = Selection.Name
                    bDone = True
                    Exit For
                End If
            Next objShape
        ElseIf ActiveSheet.Type = -4100 Then
            strStackBook(iWhereNow) = ActiveWorkbook.Name
            strStackSheet(iWhereNow) = _
            ActiveWorkbook.ActiveChart.Name
            strStackRange(iWhereNow) = "CHARTSHEET"
            strStackCell(iWhereNow) = _
            ActiveWorkbook.ActiveChart.Name
            bDone = True
        End If
        If Not bDone Then Beep
    End Select
    CommandBars("BackNext").Controls(1).Enabled = True
    CommandBars("BackNext").Controls(4).Enabled = True
End Sub
```

A few things have changed since Chapter 4: First, the procedure now knows to check whether the current selection is within a standard worksheet or a chart sheet. If it is a chart sheet, we need to record that fact; but because chart sheets contain Chart objects the way embedded charts contain Chart objects, we need something to distinguish one from the other. So we cheated: Whenever a chart sheet position is being recorded (ActiveSheet.Type = -4100), the raw string literal "CHARTSHEET" is assigned to the stack variable that generally records ranges.

At the end of the revised procedure, two of the controls in the toolbar are turned on. The only way to directly refer to individual members of the Controls collection is by their index numeral; they have no names of their own. The order always proceeds from left to right for horizontal toolbars, from the top down for vertical toolbars. So Controls(1) is the "Back" button, which we can now turn on because the user now has something to go back to; and Controls(4) is the "Clear" button, which works now because there is something to be cleared.

The handler procedure that returns the cell indicator back to the previously recorded range appears in Listing 11-3.

Listing 11-3: Sending the indicator back where it came from.

```
Private Sub GoBack()
    If iWhereNow > 1 Then
        If iWhereNow = iShadows + 1 Then CollectShadow
        If bJustMark Then
            iWhereNow = iWhereNow - 2
        Else
            iWhereNow = iWhereNow - 1
        End If
        ReturnToShadow iWhereNow
        CommandBars("BackNext").Controls(3).Enabled = True
        If iWhereNow = 1 Then
            CommandBars("BackNext").Controls(1).Enabled = False
        End If
    End If
    bJustMark = False
End Sub
```

The procedure that takes the user back to the most recently stored location, Private Sub GoBack(), may be the one most frequently executed. Variable iWhereNow was declared Public, so both the workbook module and the independent Console module will recognize it. Back at Private Sub Workbook_Open() in the ThisWorkbook module, iWhereNow was set to an initial value of 1, and will never be decremented below that value. Variable iWhereNow will equal 1 even when iShadows, the number of stored locations, is 0.

If iWhereNow equals 1 at the time Private Sub GoBack() starts, there's nothing to go back to. Otherwise, one of the important features that a user will expect of this toolbar without even knowing that she expects it, will be the ability to return to that point from which the browsing commenced in the first place. So when the internal cursor is at the end of the list (`iWhereNow = iShadows + 1`), meaning that browsing has not yet begun, the current location is "pushed" onto the stacks automatically with the call to `Public Sub CollectShadow()`. Recall from Chapter 4, in stack mechanics, "pushing" places a value onto the top of the stack and "popping" takes it off the stack.

The Boolean variable `bJustMark` is present for only one reason, which may seem trivial, although it does become important later: If the user clicked on the Mark button to store the current location, and then clicked on the Back button immediately afterward without moving the cell pointer first, the procedure would normally move the cell pointer from where it is now. . . to where it is now, which was the last recorded position. To the user, that would seem wrong; she would have to click twice to get the pointer to move. So `bJustMark` is a flag variable that registers True if the user has just clicked on the Mark button; if the user does anything else first, it blinks out to False. If the user did just click on Mark, then `iWhereNow` will need to hop over two positions to take the cell pointer to where the user expects it to be; otherwise, it only needs to move back one. That's the function of the `If bJustMark Then` loop clause.

Once `Private Sub GoBack()` has moved `iWhereNow` to where it needs to be, the call is placed to `Private Sub ReturnToShadow()`, which recalls the designated shadow location and places the cell pointer there. `Controls(3)`, which is the Next button, is then turned on; and if `iWhereNow` has backed up to the beginning of the list, `Controls(1)` — the Back button — is turned off. The caption goes gray when a button is turned off, so the user can clearly see she has reached a border. Finally, `bJustMark` is turned off to let future procedures know that the user clicked on something other than Mark.

Handling the request to mark a location is no big deal, as Listing 11-4 indicates:

Listing 11-4: Triggering the process that records a shadow location.

```
Private Sub MarkThis()
    CollectShadow
    iWhereNow = iWhereNow + 1
    bJustMark = True
End Sub
```

This procedure simply places the call to `Sub CollectShadow()`, advances `iWhereNow` to the next point, and turns `bJustMark` on.

Moving the indicator forward in the shadow list, after it has already moved back one or more positions, is a job for the procedure in Listing 11-5:

Listing 11-5: Making the U-turn and heading forward once again.

```
Private Sub GoForth()
```

```
    If iWhereNow <= iShadows Then
        iWhereNow = iWhereNow + 1
        ReturnToShadow iWhereNow
        If iWhereNow = iShadows + 1 Then
            CommandBars("BackNext").Controls(3).Enabled = False
        End If
        If iWhereNow > 1 Then
            CommandBars("BackNext").Controls(1).Enabled = True
        End If
    End If
    bJustMark = False
End Sub
```

Private Sub GoForth() is almost a logical converse of Private Sub GoBack(), advancing iWhereNow if there's space ahead of it in the list, then turning off the Next button if it encounters the rightmost end of the list, again turning on the Back button, and turning off bJustMark.

The job of the fourth button in the toolbar is to reset all current conditions and drop the current recorded list in memory, as Listing 11-6 shows:

Listing 11-6: Dropping everything and starting over from shadow one.

```
Private Sub ClearAll()
    iShadows = 0
    iWhereNow = 1
    ReDim strSelection(iShadows), strStackCell(iShadows), _
      strStackRange(iShadows), strStackSheet(iShadows), _
      strStackBook(iShadows)
    CommandBars("BackNext").Controls(1).Enabled = False
    CommandBars("BackNext").Controls(3).Enabled = False
    CommandBars("BackNext").Controls(4).Enabled = False
End Sub
```

Private Sub ClearAll() clears all of the stacks and resets all of the pointers. Here is proof that you can effectively re-dimension your dynamic array variables with a length of 0 — the value of iShadows at the time the ReDim statement is executed — without killing the array references. Once that's done, the procedure turns off all the buttons except for Mark.

The procedure that moves the cell pointer to where it needs to be is Private Sub ReturnToShadow(), a revision of its counterpart Private Sub GoBackToShadow() from Chapter 4. Listing 11-7 shows the new version.

Listing 11-7: Returning the cell pointer to any recalled position.

```
Private Sub ReturnToShadow(iWhich As Integer)
    Dim objBook As Workbook, objSheet As Worksheet, _
     objShape As Shape
    Dim bDone As Boolean
    If iShadows > 0 Then
        For Each objBook In Workbooks
            If objBook.Name = strStackBook(iWhich) Then
                Workbooks(strStackBook(iWhich)).Activate
                If strStackRange(iWhich) = "CHARTSHEET" Then
                    ActiveWorkbook.Charts(strStackCell(iWhich)) _
                     .Activate
                Else
                    For Each objSheet In Worksheets
                        If objSheet.Name = strStackSheet(iWhich) _
                        Then
                            ActiveWorkbook.Worksheets _
                                (strStackSheet(iWhich)).Activate
                            Select Case strSelection(iWhich)
                                Case "Range"
                                    Range(strStackRange(iWhich)) _
                                    .Select
                                    Range(strStackCell(iWhich)) _
                                    .Activate
                                Case "ChartArea"
                                    Worksheets _
                                    (strStackSheet(iWhich)) _
                                    .ChartObjects _
                                    (strStackRange(iWhich)) _
                                    .Activate
                                Case "OLEObject"
                                    Worksheets _
                                    (strStackSheet(iWhich)) _
                                    .OLEObjects _
                                    (strStackRange(iWhich)) _
                                    .Activate
                                Case Else
                                    For Each objShape In _
                                    ActiveSheet.Shapes
                                        If objShape.Name = _
                                        strStackRange(iWhich) _
                                        Then _
                                            objShape.Select
                                        End If
```

```
                            Next objShape
                        End Select
                        bDone = True
                    End If
                Next objSheet
            End If
        End If
    Next objBook
    If iWhereNow = iShadows Then
        CommandBars("BackNext").Controls(3).Enabled = False
    ElseIf iWhereNow <= iShadows Then
        CommandBars("BackNext").Controls(3).Enabled = True
    End If
    End If
    If Not bDone Then Beep
End Sub
```

There are only a few changes here from the version in Chapter 4 to take note of. First of all, a new conditional clause checks to see whether the recorded region is a chart sheet (remember that "CHARTSHEET" literal in Listing 11-2), before it goes checking for other types. Toward the end, the value of iWhereNow is checked to see if it has bumped against the edge of the stack yet, and turns off the Next button if it has, or on if it has not.

Only a few more unsettled matters to be covered: The project needs to turn off the bJustMark flag whenever the user does something, *anything*, between clicking on Mark and clicking on Back. Determining whether the user has done *anything* is the work of event procedures. But these procedures need to rely not on a specific workbook or worksheet, but on the Application object. Why? Because to the user should not have to amend her own work with VBA code each time she creates a new worksheet; the user should not have to be indoctrinated into the realm of VBA programming if she doesn't want to be. So within Private Sub Workbook_Open(), you'll find the instruction Set appThis = Excel.Application written near the very top. From that point on, appThis represents the Application class for the workbook module. This instruction makes way for the event procedures shown in Listing 11-8.

Listing 11-8: Event procedures for simple housekeeping.

```
Private Sub appThis_SheetChange(ByVal Sh As Object, _
 ByVal Target As Excel.Range)
    bJustMark = False
End Sub


Private Sub appThis_SheetSelectionChange(ByVal Sh As Object, _
 ByVal Target As Excel.Range)
    bJustMark = False
End Sub
```

These procedures turn bJustMark off whenever the user moves the cell pointer or types anything new into a cell, and that is all that these procedures need to do. Yet having these procedures available is invaluable to us; without them we would have had to introduce into the project a non-sensible way to work.

Finally, within the ThisWorkbook module, we need this last simple shutdown operation, shown in Listing 11-9.

Listing 11-9: Getting rid of the temporary toolbar for next time.

```
Private Sub Workbook_BeforeClose(Cancel As Boolean)
    Application.CommandBars("BackNext").Delete
End Sub
```

All this does is makes certain that BackNext doesn't become a permanent feature of Excel, because Excel will remember new toolbars even into the next session. If you *want* Excel to remember this new toolbar, you may leave this procedure out entirely.

VBA procedures can be linked directly to new or existing Excel toolbars. The Excel object library maintains a CommandBars collection that describes all of the toolbars the application has ever used. An .Add method brings in a new toolbar, that can be described entirely in code. Handler procedures, instead of event procedures, are employed to respond to the user operating added toolbars or toolbar controls; this replaces the need for the user to link controls to macros. The names of these handler procedures are assigned as string literals to the .OnAction properties of the indexed Controls contained within the CommandBars collection.

The VBA Module as Installable Component

Up to this point, you may be wondering, do we truly expect the user to have to bring in a new workbook or template each time just so she can have this cute toolbar? What we really want is for this toolbar to appear to be integrated into Excel, so the user doesn't have to think about the workbook to which the VBA code belongs. But doesn't this mean the workspace is cluttered with an extra workbook that, besides being the bearer of VBA code, has no other practical purpose? Not if we work this out properly, by making our project into an add-in workbook.

Registering a project to load and run automatically

Most *add-ins* in Microsoft Office 2000 are compiled programs supplied by dynamic link libraries, and that act as dynamically installed COM components. A VBA add-in is a standard project that masquerades as a dynamically installed component. When you construct a VBA program to serve as an add-in, you accomplish the following:

♦ You eliminate the need to designate and deploy a "startup template." This relieves you from having to write startup code that might or might not be used in startup templates, whose code checks whether it is really being executed in a startup capacity.

♦ Code belonging to an add-in project can be loaded in at startup and executed as soon as possible without user intervention. Neither the application nor VBA will be available to the user until the add-in is ready to cede control back to that application.

♦ Objects and variables declared Public by the add-in project are accessible by other visible (that is, *real*) workbooks and other VBA projects. Public procedures may be contacted from VBA projects and, in the case of Excel, from active formulas in the worksheet.

There are a few steps involved into making an Excel VBA project into an auto-loading, auto-running system, none of which involves VBA instructions, and some of which involve interacting with the Excel application. Here is the process:

1. In the VBA Projects window, click on the name of the document module for the project. In Excel, this is the ThisWorkbook module (not the general module, but the one at the bottom of the group "Microsoft Excel Objects").

2. In the Properties window, change the .IsAddIn property for ThisWorkbook to True.

3. Save the project, giving it a filename that will identify the add-in among other add-in names – in other words, refrain from using abbreviations that the user will not recognize. Your project is now an add-in. Next, Excel has to recognize it as one of its own.

4. From Excel's Tools menu, click on Add-ins. Excel will bring up a list of *known* add-ins – that is, components that Excel has seen before. Your new add-in will *not* be in this list, so click on Browse.

5. From the file selector, find the .XLA file where your add-in was stored, choose that, and click on OK. This enrolls the add-in in the list.

6. Now find the name again in the Add-ins list — it should appear there this time — then check the box beside that name and click on OK.

At this point, Excel knows to load in this project every time it starts up. As a result, the `Private Sub Workbook_Open()` procedure — which is geared to be executed immediately when the workbook is opened — will be executed as soon as the add-in is loaded. This does change the makeup of the add-in project just slightly: The `Workbook_Open` and `Workbook_BeforeClose` events are now basically equivalent to "application startup" and "application shutdown" procedures, respectively. Not even Excel's own `Application` object generates events that occur exactly at startup and exactly at shutdown.

In Depth: Distributing Functionality That Cannot Stand Alone

A complex VBA project that requires more than one Office 2000 application to be installed, plus the services of one or more of Microsoft's so-called *shared components*, plus any number of extra fonts and drop-in controls, tends to be tailored to the system on which it was originated. It worked on your system while you were developing it, so since this is for Office 2000, shouldn't it work on everyone else's?

It isn't very likely that a major VBA exercise composed on one system can be transplanted to some other system with the expectation that it will work or even perform in the same manner. The Windows setup on most users' systems tends to become, shall we say, *personalized* over time. Simply because you have some resource available to you on your system does not mean that all of your users have that same resource, or that they even have the means to attain that resource. And as some of your users customize their own systems, thereby changing or replacing some critical resources, while other users leave their systems more standardized, you may find yourself having to simultaneously support two or more sets of identically-named system resources. A custom ActiveX control, a specialized font, or the presence of some other application or "in-process server" used by your VBA project needs some way to be transported to your users' systems.

Part of the problem concerns the fact that a VBA project is not, at its core, an encapsulated element of executable code like any other program you may write. You're not giving away something that shows up in Windows Explorer as an .EXE file with its own icon that a user might double-click to run. Instead, a VBA project is an intrinsic part of a document or some other data product, or of the template used within the O2K application in the production of that product. You're distributing functionality that your users may not know they need, and even after it's been installed, might not even know they have. A VBA project is that much more shy, if you will, than your ordinary redistributable application.

If this were a Visual Basic 6.0 project, you could compile your source code into a stand-alone .EXE file. This file could contain so-called *p-code* or "processor code" that consists of the rudimentary symbols needed by a certain dynamic link library, MSVBVM60.DLL, to recognize your instructions and run your application. Beginning with VB version 5.0, it is now possible for you to build true, stand-alone executable code for your .EXE file that doesn't require the presence of the VB run-time dynamic link library. But as I've said so many times before, VBA is not Visual Basic... *per se*. The VBA module does not stand alone, in an Explorer window or anywhere else. It is a melded part of one of the data products of an Office 2000 application. So in order for you to distribute the functionality of a VBA module, it has to be joined with the container of that data product, even if that container is otherwise quite empty.

Packaging redistributable code for Access

A VBA project made into a redistributable package must make certain assumptions about the nature of the data that makes up a good part of that package. Consider a module or set of modules for Access 2000, for instance. A majority of the ideas for a VBA project that you might come up with in your head probably concern actions that can take place with respect to a particular database or structure of database (at least, this is true for my own head). In other words, most of the extended functionality we may ever conceive for Access concerns specific databases or database schemas. While a Word 2000 template aids the user in composing a multitude of documents based on a specific style, most Access 2000 users operate a *builder* (Access' term for the basis of a database) to devise the *single* database that the business will continually use for its intended purpose. The Access user doesn't borrow a builder to make cookie-cutter copies of multiple databases with the same type because a business doesn't need multiple databases of the same type – usually just one.

The type of VBA module you would want to redistribute to Access users as an all-purpose device issued *for that module's own sake* (rather than to aid in the processing of a specific existing database), would be an *add-in* that works like a wizard or a builder that aids the Access user in developing a new database or maintaining any other existing database that it happens to encounter. An Access add-in is packaged within an .MDA file, which is classified as an *Access library database.* The difference between this and an ordinary Access database is that the .MDA file is designed to contain routines that are addressable from the other VBA modules that belong to dedicated Access databases. Many different Access databases can utilize the VBA modules packaged within a library database. But a library database, while it is a library, is also still a database – which means that it has a database schema stored with it, even if it's blank. It isn't a stand-alone executable file.

If the library database isn't to be designed to address a database with a particular schema (because a business or a group of network users don't generally use more than one database with the same schema), then it probably should be designed to ascertain the schema of whatever database it will be applied to. This means that the library database (blank or not) should be designed to be "database-neutral," learning about the characteristics of the active database on which it will operate by means of polling its object properties.

What's "normal" about the Word template

A VBA module for Word 2000, by comparison, is often more applicable to the operation of the Word program as a whole, as much as it can be applied to the construction of any one type of document. It's easy to imagine, for instance, a simple Word module that cross-references article references and generates bibliographies automatically, or that checks for the presence of repetitive phrases in the body of a document's text (actually, the grammar checker already has a similar feature, although it comes complete with a system for patronizing its user). A document does not have to be styled in any particular way for this functionality to work. All added Word functionality has some global significance, if you will, to Word as a program unto itself.

Which leads us to Word's contextual problem: Any redistributable VBA projects that you build for Word are bound to a separate template file. To make these VBA projects apply to the application at large, they need to be attached to Word's Normal template. This is the template that Word loads automatically when it starts up and brings into the workspace a blank "Document1." It is also the template that Word applies by default to a new document that is generated when the user clicks on the New button in the toolbar or presses Ctrl+N.

 You can't install a Normal template directly into Word without overriding the old one, thereby eliminating any extended global functionality that previously existed.

To bring new pre-existent functionality into the Normal template, a user has to bring up Word's Organizer feature, open the Normal template and the VBA module template, and then manually transport the modules *by name* into Normal. This assumes that the user is informed in advance of your module's procedure names – and if you think about it, why should the user be informed in advance?

The way around this problem is to deploy a command button that is embedded within your *document* (remember, you can do that), and associate that button with a simple procedure that copies the new module into the user's existing Normal template without her having to run his copy of Organizer directly. The procedure is a simple one:

```
Private Sub ImportButton_Click()
    Application.OrganizerCopy Source:="New Macros.dot", _
       Destination:="Normal.dot", Name:="Citation", _
       Object:=wdOrganizerObjectProjectItems
End Sub
```

Here, the .Name property of the button on the document is ImportButton, the document template that contains the incoming template is New Macros.dot, and the name of the incoming "macro" is Citation. The .OrganizerCopy method is recognized by Word's Application object. The Source: and Destination: parameters are not full paths here, so this particular instruction assumes that both templates can be accessed from the same directory. Of course, these parameters can be modified to reflect the full path and filename of either or both files.

Packaging and PowerPoint

The whole point of a PowerPoint presentation is to be operable from a computer with a projector for its monitor, anywhere, at any time, regardless of whether the projecting computer actually has PowerPoint installed. This projection package (had enough alliteration yet?) is structurally somewhat different than PowerPoint's native .PPT file, which in a sense represents the work in progress.

When a PowerPoint presentation contains an ActiveX control that's contained by a slide, the program component that runs that ActiveX control is packaged as part of PowerPoint's "Pack and Go" version of the presentation. But when a presentation calls a PowerPoint VBA form module, the ActiveX component for UserForm (FM20.DLL) and the other general controls in the suite, plus any other controls the form may happen to contain, are not packaged with the "Pack and Go" .PPZ file. In other words, **when you distribute a VBA form module associated with PowerPoint, packaged or not, the module expects the controls to which it refers to already be installed on the system running the module.**

At Present: PowerPoint's "Pack and Go"

If you've ever programmed with a full-scale Visual Basic interpreter, you're familiar with developing an .FRM or .BAS file while you're writing the program, and saving it to a compiled .EXE file later. In a figuratively similar sense, PowerPoint's "project" is its own native .PPT file, while its "compiled" form comes in the form of a .PPZ file. When the user's presentation is in a complete and operable form, she "compiles" it by selecting Pack and Go from the File menu, and entering a separate filename in the dialog box. PowerPoint compresses into one file, in a manner similar to "zipping," all of the files that comprise the presentation, including the .PPT file and any graphics, fonts, and animations that accompany it.

What isn't obvious on the surface (and what isn't even documented) is the fact that that the .PPZ package also contains the .OCX files — the executable libraries — of all the ActiveX controls that may have been dropped into the presentation, along with an .INF file that acts as a setup script. This script is executed when the user launches the PNGSETUP.EXE file that accompanies the .PPZ file. This short executable is not packaged with the .PPZ file; its entire job is to be visible to the user, and to un-package and install all of the presentation's components, even if those components end up in the \WINDOWS\SYSTEM subdirectory.

Composing the Setup Routine

If you have the Developer edition of Office 2000 (ODE), you have a tool available for distributing VBA functionality so that the user *will* have all the same components you do (as long as you're sure to point out which ones they are). This tool is the Setup Wizard, and it is actually an Access library database. However, once you've installed the ODE Tools CD, you'll find the Setup Wizard enrolled in the Microsoft ODE Tools division of the Programs menu. When you launch it, the first dialog you'll see appears in Figure 11-1.

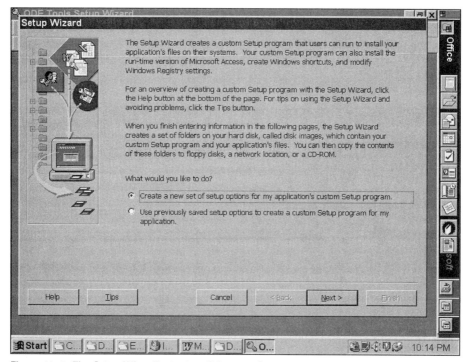

Setup Wizard

The Setup Wizard creates a custom Setup program that users can run to install your application's files on their systems. Your custom Setup program can also install the run-time version of Microsoft Access, create Windows shortcuts, and modify Windows Registry settings.

For an overview of creating a custom Setup program with the Setup Wizard, click the Help button at the bottom of the page. For tips on using the Setup Wizard and avoiding problems, click the Tips button.

When you finish entering information in the following pages, the Setup Wizard creates a set of folders on your hard disk, called disk images, which contain your custom Setup program and your application's files. You can then copy the contents of these folders to floppy disks, a network location, or a CD-ROM.

What would you like to do?

○ Create a new set of setup options for my application's custom Setup program.

○ Use previously saved setup options to create a custom Setup program for my application.

[Help]   [Tips]   [Cancel]   [< Back]   [Next >]   [Finish]

Figure 11-2: The Setup Wizard's startup dialog panel.

What the documentation fails to mention – for reasons that may become embarrassingly obvious in just a moment – is that the Setup Wizard program was originally intended for use exclusively with Access. To proceed to the part of this wizard where you build a setup script, you leave the option marked **Create a new set of setup options for my application's custom Setup program,** then click on Next. What you'll see next is the panel that appears in Figure 11-2, shown here with a few selections added.

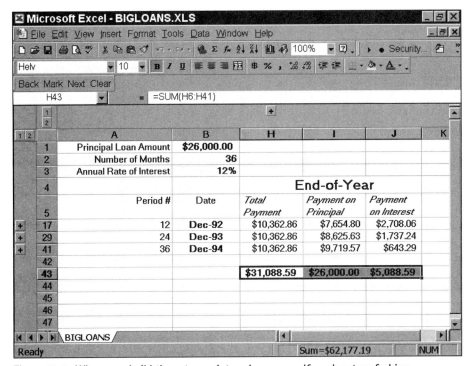

Figure 11-3: Where you build the setup script. . . in a non–self-explanatory fashion.

The list at the top marked List of Files will contain the filenames of all the files you're placing into the setup package, in the order in which they will be unpacked during the setup process on the user's end. Here is how you add files to this list and set their setup specifications:

1. Begin by clicking on Add. The standard Windows file selector box will be displayed.

2. At this point, the file selector is set up to display by default the components of an Access runtime database. Now, this is fairly convenient, if you're actually packaging an Access application. But for this example, we're building the setup file for a Word template that includes a VBA form module. The first file you choose should be the main focus of the setup, which in this example would be the template file.

3. In the File Properties frame, the Destination Path field represents the location where the unpackaged file will end up on the user's system. Here, the Setup Wizard recognizes symbols that act like string variables, standing in place of those setup parameters that the user chooses for herself. The three symbols in the Wizard's vernacular are as follows:

$(AppPath) – The location where the user has chosen the "main application," or the central files that make up the distribution package, to be installed. This assumes, of course, that the user has been informed as to where certain templates *should* go in order to be accessible (for instance, the \TEMPLATES directory of Office 97). Any subdirectory of $(AppPath) to be used or created by the setup program can be added to the end of this symbol; for example, $(AppPath)\USER.

$(WinPath) – The location on the user's system where Windows is installed.

$(WinSysPath) – The location on the user's system where the \SYSTEM folder of Windows is installed (generally \WINDOWS\SYSTEM).

4. If the file you've just added to the list is the *central* file of the installation (for instance, the template file as opposed to any associated files such as .DLLs), then check the box marked Set As Application's Main File.

5. The Overwrite Existing File list sets the option for how the setup program is to act if it encounters a file of the same name, in the same location as the file it's trying to install. Your choices here are Older (overwrite the file only if its timestamp is older than the setup version), Always (overwrite the file in any case), and Never (don't overwrite at all).

6. The Component Name list refers to the "grouping" of options given to the user of the setup program, where the files in this list will appear. **You only have one choice here,** and that's "Application." You cannot change this entry, even though it appears to be a viable option.

7. Repeat this process for as many files as you intend to package.

8. To save this list in a separate .MDT database template for use in building a future setup script, click on Save and type the name of the new template file in the dialog box.

9. To proceed to the next stage, click on Next. Figure 11-3 shows the dialog box that appears.

10. If you want to place a shortcut to this package someplace on the user's system – generally on the Desktop – click on Add. When the controls for the General Shortcut Properties become enabled, enter the text that is to appear beneath the shortcut icon in the field marked Description.

11. To give this shortcut a custom icon, click on the ellipsis button beside the field marked Icon File, and choose an icon from the file selector.

12. Leave all the other options here as they are. Frankly, they do not pertain to any of our objectives at present. Just click on Next, and you'll see the Registry Values portion of the setup routine, shown in Figure 11-4.

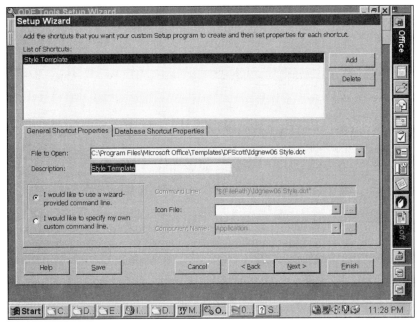

Figure 11-4: The parameters for a shortcut icon are entered here.

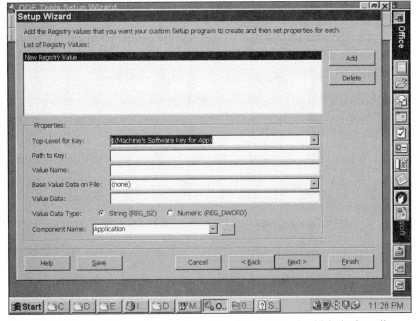

Figure 11-5: The Registry entries portion of the Setup Wizard, which don't really apply to us.

13. **Simple VBA projects do not need to alter any values in the Windows System Registry in order to run.** So this panel doesn't apply to us; it applies to people who are using this Setup Wizard to build an installation routine for an Access database. Just click on Next to proceed. The next panel you'll see is shown in Figure 11.5.

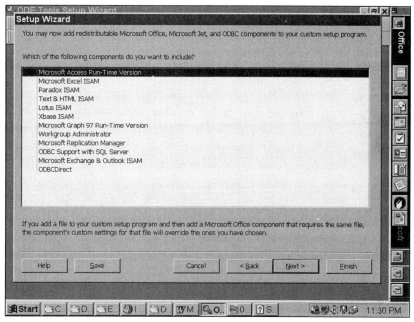

Figure 11-6: Adding redistributable Microsoft components to the list.

14. If you haven't already added the filenames for these redistributable Microsoft-brand components to the setup list, you have the option here of adding these components, which Microsoft lets you freely give away. Again, many of them pertain to run-time Access databases; but "Microsoft Graph Run-Time Version," for example, is a component which may play a role in the layout of a Word document, Excel worksheet, or PowerPoint presentation. Choose any of the components you need from this list, and then click on Finish.

15. If you haven't saved the template already (step 8), you're given the opportunity to do so here. Click on Yes or No. The Setup routine will begin the process of building "disk images," which consist of one or more groups of files of no more than 1.44Mb per group, capable of being saved to a sequence of floppy diskettes. The Setup Wizard will tell you everything was successful. Click on OK to exit the Wizard.

Like all VBA form modules for all O2K applications, you will need to include the FM20.DLL file in the setup. All installation routines for all versions of Office 2000 do install FM20.DLL automatically; but users who purchased just one of the applications by itself (the "home" edition of Word, for instance) may have chosen not to install VBA. So you can't merely assume FM20.DLL is present just because your user has *one* Office application. You will need to add it to your Files list (step 2 in the process above), then set its install location to $(WinSysPath) (step 3) to ensure that the file is placed in the \SYSTEM subdirectory. Make sure you set the Overwrite Existing File option (step 5) to Older, so the setup program will leave FM20.DLL alone if it's already present.

 VBA projects are not designed to be stand-alone entities; they are intrinsic parts of templates or documents used in the construction of Office 2000 data. As such, they are *extensions* to the data document package, rather than a package in and of themselves. You can use the VBA editor program to save your source code to a separate file; but then you'd need to educate your users on how to import that source code into their own templates, and that might be excessively difficult. Instead, you will want to craft ways of making your VBA functionality easy for the user to experiment with, and then to adopt. One way to accomplish this is to build a control into the document portion of the document template, whose _Click event procedure initiates a process that copies the *other* included VBA modules in the template to the current document or to the Normal template.

In Theory: Wires and Lights in a Box

Over the last eight years, Visual Basic has developed into an elaborate language whose prime purpose has become to facilitate other software components. You've seen how VBA relies on the Forms 2.0 dynamic link library to provide it with the basic ActiveX controls necessary for a module to communicate with its user. And while a VBA program can create, manipulate, and otherwise manage a massive database, the language does not have its own modern facilities for handling data, nor should it really. These facilities are provided to it by another component: the Jet database engine, which is utilized by VBA modules written for Access and Excel. All the facilities maintained by VBA for graphics and sound (what little sound there is) are provided by ActiveX controls — which are, officially, components. Were it not for COM components, every version of Visual Basic wouldn't be much more than an overloaded macro interpreter.

On the flip side, what is COM without Visual Basic? At the heart of the entire COM methodology are properties, methods, and events — which are tools of VB, not C++. Although COM's Interface Development Language (IDL) is actually a superset of the C++ vocabulary, the symbolism brought forth through the implementation of the interface is best expressed in Visual Basic. So while C++ is still the foundation of the system, Visual Basic is the focus of developers' attention. Intranet applications that involve Active Server Pages, Internet Information Server, and Microsoft Transaction Server are best modeled today on a three-tier implementation platform based in principle on the programming model of Visual Basic. It only makes sense that Microsoft technology should be rooted somewhat in the technology of Microsoft. And while we know full well that perfectly capable ActiveX controls can be created using Visual C++ with Microsoft's Active Template Library, all of the marketing effort and all of the evangelism and politicking is centered around VB. So although ActiveX was supposed to be powered solely by Windows well into the next millennium, it would appear the technology will be driven by VB.

Is this necessarily a good thing? The theory behind Sun's Java programming language is that it is worth the headaches that accompany using a slow and cumbersome high-level language in managing data-intensive applications, just for developers to enjoy the benefits of cross-platform development. For Visual Basic to successfully compete on all levels with Java, it must (truly) adopt a cross-platform approach. Now that Microsoft and Apple have struck an accord, this could happen; but at press time, the back burner upon which the Visual Basic for Macintosh project has perennially rested was stone cold. But what would a "VB-Mac" be anyway? Of course, VBA exists on the Macintosh platform now, thanks to the success of Office 98 there. But if the full Visual Basic system is truly a mechanism for facilitating Windows component controls, then without the Windows component controls (it's a Mac, remember?), what good is the language? What can it possibly do on the Mac on its own? The answer to these questions supposedly lies in creating component software for the Mac beforehand — an extension of Microsoft's so-called "Active Platform" into the realm of Macintosh. And UNIX, too, once someone tells Microsoft what *their* "X" stands for.

Now consider this: If Microsoft were to reinvent the model of component software for the Mac, it won't be — it can't be — the same type of component software we use in Windows. The Macintosh concept of component architecture is already in place in MacOS 8.5, and Apple's conversational model for component communication may as well be in another dimension. Perhaps it could emulate COM/OLE/ActiveX, but that's as far as it could go; and with Apple having dropped its plans to found the development of the first complete edition of the OpenDoc component standard, that's as far as it *can* go. So anything Microsoft cooks up for the Mac will be something that couldn't possibly be part of Apple's technology plans. (Most Mac users I know will tell me the only thing Microsoft wants to cook up for Apple strongly resembles a cobbler.)

The concept of "cross-platform development" generally entails building bridges between platforms, which implies not forcing developers to take leaps of faith from one platform to the next. Java is on its way to becoming the cross-platform tool whose champions are too enamored with the idea of *beating* Windows to take the next step and *embrace* Windows. This is why throughout Java's short history, the press has compared it *against* Windows, as if Java were an operating *system* now. The bridge has somehow *become* the platform; it's out there floating on its own. . . Methinks I spot a new island. We've been to islands before. Remember HyperCard?

The ideal of component software is that tightly woven cocoons of code may be trained to connect to one another so that, between them, the collection of bundles may provide the user with unique and singularly useful functionality. To achieve this ideal requires the principle of communications and connectivity to be in play within and between the platforms that comprise corporate boardrooms, as well as those which comprise operating systems and technologies. This broader and better ideal is a fruitless topic of discussion unless and until the corporations that devise new technologies start utilizing their own communications models to retrain themselves in the simple art of saying "Hi" to each other.

The broadcast journalist Edward R. Murrow, in a speech late in his life, made a statement about television that I believe applies in this context to computing. It is a medium that can inform, can educate, and can even inspire. But it can only do so to the degree that the people who maintain this medium find it in their souls to make such efforts. Otherwise, it is nothing more than wires and lights in a box.

In Brief

♦ An add-in program can appear to make permanent modifications in the functionality of Excel and Access.

♦ Office 2000 maintains its own Office object library, within which the `CommandBars` collection appears. This collection contains and describes the controls that appear in the menu bars and toolbars of an O2K application.

♦ An instance of an object can only be declared `WithEvents` from inside of an object module. Only an object module may maintain event procedures for that object, because Windows recognizes that module at run time as though it were a COM component.

♦ Handler procedures for controls in a `CommandBar` class object may only appear in a general module, in order that the names of those procedures may be visible to the component that maintains the toolbar foundations.

♦ The Setup Wizard may be used to generate a compressed package for redistributing files belonging to a VBA project. This wizard makes it possible for projects on remote systems to be installed automatically, with files (especially ActiveX controls) being placed exactly where they are needed, and with automatic functionality set to take over control of the O2K application at startup.

Part II

THE OFFICE 2000 PLATFORMS

Chapter 12

The Word 2000 Object Library

IN THIS CHAPTER

◆ Identifying the lead players in Word 2000's object library

◆ Writing small, everyday procedures

◆ Why the cursor doesn't have to be automated for every procedure

◆ Choosing the process model that best fits the task at hand

◆ The components of a document as collection objects

◆ Differentiating between the selection and ranges

◆ Phrasing direct references to textual contents

◆ Addressing Word 2000 bookmark and AutoText objects

◆ Programming and launching a quest for text with the `Find` object

THE CONCEPTUAL SEPARATION between developing a macro and developing a program is most apparent in Word 2000 programming, perhaps more so than in any other Office 2000 application. Regardless of the fact that Microsoft still chooses to use the term "macro" when referring to a standard public procedure in Word's own menus, a VBA module addresses Word as an application in a way that an individual user cannot. Word VBA is more figurative. It does not look upon its own role as that of a substitute editor of the document; for that reason, its instructions do not mimic the native commands provided to the user of the application. Instead, the Word object library provides VBA with a rich set of tools with which a document may be independently addressed, analyzed, and manipulated. As a result, the programmer of Word VBA may devise new functionality that was not present in the original application, and could not be duplicated through the use of some existing facilities.

The Everyday Word 2000 Project

When addressing Word through VBA, you will be referencing the bodies or constituents of five main objects, which play the lead roles in the Word 2000 object library. They are as follows:

◆ `Application` refers to an instance of the Word 2000 automation server. It represents the functions carried out by the program, often as the user perceives them. Like "the great and powerful Oz," `Application` is ever-present, and keeps silent until someone makes a very important request of it.

◆ `Documents` refers to the collection of one or more documents being edited by the Word automation server. Naturally, the members of this collection are of the `Document` class. `ActiveDocument` refers to the document that currently has the focus, so as a reference, it is actually independent of the `Documents` collection. But when you address a document in the collection by its name (actually, by its filename) or by its index number, you are referring to it as an item in the collection — as one item in a team rather than as an independent entity — for instance, `Documents("4Qtr99Sales.doc")`. Any document whose characteristics — such as textual contents and paragraph formatting — can be directly addressable by VBA, must be what Word considers an "open" document, and what the object library considers a member of the `Documents` collection. Even the document referred to by `ActiveDocument` is a member, even though the address itself is independent of the collection object.

◆ `Windows` refers not to the operating system, but to the collection of open window devices in the Word environment. With Word 2000, each open document window is now represented by its own independent icon in the Windows (operating system) taskbar. Those aspects of Word that focus on how you use the document, as opposed to what that document may contain, are represented by `Window` class objects. The `ActiveWindow` object represents the currently active device containing the document that the user is editing. The `Selection` object is officially a constituent of `ActiveWindow`, although this antecedent need not be stated when referring to `Selection`. An individual member of the `Windows` collection may be addressed by its index number (in the collection, not in the Word environment) or by the filename that appears in its title bar caption — for instance, `Windows("LetterManager.dot")`. The `View` object is one other notable constituent of the `Window` class, and represents all the alterable characteristics of how the user sees the document in a window, including magnification factor, full-screen mode, and whether paragraph marks are shown.

◆ `Range` refers to the grouping of text within a document between two specific characters. `ActiveDocument.Range`, for instance, represents the sequence of characters that constitutes the main body of the text of ActiveDocument. But docThis.Range(1, 100) refers to the first 100 characters of the document referenced by docThis. So a Range or Range class object can either be explicit about the ground it covers, or its purview can be implied by its own antecedent.

◆ Selection is something of a rogue. It represents whatever data element is presently highlighted in the document. By itself, Selection refers to the cursor in the active window; but technically, it's a constituent of the Windows collection (not Windows the operating system, but Windows, plural for Window). Because Word saves the cursor locations for all *inactive* documents, each Window has its own associated Selection object. Also, because the highlighted element can be anything the user is able to click on or point to with the mouse that is not a program control, the class for the Selection object at any one time can be almost any Word class. Thus, it becomes necessary for you to write instructions that test what the current Selection object class truly is, before your instructions address some property or method that is invalid for the present class. If the "selected" object is a Chart rather than a Range of text, then the valid subordinate terms of the Selection object are constituents of the Chart class rather than the Range class.

These are the five main objects in the Word 2000 object library. Their relative bearing upon one another is symbolized by Figure 12-1. All other objects that are not subordinate to these are ancillary.

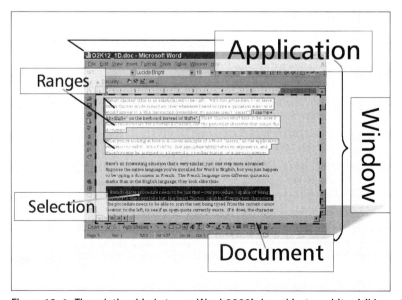

Figure 12-1: The relationship between Word 2000's key objects and its visible parts.

The Selection object is a classic example of how the key objects in the Word 2000 object library are phrased. Its quirkiness lies in how it is utilized by the VBA procedure, not in how it is written within an instruction. Here are the parts of the ordinary Selection object:

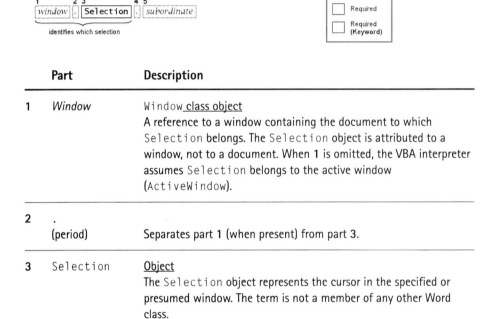

Part		Description
1	*Window*	Window class object A reference to a window containing the document to which Selection belongs. The Selection object is attributed to a window, not to a document. When **1** is omitted, the VBA interpreter assumes Selection belongs to the active window (ActiveWindow).
2	. (period)	Separates part **1** (when present) from part **3**.
3	Selection	Object The Selection object represents the cursor in the specified or presumed window. The term is not a member of any other Word class.
4	. (period)	Separates part **3** from part **5** (when present).
5	*Subordinate*	Object, method, or property A term associated with the Selection object. For instance, Selection.Range represents the area of text currently highlighted by the cursor.

At Present: What Cursor?

In Word 2000, after the user drags the mouse pointer over a region of text, that region is shown in reverse, but the cursor does not continue to blink. If the user were to type text at this point, by default, what the user types *replaces* the text that's currently highlighted (a mode of operation brought over from Macintosh). Consequently, any VBA instruction that enters data into the active document with text highlighted will also replace that text.

Traditionally, the *cursor* in programming has been a pointer to the element that is the object of some pending operation. In database terminology, with respect to sequential access (where a table is being read into active memory one record at a time), a cursor is said to point to the next record to be read. Most word processor architects have used the term to refer to the point where freshly typed characters show up in a document. But Microsoft doesn't use the term cursor in that way, if at all. Instead, Microsoft calls the blinking vertical line the "insertion point;" critics complain this phrase confuses new users by calling a line a point. So this book refers to the classic cursor, holding true to a belief that it's better to leave old problems solved.

The most commonplace tasks are often the smallest

The truth about programming with Microsoft Word on a day-to-day basis is that most of it is unexciting, uneventful, somewhat less than groundbreaking, and frankly mundane. Editing out unwanted characters, reformatting text originated elsewhere, automating long tasks, and — my personal favorite — compensating for bugs and deficiencies. This book discusses some extensively involved projects that add features to Office 2000 applications; but much of the time — especially with Word — you'll find your "projects" are really of the type that consume a full half hour of your time, and which will inevitably amount to exactly 16 per workday.

VBA's unfamiliar quotations

A trip through the Normal template in my copy of Word is a bit like rummaging through my top desk drawer. If I stare at its contents for long enough, I realize how useful some of these items might eventually become, and then stop myself from throwing much of it out. After long examination, I'm surprised to find that many of the most executed procedures on my system are the smallest and simplest. Here is perhaps the single most executed procedure I own:

```
Public Sub TypeOldQuote()
    Selection.InsertAfter Chr$(34)
    Selection.Collapse wdCollapseEnd
End Sub
```

This little gem simply types one of the "old-style quotation marks" (this is an example) common to people who still use typewriters. They're the straight quotes, not Word's "Smart Quotes" (this is an example) with the curls. With this procedure, I can leave Smart Quotes mode turned on; then whenever I need to type a quotation mark as it would appear in a VBA instruction (remember, its quotes aren't "smart"), I can type Alt+Shift+" on the keyboard instead of Shift+". Smart Quotes won't kick in because it scans the keyboard for a certain keystroke, not the particular character that enters the document.

What you're seeing here is a classic example of a Word "macro," as the application continues to call it. It's a `Public Sub` procedure that takes no arguments, and therefore may be assigned to a keystroke, a toolbar button, or a menu command.

Here's an interesting situation that's very similar, just one step more advanced: Suppose the native language you've installed for Word is English, but you just happen to be typing a document in French. The French language uses different quotation marks than in the English language; they look «like this».

A French quote procedure needs to be just that — *one* procedure, capable of being attached to one keystroke but, like Smart Quotes, capable of typing two characters. The procedure needs to be able to scan the text being typed from the current cursor location to the left, to see if an open-quote currently exists. If it does, the character that's entered needs to be a close-quote; but if it doesn't, or if it encounters a close-quote before it sees an open-quote, then the procedure should enter an open-quote. Listing 12-1 presents this little gem:

Listing 12-1: Les points du citation huppé.

```
Public Sub TypeFrenchQuote()
    Dim rngSearch As Range

    Set rngSearch = _
    ActiveDocument.Range(ActiveDocument.Range.Start, _
    Selection.Range.End)
    With rngSearch.Find
        .ClearFormatting
        .Text = "[«»]"
        .Forward = False
        .MatchWildcards = True
        If .Execute Then
            If rngSearch.Text = Chr$(171) Then
                Selection.InsertAfter Chr$(187)
```

```
            Else
                Selection.InsertAfter Chr$(171)
            End If
        Else
            Selection.InsertAfter Chr$(171)
        End If
    End With
    Selection.Collapse wdCollapseEnd
End Sub
```

This procedure begins by establishing a range, or Range class object, which is Word's mechanism for referring to any region of text without using the cursor. Finding any text within a Word document requires a formal search process, or something that Word VBA represents with a Find object. A Find object is a constituent of any other object that can represent a passage of text in a document – for instance, a Range class object, or Selection. The range of the search established here begins at the start of the document itself (ActiveDocument.Range.Start) and ends at the point where the cursor is about to insert text (Selection.Range.End). The characteristics of the search process are the properties of the Find object. For instance, the setting .Forward = False has the search process proceed in the opposite direction of forward, from the end of the range working back. The .Execute method returns a True/False value, so it can be used by itself as the test expression in If .Execute Then...

The .InsertAfter method of the Selection object is responsible for inserting the character into the document. This isn't the same as just typing it, though; the cursor is extended so that it's highlighting whatever text VBA is entering. For that reason, the Selection.Collapse instruction has Word unhighlight the text when it's through with the insertion. The constant wdCollapseEnd tells the cursor to locate itself at the end of the highlighted portion.

Utilizing an embedded field code to "overscore" text

Beginning with Word 97, you have the ability to take any single word or passage of text and draw a box or boxes around just that passage, and not the entire paragraph. But since Version 1.0, Word for Windows has allowed you to "overline" or "overscore" text – the opposite of underlining it. Why would anyone want to do this? It's decorative, especially for single-line paragraph headings, and categories for table columns. But for some, it's a necessity; for instance, in electrical notation, an overscore over a character is used to indicate a particular line held in a "high state."

The trick to overscoring a line is to invoke Word's equation formatting system from deep within its bowels. No, this isn't Equation Editor that I'm talking about; it's a graphical formatting system that's been part of Simonyi's Word engine since the beginning. A VBA procedure can take a highlighted passage and wrap that passage in one of Word's *field codes,* which represent embedded instructions from the document to the word processor. The field code system was Word's original interpreter, and might have been the only one it had, had WordBasic not been invented.

Listing 12-2 shows how this "macro" procedure evaluates the contents of the selected text, searches for characters that will throw off the field code system, and replaces them.

Listing 12-2: The "overscore" procedure, which invokes some ancient Word code.

```
Public Sub Overscore()
    Dim rngThis As Range

    If Right$(Selection.Range.Text, 1) = Chr$(13) Then
        Selection.MoveLeft Unit:=wdCharacter, Count:=1, _
        Extend:=wdExtend
    End If
    Set rngThis = Selection.Range
    With rngThis.Find
        .ClearFormatting
        .Text = "^p"
        .Replacement.Text = " "
        If .Execute Then
            ActiveDocument.Range(Start:=Selection.Range.Start, _
            End:=rngThis.End - 1).Select
            Set rngThis = Selection.Range
        .Text = ","
        .Replacement.Text = "\,"
        .Execute Replace:=wdReplaceAll
        End If
    End With
    Selection.Fields.Add Range:=Selection.Range, _
     Type:=wdFieldEmpty, Text:= _
     "EQ \x \to(" & Trim$(rngThis.Text) & ")", _
     PreserveFormatting:=False
End Sub
```

A field code is an odd looking instruction. It does utilize a keyword and parameter system, although most of its keywords are more telling of their purpose than EQ, which stands for, "Format the following as an equation."

The two characters that cannot appear in field codes are the carriage return and the comma. After the Range class object rngThis is set up to point to the currently highlighted text range Selection.Range, two searches take place for these characters. If the carriage return (coded as "^p" in the language of Word's find-and-replace system) is present, then the highlight needs to be bumped to just the first line. It wouldn't look good to overscore more than one adjacent line anyway. If the comma is found, it's replaced with a backslash and comma, which Word's display system will format as just a comma from the user's point of view.

The `Selection.Fields.Add` instruction is a marvelous example of how Word VBA symbolizes the different *things* that a whole or part of a document may contain. **Any passage of text, no matter how recently ascertained, is presumed to have its own collections of contained or embedded objects.** So `Selection.Fields` refers to the collection of field codes contained within whatever text is currently highlighted. You don't have to do any programming on your own to establish what those fields are. If you just now have highlighted a passage, and you happen to run over a field code, it's part of the collection. If there are no contained field codes, the property `Selection.Fields.Count` yields 0.

If the `Selection.Fields.Add` instruction has been executed, we can assume there's text being highlighted. So the addition of the field code will occur *on top of* the highlighted passage, therefore overwriting it. When you type characters into your Word document, after having highlighted a passage first, that passage is overwritten. Manipulating the `Selection` object in VBA works no differently. But note that in Word VBA, you don't have to cut a passage or explicitly delete it first before overwriting it, as an old-style macro might do.

Word can reformat numerals from Arabic to Roman

One of the other interesting tricks embedded deep within Word is the capability to generate Roman numerals when Arabic numerals are typed. Listing 12-3 presents a procedure that lets you highlight an Arabic numeral, invoke a command, and watch it recede into humankind's distant past.

Listing 12-3: Reformatting an Arabic numeral as Roman.

```
Public Sub Romanesque()
    If Selection.Range.End - Selection.Range.Start = 0 Then _
    Exit Sub
    If Selection.Words(Selection.Words.Count).Text = Chr$(13) Then
        Selection.Words(Selection.Words.Count - 1).Select
    Else
        Selection.Words(Selection.Words.Count).Select
    End If
    If IsNumeric(Selection.Range.Text) Then
        Selection.Fields.Add Range:=Selection.Range, _
        Type:=wdFieldEmpty, Text:= "= \* Roman " & _
        Selection.Range.Text, PreserveFormatting:=True
    End If
End Sub
```

The way this procedure works is to try to avoid error, and also to bug the user about having done something "wrong." If the user has highlighted no text at all, then the position where the `Selection` object stops (`Selection.Range.End`) will be the same place where it begins (`Selection.Range.Start`). When you subtract the latter from the former, the result would be 0 rather than a positive amount. If 0 truly is the result, then `Exit Sub` terminates this procedure without punishing the user.

Generally, the user will be expected to have only highlighted the Arabic numeral before invoking this procedure; but let's say that, by accident, there's other text in the highlight. It's reasonable to assume that this extra text would be at the *beginning*, since users tend to highlight text using the mouse in the direction they read it — from left to right. So the procedure highlights the last "word," or member of the `Words` collection, before proceeding. Remember, passages of text are presumed to have their own collections, and `Words` is one of them — so is `Paragraphs` and `Sentences`, by the way.

Because Word 2000 has a nasty habit of counting the carriage return character `Chr$(13)` as a word (perhaps some author working on staff at Microsoft got paid by the word), this procedure checks first to see if the last word highlighted is a carriage return. If it is, the selection is narrowed to the *real* word prior to it, otherwise the selection is narrowed to the final member of `Words` in the region. The property `Selection.Range.Text` represents the textual contents of this region. This text gets tacked onto the end of the field code during the insertion process.

First-Stage Programming: Automating Processes

If you picture in your mind the process of composing a Word document as though it were the construction of a building, the individual Word commands can be perceived as manual laborers, following orders from the system at large and doing their jobs in the only way they know how, without asking why. VBA is not a laborer in this model. It is more of an architect. It devises new structures that the individual commands can then work together to produce. It is not a manager of these commands, like some drill sergeant directing which individual does what job when. It is instead an engineer of a better vision of the completed product. The commands themselves may be augmented or supplemented, but they are not altogether changed, nor are they marshaled into a preset sequence.

This changes the overall mission of the Word background program from that of accelerating the user's job to that of building a new model for that job.

What VBA records often differs from a program

The conventional macro records and recites the processes that a user would take to perform a task that the application's existing commands already make feasible. But what can be recorded and what can be *programmed* are often two entirely different matters. Perhaps the simplest example of this principle involves the act of closing a document. Let's say for the sake of argument that the document being closed is *other* than the one that is currently active, and that all document windows are presently maximized. If you use the macro recorder to take note of the *user's* view of the document closing process, this is what could be recorded:

```
Windows(1).Activate
ActiveWindow.Close
```

To close a document in Word 2000, the user must first invoke its associated window by clicking on its button in the task bar, thereby making that window active and making the big "X" close box represent the document in that window. The user then clicks on this "X" to close the document (in previous versions of Word, this big "X" closed the entire application). This recorded macro recites these precise steps. A programmer studying the Word object library would find an easy way to optimize this process, by simply invoking the .Close method for the indexed window without making that window active first:

```
Windows(1).Close
```

One step in the process is saved. But this instruction makes a dangerous assumption: How are we to know if the window numbered 1 is really the one that ought to be closed? Word 2000 sorts the "Window" list (represented by the Windows() array) alphabetically; so window #1 is guaranteed to contain the document whose title falls earliest in alphabetical order. Why, then, would it ever be necessary to close the window with the earliest alphabetical title; if the macro recorder were recording the *user's* process rather than its own, it would have taken account of some article of data more critical to the operation at hand. A VBA programmer would spot this data deficiency right off and replace this instruction with one more suitable to a genuine task:

```
Documents(strTitle).Close
```

where strTitle is a string variable representing the ascertained title for the document we truly want to close. It will serve as an index for the Documents() array. You see, it's more important to us that we close a document, not a window; whereas from Word's perspective, the difference is immaterial.

The process model defines how VBA goes about its task

The way that programming a Word macro has worked historically, you write the commands in sequence that have the cursor move about the document and insert text, in the same order that those commands would be invoked by the user in the course of everyday work. As we've established, a Word VBA program does not have to model the course of everyday work as it goes about its task. It can, but it doesn't have to. A recorded Word 2000 "macro," for the most part, does mimic the commands that the user enters into the recorder. But an original VBA program does not have to be written to mimic the way the recorder would receive commands.To explain in further detail: When a word processor user edits a document, he generally invokes commands pertaining to one part of a document at a time, using the highlighter to select that part before proceeding. There's a common order of events the user invokes here: First place the cursor, then select the command. For instance, first highlight a word, then delete it. Or, first place the cursor between the two segments that will border a new table, then insert the table. A conventional macro records precisely these sequences; so if you base your concept of how a VBA module should be programmed on how a macro is recorded, you might get the idea that all text manipulation objects depend on the placement of the cursor.

With the Word 2000 object library, document manipulation is no longer necessarily bound to the operation of the cursor. It can be, but it doesn't have to be; and in many situations, you'll find it more efficient to leave the cursor alone.

So what are the different ways in which a Word VBA program may be written, and which way is the most efficient? To help you decide the answer to that for yourself, our next example presents a relatively simple task, which we'll expand upon later: Here, the objective is for the program to create a new document that contains all of the headings from an open document, sorted in alphabetical order.

In all programming, the *process model* defines how the programmer chooses to represent the elements of his task, and how the program goes about executing that task. This example exploits two such models, which I call the *cursor-dependent* and *cursor-independent* models. You will be able to spot the differences right away.

We'll start with the cursor-dependent version, which has us adopt the mindset of a macro programmer. The process model for this version manipulates two cursors: one for the document containing the headings, the other for the document that will contain the sorted copies of those headings. Listing 12-4 shows the single procedure that performs the entire job:

Listing 12-4: A cursor-dependent procedure that copies and sorts document headings.

```
Public Sub PresentSortedHeadingsBySelection()
    Dim docThis As Document, docThat As Document
    Dim iHowMany As Integer

    ActiveDocument.ShowRevisions = False

    Set docThis = ActiveDocument
```

```
Documents.Add
Set docThat = ActiveDocument
docThis.Activate

With Selection
    .HomeKey Unit:=wdStory, Extend:=wdMove
    Do
        iHowMany = .EndOf(Unit:=wdParagraph, Extend:=wdExtend)
        If Not .Style Is Nothing Then
            If Left$(.Style, 8) = "Heading " Then
                .Copy
                docThat.Activate
                Selection.Paste
                docThis.Activate
            End If
        End If
        .Collapse Direction:=wdCollapseEnd
    Loop Until .End = docThis.Content.End - 1
End With

docThat.Activate
Selection.Sort ExcludeHeader:=False, _
 FieldNumber:="Paragraphs", _
 SortFieldType:=wdSortFieldAlphanumeric, _
 SortOrder:=wdSortOrderAscending
End Sub
```

The procedure begins by declaring two object variables, docThis and docThat. These variables will point to the current document, and the new one that the procedure will generate, respectively. Variable iHowMany won't have any major purpose for this procedure, as you'll see momentarily.

The perils of mixing the Clipboard with revision viewing

In the first *procedural* (i.e., non-declarative) instruction, the "view revisions" mode of Word 2000 is set to "off," by setting the .ViewRevisions property of the ActiveDocument object to False. We did this because we will be using the System Clipboard in an automated fashion; and if the cursor happens to be highlighting a paragraph that is marked as having been entirely deleted by a registered editor of that document, an error will be generated and the procedure will shut down. We avoid any situation where VBA attempts to copy to the Clipboard a visible but deleted paragraph, by shutting down "View revisions on screen" altogether.

Next, variable `docThis` is set to point to whichever document is currently active when the procedure starts — represented by the Word 2000 global object `ActiveDocument`. A new, blank document is generated by invoking the method `Documents.Add`. Here, `.Add` is a method of Word's `Documents` collection. If you supply no arguments to this method — and here, there are none — the newly generated document will be blank, and based on Word's Normal template. The result of `Documents.Add` is the same as if the user clicked on the new document button, with the blank sheet of paper icon, in Word's Standard toolbar. Once this new document is created, of course, it becomes the active document; so variable `docThat` is set to point to it. Then `docThis` — which points to the document we started with — is reactivated.

One of the telltale signs that a Word VBA program uses a cursor-dependent process model is in how you can see each edit as it takes place, at least in the beginning. As the editing process starts to take place in a region of the document that isn't visible in a window, that window is no longer updated until the program is completed. Fewer window updates results in a much faster run time.

Notice in Listing 12-4 that the principal object in the procedure is `Selection`. You can spot this by its prominent placement in the `With` clause. Now that `Selection` is the default object in this clause, the term itself doesn't have to be spelled out explicitly for each instruction that refers to it. Instead, the dot (.) that would normally separate the term from its subordinate is left dangling to the left of the subordinate term. So the `.HomeKey` term, which constitutes the first instruction in the `With` clause, is identifiable as a method of the default object `Selection`.

Nested inside the `With` clause is a `Do-Loop` clause whose condition appears at the bottom. The point of this loop is to establish a way to tell the interpreter, "Keep going until you reach the end." "The end," in this case, is `docThis.Content.End` — for Word 2000, the end of the entirety of the document pointed to by `docThis`. This procedure will continue to highlight paragraphs as it comes upon them. After the instructions inside the loop clause have checked whether or not the highlighted paragraph is a heading, the condition at the end of the loop checks whether the tail end of the highlighted portion is one less than the official end of the document (`docThis.Content.End - 1`). This is important, because the `.EndOf` method — which steps the cursor paragraph by paragraph through the document — has no mechanism of its own to tell it when to stop. If there were no paragraphs ahead of it, the `.EndOf` method could easily step forward into the end-of-document marker (a code 13, which Word treats as an official paragraph), realize it wasn't a paragraph, and step back to the point where it was. After which, the next iteration of the `.EndOf` method would step the cursor right back to the code 13 again. So one character behind the code 13 is officially as far as we should go.

The `.endOf` method of Word's `Selection` object moves the cursor to the end of some element. By default (without any arguments or named `Unit:` parameter), the method would take the cursor to the end of the current word; so we supply the `wdParagraph` constant as the method's `Unit:` parameter. Also, we set the `Extend:` parameter to constant `wdExtend`, so that the cursor will highlight whatever it passes over. Remember, the .HomeKey method at the beginning of the procedure started us at the top of the document; as a result, whatever this .EndOf instruction tells the cursor to pass over must be an entire paragraph, since wdParagraph is the supplied parameter.

How not to compare an object to Nothing

The next conditional clause looks on its face like bad English. If Not .Style Is Nothing Then checks whether the paragraph style for the currently highlighted region is officially a style. The reason for this awkward looking formation – which would get me kicked out of third-grade English – is that the true condition being tested is in the "inside" of the statement: .Style Is Nothing. This condition will be true if whatever the cursor crosses over isn't really a paragraph. The state we want is for the condition to be False (with a capital "F") so the Not operator is placed before the condition .Style Is Nothing. Never mind that the instruction reads poorly as English; it reads correctly as VBA.

The reason we need to compare Selection.Style to Nothing in the first place is to avoid an error condition at the next instruction, which compares the first eight characters of the paragraph style name to the literal "Heading ". When the cursor isn't highlighting a real paragraph, the Style constituent object of Selection doesn't refer to anything either. So a reference to Style.Text would generate an error. Fine, but where's the .Text property in Listing 12-14? It's the default property of Style in the condition Left$(.Style, 8) = "Heading ". We could have written Left$(.Style.Text, 8) = "Heading " and accomplished the same thing. The reference to the .Text property, even though it's invisible here, would be erroneous if the cursor isn't highlighting a real paragraph. So we eliminate that possibility first with If Not .Style Is Nothing, before comparing the property to the literal.

Before we go on, if you'll allow me to run the risk of becoming dangerously close to paraphrasing a certain president, what is the meaning of the word Is in the first condition? Couldn't we have used an = operator instead? With regard to Nothing – which refers to the non-existence of an object – no. When comparing an object or object reference to Nothing, your operator must be Is.

The "business end" of the procedure in Listing 12-4 is the most heavily nested portion, which begins with the instruction .Copy. This instruction is only reached if the highlighted paragraph is officially a heading – any of Word's built-in styles "Heading 1" through "Heading 9." The .Copy method simply places the highlighted text on the System Clipboard. The next three instructions activate the new document, paste the contents of the Clipboard (thereby moving that document's cursor down the page) and reactivating the original document, in that order.

If Selection is the default object for the With clause, then how come the Selection.Paste instruction appears to mention it exclusively? Because in this particular case, we're not referring to the same Selection object. When written by itself, Selection is treated as a constituent of the ActiveWindow global. After the instruction docThat.Activate is executed, the active selection is no longer the one being referred to by the With clause. So the term here is explicitly specified.

The purpose of the .Collapse instruction, which falls outside of the double-negative conditional clause, is to leave the cursor at the end of the paragraph while turning the highlighting off. This way, the next iteration of .EndOf will start a new extension from the point of "collapse" to the end of the next paragraph. Without the .Collapse instruction being there, the next .EndOf will continue the extension into the next paragraph, resulting in two paragraphs highlighted, then three, then four, and so on.

When the With clause is exited, the new document contains all the headers from the old document, and only the headers. You'll recall that we wanted those headers sorted in alphabetical order. This is what the final instructions in the procedure in Listing 12-4 do. First, the new document docThat is activated, then the Sort method rearranges all of the paragraphs in the document in alphabetical order, by virtue of the settings of four of that method's many parameters. The Selection term was written explicitly here because we're *outside* of the With clause, where Selection was the default object. How did the .Sort method know to sort the entire document, if .Sort is a method of the Selection object, and at this point, the cursor is at the end of the document highlighting no text at all? Because when the cursor highlights no text at all, the .Sort method presumes you mean to sort the entire document – even though it's a subordinate term of the Selection object. The Document class in Word 2000 does not support a .Sort method, but the Range class does. So we could have written the instruction as docThat.Content.Sort and accomplished the same results, since Content is a Range class object in the Word 2000 library.

Range enables any text to be addressed at any time

Let's set the cursor-dependent Listing 12-4 aside for a moment, and examine an entirely different procedure which uses a cursor-independent process model that performs the same job. Any part of a Word 2000 document, or the document as a whole, may be addressed as a Range class object. The cursor doesn't have to be there, and the user doesn't have to be trying to highlight it first. Your VBA code does need to know something about the structure or content of the document before it can address a specific region of text as a Range class object – for instance, whether the region is the third paragraph, or the sentence at the end, or the fifth through twelfth characters. By contrast, with the Selection object, you do have the luxury of being able to browse through a document part by part, have the cursor highlight each part along the way, and then make some judgment about its content. With the Range class, you should know something about the content beforehand.

For a procedure that uses only Range class objects to generate a new document full of sorted headings copied from another document, we can make some assumptions about that other document's content: It's full of paragraphs, and some of those paragraphs have named styles that are formally coded as headings. Listing 12-5 shows a procedure that scans each paragraph of a document by its index number. The way it copies the qualifying heading paragraphs to the new document does not involve the Clipboard. Instead, it involves using equations to set the contents of one range to equal the contents of another.

Listing 12-5: A cursor-independent procedure that copies and sorts document headings.

```
Public Sub PresentSortedHeadingsByRange()
    Dim docThis As Document, docThat As Document
    Dim rngSearch As Range, paraThis As Paragraph
    Dim lPara As Long

    Set docThis = ActiveDocument
    Set docThat = Documents.Add

    If Selection.Paragraphs.Count > 1 Then
        Set rngSearch = Selection.Range
    Else
        Set rngSearch = docThis.Range
    End If

    For Each paraThis In rngSearch.Paragraphs
        If Not paraThis.Style Is Nothing Then
            If Left$(paraThis.Style, 8) = "Heading " Then
                lPara = lPara + 1
                docThat.Paragraphs(lPara).Range = paraThis.Range
                docThat.Paragraphs(lPara).Style = paraThis.Style
            End If
        End If
    Next paraThis

    docThat.Content.Sort ExcludeHeader:=False, _
      FieldNumber:="Paragraphs", _
      SortFieldType:=wdSortFieldAlphanumeric, _
      SortOrder:=wdSortOrderAscending
End Sub
```

This new procedure uses a few more variables. First, variable rngSearch is declared as a Range class object, which will represent the total area of the document from which heading paragraphs will be copied. Next, paraThis is a Paragraph class object that will step through each paragraph in the document from top to bottom in search of headings. This variable will do the job that Selection did in the cursor-dependent version of the procedure, only it will work much quicker.

On Point

If you're joining us late, perhaps you may be asking, "What is a 'class object?'" Truth is, there's no such thing. When I say, "Paragraph class object," the word "class" is an adjective, not a noun. It fulfills the same role in that phrase as the word "brand" fulfills in "Jell-O brand gelatin." A class describes an object, and many objects may be described by one class. Chapter 9 goes into details about how classes work and how new classes may be defined using VBA code. Chapter 8 fills in some of the background of why classes exist in Windows, and also presents the many fruity flavors of the Component Object Model.

We were able to strike two instructions from the part of the procedure that creates the new document and registers both old and new, with the addition of Set docThat = Documents.Add. By itself, Documents.Add may be written as its own instruction. But when it is assigned to a variable by way of an obvious expression of assignment using the Set statement, Documents.Add represents the newly created document. In other words, think of Documents.Add as a function that returns a value – in this case, a pointer to an object. Like any other VBA intrinsic function, Documents.Add can be "assigned" to a pointer variable to the left of the = operator.

In Listing 12-4, immediately after the Document.Add instruction, we used a method docThis.Activate to place the focus back on the original document. The reason for doing this was because the Selection object – which became the focus of the With clause – refers by default to the cursor for the *active* document. After Document.Add, the focus is on the *new* document, so we needed to switch back. But in Listing 12-5, no such switch was necessary. The reason here is because, whenever we refer to a Range class object such as variable paraThis or a member of the Paragraphs collection, we explicitly refer to the "owner" of that range – either docThis or docThat. Neither document pointed to by these variables needs to be active or have the focus in order for it to be *explicitly* addressed in this fashion.

In the conditional clause that follows the Documents.Add instruction in Listing 12-5, the Selection object makes a cameo appearance. Here, it's used to judge in advance what the user means for the procedure to do: copy and sort headings from the entire document, or just the portion of it that's highlighted. The property Selection.Paragraphs.Count never returns a value lesser than 1. So if the user isn't highlighting any text, the .Count property will still return 1. The key to judging whether the user has selected any specific paragraphs from the document lies in recognizing that "paragraphs" is a plurality. If the user has selected *paragraphs*, that probably means he has highlighted a number greater than 1. Thus the focus of the conditional clause If Selection.Paragraphs.Count > 1. When the user has indicated paragraphs, Selection.Range represents them, so that range is assigned to rngSearch. (Yes, Selection has its own Range constituent.) When the cursor is simply a blinking vertical line, `rngSearch` is set to point to the entire document, represented by `docThis.Range`. Many classes of objects in Word have their own `Range` constituents, including the `Document` and `Paragraph` classes featured in this procedure.

The `For Each...Next` loop clause is responsible for stepping through each paragraph in the main document `docThis`. You do not have to know how many paragraphs there are in the document to set up this loop, or create some variable that polls that number from the Word object library. The `rngSearch.Paragraphs` collection knows how many elements are contained within it; the `For Each` statement relies upon the collection for that count. If `For Each` were not part of the VBA vernacular, we'd have to set up a loop clause with an explicit index with a statement like `For lCount = 1 to rngSearch.Paragraphs.Count`, and then follow that statement with `Set paraThis = rngSearch.Paragraphs(lCount)`. So `For Each` automatically reduces the size of the loop clause by one instruction.

While the loop clause does keep track of which paragraph in `docThis` is being examined, it does have to maintain an independent variable `lPara` representing which paragraph in `docThat` will receive the copied heading. Notice how the copy is made here: The contents of the `Range` constituent of the recipient paragraph are set to equal those of the paragraph in `docThis` where a heading is discovered. This process is a bit tricky, but it does have its conveniences, so I'll describe it slowly: When a heading is found, `paraThis.Range` refers to the area of the original document occupied by that heading. Meanwhile, `docThat.Paragraphs(lPara).Range` points to the specific paragraph that will contain the copied heading. Each time a heading is found, variable `lPara` is incremented, so that it may be used as the index for the `Paragraphs` collection of `docThat`.

Now, the instruction `docThat.Paragraphs(lPara).Range = paraThis.Range` does not actually set one *range* to equal the other *range*, even though that's how it looks. Remember, the default property of an object is the one that's referenced when a property term is *omitted*. On both sides of the equation, property terms are omitted from both `docThat.Paragraphs(lPara).Range` and `paraThis.Range`. Both sides are actually referring to the default property of `Range`, which is `.Text`. So in actuality, the `.Text` property of the recipient paragraph is being set to equal the `.Text` property of the source paragraph, even though the term `.Text` appears nowhere in the instruction.

Because this instruction involves just the `.Text` property, the copy paragraph doesn't retain the heading style of the source paragraph. So the very next instruction appears to set the `.Style` property of the copy to the `.Style` of the source. But the same trick that worked for the previous instruction works here as well: `Style` is a constituent object of the `Paragraphs` collection. Its default property is `.Name`, which is the string that identifies the style in Word 2000's Formatting toolbar. The instruction, therefore, assigns the name of the source paragraph's style to that of the copy paragraph. As a result, the paragraph receiving the copied style *name* has its style changed to the paragraph style represented by that name. This isn't exactly the same as a paragraph receiving precisely the same style as another paragraph; it simply allows the receiving paragraph to *reference* a the name of a stored style used by another paragraph. Of course, if two styles in two documents are different by definition but alike by name, the change in style in the receiving paragraph will continue to reflect that difference.

Sequential versus random access programming in Word

There's more going on behind the scenes of this procedure than just two sets of omitted properties. A Word 2000 document contains a finite number of paragraphs, but never any fewer than one, even if that initial paragraph is empty. When the `For Each…Next` loop clause is reiterated, the `lPara` index will point to a later paragraph in the copy document. But where does this later paragraph come from? It actually gets inserted when `docThat.Paragraphs(lPara).Range` receives the copy paragraph. The reason is because the contents of `paraThis.Range` include a carriage return character (code 13) at the very end. When that character gets copied into `docThat`, it creates a new paragraph, since code 13 is the same character that is entered into a document when the user types a carriage return. The result is that the copying of the text creates the paragraph position for the next copy operation.

The final difference here is almost a cosmetic one: To sort each of the paragraphs in the copy document, we invoked the `.Sort` method of `docThat.Content`. The `.Content` property of `docThat` is actually a `Range` class object that at all times refers to "the entire document." The term `docThat.Range` without arguments also refers to the entire document, but `Content` helps put a point on it.

In practice, the cursor independent procedure in Listing 12-5 will be executed in much less time than the cursor dependent one in Listing 12-4. Addressing specific portions of a document as `Range` class objects is simply a more effective way to program, provided you can draw enough assumptions in advance about the structure of the document – for instance, that what your procedure is hunting for may be found in the style code of a paragraph. If you've ever programmed a database manager that uses both sequential and random access methods for acquiring records, perhaps you've spotted some striking similarities in the two ways of programming with Word VBA. In a sequential access scheme, you move what truly is called a *cursor* through a data table record by record, like your thumb flipping through a Rolodex. Programming with Word's own cursor by way of the `Selection` object is strikingly similar; you move the cursor through the document, and you indirectly address whatever that cursor happens to pass over. In a random access scheme, you address any record by its index or by some key field. The counterpart to random access in Word VBA is the capability to address any character, any sentence, any paragraph, or any region of text whatsoever by its index number, or in certain circumstances, by some other identifying tag.

A window should be activated before its cursor is addressed

It would seem that a procedure with fewer instructions would be executed faster than one with more instructions. But in the case of a procedure that simultaneously tracks two cursors, for some reason, this otherwise fundamental law of efficiency is thrown out the Window class object, as it were. For instance, you could attempt to speed up Listing 12-4 by eliminating the .Activate methods prior to the .Copy and .Paste operations. Technically, a document does not have to be made active before your VBA code can address its cursor. So the most heavily nested conditional clause in Listing 12-4 could be shortened to the following:

```
If Left$(.Style, 8) = "Heading " Then
    .Copy
    docThat.ActiveWindow.Selection.Paste
End If
```

To accomplish this, the .Paste instruction had to be lengthened to docThat.ActiveWindow.Selection.Paste, which means, "paste the current contents of the Clipboard at the current cursor location of the main window that belongs to document docThat." Previously, the instruction was merely Selection.Paste, but it had to be changed because, without docThat.Activate to give the focus to the copy document, Selection.Paste would refer to the *source* document docThis, not the copy.

In practice, without the .Activate instructions present, Word 2000 took far longer to process its instructions. Apparently the word processor engine has difficulty manipulating a cursor belonging to a window that is not active – or more accurately, that does not have the focus. By "far longer," I mean as much as three minutes as opposed to two seconds, and that is not an exaggeration. So as a rule, **always make certain the window containing a cursor is active before you address that cursor.**

The differences in working with the two process models becomes more evident as you develop these procedures into programs with practical purposes. Good programming is carried out in stages. When conceiving what you want your final program to do, you break down the main job into modular processes – one of the true purposes of procedures in programming. You create your program by making one process work, then building onto it. Finding all the headings in a document, then copying them into another document and sorting them, may have some practical purpose in your everyday work, but I won't bet on it. Later in this chapter, you'll see both process models for this job developed gradually into more practical purposes, and along the way, you'll learn more of the benefits and pitfalls of these two models.

In Depth: What the Paragraphs Collection Truly Represents

When Selection represents real text, a handful of collection objects become subordinate to it, among them Paragraphs. Digitally defined, a paragraph is a series of characters bordered at both sides by either a carriage return (code 13) or an end-of-document or end-of-area marker (code 7), one such marker appearing at the end of the contents of a table cell. A Paragraph class object takes on the chief characteristics common to each Word 2000 paragraph. Without the array index, however, Paragraphs refers to the collection as a whole, and the .Count property is an integer representing how many paragraphs are in that collection.

If this book were a mere reiteration of what has been published heretofore, I would leave the definition of paragraphs at this point. However, what isn't obvious to the programmer is that a Paragraph class object can be something less than a paragraph *per se*. For instance, if the user has highlighted only one word in the middle of a paragraph, the property Selection. Paragraphs.Count will return 1. The property will return greater than 1 if the highlight spans over portions (if not entireties) of two adjacent paragraphs. So if the first portion of the highlight is the last sentence of a paragraph, and the remaining portion is the first sentence of an adjacent paragraph, then Selection.Paragraphs.Count will return 2, even when the highlight does not span over any one entire paragraph. However, the property will never return 0, even if the cursor highlights no text at all; the return value is never any lesser than 1. The rule to remember here is this: The Paragraphs collection takes into account parts of paragraphs as well as whole ones, and any part of a paragraph is counted as a whole.

So what's the point of the Selection.Paragraphs collection if it overlooks whether highlighted portions are indeed paragraphs? The collection can tell you how many paragraphs' boundaries are crossed over by the highlighted area of text. As a measure of how many paragraphs supply characters to the Selection object, this collection does start to make sense. Suppose the user were to highlight a single word and the .Count property were capable of returning a zero value. Since this would be the same result if there were no text highlighted at all, 0 could no longer be counted on as a resource for determining when *no* text is highlighted at all. So Selection.Paragraphs can be of some benefit to you, as long as you recognize that it registers how many different paragraphs' boundaries are transgressed by the cursor.

On Point

The key objects in the Word 2000 object library are Application (generally implied, unless some other application owns the current instance of the VBA interpreter), the Documents collection, Range, and Selection. The Documents collection maintains the set of documents currently open in the word processor. These documents are represented individually by Document class objects. Documents are generally addressed as members of the Documents collection rather than as individual objects in their own right, although Document class object-reference variables can be declared and set to refer to these documents indirectly. The ActiveDocument term always refers to the Word document whose window currently has the focus.

How the Range class and Range object work

The Word 2000 object library views a *range* as any sequence of *textual* characters with a defined beginning and end. These defined points are simple fence posts, so when you write Range(Start:=*x*, End:=*y*), the library returns an object representing the characteristics of the text between character #*x* and #*y*, where the first character is numbered 0. (With respect to the *file* to which the active document is bound, the characters that comprise the header and formatting data are not counted – just the characters that the user actually *sees* in the open window.) When we say "characteristics," we're referring to the primary attributes that comprise the text as it appears on screen, one of which happens to be the characters themselves. The .Text property of a Range class object refers to those characters. Meanwhile, such other constituents as .Font and .Style refer to the formatting applied to those characters.

Any region of text that you define as a Range class object is independent of the text the user may have highlighted (the Selection object). So as you've seen, this versatile Range object can be used as an all-purpose identifier of textual regions, and you may declare as many such objects as your procedure may require. The term Range shows up in the Word library in two places:

◆ As a constituent object of a Document class object or of Selection, Range represents the characteristics of a *specified* region of text belonging to the antecedent object. These specifications are supplied as arguments, denoting the indexes for the first and last characters in the range. Whatever method you use to derive a character index is acceptable as long as its final result yields a valid integer; so you can use library terms to address an index indirectly. For instance, you can make a Range object refer to "all the text between the second and fifth paragraphs following the location of the first bookmark." You'll see how momentarily.

♦ With respect to a textual *element object* that is itself *not* a Range class object (for instance, a member of the Documents collection, or the Rows or Columns collection of a table), the .Range property represents the region of text that makes up the body of that element. Some element object collections, such as Sentences and Words, are already Range class objects, and thus already have all the constituent terms associated with a Range object. In this case, the term doesn't take any arguments; the element with which it's associated serves alone to define the breadth of the range.

The Range term is formed a bit differently than ordinary objects in the Word 2000 object library, so here is a closer look at how an instruction involving Range is phrased:

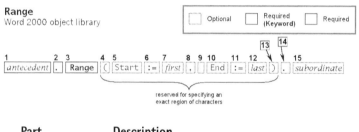

	Part	Description
1	*antecedent*	<u>Object</u> An object, a reference to an object, or a member of an object class collection, which maintains a range as one of its subordinates. Generally, a Document class object or a Selection object maintains a range.
2	. (period)	Separates the antecedent object (part **1**) from the main object (part **3**).
3	Range	<u>Constituent object</u> Represents the general characteristics of a region of text. This region encompasses all text between two points. When those points are not designated, they are assumed to be the natural start and end of the text maintained by the antecedent (part **1**).
4	((left parenthesis)	Begins the arguments list.

	Part	Description
5	Start	Parameter Optional identification for part **7**. When omitted, the argument is supplied in the first position in the list. When parameter names are used, the order of the `Start:=` and `End:=` arguments may be reversed, if you ever see a need to do so. If you state part **5**, you must also state part **10**.
6	`:=`	Associates the parameter name (part **5**) with the argument (part **7**).
7	*first*	Long integer A whole number value that uniquely identifies the beginning character position in the range. Parameters may be specified here when the `Range` class object is being assigned not to point to any previously defined range, or any standard range such as `ActiveDocument.Content`.
8	`,` (comma)	Separates arguments in the list.
9	(space)	
10	End	Parameter Optional identification for part **12**.
11	`:=`	Associates the parameter name (part **10**) with the argument (part **12**).
12	*end_char*	Long integer A whole number value that uniquely identifies the ending character position in the range.
13	`)` (right parenthesis)	Terminates the arguments list.
14	`.` (period)	
15	*subordinate*	Object, method, or property A term associated with the `Range` object that represents some aspect or function of the range, or some function that may be applied to the range.

Table 12-1 provides examples of how Range can be used to build objects that represent the characteristics of particular portions of text in a document. In some of these examples, Range appears more than once, whereas in others, the term itself doesn't appear at all, but is implied by way of a Range class object. In these examples, docThis is presumed to be an object variable declared earlier As Document, and assigned to refer to an open member of the Documents collection using the Set statement.

TABLE 12-1 VARIOUS TEXTUAL ELEMENT REFERENCES USING RANGE

Region of Text Being Referenced	Object Reference
The text of the second paragraph of the document	docThis.Paragraphs(2).Range.Text The Paragraphs collection maintains properties and constituents that are peculiar to paragraphs in a document, such as Borders and DropCap. Because paragraphs are different than your ordinary range, a Paragraph class object is not the same as a Range class object. However, it does maintain its own Range class constituent.
The text of the second sentence of the document	docThis.Sentences(2).Text By comparison, the Sentences collection is a grouping of Range class objects already, so it doesn't require a Range constituent.
The text of the first sentence in the second paragraph of the document	docThis.Paragraphs(2).Range _ .Sentences(1).Text The Sentences object is a collection of Range class objects, but it needs an antecedent that maintains a list of sentences in order to resolve for which textual element it is to count sentences. A Document class object (for this example, docThis was declared as one) does count sentences, but a Paragraph class object does not. The bridge between the Paragraphs and Sentences collections here has to be the Range constituent of Paragraphs.

Region of Text Being Referenced	Object Reference
The name of the font used in the first row of the second table in the document	`docThis.Tables(12).Rows(1).Range _.Font.Name` Tables in Word 2000 are not considered textual elements by the application, but instead formal containers for textual elements. So the `Rows` collection uses a `Range` object as a bridge between itself and its textual contents.
The number of words in the fourth paragraph of the document	`docThis.Paragraphs(4).Range.Words.Count` The `Words` collection groups another set of `Range` class objects together, so `Range` is needed again as a bridge between `Words` and `Paragraphs`. **Caution:** Word 2000 treats a carriage return as a word (strange but true), so a range that contains three words and concludes with a carriage return will generate a `Words.Count` value of 4.
The number of words belonging	`docThis.Bookmarks("Address").Range _.Words.Count` The `Bookmarks` collection contains `Bookmark` class objects that may be addressed by name as well as by index number (see sidebar below).

The text of the twelfth sentence in the area between the fourth paragraph of the document, and the next-to-last paragraph.	`docThis.Range(docThis.Paragraphs(4) _`
	`.Range.Start, docThis.Paragraphs _`
	`(docThis.Paragraphs.Count - 1).Range _`
	`.End).Sentences(12).Text`
	
	Nondescript regions of text within a document are marked using a `Range` object that operates as a function and that receives two arguments. These arguments represent the ordinal position, with respect to the document, of the first character in the range and the last character, in that order. Their objective is to describe these characters' positions as they relate to other, more specific elements of the document — milestones, if you will. Two other `Range` objects play roles here, and the `.Start` and `.End` properties of `Range` are invoked to return the character position of the beginning of the fourth paragraph, and the end of the next to last paragraph, respectively.

At Present: What's a Bookmark without a Book?

Word 2000 defines a *bookmark* as a region of text within a document that can be recorded, given a name, and later recalled from a database using that name. Some word processors have used the same or similar term to refer to a *point* in the text that can be recalled by name — not a passage or a region, but some spot such as a page number or a paragraph index. In Netscape Navigator, a "bookmark" points to an entry in a local database of frequently visited World Wide Web addresses. In Word, a bookmark points to a text range. Generally, this range consists of an excerpt or a passage of some length, though it may refer to a cursor position (technically, a range of zero length). As a result, the Bookmarks collection in the object library contains members that all refer to textual regions, but not ranges — or, more accurately, not Range class objects. The reason is that a Bookmark class object has a few characteristics that separate it from your run-of-the-mill text range — not many, just some. For instance, a bookmark can be named with alphanumeric characters, whereas a range cannot; so a Bookmark class object maintains a .Name property.

If there's such a thing in Word as a bookmark, you might be wondering, does the application recognize a "book" or "book object?" Not really. The user can write a very, very large document that just happens to be the manuscript of an entire book, but Word will treat it logically as a document, like any other. However, the user may instead write several independent documents, and then build a so-called *master document* that collects them together. In this situation, each of the subordinate documents, or *subdocuments*, would have its own file and the master document would have its own file. The Document class object that refers to the master document would maintain a subordinate collection called Subdocuments, which coordinates all the components of the master. In that case, a master document could be treated as a sort of "book object," even though there is no "Book" term in Word 2000.

Many of the examples in Table 12-1 used discrete indexes to reference textual elements. In many real-world cases, you will be using integer variables in their place, since there will most likely be very few types of documents that you or your business will ever generate in which "the fourth paragraph" has exactly the same meaning or purpose each time. But we did use those discrete indexes here to make it easier for you to comprehend the examples.

Second-Stage Programming: Integrating Processes

Returning now to our ongoing example of producing sorted document headings: Suppose we start to give the document that contains copies of document headings some practical functionality: Say this copy document is to act as an index for the main document. Each heading could act as a hyperlink that, when clicked on, takes the user to the corresponding heading in the main document. What we'd like to do, therefore, is copy each heading and then convert it to a hyperlink.

Listing 12-6 shows a revised version of Listing 12-4. It continues to use the cursor-dependent process model. I could say, "Note the extent of the revisions," but that extent obviously deserves more than just a note.

Listing 12-6: A revised cursor-dependent procedure that generates sorted hyperlinks.

```
Public Sub PresentSortedHeadingsBySelectionHyperlinked()
    Dim winThis As Window, winThat As Window
    Dim strMark() As String, strName As String
    Dim lPara As Long
    Dim iHowMany As Integer

    Application.ScreenUpdating = False
    ActiveDocument.ShowRevisions = False

    Set winThis = ActiveWindow
    Documents.Add
    Set winThat = ActiveWindow
    winThis.Activate

    If winThis.Document.Path = "" Then
        winThis.Document.Save
    End If
    strName = winThis.Document.FullName

    With winThis.Selection
        .HomeKey Unit:=wdStory, Extend:=wdMove
        Do
            iHowMany = .EndOf(Unit:=wdParagraph, Extend:=wdExtend)
            If Not .Style Is Nothing Then
                If Left$(.Style, 8) = "Heading " Then
                    .Copy
                    winThat.Activate
                    With winThat.Selection
```

Continued

Listing 12-6: A revised cursor-dependent procedure that generates sorted hyperlinks *(Continued)*

```
                            .Paste
                            lPara = lPara + 1
                            ReDim Preserve strMark(lPara)
                            strMark(lPara) = "_InterDex_" & _
                             Format$(lPara, "0000")
                            winThis.Document.Bookmarks.Add _
                             Name:=strMark(lPara), _
                             Range:=winThis.Selection.Range
                            .MoveUp Unit:=wdParagraph, _
                             Extend:=wdExtend
                            winThat.Document.Hyperlinks.Add _
                             (Anchor:=.Range, Address:=strName, _
                             SubAddress:=strMark(lPara), _
                             ScreenTip:="", _
                             TextToDisplay:=Left$ _
                             (winThis.Selection.Range.Text, _
                             Len(winThis.Selection.Range.Text) - 1)) _
                             .Range.Select
                            .Style = winThis.Selection.Style
                            .Collapse wdCollapseEnd
                            .TypeParagraph
                        End With
                        winThis.Activate
                    End If
                End If
                .Collapse Direction:=wdCollapseEnd
            Loop Until .End = winThis.Document.Content.End - 1
        End With

        winThat.Activate
        Selection.TypeBackspace       'gets rid of the excess blank
                                      ' paragraph
        Selection.Sort ExcludeHeader:=False, _
         FieldNumber:="Paragraphs", _
         SortFieldType:=wdSortFieldAlphanumeric, _
         SortOrder:=wdSortOrderAscending
    End Sub
```

Managing how Word updates its window during execution

The instruction `Application.ScreenUpdating = False` may not speed up the procedure as much as you might think it would, but what it does accomplish — especially in the case of this procedure, which switches windows back and forth — is an elimination of bothersome screen flicker. Consider this instruction this book's contribution to the health of your eyesight. Do keep in mind, though, that if you have to break this procedure in mid-execution, screen updating will still be turned off. As a result, your Word 2000 application window could look like it has just crashed, since it will appear to contain parts of other windows. In such a situation, you'll need to go into VBA's Immediate Window and type `ScreenUpdating = True` to get the Word window to look right again. Screen updating is always turned back on automatically when a VBA program ends.

The first major change in Listing 12-6 from Listing 12-4 is the replacement of `docThis` and `docThat` with `winThis` and `winThat`. Because this procedure relies upon two `Selection` objects, it only makes sense to address the source of those objects when identifying them. The `Selection` object in the Word 2000 object library is a constituent of the `Window` class, not the `Document` class. Distinguishing between cursors became absolutely necessary for this procedure, especially because one `Selection` object takes over for the other as the default object on several occasions during the run of this procedure. Besides, a window may be activated with the `.Activate` method just as easily as a document.

Verifying whether a document has ever been saved

The second change is the addition of a new conditional clause near the top that tests the `.Path` property of the document belonging to window `winThis`. If the document has never been saved in its history, its `.Path` property will be an empty string (`""`). In that event, the `.Save` method brings up a dialog box for the user to enter the filename of his choice. Once that's done, the name of that file is assigned to string variable `strName`. The reason for this assignment is because each hyperlink in Word keeps a separate tab on the name of the document to which it is anchored. By the way, you might think the `.Saved` property of `winThis.Document` would have been more appropriate to test whether a document has been saved in its history. But this property actually reports whether a document has been *changed* since it was last saved to disk. So if the user loaded this document from disk, and added to it or removed from it as much as a single character, the `.Saved` property would read False.

Nesting of With clauses for swapping of default objects

There's a peculiar way in which we use With clauses in Listing 12-6 — notice there are two. Often when one With clause is nested within another, its purpose is to change the default object to a constituent of the default object in the containing clause. Here, however, the nested clause's purpose is different: to swap the default object over to the Selection object in the copy document's window, so that it may be swapped back to the Selection object in the source document's window once the nested clause has completed execution. It was important here that we specified the parent windows for the Selection objects in With winThis.Selection and With winThat.Selection because we are addressing two different Selection objects equally. Earlier in Listing 12-4, we used the .Activate method to have Word designate docThis as the active document before addressing its Selection object by default. Here, we cannot afford a single default Selection object because we're addressing two — as a result, the .Activate method becomes unnecessary. It does show up at the end of the listing, though, just prior to the sort operation, because there we *are* addressing the default "owner" of the Selection object.

Hyperlinks in Word require bookmarks

All of the hyperlinks that belong to a document are represented by the Hyperlinks collection, which is a constituent of the Document class object that represents that document. Although Word 2000 does support HTML as an alternate document format, it is not that word processor's native format. So when a hyperlink requires the point in a document that is brought up when the user clicks on that hyperlink, the point is represented by a Range class object that is given its own exclusive bookmark. For future use, the names for all the bookmarks generated by this procedure are kept in a dynamic array strMark(), which is extended by one element using ReDim Preserve each time a new bookmark is generated. The exclusivity of the names for each bookmark is guaranteed by copying the value of the lPara variable into a four-digit number that is tacked onto the end of a string that is just too weird-sounding ever to be duplicated by accident, "_InterDex_". The reason for the underscore (_) character is so that Word will treat the bookmark as "hidden," causing it by default not to show up in its Bookmarks dialog box list.

The phrase winThis.Document may be interpreted as "the document contained within the window pointed to by winThis." This phrase is used to convert our window reference winThis back into a document — thus substituting for docThis in the previous edition — in order to address the document's Bookmarks and Hyperlinks collections. First the bookmark is created with the Bookmarks.Add method, in keeping with the Word library's consistent use of .Add to append a member to a collection. Later, the name of that bookmark is recalled as the SubAddress: parameter for the Hyperlinks.Add method.

Getting a hyperlink to say what you want it to say

Another fitting name for this segment is "World Class Hyperlink Wrestling." When a Word 2000 hyperlink is initialized by VBA and entered into a document, it has a handful of peculiar characteristics:

♦ All of its text is displayed with one character style; thus, if part of a hyperlink is italic, *all* of it is italic.

♦ VBA always gives a hyperlink that consumes an entire paragraph the Normal style, regardless of whether its text was formatted using some other style.

♦ However, a VBA paragraph does not appear exactly like a Normal one. It will be underlined, and its text color will be whatever color is set up in Internet Explorer (you read correctly, not Word 2000) for hyperlinks – by default, bright blue.

♦ There is no way for either the user or VBA to place the cursor in the middle of a hyperlink. When the user clicks on it, he is immediately taken to the destination of the link. When he comes back to the hyperlink document, the cursor rests at the *end* of the hyperlink text, even if he had clicked in the *middle* of it.

♦ The default text of a hyperlink is the filename (or URL, in the case of an HTML document) of its destination. When a user creates a hyperlink in Word 2000 manually, it contains whatever text was highlighted by the user. This way, the user can say to Word, in effect, "Take *this* text and make it into a hyperlink." But when a hyperlink is created in VBA, whatever text it is to contain instead of the filename of its destination, must be supplied to the `Hyperlinks.Add` method by way of the `TextToDisplay:` parameter.

Making our automated hyperlinks appear in the proper place and read the proper text was an extremely tricky maneuver with the cursor-dependent model. In Word VBA, **no text needs to be highlighted before a hyperlink is created; and if text is highlighted, there is no automatic mechanism for VBA to assume that the highlighted text is to be contained in the new hyperlink.** When I originally designed this procedure, at one point, I had come to the conclusion that, since the text contained within the hyperlink is supplied by a parameter anyway, there was no need to continue copying it from the source document and pasting it into the copy document. The pasted text would be written over anyway. But in practice, each hyperlink added to the document after the first one tended to overwrite the previous one, most likely because the cursor treats a hyperlink as a single object rather than a collection of characters — more like an embedded object. (The secret here is, a hyperlink *is* an embedded object). After depositing the new hyperlink on the page, the cursor rests against the right edge of the hyperlink, still effectively within its "boundaries." When the new hyperlink is deposited, because Word perceives the cursor to be within the old hyperlink's boundaries, the old one is overwritten.

The way for the procedure to respond to this is by generating some artificial text between the hyperlinks – at the very least, an extra carriage return (code 13). But as long as the hyperlink adds one such code already, the result of this would be too large of a vertical gap between hyperlinks. The solution adopted in Listing 12-6 is tricky, and was only discovered through trial-and-error:

1. I reinserted the `.Paste` method back into the `With winThat.Selection` clause, so that the text that each new hyperlink will absorb will appear someplace in its own document, and will not get lost in some other document.

2. After the bookmark is generated, a `.MoveUp` instruction turns extend mode for the cursor on (`Extend:=wdExtend`) and hikes the cursor up one paragraph (`Unit:=wdParagraph`). This effectively covers up the paragraph that was just pasted in, so that when the new hyperlink is added, it overwrites this paragraph. (During the first iteration of the loop, there's no paragraph to cover up, so `.MoveUp` simply bumps the cursor against the upper edge of the document without error.)

3. The `Hyperlinks.Add` instruction inserts the new hyperlink, setting its text to all the characters that are presently highlighted (`winThis.Selection.Range.Text`) except for the final one, which is a carriage return (code 13). This way, only the visible text gets inserted. The three critical parameters for the `Hyperlinks.Add` method are: `Anchor:` which defines the location in this document *after which* the hyperlink will appear; `SubAddress:` which defines the bookmark which Word will pull up after the user clicks on the hyperlink; and `TextToDisplay:` which contains the text of the hyperlink. Note that since this last parameter is a string, it may not contain any internal formatting.

4. The `Hyperlinks.Add` instruction is rephrased using a function syntax, where all its parameters are encased in parentheses. The reason is so it may return a `Hyperlink` class object for one purpose only: so that we may address its `Range` constituent and highlight its own text with the `.Select` method. This saves us having to create an object variable like `hypThis`, set the variable to point to the new hyperlink with the `Set` statement, and then write `hypThis.Range.Select` separately.

5. With the hyperlink highlighted, the instruction `.Style = winThis.Selection.Style` assigns the style of the heading in the source document to the hyperlink. It remains a hyperlink, although it loses its traditional blue underlined text. In practice, this loss may be a preferable tradeoff, since leaving the hyperlink as it is often results in that hyperlink having some other style. Where this new style comes from, who knows, but it belongs to neither a heading nor to Normal text.

6. The restyled region is unselected by invoking the .Collapse instruction. The single argument wdCollapseEnd is a constant that has the cursor rest to the right of the formerly highlighted region. The reason we do this is so the next instruction does not overwrite the region.

7. The .TypeParagraph instruction inserts a code 13, taking the cursor to the next line and making it ready for the next hyperlink. The method in this instruction could fool you; it doesn't mean, "Type a paragraph full of text." Instead it means, "Type a paragraph *mark*." Think of it as though you were taking recorded dictation from an old Dictaphone machine, and the speaker said the word, "Paragraph!" generally meaning, "*end* of paragraph."

When the loop clause is finally exited, there will be an excess blank paragraph at the end of the document, having been scooted along the way since the beginning of the procedure. The blank paragraph is nothing more than an extra code 13. But if it's allowed to remain at the end, the Selection.Sort method will count that paragraph as a sortable entry, and dutifully place the sorted paragraph at the very *beginning* of the text. (In sort methodologies, empty text falls before non-empty text.) So to get rid of the excess paragraph, window winThat is reactivated, and Selection.TypeBackspace moves the cursor back one character from the end of the document, taking out the code 13 with it.

 Chapter 13 covers all the essential methods for moving the cursor (the Selection object) and inserting text at the current cursor location. It also compares these methods with their counterparts in the earlier WordBasic language, which was part of Microsoft Word through Office 95.

Updating the cursor independent version of the heading sorter procedure from Listing 12-5 proved to be much simpler than having to blindly discover how and where to hike the cursor up or down one character or paragraph, in Listing 12-6. Now that you've seen the .Add method instructions in play once already, you should be able to spot the critical improvements to the procedure in Listing 12-7.

Listing 12-7: A revised cursor-independent procedure that generates sorted hyperlinks.

```
Public Sub PresentSortedHeadingsByRangeHyperlinked()
    Dim docThis As Document, docThat As Document
    Dim rngSearch As Range, paraThis As Paragraph
    Dim strMark() As String, strName As String
    Dim lPara As Long

    Application.ScreenUpdating = False
```

```
    ActiveDocument.ShowRevisions = False

    Set docThis = ActiveDocument
    Set docThat = Documents.Add

    If Selection.Paragraphs.Count > 1 Then
        Set rngSearch = Selection.Range
    Else
        Set rngSearch = docThis.Content
    End If

    If docThis.Path = "" Then
        docThis.Save
    End If
    strName = docThis.FullName

    For Each paraThis In rngSearch.Paragraphs
        If Not paraThis.Style Is Nothing Then
            If Left$(paraThis.Style, 8) = "Heading " Then
                lPara = lPara + 1
                docThat.Paragraphs(lPara).Range = paraThis.Range
                ReDim Preserve strMark(lPara)
                strMark(lPara) = "_InterDex_" & Format$(lPara, _
                 "0000")
                docThis.Bookmarks.Add Name:=strMark(lPara), _
                 Range:=paraThis.Range
                docThat.Hyperlinks.Add _
                 Anchor:=docThat.Paragraphs(lPara).Range, _
                 Address:=strName, SubAddress:=strMark(lPara), _
                 ScreenTip:="", TextToDisplay:=Left$ _
                 (docThat.Paragraphs(lPara).Range.Text, _
                 Len(docThat.Paragraphs(lPara).Range.Text) - 1)
                docThat.Paragraphs(lPara).Style = paraThis.Style
                docThat.Paragraphs.Add
            End If
        End If
    Next paraThis

    docThat.Paragraphs(docThat.Paragraphs.Count).Range.Delete
    docThat.Content.Sort ExcludeHeader:=False, _
     FieldNumber:="Paragraphs", _
     SortFieldType:=wdSortFieldAlphanumeric, _
     SortOrder:=wdSortOrderAscending
End Sub
```

Word 2000 permits the creation of multiple bookmarks whose associated ranges overlap, or perhaps even duplicate, one another. As a result, you should be careful how many times you execute the procedure in Listing 12-7 on a single document, because Word will not automatically remove an identical bookmark whenever it adds a new one.

Here, we've made some of the same general improvements, such as testing whether the document has been saved at least once before generating bookmarks. But note the relative simplicity in which the hyperlink handling instructions were added to the innermost conditional clause in the loop:

1. The bookmark is generated, and its range is set to that of the paragraph `paraThis` currently under examination.

2. The hyperlink is generated, and its `SubAddress:` parameter is set to the name of that bookmark. The `Left$()` function is used here also, to remove the rightmost code 13 from the text of the hyperlink.

3. The `.Style` assignment makes the appropriate style change to the hyperlink.

4. The instruction `docThat.Paragraphs.Add` places a new paragraph at the end of the collection – effectively, at the end of the document. This has the same effect as `Selection.TypeParagraph` in the cursor dependent procedure. Now, we just got through eliminating a code 13 from the hyperlink text; why would we want to add one here? Because this code 13 will not be part of the hyperlink. It will simply make room for the next iteration of the loop, so that `Paragraphs(1Para)` points to a real range. If the code 13 from the hyperlink were left in, because Word 2000 treats all hyperlinks as contiguous units, it could not be deleted. So there would be an extra line of blank space in the copy document acting as part of the hyperlink.

The way this procedure gets rid of that excess paragraph mark is by addressing its final paragraph as a `Range` object, and then deleting that range. The index for the final paragraph of a document is always `Paragraphs.Count`. So the reference to `docThat.Paragraphs(docThat.Paragraphs.Count)` is not all that redundant after all. Translated loosely into English, it refers to "the paragraph in document `docThat` whose index happens to be the number of the last paragraph in document `docThat`."

The revised role of the cursor object

When you consider the relative versatility of the `Range` object, you may be find yourself asking, why program using the macro-inspired cursor-dependent model at all? (Just don't ask this aloud, or someone might get the wrong impression about what you do for a living.) In the early Word for Windows macros, the "insertion point" was used not only as the tool for acquiring text from the document, but also for writing new text to that document. This made sense. After all, the user had to check the position of the cursor before he could enter text into the document, so why wouldn't the macro interpreter have to use the same methodology?

Under the new, more object-oriented Word 2000 model, the `Range` object makes the entire contents of the document equally and immediately accessible to the VBA program, without it having to move or otherwise manipulate the cursor. So what bearing does the cursor have on the VBA interpreter? The `Selection` object, which represents the cursor, can be moved about the document, and with a surprising new degree of agility. But having the program move the cursor becomes less and less necessary, because `Range` can now refer to just about any part of the document at any time. `Selection` thus becomes an indicator of something that the user wants. Remember that a VBA module is invoked generally in response to a command, or some other user-generated event. The position of the cursor at the time that command is generated may be crucial to determining what it is the user wants, and where the user wants it.

In the example procedures you've seen in this chapter thus far, the user is never asked to supply any information about the highlighted paragraphs to be sorted, although the procedures do check whether there is a highlighted region to be sorted. One of the drawbacks of the cursor-independent process model is that there isn't enough built-in logic in the `Range` object alone for it to represent, for instance, a noncontiguous, or broken, textual region. So you cannot, for instance, refer to "all the text in a range that is formatted with a given style," or "all the text in a range that's italicized."

Third–Stage Programming: Algorithmic Logic

Listings 12-4 through 12-7 utilized the `.Sort` method of the Word 2000 object library to sort each paragraph in the newly generated document containing copies of another document's headings, in ascending alphanumerical order. This method is convenient when you intend to sort the contents of the entire document, or perhaps one contiguous range within that document. Suppose, however, we have other intentions for the sorted headings document. Perhaps the copied headings are to serve as headings themselves, say, for statistics regarding the contents of the text beneath the corresponding heading in the main document.

This addition changes many of the fundamentals of how the procedure will work, and manages to shine a bright spotlight on the advantages and deficiencies of both process models. Our procedure now has two purposes: It continues to search for heading paragraphs. But any paragraph that doesn't count as a heading is treated as subordinate to that heading, and becomes eligible for being counted statistically. The procedure will place a call to a utility procedure elsewhere in the same VBA module – a Private Sub procedure that performs the sorting process that can no longer be handled by the .Sort method. The reason .Sort won't work now is because there will be other text scattered intermittently throughout the document containing statistical data, and that should not be shifted to some other position.

Our procedure is based largely on the cursor independent process model exploited in Listing 12-7, though toward the end, it makes use of the Selection object. The body of the procedure has been split into two parts – one that collects the data about the source document, and the other that produces the contents of the copy document. For this segment, we'll split Listing 12-8 into two parts, and discuss each one individually. We'll begin with Part 1, which now gathers data about the other paragraphs it passes over, and stores that data in dynamic arrays:

Listing 12–8: Developing our hyperlinked document into a statistical reference.

Part 1

```
Public Sub ParaStats()
    Dim docThis As Document, docThat As Document
    Dim rngSearch As Range, rngAnalysis() As Range, _
     paraThis As Paragraph
    Dim cmtThis As Comment
    Dim strArray() As String, strMark() As String
    Dim strName As String, strInsert As String
    Dim lPlace() As Long, lIndex() As Long
    Dim lPara As Long, lCount As Long, lWhich As Long
    Dim lX As Long, bTrack As Boolean, bProg As Boolean

    ActiveDocument.ShowRevisions = False
    Set docThis = ActiveDocument
    Set docThat = Documents.Add

    Application.ScreenUpdating = False
    bTrack = docThis.TrackRevisions
    docThis.TrackRevisions = False

    If Selection.Paragraphs.Count > 1 Then
        Set rngSearch = Selection.Range
```

Continued

Listing 12-8: Developing our hyperlinked document into a statistical reference. *(Continued)*

```
Else
    Set rngSearch = docThis.Content
End If

If docThis.Path = "" Then
    docThis.Save
End If
strName = docThis.FullName

For Each paraThis In rngSearch.Paragraphs
    lCount = lCount + 1
    If Not paraThis.Style Is Nothing Then
        If Left$(paraThis.Style, 8) = "Heading " Then
            lPara = lPara + 1
            ReDim Preserve strArray(lPara), lIndex(lPara), _
            lPlace(lPara), strMark(lPara)
            strArray(lPara) = Left$(paraThis.Range.Text, _
            Len(paraThis.Range.Text) - 1)
            lIndex(lPara) = lPara
            lPlace(lPara) = lCount
            strMark(lPara) = "_InterDex_" & Format$(lPara, _
            "0000")
            docThis.Bookmarks.Add Name:=strMark(lPara), _
            Range:=paraThis.Range
            bProg = False
        ElseIf lPara > 0 Then
            If bProg = False Then
                ReDim Preserve rngAnalysis(lPara)
                Set rngAnalysis(lPara) = paraThis.Range
                bProg = True
                lWhich = lPara
            Else
                rngAnalysis(lWhich).End = paraThis.Range.End
            End If
        End If
    End If
Next paraThis
```

In previous editions of this procedure, variable lPara has served as an index for the headings being copied, and for the strMark() array. This array has contained the names of bookmarks that serve as the destinations for the hyperlinks. For Public Sub ParaStats(), four more arrays have been added to contain the following:

strArray()   The text that will appear in each bookmark.

lIndex()   An index array that is preloaded with whole numbers in
                     sequence – 1, 2, 3, et al. As the utility procedure sorts
                     strArray() into ascending alphanumerical order, the
                     corresponding entries in lIndex() are shuffled likewise.
                     The result is that lIndex() becomes a cross reference list.
                     When you refer to this array using an integer representing
                     the paragraph number of a hyperlink in the sorted list, the
                     value returned equals the relative location of that entry in
                     the *unsorted* list – that is, the order in which the heading on
                     which the hyperlink is based, was encountered. Using this
                     array, Part 2 of this listing will produce the sorted list of
                     headings, using the unsorted list as a basis.

lPlace()   The paragraph number of the headings as they are encountered
                     in the source document.

rngAnalysis()   A series of Range class objects that will represent all of the
                     text *in-between* the headings. As non-heading paragraphs are
                     encountered, the range for this in-between text is extended.
                     Each range in this array will be assessed later for statistical
                     data, such as how many recorded revisions were made to the
                     text therein.

Part 1's main conditional clause now has two parts: one that is executed if the
examined paragraph paraThis is a heading, and the other that is executed if it is
not. If paraThis is a heading, the four dynamic arrays strArray(), lIndex(),
lPlace(), and strMark() are all extended in length by one element. This element
is tacked onto the end of these arrays without disturbing their existing contents, by
virtue of the Preserve qualifier in the ReDim statement. Then the newest element of
strArray() is assigned the text in paraThis, minus the trailing code 13. Array
lIndex() is given the ordinal number of the newly discovered heading, lPara. This
makes the contents of lIndex() at first equal 1, 2, 3, and so on – which, believe it
or not, is exactly what we want.

Next, lPlace() is given the ordinal number of paragraph paraThis in the
source document. Here, the number is represented by lCount. Notice that this is a
long integer variable just like any other. It would be nice if we had some way of
addressing "the index number of *this* paragraph." But in order to supply Word VBA
with an identity for "*this* paragraph," the very thing it would need is the very thing
we're trying to find – an index number. **In Word VBA, there is no function or
method which returns the ordinal number for any given word, sentence, or
paragraph of a document.** This may seem odd at first, until you realize that, in
order to give VBA this so-called "given" word, sentence, or paragraph, you would
need to have on hand some identifying characteristic for it.

Next, the bookmark is created as before by generating a name for it, assigning that name to the `strMark()` array, and referencing that array for the `Name:` parameter of the `Bookmarks.Add` method. Immediately afterward, a Boolean variable `bProg` is set to `False`. This variable will act as a signal later, telling the second part of this conditional clause to begin recording the range of in-between paragraphs.

The second half of the main conditional clause in Listing 12-8, Part 1, is indicated by `ElseIf lPara > 0 Then`. VBA won't check whether the running tally of discovered headings `lPara` is indeed greater than 0 unless the main condition `If Left$(paraThis.Style, 8) = "Heading "` evaluates False. Had we written `Else` by itself to lead in the "otherwise" portion of the conditional clause, the instructions contained within that portion would begin counting paragraphs that don't belong to any heading. It's important that the final product of this procedure look like a report of the text contained beneath clearly defined headings.

The `ElseIf` portion contains a conditional clause of its own. If `bProg = False` evaluates True, then the current paragraph `paraThis` must be the first one beneath an identified heading. In that case, the dynamic array `rngAnalysis()` is extended by one element, which is then loaded with the `Range` constituent of the `Paragraph` class object `paraThis`. The `Range` class carries with it all of the essential data you would ever need about the text contained within the range. So we can skip the actual assessment of how many paragraphs, sentences, and revisions the range contains until later, when the full extent of the range has been established.

Changing the boundaries of an established textual range

The boundaries of a range of text represented by a `Range` class object are considered rubber. Your VBA code may reset these boundaries manually, by setting the `.Start` and `.End` properties of the range to valid numbers. When the recording process for an "in-between" range begins, the reference `rngAnalysis(lPara)` refers only to the boundaries of paragraph `paraThis`. Then, Boolean variable `bProg` is set to `True`, and long integer `lWhich` is assigned the current value of `lPara` so that this value may be safely recalled later, when the range needs to be extended. As adjacent "in-between" paragraphs are located, the `.End` property of the range currently being recorded `rngAnalysis(lWhich)` is overwritten with the `.End` property of the newly found paragraph. The `.Start` and `.End` properties both contain character numbers, where 1 is the first character in the given range. So if `paraThis` refers to the final paragraph in the document, `docThis.Range.End` and `paraThis.Range.End` will most likely not be equal to one another, unless the entire document is only one paragraph in length.

In Part 2 of Listing 12-8, a separate loop clause provides a count for each element of the five arrays, starting once again at the very beginning:

Part 2

```
docThat.Paragraphs(docThat.Paragraphs.Count).Range.Delete
If UBound(strArray) > 0 Then
    BubbleSortIndexed strArray(), lIndex()
    For lX = 1 To lPara
        docThat.Hyperlinks.Add _
         (Anchor:=docThat.Paragraphs _
         (docThat.Paragraphs.Count).Range, _
         Address:=strName, SubAddress:=strMark(lIndex(lX)), _
         ScreenTip:="", _
         TextToDisplay:=strArray(lX)).Range.Select
        With docThat.ActiveWindow.Selection
            .Style = docThis.Paragraphs(lPlace(lX)).Style
            .InsertParagraphAfter
            .Collapse wdCollapseRight
            .Style = "Normal"
            strInsert = "Paragraphs: " & _
             Str$(rngAnalysis(lX).Paragraphs.Count)
            .InsertAfter strInsert
            .InsertParagraphAfter
            .Collapse wdCollapseRight
            strInsert = "Sentences: " & _
             Str$(rngAnalysis(lX).Sentences.Count)
            .InsertAfter strInsert
            .InsertParagraphAfter
            .Collapse wdCollapseRight
            strInsert = "Revisions: " & _
             Str$(rngAnalysis(lX).Revisions.Count)
            .InsertAfter strInsert
            .InsertParagraphAfter
            .Collapse wdCollapseRight
            If rngAnalysis(lX).Comments.Count > 0 Then
                .Font.Underline = wdUnderlineThick
                .InsertAfter "Comments:"
                .InsertParagraphAfter
                .Collapse wdCollapseRight
                .Font.Underline = wdUnderlineNone
                For Each cmtThis In rngAnalysis(lX).Comments
                    strInsert = cmtThis.Author & ":  "
                    .Font.Italic = True
                    .InsertAfter strInsert
                    .Font.Italic = False
                    .InsertAfter cmtThis.Range.Text
                    .InsertParagraphAfter
```

```
                        .Collapse wdCollapseRight
                    Next cmtThis
                End If
                .InsertParagraphAfter
            End With
        Next lX
    End If


    docThis.TrackRevisions = bTrack
End Sub
```

Don't let the size of this part of `Public Sub ParaStats()` frighten you; toward the end, in the report generation phase, it gets easier to understand. Part 2 begins by eliminating that pesky extra blank paragraph from the end of the copy document `docThat`. Next, as long as `strArray()` contains anything at all, a call is placed to a private procedure `BubbleSortIndexed()`. This procedure is passed two arrays: `strArray()` which contains the text of the located headings, and `lIndex()` whose contents will be shuffled the same way the contents of `strArray()` are shuffled.

In Chapter 3, you were introduced to a simple sort algorithm procedure `Private Sub BubbleSort()`, whose simple purpose was to sort a string array alphabetically. `Private Sub BubbleSortIndexed()` (whose listing will be presented in a few paragraphs) does exactly the same thing, although it also rearranges the order of a second long integer index array in tandem with the string array. *Indexing* is easily the most elementary efficiency technique in all of computing. As the string array `strArray()` is being compiled, a supplemental integer array is also being put together, whose values for now are equivalent to their subscripts. Why this redundancy? `Private Sub BubbleSortIndexed()` will accept both arrays as its arguments. When the procedure receives the integer array, its values will read in sequence: 1, 2, 3 . . . and so on. But once it's through, the array will reflect the index numerals of the swapped paragraphs in their new positions. As pairs of entries in `strArray()` are swapped with one another, so are corresponding pairs of entries in the equivalently sized `iIndex()`. So the calling procedure may see an array looking more like: 153, 92, 12 . . . reflecting the new positions of the originally indexed paragraphs.

It is here in Part 2 that the hyperlink is generated for each heading. A separate, conventional `For . . . Next` loop clause counts from 1 to the number of the last recorded heading `lPara`, and keeps that count in variable `lX`. Instead of pasting in text copied from the Clipboard, or setting an initial range to have the same text as the corresponding range in the source document — as prior procedures in this chapter have done — the `Hyperlinks.Add` instruction in Listing 12-8, Part 2, takes its bookmark locations and display text parameters straight from the dynamic arrays. The `TextToDisplay:` parameter is taken directly from `strArray()`, whose member string is referenced using simply `lX` as a subscript. Remember, after the call to `Private Sub BubbleSortIndexed()`, the `strArray()` array is perfectly sorted, so referencing that array with just the count variable `lX` is correct. However, array `strMark()` was not sorted likewise, so its contents reflect the original order in which bookmarks were generated by Part 1. So the entry in `strMark()` that corresponds to `strArray(lX)` is referenced using `lIndex(lX)` as a cross-reference value rather than `lX` by itself. If `lX` reflects a sorted location of an element, then `lIndex(lX)` reflects the *original* location for the same element.

Later, in order to reference the `.Style` property of the original heading, Part 2 has to know the original location of the heading paragraph in order that its style may be looked up. So a similar cross-reference takes place here. Array `lPlace()` contains the ordinal number of the heading paragraph in the original document. To cross-reference that paragraph, `lPlace(lX)` is supplied as the index for the `Paragraphs` collection. The result is that a specific paragraph is returned, whose `.Style` property may then be polled.

Insertion methods directly manipulate the cursor

From here on out, procedure `Public Sub ParaStats()` starts to look like a real macro. To generate information for a report, including the "Paragraphs," "Sentences," "Revisions," and "Comments" labels, the cursor within the window for `docThat` is manipulated directly, using methods of the `Selection` object. (So much for cursor independence.) The textual contents of the statistical data are generated by grafting the string-converted form of the `.Count` properties of the `Paragraphs`, `Sentences`, and `Revisions` collections, to the literal text that introduces them in the report, and assigning the result to string variable `strInsert`. This string is then typed out into the document by way of the `.InsertAfter` method. The "After" in this case means "after the current cursor location." By comparison, the `.InsertBefore` method generates text to the left of the cursor, generally thereby bumping the cursor to the right. Any text you enter into a document with `.InsertAfter` becomes automatically highlighted; and the `.InsertParagraphAfter` method performs the same job as if we had written `.InsertAfter Chr$(13)`. So both the inserted text and the inserted code 13 are highlighted. This is not what we want, so the `.Collapse` method is employed to un-highlight the text, and leave the cursor to the right of the formerly selected region. This leaves the cursor at the beginning of a fresh, new line, which is exactly what we want going into whatever instruction follows `.Collapse wdCollapseRight`.

Any given range supports any number of comments

In Word 2000, a comment is a separate annotation that's attributed to a passage without having to appear at, near, or in the vicinity of that passage. In fact, comments appear in a separate pane, and may be code-marked with the initials of their authors. This way, any number of editors may comment on a document without disturbing it . . . at least not any more than they do in the revision process anyway. (Perhaps I should be careful here . . .)

If any given region of text representable by a `Range` class object has comments attributed to it, then those comments may be retrieved as members of the `Comments` constituent of that `Range` object. For this procedure, we wanted to print out the comments belonging to a range of "in-between" paragraphs only if there were any comments. So `rngAnalysis(1X).Comments.Count` is checked first, and will only proceed to label the "Comments" section if that count is greater than 0. After a label is generated, a `For Each ... Next` loop counts through each of the comments in the range. (It's perfectly fine if there's only one comment; the loop clause won't complain if it doesn't actually get a chance to reiterate itself.)

A comment from the perspective of the Word 2000 object library is a formal `Range` class object enveloped with some other important data, such as the author of the comment, who is represented by the `.Author` property. So the procedure prints out `cmtThis.Author`—the name of the comment's author—followed by the text of the comment itself, `cmtThis.Range.Text`.

The final instruction in this procedure, `docThis.TrackRevisions = bTrack`, is a bug avoidance mechanism. In the beginning of the procedure (in Part 1), `bTrack` was set to the current state of Word's "Track Revisions" mode. It needs to be shut off in order to prevent references to `paraThis.Range.Text` to accidentally contain text in the revision state that is marked as deleted. The final instruction sets the mode back to the state represented by `bTrack`—whatever state it was in when the procedure started.

The indexed sort procedure

As we mentioned earlier, Part 2 of Listing 12-8 places a procedure call to `Private Sub BubbleSortIndexed()`, which appears in Listing 12-9:

Listing 12-9: A revised sort procedure that generates a cross-reference array.

```
Private Sub BubbleSortIndexed(strArray() As String, _
 lIndex() As Long)
    Dim j As Long, k As Long, l As Long, n As Long, t$
    Dim t2 As Long

    n = UBound(strArray)
    For l = 1 To n
        j = l
        For k = j + 1 To n
            If strArray(k) <= strArray(j) Then
                j = k
            End If
        Next k
        If l <> j Then
```

```
            t$ = strArray(j)
            t2 = lIndex(j)
            strArray(j) = strArray(l)
            lIndex(j) = lIndex(l)
            strArray(l) = t$
            lIndex(l) = t2
        End If
    Next l
End Sub
```

The differences between this procedure and Chapter 3's `Private Sub BubbleSort()` are to be found in the final conditional clause: The swap between units j and l of the string array is mimicked by units j and l of the index array. Otherwise, the body of the procedure remains the same.

My technical editor asks me from time to time, why do I choose to use single-letter variables and type identifier characters – such as the one in t$ above – in my algorithm procedures, but no place else? Isn't this simply inconsistent? It certainly is. I've been using these algorithms in my own programming for almost two decades, and they tend to resemble the form in which they originally appeared. In fact, I tend to recite BubbleSort procedures from memory. To quote the renowned mystic and soothsayer, Bugs Bunny, "Scary, ain't it?"

The major distinguishing factor between programming WordBasic macros and programming VBA procedures for Word 2000 concerns the principle of whom, or what, the programmer is addressing when telling the application what to do. The central terms in the WordBasic vocabulary were comprised of command *verbs* (FormatStyles, ShowHeading7, Seek), while the central terms in the Word 2000 object library are objects. Most of Word 2000's objects are nouns (Styles, Paragraphs, ActiveDocument), but one clear exception is the Find object. Although Find is, in English grammar, a verb, it is not a method in Word 2000; although rngSearch.Find looks like a method, it's actually an object that supports its own methods.

The Find object represents the criteria for a Word 2000 textual search. The characteristics of the search are the properties for this object. For instance, Find.Text represents the textual subject, if you will, of the search, and Find.Style represents any exclusive named style of paragraph or character that Word will be searching for. The search process doesn't take place until the Find.Execute method is executed.

To who does the Find object belong? Historically, a text search process moves the cursor through the document as the search progresses; but the textual engine of Word 2000 is fundamentally different in that **searches may be launched independently of the cursor.** The Selection object – which represents the cursor – does maintain its own Find object, and any searches that are executed using Selection.Find do move the cursor as they progress. But every Range class object can also have its own independent search process, which does not move the cursor and does not alter any other `Find` object.

A leisurely stroll through a search process

Here's how a search process works using the `Find` object, step by step:

1. First, the area being searched is defined. For `Selection.Find`, this area extends from the current cursor position to the border of the document or of the highlighted region, whichever comes first, in the specified direction of the search. By default, the property `Find.Forward` is set to `True`, which means that the search progresses *down* the document instead of up. For a `Range` class object, the `Find` method's boundaries are set to the region in between the character numerals pointed to by the `.Start` and `.End` properties of the range.

2. Generally, a `With` block is established, naming `Find` as the default object. This makes it easier not only to write instructions involving the `Find` object, but also for the human reader of the source code to identify the subject of the instructions.

3. Within the `With` block, properties of the `Find` object representing the characteristics of the search, may be set. Most commonly, the `.Text` property is set to a string that acts as the target of the search. The rules governing the contents of this string are the same as those employed for the Find dialog box in Word 2000. If a `.Text` property is not specified, the `Find` object will presume the target of the search does not involve text, but instead involves formatting, such as the `.Style` property.

4. If a replacement is to take place for each item found that matches the characteristics of the `Find` object, then `Find`'s subordinate `Replacement` object is used to specify the characteristics of whatever text or formatting will be substituted for the found object. For instance, `Find.Replacement. Text` will hold the text that will be substituted in place of the found text, in one or more instances. The `Replacement` object, if there is to be one, is defined prior to the execution of the search; so you can't `.Execute` the `Find` object and expect to have the module define a `Replacement` at the time the search turns up something.

5. The `Find.Execute` method starts the actual search process. If you did not specify parameters for the search earlier (steps 3 and 4), you can do so here within the optional arguments for the method; otherwise, if you leave out the arguments, the `.Execute` method assumes the `Find` property settings stated earlier. One of the common arguments for the `.Execute` method is `Replace:=wdReplaceAll`, which instructs the interpreter to go

ahead and apply the `Replacement` object characteristics to all found text without stopping to ask directions.

6. When `Selection.Find` scores a "hit," unless you specified `Replace:=wdReplaceAll`, the found portion will automatically be highlighted, and that portion becomes the `Selection` object. The same search process can be executed again from this point if the interpreter comes across the `.Execute` method once again, and the process will continue from the current cursor location toward the boundary of the document. Similarly, when `Find` for a `Range` class object scores a "hit," the `Range` class object *becomes* the found portion. At this particular point in time, when your module makes reference to the `Range` class object that owns the `Find`, that range is not presently the scope of the search, but is, instead, the region where the text was found. This is tricky, but it's for a reason. The range reference can be used to refer to the found text, to change it, to alter its formatting, to copy it somewhere, to record it within an array, or perform some other operation on it, just as you would for the `Selection` object when it scores a hit.

7. It gets trickier: When executing a reiterative search using `Find.Execute` in a loop clause, the original region of the search (the initial setting for the `Range` class object) is re-attained. If another "hit" is scored, the `Range` class object refers to the newly retrieved text region. At the end of the search process, the `Range` class object refers to the last "hit" region. If the search process never scored a hit, the `Range` class object refers to all of the original search area. By stark contrast, if the search process is non-reiterative, and `Replace:=wdReplaceAll` was specified as a parameter of the search, the boundaries of the object that owns the `Find` never change.

Augmenting search algorithms with the Find object

In Chapter 2, you were introduced to `Sub PeriodSpaceSpace()`, a Word 2000 procedure that alters a document so that if it were formatted with two spaces separating its sentences, it would become formatted with only one space, and vice versa. In two places in that procedure, `Find` objects were established within `With` clauses, the purpose of both being to find one separator type and replace it with the other wherever it appears.

Knowing what we know now about how `Find` objects work, we can modify that procedure to be more practical. After all, not all sentences end with periods. Listing 12-10 presents a modified form of that first procedure, retrofitted with the capability to search for anything used to generally terminate a sentence.

Listing 12-10: The revised sentence division procedure, aka "The Terminator."

```
Public Sub OneSpaceTwoSpace()
    Dim bEOF As Boolean
    Dim iCount As Integer, x As Integer, iCmp As Integer

    With ActiveDocument.Content.Find
        .Text = "[.\?\!]  (<[A-Z])"
        .Forward = True
        .MatchWildcards = True

        For x = 1 To 5
            If .Execute Then
                iCount = iCount + 1
            Else
                bEOF = True
                Exit For
            End If
        Next x
    End With

    If bEOF Then
        iCmp = x
    Else
        iCmp = 5
    End If

    With ActiveDocument.Content.Find
        .Forward = True
        .MatchWildcards = True

        If iCount = iCmp Then
            .Text = "([.\?\!]) (<[A-Z])"
            .Replacement.Text = "\1 \2"
            .Execute Replace:=wdReplaceAll
            .Text = "([.\?\!])([" & Chr$(34) _
                & "^0147\)\]\}]) (<[A-Z])"
            .Replacement.Text = "\1\2 \3"
            .Execute Replace:=wdReplaceAll
        Else
            .Text = "([.\?\!]) (<[A-Z])"
            .Replacement.Text = "\1  \2"
            .Execute Replace:=wdReplaceAll
```

```
            .Text = "([.\?\!])([" & Chr$(34) _
            & "^0147\)\]\}]) (<[A-Z])"
            .Replacement.Text = "\1\2  \3"
            .Execute Replace:=wdReplaceAll
        End If
    End With
End Sub
```

Here, the first Find object is used to test the waters, to determine whether the first five sentences are separated with two spaces. Based on what this first Find object turns up, it knows whether to change the document from one-space separation to two, or from two-space to one. The revised replacement section adds a few elements to the search. Word 2000 has no wildcard characters that mean "find *zero* or more instances of this character." So the search for sentences that end with common punctuation, but are separated from the spaces by a close parenthesis, a close quote (either code 34 or code 147), or some type of bracket closure has to be made a separate search.

 A Range class object refers to any division or subdivision of the text of a document. Meanwhile, the Selection object (of which there is only one per window) represents the text that is currently being highlighted, or about to be manipulated, by the cursor. Unlike earlier versions of Word, the cursor is not the only tool available to you for manipulating text in a document, nor is it even the primary tool. Your VBA module can assign text directly to a Range class object or to a reference to one of these objects, and the corresponding document will be changed in turn.

Mixing the process models

Suppose the user writes documents within which he frequently includes bibliographic references, perhaps in the midst of other paragraphs, or perhaps in footnotes along the bottom edge of pages. A Word VBA procedure could be written that detects these bibliographic references (assuming they're in isolated paragraphs) and copies them to a collective bibliography page. The tool that the module would use to detect whether a paragraph is bibliographic, would be the name of the style applied to that paragraph; in this case, the user is trusted to utilize the "Bibliography" style exclusively for such paragraphs.

In cases where conditional logic is involved in evaluating whether a text element or range qualifies for an operation, we need some way of stepping through all of the elements and testing each one in succession. A macro writing veteran would think in this way: First, drop the cursor at the top of the document, then write a never-ending loop that searches for a paragraph with the "Bibliography" style. When the loop finds one, highlight that paragraph, copy it to the Clipboard, then paste it into a specified section at the end of the document or within another document altogether. When the loop fails to find a new paragraph, force an exit from the loop, then have the cursor highlight the section with the copied bibliographies, and feed that section to the paragraph sorting procedure.

It's a working model, but in light of recent developments, it isn't as efficient as it can be. With the Word 2000 object library in place, we can leave the cursor right where it is – in fact, we can have it act as a placeholder for the spot where the sorted bibliography paragraphs should be placed. We can use a Range object to define the area of the search, and then use objects independent of the cursor to launch a search for the paragraphs in question. Once they are located, we don't need the Clipboard to move them from place to place; keep in mind that we're not trying to mimic here what the user would do if he were performing the job manually. Listing 12-11 shows a working model of this procedure. Notice here, however, the limited though still important role of the Selection object.

Listing 12-11: The bibliography collection procedure.

```
Public Sub SortCertainParaSel()
    Dim rngSearch As Range
    Dim strArray() As String, iIndex() As Integer
    Dim iCount As Integer, iX As Integer
    Dim colParaBlock As New Collection

    Set rngSearch = ActiveDocument.Range

    With rngSearch.Find
        .ClearFormatting
        .Text = ""
        .Style = ActiveDocument.Styles("Bibliography")
        While .Execute
            iCount = iCount + 1
            ReDim Preserve strArray(iCount), iIndex(iCount)
            strArray(iCount) = rngSearch.Text
            iIndex(iCount) = iCount
            colParaBlock.Add rngSearch.Paragraphs(1)
        Wend
    End With

    BubbleSortIndexed strArray(), iIndex()

    If UBound(strArray) > 0 Then
```

```
        For iX = 1 To iCount
            colParaBlock.item(iIndex(iX)).Range.Copy
            Selection.Paste
        Next iX
    End If
End Sub
```

A few new techniques have been introduced here, so I'll describe Listing 12-11 slowly. Object variable rngSearch is set to the full extent of the current document. We'll assume for this particular version of the procedure that the document being searched, and the document that will contain the sorted bibliography, are the same document.

Reiterated searches should encompass defined ranges

The parameters of the search are first preloaded into the Find object belonging to rngSearch, a Range class object. In Word 2000, executing a search operation or a search-and-replace operation involves manipulating the Find object that is the subordinate of the search area's Range class object, or of the Selection object. The entire body of a document can be addressed as a range; Word provides a special subordinate to the Document class, called Content, that identifies just the main body of text in the document, not counting the header and footer regions or annotations. So the area of the search may be stated as Set rngSearch = ActiveDocument. Content. But the native Range subordinate of a Document class object refers to exactly that same area. When you use the Find object that is the subordinate of Selection, your search range is unofficially, though generally, the entire document anyway, because when a Selection.Find process locates whatever it is set to look for, the range of Selection is reset to encompass the found item. Thus, if you were to use Selection as a tool for the Find operation here, you'd find what you were looking for, *but you would lose where you found it* – defeating the whole point of the search. You could not then search for something else within the same region of text, without resetting Selection to refer to that region. So if you plan on subdividing the document and looking for something in a defined subregion, use a Range reference to identify that region rather than Selection.

Before the search process begins in Listing 12-11, there is one maintenance instruction and two search parameters. The .ClearFormatting method is a measure of prudence. Each time a new Find object is set up for a certain range or for Selection, any new properties of the search are added to the existing properties of that same search. There can be several Find objects in existence simultaneously,

---

At Present: Character Styles versus Paragraph Styles

Word 2000, unlike some other word processors, has two different classifications for named *styles* applied within documents:

* A *paragraph style* includes the necessary characteristics for formatting a long sequence of text — such as how much leading to apply between each line or raster, and what margins and tab stops are to be applied.

* A *character style* includes a subset of the characteristics of a paragraph style, limited specifically to those necessary to print at least one letter or number — for instance, what font to use, what weight for the strokes, and whether to underline.

Both classifications are listed together in Word's single styles drop-down list box on its Formatting toolbar; and styles of both classifications share the object library's Styles collection.

---

but each one has an "owner;" and the properties of each owner's Find objects are not automatically cleared once the previously executed search has completed. So any new property settings are added to the old ones. Although rngSearch was created for the express purposes of this procedure, future builds of any modules that use this procedure may borrow rngSearch for their own purposes. Thus it makes sense to clear any existing parameters now before the search begins, using the .ClearFormatting method plus the instruction that follows it, .Text = "", which clears any target text that may be in existence.

The names given to all of the paragraph and character styles for a Word document are represented by the Styles collection of the Document class object. Here, ActiveDocument.Styles("Bibliography") refers to the style named "Bibliography" for the currently open document, not a style by the same name within any other document or template.

Next in Listing 12-11, notice an old-style While...Wend loop clause that runs a series of consecutive executions of the specified Find. The loop automatically drops out if the search ever fails, because the .Execute method returns a value of True if it finds what it's looking for (that is, if it "scores a hit"), and False if the search fails. Conceivably, you could write a conditional clause that begins If .Execute Then... and be assured that the instructions in the true portion of the clause would only be executed if Word finds what you've told it to look for.

A Paragraph object omits internal formatting

In Listing 12-11, the familiar strArray() and iIndex() arrays used by the paragraph sorting procedure Private Sub BubbleSortIndexed() are dynamic. The

ReDim Preserve statement has their sizes increased by one each time the .Execute method comes across a new bibliographic paragraph. But notice something else that's new toward the end of the While...Wend loop: our very own Collection class object, colParaBlock, to hold the actual paragraphs that match the search criteria. Remember, strArray() is a string array which, in VBA and all other BASIC language derivatives, is comprised of raw text. The paragraph sorting procedure can make use of this raw text, since it doesn't need all the extra formatting for it to do its job. But one of the elements that distinguishes a formal bibliographic paragraph, using the rules of the *Chicago Manual of Style* (to which many professional writers and layout specialists as "The Orange Brick"), is that the name of the book being mentioned in the paragraph is *italicized*. Italics is one of the main formatting features lost in the conversion to raw text; so if we relied upon strArray() as the source of the *copied* paragraphs also, we would lose the formatting in the copy. So a Collection class object that will manage the paragraphs independently, is declared near the top of the procedure using Dim colParaBlock As New Collection. (If the New term had been left out, a Set statement would have been required later to point colParaBlock toward an existing collection; and we do not want a reference to an *existing* collection.)

A Collection class object is a generic collection; it really doesn't have any exclusive characteristics, nor can it be given any since it cannot be delegated its own class. However, the characteristics of one of the objects assigned to the collection through the .Add method can be accessed through a bridge property .Item. For example, in Listing 12-11, each located bibliography paragraph is added to colParaBlock using the .Add method. Later, when a cross-referenced member of this collection is recalled, that member will contain all the exclusive formatting that belongs to the original paragraphs, including such peculiar features as *partial* italics or underline.

The Clipboard copies internally formatted text

This is where things turn a bit retrograde on us at the last minute: We want the copied bibliography paragraphs to have *all* of the same formatting as the original. Although the Word 2000 object library gives us several methods for copying ranges to new locations – among them, the .InsertAfter and .InsertBefore methods for the Selection object; and my personal favorite, simply assigning the new text directly to Selection.Text with a simple assignment expression – none of these methods retains the precise formatting of the original paragraphs. This formatting is necessary for a bibliography page to be legitimate in the eyes of English professors.

One of the few ways we can copy the text and retain the formatting is if we use the Windows System Clipboard as a conduit, and invoke the old methods .Copy and .Paste. In Listing 12-11, the .Copy method was used in succession to place a cross-referenced paragraph range on the Clipboard; Selection.Paste then takes it off. The precise formatting does come along with the paste, but at a price: Word has to communicate with the Clipboard *remotely*, because the Clipboard is an independent process managed by Windows' USER32 library at the core of the operating system. So a lot of time is expended initiating each communication and shutting it down, initiating it again and shutting that down, and so on. (This is one reason why the cursor-dependent examples in Listings 12-4 and 12-6 were slower than their cursor-independent counterparts.)

AutoText manages clips of internally formatted text

The other process available to us for copying all the text and the formatting is somewhat more elaborate, but a bit faster in execution. Strangely enough, it involves using Word 2000's own Normal document template as a conduit for shuttling paragraphs from point to point. The text gets copied to a collection maintained by the NormalTemplate object, called AutoTextEntries. Listing 12-12 shows the significant changes this underhanded process makes to our procedure.

Listing 12-12: Using AutoText as a fully formatted textual conduit.

```
Public Sub SortCertainParaSel2()
    Dim rngSearch As Range
    Dim strArray() As String, iIndex() As Integer, _
     strParaIndex() As String
    Dim iCount As Integer, iX As Integer
    Dim strPara As String

    Set rngSearch = ActiveDocument.Range

    With rngSearch.Find
        .ClearFormatting
        .Text = ""
        .Style = ActiveDocument.Styles("Bibliography")
        While .Execute
            iCount = iCount + 1
            ReDim Preserve strArray(iCount), iIndex(iCount), _
          strParaIndex(iCount)
            strArray(iCount) = rngSearch.Text
            iIndex(iCount) = iCount
            strPara = "Para" & Str$(iCount)
            strParaIndex(iCount) = strPara
            NormalTemplate.AutoTextEntries.Add strPara, _
          rngSearch.Paragraphs(1).Range
```

At Present: The Mechanics of Word's AutoText

In Word 2000, an *AutoText* entry is a passage of text — perhaps a "boilerplate" message, or a commonly used disclaimer — that is stored with one of the document templates on which a document is based, either Normal or an exclusive template. This passage is keyed by name, so when you go into the dialog box that lists available AutoText entries (Insert → AutoText → AutoText), you can see the names for all of these entries, choose one of them, and thereby enter its associated text directly into the document. Another way to produce AutoText is to type the name of the AutoText entry directly into the document, then press F3 to replace that name with the text of the entry itself. Alternately, you can place a reference to the AutoText entry instead as a *field code*; this way, the text does appear in the final printing, but it doesn't get entirely copied to the document file — something like a "link," except OLE is not involved.

```
        Wend
    End With

    If UBound(strArray) > 0 Then
        BubbleSortIndexed strArray(), iIndex()
        For iX = 1 To iCount
          NormalTemplate.AutoTextEntries _
            (strParaIndex(iIndex(iX))).Insert _
            Where:=Selection.Range, RichText:=True
          NormalTemplate.AutoTextEntries _
            (strParaIndex(iIndex(iX))).Delete
        Next iX
    End If
End Sub
```

The AutoText system makes itself convenient to you, the VBA programmer, because it is one of Word's only systems for recording a block of text plus its *precise* formatting. To explain: Assume the paragraph you're reading now is part of a Word document (and just by coincidence, it once was) and is being referred to by an object reference, rngPara. A Range class object maintains its own Boolean properties, .Bold, .Italic, and .Underline, which are set to True if the *entire* range is bold-faced, italicized, or underlined. But this particular paragraph is not entirely any one of these states; the words "*precise*" and "*entire*" are both uniquely italicized, and the various VBA terms are printed using their own exclusive monospace font. The Range class object has no way to store this information along with the body of the text itself; so a copied version of rngPara.Text will contain the words "precise," "entire," and ".Italic" without any special treatment applied to them.

Why is this the case? Because the way Word views a document *in its own memory*, the codes that have it format a single word differently from the rest of the paragraph are not stored right beside the word itself. Instead, these codes are part of a database which is stored within the header of the document file. The fact that all this information is within one database for each document is partly what makes Word work so fast and so well. You see, it has to make preparations beforehand for any text that might be formatted in a peculiar fashion, because this formatting might adversely affect the positioning of adjacent text in a paragraph. If Word were only to encounter a special italicizing code *when it came time to apply that code*, Word would have to *rethink* its approach to the formatting of the entire paragraph. (I can just hear the Simonyi engine saying to itself, "Now he tells me! First, he says he wants it *this* way, now he wants it *that* way . . . ")

So VBA and the Word 2000 object library are hindered just a bit as to the level of access they are given to the real contents of the document. Nowhere in the library is there any object that refers to this magical database header, nor are there any tools offered with which even the most fastidious programmer may hack into it. This is why Listing 12-12 uses the strange, but effective, option of borrowing from AutoText to copy multiple paragraphs in such a way that their original formatting is maintained.

Managing AutoText entries through VBA

In Listing 12-12, the While...Wend loop is responsible for recording the found bibliography paragraphs as unique AutoText entries. Although Word maintains an AutoTextEntries collection for every entry in a document, Word can't treat this like an ordinary collection, because every entry must have its own *name*. Here, a name is an alphanumeric string, whose true purpose is to make AutoText entries identifiable by the user; but since the user won't be seeing these entries, what we choose to call them is immaterial except for the fact that may not all be given the same name. So a string variable strPara was declared to hold an exclusive name for each new entry. The exclusive name is generated with the expression strPara = "Para" & Str$(iCount). You may remember that iCount is the integer which holds the number of bibliography paragraphs found thus far; we'll borrow from that number by using the Str$() function to derive a string from it, and then attach it to the prefix Para. (If there's already an AutoText entry named Para 1 or Para 2, that entry will be overwritten by the new one, with no error condition generated to inform anyone that it happened. Thus, it's important that names are generated that the user wouldn't think of on his own.) An array variable strParaIndex() was also declared that will retain the names generated for the AutoText entries, because they'll each be recalled by name later.

On Point

The key objects in the Word 2000 object library are `Application` (generally implied, unless some other application owns the current instance of the VBA interpreter), the `Documents` collection, `Range`, and `Selection`. The `Documents` collection maintains the set of documents currently open in the word processor. These documents are represented individually by `Document` class objects. Documents are generally addressed as members of the `Documents` collection rather than as individual objects in their own right, although `Document` class object reference variables can be declared and set to refer to these documents indirectly. The `ActiveDocument` term always refers to the Word document whose window currently has the focus.

A `Range` class object refers to any division or subdivision of the text of a document. Meanwhile, the `Selection` object (of which there is only one per window) represents the text that is currently being highlighted, or about to be manipulated, by the cursor. Unlike earlier versions of Word, the cursor is not the only tool you have available to you for manipulating text in a document, nor is it even the primary tool. Your VBA module can assign text directly to a `Range` class object or to a reference to one of these objects, and the corresponding document will be changed in turn.

The main collection objects maintained by the `Document` class are `Paragraphs`, `Sentences`, `Words`, and `Characters`. These collections reflect the visible contents of the main body of their antecedent document. All entries in this collection are indexed by number beginning, appropriately enough, with 1; so `docThis.Paragraphs(1)` refers to the first (visible) paragraph of a document referred to by the variable `docThis`. The `Words` and `Characters` collection also include the basic ASCII formatting codes, such as carriage returns, as individual members. Inclusion of these codes proves useful in disseminating the construction of any document, though a hindrance in determining the true word or character count of any *portion* of a document. Word 2000 does provide a `Selection.Information` collection and a `BuiltInDocumentProperties` property of a `Document` class object, for eliciting information from the word processor about the true element counts for any *entire* document. For counting elements in *portions* of a document, it becomes necessary to write code that separates the grain from the chaff, if you will.

The conditional clause uses the VBA intrinsic function `UBound()` to check whether the array `strArray` contains any entries whatsoever. (Here, `strArray` is expressed without the parentheses because `UBound()` only requires the array name for its sole argument.) If the array is empty, there are no bibliography paragraphs to be sorted anyway. If it's not empty, then the sort procedure is called, and a loop clause cross-references the sorted list of AutoText entries by name, recalling these names from the `strParaIndex()` array. The `.Insert` method copies an AutoText entry to the specified location — in this case, the region represented by the cursor,

`Selection.Range`. Notice the parameter `RichText:=True`, which directs AutoText to leave the exclusive formatting intact. After each entry is inserted, the next instruction — which contains the `.Delete` method — subsequently removes it from the AutoText collection; the user has no further need for it, and neither do you. Deleting the AutoText entry from the template does not eliminate the text from the page; once it's copied in, it's fixed there. In other words, the copied text isn't a field code reference (an application-specific link) to the original text appearing elsewhere.

In Theory: Whither hypertext?

My mother used to tell me, quite nicely, that I kept a messy desk partly because I infrequently needed reassurance that whatever it was that I was doing had some modicum of importance to it. A clean desk is, for me, a portent of inactivity, at least insofar as my own affairs are concerned. If I ever find my desk clean, even if it is I who put it that way, I begin to wonder if perhaps I had died.

The original purpose of hypertext was to give the authors of digital documents some vehicle with which to easily connect passages of non-adjacent text that shared some logical context with one another. Why make the user have to cross-reference another document with a selector dialog and a scroll bar? If computing is to be a convenience to anyone, perhaps it should be accomplished with *fewer*, not greater, tools. Clicking on an underlined passage and letting the window take you to a page with greater depth of detail about the subject of that passage, just makes too much sense. The very first Internet hypertext documents were exchanged between physicists, who used the tool as a way to link together the various treatises and propositions they were concocting at the time about muons, superstrings, and the strange quark.

When hypertext first became the next "big thing" in computing, manufacturers worked hard to incorporate as much of it into everyday computer work as possible. Hypertext became the engine that ran the new Help systems, word processors such as Microsoft Word became endowed with hypertextual capabilities, and the term itself became the "HT" in "HTTP," the protocol that drives the World Wide Web. And to help hypertext "pay off," the corporations who first got their hands on hypertext used as much of it as possible.

As a result, the first publicly accessible hypertext documents looked something like...well, like my desk. An amalgamation of mass media collected from every conceivable source — logical, physical, virtual, and metaphysical — some of it actually making some bit of sense. Still, they were interesting experiments, because some people — many of them *not* physicists — were examining for the first time the concept of lexical contexts and the ways that text conveys information to people.

All of which led to some very interesting discussions. For instance, is the nature of textual information necessarily sequential? With the Web model of information, a reader would find herself "browsing" through facts in no particular order. A writer of this information, meanwhile, is accustomed to coordinating facts in his mind and transferring that order to paper (or, in this case, to the screen). If the order in which a reader assembles facts in her own mind is different from the order in which the author presented them, is there some bit of information that gets lost as a result? Or is there perhaps some information that the reader *gains* that perhaps the author himself did not foresee?

As you've seen demonstrated here, today's Word 2000 word processor has built-in capabilities for generating hypertext links, which take the reader to a designated position in another Word document or HTML file. (The menu command is Insert → Hyperlink, and from there, the dialogs are quite descriptive.) Not that hyperlinks have anything to do with the way the document is *printed*. For another reader to enjoy the contextual relations you've devised, that reader either requires her own copy of Word 2000, or you should save your document as an HTML file so she can use her Web browser to read it. But now that you have that capability, the question arises, what can you really *do* with it? Historically, a word processor of the caliber of Word 2000 has been used to generate *printed* business documents. The application has yet to find a real niche as a console for the projection of hypertextual digital text, even now that Microsoft has been touting Dynamic HTML as Word's "alternate format." You could write the Web address for someone's home page into your Word document, and Word would be smart enough to generate a hyperlink based on that `http://` URL. But the esoteric joy of experimenting with the meanings behind meanings, ends up entirely unexplored. Which is quite alright by the standards of certain business administrators who don't have time calculated in their budgets for the study of semantics.

With the advent of "drop-in" objects on the Web page, flashy push buttons, scrolling stock tickers, and the now-irrepressible animated billboard upon which the modern Internet economy is based, the need for text that links to other text, at least with regard to the Internet, has become quite ancillary. The common Web site – in a sense, the by-product of some interested parties' quest to understand meanings behind meanings – has become . . . well, you could say, *busy*. Perhaps a bit cluttered. My mother says there's a reason for that.

In Brief

◆ The five principal objects in the Word 2000 object library are `Application` (which represents the automation server), `Documents` (which represents the collection of loaded document files), `Windows` (which represents the on-screen devices with which documents are edited), `Range` (which represents any contiguous passage of text), and `Selection` (which represents the current location of the cursor).

◆ Any contiguous passage of text describable by a `Range` or `Document` class object or by `Selection` is considered to have its own set of collection objects that represent its contents. `Paragraphs`, `Sentences`, and `Words` are all considered members of these collections, as well as features of the word processor such as `Fields` and `Bookmarks`.

♦ No longer does text within a Word 2000 document have to be manipulated in code solely by the cursor. `Range` class objects are easy to establish and are independent of the cursor. However, polling the `Selection` object is still critical for determining which text passage the user is referring to when invoking a "macro."

♦ The `.Text` properties of `Range` class objects take into account the characters that belong to a passage, but not their formatting. Word's only representative of formatted text independent of a document, is an entry in the AutoText database for a document's template.

♦ The `Find` object is representative of a search process within `Range` class objects as well as `Selection`. Its properties represent characteristics of the search operation. Besides what text to look for, characteristics include the direction in which the search is to proceed, whether the search is case sensitive, and what text, if any, shall replace the located passages.

Chapter 13

Migrating from WordBasic to VBA

IN THIS CHAPTER

◆ Manipulating the `Selection` object directly

◆ Formatting and typesetting instructions

◆ Looking into the `Font`, `ParagraphFormat`, and `Style` objects

◆ Automating the cursor

◆ Programming simple and complex search and replace operations

◆ Adding and removing text through instructions

◆ Maintaining the contents of the Word workspace

IF YOU'RE A veteran programmer of WordBasic, the macro language that was shipped with Word versions 1.x, 2.x, 6, and 7 (what happened to 3 through 5?), then this chapter may very well be the first part of this book that you read. However, even if you haven't programmed with any prior Word language to this point, **don't skip this chapter.** I discuss a number of subjects in this chapter that have not been covered up to this point.

Paradigm Shift

Programming with Visual Basic for Applications and the Word 2000 object library is as different from programming with Word 7.0's WordBasic as Pascal is from C++. Any *similarities* you may draw between the two are all on the surface, and tend to disappear the deeper you get into the subject. The VBA Help file might have given you the impression that your familiar WordBasic keywords now have synonyms in the new object library. The dangling braided cord on an ornate sword is called by the French *une porte-épée*, and by the English "a frog." Even synonyms have their own exclusive contexts, and if you don't understand them, you cannot comprehend the ways in which those synonyms do relate to one another.

A VBA procedure is not a remote controller

Perhaps the most important contextual difference between a VBA procedure and a WordBasic macro is that a VBA procedure or module is not designed to remotely control the application to which it belongs. At first, this might seem a little odd because, evidently, the terms you use in writing a VBA project contain several hundred keywords that directly address Word 2000. But not one of those terms is actually a native part of the VBA vocabulary. Instead, these terms are linked into the VBA interpreter by means of the Word 2000 object library, which is a separate file that lists the terms that VBA may use when addressing Word.

So isn't the VBA system officially remote control? Not really. "Remote control" implies that the application is being operated with the same tools that are available to the user. The control that a VBA programmer is given is *direct*, not remote. You may have noticed that a majority of the WordBasic keywords are based directly on menu commands. Obviously, a WordBasic macro is designed to follow, for the most part, the same steps that a human user would take to accomplish a given task with the word processor. Many of the statistics applicable to a document were obtained in WordBasic by "dimensioning" one of Word 7.0's dialog boxes, allowing Word to think it is displaying said box, then using the statement `GetCurValues` to dump the values from the invisible text boxes into a sort of object variable. So the WordBasic macro even assumes that if the user is not able to perform a task without pulling up the appropriate dialog, then neither should the macro interpreter.

Rather than try to mimic the behavior of a user going through the motions of performing some task, the VBA procedure plays the role of an accessory to the application. The user interacts with the VBA program rather than that program interacting on behalf of the user with the Word application. You'll find the newer model to be significantly more sensible. As an extension of the application rather than of the user, the VBA program is more seamlessly integrated into the Word 2000 environment.

Structural changes: The end of Sub MAIN

The WordBasic macro was structured around the performance of *one task*. This one task was given a name, and Microsoft's suggestion was that you pick a name that implies the position of that macro on the Word application menu. For instance, `ViewReplaceIcons` would suggest the presence of a "Replace Icons" command accessible from the View menu. The macro interpreter, upon receiving the command, would initiate a procedure that was always called `Sub MAIN`. Late in the development of WordBasic, it became possible for `Sub MAIN` to place calls to other procedures and pass arguments to those procedures; and later still, those procedures could be located in separate "library" macros. You could define a library macro as a set of procedures that contained no `Sub MAIN`. But with respect to the "interface," if you will, between the WordBasic macro and the Word application, there was either *one* macro entry point — `Sub MAIN` — or there were *zero* entry points.

The Word VBA project is designed to "plug into" the application at various points. This way, its modules and contained procedures may provide the user with a set of functionality options without having to confine all of those options to just one menu command or keystroke. Gone is the necessity to name one of the procedures in the macro Sub MAIN. In its place is the requirement to declare at least one of the procedures in the VBA module Public, as in Public Sub ViewReplaceIcons(). **The names that the user sees when he selects Macros from the Macro list under the Tools menu in Word 2000 are from a list of available** Public Sub **procedures in so-called general modules, not the names of modules that contain macros.** A general module may contain more than one Public Sub procedure, including any number of Public Function procedures, whose purpose is to return a calculated value to the part of the module that calls it. Public Function procedures are not available to the user, however, since the user would have no mechanism for passing arguments to the procedure, nor is the user expected to have a spare variable at the ready for receiving the result.

In VBA, a general module is a distinct entity from an *object module*. VBA has three kinds of object modules: one that represents *forms* (Word VBA's replacement for the old custom dialog boxes), another that represents each Word document (ThisDocument), and the class module that provides a mechanism for portable component-oriented functionality. The true difference between a general module and an object module is that, at run-time, an object module behaves like a Windows COM component, with its own rules of interfacing with other components and broadcasting its own events. A general module, by contrast, is merely a scroll with some executable source code in it.

If you leave off the Public designation from a procedure, the VBA interpreter assumes it to be public anyway. So to remove a procedure from view of the user, you explicitly declare it Private. This designation also renders the procedure inaccessible from other modules, which gives you a means for "exposing," to use the Microsoft term, only those procedures that you want the rest of the world to be able to utilize.

Replacing dialog functions with form modules

The WordBasic macro permitted you to generate "custom dialogs," which were controls loaded with the contents of WordBasic variables. Although you could use a program called Dialog Editor, the purpose of that accessory program was to generate the WordBasic instructions that told the macro, at run time, how to assemble your dialog panel. From one of my favorite Word 7.0 macros, Listing 13-1 presents the instructions for the dialog panel that mimicked the "View Header/Footer" dialog of Word 2.0.

Listing 13-1: An old **WordBasic** procedure for generating a dialog box.

```
Sub MainDialog
        Begin Dialog UserDialog 484, 175, "Header/Footer", ●
    .DialogFunction
                Text 10, 6, 117, 13, "Header/Foote&r:", .tType      '0
                ListBox 11, 22, 265, 89, Type$(), .lbType '1
                CheckBox 12, 125, 176, 16, "Different First &Page", ●
    .chbFirstPage   '2
                CheckBox 12, 148, 260, 16, "&Different Odd and Even ●
    Pages", .chbOddAndEvenPages   '3
                OKButton 307, 12, 148, 21, .pbOK      '4
                CancelButton 307, 36, 148, 21, .pbCancel   '5
                PushButton 307, 64, 148, 21, "Page &Numbers...", ●
      .pbPageNumbers       '6
                GroupBox 289, 104, 184, 65, "From Edge", .gbDistance
    '7
                Text 301, 123, 61, 13, "&Header:", .tHeaderDistance
    '8
                TextBox 370, 121, 91, 18, .tbHeaderDistance       '9
                Text 301, 147, 55, 13, "&Footer:", .tFooterDistance
    '10
                TextBox 370, 144, 91, 18, .tbFooterDistance       '11
        End Dialog
        Dim dlg As UserDialog
        x = Dialog(dlg)
End Sub
```

The Word 7.0 macro would define a custom dialog by means of a so-called Dialog block (what we would today call a "clause"). Here, the block defined a dialog panel with the UserDialog classification. All of the controls that comprised this dialog were declared here by designating their upper left corner coordinates, followed by their width and height, their textual contents if they had any, and their control names with which the rest of the macro could refer to them. Once constructed, UserDialog became the class name for the dialog panel, and an object variable dlg was declared that would collectively represent all the values maintained by the dialog panel, though only for purposes of the very next instruction. Finally, the Dialog() function was used to bring the dialog panel to the screen. Here, variable x was a dummy, and could logically have been used to determine whether the dialog panel successfully made it to the screen.

At the top of the procedure, the Begin Dialog statement named a function DialogFunction, which would act as the "handler" for this dialog. Whenever the user activated anything on this panel while it was on the screen, Function DialogFunction() was called, and was given the name and associated value of the activated control. It was then up to this handler function alone to determine, based on the name and value of the control, what it was that the user was directing the dialog panel to do. Remember, each time the user activated the panel, this one function procedure was called as a result; the fact that this procedure was called did not necessarily impart any information to the programmer as to *why* it was called. So the programmer had to employ a lot of `Select Case` logic to determine the active status of the dialog panel each time.

The structure of VBA and the Word 2000 object library in producing and handling programmer-defined dialog panels is fundamentally different from that of WordBasic. There is near zero correlation between these two models of the Word background program. With VBA, all dialog panels belong to their own modules. These are the *form modules*, which were introduced in Chapter 5. More importantly, the identity and positioning of controls within a VBA form (dialog panel) do not translate into instructions. In other words, there is no equivalent of the `Begin Dialog...End Dialog` block from WordBasic. When you use the VBA environment to build a dialog panel, just dragging its controls into place and shaping them the way you need them to appear at startup is enough to define the dialog for VBA. The VBA interpreter records what you have done within its own internal database, and doesn't need to render an account of what you've done within separate instructions. If you need to change the dialog, you can move the controls around and add and subtract features as necessary, rather than tinker with clumsy instructions in your mind.

A form module is separate from the modules that call it and that are linked to Word 2000. So it is up to a `Public Sub` procedure in a general module that is accessible to the user – that has a hook to the application somewhere – to execute an instruction that contains the `.Show` method, and that names that form (dialog panel). This `.Show` instruction passes control to the form module, but does not name any specific procedure within that module that is to be executed first. What does get executed first is the procedure associated with the *event* of form initialization. You see, each control within a form, including the form itself, has a number of named events that trigger the execution of procedures specifically named for them. (Chapter 2 introduces the topic of event procedures.) `Private Sub UserForm_Initialize()` is the name of the procedure that is always executed first within a form module, if it's present. Its execution takes place *prior* to the form or any of its controls actually being seen; so you can preset some of the conditions for the form's execution out of sight of the user. By the way, in the context of a form module, `UserForm` is always the name with which it refers to its own class, so `UserForm` is the name applied to the module's event procedures; whereas, whatever name you give to the form arbitrarily is used in the `.Show` method *outside* of the form module.

By contrast with the `.Show` method, VBA does maintain the `Load` statement as a mechanism for loading a designated form into memory *without* displaying it. Both the `Load` statement and any other instruction that makes reference to a form that has not been loaded and made active, will result in that form being loaded into memory and its `_Initialize` event procedure being shown, *but not made active and visible to the user.*

The truth about "conversion"

If the old UserDialog and the new UserForm are so fundamentally different from one another, why is it that when Word 2000 loads an old Word 6.0 or 7.0 template and, without asking first, converts its macros to run in Word 2000, those macros generally run just fine? I've read more than one nationally published review praising the capabilities of the macro conversion process. If the converter does such a good job, why should you even have to consider writing replacements for your old macros?

The old macros may still work for a reason you might not expect: **WordBasic is still a component shipped with Word 2000.** The old macros work because VBA converts their old instructions into component-lexicon-style calls placed to the WordBasic component. For example, Listing 13-2 shows how Word VBA treated the dialog definition instructions from Listing 13-1 during its conversion process.

Listing 13-2: The "converted" macro procedure.

```
Private Sub MainDialog()
Dim x
    WordBasic.BeginDialog 484, 175, "Header/Footer", _
  "NormalViewHeaderFooter.DialogFunction"
        WordBasic.Text 10, 6, 117, 13, "Header/Foote&r:", _
         "tType"    '0
        WordBasic.ListBox 11, 22, 265, 89, Type___$(), _
         "lbType"   '1
        WordBasic.CheckBox 12, 125, 176, 16, _
         "Different First &Page", "chbFirstPage"    '2
        WordBasic.CheckBox 12, 148, 260, 16, _
         "&Different Odd and Even Pages", "chbOddAndEvenPages" '3
        WordBasic.OKButton 307, 12, 148, 21, "pbOK" '4
        WordBasic.CancelButton 307, 36, 148, 21, "pbCancel" '5
        WordBasic.PushButton 307, 64, 148, 21, _
         "Page &Numbers...", "pbPageNumbers" '6
        WordBasic.GroupBox 289, 104, 184, 65, "From Edge", _
       "gbDistance" '7
        WordBasic.Text 301, 123, 61, 13, "&Header:", _
       "tHeaderDistance" '8
        WordBasic.TextBox 370, 121, 91, 18, "tbHeaderDistance" '9
        WordBasic.Text 301, 147, 55, 13, "&Footer:", _
       "tFooterDistance" '10
        WordBasic.TextBox 370, 144, 91, 18, "tbFooterDistance" '11
    WordBasic.EndDialog
    Dim dlg As Object: Set dlg = WordBasic.CurValues.UserDialog
    x = WordBasic.Dialog.UserDialog(dlg)
End Sub
```

Essentially, it is the same procedure, though the converted instructions merely address WordBasic remotely. It is the WordBasic component, registered within the OLE System Registry, which handles the job of assembling the UserDialog panel. Before you get the idea that VBA converted this procedure blindly, take a look at some of the smart things it did add: The two variables utilized by the procedure are now declared, and dlg is given the correct type As Object. Since the old Dialog() function itself is now no longer adequate as a mechanism for calling the procedure mentioned in the Dialog block, VBA now knows to pass a function call UserDialog(dlg) to WordBasic's Dialog component.

So the changes that were made to make the old structure conform even in the slightest bit, do make some sense. But perhaps Listing 13-2 does give you the (proper) notion that continuing to address WordBasic yourself through VBA is more than a bit cumbersome. You can't exactly follow WordBasic's old rules – note the case with the replaced Dialog() function call. And what rules you can follow, and which ones you cannot, are not documented anyplace; I could try to document them in this chapter, but I feel I would be performing a disservice to you. Just be comforted by the knowledge that your Word 6.0 and Word 7.0 macros should continue to work properly in Word 2000, during the time you're rebuilding them into VBA procedures.

What gets recorded and what happens to it

You may have become accustomed to recording all or part of a WordBasic macro, even if you're just recording a portion of the program that you intend to embellish later. How do I know this? Well. . .okay, guilty as charged. Surely we can agree that programming the cursor by hand to scoot down one paragraph, to the right one word, turn extension on, slide right four characters, then cut the selection to the Clipboard, move the cursor to the head of the document, make certain the cursor isn't in Character Heck, then paste... is not exactly the type of material that makes for an interesting Friday evening. Recording the macro and then going through the motions has historically been a much easier way to go about laying the groundwork for the manipulation of characters in a document.

But as Chapter 12 demonstrated, procedures in the VBA module do not have to manipulate characters within a document solely with the cursor. At all times, all of the characters within a document can be addressed, as a whole or partitioned, as *objects*. Your knowledge of the contents of a document are no longer restricted to the contents of Selection$, the persistent variable that used to mirror the text under the cursor. With WordBasic, you could not gain knowledge of any part of your document unless you selected a specific part first; and sometimes, in order to know what to select, you had to know what was in its vicinity, which meant you had to select that first. With the Word 2000 object library, all of the Characters, Words, Sentences, and Paragraphs are addressable at all times, regardless of whether they're selected. Furthermore, the Range term gives you the capability of reading into a variable the raw text of any part or all of the document, again without regard to the cursor.

Nonetheless, **these direct addressing techniques are not what gets recorded by the VBA macro recorder.** Instead, the recorder takes note of how you move the cursor, as the WordBasic macro recorder once did, except using VBA instructions. So if you plan to use the more efficient method for addressing parts of your Word 2000 document, you do not need, nor should you want, to borrow the services of the macro recorder.

It's also important to note here that the Word 2000 recorded macro is stored as a procedure within a module named NewMacros that is already allocated within the Normal template. Naturally, those procedures don't place any calls to other procedures, because there's nothing a user can do to "call" a procedure that can get recorded. So the recorded procedure is more of a sequence than a structure.

What Changed and Why

The remainder of this chapter is devoted to how operations that you performed in WordBasic translate — and fail to translate — to Word VBA.

Moving the cursor

With today's Word VBA project, you will find yourself manipulating the cursor position less often in order to determine the contents of your document, but perhaps just as often to detect and position where you want *added* text to appear. In the Word 2000 object library, there are about four or five ways to direct the cursor to do exactly the same thing, whereas there may have been one, perhaps two, corresponding instructions in WordBasic.

The way object library instructions are phrased, they end up being somewhat longer than their predecessors. One reason is that Word 2000 *constants* are often used in place of straight integers to represent a setting or characteristic. For example, wdCharacter is a constant that directs the .MoveLeft and .MoveRight methods (described below) to move the cursor, counting each character, rather than each word or paragraph, as it goes along. You could write 1 instead, for that is the value to which wdCharacter is permanently set; but if you were to get into that habit, you would have to look up all the settings integers yourself. The hope is that you'll remember wdCharacter more readily than you would remember that 1 means to count by characters.

The other reason Word 2000 instructions are generally longer is that most instructions are phrased as addresses to specific objects rather than to the word processor as a whole. When you're moving the cursor or ascertaining its contents, you start by directing your instruction to the object Selection. From there, you add a period and follow that with the *method* term that represents the action you intend to perform. There are fewer method terms in the Word 2000 object library than there were keywords in WordBasic, primarily because each WordBasic keyword that didn't represent a menu command generally represented both what the interpreter was supposed to do *and* the characteristics of how it was supposed to do it. So CharLeft, LineDown, and ParaUp were all separate commands that were capable of "speaking" entirely for themselves in WordBasic. In Word 2000, by contrast, you must specify *what* the subject of the operation is, *which one* is the operation it is to perform, and *how* it is to perform that operation, in separate terms that comprise the instruction.

Table 13-1 shows examples of some of the most commonly used WordBasic terms, along with their new Word 2000 counterpart operations.

TABLE 13-1A MOVING THE CURSOR ONE OR MORE CHARACTERS

WordBasic for Word 7.0

```
CharLeft
CharRight
```

EXAMPLES:

```
CharRight 1
bSuccess = CharLeft(12, 1)
```

The first instruction moves the cursor one character to the right. By omitting the second argument from that instruction, the selection is *not* extended. Written as a function, these instructions return a True/False value indicating their success.

VBA/Word 2000 Object Library

```
.MoveLeft
.MoveRight
```

EXAMPLES:

```
Selection.MoveRight wdCharacter, 1
bSuccess = Selection.MoveLeft _
 (Unit:=wdCharacter, Count:=12, _
 Extend:=wdExtend)
```

Word 2000 uses a more generalized set of instructions: the methods .MoveLeft and .MoveRight, which imply that the cursor is to be moved, but do not imply how. That question is answered by the first argument, which here is a constant wdCharacter that stands for "by characters," as opposed to "by words" or "by paragraphs." The second instruction demonstrates both how the method may be addressed as a function, and how arguments may be presented in named format. The Extend:= argument may be set to either wdExtend or wdMove; when omitted, it's assumed that you only intend to move the cursor without extending the selection.

Continued

TABLE 13-1A **MOVING THE CURSOR ONE OR MORE CHARACTERS** *(continued)*

One other method available to you that's more generic in nature is .Move, which works about as well as .MoveLeft or .MoveRight except that .Move cannot extend the selection. For example:

```
Selection.Move _
 Unit:=wdCharacter, Count:=-12
```

This instruction moves the cursor *left* 12 characters, using a negative number to signify "left."

TABLE 13-1B **MOVING THE CURSOR UP OR DOWN LINES OF TEXT**

WordBasic for Word 7.0

```
LineDown
LineUp
```

EXAMPLES:

```
LineUp
bSuccess = LineDown(6, 1)
```

When arguments were omitted, WordBasic assumed that the cursor should be moved one unit, and that the selection should not be extended.

VBA/Word 2000 Object Library

```
.MoveDown
.MoveUp
```

EXAMPLES:

```
Selection.MoveUp
bSuccess = .MoveDown _
 (Unit:=wdLine, Count:=6, _
 Extend:=wdExtend)
```

When all arguments are omitted, the VBA interpreter assumes that the units in question are lines, that the number of such units is 1, and that the selection is not to be extended.

TABLE **13-1c** MOVING THE CURSOR TO THE NEXT OR PREVIOUS PAGE

WordBasic for Word 7.0

```
GoToNextPage
GoToPreviousPage
```

EXAMPLES:

```
GoToNextPage

GoToPreviousPage
```

VBA/Word 2000 Object Library

```
.GoTo
```

EXAMPLES:

```
Selection.GoTo(wdGoToPage, _
 wdGoToNext)
Selection.GoTo _
 (Which:=wdGoToPage, _
 What:=GoToPrevious)
```

In Word 2000, the .GoTo method (not to be confused with the VBA GoTo statement) takes the cursor to a designated "landmark," such as "the previous page" or "three bookmarks from this point." The constant wdGoToPage is used here to designate that the method is to count off by pages, rather than some other element such as tables or lines.

TABLE **13-1d** MOVING THE CURSOR TO ONE EDGE OF THE LINE OF TEXT

WordBasic for Word 7.0

```
EndOfLine
StartOfLine
```

EXAMPLES:

```
StartOfLine
bSuccess = EndOfLine(1)
```

Notice how in WordBasic instructions, the fact that you were addressing the cursor (or cursor position) was presumed rather than explicitly stated.

Continued

TABLE **13-1**ᴅ **MOVING THE CURSOR TO ONE EDGE OF THE LINE OF TEXT** *(continued)*

VBA/Word 2000 Object Library

```
.EndOf
.StartOf
```

EXAMPLES:

```
Selection.StartOf wdLine
bSuccess = Selection.EndOf _
 (Unit:=wdLine, Extend:=wdExtend)
```

Here, `wdLine` serves as a constant that resolves the question, "End of *what*?" The `.EndOf` and `.StartOf` methods take the cursor to the edge of any of the following: character, word, sentence, paragraph, section, "story" (main body of a document's content), cell, column, row, table. The necessary constant for the `Unit:=` argument is prefixed with `wd`, and is followed by the name of the document element just as you see it in the list above, first letter capitalized.

```
.EndKey
.HomeKey
```

EXAMPLES:

```
Selection.HomeKey wdLine
bSuccess = Selection.EndKey _
 (Unit:=wdLine, Extend:=wdExtend)
```

For no particular reason, there is another pair of methods you can use for exactly the same purpose, whose syntax for this task are basically the same. The `.HomeKey` and `.EndKey` methods are said to simulate the functionality of the Home and End keys in the current context; however, no other keys have been so simulated in Word 2000.

TABLE **13-1**ᴇ **RETURNING TO A PREVIOUS CURSOR LOCATION**

WordBasic for Word 7.0

GoBack

Returns the cursor to the most recent previously recorded position in the document.

VBA/Word 2000 Object Library

GoBack

Well, here's a surprise: something that hasn't changed! In Word 2000, `.GoBack` is a method of the `Application` object. Since `Application` is a global, both it and the separating dot may be omitted from the instruction.

TABLE 13-1F MOVING THE CURSOR TO THE TOP OF AN ADJACENT PARAGRAPH

WordBasic for Word 7.0

```
ParaDown
ParaUp
```

EXAMPLES:

```
ParaUp 2
bSuccess = ParaDown()
```

For a WordBasic keyword acting as a function, parentheses were required even when arguments were omitted.

VBA/Word 2000 Object Library

```
.MoveDown
.MoveUp
```

EXAMPLES:

```
Selection.MoveUp wdParagraph, 2
bSuccess = Selection.MoveDown
```

For a Word 2000 term acting as a function, when arguments are omitted, the parentheses may be omitted as well, or left in.

TABLE 13-1G MOVING THE CURSOR TO THE TOP OR BOTTOM OF THE DOCUMENT

WordBasic for Word 7.0

```
StartOfDocument
EndOfDocument
```

EXAMPLES:

```
EndOfDocument 1
StartOfDocument
```

The second example includes an optional argument that, when set to a non-zero value (1 generally suffices), extends the cursor selection from its previous position to the beginning of the document.

Continued

TABLE **13-1**G *(continued)*

VBA/Word 2000 Object Library

`.HomeKey`
`.EndKey`

EXAMPLES:

```
Selection.EndKey wdStory, wdExtend
Selection.GoTo wdGoToLine, _
 wdGoToAbsolute, 1, wdMove
```

The `.HomeKey` and `.EndKey` methods are basically synonymous with the `.StartOf` and `.EndOf` methods, except that the former pair is limited to working only within those contexts in which the real Home and End keys are operative: the current "story" (body of text), line, row, or column. `.StartOf` and `.EndOf` will work for such ranges as sections, paragraphs, sentences, and words.

As the second example demonstrates, however, both pairs of terms share a context problem: If the cursor is currently within the headers or footers area, or any other region other than the "main story," `.HomeKey`, `.EndKey`, `.StartOf`, and `.EndOf` will only move the cursor within that region, not out of that region. On the other hand, *though it is not supposed to work this way*, using the `.GoTo` method to direct the cursor to move to absolute line #1, as shown in the example above, will move the cursor to the first line in the main body of the document — the same location to which `StartOfDocument` moved the cursor in WordBasic.

At Present: What's the "Story"?

Intermittently throughout the Word 2000 object library, you'll find object terms and some constants that make reference to something called the *story*. Originally, this element was supposed to be defined as the main body of text in the document. As such, a document's story would be distinct from its headers or footers, its footnotes, its annotations, and such items as included graphics and page numbers.

Somewhere along the line in the development of the application, this basic meaning became entirely lost. It so happens now that any one document has, by its very nature, *more than one* story region. The entire body of a document's footnotes, for example, taken collectively, is called the *footnote story*; and the body of a document's footers is called its *footer story*. Meanwhile, the main body of text is called the *main text story*. Why? Certain Word 2000 object library instructions draw distinctions between the common elements of a document, and "stories" define those distinctions. Certain other instructions draw similar distinctions between those same elements, and "stories" do *not* define those distinctions.

Elsewhere in the Word 2000 object library is a term `Content`, which refers to the main body of the document and is probably, for most intents and purposes, identical to the "main story." In fact, within the `StoryRanges` collection that represents all of a document's story areas grouped together, the member whose associated constant is `wdMainTextStory` has the same range as `Content`. Thus, `docThis.Content` and `docThis.StoryRanges(wdMainTextStory)` refer to the same area.

Inserting text

The Word 2000 object library does contain instructions that parallel their WordBasic counterparts, and whose purpose is to insert text or other materials at the current cursor location. However, the methodology for inserting text in Word 2000 goes somewhat deeper than these relatively simple parallel instructions let on. As I mentioned earlier, each document's main body of text and other elements (what Word 2000 calls "stories") are addressable at all times as objects. Such regions may be referred to as "the first hundred characters" or "the last paragraph" without having to send the cursor out toward them to try to discover where their boundaries lie. Those methodologies will be discussed later in this segment; for now, Table 13-2 shows those terms that are parallel to the old WordBasic text insertion keywords.

TABLE **13-2A** ADDING TEXT AT THE CURRENT CURSOR LOCATION

WordBasic for Word 7.0

`Insert`

EXAMPLES:

```
Insert "IDG Books"
Insert FileName$
```

The `Insert` statement was the lead keyword for entering strings or literal text at the current cursor location.

Continued

TABLE **13-2A** ADDING TEXT AT THE CURRENT CURSOR LOCATION *(continued)*

VBA/Word 2000 Object Library

`.InsertAfter`

<u>EXAMPLES:</u>

```
Selection.InsertAfter "IDG Books"
ActiveWindow.Selection.InsertAfter _
 Text:=strAccession
```

The `.InsertAfter` method enters text at the cursor represented by `Selection`, and then extends the selection so that it encompasses the new text. Any text that may already have been highlighted remains in the document, with the inserted text appearing to the *right* of the existing text.

`.TypeText`

<u>EXAMPLES:</u>

```
Selection.TypeText strFileName
ActiveWindow.Selection.TypeText _
 Text:="Yours sincerely,"
```

This method enters text into the document exactly as though the user typed it in, making this the functional equivalent of WordBasic's `Insert` statement. If Word 2000 is currently set up so that text that the user would type *overwrites* existing text, then the text that comprises the argument of the `.TypeText` method *will* overwrite existing text at the cursor location. The instruction which sets this mode is:

```
Application.Options. _
 ReplaceSelection = True
```

By contrast, the same text applied to the `.InsertAfter` method will *not* overwrite the existing text, but instead will add the new text to the right of the existing text, and extend the selection area to cover the new text. It may be necessary to use the

`Collapse` method to turn `selection` off and proceed.

`.InsertBefore`

<u>EXAMPLES:</u>

```
Selection.InsertBefore strWhatever
ActiveWindow.Selection.InsertBefore _
 "pre-"
```

This method is very similar to `.InsertAfter`, except that the inserted text will appear to the *left* of the current cursor location or selected region.

TABLE 13-2B **ADDING A CARRIAGE RETURN**

WordBasic for Word 7.0

```
InsertPara
```

EXAMPLE:

```
InsertPara
```

This instruction took no arguments, and was effectively the same as `Insert Chr$(13)`.

VBA/Word 2000 Object Library

```
.InsertParagraph
.TypeParagraph
```

EXAMPLES:

```
Selection.InsertParagraph
Selection.TypeParagraph
```

Again, the differences between these two methods seem minute until you find yourself in a situation where specifics become important. The `.InsertParagraph` method adds a carriage return *after* the current cursor position, but leaves the cursor where it is. The cursor would need to move down (`Selection.MoveDown wdParagraph`) to travel into this paragraph area. Meanwhile, the `.TypeParagraph` method adds the carriage return just as if the user had typed it, moving the cursor along with it.

```
.InsertParagraphAfter
.InsertParagraphBefore
```

EXAMPLES:

```
Selection.InsertParagraphAfter
Selection.InsertParagraphBefore
```

If no text is currently selected (in other words, if the `Selection` object is empty) then both of these methods have the same effect as `.InsertParagraph`. But if text is selected, then with `.InsertParagraphAfter`, the carriage return is added at the end of the selection while the remainder of the selection remains as is; for `.InsertParagraphBefore`, the only difference is that the carriage return is placed at the beginning. But `.InsertParagraph` deletes the selection before adding the carriage return, just as if the user had selected that text and pressed Enter.

Continued

Table **13-2b** **ADDING A CARRIAGE RETURN** *(continued)*

Note: None of these methods inserts a paragraph of text. Instead, they inserts a carriage return, or what has also been called a "paragraph mark." Imagine, if you will, a typist taking dictation from a Dictaphone. When the typist hears the narrator say, "Paragraph!" he responds by ending the current paragraph and returning the carriage to Column 1. This is what we mean by "carriage return." Elsewhere in the book, you'll find a carriage return character also referred to as a "code 13," referring to the ASCII numeral assigned to that character.

Table **13-2c** **INDICATING ("SELECTING") TEXT**

WordBasic for Word 7.0

```
ExtendSelection
```

EXAMPLES:

```
ExtendSelection
ExtendSelection "."
```

This keyword *toggled* the selection mode of the cursor on and off, like a light switch. The user normally turns on "selection mode" by holding down the left mouse button as she drags the pointer. The second example extends the cursor from its current position up to and including the next instance of a period.

The primary reason a macro would execute this instruction is so that the normal cursor movement statements could be used next to actually extend the selection as it moved.

VBA/Word 2000 Object Library

```
.Extend
```

EXAMPLES:

```
Selection.Extend
Selection.Extend "."
```

This is perhaps the instruction that lost the least in the translation to Word 2000. Because the architects of Word 2000 had to change *something*, they altered the instruction so that if your procedure executes it repeatedly, it does something else each time. With the second iteration, `.Extend` moves the selection to encompass the current word; with the third, the current sentence; with the fourth, the current paragraph; and with the fifth, the whole document.

If one instruction in your procedure is `Selection.Extend`, and the following one is `Selection.MoveRight wdCharacter, 1`, the character passed over by the cursor will be selected.

TABLE **13-2**D REMOVING SELECTED TEXT

WordBasic for Word 7.0

```
EditClear
```

EXAMPLES:

```
EditClear

If Len(Selection$()) > 1 Then
    CharRight
    EditClear 12
End If
```

The first example deletes whatever text is currently selected by the cursor. The second example, however, tells the macro interpreter to delete 12 characters; but to do that it must first make certain no text is selected. If that's true, `CharRight` will knock the cursor to the right of the selection first, before making the deletion.

VBA/Word 2000 Object Library

```
.Delete
```

EXAMPLES:

```
Selection.Delete

If Selection.Characters.Count _
 > 1 Then
    Selection.Collapse _
     wdCollapseEnd
    Selection.Delete 12
End If
```

In Word 2000, `Characters` is a collection object that is applicable to any object that maintains its own textual range, including `Selection`. So `Characters.Count` refers to the number of characters in the range — which, in the case of `Selection`, is never 0. This is because the "selection" is always considered to include, at the very least, the character to the right of the blinking cursor.

TABLE 13-2E UTILIZING THE CLIPBOARD

WordBasic for Word 7.0

```
EditCut
EditCopy
EditPaste
```

These statements, written on lines by themselves with no arguments, operated on text at the current cursor location. Any selected text was overwritten during a paste operation.

VBA/Word 2000 Object Library

```
Selection.Cut
Selection.Copy
Selection.Paste
```

The equivalent methods in Word 2000 VBA involve the `Selection` object. However, any textual range may be the subject of a Clipboard operation; for example, `ActiveDocument.Range.Copy` places the entire raw text of the document on the Clipboard; no selection is necessary.

Word 2000 shuttles text using assignment expressions

Perhaps the most convenient method available to the Word 7.0 WordBasic programmer for moving text between two points in the document, or between other open documents, involved a statement called `MoveText`. It was perhaps a bit unusual in formation, but it was about as direct as the old cursor-dependent model of programming could handle. Here's how it worked: First the macro toggled selection mode on with `ExtendSelection`, then it moved the cursor over the text to be moved. With the selection area ready, `MoveText` would be invoked on a line by itself, *without arguments*. Next, the cursor was moved to the destination location, and then the rather quaint instruction `OK` (again, no arguments) was invoked on a line by itself. The text in the selected area would be moved from its prior location to the current location. The `CopyText` statement could be used instead to leave the original text behind. The Windows Clipboard was not involved in this operation; no text was copied to the Clipboard nor pasted from it. This resulted in the move or copy process being significantly expedited.

The reason that the `MoveText`/`CopyText` statement pair and their corresponding `OK` statements (which marked the point of their real execution) were split from one another was because Word 7.0 and its forebears were generally only capable of "seeing" the text under the cursor. So it became necessary at that time to have the macro interpreter *shadow* the cursor location, because there were no object variables capable of simultaneously storing a region's contents and its location. `MoveText` and `CopyText` actually shadowed the cursor location, while `OK` released the shadow and finally processed the directive.

The Word VBA method — or rather, *methods* — for moving and copying text without the Clipboard being involved, are faster than the WordBasic method and far more sensible. If you know what you're doing, you can perform the entire textual transfer — from finding the text, to finding its new location, to performing the move — in one instruction. Granted, it's a longer instruction, but it doesn't waste time. Here is the theory behind the new operation, point by point:

- Every document has an object associated with it that represents its raw textual contents — its *native range*, if you will. The various obvious elements of that document — including its paragraphs, sentences, and individual words — are also addressable as objects, and they too have their own native textual ranges.

- Meanwhile, the text between any two-character locations is also addressable as an object. It is the `Range` object that is used in a variety of ways to address these textual regions. So at any time, you can use objects to symbolize such regions as "the third paragraph," or "the first 1000 characters." With some clever realignment of these objects, you can address "the third paragraph in the second section," or "the first 1000 characters after the end of the first table."

- The cursor is represented at all times by the `Selection` object, and all active document windows have a cursor of their own. The text which is currently being "selected" (highlighted in reverse text) by that cursor is addressable as `Selection.Range`. In this form, not only can the text highlighted by the cursor be read into a variable, but **text may also be written to the `Selection.Range` object, thereby changing its contents.** An expression of assignment is used to make the current cursor selection range, whatever its length may be, "equivalent to" the contents of a string variable or a string literal, whatever *its* length may be.

- **The cursor is not required for textual manipulation operations.** It is still available, though not always entirely necessary. Instead, the `Range` subordinate object that belongs to the `Document` class object associated with the document being altered is assigned new textual contents through a string variable or string literal, again using an expression of assignment.

The way the `Selection` object is designed, developing a procedure or module that operates a document no longer needs to mimic the precise way a human user would perform the same functions, especially because `Selection` (as well as `Range` class objects) may represent any region of text without it having to be clipped to the Clipboard first. Textual contents may be placed within a region represented by `Selection`, or by an independent `Range` class object, simply by assigning that text to the region by way of an expression of assignment — just as though you were assigning data to a variable.

Chapter 14 discusses in detail the use of *collection objects* such as `Paragraphs` and `Words` to represent, in numerical order, the succession of elements in the main body of a document. For instance, `ActiveDocument.Paragraphs(3)` represents the third paragraph in the document that currently has the focus (the one whose cursor is blinking). Because a paragraph is a complex object that represents formatting as well as content, the text within a paragraph is represented by its `Range` constituent — so the text in the third paragraph is `ActiveDocument.Paragraphs(3).Range.Text`. To replace this paragraph with any text at all, you could simply write an instruction similar to this:

```
ActiveDocument.Paragraphs(3).Range.Text = strBoilerplate3
```

Notice that the cursor — represented in Word 2000 by the `Selection` object — plays no role here. Notice also that whether the lengths of `.Range.Text` and `strBoilerplate3` match is inconsequential; their lengths do not have to match for one to be substituted for another.

If your text replacement mission isn't so specific in nature — for instance, if your aim is not to replace "the *third* paragraph of the document" — you could launch a `Find` object to locate the start and end points of the area to be replaced based on their textual content, and then address that region as a `Range` object. Which brings us directly to our next subject.

Search and replace operations

The newcomer to object-oriented thinking may wonder, why did Microsoft develop a Word 2000 search-and-replace operation into an *object*? The answer concerns this fundamental concept of programming: All programs are processes, and processes represent *actions*, not things. Objects are bestowed that name to lend them some sense of tangibility to the programmer, not to cast them in some sort of physical mold. So the process of *finding* text is actually the perfect candidate for an object.

In the Word 2000 object library, the `Find` object represents the agent of a search and replace operation. You give this agent instructions one at a time until it has all the specifications it needs to do its job; then you use the `.Execute` method to send it on its way. This is altogether different from the methodology employed by WordBasic.

Every `Range` class object has an available `Find` subordinate, which lets you set up a detailed search within any addressable region of a document. For instance, you may restrict the search to the first three paragraphs by setting up the `Find` object within a clause that begins with this instruction:

```
With ActiveDocument.Range(ActiveDocument.Paragraphs(1).Range _
  .Start, ActiveDocument.Paragraphs(3).Range.End).Find
```

The `.Start` property refers to the first character of a range, and the `.End` property refers to the final character. These properties are used above to designate the beginning and end of the area of the search.

Chapter 12 describes how a `Find` process is carried out, step by step. For a more detailed example, consider the following: Although Word 2000 now has provisions for viewing HTML-formatted text (some of which involve borrowing the engine of Internet Explorer), it does not recognize HTML *tags* — those hidden parts of the document that are bordered with carets, as in `<BODY>` and `</P>` — as objects in and of themselves. Suppose you needed a simple procedure to find all HTML tags in your document and render them as *hidden text*. In Word 2000, hidden text is text that does not appear until the user chooses "View Hidden Text" from the Tools → Options → View menu. Making existing text hidden can be considered an official *replacement*, as Listing 13-3 demonstrates.

Listing 13-3: An ordinary Find process whose aim is to change formatting.

```
Public Sub FindHTMLTags()
    With ActiveDocument.Range.Find
        .ClearFormatting
        .MatchWildcards = True
        .Forward = True
        .Text = "\<*\>"
        .Format = True
        With .Replacement
            .ClearFormatting
            .Font.Hidden = True
            .Text = ""
        End With
        .Execute Replace:=wdReplaceAll
    End With
End Sub
```

Here, the .MatchWildcards property refers to whether Word 2000 executes its search more symbolically. The .Text of the search shows that we're looking for "anything in-between two opposite caret marks." The asterisk stands for "anything" just like it would for a DOS filename. Backslashes appear before the carets to prevent Word 2000 from treating them as search *symbols*, which would make them be misinterpreted as meaning "a word that begins with an asterisk and ends with nothing." (Quite poetic, actually.)

The Replacement object is a subordinate of Find, and is only used when a replacement is to be made. It is similar to a Range class object, but it doesn't refer to any specific text in the document yet, because it officially has yet to find that text. Besides, Replacement has some unique characteristics, as you'll see later in this chapter. Here, we invoked Replacement to demonstrate how we can direct that object to make changes to the found text region. Notice the replacement doesn't necessarily have to contain *text*; in this case, Replacement.Text was set to an empty string "" to ensure that the found text was *not* replaced with other text. All we want is a change to the *formatting* of the found text.

Under normal circumstances, setting Replacement.Text to a null string would have Word 2000 replace any found passage of text with nothing – the equivalent of deleting that text. But these are not normal circumstances, since the .MatchWildcards property in this instance has been set to True. In this mode of operation, some characters belonging to both Find.Text and Find.Replacement. Text serve as syntax directives to the word processor, and not as characters to be matched themselves. With this mode set to True, an empty string doesn't mean nothing (pardon the double-negative), but instead means "leave the replacement process alone." Notice also the text that is being searched for is phrased using the comic book swear word "\<*\>". Generally, the < and > are wildcard characters that tell Word 2000 to look for a word that starts with the next character, or that ends with the next character, respectively. But here, these characters are preceded with \ backslashes, which are overriding directives to Word 2000 to treat the characters that follow them as true characters. So the search is for the left caret and the right caret, with the * asterisk acting as a wildcard for "anything in between."

Once everything is set up, the .Execute method launches the search process. Here, the method does take one argument, Replace:=wdReplaceAll, which starts the search as though the user had clicked on the Replace All button in the Find dialog box.

Now, let's change the parameters of our mission a bit. Suppose rather than just replace everything in sight, we want Word 2000 to perform some operation on each instance of the found text that is far outside the scope of a simple find-and-replace operation. In this expansion of the previous example, the range containing each found HTML tag is enrolled within a module-level collection object, HTMLTags.

It's relatively easy for you to set up your own collection object that takes HTML tags, text ranges, or any other object classes into account and enumerates them. Within the Declarations section of your general (non-object) module, you will require this declaration:

```
Public HTMLTags As New Collection
```

The Declarations section is the location for all *shared variables*, as WordBasic used to call them, between the procedures in a module. It is our more civilized and mature term for what others have so unappreciatively deemed "the top." By declaring the HTMLTags variable As New Collection, there's no need to Set that variable to refer to any collection object that already exists. There's also no need to declare the collection itself as being of any specific type; in fact the members of a collection do not actually have to have the same type (although choosing to randomize the types of collection members is impractical). The New portion of the declaration brings that collection into existence.

With those two declarations set up, you would then include the procedure in Listing 13-4 within one of the modules belonging to either the Normal template or to one of the exclusive templates that will be handling HTML text.

Listing 13-4: A complex Find object used in gathering a new collection.

```
Public Sub EnrollHTMLTags()
    Dim rngDoc As Range
    Set rngDoc = ActiveDocument.Range
    With rngDoc.Find
        .ClearFormatting
        .MatchWildcards = True
        .Forward = True
        .Text = "\<*\>"
        .Format = True
        With .Replacement
            .ClearFormatting
            .Font.Hidden = True
            .Text = ""
        End With
        While .Execute(Replace:=wdReplaceOne)
            HTMLTags.Add rngDoc
            rngDoc.Collapse wdCollapseEnd
        Wend
    End With
    MsgBox Str$(HTMLTags.Count)
End Sub
```

The major change in Listing 13-4 from Listing 13-3 is the addition of a While...Wend loop clause that accounts for a succession of single searches rather than one broad search for everything. Again, .Execute is the method of the Find object that formally launches the search. But this time, the argument I specified is Replace:=wdReplaceOne, which tells Word 2000 to stop after the first spotting of the target text. The argument was phrased within parentheses here because .Execute is stated in the context of a *function* and not an ordinary method. The loop clause will automatically terminate when there are no more instances of Find.Text to be acquired. Execution is suspended until the search turns up something, or turns up nothing. What it does turn up is represented as a flag integer – a 1 or a 0. This way, a 0 can be treated by the `While...Wend` loop as a False finding, causing the loop to drop out.

Three ways to set up a text search process

The other possible setting for the `Replace:` parameter of the `Find` object is `wdReplaceAll`, which executes the entire search-and-replace process in one fell swoop. If we were to have used that parameter here, we would not have had occasion to enroll each element of the found text into the `HTMLTags` collection. For that reason, the `While...Wend` loop is necessary.

There are three ways in which a multiple `Find` operation may proceed, especially with regard to replacing located regions:

1. With the **reiterative method**, which you saw in Listings 13-3 and 13-4, the properties of `Find` and `Find.Replacement` are individually set beforehand, and targeted text is retrieved one item at a time, by way of stating `.Execute` within a `While...Wend` loop clause. (A `Do While` loop clause will work just as well.)

2. With the **express method**, one of the parameters of the `.Execute` method is stated in this instruction:

   ```
   .Execute Replace:=wdReplaceAll
   ```

   Here, `wdReplaceAll` is a constant that makes the search process work as though the user clicked on the Replace All button in the Find dialog box. With this parameter set, the `.Execute` method need only be executed once, and need not be placed within a loop clause.

3. With the **conventional method**, all of the properties of the `Find` object are expressed as parameters (or arguments, if you leave the names off) to the `.Execute` method. It makes for an unruly instruction, but a *single* one. For example, many of the properties from the `Find` object in Listing 13-4 could have instead been expressed as parameters of the `.Execute` method, like so:

   ```
   While .Execute(FindText:="\<*\>", MatchWildcards:=True, _
       Forward:=True, ReplaceWith:="", Replace:=wdReplaceOne)
   ```

The object that is the "owner" or antecedent of the `Find` object specifies the boundaries of the region being searched – simply put, where the search begins in the document and where it ends. This owner may be a `Document` class object, a `Range` class object, or `Selection` (the cursor). You'll recall from Chapter 12 that each window maintains its own cursor location and selection, though Word considers only one of these cursors to be "active" at any one time. Your VBA code may address any window's cursor directly, as in `Windows(1).Selection`, without necessarily rendering that that window "active." In other words, just because you're doing something with one window's cursor does not mean that window has to be displayed, nor that the user has to see everything that you're doing with that cursor. So a `Selection.Find` process can be entirely clandestine, especially if you determine beforehand that the window to which your particular `Selection` object belongs is *not* active, with a condition like `If Windows(1).Active = False`...

When you begin a repetitive or reiterative search, the boundaries of the process are taken from the native range of the owner and assigned to its `Find` object. This object will remember the region boundaries throughout the search. However, when you use a reference to `Range` class object as the owner — in other words, a variable that you have declared in advance `As Range` — then when the search process turns up what it's looking for, that object will refer to the located text, not to the original boundaries of the search. If you want to do anything to the located text other than simply replace it — such as italicize it, or copy it into a buffer or a collection — your original `Range` class object gives you a handle on that text. When the reiterative search concludes, the `Range` object will continue to refer to the last passage found, unless it did not turn up anything — in which case, it continues to refer to the original boundaries of the search. So suppose you declare an independent reference such as `rngThis`, then `Set` its boundaries to the first three paragraphs, and *then* address `rngThis.Find` where `rngThis` becomes the "owner" of the `Find` object. With each new iteration of the loop clause bound by `While .Execute`, the VBA interpreter will recall the original boundaries so VBA knows precisely where to end.

In cases where you're only searching for one instance of a text string, you could address your `Find` object using a very specific antecedent and get away with it, and execute the find within the same massive instruction, like this:

```
ActiveDocument.Range(ActiveDocument.Paragraphs(1).Range.Start, _
  ActiveDocument.Paragraphs(3).Range.End).Find.Execute _
  (FindText:="\<*\>", MatchWildcards:=True, Forward:=True, _
  ReplaceWith:="")
```

While this may seem like a quick and dirty way to approach the problem of a search operation, it presents a problem when you try to embed this search within a loop clause: The VBA interpreter will literally forget the original boundaries of the search and go on to search the rest of the document as though those boundaries were `ActiveDocument.Range` to begin with.

The `.Add` instruction in Listing 13-4 takes the `Range` class object `rngDoc`, once the HTML tag has been found, and adds it to the ongoing collection `HTMLTags`. But isn't `rngDoc` set to `ActiveDocument.Range`? It was when the `Find` process started. However, at this point, we can assume that the process turned up what it was looking for. Now, `rngDoc` is set to the boundaries of just that target. Why? To give us a handle on the target, thus enabling us to copy it to a string, to the Clipboard, or to another variable, or otherwise add it to a collection as we've done here. But what happens when `While.Execute` is executed the next time around? If the search process locates text, `rngDoc` points to the located text; if it doesn't, it continues to point to the previously found passage. The original `rngDoc` boundaries are lost if and only if the search process locates text.

Stranger yet is the instruction that had to be added to this procedure to prevent it from halting prematurely. The instruction `rngDoc.Collapse wdCollapseEnd` has the boundaries of `rngDoc` "collapse" on its own end, so that its start point and its end point are the same. Why would I want to do that? Because for some reason, when the text of `rngDoc` is made hidden, the range flies off into never-never-land upon reiteration of the search. Doing something silly, such as collapsing the range first, seems to knock it back into reality before beginning the next iteration. I discovered this debugging solution quite by accident, after having tried about 40 other methods.

Maintaining `rngDoc` — or whatever `Range` class object may be the owner of the find — becomes more difficult when the range of the search is a *subset* of the main body of the document. Here, the document may be represented by a `Document` class object set to refer to a document in memory, or by `ActiveDocument`. When the `While .Execute` loop clause is reiterated, the range of the search *always* changes to encompass the main body of the document, even if that isn't how the range was initialized. So to restrict the range of the search to a smaller area, another range variable needs to be implemented whose boundaries do not change as a result of finding text. This second reference will maintain the restriction to the boundaries originally set for both it and the first reference.

So our example is extended once more, with the assumption that the test document contains two or more *sections* (divided by section breaks), and that the subset of the main document is the second section of the document, `Sections(2)`. Listing 13-5 shows how the search range and the regulator range may now be managed separately.

Listing 13-5: Making the independent range follow the rules.

```
Public Sub EnrollHTMLTags()
    Dim rngSearch As Range, rngBounds As Range

    Set rngSearch = ActiveDocument.Sections(2).Range
    Set rngBounds = ActiveDocument.Sections(2).Range
    With rngSearch.Find
        .ClearFormatting
        .MatchWildcards = True
        .Forward = True
        .Text = "\<*\>"
        .Format = True
        With .Replacement
            .ClearFormatting
            .Font.Hidden = True
            .Text = ""
        End With
        Do
            If .Execute Then
                If rngSearch.End < rngBounds.End Then
                    HTMLTags.Add rngSearch
                Else
```

```
                Exit Do
            End If
        Else
                Exit Do
        End If
    Loop
    End With
    MsgBox Str$(HTMLTags.Count)
End Sub
```

Here `Range` class references `rngSearch` and `rngBounds` (its guardian) are set to refer to exactly the same range. Why didn't we just `Set rngBounds = rngSearch`? Because that would have made the two ranges the same, so that when `rngSearch` changed, so would `rngBounds`. The whole point of having two ranges is so that one range can be used to guide the other, not mimic it.

Gone is our `While...Wend` loop and in its place is an indefinite `Do...Loop` clause. I call it "indefinite" because it has no built-in logic that would terminate it upon a condition; unless execution encounters an `Exit Do` statement, this clause could go on forever. But it won't because it's designed to stop when either the original search boundaries have been exceeded, or there's nothing left to find.

If the `.Execute` method is successful, the first check is whether the found text is out of our original bounds – which is an entirely feasible evaluation today, given how Word 2000 currently works. If we're within bounds, the range is added to `HTMLTags`; if we're out of bounds, the loop is exited. On the other hand, if the `.Execute` method was not successful to begin with, the loop is exited there as well.

Why go through all this trouble declaring two range objects, when a `Find` operation owned by `Selection` doesn't have these problems? Because the user's placement of the cursor at its present location might hold some purpose. In Chapter 14, I'll demonstrate that when the cursor is absolutely necessary for an operation, it takes the creation of a false bookmark to hold the prior location of `Selection.Range` and to return the cursor to that range once the module concludes. If a procedure moves the cursor for its own purposes and doesn't put it back where it was found, the user is left to hunt for it himself. Besides, the current cursor location may be an important place for a procedure to write its results – that is, if they are to be part of the final document.

How Word 2000 replaces WordBasic's EditFind instruction

The way that WordBasic used to handle search-and-replace operations involved primarily one instruction. Granted, this instruction became long and often unwieldy, but it was one instruction nonetheless: `EditFind`. Table 13-3 shows the constituents of Word 2000's modern `Find` object and its subordinate, the `Replacement` object. Table 13-3 also shows the WordBasic keyword that the new term replaces.

TABLE 13-3 TERMS ASSOCIATED WITH THE FIND AND REPLACEMENT OBJECTS

Word 2000 Term	Definition
.ClearFormatting†	**(Method)** Resets existing formatting settings prior to reprogramming a new Find object, lest those settings be used unwittingly by the new object. The reason for the existence of this method is because **Word 2000 retains the settings for the previous search process whenever a new search process is begun.** This is true regardless of what object effectively owns the search; so if a Selection.Find process sets a property such as .Format to True (so that the search includes particular text formatting), then even if the next Find process belongs to a Range class object, its .Format setting will also be True. Only when there has been no previous search process during the Word 2000 session will the .Format property be set to its default of False automatically; and there's no way for you to know confidently whether the user has engaged a search process on her own. For that reason, .ClearFormatting becomes an essential method to almost any search process. **WordBasic equivalent:** EditFindClearFormatting
.Execute	**(Method)** Initiates the search process represented by the Find object. This method may take a wide number of arguments, most of which correspond directly to the properties listed in this table (even when the arguments' and properties' names do not match). Parameter equivalents are listed throughout this table. The one unique parameter that .Execute passes that is not listed elsewhere in this table, is Replace:=. This parameter is set to a constant representing how many replacements are to be made, if any. Possible settings are wdReplaceAll, which suspends execution until all replacements are complete; wdReplaceOne, which replaces the first instance of the target text that is found; and wdReplaceNone, which puts the replacement process on hold. Even if you use a With block to set all of Find's properties rather than address them as arguments, you may still pass this one parameter as an argument through the .Execute method. **WordBasic equivalent:** EditFind
.Font†	**(Constituent)** Represents the characteristics of the characters of text for which the Find process is to search. Any text that does not match these characteristics is not counted as found and is discarded.

Word 2000 Term	Definition
	WordBasic equivalent: The EditFindFont keyword was used prior to EditFind, in searches where typefaces were involved, to specify the characteristics of the text for which EditFind would launch the search.
.Format	**(Property)** A Boolean value that denotes whether typesetting features are to be considered during the search process. **Default setting:** False
	.Execute method parameter: Format:=
	WordBasic equivalent: The .Format argument of the EditFind statement. In this case, an EditFindStyle statement was used prior to EditFind to specify the style name for the target text.
.Forward	**(Property)** A Boolean value that represents the relative direction of the search through the document. **Default setting:** True
	.Execute method parameter: Forward:=
	WordBasic equivalent: The .Direction parameter of the EditFind statement.
.Found	**(Property)** A flag that denotes whether the search process has found *one* instance of the target text. The property is designed to be used following the completion of an .Execute method.

Example:

```
Do
    .Execute
    If .Found Then
        If rngSearch.End < _
        rngBounds.End Then
            HTMLTags.Add rngSearch
        Else
            Exit Do
        End If
    Else
        Exit Do
    End If
Loop
```

Continued

TABLE 13-3 TERMS ASSOCIATED WITH THE FIND AND REPLACEMENT OBJECTS.
(continued)

Word 2000 Term	Definition
	This demonstrates an alternate method for determining whether a Find process was successful, borrowing from the Do...Loop clause employed in Listing 13-5. Here, the .Execute method is stated by itself, like a statement. The .Found property is used as the basis of the conditional clause.
	WordBasic equivalent: The EditFindFound() function, which returned a Boolean value denoting the success of the operation.
.Frame†	**(Constituent)** Represents the characteristics of a frame, which in Word 2000 is a "floating" object where text and other objects are contained. The characteristics of this Frame class object are set to those to which the Find process is to restrict its search. Text whose frame does not meet these characteristics, or text falling outside a frame, is not counted as found and is discarded.
	WordBasic equivalent: WordBasic did make attempts to support the EditFindFrame statement, which was to be used prior to EditFind when the target text was to be included in a frame. However, the statement was not functional in Word 7.0.
.Highlight†	**(Property)** A Boolean value that denotes whether the Find process is to restrict its search to textual passages that have been given colored highlighting. This is different from the "background pattern" for the text, which is considered part of its bordering. **Default setting:** False
	WordBasic equivalent: The EditFindHighlight statement was used prior to an EditFind statement whose .Format argument was set to True. EditFindHighlight passed no arguments.
.MatchAllWordForms	**(Property)** A Boolean value that designates whether the Find process is allowed to search for alternate forms of any of the words in its .Text property. For instance, if get appears in Find.Text and .MatchAllWordForms is True, then the Find process may search also for such forms as got and gotten.
	Note: Setting this property to True overrides a True setting for the .MatchWildcards property.
	.Execute method parameter: MatchAllWordForms:=
	WordBasic equivalent: The .FindAllWordForms parameter of the EditFind statement.

Word 2000 Term	Definition
.MatchCase	**(Property)** A Boolean value that designates whether the case of characters in Find.Text (the subject of the search) is to be treated exactly as they appear (True), or whether they may be exchanged for their alternate case (False). **Default setting:** False
	Note: Setting this property to True overrides a True setting for the .MatchWildcards property.
	.Execute **method parameter:** MatchCase:=
	WordBasic equivalent: The .MatchCase parameter of the EditFind statement.
.MatchSoundsLike	**(Property)** A Boolean value that designates whether the Find process is allowed to search for homonyms of words that may appear in its .Text property. **Default setting:** False
	Note: Setting this property to True overrides a True setting for the .MatchWildcards property.
	Execute **method parameter:** MatchSoundsLike:=
	WordBasic equivalent: The .SoundsLike parameter of the EditFind statement.
.MatchWholeWord	**(Property)** A Boolean value that designates whether the Find process is to restrict its search to those words in Find.Text in the context of whole words, and not as characters that may appear in sequence in the context of other words. **Default setting:** False
	Note: Setting this property to True overrides a True setting for the .MatchWildcards property.
	.Execute **method parameter:** MatchWholeWord:=
	WordBasic equivalent: The .WholeWord parameter of the EditFind statement.
.MatchWildcards	**(Property)** A Boolean value that denotes whether the Find process is to interpret its .Text property as containing "wildcards," or symbols that represent directives to the word processor. For example, the wildcard <VB has Word search for words that begin (left caret) with the capital letters "VB."

Continued

TABLE 13-3 TERMS ASSOCIATED WITH THE FIND AND REPLACEMENT OBJECTS.
    (continued)

Word 2000 Term	Definition
	Note: Standard letters (i.e., not code letters) used within wildcard search phrases are treated case-sensitively at all times; so a search for `<TH` will find "THX" but will skip "the."
	Note: Setting this property to `True` overrides `True` settings for the properties `.MatchAllWordForms`, `.MatchCase`, `.MatchSoundsLike`, and `.MatchWholeWord`.
	`.Execute` **method parameter:** `MatchWildcards:=`
	WordBasic equivalent: The `.PatternMatch` parameter of the `EditFind` statement.
`.ParagraphFormat†`	**(Constituent)** Represents the characteristics of any typesetting characteristics and formatting given to the paragraph containing the text for which the `Find` process is to search. Any text that is not contained within a paragraph whose formatting is represented by this object is not counted as found, and is discarded.
	WordBasic equivalent: The `EditFindPara` statement was used prior to `EditFind` in search operations where the formatting of the paragraph containing the target text was important. `EditFindPara` would specify the characteristics of the paragraph, then `EditFind` would initiate the search.
`.Replacement`	**(Constituent)** Represents the contents and all characteristics to be applied to text that are to substitute for the found text, if any. Subordinate terms for the `Replacement` object appear in this table, and are marked with a dagger (†) symbol.
	`.Execute` **method parameter:** `ReplaceText:=`
	WordBasic equivalent: The `.Replace` parameter of the `EditFind` statement.
`.Style†`	**(Property)** Represents the style code or name given to the text for which the `Find` process is to search. Any text whose attributed style is not that listed by the `.Style` property is not counted as found and is discarded.
	WordBasic equivalent: In situations where the style name of the paragraph containing the text was important, the `EditFindStyle` statement was executed first and passed the style name as its sole argument. Then the `EditFind` statement was executed, making certain to set the `.Format` argument to `1`.

Word 2000 Term	Definition
`.Text`†	**(Property)** Set to a string literal or contents of a string variable. The `.Text` property contains the text, plus any symbols that may apply, for which the `Find` process is to search.
	`.Execute` **method parameter:** `FindText:=`
	WordBasic equivalent: The `.Find` parameter of the `EditFind` statement.
`.Wrap`	**(Property)** An integer that designates the behavior of the cursor when the `Find` process encounters the boundary of the search range. If a `Range` class object is the owner of the `Find`, then the `.Wrap` property setting is evaluated once the VBA interpreter has reset those boundaries to those of the original search area.
	Possible settings:
	`wdFindAsk` – Designates that the interpreter should inform the user when the search has reached its boundary.
	`wdFindContinue` – **(Default)** Designates that once the search has reached the end of its designated range, the search is to continue from the beginning of the range until it reaches the point at which the search commenced.
	`wdFindStop` – Designates that the search process is to stop once one of the boundaries has been reached.
	`.Execute` **method parameter:** `Wrap:=`
	WordBasic equivalent: The `.Wrap` parameter of the `EditFind` statement.

† Indicates that the term is also a constituent of the `Replacement` object.

Even though VBA treats each `Find` object as a separate entity from each other `Find` object, Word 2000 maintains only one search-and-replace system. **Word 2000 maintains the attributes of any prior search for the next search.** So, even if one operation performed by your procedure was a `Selection.Find` and the next belonged to a `Range` class object, the attributes of the `Selection.Find` process become the default attributes of the next search. Any attributes that your code does not set explicitly remain as they were. It becomes important, therefore, whenever you intend to initialize a fresh search rather than amend the previous one, to use the `.ClearFormatting` method to clean the existing formatting attributes, and to set `Replacement.Text` to `""` if you don't plan to replace any found text.

In Depth: Of Naming Arguments and Passing Parameters

The convention I've used throughout this book is that a *parameter* is a named argument given to a function or method. If the name isn't explicitly specified, I simply call it an argument. In Word 2000, you can specify the entire search and replacement criteria in one instruction, as you did in WordBasic. But today, the way you name and pass a parameter as an argument is different. With the old `EditFind` statement, named parameters were preceded with a period, as in this example:

```
EditFind .Text = "thier", .Replace = "their"
```

With VBA, named arguments are passed almost like value settings in Pascal:

```
Selection.Find.Execute FindText:="thier", ReplaceWith:="their"
```

In earlier examples, when I set up `With` clauses that defined the `Find` object as the default, these terms were methods, constituents, and properties, and were indeed preceded by periods, as in `.Text = "thier"`. But in the context of an `.Execute` method written in long form, the characteristics of the operation that you are setting are not properties, but arguments. They accomplish the same thing, but by different means — which is a common policy among Microsoft programming products these days.

The `Find` object represents the process of searching for, and possibly replacing, passages of text. It is a constituent of the `Document` class (which includes `ActiveDocument`), of the `Range` class, and of `Selection`. A search-and-replace operation may be established by assigning properties to this object, then invoking the `Find.Execute` method. When a `Range` class object is the owner of that method, then that object's reference will change to refer to the found text, if text has been found.

Addressing the typeface used for a range

The way Word 2000 interprets characters, all of the formatting characteristics that are specific to those characters *alone* — aside from the formatting of its containing paragraph or the border graphics — are maintained by the collective `Font` object. Whether text is italicized is determined by polling the `Font` object for its respective range. For instance, `rngThis.Font.Italic` returns `True` if the selected text, or the word over which the cursor currently resides, is italicized. Whether text is under-lined is also determined by polling its range's `Font` object, even though, conceptually speaking, whether there's a line *beneath* the character has little or nothing to do with its typeface.

The Font object is a constituent of both Range class objects and Selection, which represents the cursor. Table 13-4 lists some of the more common terms used to refer to the characteristics of characters.

TABLE 13-4A SPECIFYING THE FONT NAME

WordBasic for Word 7.0

```
Font$
```

VBA/Word 2000 Object Library

```
Font.Name
```

TABLE 13-4B REFERRING TO THE TYPESTYLE OF A GIVEN RANGE

WordBasic for Word 7.0

```
Bold
Italic
Underline
WordUnderline
DoubleUnderline
Strikethrough
Highlight
```

To set the cursor to type this character format or to change the character format of the text under the cursor, WordBasic used one of these keywords phrased as a statement, with a 1 or 0 passed as an argument. To determine what character formatting the cursor was ready to type, one of these keywords was phrased as a function, returning a signed integer value denoting whether all (1), part (-1), or none (0) of the indicated text bore that formatting.

VBA/Word 2000 Object Library

```
Font.Bold
Font.Italic
Font.Underline = wdUnderlineSingle
Font.Underline = wdUnderlineWords
Font.Underline = wdUnderlineDouble
Font.StrikeThrough
Font.Highlight
```

Continued

TABLE **13-4B** REFERRING TO THE TYPESTYLE OF A GIVEN RANGE *(continued)*

In Word 2000, the various properties important to the characteristics of characters are bound together by the `Font` object. There the single `.Underline` property may be set to any one of a varying number of constants, which represent the type of underscoring given to the text range, including dotted and dashed lines.

TABLE **13-4C** INCREASING OR DECREASING THE FONT SIZE FOR A GIVEN RANGE

WordBasic for Word 7.0

```
GrowFont
ShrinkFont
```

VBA/Word 2000 Object Library

```
Font.Grow
Font.Shrink
```

Like their WordBasic counterparts, these methods increase and decrease, respectively, the size of text represented by the antecedent range or cursor, by one point (supposedly $\frac{1}{72}$ inch, though not all fonts utilize points in exactly the same way).

TABLE **13-4D** RETRIEVING THE FONT COUNT FOR THE APPLICATION

WordBasic for Word 7.0

```
CountFonts()
```

Returns the number of typeface *families* currently enrolled in the Windows Fonts Control Panel, and thus in the word processor (see right).

VBA/Word 2000 Object Library

```
Application.FontNames.Count
```

With Word 2000, `FontNames` is an ordinary collection object that lists the names of *typefaces* available to Word. Typefaces in this case are font families; so even though "Arial," "Arial Bold," and "Arial Bold Italic" are three different TrueType font files, they are enrolled within Word 2000 as the same font.

Accessing paragraph formatting

Keeping in the spirit of rebuilding everything into objects, Word 2000 has devised a class of object called `ParagraphFormat` that maintains the typesetting characteristics that the word processor applies to any one paragraph. **A paragraph format describes the typeset attributes of a paragraph in a document.** By itself, it relates to the characteristics of a real paragraph in a real document, not a paragraph that the user might compose later. As a constituent of the `Style` object (yes, Virginia, there is another object), `ParagraphFormat` describes the characteristics that *will be attributed* to any paragraph to which that style is assigned.

All versions of Microsoft Word have, since the beginning, recognized four distinct categories of formatting that pertain to the appearance of text in a document:

♦ **Character formatting** pertains to the placement, arrangement, and appearance of characters on the text lines (rasters) already apportioned for them. The type of characters used and the space applied between characters are considered elements of character formatting.

♦ **Paragraph formatting** pertains to the situation of text lines on the page. This includes their margins relative to the space already apportioned for them on the page, plus the amount of leading (vertical separating space) between lines of text, and the placement of tab stops along each line. For contextual purposes, this now also includes such features as bulleting, enumeration, and outline tier placement.

♦ **Border formatting** in Microsoft Word refers not only to the weight and color of lines drawn around or between paragraphs, but also to the color and patterns given to the background area behind characters.

♦ **Document formatting** pertains to the areas of each page of the document apportioned to the main textual elements, or "stories," including the main body of text, header and footer regions, and footnote regions. A document may be subdivided into sections, each of which has its own set of document formatting characteristics; but the document formatting for any one file consists of the collection of all section formats.

The way the common Word user creates a new paragraph style is by building a prototype for that style in a document, giving it the attributes needed to distinguish it from others in the active templates, then indicating the prototype and asking Word to apply a style whose name it does not yet recognize. Word gets the hint and generates a new style entry, using the indicated text as a basis.

Neither WordBasic nor Word 2000 VBA generates new paragraph styles in exactly that way, even when they are recording the user's own actions. WordBasic was very straightforward, using single, multiple-attribute statements for each of the four categories listed above: `FormatDefineStyleFont`, `FormatDefineStylePara`, `FormatDefineStyleBorders`, and `FilePageSetup`. The names of these statements came from the position on the menu bar where their corresponding commands could be found. A new format or style was called into existence and defined using one of these statements.

With Word 2000, you do take a few more steps. A `Style` class object defines the characteristics of a paragraph or character style in Word 2000. For it to be complete, it must be comprised of a constituent `Font` object that defines the typeface and treatment of characters in the style, and a `ParagraphFormat` object that defines the treatment of text lines and margins. **The main `Style` object and its constituent objects must exist before their properties can be set.** This seems logical enough, but there's a realization that comes from this: Word 2000 has you add the `Style` class object first, and then build it into something usable. So for a brief time, a style exists among the current document or template styles collection that is essentially null.

It's important to note that **styles and formats are not necessarily complete listings of all of the attributes that comprise them.** When you record a macro in which you define a style or format, all of the attributes are recorded, regardless of whether you made any changes to those attributes during the recording. But when you write your own procedure that defines a style but leave attributes out of the definition, that omission is treated as a directive to Word to apply the attributes for the text under the cursor to the style you're defining. (The exception is when you redefine the paragraph style called Normal, which must contain a full set of attributes.) So when you write a `With` clause that pertains to a `ParagraphFormat` class object, the properties you leave out will be those that Word leaves as is when it applies that format later to a region of text. This may be what you want. It may be quite practical for you to have a paragraph style that does nothing but squeeze the margins inward one-half inch, while leaving the font and leading as they are.

So here is the order of events that should take place for your Word 2000 VBA procedure to define a new style (although the Word 2000 macro recorder does things a bit differently, this method is a bit more efficient):

1. The new, null style must first be added to the `Styles` collection for the document, with an instruction like this:

   ```
   docThis.Styles.Add Name:="NewStyle",
   Type:=wdStyleTypeParagraph
   ```

   Here, `docThis` is an object reference to a `Document` class object, though `ActiveDocument` would do nicely here as well. `"NewStyle"` is the name given to an example `Style` class object.

2. The main `With` clause is defined listing `docThis.Styles("NewStyle")` as the default object. There are relatively few properties specific to the `Style` object alone that may need to be set at this time.

3. A secondary With clause is defined listing .Font as the default object, the leading period referring the object back to docThis.Styles("NewStyle"). The Font constituent of the Style class object lists attributes that pertain to the default character format for the style. Setting the properties of the Font object establishes those characteristics.

4. Another secondary With clause is defined outside of With .Font, but inside With docThis.Styles("NewStyle"), this time listing .ParagraphFormat as the default object. The ParagraphFormat constituent of a Style class object lists attributes that pertain to how the text lines for the style are typeset. Setting the properties of the ParagraphFormat object establishes those characteristics.

5. You may require third-level With clauses for the .Shading, .Borders, and .Frame constituents of the ParagraphFormat object. Shading addresses the foreground and background colors that are blended together to form the pattern behind the text (VB6 programmers: *not* the text color, but a separate hue known as the foreground color). Borders addresses the color and weight of line used for any borderlines around the text and between its paragraph boundaries, if any. Frame is only used if a paragraph being given this style is to appear in an independent, floating frame.

Listing 13-6 shows a fragment of a procedure that defines, as completely as possible, a new Style class object and adds it to the active document. Here, you'll see the five-step process outlined above put into practice.

Listing 13-6: A complete Word 2000 definition of a new style.

```
ActiveDocument.Styles.Add Name:="MainBodyText", _
  Type:=wdStyleTypeParagraph
With ActiveDocument.Styles("MainBodyText")
    .LanguageID = wdEnglishUS
    .Frame.Delete
    With .Font
        .Name = "Lucida Bright"
        .Size = 11
        .Bold = False
        .Italic = False
        .Underline = wdUnderlineNone
        .StrikeThrough = False
        .DoubleStrikeThrough = False
        .Outline = False
        .Emboss = False
        .Shadow = False
        .Hidden = False
        .SmallCaps = False
```

```
            .AllCaps = False
            .ColorIndex = wdAuto
            .Engrave = False
            .Superscript = False
            .Subscript = False
            .Spacing = 0.2
            .Scaling = 100
            .Kerning = 10
            .Animation = wdAnimationNone
        End With
        With .ParagraphFormat
            .LeftIndent = InchesToPoints(0)
            .RightIndent = InchesToPoints(0)
            .SpaceBefore = 0
            .SpaceAfter = 12
            .LineSpacingRule = wdLineSpaceAtLeast
            .LineSpacing = 16
            .Alignment = wdAlignParagraphLeft
            .WidowControl = True
            .KeepWithNext = False
            .KeepTogether = False
            .PageBreakBefore = False
            .NoLineNumber = False
            .Hyphenation = True
            .FirstLineIndent = InchesToPoints(0)
            .OutlineLevel = wdOutlineLevelBodyText
            .TabStops.ClearAll
            With .Shading
                .Texture = wdTextureNone
                .ForegroundPatternColorIndex = wdAuto
                .BackgroundPatternColorIndex = wdAuto
            End With
            With .Borders
                .item(wdBorderLeft).LineStyle = wdLineStyleNone
                .item(wdBorderRight).LineStyle = wdLineStyleNone
                .item(wdBorderTop).LineStyle = wdLineStyleNone
                .item(wdBorderBottom).LineStyle = wdLineStyleNone
                .DistanceFromTop = 1
                .DistanceFromLeft = 4
                .DistanceFromBottom = 1
                .DistanceFromRight = 4
                .Shadow = False
            End With
        End With
    End With
End With
```

A few items of note here: Since this particular paragraph format is not designed to be placed within a floating frame, the instruction `.Frame.Delete` removes the paragraph given this style from any frame that the cursor may presently inhabit. Also, notice in the `With` `.Font` clause, the presence of the properties `.Outline`, `.Emboss`, and `.Shadow`. These are three entirely new special textual effects for Word 2000.

In WordBasic, the way you applied an already defined style to a region of text was to first manipulate the cursor so that it selected that region, and then to use the `Style` statement, naming the paragraph style in quotation marks. Simple in explanation, complex in execution. With Word 2000 VBA, the `Style` object applies to any region of text belonging to a document, which includes `Selection`, but also includes `Range` class objects in all their various forms. To apply the style named `"NewStyle"` to a given range `rngThis`, you'd invoke the instruction `rngThis.Style = "NewStyle"`. (You could also, as some documentation states, write `rngThis.Style = ActiveDocument.Styles("NewStyle")`, but if you think about it, what's the point of writing it out longhand?) Keep in mind that a paragraph style is applied to the *whole* paragraph that contains any part of the range being reformatted. So if `Selection` is the object in question here, and selected text spans parts of two paragraphs, an assignment such as this affects both paragraphs. On the other hand, if the style is a *character* style only (defined from the beginning by using the constant `wdStyleTypeCharacter` instead of `wdStyleTypeParagraph`), where paragraph formatting does not apply, the style change only takes effect within the boundaries of the range and not outside.

Maintaining the document files

Finally, Table 13-5 covers the instructions used to open and close documents.

TABLE **13–5A** **OPENING AN EXISTING DOCUMENT**

WordBasic for Word 7.0

```
FileOpen
```

EXAMPLES:

```
FileOpen .Name = š
 "C:\Docs\02K13_1D.DOC"

FileOpen .Name = "Q1SUM.DOC", š
 .ReadOnly = 1
```

Continued

TABLE 13-5A **OPENING AN EXISTING DOCUMENT** *(continued)*

VBA/Word 2000 Object Library

.Open

EXAMPLES:

```
Documents.Open _
"C:\Docs\02K13_1D.DOC"

Documents.Open _
 FileName:="Q1SUM.DOC", _
 ReadOnly:=1
```

The antecedent object being addressed here is the Documents collection, which is a constituent of Application (which may itself always be omitted). The first argument recognized in the .Open method's native sequence is the FileName: parameter, and it is the only required parameter. For that reason, the naming of the parameter can be omitted.

TABLE 13-5B **SAVING A DOCUMENT OR DOCUMENTS**

WordBasic for Word 7.0

```
FileSave
FileSaveAll
```

EXAMPLES:
```
FileSave
FileSaveAll
```

The first example saved to disk whatever document currently had the focus (the blinking cursor).

VBA/Word 2000 Object Library

.Save

EXAMPLES:
```
ActiveDocument.Save
Documents.Save
```

VBA/Word 2000 Object Library

With Word 2000, it becomes necessary to explicitly state which document or documents you are saving; the `.Save` method makes no assumptions. If you are saving the document that currently has the focus, you need to say so by writing `ActiveDocument.Save`. Otherwise, you can save any open document by referring to it as an indexed member of the `Documents` collection — for instance, `Documents("Q1SUM.DOC").Save`. If you refer to the entire `Documents` collection without any indexed members, the `.Save` method saves all the open documents.

TABLE **13-5c** CLOSING A DOCUMENT OR DOCUMENTS

WordBasic for Word 7.0

```
FileClose
FileCloseAll
```

EXAMPLES:

```
FileClose
FileCloseAll 1
```

The 1 passed as an argument to `FileCloseAll` had the interpreter save all the documents before closing, without asking the user's permission first.

VBA/Word 2000 Object Library

```
.Close
```

EXAMPLES:

```
ActiveDocument.Close
Documents.Close wdSaveChanges
```

The `.Close` method has a similar mode of operation to `.Save`. If you refer to one `Document` class object, and that one is open, it gets closed. If you refer to the entire `Documents` collection, they all get closed. The `wdSaveChanges` constant obviously tells the interpreter here to save all documents before closing.

In Theory: The Forgotten BASIC

QBASIC was the last edition of an interpreter that was part of every version of MS-DOS up to version 7. It might not have been an "integral" part from the point of view of DOS users, but QBASIC was there. It was perhaps the single most *disused* program ever distributed – maybe less than one percent of the people who installed MS-DOS ever made use of the thing.

Aside from QBASIC, however, it's believed that the single most distributed BASIC interpreter in the year 1990 was WordBasic. For the longest time, it seemed, WordBasic was the only BASIC available for Microsoft Windows. As a result, innovative tinkerers during that time were writing and distributing WordBasic applications that required Word for Windows to be installed, but otherwise had little or nothing to do with the operation of a word processor.

It probably cannot be said that WordBasic was the forerunner to Visual Basic, otherwise much of this chapter would not have been written in a distinctively comparative two-column format. As an early initiate to Visual Basic since before the product first hit the shelves, I noticed right away that Microsoft was steering clear of many of the design decisions that WordBasic put forth. First and foremost was the way dialog panels worked.

In WordBasic, you designed dialog panels by writing textual instructions. This made perfect sense to those of us who, even by the time WordBasic was introduced, had already been programming in BASIC for a decade. The programming language at that time was just that – a *language*, not an *environment*. Back then, the back panel of the dialog box was declared with instructions that had statements and arguments. Controls were then declared with separate sets of arguments inside a clause that was bound by the background instruction. As you ran your program, you saw WordBasic construct your dialog panel one instruction at a time. And you didn't need breakpoints or other fancy debugging tools to watch this process happen, because you had the perfect debugging tool for such matters right in front of you: a very slow computer running an astonishingly slow operating environment. Windows was a *slug*.

But even in WordBasic, a few interesting ideas took root, and came into full fruition in Visual Basic. From time to time, a WordBasic macro might need to bring up a dialog panel that belonged to Word's own repertoire. To do this, you declared a variable and set it to refer to the standard dialog by name. This was the beginning of the *object reference* in BASIC; this hadn't been done before. The use of a *name* (not a character like $ or %) to refer to the type of a variable was also a new thing for those of us who had already been programming in BASIC for over a decade. I stared at `Dim dlgrec As FileOpen` for the first time in 1988 and was bewildered.

Also, WordBasic introduced the world to a radical new concept that, even when it was explained at the first developers' conferences, didn't make immediate sense to everyone. WordBasic used the `Declare` statement, with almost exactly the same format as VB's and VBA's implementation today, to introduce an external function from a dynamic link library to the WordBasic macro. The concept of being able to tap directly into Windows from something as trivial as a text formatting menu command was wildly fascinating to me, and it was totally lost on most of the rest of the computing press at the time.

WordBasic held on as a viable complementary product to Word until as late as the first quarter of 1997, when it was finally replaced by Visual Basic for

Applications in Word 97. It was the last of a style of interpreter that bridged the gap between the alphanumeric era of computing and the graphical era. It marked the end of the critical transition in computing between command-oriented and object-oriented functionality. And while WordBasic certainly did not lead us in the direction of object-oriented wisdom, in the period when objects were all around us, everywhere we programmers looked in the configuration space that represents the place we work in our minds, WordBasic was the last light we saw glimmering from the shores of the old world as we sailed on.

In Brief

- ◆ Word 2000 projects range in scope from single procedures to complex modular systems with object-oriented interfacing. As such, they shed the scroll-like procedural model that was the basis for WordBasic programming.

- ◆ Instructions that address the cursor and tell it to move or select text are directed toward the `Selection` object in Word 2000.

- ◆ A `Find` object is a constituent of a range or some other representative of text in a document.

- ◆ In Word 2000, the active typeface is represented not by an aspect of the cursor, but by an independent `Font` object.

- ◆ A paragraph style and a character style are both represented by explicit and replete hierarchies of objects and constituents, rooted in the `Style` class.

Chapter 14

Force-Feeding Word 2000

IN THIS CHAPTER

- ◆ The components of a document as collection objects

- ◆ Differentiating between the selection and ranges

- ◆ Phrasing direct references to textual contents

- ◆ Addressing Word 2000 bookmark and AutoText objects

- ◆ Using collection properties to sort their elements

- ◆ Declaring and loading independent collections

- ◆ Compiling statistics on open documents by using, then correcting, Word's concurrent information

- ◆ Polling a document's properties through `Selection.Information()` and `.BuiltInDocumentProperties`

- ◆ Utilizing the MultiPage Forms 2.0 control in a `UserForm` module

- ◆ Using `.GoTo` and `.Move` to manipulate the cursor

- ◆ Distinguishing between true and false entries in the `Words` collection

- ◆ Adding a binary search algorithm

- ◆ Managing a form's initialization and termination through event procedures

IN THE OCTOBER 1997 issue of *Byte* magazine, veteran Chaos Manor columnist (and my hero) Jerry Pournelle made a suggestion concerning future revisions to Microsoft Word. First, he mentioned how Word's optional white-on-blue text display mode — accessible from Tools → Options → General — was added to the product at his request. (I personally, uh, *know* of at least one other request that was made for that specific feature, but I imagine Jerry's was the one that was laminated and framed.) Then Jerry made an open request for one other feature: Could Word's document statistics account for such items as words, lines, and paragraphs that fall *before* the cursor location and *after* the cursor?

Why would such a feature be helpful? Well, the way Jerry writes his columns and other works (he co-authors science fiction blockbusters with Larry Niven), he copies his outline and notes into the document first. Then, he weaves portions of those notes into the draft in progress, working top-to-bottom. As a result, his documents have two unofficial sections: the draft portion at the beginning, and the notes/outline portion at the end. With his prior word processor, Symantec Q& A Write, Jerry could place his cursor at the borderline between his two sections, and after hitting Ctrl+F3, the statistics dialog would give him word and line counts before and after the cursor. Couldn't Word 2000 do the same? Should be a simple addition, right?

I took it upon myself to fulfill Jerry's wishes in lieu of Microsoft. The approach I took at first was to trust the Word object library's running tally of words, sentences, and paragraphs for any given range or selected area. I then easily subdivided the document into three ranges: text before the cursor, selected by the cursor, and after the cursor. Those divisions having been made, the element counts should tell me precisely what exists within those divisions, and I could then just render the results in a `UserForm` object.

One rule of programming that you should regard closely and often is that any programming task that you undertake that has the word "Microsoft" associated with it in part or whole, will probably be more difficult than it seems at first. The reason doesn't necessarily have anything to do with the relative quality of the programming language or environment, or the characteristics of the operating system. It has more to do with the fact that Microsoft encompasses so many different departments, paradigms, and schools of thought in one massive melting pot of mnemonics, models, and schematics, such that any project you undertake is likely to address more than one way of thinking. As a result, you're likely to spend more time reconciling than you are creating.

Analyzing the Parts of a Document

Here's our goal: We want a dialog box that shows the Pournelle-inspired statistics for all the open documents in Word 2000. A MultiPage control will be used to display each document's statistics in independent panels, with visible tabs that the user can click on to pull up the statistics for any open document. Figure 14-1 shows the finished product, which looks quite like the way I had planned it to look from the beginning.

The finished product does hide quite nicely some of the trouble it took to actually produce the module. To try to spare you some of the same trouble, I'd like to share with you the details of the debugged product.

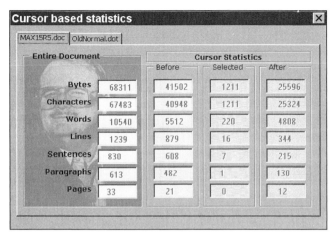

Figure 14-1: The completed cursor-based statistics form.

Planning controls for indeterminate pages

A MultiPage control, as you saw in Chapter 7, is a container for a handful of independent containers of other controls. At design time, you can set the number of panels (Page objects) that MultiPage will house, and invoke other controls and assign them to the separate panels. But in this situation, you, the programmer, cannot know in advance how many documents will have been opened in Word 2000, so the number of panels that MultiPage will house at any one time is variable. This means that MultiPage Page objects will have to build themselves at run time, *after* the user has invoked the procedure that spawns the form.

To solve this problem, I took the easy way out: I designed all the panels so that they contain identical controls to one another's. The procedure won't be wasting time in determining how best to lay out some particular arrangement of new controls. Instead, the system I came up with is to build one panel at design time, and use that panel as a template for the generation of as many new panels as are required later.

This is not an easy task. Listing 14-1 shows the procedure that the main form module will always execute *first*, Private Sub UserForm_Initialize(). As with any UserForm-based form module, the _Initialize event is recognized first. The code here is executed before the user ever sees the form; so we have a window of opportunity to arrange MultiPage out of sight of the user.

Listing 14-1: The MultiPage control is arranged prior to being seen.

```
Private Sub UserForm_Initialize()
    Dim strPage As String, winDer As Window, ctrlThis As Control
    Dim iCtrl As Integer

    ReDim ctrlRef(Windows.Count, _
     mpDocStats.Pages(0).Controls.Count)

    Set docRecall = ActiveDocument

    For Each winDer In Windows
        winDer.Document.Bookmarks.Add _
      Range:=winDer.Selection.Range, _
      Name:="RecallSelectionObject"
        strPage = "mps" & Str$(winDer.Index)
        mpDocStats.Pages.Add strPage, winDer.Document.Name
        mpDocStats.Pages("Page1").Controls.Copy
        mpDocStats.Pages(strPage).Paste
        iCtrl = 0
        For Each ctrlThis In mpDocStats.Pages(strPage).Controls
            Set ctrlRef(winDer.Index, iCtrl) = ctrlThis
            iCtrl = iCtrl + 1
        Next ctrlThis
    Next winDer

    mpDocStats.Pages.Remove "Page1"
    mpDocStats.Value = ActiveWindow.Index - 1
    ComputeStats ActiveWindow.Index - 1
    bActive = True
End Sub
```

The determinant of how many MultiPage panels (Page objects) will be generated is how many active document windows there are in Word 2000. The Windows collection does not represent the operating system; instead, it represents the plurality of document windows currently open in Word. The object reference winDer ("*der*" meaning "this" in German, and "winder" being how we pronounced "window" back home) will refer successively to each active window in the Windows collection by virtue of the For Each...Next loop clause.

We'll talk about the Bookmarks instruction in a bit. First, each newly invoked Page object must have its own unique name. To generate one that will point to the window whose document is being accounted for, we create a string strPage comprised of a prefix mps followed by the index numeral of the associated window, borrowed from winDer.Index, converted to a string using the intrinsic function Str$() because names are strings that cannot be made up of real numbers.

The `Pages` collection contains all the panels that are being maintained by the MultiPage control, whose `.Name` property here is `mpDocStats`. The `.Add` method brings a new `Page` object into the control and adds it to the collection. The two arguments *required* by the `.Add` method are the name with which the panel will be referenced later and the caption that will appear in the visible tab for the panel. The term `winDer.Document.Name` refers to the name (actually the filename) of the document that currently appears in the window being referenced by `winDer`.

In the instruction following the `.Add` method, you see how a named panel is referenced. Notice the indirectness of the reference to `"Page1"`; the name does not act as the page's exclusive address, as in **mpDocStats.Page1.Controls**. Instead, the name is put in quotation marks, and serves as an alternate index for a member of the `Pages` collection. `"Page1"` is the name of the template panel on which all the other panels are based. In the instruction that follows, `strPage` stands in as the reference to the panel being built. Notice here that we're performing a `.Copy` and `.Paste` maneuver, involving the `Controls` collection that belongs to `Pages("Page1")`. Yes, we're using the System Clipboard. This is the only method available to us for "cloning" controls; actually, it's the same method that a programmer would use for copying controls at design time, only involving instructions rather than menu commands. Notice that the term `Controls` term is necessary for the `.Copy` method to know what is being copied; but `.Paste` does not require the same antecedent, because `.Paste` performs a paste on whatever happens to be on the Clipboard at the time.

Once duplicates of the `Page1` controls have been pasted into the new panel, the next order of business is to give them names with which we can refer to them. If you read some of the documentation, you might have gathered that you can change the `.Name` properties of the duplicate controls directly, using instructions that would be illegal for any other type of control. For instance, assuming `ctrlThis` referred to one of the controls in the new panel's `Controls` collection, you could write: `ctrlThis.Name = "Readout" & LTrim$(Str$(iCtrl))`, where `iCtrl` is an index numeral. You would then have a control with a name like `Readout1`, and then later you could write an instruction `Readout1.Text = Str$(docThis.Sentences.Count)`. These would all be legitimate instructions. Something out there called `Readout1` does maintain a `.Text` property. Trouble is, that something doesn't seem to be any real control. For whatever reason, the block of memory that Forms 2.0 apportions for `Readout1` doesn't relate to any real control anywhere, despite the fact that earlier, a real reference `ctrlThis` referred to it.

The only way to access individual duplicate controls in a MultiPage panel is by way of an object variable set to refer to it indirectly. Here, we've created an array of object references, called `ctrlRef()`, declared within the Declarations section of the VBA module, shown here:

```
Dim ctrlRef() As Control
Dim docRecall As Document
Dim bActive As Boolean
```

Declaring an object variable As Control makes it possible for that variable to refer indirectly to a control. Because you can't give a MultiPage clone control a real name (or, more accurately, because whatever you're really giving the name to doesn't exist), the ctrlRef() array is necessary here to refer to the entire set of clone controls for each page. This will be a two-dimensional dynamic array whose bounds are set at the top of Private Sub UserForm_Initialize() (Listing 14-1).

Envisioning a control set within a 2D array

We haven't done much with two-dimensional arrays up to this point, so I'll explain their purpose from the beginning: Imagine a two-dimensional array like a table, such as the one you'd find in a spreadsheet. Each cell in the table is accessed using a pair of identifiers — one for rows, one for columns. For a VBA two-dimensional array, you can imagine whichever identifier you want for row and whichever for column; but perhaps now you have a better idea of the construction of such an array. Imagine ctrlRef() as having as many "cells" wide as there are open windows (Windows.Count), and as many "cells" long as there are controls in the template panel (mpDocStats.Pages(0).Controls.Count).

So the interior For Each...Next loop clause loops through all of the controls in the newly created panel, and assigns one column, if you will, of the ctrlRef() array to refer to the set of clone controls in one of the new pages. The loop clause ticks down that column one at a time in succession, using the iCtrl integer here to count the specific cell that is being attributed to ctrlThis at the time. (Variable iCtrl is set to 0 prior to the loop, because it's going to be used again later and it needs to be "refreshed" at that time.) Later, since ctrlRef() is a module-level array (we declared it in the Declarations section at the top of the module), we can refer to the controls within each panel of the MultiPage control using the index number of the window for the document being scanned (which corresponds to the index number in the Pages collection) and the control number as identifiers.

Back to where we left off in Listing 14-1: The .Remove method deletes the panel named Page1 from the collection. Why couldn't we just leave Page1 there and have it refer to one of the open documents, since it looks like all the other panels anyway? We could, but it would be a more elaborate process than the one we've chosen. We'd need one block of code to refer one column of ctrlRef() controls to Page1, and a duplicate code block to refer the rest of the columns to successive panels *if* there's more than one document open . . . you can see the mess we'd be getting ourselves into.

What's bActive for? We need a module-level Boolean variable in place to squelch certain unscheduled calls to the _Change event procedure. (This is the type of programming that you just don't conjure up in the first build.) Our form module uses the mpDocStats_Change event to denote when the user clicks on one of the tabs in the MultiPage control. Unfortunately, this event "fires" whenever something changes the active panel, thereby changing the .Value property of the MultiPage control. Removing Page1 makes this event "fire" before we're ready for it; so bActive serves as a flag that indicates whether we're ready or not. We are officially ready when mpDocStats.Value is set to officially point to the index of the active window, minus one because MultiPage's "number one" is 0, not 1. The _Change event procedure below scans the bActive variable prior to executing its main directive:

```
Private Sub mpDocStats_Change()
    If bActive Then ComputeStats mpDocStats.SelectedItem.Index
End Sub
```

If bActive is False, the _Change event procedure does nothing. Otherwise, if we're clear to work, the .Index of the chosen MultiPage panel is passed to Private Sub ComputeStats(), which analyzes the associated document.

The _Click event doesn't always work

Why are we relying on MultiPage's _Change event rather than its _Click event to tell us when the user has clicked on one of the tabs? Because there is a bug in the MultiPage control (Microsoft knows about it) where if the tabs area becomes more than one row tall, any clicks on the second row do not generate _Click events. Normally, this would render the second row and all rows thereafter inaccessible to the user. But luckily, the MultiPage control is devised in a non-standard manner. MultiPage does not use an exclusive property like .ActiveControl to determine which panel has the focus at any one time. Instead, it uses the more generic .Value property, which is set at run time to the index number of the visible Page object. You may set this .Value property yourself to manually change the visible panel. But the upshot of using the .Value property is that the _Change event, as for most other controls, reacts to any changes to that property. So whenever .Value changes, _Change fires.

Luckily, when the user clicks on *any* row of tabs in the MultiPage control, the _Change event is recognized. On the other side of the spectrum of luck, anything else that the user or program may do that affects the .Value property also activates the _Change event. So we need the bActive variable as a sort of "gate," that enables us to open up formal processing of the event procedure at the time we designate.

Preparing to count real and not-so-real elements

We now begin our listing of this monstrosity of a procedure, but be advised that we'll be presenting this procedure in parts, so that we can go over the details without you having to flip back and forth between too many pages. Listing 14-2 shows the preparatory instructions:

Listing 14-2: The main document analysis procedure, preparations section.

Part 1

```
Private Sub ComputeStats(lPage As Long)
    Dim strTitle As String, docThis As Document, winDer As Window
    Dim rngBefore As Range, rngAt As Range, rngAfter As Range, _
    rngAll As Range
    Dim selThis As Selection
    Dim lCharsBefore As Long, lCharsAt As Long, lCharsAfter As _
    Long
    Dim lWordsBefore As Long, lWordsAt As Long, lWordsAfter As _
    Long
    Dim lLinesBefore As Long, lLinesAt As Long, lLinesAfter As _
    Long
    Dim iPagesBefore As Integer, iPagesAt As Integer, _
    iPagesAfter As Integer
    Dim rngWord As Range, strThis As String, _
    iLPageNo As Integer, iRPageNo As Integer
    Dim charThis As String, rngCount As Range
    Dim lPageLines() As Long, lPageFinalChar() As Long, iPages _
    As Integer, iCount As Integer

    Application.ScreenUpdating = False

    strTitle = mpDocStats.Pages(lPage).Caption
    Set docThis = Documents(strTitle)
    Set winDer = Windows(lPage + 1)

    If winDer.Selection.Range.Start > 1 Then
        Set rngBefore = docThis.Range(docThis.Range.Start, _
        winDer.Selection.Range.Start - 1)
    Else
        Set rngBefore = docThis.Range(docThis.Range.Start, _
        winDer.Selection.Range.Start)
    End If
    Set rngAt = winDer.Selection.Range
    If winDer.Selection.Range.End < docThis.Range.End Then
        If winDer.Selection.Range.End = docThis.Range.End - 1 Then
            Set rngAfter = docThis.Range _
            (winDer.Selection.Range.End, docThis.Range.End)
        Else
            Set rngAfter = docThis.Range(winDer.Selection _
            .Range.End + 1, docThis.Range.End)
        End If
    Else
```

```
        Set rngAfter = docThis.Range(winDer.Selection.Range _
          .End, docThis.Range.End)
    End If
    Set rngAll = docThis.Range
    Set selThis = winDer.Selection
```

The purpose of this procedure is to analyze the data that Word 2000 generates about certain elements of a document, and systematically *correct* them. That's right – the numbers the Word object library generates, if you view them outside of their programming-based context, are inaccurate, and at times incorrect. Case in point: The `Selection` object always returns a `.Words.Count` of 1, regardless of whether a word is actually highlighted at the time. Why is this the case? Is this some kind of bug? Not at all. It may be helpful *in some other scenario* to know what word the cursor is presently hanging over, if any. In that case, `Selection.Words(1).Count` would return that word. So there's a good reason for what appears, from the point of view of our present project, to be an inaccuracy. But multiply the `Words` problem by so many `Characters` and so many more `Paragraphs`, and you'll get a better idea of the problem this procedure faces head-on.

The sets of variables being declared here, with the suffixes `Before`, `At`, and `After`, will hold the corrected numbers ascertained by this procedure. Some of the other object variables with the `-This` suffix will be used as temporary references, especially to one item in a set. The dynamic arrays `lPageLines()` and `lPageFinalChar()` will be used later in ascertaining just how many *lines* (what professional typesetters call "rasters") there are in the active document. You may have noticed that "Lines" is not one of the categories maintained by the Word 2000 object library. So if the number of lines in your document is something in which you happen to be interested – and many magazine editors are – then you'll be thankful for these arrays . . . in the end.

One of Word's more interesting rules is that **you cannot manually establish a `Range` class object whose `Start:` and `End:` parameters are set to equal values** – at least, not without generating an error. So we use a group of conditional clauses to make certain that the `rngBefore` and `rngAfter` ranges have `Range` boundaries that are at least one character separated from one another, if only for the sake of argument (pun intended). Word could crash (yes, I use that word literally) if a `Range` class object is manually established with zero length.

Temporarily halting screen updates for faster execution

The first operative instruction of Listing 14-2, past the variable declarations, is `Application.ScreenUpdating = False`. This will speed things up a bit by canceling the paint events that Word sends to the operating system to redraw its own window. We can – in fact, we have to – reset the `.ScreenUpdating` procedure to `True` when the procedure is done and screen updates are warranted once again.

Next, the main range object references are set. We'll be using these variables docThis, winDer, rngBefore, rngAt, rngAfter, rngAll, and selThis as shorthand for their longer forms, which you can see to the right of the = operator in each instruction. The range rngBefore covers all the characters from the start of the document docThis.Range.Start to the character just before the start of the cursor point, which is winDer.Selection.Range.Start - 1 if the selection is in the middle of the document, and winDerSelection.Range.Start if the selection is at the beginning. In the case where there are no obvious characters before or after the selected area, the ranges "before" and "after" that area still exist, if you don't mind them being one character long.

You may be wondering, since the cursor in Word is a line that comes *between* two characters, when there is no text "selected," what exactly is the "selected" character? It's the character just to the *right* of the line. The range reference rngAt will mirror the selected characters (there will always be at least one), and rngAfter will refer to everything from the character just after the selection range, up to the end of the document.

Listing 14-3 continues Private Sub ComputeStats() with the instruction block that deals with where pages truly *end*:

Listing 14-3: Preparing for a faster, more realistic, line count.

Part 2

```
iPages = docThis.BuiltInDocumentProperties("Number of Pages")
ReDim lPageLines(iPages), lPageFinalChar(iPages)
If iPages > 1 Then
    For iCount = 1 To iPages - 1
        Set rngCount = rngAll.GoTo(What:=wdGoToPage, _
    Count:=iCount + 1)
        rngCount.Move wdCharacter, -1
        lPageLines(iCount) = _
    rngCount.Information(wdFirstCharacterLineNumber)
        lPageFinalChar(iCount) = rngCount.End
    Next iCount
End If
Set rngCount = rngAll
rngCount.Start = docThis.Range.End
lPageLines(iPages) = _
rngCount.Information(wdFirstCharacterLineNumber)
lPageFinalChar(iPages) = rngCount.End
```

The purpose of this part of the procedure is to generate internal summaries of how many lines there are in each page, and the ordinal character numerals at the end of each page with respect to the whole document. The reason we need these is to calculate a true line count, and to do so faster than if we were to step through each line of the entire document – which could consume minutes of the user's time, even on a fast machine.

Obtaining a document's built-in properties

We start by relying on Word's internal count of the number of pages in the document, which we do know to be flawlessly correct. We acquire this count by addressing a fairly long though straightforward collection of internal properties that Word concurrently maintains for each document. The collection is called `BuiltIn DocumentProperties`, and it contains `DocumentProperty` class objects that reveal something important about the associated document. (Remember, `docThis` is a shorthand pointer to the document currently being studied.) Each document property is addressable by full name, and `"Number of Pages"` obviously refers to the document's page count. This integer is here assigned to the variable `iPages`, which acts from here on out as the document's page count representative. Our lines-per-page and final-character-numeral dynamic arrays `lPageLines()` and `lPageFinal Char()` are both reset and given `iPages` number of elements.

Why do we need the numeral of the final character in each page? Later on, we'll have a situation where we have a lone character numeral, and we need to know on which page that character falls. Using an algorithmic search technique (which you'll see demonstrated later), we can position that lone numeral before the nearest final character numeral in `lPageFinalChar()`, and the index of that numeral in the array will be the page number where the character falls. Why do we need an array with the number of lines per page? Word can tell us how many lines there are in a page without us having to step through each line individually. When it comes time later to find out how many lines are covered by a given range, we can ascertain whether that range covers entire pages, and borrow those pages' line counts in summing up the total number of lines. This is a big performance boost to the module and, although it consumes more instruction lines, it does aid in its overall efficiency.

Moving ranges and the selection with .GoTo

The way we determine the final character numeral for each page quickly is by having Word take us – or more accurately, take `rngCount` – to the page *after* the one we're counting for, by dialing up that page using the `.GoTo` method. BASIC veterans, `.GoTo` **is not a branching statement.** It's a directive to Word to set the named range `rngCount` to point to a particular spot within another stated range – in this case, `rngAll`, which points to the entire document. For this `.GoTo` method, we're using named arguments; `What:=` tells Word what category of element to be searching through, and `Count:=` designates which of those elements in the set it should find. By default, `.GoTo` takes `rngCount` to the *beginning* of whatsoever `What:=` it names; so the beginning of the page *after* the one we're interested in should be adjacent to the one we really need: the final character in the *previous* page. So with the `.Move` method, we have `rngCount` move back one, with `wdCharacter` answering the question, "One *what?*" One character. "Back" is symbolized here by the *negative* before the 1; a positive 1 would mean one *forward*. By the way, wdGoToPage and wdCharacter are *constants*, which are terms that substitute for values. In these cases, you could have written 1 and 1, respectively, in place of the constants. But would you have remembered what the 1 stood for in each case, as easily as you might recall wdGoToPage or wdCharacter; and would you be able to recall what the 1's mean when you look over this source code in, say, six months' time?

At Present: Whose Line Is It anyway?

In the era of non-proportional character sets, the length of a *line* of text in a word processor document was a fixed amount — usually 78 characters, give or take a few. But not only do proportionally-spaced fonts make it more difficult to determine the length and position of a line of text, but the characteristics of the *device context* responsible for rendering the line only serve to compound the problem. In Windows, a device context contains the data with which characters are plotted. Both the screen and printer have their own device contexts; individual applications such as word processors, which can see things a bit differently than Windows itself, also have their own device contexts.

In Word 2000's so-called "Normal" view mode, text that the user sees is rendered using the application's own native device context. This means that all information about available resolution, margins, and leeway for kerning is based on the application's own data concerning rendering to the *screen*. But when the user chooses so-called "Page Layout" mode, Word switches device contexts, and maps the device context of the *printer* onto that of the *screen*. The result is a closer approximation of how the printed text will appear. What this means is that the characteristics of the plotting device change and, often as a result, the characteristics of a simple line of text change as well. By adding just a few points of resolution, a word once wrapped will suddenly not be wrapped, changing the layout of an entire paragraph, and possibly affecting how much text in successive paragraphs is placed in the current page. This is why a document that Word is "Printing" to the designated fax machine may have one more page than the same document printed to a laser printer, even though that extra page may be comprised of just one line followed by a bunch of white space.

So how long is a line of text really? It isn't entirely possible for a VBA module to determine that; the user just has to keep in mind that with the changing nature of Windows' device contexts, a line is a variable thing.

Still in Listing 14-3: With rngCount moved back to where we want it, we have access to another peculiar property .Information that gives us data about any of several facts: whether Caps Lock is turned on, for instance, or whether the range is within the header or footer area of the page. In this case, by passing the not-exactly-self-explanatory constant wdFirstCharacterLineNumber to the .Information property, the value returned is the number of *lines* in the page where the first character of the range currently resides – in this case, right at the end of the page. At that point, we also retrieve the character numeral rngCount.End, and assign it to the lPageFinalChar() array.

In the case of the final page in the document, we can't have Word take rngCount to "the page after that" and back up one. Actually, we could try, and we would *not* generate an error condition. The trouble is, rngCount would be placed at the top of the *real* last page, and we wouldn't know that unless we were to compare this position with the one it had in the previous iteration of the loop. So for the last page, as well as for all documents that have just one page in the first place, we reset rngCount to point to the entire document, which will let us use docThis.Range.End as a reference to the absolute final character of the document.

Now, we use all this information we've gathered to help us ascertain the total number of lines of text in all three ranges. We start using this information in Listing 14-4.

Listing 14-4: Beginning the process of counting lines in the regions.

Part 3

```
iLPageNo = BinSearch(lPageFinalChar(), rngAt.Start)
For iCount = 1 To iLPageNo
    lLinesBefore = lLinesBefore + lPageLines(iCount)
Next iCount
iRPageNo = BinSearch(lPageFinalChar(), rngAt.End)
For iCount = iRPageNo To iPages
    lLinesAfter = lLinesAfter + lPageLines(iCount)
Next iCount
```

Elsewhere in the module, I've written a procedure Private Function BinSearch() that uses the array of final character numbers as a guide to tell us what page a given character number resides on. Word 2000 has no such function of its own; you can't give it a number, and have it tell you, "Ah, that's on page 18!" What we need here are two page numbers, one for the beginning of the selection range rngAt.Start, and one for the end rngAt.End.

Word 2000 does not account for lines of text

We need to know these things because **Word has no function that counts the number of text lines in** *any* **given range.** So as a "next-best" measure, we take all the pages from the beginning of the document up until the page with the start of the selection range, plus all the pages from the end of the selection range up until the end of the document, and sum their numbers-of-lines together. This leaves us with approximate values in `lLinesBefore` and `lLinesAfter`, which, although incorrect for now, will be adjusted later when we step through just those lines that overlap into the selection range. This process comes next, as shown in Listing 14-5.

Listing 14-5: Focusing in on accurate line counts.

Part 4

```
selThis.Collapse wdCollapseStart
If iRPageNo <> iLPageNo Then
    Do
        selThis.Range = selThis.GoTo(What:=wdGoToLine, _
      Which:=wdGoToRelative, Count:=1)
        If selThis.End > lPageFinalChar(iLPageNo) Then
            Exit Do
        Else
            lLinesAt = lLinesAt + 1
            lLinesBefore = lLinesBefore - 1
        End If
    Loop
    docThis.Bookmarks("RecallSelectionObject").Select
    selThis.Collapse wdCollapseEnd
    Do
        selThis.Range = selThis.GoTo(What:=wdGoToLine, _
      Which:=wdGoToPrevious)
        If selThis.Start < lPageFinalChar(iRPageNo - 1) _
        + 1 Then
            Exit Do
        Else
            lLinesAt = lLinesAt + 1
            lLinesAfter = lLinesAfter - 1
        End If
    Loop
    If iRPageNo - iLPageNo > 1 Then
        For iCount = iLPageNo + 1 To iRPageNo - 1
            lLinesAt = lLinesAt + lPageLines(iCount)
        Next iCount
    End If
Else
```

```
    Do
        selThis.Range = selThis.GoTo(What:=wdGoToLine, _
    Which:=wdGoToRelative, Count:=1)
        If selThis.End > rngAt.End Then
            Exit Do
        Else
            lLinesAt = lLinesAt + 1
            lLinesBefore = lLinesBefore - 1
            lLinesAfter = lLinesAfter - 1
        End If
    Loop
End If
docThis.GoTo What:=wdGoToBookmark, _
  Name:="RecallSelectionObject"
```

Up to this point we preferred using Range objects rather than Selection for determining lengths and amounts. But due to the makeup of the model Word uses for building documents, **lines of text are not elements integral to the construction of a Word document.** What happens is that the characters that belong to *paragraphs* fall in place, and whatever rows they may happen to fall in are where their lines end up. So there is no line-feed character (or code 9, as we used to call it) that designates the precise boundary between one line and another, the way that a carriage return (code 13) designates the end of a paragraph. A paragraph is merely a stream of characters from beginning to code 13, without any real structural divisions to comprise it. (Word does maintain a Sentences collection, although its contents are assembled separately, and are not crucial to the contents of the Paragraphs collection.)

Because there are no codes that act as boundaries between lines of text, the contents of any Range class object tell us nothing about lines whatsoever. We can only determine the length and constitution of a line of text in the context of how it is typeset in the current document; and quite a bit more data is involved there than simply the characters in the Range. **Only the Selection object can give us any information about a line of text, because unlike a Range class object, Selection exists in the context of the fully typeset page.** So we have to use Selection in this instance to count those lines that constitute *partial pages* in a range of characters. We've already counted too many lines for lLinesBefore and lLinesAfter; we need to step line-by-line from the edges of the rngBefore and rngAfter ranges to the nearest page boundaries in order to lop off those extraneous lines. Those same lines are part of the range in the middle, rngAt, which accounts for the original selection area, so we give those lopped off lines right back to rngAt. Because we're using the Selection object to do the line counting for us, we need rngAt to act as its stand-in, representing the range of text that the user originally selected.

How and why to collapse a range

We begin by "collapsing" the selection, represented by selThis, like a slinky-toy that has been let go of at one end. In this case, we collapse it to its own beginning so that its .Start is where it was before, but its .End is where its .Start is. No text is highlighted at this point. The reason we do this is because playing with Selection can be like playing with fire. When you Set a Range class object, you're merely changing its boundaries; but when you Set the Selection object, you're changing the textual contents of the region previously represented by Selection, *if* any text is selected at the time. **To change the boundaries of Selection without altering its textual contents in so doing, collapse the object first using the .Collapse method.**

Next, the main conditional test, If iRPageNo <> iLPageNo, tests whether the beginning of the selected range and the end of that range lie on two separate pages. If they do, we need to account for the selection range in a different way: counting from both ends of the selection range towards the page boundary between those ends.

The first Do...Loop clause steps selThis through each line from where the selection range originally started to the final character number of the page where the start of the selection resides, lPageFinalChar(iLPageNo). The .GoTo method is used again to step through lines, this time with an added argument Which:=wdGoToRelative, which has the method interpret Count:=1 as "one line forward" rather than "to the first line." With each line counted, 1 is added to lLinesAt (the number of selected lines), and 1 is subtracted from lLinesBefore (the overestimated number of lines in the range before the selection). When selThis transgresses over the page boundary, Exit Do has us drop out of the loop. The next Do...Loop clause repeats the operation on the other side of the selection, from the end counting back to the start of the page.

Using bookmarks to maintain the user selection

In between the loops, we recall a certain bookmark with the following instruction:

```
docThis.GoTo What:=wdGoToBookmark, Name:="RecallSelectionObject"
```

Another use for the .GoTo method is here revealed. Back in Private Sub UserForm_Initialize(), you saw this particular bookmark being created. The reason for its existence is to provide a reliable way to record and recall the area selected by the user, because we need to move Selection around in order to ascertain where the lines are. We cannot just use a shadow variable for selThis and recall that variable using an instruction like Set selThis = selShadow, because **setting a selection object to refer to another valid selection object copies the contents of that other object into the selection area.** What would that matter, if what was being copied was the same as what was there before? **The existing selection** area is not overwritten, so the copy scoots the original text to the right, resulting in two editions of the selected text. Of course, that's bad. So we needed a mechanism *outside* of the purview of the document for storing the selection area, and that became a bookmark. Each open document is given its own selection bookmark called `"RecallSelectionObject"`, a title that hopefully the user would not have already come up with for another purpose.

What is the real difference between AutoText, which we examined in Chapter 12, and the bookmark system? Both are databases, both keep track of ranges of text, and both systems are keyed by arbitrarily given names for each entry. But the text of a bookmark exists *within the document* and is visible to the user, while the text of an AutoText entry exists *within the template* and is invisible to anyone except the editor of AutoText entries, up until the user recalls one and copies it to his document.

Once both ends of `selThis` have been stepped inward toward their nearest page boundaries, the next thing to check is whether there are any whole pages in-between those boundaries, or are those boundaries in fact the same one? If the selection range involves more than two pages, then `iRPageNo - iLPageNo` will yield a value greater than 1. In that case, all the pages in between are accounted for, and their numbers of lines are added to `lLinesAt`. Why isn't anything being subtracted here as well? Because the original estimate of line count could only have overlapped by *parts* of two pages on either end, not by whole page amounts.

The `Else` portion of the main conditional clause is executed only if the selection area fits nicely on the same page. In that case, we step `selThis` through each line of the selection area (it will already have been collapsed beforehand), each time adding one line to `lLinesAt` and subtracting one from both `lLinesBefore` and `lLinesAfter`, which would both have accounted for this page. Once `selThis` has stepped out of the bounds of `rngAt`, then we drop out of the loop. Wait a minute; didn't I just get through saying that you can't have a safe shadow variable for the selection area? What's `rngAt` doing then; isn't it pointing to the area previously selected by the user? It is, but we won't be using `rngAt` to reposition the boundaries of `Selection.Range`; that's the dangerous part. We'll rely on the `docThis.GoTo` instruction to do that for us.

When are Words not really words?

Now that we have three accurate line counts, we turn our attention to Word 2000's tally of `Words` and `Characters`. It would be inaccurate for us to say that the `Characters` collection contains all of the characters that comprise a document. We know this statement to be false, because the header information of a document file that describes how text is to be typeset is not included in `Characters`; and the line feeds (code 9) that Word generates on the fly are also absent from the collection. Carriage returns, manual line and page breaks, section breaks, and the lower boundary of a table cell (code 7 in Word) are characters that are present in the `Characters` collection.

To a programmer studying the construction of a document, the presence of these characters may be a convenience. However, the *author* of a document is probably not as interested in the presence of these internal codes, and may instead be more curious as to how many *legible* characters her document contains. So for an application such as ours, it's important that we have a way to weed out unwanted and unsightly (literally) characters from the tally. But it's also important that we apply the same diligence to cleaning the tally of `Words` as we do to that of `Characters`. The reason is that Word 2000 treats boundary codes, such as carriage returns, as *separate words*.

You may be asking, as I did at first, *is this a convenience to anyone?* If you as programmer are interested in the words that a document contains, wouldn't you be more interested in them for their "word-ness" rather than for their contribution to Word 2000, the word processor? Perhaps so; but then if you are, you would also be interested in the point in which the context of those words shifts, and that point is generally a paragraph break. So having a code 13 be counted as a whole word can be a legitimate convenience. . . except in this situation, where we have to provide information to the *user*, and paragraph breaks are not words in whatever context she may happen to be thinking.

Listing 14-6 shows the method I settled on for finding words that are not words. There's no algorithmic beauty to this part of `Private Sub ComputeStats()`; it's just a quick-and-dirty non-word finder, which is, unfortunately, the fastest routine I could come up with, for reasons that I'll explain in a moment.

Listing 14–6: Searching for words that aren't words, General Sherman style.

Part 5

```
lCharsBefore = rngBefore.Characters.Count
lWordsBefore = rngBefore.Words.Count
For Each rngWord In rngBefore.Words
    strThis = rngWord.Text
    If Asc(strThis) < 14 Then
        Select Case Asc(strThis)
            Case 13
                lCharsBefore = lCharsBefore - 1
                lWordsBefore = lWordsBefore - 1
                If Asc(Right$(rngWord.Text, 1)) = 7 Then
                    lCharsBefore = lCharsBefore - 1
                End If
            Case Else
```

```
                    lCharsBefore = lCharsBefore - 1
                    lWordsBefore = lWordsBefore - 1
            End Select
        End If
    Next rngWord


    lCharsAfter = rngAfter.Characters.Count
    lWordsAfter = rngAfter.Words.Count
    For Each rngWord In rngAfter.Words
        strThis = rngWord.Text
        If Asc(strThis) < 14 Then
            Select Case Asc(strThis)
                Case 13
                    lCharsAfter = lCharsAfter - 1
                    lWordsAfter = lWordsAfter - 1
                    If Asc(Right$(rngWord.Text, 1)) = 7 Then
                        lCharsAfter = lCharsAfter - 1
                    End If
                Case Else
                    lCharsAfter = lCharsAfter - 1
                    lWordsAfter = lWordsAfter - 1
            End Select
        End If
    Next rngWord
```

We start by gathering Word 2000's counts of the total Characters and Words, codes included, belonging to rngBefore, the range of characters preceding the cursor. An object reference rngWord will cycle through each word in the range, searching for "words" whose initial character is an obvious code (Asc(strThis) < 14). When the argument to the Asc() function is a long string rather than a single character, the ASCII (ANSI) character code it returns belongs to the first character of the string; so Asc(strThis) would be the same as Asc(Left$(strThis, 1)).

Why couldn't we have launched a Word 2000 find operation for these non-word codes? In an earlier build of this module, I did program a Find object, but for it to work, I had to program separate searches for each individual code. The result was that although the single Find operation was faster than the process in Listing 14-6, all of the Find operations put together ended up being slower. So I opted for this slightly faster, less pretty method. Here, the Words in each entire range are searched in succession for codes and, when they are found, 1 is subtracted from the original estimates of both characters and words. In the case of a table cell boundary, Word adds a code 7 following a code 13, and treats the resulting pair as a single Word object. Still, the code 7 is one more non-character character; so in the case of a code 13 (Case 13), the final character of rngWord is tested for the presence of a code 7 and, if it's found, another character is removed from the running tally.

For counting the words within the selection area, I modified this process a bit. There will be situations in which the beginning of a selection falls in the *middle* of a word, and the end of that selection may fall in the middle of another word. In such a case, Word 2000 treats the "middle" words as words; so even if the selection area encompasses two whole words and two half-words, Selection.Words.Count will return 4. To the user, this wouldn't make much sense, so it's important that we try to determine whether the characters at either end of the selection are really words. Listing 14-7 shows the methodology I chose.

Listing 14–7: Lopping off half-words from both ends of the selection range.

Part 6

```
lCharsAt = rngAt.Characters.Count
If Selection.Words.Count > 1 Then
    lWordsAt = Selection.Words.Count
    If Left$(Selection.Text, Len(Selection.Words(1).Text)) _
    <> Selection.Words(1).Text Then
        lWordsAt = lWordsAt - 1
        rngAt.Start = Selection.Words(2).Start
    End If

    If Right$(RTrim$(Selection.Text), _
    Len(RTrim$(Selection.Words(Selection.Words.Count) _
      .Text)))<> RTrim$(Selection.Text) Then
        lWordsAt = lWordsAt - 1
        rngAt.End = Selection.Words(Selection.Words.Count _
          - 1).End
    End If

    If lWordsAt < 0 Then lWordsAt = 0
Else
    If rngAt.Text = Selection.Words(1).Text Then
        lWordsAt = 1
    End If
End If
```

My theory here is that the routine will only be able to detect when a "word" is really a half-word when it has first gathered all of the edge characters together up until the word break character, which is generally a space but could also be punctuation or a code. Next, these characters gathered together are compared against what Word 2000 perceives to be the entire word; and if they do *not* match, then the selected area is indeed a half-word. Remember, Selection.Words(1).Text and Selection.Words(Selection.Words.Count).Text will both return whole words, even when the beginning and end of the selection range fall in-between a word.

There's a conditional clause here with a large True side and a small False side. The True side is executed if Word 2000 counts more than one word in `Selection.Words.Count`, which means at the very least that the selection area has crossed over at least one space (code 32). We don't know yet whether this means there's a half-word selected. So we begin by loading `lWordsAt` with Word 2000's estimate of the number of words in the selection area. Next, we create a sort of "cookie cutter," using `Len(Selection.Words(1).Text)` as a model, whose width will be the number of characters in the first presumed `Word` object in the selection area. The cookie cutter is then used to extract the same number of characters from the front of `Selection.Text` using the `Left$` function. The resulting extraction is compared against the first word in the `Words` collection, `Selection.Words(1).Text`. Notice the logical operator in place here is `<>`; we're comparing one to the other for the *lack* of a match. If there is no match, then 1 is subtracted from the tally variable `lWordsAt`, and `rngAt` is adjusted to point to the beginning of the *second* word in the collection.

Next, the mirror image of the same operation is applied to the right side of the selection range. For this side, we use the `RTrim$()` intrinsic function to lop off the trailing space because **Word 2000 always counts the trailing space as part of the word object, unless its corresponding word in the text is followed by punctuation.** Word 2000 does *not* count punctuation as part of the word (lowercase "w") object. Nonetheless, `RTrim$()` is harmless if the string being trimmed does not have any trailing spaces. If the cookie cutter here, `Right$()`, extracts a string that does *not* match, then once again 1 is subtracted from `lWordsAt`, then the end of the mirror of the selection range `rngAt` is adjusted to the end of the next-to-last official word in the collection. At this point, `rngAt` should contain only whole words.

The False side of the conditional clause is executed when `Selection.Words.Count` returns a 1. This can happen in either of two cases: (a) when one word is highlighted by the cursor, or (b) when *no* words are highlighted by the cursor. So we perform a simple check of `rngAt.Text`, to see if it's equivalent to `Selection.Words(1).Text`; that is, if it's really a word. If it *is*, then `lWordsAt` is set to 1. Otherwise, the variable is left as is, and with no other assignment expression having operated on `lWordsAt` to this point, it will equal 0.

Next, with the borders of `rngAt` having been adjusted to the boundaries of real words, we can then perform our now familiar check of the range for the presence of code characters; and for each code found, one word and one character are removed from the running tallies. Listing 14-8 shows this part of the procedure:

Listing 14-8: Removing non-words from the current word count.

Part 7

```
For Each rngWord In rngAt.Words
    Select Case Asc(Right$(rngWord.Text, 1))
        Case Is < 14
            lWordsAt = lWordsAt - 1
```

Continued

Listing 14-8: Removing non-words from the current word count. *(Continued)*

```
Case 63    '?
    lWordsAt = lWordsAt - 1
Case 33    '!
    lWordsAt = lWordsAt - 1
Case 46    '. (period)
    lWordsAt = lWordsAt - 1
Case 44    ', (comma)
    lWordsAt = lWordsAt - 1
Case 58    ':
    lWordsAt = lWordsAt - 1
Case 59    ';
    lWordsAt = lWordsAt - 1
Case 45    '-
    If rngWord.Text = "—" Then
        lWordsAt = lWordsAt - 1
    ElseIf Asc(Right$(rngWord.Text, 2)) <> 32 Then
        lWordsAt = lWordsAt - 2
    End If
Case 32    ' (space)
    Select Case Asc(Right$(rngWord.Text, 2))
        Case 32
            If bTrimmedOnce = False Then
                lWordsAt = lWordsAt - 1
            End If
        Case 63
            lWordsAt = lWordsAt - 1
        Case 33
            lWordsAt = lWordsAt - 1
        Case 46
            lWordsAt = lWordsAt - 1
        Case 44
            lWordsAt = lWordsAt - 1
        Case 58
            lWordsAt = lWordsAt - 1
        Case 59
            lWordsAt = lWordsAt - 1
    End Select
End Select
Next rngWord
```

The key to getting the non-words out of there is to examine the rightmost character in the non-word member of the rngAt.Words collection (the only character in most cases, where the non-word is one character in width anyway). If the character in question is a dash (-), then we first need to check whether the word in question is a double-dash (–), which Word 2000 treats as a word. If it's not a double-dash, then we need to check the character just behind the dash to see if it's not a space. If it isn't, then the dash is being used for a hyphenated word, and should then be discounted. If the final character is a space, then the character just before it needs to be examined for the same reasons as before.

We're coming into the homestretch now. The next bit of housekeeping involves correcting the count of the number of whole pages encompassed by the three regions of interest. Listing 14-9 shows that part of the procedure.

Listing 14-9: Adjusting the page counts for whole pages covered.

Part 8

```
iPagesBefore = BinSearch(lPageFinalChar(), rngAt.Start)
iPagesAfter = iPages - BinSearch(lPageFinalChar(), rngAt.End)
iPagesAt = iRPageNo - iLPageNo
```

Using our private function named `BinSearch()`, we find out what pages the adjusted selection area boundaries fall within. If the selection crosses a page boundary, then `iRPageNo` will be greater than `iLPageNo`, so subtracting the latter from the former will yield a positive number for `iPagesAt`.

Learning where Forms 2.0 copied the clone controls

Finally (you knew there would be an end to this, you were just wondering when), as Listing 14-10 shows, we have finalized data that we can display to the user. Using the `ctrlRef()` array to refer to the individual text box controls in the active MultiPage panel, we write the final values into the text boxes by number.

Listing 14-10: Writing the final values to the MultiPage panel.

Part 9

```
ctrlRef(winDer.Index, 1).Text = Str$(docThis.Characters.Count)
ctrlRef(winDer.Index, 2).Text = Str$(lCharsBefore + lCharsAt _
 + lCharsAfter)
ctrlRef(winDer.Index, 3).Text = Str$(lWordsBefore + lWordsAt _
 + lWordsAfter)
ctrlRef(winDer.Index, 4).Text = Str$(lLinesBefore + lLinesAt _
  + lLinesAfter)
ctrlRef(winDer.Index, 5).Text = Str$(docThis.Sentences.Count)
ctrlRef(winDer.Index, 6).Text = Str$(docThis.Paragraphs.Count)
ctrlRef(winDer.Index, 7).Text = _
 docThis.BuiltInDocumentProperties("Number of Pages")
```

Continued

Listing 14-10: Writing the final values to the MultiPage panel. *(Continued)*

```
ctrlRef(winDer.Index, 16).Text = _
  Str$(rngBefore.Characters.Count)
ctrlRef(winDer.Index, 17).Text = Str$(lCharsBefore)
ctrlRef(winDer.Index, 18).Text = Str$(lWordsBefore)
ctrlRef(winDer.Index, 19).Text = Str$(lLinesBefore)
ctrlRef(winDer.Index, 20).Text = _
  Str$(rngBefore.Sentences.Count)
ctrlRef(winDer.Index, 21).Text = _
  Str$(rngBefore.Paragraphs.Count)
ctrlRef(winDer.Index, 22).Text = Str$(iPagesBefore)

ctrlRef(winDer.Index, 32).Text = Str$(rngAt.Characters.Count)
ctrlRef(winDer.Index, 33).Text = Str$(lCharsAt)
ctrlRef(winDer.Index, 34).Text = Str$(lWordsAt)
ctrlRef(winDer.Index, 35).Text = Str$(lLinesAt)
ctrlRef(winDer.Index, 36).Text = Str$(rngAt.Sentences.Count)
ctrlRef(winDer.Index, 37).Text = Str$(rngAt.Paragraphs.Count)
ctrlRef(winDer.Index, 38).Text = Str$(iPagesAt)

ctrlRef(winDer.Index, 24).Text = _
  Str$(rngAfter.Characters.Count)
ctrlRef(winDer.Index, 25).Text = Str$(lCharsAfter)
ctrlRef(winDer.Index, 26).Text = Str$(lWordsAfter)
ctrlRef(winDer.Index, 27).Text = Str$(lLinesAfter)
ctrlRef(winDer.Index, 28).Text =
  Str$(rngAfter.Sentences.Count)
ctrlRef(winDer.Index, 29).Text = _
  Str$(rngAfter.Paragraphs.Count)
ctrlRef(winDer.Index, 30).Text = Str$(iPagesAfter)

  Application.ScreenUpdating = True
End Sub
```

Throughout this set of instructions, `winDer.Index` refers to the index number of the active window that contains the document being scanned. But each of the numerals used as the second identifier for `ctrlRef()` refers to one of the text boxes that were created during the copy-and-paste process back in `Private Sub UserForm_Initialize()`. How did we know which numeral refers to what control? Trial and error.

The only way you as programmer can get any kind of handle on the number that Forms 2.0 gives to cloned controls is if you very, very carefully build the template panel, making sure to enter new controls in a pre-defined pattern. The pattern I chose was to build a frame, then enter the text boxes, then enter the labels for those text boxes (for the first frame), then enter the next frame and put boxes into it, and then do the same for the remaining two frames. Even having done that, Forms 2.0 swapped the running order of the third and fourth frames so that the third frame's text boxes were numbered 32 through 38 and the fourth frame's were numbered 24 through 30.

The downside of this little quirk in Forms 2.0 is this: Even if you copy the form modeled in Figure 14-1 as closely as you can when devising your own form, and even if you copy Listing 14-10 to the letter, your own data may go into the wrong text boxes. You'll need to do your own debugging with a document whose construction you're already familiar with, and probably change the numerals in the `ctrlRef()` references around until the data you see is where you expect it to be.

Of sentences, paragraphs, and "fuzzification"

To clear up one matter of potential contention before we continue: Why didn't we use the same type of logic used in determining whether whole *words* have been selected to weed out half-*sentences* and half-*paragraphs*? If you think about it (and if you're involved with the Word 2000 object model for any length of time, you find yourself thinking about it in your sleep), the definition of a *word* is a rather concrete thing. It's a series of letters, the oddball digit or two, and the occasional apostrophe, surrounded by spaces. We could "fuzzify" the definition of a word a bit if this were a book by Noam Chomsky; but for the purposes of programming, a word is a fairly cut-and-dried thing.

A sentence, however, is not such a clear thing. In an ordinary essay, a sentence could be easily identified as a series of words whose initial character was capitalized, and whose closing punctuation was a period, a question mark, or an exclamation point. If it were anything else, the English professor would probably grade you down a notch. But for the purposes of general formatting, just what is a sentence and what isn't? The upcoming header in this book — a "B-level," as we say in publishing — is "Programming a binary search." Now, is that a sentence or is it not? Word's object model says it is, but that's only because it makes no judgments about syntax. English grammar would say it's not, because the verb form "Programming" is really a participle rather than a transitive or intransitive verb.

Suppose we were to make a rule discounting all headers as real sentences. We could then write code that searched for the use of a style named "Heading *x*" in each document, and however many sentences Word 2000 thought it found there, subtract that number from the running tally. But then, what about some of the fuzzier elements? Have you noticed that bulleted lists, the way IDG Books typesets them, omit the final periods even if the lists contain what would otherwise be considered whole sentences? So we can't make a rule for Word 2000 that states that all "true" sentences end with punctuation — at least, not a rule with which IDG Books would be pleased. Finally, consider our multiple citations of VBA instructions within a document such as this chapter. Could we write a rule that states that a single "paragraph" that contains, for our purposes, a citation of a VBA instruction counts as a "sentence?" Is it more important to the user to *count* each citation as a sentence or to *discount* it? And aren't we mixing our definitions of "paragraph" and "sentence" in any event?

With all these issues in play simultaneously, I thought it best to leave the matter of Sentences and Paragraphs precisely where Word 2000 left it: fuzzy. The counts returned by the cursor-based statistics module are of sentences and paragraphs the way Word defines them.

Programming a binary search

At four points in Private Sub ComputeStats(), a function is called that returns the page number that contains a certain numbered character. What the procedure actually does is perform a simple *binary search*, which is an algorithmic search process for sorted lists.

When the list your program is searching through is sorted – numerically or alphabetically, ascending or descending order – you can employ a binary search to locate one item in the list with a minimum amount of trials. To better understand this, imagine a set of people's addresses written on Rolodex cards. If you were looking for just one name, and your stack of cards was an unsorted mess, you might have to search through the stack one at a time, in succession, until you ran across the item that you were looking for some hours later. With a sorted card stack, normally the letter partition cards would serve as guideposts to help you obtain a starting point for your search.

An ordinary sorted computer list has no such guideposts; in fact, the procedure that searches through a list generally knows nothing about the list beforehand other than its length and the fact that it is sorted. So the binary search algorithm takes those few facts and proceeds like this: Start in the *middle* of the list. If the entry found there isn't the target of the search (and it rarely is), decide whether the target falls before this entry or after. Exclude all those entries in the *opposite* direction from any further search; we know now that none of those contain the target. Having divided the list in half, jump to the middle of the remaining portion of the list. Then perform the before-or-after check again. Eventually the algorithm finds its target – or, in the case of our page finder, the page number whose final character is nearest to the target – and "eventually" is not as long as you might think. In fact, the maximum number of trials a binary search algorithm will require to find a unique entry in any given sorted set, is equal to the base-2 logarithm of the length of the set. For a set of 128 entries, the algorithm will require no more than 7 trials. Listing 14-11 shows our particular permutation of the binary search algorithm.

Listing 14-11: The binary search algorithm finds the page containing a character.

```
Private Function BinSearch(varData() As Long, s As Long)
    Dim t As Variant, i As Long, l As Long, o As Long

    r = UBound(varData)
    i = Int(r / 2)
    l = 1
```

```
    Do
        t = varData(i)
        If t = s Then
            BinSearch = i + 1
            Exit Do
        ElseIf t < s Then
            l = i
        Else
            r = i
        End If
        o = i
        i = l + Int((r - l) / 2)
        If i = o Then
            If varData(i) < s Then
                BinSearch = i + 1
            Else
                BinSearch = i
            End If
            Exit Do
        End If
    Loop
End Function
```

Following the classic style of algorithmic procedures, I use the old single-letter variables that have been associated with this and other procedures for decades. Variable r starts off with the length of the incoming sorted array, returned using the intrinsic function UBound(varData). This will be the "right" bounds of the array (r for "right"). Notice that in passing the array varData() as an argument to UBound(), the empty parentheses are omitted. Variable i represents the position of the entry in the list currently being scanned. Variable l represents, obviously, the *left* bounds of the array, which of course start at position 1.

The Do...Loop clause continues execution for as long as the contents of the entry being scanned (represented by t) fail to match the contents being searched for (represented by the argument s). After t is assigned the contents of the list at position i, t is compared to the subject of the search s. In the case of a lack of match, the search boundaries in the direction of the target of the search are moved back to i, then i is moved to the middle of the remaining portion of the list.

If we knew in advance that the target of the search would have a *matching* entry in the list, that is all the logic we would need for the binary search. But in this case, we need to execute a match when the search has turned up the *nearest* final character number. How do we know when the search is as near as it can get? When the search boundaries can no longer be divided in half, as we find out when o is used to store the old position of i, then i is moved by an amount rounded off to the nearest integer, and that integer happens to be 0. Variable i is then compared to o and when i appears to have stayed the same, the procedure concludes that this is as close as we're going to get.

Using the _Terminate event for a wrap-up

The first event recognized by a `UserForm`-based form module is `_Initialize`, so the first event procedure executed is `Private Sub UserForm_Initialize()`. On the other end of the module, the final event that the form recognizes is `_Terminate`; so the procedure `Private Sub UserForm_Terminate()` can be used as a container for the shutdown process for the form module. Listing 14-12 shows the procedure I wrote for the cursor-based statistics form.

Listing 14-12: The form module's final procedure.

```
Private Sub UserForm_Terminate()
    Dim docThis As Document

    docRecall.Activate
    docThis.GoTo What:=wdGoToBookmark, _
     Name:="RecallSelectionObject"
    For Each docThis In Documents
        docThis.Bookmarks("RecallSelectionObject").Delete
    Next docThis
End Sub
```

The cleanup process here mainly involves the removal of some unsightly and unwanted bookmarks. Each open document was given a bookmark with the same name; they won't overlap or overwrite one another because bookmarks are specific to individual documents, not to the entire application. First, after the document and selection that originally inhabited the application's main window are called back, `docThis` steps through each open document and removes the housekeeping bookmark using the `.Delete` method of the `Bookmarks` collection.

Making the form module available to the user

All form modules are considered private in scope by VBA. This means that, in Word 2000's list of "macros," the procedure that initiates the form module — `Private Sub UserForm_Initialize()` — is noticeably absent. (By the way, you might have noticed that the initial procedures for all form modules have the exact same name. So you can imagine what confusion there would be if all form modules' initial procedures showed up in the Macros list.) This is because a "native" Word 2000 VBA procedure is *not* a form module. Instead, Word expects to be able to directly run procedures from within the modules listed in the Projects window under the subheading of "Modules" for both the Normal and specialized templates.

The names for the *procedures* in those modules, not the names of the modules, are what are shown in Word 2000's Macros list.

So you need a general procedure in a general module, whose purposes are to be accessible to the Macros list and to Word's toolbars and menus, and to launch the form module. In the programming department, here is all you need to write:

```
Public Sub ViewCursorBasedStats()
    frmJerryStats.Show
End Sub
```

The .Show method for the form loads it from storage and calls it into existence. From there, the form module can handle the job of establishing itself and shutting itself down.

How revisions and marked deletions change the picture

For documents such as the one I'm writing now, which are passed around from person to person with comments and deletions specially marked, text which is "marked as deleted" (part of one editor's suggestion) is not actually removed from the document. As a result, that text could still show up within the Word 2000 object model's main collections, including Paragraphs and Words. As I heard someone say on a TV chat show once, this throws a significant rat into the ointment.

If a person editing the document is having Word "track revisions," but isn't displaying those revisions at the time, any text "marked as deleted" *will not appear* within the Paragraphs and other collections. However, if the user has "Highlight Changes" turned on, any text "marked as deleted" *will* appear within those collections. So the contents of those collections will always reflect what the user sees on screen, and that is good news. However, it's impossible going by the collections contents alone for you as programmer to distinguish marked-as-deleted text from unmarked text.

If your module is concerned with revisions, Word does maintain a Revisions collection, which we'll discuss in detail at another time. You may have to rely on this collection to provide you not only with revision information but with vital statistics about a version-controlled document as well.

Chaos Manor is alive and well

By the way, I named my version of the cursor-based statistics form frmJerryStats in honor of Dr. Pournelle, whose column represented the everyman computer user for almost a quarter-century. The final printed issue of *Byte* magazine made its way unceremoniously onto the newsstands in June 1998. At that time, the magazine's new owner — which had recently acquired the title from McGraw-Hill — had promised to renovate and renew this great masthead. What wasn't known at the time is that this renewal would take place on-line..

Byte.com is the new home for all of *Byte* magazine, including as many of its writers as the new publishers have managed to retain, including Senior Editor Pournelle. (At least online, the magazine won't have to endure *Byte* magazine's old six-month lead time.) Naturally, the URL for the new site is `http://byte.com`, which is the new home for Jerry's "Chaos Manor" column, and also the source of the old printed magazine's back issues since 1994. Jerry's thoughts and opinions on topics that may or may not include computing, appear at `http://www.intellectualcapital.com`. His own Web site has precisely the address you guessed it has: `http://www.jerrypournelle.com`. At any of these sites, you'll find how Pournelle has mastered the art of the essay, and in so doing perhaps get a few hints as to why I admire the man. While maintaining a solid Web presence, Jerry is still co-authoring the world's most thoughtful science fiction along with Larry Niven, and is currently Chairman of the US Civilian Advisory Council on National Space Policy.

In Theory: Progress versus Itself

The last two decades of the computing industry is replete with stories of two-way battles. The first that I had the pleasure to cover as it was happening, was the battle between the Atari ST and the Commodore Amiga. Soon after, I would cover Apple vs. Digital Research, IBM vs. Apple, Intel vs. Motorola, Microsoft vs. Lotus, Lotus vs. Borland, Microsoft vs. Apple, IBM vs. Microsoft, Microsoft vs. Netscape, NeXT vs. everybody, everybody vs. National Semiconductor, Apple vs. Apple, and the one which has recently given me no end of amazement, United States of America vs. Microsoft. (Or is it Microsoft vs. United States?)

One lesson I have learned about the Great Two-way Battles of Computing is that they tend never to decisively end, and there never seems to be a clear victor. Instead, the battles fizzle out, generally there are out-of-court settlements, then the battle lines are redrawn and, like hostile square dancers, new pairs of companies agree to be enemies with one another. The same music starts up again, and strangely enough, little is ever resolved.

Part of the reason for these inconsistencies – some of which have been the focus of this chapter – is the reversal of priorities that always takes place in the midst of these two-way battles. The need to be "one-up" overshadows the need to think things out. A product is released in "beta," and its follow-up is then called "beta," followed by "beta." Then there's the inevitable release candidates, followed by the golden release candidates, and finally "beta." The "beta testers," throughout this time, are doing their job and acknowledging the problems with the product; but their warnings are often unheeded, for fear that the presence of bugs might make the product, and therefore the company, look bad.

It is as though a war is being fought by two divisions of infantrymen, driving tanks that are being constructed as they are driven. Each division is relying on its tank commander to lead the way forward; yet in the confines of his half-built contraption, the gauges often read the wrong amounts and the compasses point the wrong way. Still, whatever the commander says goes, even if the direction set by the point tanks lead the infantrymen into, or over, a cliff. Any one infantryman who notices this cliff is sent, rather than to the commander, to the morale officer instead, who gives that man a lesson on making statements that could make the troops feel bad.

It's a statement I made over what passed for the Internet ten years ago, and I'll repeat it here: If you think that globally interconnected computing is interesting now, just wait until it gets out of beta. If that event is ever going to happen, the commanders who set the course are going to have to heed the warnings of the troops in the field, and stop relying so heavily on their own faulty gauges.

In Brief

- When programming a form module that uses a MultiPage control, you will need to declare a private form-level dynamic or fixed array `As Control`, and set its members to refer to those ActiveX controls that may be duplicated in the various pages.

- A manually defined `Range` class object in Word must refer to a positive, non-zero-length passage of text.

- Word 2000 maintains a `BuiltInDocumentProperties` collection whose members – which are addressable by name – contain the pertinent information about a document that the user may find by selecting File → Properties.

- A bookmark is a recorded location in a Word 2000 document. Word maintains a `Bookmarks` collection whose members may be addressed by name, such a name having been created arbitrarily beforehand.

- The Word 2000 Object Library maintains collections for `Paragraphs`, `Sentences`, and `Words` contained within a document, each of whose members are `Range` class objects. However, many of the members of the `Words` collection are not truly words but punctuation and carriage returns. A significantly lengthy procedure is necessary to filter such non-words out of the analysis to result in a correct assessment of a document's word count.

Chapter 15

The Program, the Presentation, and PowerPoint

IN THIS CHAPTER

◆ The two root object classes of the PowerPoint library, `Presentation` and `DocumentWindow`

◆ Differentiating between slides, shapes, and ranges

◆ Manipulating the aspects of PowerPoint's `Selection` object

◆ Slides and slide masters

◆ Making PowerPoint the tool of another Office 2000 application

◆ Generating new slides and slide objects automatically

◆ The peculiarities of PowerPoint's `TextRange` class

FROM A STRUCTURAL STANDPOINT, Microsoft PowerPoint is a surprisingly, often refreshingly, simple program. Its purpose in life is straightforward: You give it a sequence of operations and it plays back that sequence. In PowerPoint's case, the "sequence of operations" is a slide show with animations. If programmers alone comprised the scope of the software market, PowerPoint could conceivably have been bundled with Word and/or Excel as an add-in. But the fact that the market perceives presentation capability as a major rather than a minor feature has mandated PowerPoint's rightful presence as a "puzzle piece" in Office 2000.

PowerPoint's functionality is, to borrow a complimentary term from the vocabulary of software designers, *flat*. Most everything that the user is given the power to do with PowerPoint is represented by menus or icons that are generally no more than two clicks away. Nothing is hidden from the user; everything's up front and readily accessible. So what would a PowerPoint VBA module actually be needed for? Apparently, not many programmers have come up with a decisive solution to this lack-of-dilemma dilemma. As a presentation manager, the application's functionality is quite determinate. The definition of a presentation in PowerPoint is so narrow, especially in comparison to Word 2000's "document" and Excel 2000's "worksheet," both of which have only whatever definition their users provide them with. From a performance standpoint, PowerPoint could arguably be enhanced in the graphics department, giving the user more capability to draw or animate directly rather than generally. But even if we agreed upon that, VBA would not be the proper implement with which to extend PowerPoint's functionality in that department, any more than we should program set logic into Access or sheet scanning capacity into Excel using VBA.

If we start to think of PowerPoint more as its "puzzle piece" logo implies – as a component of a larger operation defined by Office 2000 – then we can perhaps perceive how PowerPoint can be used in a more integrated fashion to meld presentation capabilities into the word processor and spreadsheet. A presenter needs correct data, and Excel or Jet may act as the provider of that data. A presenter needs a way to tie in her oral presentation with the written text of her speech, and Word may act as the mechanism for maintaining continuity. PowerPoint VBA's exploitable features appear to lie in its accessibility to the other Office components.

The PowerPoint Toybox

As with the libraries of Word and Excel, the default object in the PowerPoint library is `Application`, which rarely has to be stated within PowerPoint's own VBA environment. There are two major subordinates that constitute the key collection objects with which you'll deal as a PowerPoint VBA programmer, both of which are addressed as collections:

◆ `Presentations` represents the final stored contents of slide shows currently loaded into the PowerPoint workspace, along with their text, animations, and imported shapes.

◆ `Windows` represents those places within the PowerPoint workspace where presentations are constructed – the stage as opposed to the show.

Both of these collections have persistent members. `ActiveWindow` refers to the window that currently has the focus, and `ActivePresentation` refers to the slide show that is under construction within that window.

You may have noticed that PowerPoint's main workspace window – represented by the `DocumentWindow` class in its object library – looks suspiciously familiar. With rulers along the top and left edges, movable toolbars along the top, and view controllers at the lower-left corner, the user might think he's really using Word, especially when he's typing the contents of his presentation into Outline view. This similarity is not an indicator that both applications are using the same engine, as a trip through the wonders of COM might have you believe. The truth is, both Word and PowerPoint were constructed using MFC, which provides the common features that an application might utilize. MFC42.DLL is a common component of the two applications, which makes the toolbars and window gadgets look and operate much the same; in other words, the window parts are not made up of ActiveX controls. But while MFC does give Word and PowerPoint this strikingly similar look and feel, these applications are based around separate automation servers. So the devices operated when the user types into the two windows are truly two programs, and you shouldn't let their similarities fool you.

PowerPoint's object library continues the distinction between the product of the application and the producer of that product — `Presentations` and `Windows`, respectively — that was established by Word 97 with `Documents` and `Windows`. But the PowerPoint library does not maintain an all-encompassing `Range` object or `Range` class that refers to any given subset of the document. In Word 97, when you specify `Selection.Range`, you're referring to whatever is currently indicated by the cursor. The class of object to which `Selection` belongs depends on whatever happens to be indicated at the time — text, graphics, table cells, an embedded OLE object. So the class to which the `Range` object in `Selection.Range` belonged was flexible.

PowerPoint's root content object is DocumentWindow

For whatever reason — perhaps to avoid confusion between windows, the things you use within a program, and Windows, the operating system — each member of PowerPoint's `Windows` collection is a `DocumentWindow` class object, not a `Window` class object like in Word. This is important in situations where you need to declare an object variable that will reference one of the open windows in the PowerPoint workspace.

Addressing the range constituent of PowerPoint's `Selection` object — a constituent of the `DocumentWindow` class — is not so flexible. In fact, `Selection` maintains three constituents with their own individual classes:

◆ `TextRange` represents the raw text of any part of the presentation in its unformatted state. `Selection.TextRange` is considered a `TextRange` class object.

◆ `SlideRange` represents the contents and *common* properties of any number of indicated slides in the presentation. `Selection.SlideRange` is considered a `SlideRange` class object.

◆ `ShapeRange` represents the rectangular regions in the plotting area for a slide, where text, graphics, or an imported object appears. `Selection.ShapeRange` is considered a `ShapeRange` class object.

What shape is a Shape?

A PowerPoint slide is a montage of cutouts containing text or graphics arranged in a visually appealing order and placed against a graphic backdrop. Figure 15-1 shows one example from a presentation given by the author some months back. Each of these cutouts are what the application calls *slide objects*, and what the PowerPoint object library calls *shapes* or Shape class objects. Why? Because Slide objects in the library are what the application calls *slides*, which are not the same as "slide objects" in that context.

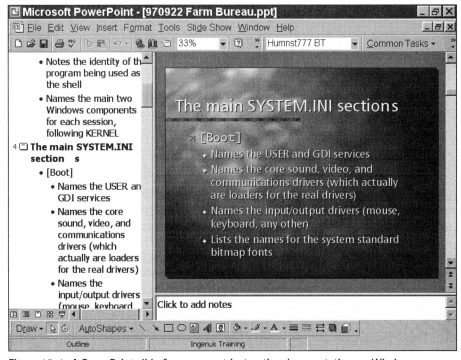

Figure 15-1: A PowerPoint slide from a recent instructional presentation on Windows.

In the Excel object library, a Shape class object represents any element of a worksheet that is imported through OLE and whose source is other than Excel. For PowerPoint, a Shape class object isn't necessarily the same thing, though it can be. Whatever the contents of a shape (slide object) happen to be at the time define the *type*, not the class, of the Shape object. So if Shapes(1) represents the first shape in the collection for the first slide (notice the first is numbered 1 here, not 0 like in Access collections) then ActivePresentation.Slides(1).Shapes(1).Type returns a long integer that represents the makeup of the contents of that shape. There's a long list of constants that represent the possible types here, though you need to poll the .Type property in order for you to correctly address the contents of a Shape class object.

Here is where things get weirder: PowerPoint perceives the *contents* of a presentation and the contents of the window where the presentation is constructed, as separate objects. In other words, you cannot attain a Slide class object by perusing the constituents of a DocumentWindow class object; a window does not contain a Slide. Nor does it contain a Shape, for that matter. What it does contain is a Selection object whose constituents are ranges by the PowerPoint definition — TextRange, SlideRange, and ShapeRange class objects. What are the differences? Well. . . extremely few, really. For the most part, they are simply different in name. And one class cannot substitute for the other. You cannot assign ActiveWindow.Selection.SlideRange to a Slide class reference variable, nor can you assign ActivePresentation.Slides(1) to a SlideRange class reference variable. Microsoft's documentation states that the Slides collection refers to all the slides, while SlideRange refers to a subset. This is not quite accurate. Both Slides and SlideRange refer to all of the slides in a show, and both terms may take a single index argument — as in Slides(2) or SlideRange(2) — that allow them to refer to a single slide in the show.

Selection's complex identity, or identity complex

PowerPoint simultaneously maintains three separate "planes of existence," if you will, all of which represent the active presentation in whole or in part: its text, its shapes, and its slides. The Selection object can reside in any one of these three planes at any one time, but in only one plane at one time. As a result, the terms you use to refer to the constituents of Selection, have — all things being equal — a 66 percent chance of being erroneous, because two times out of three it's possible that the terms you use are not constituents of Selection *at the moment.*

When PowerPoint is in Normal view, Outline view, or Slide view, the user is capable of indicating text with the cursor, either from the outline along the left pane or the slide window in the upper right pane. (These three views actually have the same contents and controls as one another, although the sizing and positioning applied to each of their sets of panes are different.) At this point in time, the text being indicated by the cursor is attainable through this reference:

```
ActiveWindow.Selection.TextRange.Text
```

Also, in any of these three views, the user may indicate a graphic object or *shape* (generally a block of text or a graphic image) in the slide pane. In this case, the shape being indicated by the cursor is attainable through this reference:

```
ActiveWindow.Selection.ShapeRange(iWhich)
```

where `iWhich` is the index for a member of the `ShapeRange` array. The total number of shapes being indicated at any one time is attainable through this reference:

```
ActiveWindow.Selection.ShapeRange.Count
```

When the shape being indicated happens to contain editable text, then `ActiveWindow.Selection.TextRange.Text` will return its contents. But when the shape is a picture, the reference generates an error. Furthermore, if the user moves the cursor out of the sample shape and into the outline along the left pane, the reference will generate another error. How can you avoid this? There is one way to learn which "plane of existence" the `Selection` object resides in, using the property `ActiveWindow.Selection.Type`. The property returns an integer: 1 if a slide; 2 if a shape; 3 if text; and 0 if nothing at all. So if you cannot be absolutely certain where the cursor is at the time the PowerPoint user invokes your VBA program, you could put a "sentry" at the gates of your procedures, throwing execution out of the procedure if the cursor is in the wrong place. In this example, execution of this procedure is terminated if the cursor indicates something other than text:

```
If ActiveWindow.Selection.Type <> 3 Then Exit Function
```

When PowerPoint is in Slide Sorter view, each slide in the presentation shows up in a "thumbnail," or miniaturized, mode. In this mode, the user chooses one or more slides from the list, then selects an operation from the menu. Here, neither text nor shapes can be indicated with the mouse, but only slides. So the only legal constituents of `Selection` under these circumstances belong to the `SlideRange` array; and the number of slides chosen at any one time may be attained through this reference:

```
ActiveWindow.Selection.SlideRange.Count
```

You may have noticed that I've been leaving in references to `ActiveWindow` in these examples. If `ActiveWindow` is a global in the PowerPoint 2000 object library, why can't we just state `Selection.Type`? It's a safety measure. At the time of this writing, PowerPoint's object library was improperly bound, and `Selection` by itself was interpreted as an object of Word. Yes, it's a bug; and yes, it has been officially reported.

The three divisions of the PowerPoint object library

PowerPoint maintains some specific and esoteric boundaries between the divisions of objects in its hierarchy. For instance, the following reference:

```
ActiveWindow.Selection.SlideRange.Shapes.Count
```

will only yield a non-erroneous result if one or part of one slide is currently being selected — in other words, if `ActiveWindow.Selection.SlideRange.Count` is 1. If two or more slides are being indicated in whole or in part, then this reference will result in an error. How, then, do you count the total number of shapes in a `SlideRange` whose number of contained slides is a variable? Through the use of this `Function` procedure, which may be placed in a general module of a PowerPoint project:

```
Public Function CountShapes(slThisRange As SlideRange)
    Dim iCount As Integer

    For Each slRange In slThisRange
        iCount = iCount + slRange.Shapes.Count
    Next slRange

    CountShapes = iCount
End Function
```

What's difficult to comprehend here is that the `SlideRange` in `ActiveWindow.Selection.SlideRange.Count` and the one in `ActiveWindow.Selection.SlideRange.Shapes.Count` are not the same. In the former, `SlideRange` is an array. It represents a multiple amount of elements, although it is not a collection in the formal sense in that it has no constituent objects. In the latter, `SlideRange` is a unit that tries to refer, by default, to the first member of this collection. You see, the `SlideRange` array has elements that are objects of class `SlideRange`. (Hey, at least you won't forget the name of both of them, will you?) Here's the rule to remember: **References to the** `-Range` **suffixed constituents of** `ActiveWindow.Selection` **will generate errors whenever** `ActiveWindow.Selection.SlideRange.Count > 1`.

The fact that the `SlideRange` class expects only a single argument makes it difficult for one to imagine how it can truly represent a *range*, or plurality, of slides the way that Word's `Range` constituent refers to a plurality of characters. The Word library phrases `Range` with two arguments, representing the beginning and end of the character grouping, and then makes the resulting term a constituent of a `Document` class object — for example, `ActiveDocument.Range(1, 100)`. With `SlideRange` there is only one argument, so there's no obvious way to phrase a "first slide/last slide" reference.

Retrieving selected text from any source

With a bit of work, we crafted a solution to the problem of retrieving the raw text indicated by the cursor regardless of the size of the selection. Listing 15-1 presents our approach to the problem, which is to treat PowerPoint with kid gloves. It tests for each of the conditions that might cause PowerPoint to lose its temper, and uses whichever text gathering technique works for the current state of affairs.

Listing 15-1: Retrieving any amount of text into a string without fear of explosion.

```
Public Function RetrieveSelectedText() As String
    Dim strCollect As String
    Dim sldThis As Slide, shpThis As Shape
    Dim iNum As Integer, lIndex As Long

    With ActiveWindow.Selection
        If ActiveWindow.View.Type = ppViewOutline Then
            RetrieveSelectedText = .TextRange.Text
            Exit Function
        ElseIf ActiveWindow.View.Type = ppViewNotesPage Then
            For Each shpThis In ActivePresentation.Slides _
            (.SlideRange(1).Name).Shapes
                If shpThis.HasTextFrame Then
                    If shpThis.TextFrame.HasText Then
                        strCollect = strCollect & _
                        shpThis.TextFrame.TextRange.Text _
                        & Chr$(13)
                    End If
                End If
            Next shpThis
            RetrieveSelectedText = strCollect
        Else
            If ActiveWindow.ActivePane.ViewType = ppViewOutline _
            Or ActiveWindow.ActivePane.ViewType = ppViewSlide _
            Then
                RetrieveSelectedText = .TextRange.Text
                Exit Function
            End If
            If .SlideRange.Count = 1 Then
                For Each shpThis In .SlideRange.Shapes
                    If shpThis.HasTextFrame Then
                        If shpThis.TextFrame.HasText Then
                            strCollect = strCollect & _
                            shpThis.TextFrame.TextRange.Text _
                            & Chr$(13)
```

```
                    End If
                End If
            Next shpThis
        Else
            For iNum = 1 To .SlideRange.Count
                lIndex = .SlideRange(iNum).SlideIndex
                Set sldThis = _
                ActivePresentation.Slides(lIndex)
                For Each shpThis In sldThis.Shapes
                    If shpThis.HasTextFrame Then
                        If shpThis.TextFrame.HasText Then
                            strCollect = strCollect & _
                            shpThis.TextFrame.TextRange _
                            .Text & Chr$(13)
                        End If
                    End If
                Next shpThis
            Next iNum
        End If
        RetrieveSelectedText = strCollect
    End If
    End With
End Function
```

As a `Function` procedure, Listing 15-1 returns a string to a variable used in an assignment expression, as in `strText = RetrieveSelectedText`. The direct approach to retrieving the text, through `ActiveWindow.Selection. TextRange. Text`, works only when PowerPoint is in Outline view, or when PowerPoint is in Normal view but the cursor is in the outline pane. So the first conditional test polls `ActiveWindow.View.Type` for the specific long integer that represents Outline view; the corresponding constant here is `ppViewOutline`. If there's a match, the text can be assigned to the `Function` name, and we can get out of here. The `View` object represents the current view of a PowerPoint window, and `.Type` is an integer representing the specific view chosen by the user. However, the `.ViewType` property of the `DocumentWindow` class represents the same element of PowerPoint; we could have omitted a period, written `ActiveWindow.ViewType`, and accomplished the same thing.

The `ElseIf` portion of the conditional clause checks whether PowerPoint is displaying its new Notes view, which is a feature made more prominent in PowerPoint 2000. It represents a printed-page version of the presentation, where each slide is printed on its own sheet, with the presenter's notes typeset below. When Notes view is active, only one slide is visible, so only one slide can be selected. We refer to that slide directly as `SlideRange(1)`. A loop clause cycles through each member of the `Shapes` collection and assigns variable `shpThis` to refer to "each member" *per se*.

Embedded conditional clauses check whether the shape has a text frame by polling its `.HasTextFrame` property. Simple enough. If that test passes, we can refer to `shpThis.TextFrame` without generating an error. We can then poll that object's `.HasText` property to see if it contains anything worthy of a `.Text` property. If that test passes, then and only then do we tack the textual contents onto the end of the collector string `strCollect`. The carriage return `Chr$(13)` is added because that character, although present in some cases, isn't actually considered part of the `.Text` property of a `TextRange` object.

Before we go on, notice how we had to refer to the `Shapes` collection in Notes view. We actually couldn't get there by way of the `ActiveWindow` object like we could for the other views without falling through a rather nasty crack in the floor of the PowerPoint object library. So we took a back door and came at `Shapes` from the other direction by rooting it in the `ActivePresentation.Slides` collection, and using the name of the slide (`.SlideRange(1).Name`) as its index.

The `Else` side of the conditional clause is executed only when we're not in Outline view or Notes view. However, in Normal view, the active pane (one of three, generally) may itself be a miniature Outline view or slide view (the cursor is inside the slide sample). In either case, we can again simply retrieve the selected text and leave.

The only possible view left that we haven't covered is Slide Sorter view, where the user chooses from all the different thumbnails. PowerPoint's behavior when only one or part of one slide is selected is different from its behavior when more than one slide is selected. The condition `If .SlideRange.Count = 1` tests whether the indicated area transcends the boundary between at least one pair of slides. If it does not (a True result), a `For Each...Next` loop clause steps through each member of the `Shapes` collection for the single selected slide. The user can indicate *part* of a slide only when she is in any of the views that don't apply to this portion of the procedure. When the user is indicating more than one slide in whatever view, she cannot indicate *part* of a shape or *part* of the text in a shape. Lucky for us, for this means we don't have to scout for parts rather than wholes – remember the trouble we went through in Chapter 14 scouting for parts of selected paragraphs, sentences, and words?

The text in a rectangular "slide object" – a `Shape` class object in the terminology of PowerPoint's object library – is, shall we say, well contained. The way the object library perceives it, the shape contains a separate frame reserved for text. The contents of this frame are perceived to be a text range, like a region on a map; but even this is not the text itself. The raw text is considered to be the property of this range. So if `shpThis` is set to point to a shape in an indicated slide, then the text within this shape is addressable after traversing three layers of objects: `shpThis.TextFrame.TextRange.Text`. To move through those three layers without tripping an alarm and perhaps notifying the Pentagon, we use the double-nested test again, involving the `.HasTextFrame` and `.HasText` properties.

If the selected area is confined to one slide, then after the selected region passes both tests, `strCollect` serves as an accumulator for the raw text of each of the shapes in that slide (`ActiveWindow.Selection.SlideRange.Shapes`). A carriage return is manually added using `Chr$(13)`, because the text of a shape does not contain a carriage return or line feed by default the way a Word 2000 `Paragraph` object does.

On the other hand, if the selection contains more than one slide, then we must be in Slide Sorter view where *one or more* slides may be selected *whole*. The `SlideRange` class is not a collection like `Slides`, nor does it have a `Slides` constituent, so there is no way to step through each `SlideRange` class object in a range the way we've become accustomed to with `For Each...Next`. Instead, you refer to a single member of the `SlideRange` *array* like you would for any other one-dimensional array. In Listing 15-1, we built a conventional `For...Next` loop clause that counts for an integer `iNum`. The loop counts from 1 to the final entry in the array, `ActiveWindow.Selection.SlideRange.Count`. With each count, the true index number of the given slide in the `SlideRange` array is obtained using the `.SlideIndex` property, then assigned to a second integer `lIndex`. Be careful to make this a long integer, because the `.SlideIndex` property returns a long value. If you assign a long-valued property to a mere `Integer` variable, VBA won't always make the proper translation for you, and a value that was supposed to be 3 will end up being some negative-nine-million-and-something value. (Can you tell I've made this mistake before?)

The reason we're obtaining the index number of each selected slide in the `SlideRange` array is because it just happens to be the same index as that used to index a member of the `Slides` collection. Remember, `SlideRange` and `Slides` refer to the same items, just by way of different root classes — `DocumentWindow` and `Presentation`, respectively. But a member of the `Slides` collection has a constituent `Shapes` collection all to itself that a member of the `SlideRange` array does not. We need to get to `Shapes` because that's where the text is located; so we rely upon the mutual index of the two pluralities as a common element that enables us to jump from one to the other. Once we've attained the `.SlideIndex` property from the slide currently being scanned, we use that same index to refer to the slide in the same position in `ActivePresentation.Slides` — which are the same slides. Now that we're referring to the `Slides` collection, we have access to its constituent `Shapes` collection, where we can take the same four steps to retrieve the text in each shape and tack it onto the end of `strCollect`.

The Selection object can only jump to slides

In Chapter 12, which dealt with Word 2000, I demonstrated that you no longer need to have your background program move the cursor around a document in order for it to address any one portion of text. PowerPoint's Outline view can fool you into thinking of a slide show as a reformatted document, since it bears some notable similarities to Word's Outline view. But PowerPoint's Outline view is in fact a reinterpretation of the contents of the slide show; the text from the slides is reorganized to look like a document outline. With PowerPoint, you cannot make use of the `Selection` object like you can in Word as an agent you can send to any point within the work in progress, absorbing whatever is under the cursor. You can have the cursor move to and select an entire slide with the instruction `ActiveWindow.View.GotoSlide` x, where x is the index number of the slide (representable by `SlideRange.SlideIndex`), but that's the limit of what you can do to move the cursor from within VBA.

On the other hand, you cannot reference a plurality of slides through the `ActivePresentation.Slides` collection, other than *all* of the slides. The lesson here is this: If you need to peruse all of the shapes in the entire presentation, you have to flip through them slide by slide.

Applying PowerPoint as a Tool

One of PowerPoint's many views is the so-called Notes Page view, which gives a way for the user to write notes or the full text of his speech and align that text with the slides in the presentation. But many presentations are based on an existing document, rather than a speech or a set of notes. For instance, testimony before a government body or panel is generally rendered in the form of a spoken summary of a much broader text, which the witness distributes to the panelists prior to the presentation. A witness or other similar presenter is more likely to use Word than PowerPoint to write this broader document because he is at least as concerned with the appearance of that document as he is the impact of his presentation.

So how can we make it easier for the witness to move from a broader body of written testimony to a more succinct body of oral testimony? From experience working with Office 2000, you may have learned that **text copied from the Outline view of Word 2000 into PowerPoint 2000 retains both its formatting and its hierarchical structure.** But the construction of a slide cannot sustain itself on text and hierarchy alone. What would be preferable to a raw cut-and-paste operation between the Outline views of two programs is a module that lent some extra logic to the process.

At Present: Mastering Slides

PowerPoint maintains a set of so-called masters that serve as dynamic templates for new items that are added to a series. A *master slide* is a boilerplate of sorts where the shapes and background that are set to appear in every new slide in the main presentation are set up beforehand in the master slide. This way, when a new slide is added, it already contains the general appearance of the master slide; most of the setup work is already done. Changes may then be made to the new slide without affecting the general style of the master.

In setting up the master slide, the user generally picks one slide object (Shape class) that shall act as the "body text" for the slide. This region can contain multiple tiers of outlined text, and PowerPoint is capable of animating each tier within a single textual region individually. So if you have one bullet point and three subordinate points, all four items can share the same slide object. The style and formatting of text in the various tiers are all determined by the settings made to dummy text typed into the master slide.

The goal: An automatic presentation generator

The purpose of our next example VBA project is to give the PowerPoint user a single push button that starts the generation of a simple presentation based on the structure of the active Word 2000 document. Any aesthetic issues regarding the appearance of all slides in the show can be handled ahead of time by the settings of the master slide; and any issues regarding one slide in particular – such as the number of columns in the body area – can be managed by the user later. For now, we want the dirty work to be done automatically. Assuming that the user has already written the treatise or deposition in Word using its built-in styles named "Heading 1," "Heading 2," and so on for paragraph heads, we can have PowerPoint VBA scan the document for the presence of hierarchical headings and move those headings into the presentation, leaving the body of the Word document's text as it stands.

Here's how the logic will work: The main procedure will scan every Word 2000 paragraph. When it finds one with a "Heading *x*" style, the procedure will start to analyze it. If the style is "Heading 1," then the procedure starts a new slide. To keep things simple – or, at the very least, simpler than they would be otherwise – each automatically generated slide will be kept to two slide object text areas: one for the slide title at the top, the other beneath it for bullet points. All of the text that goes into the lower region will have "Heading" styles ranging from 2 on.

Into this logic, we inject a couple of bonus features: First, we want the same VBA module to scan each *non*-"Heading *x*" paragraph for the presence of specially marked sentences – excerpts from the body text. When it finds these sentences, the module treats them as though they were "Heading 3." This way, if passages from the main paragraphs are worthy of being projected as part of the show, the author can give these passages a special Word 2000 character style (as opposed to a paragraph style) that does not change their appearance in the printed text (or at least, does not have to) but that does mark those passages for the sake of PowerPoint VBA.

Secondly, we need the PowerPoint VBA project to be capable of determining for itself at what point the text in the lower region is overflowing its boundaries, and when it is time to generate a new slide to pick up the overflow. By default, text added to a PowerPoint slide can overflow the visible region of the slide without the application having anything to say about it one way or the other. Without knowing it, the VBA project could generate contents that are too tall for one slide. We need some way for a procedure to detect when a slide starts becoming larger than it should be, so that it can interrupt and start a new slide. (Word seems to have no trouble generating new pages when the old ones start to overflow, but PowerPoint is not as adept.)

A few extra months on the drawing board

The listings we'll show here are the results of a significant amount of trial-and-error programming. Several approaches to this main goal were tried, adapted, re-adapted, scrapped, and un-scrapped. Let the record show that the final methodology adopted by this module is not very indicative of the first methodology attempted.

To make this functionality a persistent part of PowerPoint (say that three times real fast), this module should be attached to a template (.POT file) and constructed as a class module. What this means is that the Declarations section of the class module needs to declare a `Public` variable for exporting its functionality to other modules – for making the class module's procedures available to the other modules in the VBA project. This module ended up consisting of one main procedure and two `Private` procedures, which it contacts. Ten years ago, these `Private` procedures would have been written as *subroutines*, which would have been contacted with a `GOSUB` statement, and which would have jumped back to the calling body with a `RETURN` statement. But because these three procedures must have access to most of the variables, those variables ended up being declared at the top of the module, along with the class module exporter. Listing 15-2 shows the Declarations section:

Listing 15-2: Module-level variables for the automatic presentation generator.

```
Public classApp As Application
Dim paraThis As Word.Paragraph
Dim rngBodyPoints() As Word.Range
Dim iHeading() As Integer, bExcerpt() As Boolean
Dim iPoints As Integer, iIndex As Integer
Dim sBodyHeight As Single
Dim bBodyInProgress As Boolean, bFirstTitle As Boolean
Dim iKeepFonts As Integer
```

Variable `classApp` serves as the "exporter" for the class module, which ties its functionality to that of Word. To make your class module work, you need to remember to give it an exclusive `.Name` property in the Properties window – not just leave it `Class1`. We named our class module `WordDocShow`. Next, we declared an importer within the Declarations section of each general module that will make use of the class library, like this:

```
Dim clsWordCon As New WordDocShow
```

We need the `New` part of the declaration to generate a *new* instance of the class, not to refer to an existing instance. . . because there is no existing instance. Also, the declaration must be a straight `Dim`, not a `Public`, since other general modules will not be able to make contact with this module's exclusive instance of `WordDocShow`.

Next, among the first executable instructions, we wrote a `Set` instruction that assigns the importer variable `clsWordCon` to point to the exporter variable in the class module, which was declared `Public` so that the general module can see it. We wrote a procedure within the general module that does just two things: It links to the class module, then it starts the main procedure in that module. It's the simplest procedure in this project:

```
Public Sub MakePresentationFromWord()
    Set clsWordCon = clsWordCon.classApp
    clsWordCon.GatherYeWordText
End Sub
```

The second instruction here is phrased in object-oriented fashion, like a method call. Variable `clsWordCon` refers to the instance of the `WordDocShow` class, and `.GatherYeWordText` (while ye may) becomes the method call, which invokes the procedure of the same name within the class module.

It's worth noting here that PowerPoint does not utilize a native object module for its presentations, the way `ThisDocument` serves as an object module for Word, and `ThisWorksheet` as an object module for Excel. What this means is that there is no component-like mechanism that responds to events generated by any specific

PowerPoint document. The only functionality you can give a PowerPoint presentation is through its template (.POT file). When a user chooses to start a "Blank Presentation" after selecting File → New, it cannot utilize VBA because a blank presentation has no template. It's out there on its own. So with PowerPoint, you are limited to crafting functionality with regards to specific categories of presentations, and not with the application as a whole.

Public declarations with another application's library

In Listing 15-2, all of the module-level object variables refer to the Word object library, not PowerPoint's. You might get the impression that this module would be better suited to running from Word VBA rather than PowerPoint VBA. True, a version of the module could be constructed for Word just as uneasily as it was for PowerPoint. But then the Word version's module-level Declarations section would probably need to include object variables referring to PowerPoint for the convenience of that particular edition of the project.

Keep in mind that PowerPoint VBA cannot automatically make use of Word's object library just because it uses the term Word in its declarations. You still have to engage the object library from the list in the References window, which is attainable by selecting References from VBA's Tools menu. You'll find Word's library listed as "Microsoft Word 9.0 Object Library."

Listing 15-3 shows the main procedure for this module, Public Sub GatherYeWordText(). It's contacted directly from the general module, where its procedure name acts like a method instruction.

Listing 15-3: The main procedure for the automatic presentation generator.

```
Public Sub GatherYeWordText(Optional iHow As Integer)
    ActiveWindow.ViewType = ppViewSlide
    If ActiveWindow.Selection.Type > 0 Then
        iIndex = _
          CInt(ActiveWindow.Selection.SlideRange.SlideIndex)
    Else
        iIndex = 0
    End If
    iKeepFonts = iHow

    Word.ActiveWindow.Document.Bookmarks.Add _
     Range:=Word.ActiveWindow.Selection.Range, _
     Name:="RecallSelectionObject"
    Word.Selection.HomeKey Unit:=wdStory, Extend:=wdMove

    For Each paraThis In Word.ActiveDocument.Paragraphs
        If Left$(paraThis.Style, 8) = "Heading " Then
```

```
    If Right$(paraThis.Style, 1) = "1" Then
        bFirstTitle = True
        If bBodyInProgress Then StreamBodyPoints
        paraThis.Range.Copy
        MakeNewSlide
    Else
        If bFirstTitle Then
            bBodyInProgress = True
            iPoints = iPoints + 1
            ReDim Preserve rngBodyPoints(iPoints), _
             iHeading(iPoints), bExcerpt(iPoints)
            Set rngBodyPoints(iPoints) = paraThis.Range
            iHeading(iPoints) = _
             Val(Right$(paraThis.Style, 1))
            bExcerpt(iPoints) = False
        End If
    End If
Else
    If bFirstTitle Then
        With paraThis.Range.Find
            .ClearFormatting
            .Style = ActiveDocument.Styles("Point")
            .MatchWildcards = True
            .Text = "<*."
            While .Execute
                bBodyInProgress = True
                paraThis.Range.Select
                With Word.Selection.Find
                    .ClearFormatting
                    .Forward = True
                    .Style = _
                     ActiveDocument.Styles("Point")
                    While .Execute
                        iPoints = iPoints + 1
                        ReDim Preserve _
                         rngBodyPoints(iPoints), _
                         iHeading(iPoints), _
                         bExcerpt(iPoints)
                        Set rngBodyPoints(iPoints) = _
                         Word.Selection.Range
                        iHeading(iPoints) = 3
                        bExcerpt(iPoints) = True
                    Wend
```

Continued

Listing 15-3: The main procedure for the automatic presentation generator. *(Continued)*

```
                    End With
                Wend
            End With
        End If
    End If
    Next paraThis
    StreamBodyPoints

    Word.ActiveDocument.Bookmarks("RecallSelectionObject").Select
    Word.ActiveDocument.Bookmarks("RecallSelectionObject").Delete
End Sub
```

The single `Optional` argument is employed when the calling body directs this procedure to retain the original fonts from the PowerPoint slide master, rather than use the fonts in the Word document. The variable that will actually be keeping track of whether to retain existing fonts is `iKeepFonts`, but since that was declared at module-level, and all of the arguments that a procedure receives are local to it, the value of the argument `iHow` is assigned to the already declared `iKeepFonts`.

`Public Sub GatherYeWordText()` starts by setting the view of the active PowerPoint window to Slide view, which is represented by the constant `ppViewSlide`. I used the `.ViewType` property rather than the `.Type` property of the `.View` object just to be different. No qualifying library name appears before `ActiveWindow`, which is a term that is also used by Word, so this VBA interpreter assumes the window in question belongs to PowerPoint.

The long, Long slide index property

Our procedure generates slides within the active presentation, rather than creating an entirely new presentation. The best way to handle the usability question, as this procedure demonstrates, is to let the user choose the point where slide generation is to begin, by making that point the active slide. Any existing slides from that position on will be pushed over to make room. For the procedure to know where to begin, we need to determine where it is that the user has placed the slide pointer. There are a handful of ways in PowerPoint to get to the index number of the active slide, the shortest of which is to poll `ActiveWindow.Selection.SlideRange.SlideIndex`. Essentially, this reference means "the index number of the first of all selected slides in the active window." VBA assumes "the first" because no argument is stated here for `SlideRange`; if an argument were present — for instance, `SlideRange(2)` — the value of that argument would denote *which* selected slide is being referred to. In Slide view, the user can only "select" one slide anyway, so any such argument would be immaterial here.

By the way, the value of the `.SlideIndex` property is always a `Long` integer, not just an `Integer`. Its value can be assigned to a variable declared `As Integer`, as long as we can guarantee that the presentation will have fewer than 65,536 slides. But in my experience with PowerPoint VBA, I discovered that sometimes – not always – such an assignment of a long integer value to a standard integer variable was unsuccessful. So for this procedure, I applied `CInt()`, an old-fashioned function from the early days of Microsoft BASIC, to the `.SlideIndex` property before assigning it to the `Integer` variable `iIndex`. The `CInt()` function performs the conversion that you should not have to perform in VBA.

The next order of business in Listing 15-3 is to have Word remember where the cursor is currently located within its active document. Later on, we'll need to make use of `Word`'s selection object to search for particular aspects of text, because a `Word.Selection.Find` object treats searches for textual attributes, as opposed to pure text, differently than does a `Range.Find` object. Because `Word.Selection` will be scooted around the document somewhat, we need to use the bookmarking method that we discussed in Chapter 14 to store the current cursor position at the start of the module, so that we can put the cursor back there at the end of the module.

The main `For Each...Next` loop clause counts through each of the paragraphs in the Word document. The interior conditional clause divides the loop clause into two main segments: one which is executed if the paragraph is a "Heading," and the other which is executed for non-headings in the search for specially marked text passages.

In the "Heading" segment, a secondary conditional clause draws the conclusion that there are really only two types of headings: those that are level 1 and those that are not. "Heading 1" paragraphs are to be used for slide titles. Thus, the purpose of this part of the procedure is to copy the "Heading 1" paragraph to the Windows clipboard so that it can be transferred to the title frame area intact, without dropping its original font or any italicized, boldfaced, or underlined text.

Reducing the strain on PowerPoint

Of the four Office 2000 object libraries, PowerPoint's is by far the least stable. This was also true for the Office 97 suite, and although PowerPoint itself has changed, its underlying object library's instability has not. Many of the actions this VBA class module takes result from the fact that the more direct approach can lead PowerPoint to crash. One way I've treated PowerPoint with kid gloves here is to have the procedure store in memory all of the text being collected for the body text of the slide until it's ready to generate that portion, at which time the slide object is generated all at once. The time for the procedure to do this is when it comes across the next "Heading 1" paragraph, which should go at the beginning of the next slide. Asking PowerPoint to do a lot at one time is apparently less stressful on it than asking it to do individual things a lot of times.

So the purpose of the Boolean variable `bBodyInProgress` is to keep track of whether text for the body text area is currently being retained in memory. If it is (`If bBodyInProgress`), then a call is placed to one of our two "subroutine" procedures,

StreamBodyPoints. This procedure will complete the current slide before starting a new one.

The Boolean variable bFirstTitle is a late addition to the program, and a result of a testing period for this VBA class module that at least approaches the proper amount. I decided on a hard-and-fast rule that no other headings or "Point" format excerpts should be recorded until this procedure has found the first "Heading 1" paragraph in the Word document. This way, I can be assured that any successive paragraphs will be pasted into a slide that is ready for them, and that has a title already drawn up for it in Shapes(1). Otherwise, without a new slide having been created with the proper layout type, the current slide would be a pre-existing one – either one drawn up by the user or a title slide generated by PowerPoint's separate title master. In this slide, Shapes(2) could be anywhere, or perhaps nonexistent; in any event, if a procedure attempted to paste text into that shape, it could wreak havoc. So bFirstTitle is one preventative measure, devised after I became an eyewitness to said havoc.

To start a new slide, first the procedure copies the "Heading 1" paragraph from the Word 2000 document, with the instruction paraThis.Range.Copy. From there, a call is placed to our other "subroutine," MakeNewSlide. The reason we have these two separate procedures is simple: They contain processes that can be initiated from more than one point in the program.

If this isn't a "Heading 1" paragraph, but we know that it is a "Heading *something*" paragraph, then we start the process of remembering bullet points for the body text area of the slide. So first we poll bFirstTitle to make certain that a proper slide exists. Next, we set bBodyInProgress to True, just in case it isn't True already. If this is the first iteration of this subclause for the current slide, we can assume iPoints – that retains the number of bullet points found thus far – is 0; either it hasn't been used to this point and is freshly initialized, or it was cleared after the contents were last dumped to the body text region. If iPoints is positive, then it's still safe to increment it here.

Each of the retained bullet points has three important elements about them that should be retained in memory. First of all, of course, is the text itself. The text plus its formatting can be stored within the Word.Range class array rngBodyPoints(). Next is the heading level, which determines the hierarchical level of the bullet point in the set; this is kept in iHeading(). Third is whether the text of the bullet point came from a "Heading" paragraph or is an excerpt from another paragraph. This last item, retained by bExcerpt(), is important because a heading paragraph copied to the clipboard is a full paragraph, complete with a carriage return at the end, while the last character of an excerpt is generally alphanumeric.

The procedure in Listing 15-3 will reuse these dynamic arrays for each slide. Variable iPoints will be used throughout the class module as a common index. The ReDim Preserve statement tacks one more entry to the end of these arrays, by virtue of the fact that iPoints is incremented just prior. The indent level for the bullet point is taken from the digit at the end of the paragraph style, `paraThis.Style`. The `Right$()` function is used to extract this single digit, 1 being the second argument to the function; then the `Val()` function is used next to convert the digit from a character into a numeral value.

Having Word search for attributes, not text

The `Else` side of the secondary conditional clause is executed only when the paragraph being scanned `paraThis` is not a heading, and is then guarded against pasting to a non-automatic slide by `bFirstTitle`. Here is where matters get extremely tricky. We need to search this non-heading paragraph for the presence of text that has been specially marked by the Word 2000 user with the character style `"Point"`. A character style, you'll recall, refers to the appearance of the typeface for a passage of text, but not to its layout with respect to the paragraph. Once that passage is found, it needs to be extracted and copied to the Windows clipboard.

To accomplish this, we had to execute the search *twice* for each successful extraction. How come? The reason has to do with a peculiarity of Word's internal operation — and here is where we digress from the topic of PowerPoint for a few paragraphs to talk about Word. You'll recall from Chapter 12 that a search or search-and-replace process is handled through Word's `Find` object. The parameters of the search are set through the object's properties, and then the process is set on its way by invoking its `.Execute` method. The cursor does not have to be involved in the search process. A search process independent of the cursor can be programmed through the `Find` constituent of any `Range` class object.

Once a `Range.Find` process locates a passage of text, the boundaries of that `Range` class object change to surround just that passage. **This boundary relocation only takes place when the** `Find` **object searches for particular text** — that is to say, when `Find.Text` has a non-null setting. When the search process looks only for formatting information or a specific style, the `Find` object will still register that it has found what it was looking for, but its boundaries will not automatically shrink to fit the text that meets the qualifications searched for.

So we have a problem: We can search a paragraph `paraThis` for the character style `"Point"`, and we can know when we have found text formatted with that style, but we cannot isolate by means of this search process alone just the text that is so formatted. The settings for `paraThis.Range` will remain just as they were. If we used a `Selection.Find` process instead, the text that matches the style qualifications *would* be indicated and isolated by the `Selection` object. But a normal `Selection.Find` process assumes we are searching through whatever text is currently selected or, in lieu of a selection, through the entire document. You cannot isolate a paragraph for `Selection.Find` until you have the cursor (or the user) select that paragraph first.

This entire procedure is structured on the capability to step through each paragraph in the document, and not search for anything in particular until we know more about that paragraph. The class of object that represents the paragraph to

VBA is the Word.Range class (or just Range for Word's own VBA interpreter). To change the search process to a Selection.Find model, we'd have to abandon stepping through paragraphs, and instead search specifically for all "Heading 1" passages, then all "Heading 2," then all "Heading 3" and so on, until finally we could search for all "Point" passages. But then after that, since each search for each type of passage looks through the *entire* document over again, the procedure would have to reorganize all the located passages into some type of order, which means we would have needed from the beginning to have built into the procedure a mechanism for remembering where a heading or other passage was found. This would have been an architectural nightmare, for more reasons other than its obvious inefficiency.

So what we do instead in Listing 15-3 is allow the Range.Find process to turn up those paragraphs that do contain "Point" excerpts somewhere in them. When one paragraph turns up, *then* we use paraThis.Range.Select to indicate that paragraph, making it the boundaries of the Selection.Find process. The second process then closes in on any excerpts styled with "Point" — there may be more than one in a paragraph — and then adds the data for each excerpt located to the three dynamic arrays.

Although the Range.Find process had its own .Text property setting, the "text" being searched for consisted entirely of Word 2000 wildcards. Word recognized this string to be made up of wildcards because the .MatchWildcards property was set to True. Why is it necessary to execute the .ClearFormatting method for both search processes? Because even though these search processes are separate, Word 2000 has only one text-finding mechanism. As you saw in Chapter 13, it does not clear its search attributes with each new search; in fact, new property settings to any Find object are treated as amendments to the previous search. The user may have been searching for text that was double-underlined; Word will remember that attribute and apply it to the next search, *unless* your procedure executes .ClearFormatting.

Notice that excerpts are arbitrarily given the heading level 3, and that bExcerpt(iPoints) is set to True so that later on the procedure knows to add the carriage return to the end of the excerpt.

To close out Public Sub GatherYeWordText(), we make one more call to Private Sub StreamBodyPoints() to flush out any body text that's still being assembled. Finally, we put the cursor back where the Word 2000 user had it, and delete the bookmark so that it doesn't clutter the document.

On Point

The PowerPoint 2000 application was not originally designed to be extensible through VBA or any other language. But the need for a rich feature set prevailed, and VBA functionality was grafted onto PowerPoint to make it fit in with the rest of the Office family. Few PowerPoint functions need to be automated for PowerPoint's sake, because in a sense, much of its functionality in the generation of presentations is either already automated or made interactive to the extent that users would not want those functions to be automated and thus made *non*interactive. But this does not leave PowerPoint VBA entirely in the cold. Its extensibility can be exploited by other O2K applications.

The root classes in PowerPoint's object library are the `Presentation` and `DocumentWindow` classes. Collections of all the current instances of those classes are `Presentations` and `Windows`. The latter is sometimes confusing, because you have to get into the habit of knocking off the `Document-` portion of the class name when referring to its collection. The `Selection` object maintained by PowerPoint is subordinate to the `DocumentWindow` class, and is retrievable through the persistent instance `ActiveWindow`. A slide within the current presentation may presently have the focus, and a "slide object" — a.k.a., `Shape` class object — may have the focus with respect to the current slide. Within that shape, a passage or paragraph of text may currently be indicated by the cursor. All three of these "selections," or aspects of the current selection, are represented as constituents of `Selection`. The currently indicated slide or slides are addressable by `ActiveWindow.Selection.SlideRange`; the shape or shapes within an indicated slide having the focus are `ActiveWindow.Selection.ShapeRange`, and the text indicated within that shape is `ActiveWindow.Selection.TextRange`.

Generating the new slide and title

One of our "subroutine" procedures calls into existence a new PowerPoint slide, places the title into the upper slide object, and prepares the lower slide object to receive bullet point text later. Listing 15-4 shows this procedure.

Listing 15-4: Automatically calling forth a new PowerPoint slide.

```
Private Sub MakeNewSlide(Optional iSameTitle As Integer)
    Static txrTitle As TextRange
    Dim sTitleHeight As Single

    iIndex = iIndex + 1
    ActivePresentation.Slides.Add Index:=iIndex, _
     Layout:=ppLayoutText
    ActiveWindow.View.GotoSlide Index:=iIndex
    sBodyHeight = ActivePresentation.Slides(iIndex) _
     .Shapes(2).Height
    ActivePresentation.Slides(iIndex).Shapes(1) _
     .TextFrame.AutoSize = ppAutoSizeShapeToFitText
    sTitleHeight = ActivePresentation.Slides(iIndex) _
     .Shapes(1).Height
    ActivePresentation.Slides(iIndex).Shapes(2) _
     .TextFrame.AutoSize = ppAutoSizeShapeToFitText
    ActivePresentation.Slides(iIndex).Shapes(1).Select
    ActiveWindow.Selection.ShapeRange.TextFrame.TextRange _
     .Characters(Start:=0, Length:=0).Select
    If iSameTitle = 1 Then txrTitle.Copy
    ActivePresentation.Slides(iIndex).Shapes(1).TextFrame _
     .TextRange.TrimText.Paste
    If iSameTitle = 0 Then Set txrTitle = _
     ActiveWindow.Selection.TextRange
    If iKeepFonts = 1 Then
        ActivePresentation.Slides(iIndex).Shapes(1).TextFrame _
        .TextRange.Font.Name = ActivePresentation.SlideMaster _
        .Shapes(1).TextFrame.TextRange.Font.Name
    End If
    ActiveWindow.Selection.ShapeRange.TextFrame.TextRange _
     .Characters(Start:=ActiveWindow.Selection.TextRange.Length, _
     Length:=1).Select
    ActiveWindow.Selection.TextRange.Text = ""
    While ActivePresentation.Slides(iIndex).Shapes(1).Height > _
     iTitleHeight
        ActivePresentation.Slides(iIndex).Shapes(1).TextFrame _
        .TextRange.Font.Size = ActivePresentation _
        .Slides(iIndex).Shapes(1).TextFrame.TextRange _
        .Font.Size - 1
    Wend
End Sub
```

With the lengths of all of these object references, the first question you must be asking is, "What happened to the `With` clauses?" Conceivably, `Active Presentation.Slides(iIndex)` could have been made the default object using a `With` clause. And in fact, I did...once. But the reason I reverted to this long form is the worst reason of all: **In long-term performance tests, PowerPoint crashed intermittently when `With` clauses were in use.** I'd rather you be able to enter the code into your computer and have it run.

Utilizing a Static variable

The first variable declared in Listing 15-4 is `txrTitle`, which is declared `Static`. We haven't had examples to this point of `Static` variables in use, so permit me, if you will, to summarize its purpose: The statement declares a variable whose value or contents will be retained, instead of discarded, when the procedure is exited. When the procedure is re-entered, the variable will pick up the same value it had when the procedure was last exited.

Variable `txrTitle` is a `TextRange` class variable (obviously PowerPoint, not Word) that will contain the text that will be used as the title of the slide. The reason we declared it `Static` is so that we could use that same title again, at some future execution of this procedure, whenever the bullet point region becomes too long for one slide and needs to be split into segments of two or more slides. When a split takes place, we can pick up `txrTitle` from the previous execution.

The procedure begins by adding one to the `iIndex` counter, then passing that counter as a parameter to the `.Add` method of the `Slides` collection. PowerPoint maintains a handful of preconstructed slide layouts for every template in its repertoire. The layout represented by the constant `ppLayoutText` is the simple two-shape layout with a title region on top and a body region below.

Newly added slides are not automatically shown or selected. I used the `.GotoSlide` method of the `View` object to move Slide view to the new slide. You'll notice that I flip root objects from instruction to instruction, between `Active Presentation` and `ActiveWindow`. This isn't because I'm fickle or changing my party affiliation in mid-term. It's because instructions having more to do with the state of the slide, as opposed to the text within the slide or selected elements within the slide, are best expressed with the `ActivePresentation` object; the rest use `ActiveWindow`.

Making shapes sensitive to stretching

Just because a `Shape` class object ("slide object") is given a certain size once it's created does not mean that text typed into that shape couldn't overflow its boundaries. With PowerPoint, textual overflow can spill into the area of other shapes, and even past the lower boundary of the slide and into neutral workspace. When this happens, however, the height of the shape containing the text does not register a change. Like a cell in an Excel worksheet, a PowerPoint shape does not expand its *borderlines* whenever text overflows outside of them.

I wanted a way for this procedure to detect when bullet points start to overflow the boundaries of the shape in which they're displayed and, in response, transfer to a new shape in a new slide. Similarly, I wanted a way for the point size of text in the title region to reduce itself when the title starts to spill over its shape's boundaries. Properties are required to notify us when boundaries have been exceeded. But the `.Width` and `.Height` properties themselves don't expand to fit an overflowing body of text, unless of course they're told to do that. So two instructions within Listing 15-4 set the `.AutoSize` property of the `TextFrame` object — which represents an invisible textual frame within a shape, and is thus a constituent of a `Shape` object — to the value represented by `ppAutoSizeShapeToFitText`. This way, when the `TextFrame` object expands, so does its containing `Shape` object. For future reference, I recorded the current `.Height` properties of both shapes into the variables `sTitleHeight` and `sBodyHeight`. These variables were declared `As Single` because `.Height` properties of PowerPoint shapes may have fractional values. With these variables in place, when text is written into the shapes, we can determine whether their current `.Height` settings have exceeded their recorded initial values. Variable `sBodyHeight` is required in the other "subroutine" procedure, so it was declared module-level, whereas `sTitleHeight` is local and required only in this procedure.

By the way, if I had wanted the title shape to be restricted to one line of text but have the text always fit that line, I could have set the `.WordWrap` property of `Shapes(1).TextFrame` to `True`. After that, I'd need to record the `.Width` property of `Shapes(1).TextFrame` rather than the `.Height` property, because text would then overflow the right edge rather than the bottom.

Positioning the cursor using textual characteristics

Next, I have to make a couple of "selections" in order to get the cursor in the right place for the paste operation. First, the `.Select` method is used to give the focus to `Shapes(1)`. This makes `Shapes(1)` effectively the same as `ActiveWindow.Selection`. Next, the cursor within the text frame of that shape is set to the very beginning using another `.Select` method. This time, the specific `Characters` collection being addressed is a constituent of the `TextRange` object. `TextRange` has a few constituent collections that make it almost "Word-like," you might say: `Characters`, `Words`, `Sentences`, and one which even we wish Word 2000 had with regard to textual length, `Lines`. Unlike with Word, however, these collections are addressable like ranges, with two parameters marking the start and length of the range. Here `Start:=0` refers to the very beginning of the text, and `Length:=0` refers to the lack of any characters being indicated by the cursor.

At the top of `Private Sub MakeNewSlide()`, the single `Optional` argument `iSameTitle` denotes whether the title for this slide is to be a new one from the Word document (0), or the same one being retained by `txrTitle` (1). If it's to be a new title, then the `.Paste` method is used to bring the title text — which would have been placed on the clipboard earlier by the instruction `paraThis.Range.Copy` in

Listing 15-3 — into the text frame, and then recorded into the `TextRange` class variable `txrTitle`. Otherwise, the former title stored in `txrTitle` is copied to the Clipboard and pasted here. If I had instead written `ActivePresentation.Slides(iIndex).Shapes(1).TextFrame.TextRange.Text = txrTitle.Text`, then the raw text would have made it into the text frame, but without any of the embellishments that the Word document author may have given the heading originally.

If you look closely at the `.Paste` instruction, you'll notice the curious term `.TrimText`. It's a method, whose purpose in this context is to remove any trailing spaces from the end of the text in the `TextRange` object. But its return value is itself a `TextRange` object, so it can be used as the antecedent for the `.Paste` method without a break in the long chain of periods. Remember, by the way, that the antecedent of a `.Paste` method always refers to the location of the *paste* — where text will be received — and not the location of the source of the text. The source, which was copied to the clipboard, is the antecedent of a prior `.Cut` or `.Copy` method. Text pasted to a region from the Clipboard retains its original formatting — which is why the Clipboard is being used in the first place.

Font objects are not transferable

Variable `iKeepFonts` holds the original `Optional` argument made by the general module's procedure in placing a call to `Public Sub GatherYeWordText()` in the class module. If it's set to 1, then evidently the calling procedure wants the typeface used by PowerPoint's slide master rather than that used by the Word document's "Heading 1" style. So the `Font.Name` property of `Shapes(1)` in the slide master is duplicated and assigned to the `Font.Name` property of `Shapes(1)` of the new slide.

Why not just assign the whole `Font` object, with all of its properties and constituents, to the `Font` object of `Shapes(1)` in the new slide? Well, try it sometime; you'll find that it won't work. The `Set` statement expects to assign the aspects of an object to a *variable*, not to an instance of another object. But why didn't the procedure go ahead and equate `Font.Size` of the slide master with `Font.Size` in the new slide while it was at it? I tried this. . . and I failed. For reasons unknown to this author, the **`Font.Size` properties of `TextRange` class objects in PowerPoint tend to return values of `-2`, no matter what their true and visible settings may be at the time**. No typeface in Windows, you can imagine, employs a point size of –2. What's more, if you assign a new size to the `.Size` property of a `TextRange` class object (hopefully to some *positive* value), you will manage to change the visible text size, but the `.Size` property of that object will still return `-2`. Go figure. Or not.

Next, Listing 15-4 does a little cleanup work: When the "Heading 1" text is first pasted into the title shape, it contains an extra character at the end that could boost the title text up one line further than it actually belongs. That character is a carriage return, which isn't necessary for `TextFrame` regions in PowerPoint except to signal the presence of a new line *after* the current one. There are relatively few cursor automation instructions in the PowerPoint library. So the only certain way to eliminate the trailing carriage return—which *will* be present in all cases—is to invoke the .Select method for the Characters collection again, this time to point to the final and highest-numbered location (ActiveWindow.Selection. TextRange.Length). The Length: argument is extended so that the cursor indicates this final carriage return (code 13) character. Then, using the Selection object as though this were in Word 2000, I assigned the text of the selection to a null string. This effectively tells the cursor, "Whatever you were indicating before, you're now indicating nothing," without moving the cursor's position. The TextRange object does maintain a .Delete method, by the way, but TextRange. Delete always means "delete *everything*," and thus would be inconvenient in this context.

Finally, the purpose of the While...Wend loop is to keep trimming the font size of text in the title frame until its shape's boundaries snap back to a value at or below its original iTitleHeight setting. The Font.Size property is decremented until that condition is accounted for.

Dumping the bullet points in succession

Getting PowerPoint to display the recorded bullet points precisely the way they are supposed to appear in PowerPoint (as opposed to Word) was a trial-and-error process that consumed most of the time in developing this VBA project. I even tried dumping the subordinate bullet points into each slide *backwards*, until I realized that this could leave one slide in the middle of the presentation with just one bullet point, while all the rest of the points belonging to the given heading would be in *successive* slides. Listing 15-5 tells the story.

Listing 15.5: Filling the body text region of the slide with bullet points.

```
Private Sub StreamBodyPoints()
    Dim iCount As Integer

    If iPoints = 0 Then Exit Sub
    ActivePresentation.Slides(CInt(iIndex)).Shapes(2).Select
    For iCount = 1 To iPoints
        rngBodyPoints(iCount).Copy
        ActiveWindow.Selection.TextRange.TrimText.Paste
        ActiveWindow.Selection.TextRange.RemovePeriods
        If iKeepFonts = 1 Then
            ActivePresentation.Slides(iIndex).Shapes(2) _
            .TextFrame.TextRange.Font.Name = ActivePresentation _
            .SlideMaster.Shapes(2).TextFrame.TextRange.Font.Name
        End If
        If bExcerpt(iCount) Then
            ActiveWindow.Selection.TextRange.IndentLevel = _
            iHeading(iCount)
```

```
            ActiveWindow.Selection.TextRange.InsertAfter Chr$(13)
        End If
        ActivePresentation.Slides(iIndex).Shapes(2).TextFrame _
         .TextRange.Characters(ActivePresentation.Slides(iIndex) _
         .Shapes(2).TextFrame.TextRange.Length + 1, 1).Select
        If ActiveWindow.Selection.ShapeRange.Height > _
        sBodyHeight Then
            If iCount < iPoints Then
                MakeNewSlide 1
                ActivePresentation.Slides(iIndex).Shapes(2).Select
            End If
        End If
    Next iCount
    bBodyInProgress = False
    ReDim rngBodyPoints(0), iHeading(0), bExcerpt(0)
    iPoints = 0
End Sub
```

The first discovery in my initial attempt to paste bullet point copies from the Clipboard into Shapes(2) was that a paste operation into a PowerPoint paragraph, during which the cursor resides in the middle or end of the paragraph, will overwrite the text in that paragraph. So if a loop clause were to paste in bullet point #1, followed by #2 and then #3, all that would remain in the shape would be #3. However, if the cursor were scooted back to the beginning of the shape, the next paste would simply force the text in the shape down a line rather than replace it. There's no documentation stating this is how PowerPoint works (until now, that is); I simply had to find this out through trial and error.

Where does a text range end?

I later learned through further trial and much further error that character codes do not denote the end of the text frame, although they do denote the end of the text *range*. What's the difference? PowerPoint does require the conventional carriage return Chr$(13) to mark the end of a paragraph; I actually have to add one of these codes manually to pasted elements that are marked as excerpts. But that addition does not cause PowerPoint to begin the next bullet point, the way pressing Enter tends to do when you're using PowerPoint without VBA. Instead, PowerPoint expects any incoming text to be added to the point just beyond the current cursor position, even if the character at that position is a code 13. PowerPoint relies upon the border of this invisible TextFrame object to tell it where a stream of text really stops.

I triggered PowerPoint into starting the next bullet point *after* the code 13 character by having it execute one of the world's largest instructions, in VBA or perhaps any other language. (We have the absence of any With blocks to credit for this colossus.) The line that begins with `ActivePresentation.Slides(iIndex)` and ends with `.Select` actually directs the cursor into trying to select a character *that does not exist*. The first parameter passed to the `Characters` collection ends with `.TextRange.Length + 1`, meaning that the cursor is being asked to count the number of characters in the text range, add one, and select that character. Logically, this should not be possible. But by forcing PowerPoint over the proverbial cliff, the cursor lands on a new line that has a new bullet point. The moral of this chapter is fast becoming, "Go figure."

Notice that `rngBodyPoints(iCount)` is the antecedent of the `.Copy` method, while the destination `ActiveWindow.Selection.TextRange` (the location of the textual cursor) is the antecedent of the `.Paste` method. It's often easy to forget that O2KOM expects you to designate *what* text is being copied, but *where* that text is being pasted to as opposed to *what* it is replacing. The antecedent of the `.Copy` method is the text being copied, while the antecedent of `.Paste` is the destination of the copied text.

Properties that correct the appearance of text

The `.TrimText` method makes another appearance here just before the `.Paste` method; it removes trailing spaces from the text range, but returns a `TextRange` class object so that `.Paste` can be attached to it. In the instruction below that is the `.RemovePeriods` method, which takes out the periods that close sentences. Most often in presentations, there are no periods at the close of a bullet point. The `.RemovePeriods` method performs a similar task as `.TrimText` but, unlike its neighbor, it does not return a `TextRange` class object. As a result, the instruction has to appear on a line by itself. It's inconsistent, but we have to deal with such matters by the hour. (Remember the moral of this chapter.)

The first conditional clause responds to the original `Optional` argument to `Public Sub GatherYeWordText()`, that being a signal stating whether the fonts from the Word document are to be kept as they are in the PowerPoint slide, or whether the font from the slide master is to be applied instead. Here again, I can only get away with assigning the setting of the `.Name` property of the slide master's `Slides(2)` to the `.Name` property of the slide under construction, because the `.Size` properties still continue to register `-2` regardless of the visible size of the text.

The second conditional clause tests whether the pasted element is an excerpt from the middle of a paragraph (`If bExcerpt(iCount)`). If it is, then it needs to be massaged a bit to make it behave more like a bullet point. First, the pasted element's `.IndentLevel` property is set to the amount remembered in `iHeading()`; this will apply the proper amount of indentation and the right bullet point defined by the slide master. Then a carriage return `Chr$(13)` is added to the end of the range using the `.InsertAfter` method.

Following The Attack of the 50-Foot VBA Instruction, `Private Sub StreamBodyPoints()` tests whether the lower boundary of `ShapeRange` have been stretched to any degree. The .Height property of ShapeRange is compared to the recorded original height setting sBodyHeight. But an interior clause tests to see whether iCount, the running tally of bullet points being written to the presentation, is still less than the total number of points as maintained in iPoints. If there are no bullet points left to paste to the slide show, then there is no reason to make a new slide.

Otherwise, as long as there are bullet points left, if the lower boundary of the shape has moved *at all*, then it's already moved enough. The call is placed to the procedure MakeNewSlide, passing to it the optional 1 argument to tell it that it is to make a new slide based on the existing title. I let the previously pasted bullet point spill over a little bit, because I know that there is enough lower margin in the slide master to allow for a little "give." Next, I used the .Select method one more time to give the focus back to Shapes(2), because Private Sub MakeNewSlide() leaves the focus with Shapes(1) (the title region) and I don't want bullet points appearing there.

In closing the procedure, bBodyInProgress is set to False as a signal that there are no more bullet points in waiting, then all of the dynamic arrays are cleared, and iPoints is reset.

Figure 15-2 shows the results of this PowerPoint VBA module, in the form of one of the slides in an automatically generated presentation. Recognize the headings?

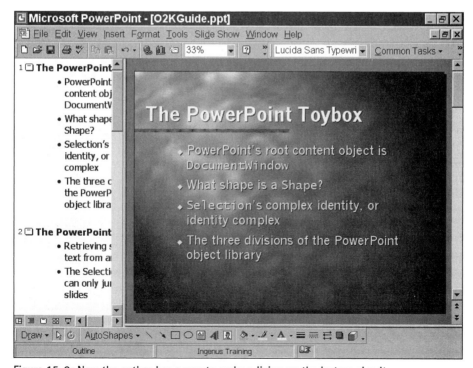

Figure 15-2: Now the author has a way to make a living on the lecture circuit.

On Point

With respect to the `Presentation` class, its persistent instance in PowerPoint 2000 is `ActivePresentation`. The main constituent of this class is the `Slides` collection. Rather than make slides, shapes, and text ranges equal subordinates, as is the case with `Selection`, in the `Presentation` class, one is the constituent of the other. So the collection of shapes within the first slide is:

`ActivePresentation.Slides(1).Shapes`

The container of text within the first shape in that collection is:

`ActivePresentation.Slides(1).Shapes(1).TextFrame`

This frame object, which doesn't show up in `ActiveWindow.Selection`, is the presumed container of text within a shape. The PowerPoint user never sees this frame, nor ever
has to deal with it herself. Its constituent is `TextRange`, which represents the formatting and contents of the text within the frame. So the raw text within a shape becomes addressable by:

`ActivePresentation.Slides(1).Shapes(1).TextFrame _`
`  .TextRange.Text`

In Theory: All the World's in Beta

Several years ago, when I first tried to make myself known to other programmers as a candidate for the deposit of any loose capital they might happen to find lying around, I made myself available to them as a beta tester. These were the days in which beta testers were *paid* – not much, but to borrow a Boolean phrase, not nothing. What I wanted to impress upon these programmers was my capability to understand the nature of their programs. True, I wanted them to like me. True, I was about as naïve as a lobbyist for campaign finance reform.

In my endeavor to be impressive, I generated some very long reports – dozens of pages supplemented by handwritten notes and a sprinkling of my curious three-dimensional drawings of programming principles suspended in Euclidean space. Everything that could possibly be wrong or out of kilter with the program in question, each point meticulously numbered and indexed. I have a strange way of making friends.

After the aftershocks wore off, many of the less instinctual responses I received were of a comparative nature. Invariably in each case, I was one of a handful of beta testers selected for the project, and everyone else reported the program to be perfect or near perfect. One gentleman, whom I remember fondly, had hired as a beta tester his colleague from a former professional programming job of more than a decade and his close friend, and then hired me as a tester for the same program because I was not only a programmer but a *Computer Shopper* correspondent. Free publicity, at one time, was a good thing. His friend extolled the program while I reduced it to so many carefully indexed bits. And then he was surprised to learn that at least most of my performance comments were indeed true. So he spent the next several months rewriting the entire program from the beginning. During that time, when *my* colleagues in the press asked him about the cause for his long delay, he simply said he was perfecting his work, and nothing further. I appreciated that. I should remember to call him sometime.

To be a beta tester today is to be a user of software, nothing more. Curious and often semi-developed new features are released into the public arena by their manufacturers in the form of "beta" products merely to stave off the possibility of anyone else doing the same first. Nothing particular is asked of the user in return, except, of course, to like the product so much that the user remembers not to buy – or more accurately, not to download for free – anything with anyone else's trademark on it. The beta product has become an advertising gimmick, a way for a manufacturer to appear to do a favor for its customers, while managing to install on millions of systems worldwide code that should not be worthy of any trademark – in some cases, so poor in design and execution that some companies would have been ashamed just six years ago for their names to be associated with it. And yet it's well reviewed, not because it works so much as that it exists. We don't appreciate the product when it crashes our computers, yet we don't seem to do much about it anymore because it was practically – or even *actually* in some cases – given to us by the manufacturer. We don't want to disturb our friendship, you see.

We could end this essay here, having made the point that the modern "beta testing" process, often involving more non-paying testers than do eventually become paying customers, has led to the rapid dissemination of bad software. But then I would have neglected a far more important point: Trademarks were at one time marks of quality. For many industries outside of computing, they still are. They stand for the workmanship and effort that individual creators and teams of dedicated laborers undertake to put forth a product worthy of our own efforts to make use of it. A product that is *tested*, long and well, is one upon which its users will come to depend, and one whose manufacturer will be reflected upon in a positive light. If a product must be tested more in order to make it work, then there should be no hesitation before continuing. The success of Gateway Computer, CNN, Columbia Sportswear, and even Starbuck's Coffee is proof that people are willing to *pay*, and even pay *well*, for a product into which people put real time and effort to perfect.

The relatively non-groundbreaking automatic presentation generator presented in this chapter took four days longer for me to produce than I had scheduled for it. In putting the prototype through just one more test, this time tweaking the operating conditions some slightly different way, I'd find something else wrong, either with my own code or with the way PowerPoint performs while that code is being executed. The result, printed here, works for most conditions under which I have tested it. And yet, I have to report, it is not perfect. After repeated use, PowerPoint VBA will eventually begin to lose track of the types of certain declared variables; and values passed to procedures that should have discrete types are instead treated as variants, often causing PowerPoint in its entirety to crash.

I can't do much about this. The problem here is not with the VBA code but with the underlying VBA interpreter. It has some faults. Perhaps you've noticed. Proper testing would have eliminated these faults. Taking heed of the plaintive cries of certain unpaid testers would have at least isolated those faults back when they first cropped up in Office 97. But Office 97 and Office 2000 were each supposedly the beneficiary of at least one year's worth of beta testing by thousands, perhaps tens of thousands, of individuals — orders of magnitude more testing *on paper* than we entrepreneurs did for any one product back in the 1980s. If there was a single forty-page brief with numbered points, indexes, and funny little 3D drawings delivered to the manufacturer by registered mail, it apparently was not read.

So what's the result of the lack of true testing on the manufacturer's part? *More testing*, on my part as well as on the part of other VBA developers. The buck was passed to us; we who write programs that support a platform are paying to compensate for the reduction or elimination of that platform's shelf price. The world is a sea of perfect developers for imperfect platforms: HTML, Java, Visual Basic, Oracle, COBOL, PowerBuilder, ASP, and SAP.

I could write this up in a letter and send it to some people I know, perhaps to impress upon them what it is that I know. But I wouldn't make many friends in so doing.

In Brief

- The two root collections in PowerPoint 2000 are Presentations and Windows. Their member objects are of the `Presentation` and `DocumentWindow` class, respectively, and their persistent instances are `ActivePresentation` and `ActiveWindow`.

- The `Selection` object is a constituent of `ActiveWindow`. Its immediate constituent at any one time is dependent upon what type of object the user has presently indicated: a passage of text (`TextRange`), one or more slides (`SlideRange`), or a shape contained in one of the slides or one of the `SlideRange` class objects (`ShapeRange`).

- Although `TextRange`, `SlideRange`, and `ShapeRange` may either be addressed as a group or enable one of its members to be addressed by way of an index, none of these are officially collections. They therefore cannot be used in `For Each …Next` clauses, because no object that would be the subject of a loop could be assigned to refer to a member of these arrays.

◆ A shape is an item deposited onto a slide that contains some visual element, be it text or graphics. The collection of all shapes belonging to a single member of one of the -Range suffixed arrays is Shapes, and is a constituent of the ShapeRange array.

◆ Because text ranges are indivisible, closed entities, there is no direct way to retrieve the textual contents of a region selected from PowerPoint's Outline view when the bounds of that region spill over the boundaries of a slide. The solution demonstrated here was to assemble a procedure that breaks larger selected regions into smaller subregions within slide boundaries, then acquires the textual contents of those subregions and splices them together.

Chapter 16

Comprehending Databases

IN THIS CHAPTER

- ◆ What we mean by "relational database"

- ◆ Why true database management is a communications process

- ◆ Jet: The under-appreciated Office 2000 component

- ◆ The mechanics of a database query

- ◆ An introduction to Open Database Connectivity (ODBC)

- ◆ Tables, records, and fields, and why they create *regulation*

- ◆ The importance of the access scheme

- ◆ A briefing on Structured Query Language (SQL) and its four main keywords

- ◆ The construction of complex queries such as joins and unions

THE HISTORY OF THE COMPUTING INDUSTRY is replete with mixed metaphors, and the modern theory of data management is now three decades old. Yet the person who conceived this model is neither a man of metaphors nor mixture, but of specificity and order. Dr. E. F. Codd, an IBM programmer since 1949, put forth a brilliant and inspired concept in a 1969 paper entitled *Derivability, Redundancy, and Consistency of Relations Stored in Large Data Banks*. Up to that time, Dr. Codd's colleagues had been working on the problem of how to represent, in an encoded fashion, the associations between some elements of data and other elements of data — their *relations*. Codd's treatises, from 1969 to now, have never been very long (far shorter than this book), and have always been written in a simple and reasonable English, mixed with a tastefully conventional math. While Codd is more of a mathematician than a programmer, nothing that Codd has ever invented concocted terminology for the sake of terminology. (Of course, there's that curious word, "tuple.")

It is said that nothing in mathematics is invented, but is instead either discovered or waiting to be discovered. If the relational model of databases is purely mathematical, as Dr. Codd would politely state that it is, then I sincerely doubt that its predicate logic predated the human race, and that Codd stumbled onto it one day while collecting fruit from the orchard. If we cannot give Codd credit for having created an entirely new tree, let us at least conclude that he grafted onto the existing tree of mathematics a branch entirely of his own making. Yet the nuances of what Codd so obviously did invent, today's programmers have still yet to discover.

The True Meaning of "Relational"

The Codd concept, on which all of his theory is based, is this: **A database is defined by its relations.** Information, you see, only has value to us when we're able to collect all of its components together in groups such that those components become cohesive through their similarities, yet identifiable through their distinctions. An item of data – a *datum* – by itself is about as meaningful as someone shouting "Ank!" in a crowd. As adept at listening as we might be, we don't truly comprehend any information within our own minds until we've defined a context for it, even if it's a metaphorical one. So for machines to have any definition of data, calculated or otherwise, their relations – the bearings of data upon other data – are defined first.

The simplest way to think of this in a modern context is to imagine the data that you type everyday into a word processor. The relations that the words have with each other are those given to them by you, the author of those words, and all of their readers, but (at least for now) by nothing inside of the computer. However, if you embed a table in your document, you've defined an area of data that both you and the computer can possibly get a handle on. Rows and columns impose a certain order to information that can be easily defined mathematically. A program can easily make an assumption that all of the elements sharing a row in a table are related to one another. But generally the process of building that table begins with inserting the framework for that table – the rows and columns themselves. So the rules for the relations are established first.

No sensible user manages a complex database through her word processor. (Not that it hasn't been tried.) But the principle of building the relations first and applying the data later applies for the most complex database operations. Many programs have been devised since the late 1960s that claim to let you just enter the data straightaway and take care of the rest of the job for themselves. But for each case, the truth is probably any of the following:

(a) The program is merely *guessing* at the structure you're implying, which means it can guess wrong;

(b) The program is probably using a strict row/column table structure, which means its relations are assumed beforehand anyway; or,

(c) The way you enter the data is probably graphical, so that you truly are programming the database structure although the program's authors would prefer you to think that you're not.

Prior to E. F. Codd's work at IBM, the whole idea of data *storage* as we understand it today – clustered, partitioned, and optimized – had yet to be invented. The rotating cores that served as both the memory *and* the data storage for the highest-speed computers of the early 1970s reminds one of the wax cylinders on which Thomas Edison etched his first phonographs. By 1978, individuals seated on their couches were using Apple IIs. The technological leap between those two periods in history is staggering, especially given the fact that its length is shorter than the interval between the time that the Windows 95 project was begun and today. What catapulted this industry so far so fast was a number of initiatives and innovations, which included the downsizing of integrated circuits and the plummeting cost of manufacturing, but which also included a new and more realistic understanding of the nature of software. All data, thus, is either a database or else white noise. All data has a fundamental structure independent of its content. That structure does nothing else but to define the relations between elements of that data which fit a category. Without this structure, data has no informational value. This was Codd's work.

In hindsight, the idea is so devastatingly simple that one inundated with the inner workings of applications and operating systems may wonder why it took ingenuity to even discover it. In practice, however, there is an art to the idea as well as a science, that is sometimes so elegant that one may wonder if someone inundated with everything that makes up modern computing would ever discover it today, given the opportunity.

In the last three decades, both engineers and marketers have endeavored to repackage the database application into some new and clever format appealing to a broader array of potential buyers. The tools which new engineers use to introduce a repackaged concept to a waiting world are generally metaphors. So let this be your warning as you enter the depths of this chapter and the two to follow. Only in the field of computing would something need to be opened before it was executed. Only in computing is a recording of one's transactions called a workspace, and the visible space in which those transactions take place called a session. Only in computing is the logical intersection between records matching a query called something as silly as a *dynaset*. It is language not to Dr. Codd's liking, as he has stated quite clearly on many occasions. But it is the language to which we must adapt if we are ever to gather the nerve or the time to change it later.

The client/server model of data

Another aspect of what Dr. Codd has helped us to understand about data is that the management of it is a communications process. Any such process can be likened to a conversation among at least two parties. There is an introduction, an establishment of a mutual topic, an exchange of information, and a termination. The client in the conversation is the agent responsible for viewing and displaying the data for the user, while the server is the agent responsible for storing and distributing that data. The distance between these two parties is insignificant to the transaction. From the database architect's point of view, that distance can be anywhere from zero (the two share the same processor, or even the same program) to infinity (the client is on a deep space station, while the server is in Armonk).

In any client/server model, it is the client that initiates the communications process. The server's primary job, therefore, is *response*. A Web server, for instance, is a respondent. A database server such as Microsoft SQL Server 7.0 (not part of

Office) has the responsibility for fielding requests from a multitude of clients. Other programs have the duty now of maintaining traffic control and "proper packet propagation" (say that *x* times real fast). **The database-oriented programs that you craft with VBA for Excel or Access are basically clients.** They make requests for existing data, produce reports on screen or in print, and post changes to databases. But they generally do not establish and initialize the database schema or its content; for most projects, you can assume those jobs are being handled by another component in the process.

Dr. Codd is not a communications engineer, so the terms and models he has employed through the years have not followed the vernacular of telephony. For Codd, there are no calls, no connections, no circuits. Yet, almost like Albert Einstein having proven the veracity of quantum theory in the attempt to disprove it, Codd happened upon a communications model for data in the search for a vehicle for his own predicate logic, because the relational model he created involves such factors as propagation of signal, traffic avoidance, and redundancy allowance – the same factors considered by the designers of digital telephony. Perhaps if Codd had worked at AT&T rather than IBM, his approach to the subject would be different. However, the conclusions that he has reached would probably be much the same.

Why is there a communications model for data?

Most modern databases inhabit computer networks. Networking follows a communications model of its own. We could state that since databases must assume they're on a network, they follow the network's communications model, and be done with much of this chapter – and as others have done, we might get away with it. Still, we would be flat wrong. In fact, the database model is entirely independent from the computer network model; they actually have to be in order for both to work.

The modern relational database management system (RDBMS) assumes a different cast of characters for its own private stage than does a network operating system. Yet the stars end up playing similar roles of clients and servers, following an old, but not yet tired, plot. While the conventional roles of operating systems in computing are to maintain order among files and to manage applications, the RDBMS is an operating system for data, perceiving not files but tables, not storage devices but databases, not accesses but transactions. The RDBMS serves as a broker for requests for particular subsets of data, placed by those clients in the system that it currently recognizes. It's entirely possible that the data server and data client could share the same processor. But when that happens, the communications model they share does not change.

A request placed by a database client to a database server is not the same type of request that a network client makes of a network server, because the operatives in the database environment do not have to be familiar with the constitution of the network. The network operating system (Windows NT, NetWare, or Windows 98 in a peer-to-peer or single-processor setting) takes account of where in the network that the database servers and clients are located; the RDBMS doesn't have to bother with that. Database transactions take place in a sort of conference call environment, where the locations of each participant are insignificant to the process. The database server is concerned with more fundamental matters – for instance, *who* the client's users are and what their specifications and privileges may be, *what* it is that these clients need to see, and *how* they need to see it. As long as the server knows each client's "number," if you will, it doesn't care what route the data takes along the way from server to client or vice versa. (World Wide Web servers work the same way.)

The transactions that take place in this communications process are what Dr. Codd has dubbed, with his usual flare for calling things as they are, *transactions*. (Don't celebrate too loudly, or someone in authority might hear you and decide to rename them something else.) Requests are placed and responded to, sometimes negatively. Updates and warnings are issued, and generally acknowledged. These are the simple transactions that take place within the system of a modern RDBMS. The transactions themselves are not what are so complex about a database system; what is complex is the process of arbitrating which of these transactions take place when, if at all.

In the private world of the RDBMS, files, directories, and drives are obscured from view, and may as well not exist. In their place are data tables, and the data produced as a result of performing logical operations on those tables. This resultant data is contained in what Microsoft calls *record sets*.

Jet is VBA's presumed database engine

Besides the client and server, there is one more major party in the database communications process, and that is the actual processor of the data itself, the *engine*. This component is responsible for maintaining and managing the data – it is the core component of the RDBMS. Microsoft Office includes its own database engine – no, not Access. It's called Jet, and it is utilized primarily by Access 2000 and to some degree by Excel 2000. (The other Office applications may address it too, but Jet's purpose with respect to them is generally ancillary.) The way Office 2000 puts Jet to use is by making it an automation server – an engine from OLE's point of view as well as the database model's. This way, OLE provides Jet with the line of communication it needs to find a way to present itself to the user. You see, Jet has no native container application; you don't see a colored puzzle piece on the front of the Office 2000 box that contains the word "Jet." Most of the time it borrows the container of Access, which has its own automation server, thank you very much. But Access' automation server is not a database engine. Instead, it is a transactional client. It knows how to handle queries directed to database engines, and to process the data it receives in response to those queries. When no other engine is available, Jet is the one it uses. This does not mean that Jet is the engine of last resort, only that it is the "default" engine for Access.

The ordinary user of Microsoft Access 2000 on his home computer is still engaging in a client/server process. It just so happens that client, server, and engine reside on the same processor. Access is still the client, while Jet serves locally as the engine. The fact that Jet resides on *this* processor rather than some other processor is insignificant to Access.

Introducing VBA into the database realm

The engine is ultimately responsible for the maintenance of the database. The server, meanwhile, is the party responsible for fielding requests from clients, and placing directives to the engine to fulfill them. Jet does not have the facilities to act as a full-scale server. On the other side of the equation, Visual Basic for Applications does not have facilities of its own for managing or even addressing data in any other fashion than in individual units. (Remember the array sorting algorithm we've employed in previous chapters? Imagine having to use procedures with that algorithm for every process that involves a database.)

As a result, when Jet is utilized as the engine for a VBA project, another party is required to make the data being managed by the Jet engine (not meant as a pun) accessible by the module. With Jet, you have your choice of three such managers, all of which are supported to some degree by Microsoft. (That degree happens to be less than 100 percent for all three, the reason for which concerns the fact that it has been more difficult than anticipated for Microsoft to cast its older software into obsolescence.) The most recent and perhaps most capable local manager for data is what Microsoft calls ActiveX Data Objects (ADO), and its objective is to put a VBA-compatible wrapper around whatever data is being addressed by the VBA module, whether it's being served by Jet or some other server. **ADO rephrases the contents of databases so that the sets that comprise a database table or record set are addressable as VBA collection objects.**

From an architectural standpoint, you may be wondering why this is a good thing. And you would not be alone, for many database architects and RDBMS engineers, including Dr. Codd, have argued against the use of procedural languages such as VBA in the data management process, often regarding such entities as intrusions into an otherwise sacrosanct realm. But SQL, for all its merits, does not address display devices – such as forms and dialog boxes – as objects, and does little or nothing to manage the process of actually *using* the database application. SQL addresses the database server, not the database user. So it has its deficiencies as well in this regard; and the successor that Dr. Codd proposes for it, RL, is no better equipped.

The key to database operations: The query

When a VBA program makes a formal request of a database manager for a view of certain data, that request is called a *query*. What distinguishes a query from an ordinary programming language instruction is that a query is capable of making generalizations, asking for data that meet exactly, or closely, or relatively closely some stated criteria, without specifying or even caring where that data is *physically* located – in memory or an array or a variable or anywhere else. A query works this way because a *person* works this way. A person doesn't care where data is stored or what it is stored in, unless that person programs the database manager to start with. A query more closely approximates what a human user would ask for in an everyday circumstance.

A query describes a subset of existing data, stating criteria that confine the values of some of that data to specific ranges and amounts. A client presents this description to the server, which responds by delivering records or other data elements that fulfill the criteria. The job of the server in responding to the query is to assemble sets of data that meet the query criteria.

All requests for data from a database are essentially queries. If a user is looking for a customer with a given name, a part with a given number, a set of blueprints for houses that cover a given range of areas, all bolts whose weights fall between two given values, or the data for a person whose psychological profile covers a wide array of given attributes, that user will, one way or another, generate a query that will be handled by the database server. As a programmer, you will at times be generating one more type of query which is far simpler, and that says something to the effect of, "Show me the fifteenth record in the table." Although it's a legitimate query, it isn't the type that a user would, or should, generate for you, because **it isn't important that the user ever know the inner structure of the database**, besides the categories of the items stored in the database (what database engineers call *fields*). The user may instead be operating a button that, to him, means, "Next record, please;" and it would then be up to your VBA module to record that he's looking at the fourteenth record now and is requesting the fifteenth, albeit indirectly.

VBA is not a database management system

Because the terms with which we must concern ourselves when we talk about database management involve such irresolute matters as the probability of change, the passage of time, and the possibility of undefined states ("gray areas"), the algebra upon which programmers normally tend to rely goes right out the window. In its place, E.F. Codd presents *predicate logic*, which deals with such matters as variable states and qualities. But the type of language Dr. Codd proposes to deal with these matters – which he calls "RL" for, you guessed it, "Relational Language," and which he proposes as a replacement for the Structured Query Language (SQL) inspired by his work, but which he himself spurns – is, by many programmers' accounts, next to impossible to implement, mainly because it takes another programming language to do it. Many SQL interpreters, for instance, are written in C++, and the better ones have a core of pure machine language. Whatever language the programmer chooses for writing the relational interpreter, like all other programming languages, it must be algebraic in nature. Yet algebra deals entirely with *static* (that is, non-changing) values, even though its key terms are called "variables." On the other hand, calculus – more in Dr. Codd's department – deals with changes, derivatives, fields, sets, and values that are far more abstract than simple algebra.

These two worlds – the common high-level programming language, like Visual Basic for Applications, and the database manager that deals with sets and relations using terms that approach predicate logic – are inherently disparate. To this point, you've seen how VBA addresses *collections* – groups of objects of the same class addressed as one entity. With Word 2000, the `Documents` collection refers to all documents currently open in the Word workspace, the `Windows` collection refers to the windows (lowercase "w") used to display those documents, and such collections as `Sentences` and `Paragraphs` refer to their textual content. All of this is data, and all of it is stored in some regulated fashion – in some sense, a database.

Aren't these essentially the same as sets? Not in the sense that an RDBMS observes sets, because you as programmer cannot employ *set logic* to address these ordinary collections. For instance, there is no VBA instruction you could craft that would directly address "all those documents that contain correspondence written to departments of Hughes Electronics," or "all those documents that contain sentences that refer to offshore drilling." Now, you could envision a complex VBA *procedure* that derives an array variable whose members are all references to `Document` class objects that appear to meet these characteristics. One way or another, a word processor can be programmed to search for such items. But there would be a massive programming effort involved just for the word processor to be able to identify the meanings of the objects of such queries, let alone launch searches for them.

For those applications more adept at locating data in a large file, such as Access 2000, **no VBA procedure that you will ever write should actually perform the job of searching the database for requested records**. Jet already performs this job well enough; and where the entire Office 2000 suite is installed, another Office application "owning" the VBA interpreter can call up the Jet engine – remember, it's an automation server too – and have it handle the data request without the user ever actually seeing it happen. The role of your VBA database-oriented project will never be to directly manage a database. That should be a relief to you. What your VBA project can do, and will often need to do, is automate the components whose job it is to directly manage databases.

Figure 16-1 depicts the "realm," in a figurative sense, where the elements of an Access 2000 VBA module reside. Here, many container programs are responsible for communicating with the RDBMS – including Access and Excel. Both rely on VBA to provide them with a reliable view of some or all of the data in the database, while VBA relies, in turn, on the RDBMS to provide it with a consistent, up-to-date view of the data. So there are quite a few parties in this conversation.

In this realm, the borders between processors and domains or contexts in the network are invisible because they simply are not important. There are several *sessions* in progress here, some of which are being maintained by the same client program. Figure 16-1 has marked four sessions in progress, A, B, C, and D. A session in the database model is like a conversation – a series of transactions between client and server. That a client may recognize more than one session simultaneously is analogous to how an operating system recognizes more than one application. Each session is piped from the client through to the server, which either relays queries through to the engine or processes those queries as the engine.

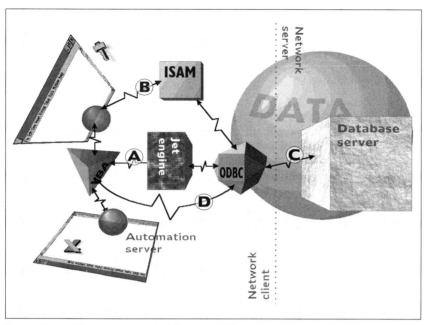

Figure 16-1: All of the players in Microsoft Office data communications.

Session A in Figure 16-1 symbolizes a connection between the client and the Jet engine, which is also Access' default server on a local system. When Jet is not acting as the local server, a separate driver may fill that role. Office 2000, as well as other applications, includes a set of *indexed sequential access manager* (ISAM) drivers that link Jet to data produced by another application, such as a table within an Excel spreadsheet, or a locally addressable database in the format of dBASE, Borland Paradox, or Microsoft FoxPro. The VBA module must specify the ISAM driver explicitly. Session B in Figure 16-1 symbolizes the client/ISAM connection.

ISAM is not another trademark, nor does it represent some proprietary technology invented just for the sake of the cute acronym. It refers to a technique for locating an entry in a database table. An ISAM driver or server uses a separate table called the *index* to look up a key number for a record. A key number is a unique entry used to identify that record, such as a serial number or purchase order number. Having found that, the index then points the server in the direction of the true record in the database, thus saving some search time. The topic of ISAM will be covered in greater detail in a few pages.

On a network, the server is generally a high-volume processor such as Microsoft SQL Server or Oracle, although Informix, Paradox, and FoxPro may also act as the network data server. Under such conditions, Jet is not involved in the slightest. But because a network data server still cannot make direct contact with VBA, it's up to Windows to provide VBA with the medium for communication between the database server and the language interpreter. In this case, it's another mouthful: a *provider* maintained by Windows and formally installed by applications such as the Office 2000 suite. In most installed editions of Windows (95, 98, and NT), this provider is called Open Database Connectivity (ODBC). The ODBC system includes another set of drivers whose purpose is to make data served from the outside world visible to programs designed to be clients (Access), and programs not designed to be clients (VBA), in such a way that the barrier between the operating system and database models is maintained. From the client's point of view, ODBC is the server, or at the very least the server's representative at large.

Microsoft is currently at work either replacing or supplementing ODBC (depending, once again, upon whom you ask) with a broader, more multilingual data service provider called OLE DB. (What, you may ask, has this service to do with OLE, especially as we've defined it in Chapter 8? OLE and OLE DB share nothing whatsoever but a trademark and a common manufacturer. Neither linking nor embedding have any bearing upon this technology.) The stated purpose of OLE DB is to make as much data as possible appear to the client to have virtually the same source and the same format. To accomplish this feat, OLE DB enlists the services of ODBC, in order for it to connect the data client to those traditional sources and formats to which that client is presently accustomed.

Historically, the Jet database engine has been used to manage the exchange of data between an Access client and a server linked through ODBC. Not that Jet adds anything particularly extraordinary to the mix, although it can act as another conduit between client and server. In Figure 16-1, Session C symbolizes the connection between the client and server that runs through both Jet and ODBC. Since the advent of DAO version 3.5, the Jet engine could be sidestepped entirely, removing one excess party from the conversation, as symbolized by Session D. Some of the functionality that Jet lends to DAO is lost in this *ODBCDirect* method; the basic query operations, however, are more succinct. (The version of DAO shipped with Office 2000 is 3.6, having been revised as recently as its once-purported successor, ADO. The latter is currently on its *second* version that has been numbered 2.1; there was one earlier 2.1 that was not widely distributed.)

None of the servers or servers' representatives in the four sessions depicted in Figure 16-1 have the capacity to make contact with VBA. Here is where Microsoft's data access models make their mark (and here is also where the Franklin Roosevelt administration begins to appear as though it didn't make thorough enough use of the alphabet). At present, Microsoft officially supports two, and actually supports three; its marketing tends to shift the spotlight between one and the other depending upon which has made the greater stride of late. The two most recent models make up Microsoft's umbrella methodology called Universal Data Access (UDA). DAO, the older of the two data access models, is provided by an object library that makes the data elements handled by Jet, ISAM drivers, and ODBC available to and addressable by VBA. Once DAO has made a database "open" to VBA, and has specified the whereabouts of the database and, in effect, its format, VBA treats DAO as the source of the database. ADO, the newer of the two models, is leaner and more object oriented. It relieves itself of some of the maintenance and oversight functions, ceding them to OLE DB and other service providers closer in the UDA umbrella model to the server. All of VBA's communication with the database up until the point it closes it, or terminates the session, is through either DAO or ADO.

RDO is the oldest of the three *truly* supported models; and while it is not officially covered by the UDA umbrella, it actually is shipped with Office 2000. RDO relies upon ODBC to an almost equivalent degree as does DAO, and does not utilize OLE DB — at least at the time of this writing. I've chosen not to concentrate on RDO in this book, not because of any inherent sense of inefficiency or obsolescence it may present — RDO shows signs of neither — but instead because I made a conscious decision not to confuse you, the reader investing patience in this chapter, with a third methodology for accomplishing basically the same thing. For similar reasons, book publishers choose not to release such titles as, "Learn Spanish, Portuguese, and Hungarian in 48 Hours."

On Point

A database is defined by its relations — by the bearing which certain data has upon other data. Logically grouping together related items of data gives that data meaning that it would not have otherwise, especially to a computer program that is incapable of discerning "meaning" lexically.

A properly engineered relational database management system utilizes a communications process. This is because such a system involves multiple parties, each of which engages in transactions, all of which take place in time. To take full account of which transaction took place between whom when, it's necessary to model these transactions as messages being sent between parties. For all database management, the central parties become identified as client and server. For Office 2000, other parties tend to act as go-betweens. For instance, the Jet engine acts not only as an OLE automation server, but also as a database server in local environments, and also as a mediator for fully featured connections between an Access-based client and a remote database server.

The Constitution of the Database

The true definition of a database is more general than you might think. Simply put, a database is any collection of digitally encoded information stored in a regular manner, and designed for retrieval in a mathematical fashion. By "regular," I don't mean "ordinary" or "normal," as the term has come to mean, thanks in large part to its presence on gas pumps. I mean "regular" in the sense that E. F. Codd uses the term: *following the rules*. If there are no rules, there is no database.

The purpose of tables

I've stated in the past that almost any computer file, including a word processor document, can be assumed to be, in an extremely loose sense, a database. When a word processor searches for words in a document, it's looking for so-called *pattern matches*, applying the search target against the patterns formed by the document's characters. It is tedious business, which would be far less tedious if the contents of the document's data were stored in some more regular fashion.

A more formalized database, as opposed to a word processor document, is comprised of sets of data of like categories, and relations that link certain items of data among these categories. For a database that contains a list of customer information, for instance, all of the street addresses, all of the postal codes, and all of the business telephone numbers comprise individual sets. All of the sets treated together is considered a *table*. Each person represented in that table has entries in all of the sets that correspond to one another. That correspondence is a group of relations among sets, the result of which is called a *record*. **Both Microsoft Jet and ODBC apply the tabular model in their management and manipulation of data.** Although not all existing databases are tabular in nature, and not all data can be modeled digitally using the tabular model, it is the most common and most pervasive model, and does describe most of the world's existing digital data.

In Chapter 3, you saw how a standard data table could be formulated in VBA through the use of multiple arrays of equal size. There, a single index numeral could be applied to refer to a record, addressing each of the arrays at the same location as though they were columns in the table, making the combined record into a row. A more formal data table can be written into an Excel 2000 spreadsheet, where each row contains a record and each column a category.

A table provides both the database and the programmers who visualize it with *regulation* – a conceptual container that brings order to the data, and in so doing gives its contents meaning. It is the placement of data within the table that defines its meaning for the sake of the database manager; the characters themselves have no meaning besides what a person might render unto them upon seeing them on screen or in a report. A word processor document has no such regulation; it doesn't require it, because its organization is largely a product of how its author chose to approach its subject matter, which is an entirely subjective process. Database regulation is by contrast far more objective: It relies on organization rather than content to provide the data with definition. Whatever data is written into the fields of a given row (or what Dr. Codd calls a *tuple*) defines the record for that row. That record exists even if those fields are empty; in Codd's logic, *null* is a value.

Columns and fields

Although a field is, in effect, the smallest area of a database table, think of the term in the sense that a farmer thinks of it: as a region or area that is to be cultivated, synonymous with "plot." **A field is the region of a record where an item of data — that is, a datum — is to appear, and represents the state, value, or contents of the category associated with a record in its given column.** A field is not its contents any more than a plot of land is its crop. Yet when a query is placed to a database server, what the query asks for are fields, not contents. Why? Because in placing a query, a *criterion* (singular for "criteria") applies to a specific field, and states a condition that the contents of records in the table must meet to respond to the query.

Any number of records may match a query's given criteria. Unless the query specifically addresses "the first record that matches these criteria," or "the *only* record that matches this criterion," or unless the access scheme in place is sequential in nature (addressing one record at any one time), the client has no idea beforehand of how many records it may receive in response to a query. In mathematical terms, we state that the size of the query response is generally *equivocal*, which comes from the Greek term meaning "talking from all sides at once," or *ambiguous*. And if the client is indeed requesting *one* record, and knows it is doing so, it is generally unaware of the precise location of that record in the database, both before the query and following it. A query is searching for records that match, approximate, or are distinct from certain criteria. Those criteria are bound to the fields where the contents of records in the table will meet the criteria.

A better understanding of ISAM

In the preceding paragraphs, I referred once again to the address scheme of the database and how it affects the results of a query. Because programming languages are based in algebra rather than predicate logic, their variables (strange that they should be called that, given what we know now) must refer to units rather than to sets.

Visual Basic for Applications is based on Microsoft Visual Basic, which, in turn, is based on BASIC, which, throughout its long history, has never been an adequate manager of data. In fact, the language didn't address *quantities* of stored data of any size until the early 1970s, when an associate of Kemeny and Kurtz, working on assignment for General Electric, devised BASIC's first data file access system. It used a purely sequential access scheme, which means simply enough that it started at the top of the file and worked its way toward the bottom in search of matching data. "Let's look at the first record, does it match? No. Okay, on to the second record. Does it match? No. On to the third . . ." and so on. This method sounds awfully arcane, so you might be surprised to note that **Visual Basic for**

Applications still uses sequential access as one of its two methods for addressing
data native to VBA. The instructions for sequential access have changed little in a
quarter century.

Notice the last part of the boldfaced sentence: "... data native to VBA." Yes, VBA
has its own native data format, which is frankly nothing but raw ANSI characters
separated with tabs or commas for delimiters. The fact that we will not be using
VBA-native data in any of the examples in this book thrills me to no end. The reason for its omission, aside from its brief mention here, is because it's inconsequential to most Office 2000 operations; whenever a VBA module truly needs its own
database, Jet is available to it. But this leaves VBA without a viable data access
scheme of its own.

One of the schemes with which Jet provides VBA is *indexed sequential access*,
the basis of ISAM, which was introduced earlier. ISAM relies on a few conditions
being met before it can work properly:

◆ **No two records in a table may be identical.** If you think about it, no
   properly conceived database table would have any need for identical
   records. Even if your table were a catalog of baseball cards, and a given
   collection contained two identical cards, both cards should be given
   unique identifiers, making their respective records unique.

◆ **At least one column of the database table must contain fields whose
   contents are unique for each record.** Generally, a serial number qualifies
   as such a column. This column serves to contain the *key field* that
   uniquely identifies each record.

For ISAM, at least one separate table is generated for each key field column. This
table is the index for the database table. It contains two and only two columns: a
duplicate of the key field column, and a separate column that records the location
of the record in the table whose key field matches the duplicate in the index. The
theory here is that because the index table is smaller, it's quicker to search through
it than through the main table. But generally, ISAM drivers "cheat" and sort the
index column, then employ a binary search instead of a sequential search (the algorithm for which was introduced in Chapter 14), which is far faster. So why isn't it
called "IBAM" rather than ISAM? Sometimes it's just too difficult to ditch a cute
acronym.

Because ISAM is a sequential method, even if it does at times employ binary
searches, it does maintain a device called the *record pointer* (also called the *cursor*
but, since we already deal with another type of cursor in Windows, we'll stick to
"record pointer"). This device points to the "current" record in a table, which is the
record most recently accessed. When records are accessed repeatedly, an ISAM driver or engine generally has the record pointer move one notch to the next record in
the table.

Often, when a form, such as an Access form or a `UserForm` object, is used as a display device for a record in a table, it utilizes a scroll bar or sliding tab as a device for indicating to the user the relative location of the form's displayed record in the table or record set. For most applications, the ordinal position of a record in a set whose size and content is variable anyway is unimportant to the user. However, as a programmer managing a process that addresses an ISAM driver, the record pointer may become important, especially in situations where the form is being directed to call up the "next" or "previous" record.

If your server is at a remote location on the network, and the connection for your session is being handled through ODBC, a record pointer may not be available to you. This is because larger-scale RDBMS systems use more sophisticated access schemes than ISAM, and therefore do not maintain "current" record pointers themselves. In other words, these RDBMS systems don't search through individual items one-at-a-time in search of a match, but instead have tools that point them in the right direction.

Why is the access scheme important?

Jet utilizes an ISAM driver when it addresses data stored under a format that's foreign to Access. What's important about this is the fact that stored data is not active data. That is to say, it isn't being managed by a server, so its accessibility to the user is handled by the operating system – in this case, Windows. So a database file being accessed by an ISAM driver is just another file. It doesn't have multiple users, generally doesn't contain multiple indexes, and certainly carries with it no guarantees of being up-to-date.

A genuine database is an active resource, whereas a data file is merely a by-product. A corporate database, managed by a main server such as SQL Server, Oracle, or Informix, teems with updates, insertions, and queries – multitudes of transactions from various sources in the network and via the Internet. A data file is an assembly of records, which may be a snapshot of some portion of a larger database, or simply something constructed on a local system from the ground up. But addressing this file is a more direct, more explicit process. Using the ISAM driver, the query criteria are stated in individual Data Access Object variables. VBA pulls up records that meet query criteria into a separate record set, which may then be scanned individually by means of VBA collection objects.

An Overview of SQL

The main tool used by the Jet engine to present a query to the server is Structured Query Language. The reason is because neither VBA nor any other algebraic programming language is efficient at phrasing queries that follow Dr. Codd's predicate logic. Because SQL (sometimes pronounced "sequel") cannot be directly embedded into the VBA language, an SQL query is phrased as a string literal, then posed as an argument to a VBA method directed to the engine component that receives and processes the query. Amid the chaos of Office 2000's thousands of associated terms necessary to make VBA work effectively with it, SQL is refreshingly and brilliantly simple to comprehend and to operate. Its vocabulary centers on just five instructions, the versatility of their phraseology making it entirely possible for the basics of SQL to be covered in a space as small as this segment of the chapter.

The central five terms in the SQL vocabulary are as follows:

SELECT   The main term – for some database engines, the *only* key term – used in phrasing a standard query. It directs the database server to retrieve the fields of certain records where the contents of those records meet the conditions covered in the stated criteria.

INSERT   Adds specific field contents, or the results of another SELECT query, into the specified table. Position is unimportant, because the order of records in a database is generally resorted for different views anyway.

UPDATE   Replaces the contents of certain stated fields in a table with specific new contents, for all those records that meet the stated criteria.

DELETE   Removes records from a table that contain fields whose contents meet the stated criteria.

CREATE   Used on rare occasions to generate an entirely new permanent table.

The process of natural SELECTion

Most queries, whether they're persistent (the views of their results are available at all times) or dynamic (the views are available on demand), utilize the SELECT statement. The result of a SELECT query is a set of records whose contents meet the stated criteria. SQL is not an access scheme; it can be used to address engines that employ address schemes that are sequential, random, indexed-sequential, or binary without having to alter its syntax to accommodate any specific scheme. The standard syntax of a SELECT statement in the format in which Jet perceives it, is as follows:

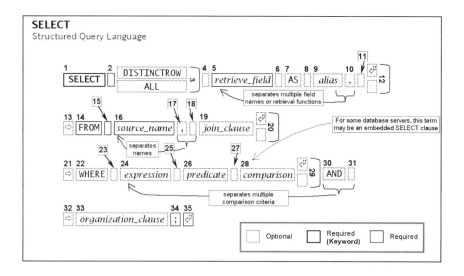

SELECT
Structured Query Language

	Part	Description
1	SELECT	<u>Statement</u> Directs the database server to prepare to retrieve records.
2	(space)	
3	DISTINCTROW ALL	<u>Qualifier</u> Substitutes for the search criteria clause (parts **17** through **25**). ALL has the database server retrieve all records belonging to the specified table or tables into a record set. DISTINCTROW (or DISTINCT in ANSI standard SQL) specifies that if the retrieval process gathers more than one identical record, only one such record is to be entered into the query record set.
4	(space)	
5	*retrieval_field*	<u>Variable</u> In most cases, this is a field name which identifies a category or column of data within a record of the specified table. If a field is being requested from a table other than that listed in *source_name* (part **16**), in order to build a record set that is a *join* of the records from two or more tables, the name of the table containing the field must be stated first and separated from *retrieval_field* by a period.

Note: You may substitute the wildcard ⋆ (asterisk) here to refer to "all fields" in each record.

6	(space)	
7	AS	Designates that the name which will exclusively refer to this retrieved field (part **5**) in the result set will be the *alias* term specified in part **9**. If *retrieval_field* (part **5**) is a field name from a table, then this designation does not affect that table; though for purposes of the retrieved result set, the *alias* name (part **9**) will refer to the column of the record where the retrieved field is located.
8	(space)	
9	*alias*	<u>Literal</u> An alternate name to be used for the retrieved field represented by part **5**. Using an alias proves helpful when the retrieval field (part **5**) is actually an SQL aggregate function of fields in the database. For example, SUM(Price) may present a result record whose value is the sum of all data in the Price field meeting the given criteria in the WHERE clause. In such a case, you could designate the retrieval field as SUM(Price) AS Total. See sidebar for details.
10	, (comma)	Separates multiple retrieval fields in a list.
11	(space)	
12	(Enter) (space)	In SQL, a statement is divided into component clauses. SQL programs tend to separate those clauses on individual lines, with subclauses of the main statement indented with tabs. For a Jet database query, carriage returns and tabs are not necessary. However, at least a space is required to separate the final term on this line from the beginning of the next clause (part **14**).
13	(Tab)	When SQL statements are divided into subclauses using carriage returns (part **12**), a Tab character is often used to indent the subclauses, making it easier for the human reader to spot their correlation to the main clause.
14	FROM	<u>Clause</u> Denotes the location of the name or names of tables (part **16**) from which records are to be extracted.
15	(space)	

16	*source_name*	For Jet's purposes, the name given to a table in an accessible database. In more complex situations, this may also be the name of a record set or view.
17	, (comma)	Separates multiple instances of source names (part **12**).
18	(space)	
19	*join_clause*	<u>Clause</u> When one record set is being assembled from the contents of two or more tables or other data sources, the product is called a *join*. The join record set is made up of fields from all sources. Here qualifiers may be stated that specify how the database server is to treat the merging of multiple records. For instance, an INNER JOIN qualifier states that only complete records may be included in the product record set, not partial records in which data was gathered from one or some of the named sources but not all.

The *join_clause* may not be separated from the final *source_name* (part **16**) in the list by any delimiter character other than a space (part **18**).

20	<u>(Enter)</u> (space)	A carriage return aids in human readability of subclauses, though is not required. At least a space is required to separate the final term on the previous line from the beginning of the WHERE clause (part **22**).
21	(Tab)	Helps to isolate subclauses; not required.
22	WHERE	<u>Clause</u> Begins the clause where query criteria are specified.
23	(space)	
24	*expression*	The comparison that takes place is phrased as an SQL *expression*. In the general phraseology of an expression, each field in the record is compared to a literal value or string, and the mathematical type of the comparison is stated by an operator. For example, Location = 'Iowa' is a legitimate SQL expression of comparison. When there is more than one table or data source (part **12**), the name of the source containing the field must be specified before the field name, the two names being separated by a period.
25	(space)	

26	*predicate* < = <= => BETWEEN EXISTS IN LIKE NULL	In database terminology, the comparison operator is called a *predicate*. Symbolic predicates are: < (less than or falls before), < (greater than or falls after), =, <>, <=, and >=. Terminological predicates are: BETWEEN (determines whether the object of the comparison falls between two stated values), EXISTS (works like a function that returns True if the SELECT statement between its parentheses returns any values), IN ("returns True" if the LIKE (tests for similarity as well as equality), and NULL ("returns True" if no such data exists for the given subject). The Boolean operators AND, OR, and NOT are available for compound comparisons.
27	(space)	
28	*comparison*	Data to which the *expression* (part 20) is being compared. To eliminate some confusion here, parts 20 through 24 form the expression of comparison; however, part 20 may itself be an expression that is being compared to the data here. Ordinarily, this would be a field name or a literal; but in versions of SQL supported by database servers that may be contacted through ODBCDirect (i.e., without Jet as the main engine), this part may be an entire SELECT statement, embedded into this one and offset from it with parentheses. Such an embedded statement for these purposes often involves the DISTINCTROW qualifier.
29	(Enter) (space)	A carriage return may be typed in order to isolate a WHERE criterion on its own line, thus improving readability, although it is not required. If you do not type a carriage return, however, then if you do have multiple criteria, a space at least is required to separate the term of the previous comparison (part 28) from the AND term (part 30). If only one criterion is provided, then neither punctuation is required.
30	AND	Collected with delimiter punctuation on either side (parts 29 and 31), separates multiple WHERE criteria from one another.
31	(space)	
32	(Tab)	Aids in human readability; not required.
33	*organization_* *clause*	<u>Clause</u> An optional portion of the statement specifying how records meeting the criteria are to be arranged. For instance, an ORDER BY clause states the name of the field to be used in sorting the record set.

34	;	
	(semicolon)	In SQL, an instruction is always terminated with a semicolon.

35	(Enter)	For an ordinary SQL program which contains multiple instructions, a carriage return is generally required to separate instructions; but for the purposes of being included within a VBA method, neither this nor any other carriage return is necessary within the SQL statement.

In Depth: Using aliases as field names in a result record set

The reason you would want to designate an alias as a handle to a result field in a SELECT statement is rarely because you dislike one of the names in the table being queried. The real reason is in order to give you a means for referring to the result of one of SQL's *aggregate functions*, as though it were a variable. SQL allows you to derive certain simple statistical data about your database tables, by means of a limited number of its own intrinsic functions. An argument for such a function is generally a field name; for example, AVG(Age) would calculate the average age of everyone represented within the returned records, assuming Age is a field name where such data is entered. The results of aggregate functions reflect all of the records returned by the SELECT query. The five such functions supported by ANSI standard SQL, and supported by Jet as well, are as follows:

AVG()	Returns the average value for the designated field in all returned records.
COUNT()	Returns the number of returned fields matching the criteria. (Since the number of returned fields is equal to the number of returned records — how could it not be? — the best argument for this function is often simply an asterisk * regardless of the field that is the subject of your query.)
MAX()	Returns the greatest value encountered for the designated field in all returned records.
MIN()	Returns the smallest value encountered for the designated field in all returned records.
SUM()	Returns the total of all entries for the designated field in all returned records.

Continued

> **In Depth: Using aliases as field names in a result record set** *(Continued)*
>
> It should be obvious at this point that the data type for any field used as an argument for an aggregate function, must be numeric.
>
> A SELECT statement that uses only aggregate functions will always return one record reflecting the result values of those functions, even if there were no records matching the WHERE criteria of that statement. Phrasing a SELECT statement that mixes aggregate function fields with straight field names is generally not allowed by the DBMS, and is not permitted by the ANSI SQL standard.

SELECT STATEMENT EXAMPLES

A simple example that I use from time to time assembles a set of records from a table of military officers:

```
SELECT Name, Rank, SerialNo
  FROM Officers
  WHERE Rank = 'Colonel'
  ORDER BY Name;
```

With an example this simple, all the rules of syntax suddenly seem transparent. It is a long instruction, but it is almost legible like a sentence, and it conveys its purpose just as easily to the human reader as it does to the database server. Here, Name, Rank, and SerialNo are field names in the table called Officers. The query is requesting a list of all colonels in the database, sorted by name. Real-world databases will be a bit more complex than the one implied here, and persons' names will most likely be split into its constituent parts.

Here's another simple example of a SELECT statement, this time using a feature you should only employ when you are certain that your result set will contain one and only one record:

```
SELECT DISTINCTROW *
  FROM Customers
  WHERE ID = '32615';
```

The asterisk (*) here stands for "every field in the table," so you're not forced to write all the field names out. Here, ID is the primary field, or key field of the Customers table. This field is used as the table's index; so both you and the DBMS know that no two customers will ever be numbered '32615'. The DISTINCTROW qualifier has the DBMS stop looking for more records that meet the criteria, after it has found the one.

Here is a somewhat more complex example: Suppose a table named `Timestamp` records the times when employees enter and leave their shifts daily. This table contains four fields, one of which is the key field that serves as the index for each entry. (Few well-normalized database schemas contain tables that are *not* indexed by key fields in this way.) The other three fields are the internal ID number for the employee, the time of entry, and the time of departure. So `Timestamp`'s field structure is comprised of `ID`, `EmployeeID`, `Enter`, and `Exit`. Suppose a second table in this same schema is named `Employees`, whose key field `ID` is used in other tables including `Timestamp` when making exclusive references to an employee.

The following `SELECT` query would generate a record set that contains the *names* of employees who clocked in during the month of February 1998:

```
SELECT Employee.[First Name], Employee.[Last Name],
 Employee.[Middle Initial], Timestamp.Enter, Timestamp.Exit
   FROM Employee INNER JOIN Timestamp
   ON Employee.ID = Timestamp.EmployeeID
   WHERE Timestamp.Enter >= #2/1/98#
    AND Timestamp.Exit <= #2/28/98#
   ORDER BY Timestamp.Enter;
```

The join takes place here for ali records where the `ID` field in `Employee` is equal to the `EmployeeID` field in `Timestamp`. But notice neither of those fields have to be included among the retrieved fields in the upper portion of the statement. The `SELECT` statement will only retrieve data in the five listed fields for those records where two *other* fields are equal to each other. This is not only legal in SQL, but quite practical. You shouldn't have to *retrieve* the ID field just because your main join condition is contingent upon it.

Toward the end of the `SELECT` statement, the `WHERE` subclause presents two conditions that serve as *filters* for the retrieved records, then the `ORDER BY` subclause sorts the result set in chronological order by date/time of entry. So the order of events in the `SELECT` statement follows exactly the natural order in which the DBMS will process the records in the result set. First, the records containing identical employee ID numbers are matched with one another. Then all the records are removed except for those concerned with the month of February 1998. Finally, the remaining records are sorted by the date and time in which the employee clocked in.

You may be asking, if tables `Employee` and `Timestamp` are both prominently listed in the `FROM` subclause, why must they be also explicitly written as though they were "antecedents" of the retrieved fields, as in `Employee.[Last Name]`? The truth is, they actually do not have to be written this way. All five retrieved fields have names that are different from one another, so the DBMS should be able to distinguish for itself the name of the containing table for each of the retrieved fields. So `SELECT [First Name], [Last Name], [Middle Initial], Enter, Exit` would have been completely legal. For that matter, the references to `Timestamp` in the `WHERE` subclause are also redundant. So again, *why are they there?* Because in this author's experience, manipulating a Jet database remotely has been a treacherous business; a previous edition of this book omitted references to certain database features which were found to be less than 80% operational, or to fail more often than one time in five. Redundancies such as these not only help the human reader to interpret the statement, they also have proven to help prevent accidents on the part of the Jet engine.

An SQL query may be built in stages

Assume we have a fully normalized database, where we allow a large number of base tables and rely upon explicit queries to provide us with derivative data. In this schema, a query that produces all of the records in a table of published articles would look like this:

```
SELECT * FROM Articles;
```

If a form were to show only those records in the `Articles` table whose date of publication is from January 1997 on, then a criterion could be added to the query statement:

```
SELECT *
  FROM Articles
  WHERE IssueDate >= #01/01/1997#;
```

Inner joins build combined sets to extract data

However, in a normalized database, all the information pertinent to particular issues (issue date on cover, date of publication, number of pages, number of copies printed) would belong to a separate table. With the cover date belonging to another table, a *join* is necessary to produce records that contain all the data from the `Articles` table, and the date of publication from a table called `Issues`:

```
SELECT Articles.*, Issues.[Cover Date]
  FROM Articles INNER JOIN Issues
  ON Articles.Issue = Issues.ID
  WHERE Issues.[Cover Date] >= #01/01/1997#;
```

The fields that comprise the records in the set produced by this query are taken from two tables. The query asks the engine to retrieve all of the fields in the `Articles` table (`Articles.*`, where the asterisk is a wildcard that stands for "all fields") plus just the `Cover Date` field from the `Cover Date` field from the `Issues` table (placed in [square brackets] because the name has a space in it). The join in this case is the matching of just those records from both tables whose issue identification numbers match. `Articles.Issue` represents the number of the issue in which the article was printed, while `Issues.ID` is the key field in the `Issues` table. A key field in a table is the field that exclusively identifies each record in that table for purposes of indexing and sorting.

The type of join here is called an `INNER JOIN` because it trims from the edges, if you will, those rows of joined records whose field values don't match the given `ON` criteria, along with those columns (fields) not specified by the `SELECT` portion of the statement. Imagine the entire record set as though it were written on paper. Fold the paper in half one way, then fold it in half again another way. The one-quarter region remaining is analogous to an inner join. The `WHERE` clause can then further reduce the contents of the record set based on criteria applied to single fields.

Outer joins combine records across tables

By comparison, an *outer join* performs a similar join operation to two or more tables without the trim. In a normalized schema, the data representing individual issues, individual articles, and their authors would be listed in separate tables. So retrieving the list of the names of all articles in an issue requires a query whose criteria addresses both tables:

```
SELECT Articles.*, Issues.*
  FROM Articles, Issues
  WHERE Articles.Issue = Issue.ID;
```

The term for this type of join, which bridges together records from two or more source tables based on the equivalence of the contents of certain fields (generally key fields) without any trimming from the outside, is *equijoin*. (Okay, so database engineering has its silly terms, too.) If we were to extend this query to join three tables, our `WHERE` criteria could form a chain, like this:

```
SELECT Articles.Headline, Issues.[Cover Date], Staff.[Last Name],
  Staff.[First Name]
  FROM Articles, Issues, Staff
  WHERE Articles.Issue = Issues.ID AND Articles.[Lead Author]
  = Staff.ID
  ORDER BY 2;
```

Here the elements of the query have been split into separate lines to make it a bit simpler to read; doing so does not affect the interpretation or outcome of the query in any way. In fact, an SQL query can have any number of carriage returns – we could have added one between Issues.ID and AND – and not have affected the query, since the database server expects the query to end with a ; semicolon.

The key fields in these tables – the ones used to exclusively identify and sort them – are named ID in the examples presented here just for convention. A key field is what Access calls a "primary key," even though it doesn't recognize secondary keys. (Other DBMS systems do, but not Access/Jet.) You can call your table's key field whatever you want, though I've gotten into the habit of always giving the name ID a numeric field that identifies a record but doesn't matter much to the user.

The previous example generated a four-column record set from records in three tables. Notice that the fields in the WHERE criteria used to extract the records do not have to match the field in the SELECT extraction set. Even though the viewer of the form or report attached to this query never sees the contents of Articles.Issue, the field is crucial to extracting the right records. The criteria only need to name certain fields of records that are being compared, but if the fields from a record pass the criteria test, the entire record passes. From there, the SELECT portion has the DBMS engine extract any fields that are to be deemed visible. Here, the two pairs being compared to one another, Articles.Issue to Issues.ID and Articles. [Lead Author] to Staff.ID, deal with identification numbers that are not of importance to the user. It's important that these fields match, but not that the user sees that they match.

Finally, the ORDER BY clause designates how the records in the set are to be sorted. This determines which record gets seen first in a form, or which record is placed at the top of a data sheet. The numeral – in this case, 2 – refers to the *second* field in the SELECT list, Issues.[Cover Date]. Some implementations of SQL let you specify the field instead of the field number, but this way just takes up less space. The default sort is descending order; to sort the list in ascending order, we could have written instead ORDER BY 2 ASC. If no sort is stated, the records in the result set will appear in the order in which they were found, which could be in some logical order from the user's perspective, though not necessarily.

Unions treat identical fields from two tables as one

If two tables in a schema have some common fields with exactly the same structure, then a record set may be constructed that combines the contents of those fields in what is called a *union*. Why would this ever be necessary? In our magazine example, suppose the publisher deals with two categories of personnel: staff or direct employees, and contractual or freelance. Tables consisting of the attributes of both categories could be kept separate from one another so that the distinction is maintained, especially for payroll purposes. But when it's necessary to build a directory of everyone hired by the company in whatever capacity, a union enables you to address several sources of data, so long as the result fields that you are blending together are of the same data type, and that each field sharing the same column in the result set has the same name.

Consider this example which generates a directory of telephone numbers from two identically structured tables, Staff and Contractual:

```
SELECT [Last Name], [First Name], [Middle Initial],
 [Business Phone]
  FROM Staff
UNION
SELECT [Last Name], [First Name], [Middle Initial],
 [Business Phone]
  FROM Contractual
  ORDER BY 1;
```

What's the difference between a union and a join? Had we asked for all eight fields, and listed the data source as FROM Staff, Contractual, then the resulting record set would have had eight fields, four of which would always be blank. Since it's unlikely for an employee to also be a contractor, one person would probably not be listed in both tables. A staff member and a contractor may conceivably share the same ID number, but that would be coincidence. So there are no mutual criteria among records in those tables upon which a join can be based. With a union, the results from one SELECT are added to the same record set as the results from another SELECT.

In Depth: What happens to data after it's SELECT-ed?

The Structured Query Language is not, by design, a *procedural* language like VBA. What this means is, SQL wasn't designed to be a language where the programmer tells the interpreter, "First, you do *this*, and then you do *that* to it, next you pull up a dialog box . . ." and so on. There are procedural derivatives of SQL — most notably the one used by Microsoft SQL Server 7.0, and Oracle's PL/SQL — but the reason for those derivatives' existence is because the language from which they are derived is not procedural by nature. Moreover, it was designed to facilitate a type of math made prominent by the work of E. F. Codd and others.

So when you examine an SQL instruction such as those used in the previous three examples, and you wonder, "What happens to that data now?" then already you're thinking procedurally — which is against the grain of standard SQL. In a few paragraphs, you'll see some SQL instructions that do specify changes to be made to the contents of a table. Because these instructions involve "actions" (Microsoft calls them "action queries") you can easily be fooled into thinking these actions are, in some sense, procedures. But in relational algebra, as opposed to procedural algebra, you have states of existence and states of change. A SELECT statement specifies a state of existence for a subset of data within a database. Think of it more as an *observation* than a directive.

Then why is it a *query*? Because there remains a process of interchange between the party making the observation (the program) and the party acknowledging it (the database manager). The program poses its observation as a request, which is indeed responded to with a retrieval process.

Most queries associated with a database are *permanently* associated with it, like a standing request. A *persistent query* is a request for data that is an intrinsic part of the database, and is responded to continually. The results of a persistent query may appear within an Access 2000 form or report. This type of query plays a role in Data Access Objects. All of the persistent queries maintained by a database are stored within a DAO collection called QueryDefs. Persistent queries for a database may be set by assigning the text of an SQL query to a member of the QueryDefs collection. By design, a persistent query is generally an SQL SELECT statement.

The concept often sounds more technical than it truly is. When you enter a record into a form on screen, the code that retrieves that record is often a persistent query. Commonly, the arrangement of the fields in the form is analogous to the arrangement of columns in a single table. But at times, depending upon how the underlying database schema has been "normalized," a form's contents may be collected from two or more tables, by means of a join operation. For instance, a form may show both the location and identity of an item in inventory, whereas location and identity may be represented in the schema by two separate tables. The join is a crucial part of the program displaying the form, though it is completely transparent to the person using the form.

The term "query" in English refers to a question, more specifically to a question in the act of being posed to another person. In database mechanics, it is a relational formula phrased like a command. The term *action query*, therefore, could only be a product of database mechanics. It refers to an SQL phrase designed to make changes to the contents of one of the tables in a database.

The "one of the tables" portion of that last sentence is more important than it appears at first. By contrast to an action query, a SELECT query (or *selection query*) may address more than one table in retrieving certain fields or records. The product of a SELECT query is a set of records – a single dynamic table in and of itself. So its *product* is a single table. An action query's *source* is a single table; and the three keywords provided by SQL for generating an action query are INSERT, UPDATE, and DELETE. Their purposes are fairly self-evident, and their syntax are all quite straightforward. We'll begin with the most oft-used of the three.:

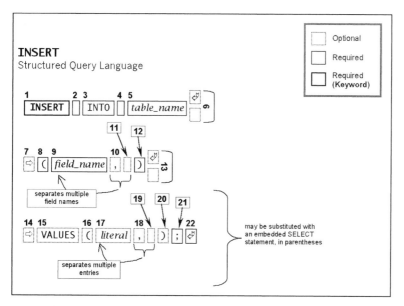

	Part	Description
1	INSERT	Statement Directs the database server to add new records to the designated table (part **5**).
2	(space)	
3	INTO	Separates the keyword (part **1**) from the table name (part **5**).
4	(space)	

5	*table_name*	<u>Literal</u> The name of the table that is to receive new records.
6	<u>(Enter)</u> (space)	A carriage return aids in human readability of subclauses, though is not required. At least a space is required to separate the table name (part **5**) from the beginning of the inserted fields list (part **8**).
7	(Tab)	Indents subclauses, making them easier to read; not required.
8	((left parenthesis)	Begins a list of field names comprising a record to be added to the table, in the order in which those fields are to appear in the record. There are two parenthetical subclauses in an INSERT statement. The first, which begins here, serves as a template for the SQL interpreter denoting where data is to be entered in a record. The second, which begins with part **16**, presents elements of data, generally as literal values, in the same order as the fields in the first list.
9	*field_name*	<u>Variable</u> The name assigned to the column of the record in the named table (part **5**) that is to receive new data (part **17**). All of the field names in this list collectively constitute a single record in the table. The order of field names in this list correlates to the order of fields in the record.

Rule: Field names containing spaces are allowed in Access; but in order to include them in an SQL statement, they must be delimited by [square brackets].

10	, (comma)	Combined with the space (part **11**), separates field names in the list.
11	(space)	
12	) (right parenthesis)	Closes the list of field names.
13	<u>(Enter)</u> (space)	A carriage return aids in human readability of subclauses, though is not required. At least a space is required to separate the end of the inserted fields list (part **13**) from the beginning of the insertion clause to follow.
14	(Tab)	Indents subclauses; not required.

15	VALUES	Denotes the beginning of the list of data to be inserted into the record, and helps separate the first list from the second.
16	((left parenthesis)	Begins the list of data being entered into the record. Note no space separates this parenthesis from part **15**.
17	*literal*	<u>Numeral or string</u> An item of data to be entered into the record for the field name whose position in the first list corresponds to the position of this item in the second list. For VBA's purposes, textual (string) data is delimited by 'single quotes' whereas numeral data requires no delimiters.
18	, (comma)	Paired with a space (part **19**), separates multiple data items in the second list.
19	(space)	
20	) (right parenthesis)	Closes the data items list.
21	;	Terminates the SQL query.
22	(Enter)	Terminates the INSERT statement.

Microsoft calls this statement INSERT INTO in its own documentation. However, the people who created the statement in the first place call it the INSERT statement. When you find references by Microsoft to INSERT INTO, they are referring to INSERT. (No reason is given why, by the same token, the deletion instruction isn't referred to as DELETE FROM.)

INSERT statement examples

Here's a simple SQL example that inserts a single record into a table. In this case, it's an inventory item:

```
INSERT INTO Inventory (ID, Category, Title, Cost, [Price Markup])
```

```
VALUES ('000242', 12, 'Trampoline', 124.90, 0.20);
```

Notice how numeral values generally do not have 'single quotes' for delimiters, but the ID number '000242' does have the quotes. In this case, the ID field is actually textual, and expects a six-digit – or more accurately, a six-character – string. Notice also two points of interest about the [Price Markup] field. First, it is a two-word field, which some database managers (DBMS) do allow, including Access. For SQL's purposes, however, the entire field name is delimited by [square brackets] because the name contains a space character. Also, note the value being assigned to [Price Markup], which reflects "20%." The true data value is two-tenths, which is less than one; but for the purposes of the DBMS, the zero is generally included to help identify the number as a numeral value, prior to the inclusion of the decimal point.

When you use the VALUES clause with the SQL INSERT statement, you're having the database server accept one new record into the named table. Another formation for the INSERT statement inserts the results of a SELECT query – however many there may be – into the named table. The result set for the SELECT query must be identical in structure (field names, field types, and any restrictions the DBMS may impose) to a record in the named table.

As an example of an embedded SELECT query in an INSERT statement, let's refer back to the Timestamp INNER JOIN example presented earlier. Suppose in the same schema that contains tables Employees and Timestamp, there is a third table Calendar whose record structure is identical to the result set of that SELECT statement. This result set may be appended in its entirety to the Calendar table by embedding the SELECT query in an INSERT statement, as follows:

```
INSERT INTO Calendar ([First Name], [Last Name], [Middle Initial],
 Enter, Exit)
  (SELECT Employee.[First Name], Employee.[Last Name],
   Employee.[Middle Initial], Timestamp.Enter, Timestamp.Exit
    FROM Employee INNER JOIN Timestamp
    ON Employee.ID = Timestamp.EmployeeID
    WHERE Timestamp.Enter >= #2/1/98#
     AND Timestamp.Exit <= #2/28/98#
    ORDER BY Timestamp.Enter);
```

Here, the field structure for Calendar is still presented explicitly. But the VALUES subclause is omitted, because explicit values are not being stated here. The only change that had to be made to the SELECT statement was a repositioning of the closing semicolon; for all SQL instructions, there is only one.

An UPDATE statement modifies existing records

In all cases, an INSERT statement generates at least one entirely new record, and places that record in a table. If existing data in a record is incorrect or invalid or outdated, an `INSERT` statement cannot correct that problem except if that record were explicitly deleted first. To use the `DELETE` statement and then the `INSERT` statement each time you wanted to perform a simple update could be the cause of significant headaches. Instead, you'll want to use one, and only one, `UPDATE` statement, whose syntax is presented below:

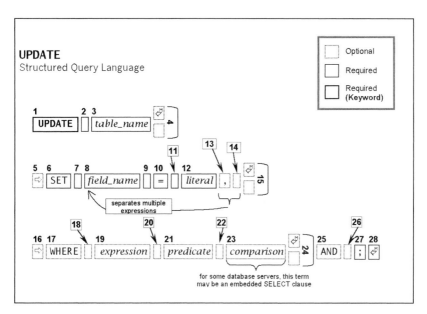

	Part	Description
1	UPDATE	Statement Directs the database server to amend certain records in the designated table (part **3**).
2	(space)	
3	*table_name*	Literal The name of the table whose records are to be changed.
4	(Enter) (space)	A carriage return aids in human readability of subclauses, though is not required. At least a space is required to separate the name of the table receiving updates (part **3**) from the beginning of the SET clause (part **6**).
5	(Tab)	Helps to isolate subclauses; not required.

6	SET	Clause Denotes the beginning of the portion of the statement where altered fields and new settings are to be listed.
7	(space)	
8	*field_name*	Variable The name of the column whose associated field name is to have its data replaced.
9	(space)	
10	=	Operator Forms an expression of assignment in which the data for each record whose field name is part **8**, is to be changed to the setting in part **12**.
11	(space)	
12	*literal*	Numeral or string The data which is to replace the existing data for the named field (part **8**), generally on the condition specified in the WHERE clause the begins with part **17**.
13	, (comma)	Paired with the space (part **14**), separates multiple expressions in the list.
14	(space)	
15	(Enter) (space)	A carriage return aids in human readability of subclauses, though is not required. At least a space is required to separate the final term on the previous line from the beginning of the WHERE clause (part **17**).
16	(Tab)	Aids in human readability of subclauses; not required.
17	WHERE	Clause Begins the clause where conditional criteria are specified. Only records that meet these criteria will have the designated fields (part **8**) updated.
18	(space)	

19 *expression*   Here, the expression most often used is a field name. The rule to remember here is that the field being referenced must belong to the designated table (part **3**).

---

20 (space)

---

21 *predicate*

=	In database terminology, the comparison operator is called a
<	*predicate*. Symbolic predicates are: < (less than or falls before), >
<=	(greater than or falls after), =, <>, <=, and >=. Terminological
=>	predicates are: BETWEEN (determines whether the object of the
>	comparison falls between two stated values), EXISTS (works like a
BETWEEN	function that returns True if the SELECT statement between its
EXISTS	parentheses returns any values), IN ("returns True" if the object of
IN	the comparison is reflected in the result of the dependent SELECT
LIKE	statement), LIKE (tests for similarity as well as equality), and NULL
NULL	("returns True" if no such data exists for the given subject). The
	Boolean operators AND, OR, and NOT are available for compound
	comparisons.

---

22 (space)

---

23 *comparison*   Data to which the *expression* (part **19**) is being compared. If the data is a field name, then that field must also belong to the designated table (part **3**). In other words, you can't perform a join operation entirely within a WHERE clause. **Update operations in SQL take place for records in one table at a time.**

---

24 (Enter)
     (space)   When multiple WHERE criteria are specified, an extra carriage return may be typed at this point to separate each criterion on its own line. If you don't type one, you do need at least a space to separate the term of comparison (part **23**) from the AND term (part **25**). If only one WHERE criterion is specified, neither of these is required.

---

25 AND   Used as a conjunction between multiple WHERE criteria, in cooperation with surrounding punctuation (parts **24** and **26**).

---

26 (space)

---

27 ;
     (semicolon)   Formally terminates the UPDATE statement.

---

28 (Enter)   Closes the instruction.

Rule: In the normal course of using SQL queries with Access, this carriage return is required. However, when posing an SQL query using VBA via DAO or ADO, the carriage return is not required; the Jet interpreter will actually add one on its own after the semicolon (part **27** of the UPDATE instruction).

UPDATE STATEMENT EXAMPLES

An extremely simple example of the UPDATE statement is the following:

```
UPDATE CustomerAccounts
  SET Credit = 0;
```

This statement will eliminate any credit applied to any people listed in the CustomerAccounts table. The DBMS assumes *any and all* people in this case because there is no WHERE clause; without filter criteria to go on, the DBMS will assume you mean *everyone.* There will be very few circumstances when you will ever need to update every record in a table all at once. Here's a practical amendment to this example:

```
UPDATE CustomerAccounts
  SET Credit = 0
  WHERE Credit < 0;
```

This statement only replaces data where a customer is shown to have "negative credit," or is actually owed money. The instruction eliminates your debt to these customers . . . at least in the database.

Here's a more complex example: Suppose you wish to issue $100 of credit for all customers who live in ZIP code 73112. This latter group may be symbolized by the following:

```
SELECT ZIPPostal
  FROM Customers
  WHERE ZIPPostal = '73112';
```

Here, the ZIPPostal field is the only one retrieved; and for the purposes of this example, it's the only one we need. We want to update only the records in

CustomerAccounts whose ZIP code is reflected in a different table, Customers, as '73112'. This may be accomplished with the following:

```
UPDATE CustomerAccounts
  SET Credit = (Credit + 100)
  WHERE CustomerID IN
    (SELECT ID, ZIPPostal
      FROM Customers
      WHERE ZIPPostal = '73112');
```

The key to how this instruction works is the IN predicate, which allows the comparison in the WHERE clause to test whether *all* of the entries for the CustomerID field match *any* of the entries in the Customers table that have the desired ZIP code. It's important to note here that not all DBMS servers will perform the arithmetic part of this operation SET Credit = (Credit + 100). However, Jet actually calls upon VBA to parse the arithmetic just as it would for an expression in a VBA program that uses VBA variables.

In this example, ID represents the key field for which the Customers table is indexed. The reason that an ID field was added to the embedded SELECT query was because the IN predicate only has the DBMS search for matches within the result set of the query, not within the entire record that matches the WHERE criteria. Had we left the selection subclause SELECT ZIPPostal . . ., then a match for CustomerID would not have been located. Here, CustomerID serves as a pointer from CustomerAccounts to each customer's entire vital statistics within Customers, eliminating the need to duplicate data such as last name or billing address.

The simple, but dangerous, DELETE statement

In SQL, you delete records by referring to the specific table to which they belong. This is important for a subtle, though profound, reason: **You cannot use SELECT to bring up a set of records from multiple tables, and have that result be deleted in one fell swoop.** In other words, you cannot use SQL to say to a DBMS, "Remember that query where you looked up all the people who overpaid their bills between March and April? Well, delete all those records pertaining to any of that business." The SQL DELETE statement addresses a single table specifically and directly.

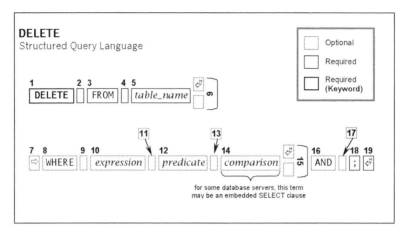

	Part	Description
1	DELETE	**Statement** Directs the database server to delete records from the designated table (part **5**).
2	(space)	
3	FROM	Separates the keyword (part **1**) from the table name (part **5**).
4	(space)	
5	*table_name*	**Literal** States the name within the active database schema of the table from which records are to be deleted. Records are always deleted in their entirety; therefore, the fields within those records do not need to be specified.
6	(Enter) (space)	A carriage return aids in human readability of subclauses, though is not required. At least a space is required to separate the name of the table where records are to be deleted (part **5**) from the beginning of the WHERE clause (part **7**).
7	WHERE	**Clause** Begins the clause where conditional criteria are specified. Only records that meet these criteria will be deleted.

8	(space)	
9	*expression*	With few exceptions, the name of a field belonging to the designated table (part **5**).
10	(space)	
11	*predicate* = < <= => > BETWEEN EXISTS IN LIKE NULL	Compares the expression (part **9**) to the subject of the comparison (part **13**). The True/False result of this comparison determines whether the record containing the field mentioned in part **9** will be marked for deletion. (Deletion takes place when all criteria are met.)
22	(space)	
23	*comparison*	Data to which the *expression* (part **19**) is being compared. If the data is a field name, then that field must also belong to the designated table (part **3**). In other words, you can't perform a join operation entirely within a WHERE clause. **Update operations in SQL take place for records in one table at a time.**
24	<u>(Enter)</u> (space)	When multiple WHERE criteria are specified, an extra carriage return may be typed at this point to separate each criterion on its own line. If you don't type one, you do need at least a space to separate the term of comparison (part **23**) from the AND term (part **25**). If only one WHERE criterion is specified, neither of these is required.
25	AND	Used as a conjunction between multiple WHERE criteria, in cooperation with surrounding punctuation (parts **24** and **26**).
26	(space)	
27	; (semicolon)	Formally terminates the UPDATE statement.

| 28 | (Enter) | Closes the instruction. |

Rule: In the normal course of using SQL queries with Access, this carriage return is required. However, when posing an SQL query using VBA via DAO or ADO, the carriage return is not required; the Jet interpreter will actually add one on its own after the semicolon (part **27** of the UPDATE instruction).

DELETE STATEMENT EXAMPLE

By nature, DELETE statements are generally very simple in and of themselves. The reason has solely to do with the fact that they are limited to deleting records from single tables based on criteria dealing only with those tables. For instance, the following deletes records from a table of customers whose last known contact was at the end of 1992:

```
DELETE FROM Customers
  WHERE DateOfContact <= #1/1/1993#;
```

Notice no fields are listed in the deletion portion of the statement; they're unnecessary. The statement always deletes entire records. Technically, you see, there's no way to truly delete (remove) a *part* of a record. The closest you can get to deleting just a field is to set its string contents to empty or its numeral contents to 0. For that, you need the UPDATE statement.

On Point

A join in SQL extracts the contents of designated fields from two or more tables, based on criteria that compare the contents of those tables to one another. Examples of indirect relations where join queries may apply are: customers who purchased a certain item, the impacts of recorded earthquakes on the economies of certain countries, the number of votes lost by a candidate to precincts where crime is not listed as the top issue in exit polls. Although a single form or report may be used to relate this data, it would not be wise to try to store individual records of these relationships in a single table because the number of records required to represent these relationships would be a product of the number of direct relations pertaining to one subject (customers, earthquakes, votes cast) multiplied by the number of direct relations pertaining to the other subject (purchases, economic performance, exit poll results).

A join query that trims the results to only those records where the indirect relationship makes sense is called an inner join. By comparison, an outer join includes records where the indirect relationship is not defined, in order to represent the fact that this relationship is indeed undefined. Representing undefined relationships requires the RDBMS to be able to store symbols for "undefined," "unknown," or null values. A union, by contrast to a join, is a combination of two subqueries whose result contains all the data pertaining to the tables referenced in both subqueries. The field names for the resulting records reflect the names for all the fields in both subqueries. Where no data exists for a field from one of the subqueries, that field is left empty.

In Theory: Renewing Old Relations

The history of computing is replete with instances in which merely adequate technology has been passed as exceptional technology under the pretext that little else exists in that technology's category with which to compare it.

Database management systems proved invaluable to computing only when it was finally realized what they truly were. No organization, save perhaps IBM and even then in its own permutation of English, professed the explicit need for such devices in the computing environment prior to their creation. The creator of the single most pervasive data format in computing is not Dr. E. F. Codd, but one C. Wayne Ratliff. He dubbed this format and its underlying system "Vulcan," after a certain science fiction hero with a penchant for recalling data off the top of his head. The explicitly stated initial purpose for "Vulcan" was to aid in the storage and recall of information copied from baseball and football cards. Since not all such cards are alike, Ratliff made it possible for the field names in his tables to be variable. Then he endowed his system with an underlying interpreted language based entirely on what he knew about database theory at the time, plus what information he lacked that he was able to fill in by approximation – the latter, by his own account, outweighing the former. On the advice of a colleague who said something to him on the order of, "Hey, you could make money off this thing!" Ratliff revised and repackaged his creation in a format more appealing to its new owners at Ashton-Tate: dBASE II.

One can only imagine how it must feel for another man's own life goal to be scored out from under him by someone else whose intentions were never as lofty to begin with. Since the proliferation of the dBASE format, E. F. Codd, the originator of the relational model – the document which many at IBM once believed would be the constitution for future operating systems – has spent much of his life backtracking. He has been demonstrating why the system that succeeded was not the one that should have, professing his 12 Rules for Database Systems to Qualify as Relational, and demonstrating why existing systems, including those that use the SQL language purportedly inspired by Codd, fail to follow those rules.

In 1987, Codd partnered with Chris J. Date to form Codd & Date, Ltd., a consulting and training firm with offices in London and San Diego. Date is the most widely published author on database technology in the world, as respected a source on database theory as is Will Durant on history and Carl Jung on psychology.

Since the founding of Codd & Date, Ltd., the database market has changed dramatically. On the low end, dBASE is a trademark of Borland International, and Borland International isn't even a trademark – in its place is something called Inprise, but something we tend to call "The Software Company Formerly Known as Borland." In the middle of the market, the key research in database technologies has not been in improving the fundamentals but in extending its Internet functionality. As a result, Lotus has effectively merged Domino with Notes (a job which, arguably, did not really require Superman) and IBM – Lotus' parent now – still has the venerable DB2, the most widely installed implementation of an SQL server. The face of DB2 was given a major overhaul in the fourth quarter of 1997, and is now optimized for network and internetwork access. But at the core, it is still DB2. On the high end, Informix, at one time an engineering powerhouse, is facing extinction as a brand name; and Oracle, the acknowledged leader of the top-of-the-line, is busy diversifying itself, having announced a partnership with Sun to develop modular computers that, the companies claim, do not require operating systems. (I suppose this makes some sense if you consider the idea behind this, as I do, to be suggestive of a lack of cogitative throughput on the part of its originators.)

Could there be an opening for an emergent, truly relational RDBMS? If so, Chris Date and Ted Codd aren't going to spoil their chances by announcing their plans to the world. No major manufacturer has expressed interest lately in an entirely new database scheme, mainly because they feel it is in their best interests to maintain the old formats for as long as possible. But this doesn't mean that some new player could not make an investment in Codd & Date's ideas, the sheer volume of which could fill some public libraries.

What would such a new relational system *be* . . . and what *wouldn't* it be? One thing is obvious: It would *not* be an OLE automation server addressed by a separate scripting language. That would violate several of Codd's 12 Rules (of which there are actually 13, if you count "Rule #0"). Among them: That the management of databases be facilitated entirely through relational capabilities (scripting languages are algebraic); unknown values or contents must be supported by null entries (Windows applications tend to address null entries in databases as empty strings, which end up at the top of a sorted list and are therefore not null), and that no other language be applied to the addressing and management of data than a relational language (so much for VBA).

What a new system *would* be, if you interpret Codd's work the way I do, is a system that is not bound to a native data format. It could employ its own native format, but it would not be restricted to that format. Furthermore, since data of all formats must be tabular (one of Codd's 12 Rules), there need be no special addressing scheme particular to any one format. Recall from earlier in this chapter, how ISAM-driven data files are treated differently from active ODBC databases. So the language used to address the data would reveal nothing about the format in which the data is stored, thus the user wouldn't have to care about formats anymore.

Which leads us to the fundamental impediment to such a system ever coming to fruition: A format-independent data processing application is contrary to the manner in which data is currently registered in Windows. This is of principal importance to the question of whether such an application could be expected to cooperate with other Windows applications, including Explorer. You see, in the Windows OLE system, *format implies ownership.* An Access 2000 database is an .MDB file, which has its own proprietary Microsoft format. In and of itself, that fact is harmless; but what makes Access 2000 *registered* in the OLE system of Windows as a database manager is the fact that its native format is the .MDB file. No other application can be registered to handle .MDB files, even if some other manufacturer of some program other than a database manager chose to use .MDB as its own associated filename extension.

In the OLE DB system, multiple database formats of every conceivable structure can be accessed through a "middleman" of sorts – an intermediary. To the client, all the accessible data appears to be of one format. That is because, in the client/server link that exists between this intermediary and the database client, the data truly is of one format. The conversion took place at the intermediary. Fine, then, problem solved . . . except for the fact that, rather than actually achieving format independence, such a system binds all known and unknown data formats and schemes to one proprietary, translatable form – the native format of the client. This is because there is still money to be made in the development of native formats.

We could end the story here, with one more roadblock imposed by Microsoft, willingly or unknowingly, against the progress of computing. Crane shot of two diligent, unfettered software engineers crouched at their desks, as we pull away from the window and over the rooftop, and watch the brilliant sun set over a magnificently framed San Diego beach. Another David and Goliath story for your collection. But I know better. This industry was built by men and women whose colossal ideas came from their own single heads, sometimes to reinvent our view of the world, sometimes to improve the way we account for our baseball cards. In any event, it was built not because the weather was fine, the world was flat, and all the people were happy. It was built because there were obstacles to be overcome, and only the hobbyists and the scientists knew what they were. You may see an impasse. I see an opportunity.

Gentlemen, whenever you're ready.

In Brief

- ◆ In the client/server model of database communication, the client initiates the transaction process. It is the server's job to act as respondent to clients rather than a catalyst of transactions.

- ◆ A database is based upon a schema that defines the relations between named elements. One instance of data whose content follows these relations is called a record. The set of all instances of data that follows these relations is called a table. A table is therefore more the product of a database than its foundation.

- ◆ When retrieving data based on one set of criteria from two or more tables, the tool SQL makes available to you is the join. The record set resulting from a join operation contains fields chosen from all the tables involved in the join process. A record set that contains absolutely all the fields is said to have been produced by an equijoin. A record set that contains all the fields from one table, and whose records match criteria that pertain to another table, is said to have been produced by an outer join. A record set that contains only those fields involved in the criteria is said to have been produced by an inner join.

- ◆ A union is a combination of data from two or more tables – a splicing together, if you will – without the use of criteria that apply to all of these tables mutually.

- ◆ The access method utilized by Jet is the Indexed Sequential Access Method (ISAM). This method maintains a "cursor" that moves through the contents of a retrieved record set like a phonograph needle over an album. The cursor may be moved forward or backward, or it can be made to search for a particular position in the record set by looking up that position in its index.

Chapter 17

Automating Data and Calculations with Excel

IN THIS CHAPTER

◆ A better understanding of Excel 2000's event-driven mechanics

◆ All of Excel's events that VBA recognizes

◆ Major events versus resonant events

◆ Applying style and color to cells logically

◆ The many ways VBA addresses a range of cells

◆ Why Excel projects often exceed the scope of just one module

◆ Linking event procedures of disparate classes via class modules

◆ Joining the object libraries of two Office 2000 applications

THE SPREADSHEET IS PERHAPS the single best idea in personal computing ever bought to fruition, arguably more so than the current graphical model presented by the Windows operating system. The spreadsheet model presents to the user a blank grid, capable in and of itself of nothing. What functionality the grid attains is equal to what the user assigns to it, in neat little bundles, at points chosen entirely by the user. It is the accountant's equivalent of the old Archer-Kit breadboards with which young hobbyists built their first crystal radio sets. All the basic mechanisms of computing are laid out neatly for the user to assemble harmlessly and without fear of combustion or catastrophe, into a working machine that the user can not only see, but, in a purely mental sense, feel.

Excel is the most mature incarnation of the idea that first took root in Dan Bricklin's and Bob Frankston's VisiCalc. Putting aside all the literary embellishment heaped on it by me (and others) through the years, Excel is a matrical calculator. For new users to be able to truly understand it, however, Excel has had to be defined in terms of what it is *not*. Excel is not a programming tool in and of itself, though many have professed their own programming skills – especially on their résumés – as having been acquired from Excel. It is not a database management system, though a significant number of real businesses in the world continue to use Excel, as well as other spreadsheet programs such as Lotus 1-2-3, for the storage of their critical data. It is not a presentation system, though millions made their investment in the first edition of the program because its pie charts were so impressive, especially with the 3D wedges. One wonders if Microsoft threw all these other application packages in with Excel, to truly do what users have tried to coerce Excel to do, simply to relieve undue stress on the poor product.

The Excel macro is no longer a recitation of the application's available commands from a recorded sequence. Instead, it has become an interpreted VBA program, capable of addressing Excel's components objectively, but also of building new functionality into the application that it does not contain by default. An Excel 2000 VBA module can enhance this system of operation in any of the following respects:

◆ It can be geared to respond to user actions in much the same way that the calculation engine already does, so that the worksheet may react in a manner that guides the user more directly, and is more conducive to fulfilling the operation at hand.

◆ It may serve as a mathematical function, rendering its results to an Excel formula.

◆ The module may act as a toolbar extension or menu command, with its own dialog box (`UserForm` object) for eliciting information from the user.

◆ It may provide supplementary functions to the user through the keyboard, such as the "Go Back" module presented as an example in Chapter 4.

◆ It may serve to rebuild the worksheet into a control panel of its own, with ActiveX controls embedded directly onto the worksheet, giving the worksheet more of the functionality of a Web page.

◆ The module can be used to automate the entry of data from a database, especially from the Jet database engine or from an ODBC driver, into a worksheet.

◆ It may serve as an *add-in workbook*, which contains all code but no visible worksheets or charts, to provide a library of functions to other modules or to Excel formulas in other workbooks.

Devising Custom Excel Functions

Perhaps the simplest VBA programs you may ever write for Excel will be *custom functions*, which are activated by references within cell formulas. The custom function is VBA's replacement for the old Excel macro. Its sole purpose is to return a single element of data — generally a numeric value — to the Excel cell formula that invokes it. Often a custom function may be as simple as a single procedure, though it certainly may make calls to other VBA procedures. But in the end, the structure that governs how the custom function works and how it progresses is a single `Public Function` procedure.

From VBA's point of view, the custom function is a `Public Function` procedure invoked in the midst of an arithmetic or logical expression. The procedure receives arguments just like any other VBA function procedure. VBA does not mandate that the procedure be structured any differently in order for it to be invoked directly from the worksheet rather than from elsewhere in VBA.

From Excel's point of view, the custom function is just another term in its repertoire. When Excel's formula interpreter encounters a foreign term, it first checks its native vocabulary to see if it matches one of its own intrinsic worksheet formulas. When it doesn't find the term there, Excel looks next to its set of installed add-ins for a match. Just before Excel concludes it's out of luck, it looks finally to the names of all the VBA `Public Function` procedures located within *general* (that is, non-object) modules for all open worksheets, including worksheet templates. Because Excel looks to all of these places for its formula names, **the name of your Excel VBA custom function need not follow any special rules of nomenclature,** other than the fact that it should not duplicate any existing Excel worksheet function.

Listing 17-1 presents an example of a custom function that utilizes a common accounting formula called the Sum of Years' Digits method of depreciation. The return value is the amount of an item's original purchase value that you would be allowed to depreciate from its actual value during a particular year of service. The function's three arguments are, in sequence, the purchase value of the item, the number of years you plan to utilize this item before its value is fully depreciated, and the specific year for which you require the depreciation amount.

Listing 17-1: A common single-procedure custom function.

```
Public Function DEPRECSDD(curAmount As Currency, iYears _
  As Integer, iWhich As Integer) As Currency
    Dim iNumerator As Integer, iDenominator As Integer
    Dim iCount As Integer

    iYears = Abs(iYears)
    iWhich = Abs(iWhich)
    If iWhich > iYears Then
        iWhich = iYears
    End If

    iNumerator = iYears - iWhich + 1
    For iCount = iYears To 1 Step -1
        iDenominator = iDenominator + iCount
    Next iCount

    DEPRECSDD = curAmount * (iNumerator / iDenominator)
End Function
```

A reference to a custom function within a worksheet formula should be treated exactly as though it were a function call in a VBA expression. Arguments are passed to the procedure within parentheses, separated by commas. Here's how a call to this function might appear within a cell:

```
=DEPRECSDD(A7, 10, 4)
```

Here is where VBA, in taking the cue from Excel's formula interpreter, is a bit more forgiving. The first argument in this instance is clearly a cell address, while the other two are literal numbers. Normally, VBA performs complete type checking when it receives arguments to a Function or Sub procedure; and in the heading for Listing 17-1, the arguments are clearly declared as types Currency, Integer, and Integer, respectively. But when the incoming argument to a custom function is a cell address – or, to put it in terms of Excel VBA, a Range class object – VBA accepts the argument as though it were the *contents* of the cell at that address rather than the address itself. So your custom function need not decipher whether an incoming argument is a reference or a *literal* – the value or string itself – before it acts on that data. That's a lot of coding you do not have to do.

Although VBA manages to achieve seamless integration with Excel with regard to formula translation, the boundaries between the two start to show with regard to error trapping. A normal Excel formula that contains only Excel's intrinsic worksheet functions is capable of rendering an error result, such as #REF! or #NAME?, clearly within the cell itself. So if a function is expecting a value for a certain argument, and the formula feeds it a string of text instead, the cell containing the formula will read #NAME? within the worksheet. When a VBA custom function comes into play within an Excel formula, if the arguments fed to the formula – whether directly or indirectly by cell address – are not of the declared type, Excel will graciously place a #VALUE! error marker in the cell. But besides type checking, suppose your formula needed to consider an argument erroneous for its own reasons, not just VBA's. There is no way for your custom function procedure to send a textual error message to the cell, like "#WHY?" or "#WHAT'S THIS MEAN?" Instead, your VBA formula will have to resort to VBA methodology, such as posting its own message box. Here's an example of a pair of VBA instructions that respond to a situation where the value of argument iThis has been found to be somehow invalid:

```
strError = "Invalid argument: " & Str$(iThis) & Chr$(13) & _
  "Result value will be invalid."
MsgBox strError
```

Of course, the problem remains that your function must still return some sort of value to the worksheet, because VBA cannot stop Excel from processing the formula except when a VBA error has been encountered. Listing 17-1 declared no "internal errors" for its own sake; after minor bits of correction such as making certain the second and third arguments are positive integers, the procedure merely presumed the arguments were valid. If, for some reason, invalid arguments of the *proper* type were entered into a custom function, it could, at best, set its own return value to 0 and exit, as in `DEPRECSDD = 0`. (`Null` would be a good alternative to 0 if you declare the `Function` procedure itself `As Variant`.)

When in doubt about how your custom function should handle arguments that aren't valid for the job at hand, and cannot be made valid, your best course of action – strangely enough – may be to just let it go. Your worksheet is in no danger of being adversely affected by a custom function. This is because **for custom function procedures only, Excel suspends all updates to worksheets, temporarily rendering them read-only for the duration of the procedure.** A custom function may not, therefore, alter the contents of its own cell or some other cell, or even any of the formatting characteristics of any range or the entire worksheet. All the worksheet's contents are locked tight until after processing of the cell formula has been completed in its entirety. So the worst that could happen is that the result of a formula might appear strange or meaningless to the user. In such a case, you do have the option of bringing up a message box explaining what's going on.

As stated earlier, when you declare an argument to a custom function procedure as one of VBA's standard types, such as `Double`, `Integer`, or `String`, if a call to this function is placed from a cell formula, and the data passed to this argument is a cell address, VBA will automatically retrieve the contents of the addressed cell without error. However, if you explicitly declare an argument to a custom function `As Range`, then Excel will expect only a cell address to be passed to it and not a literal value or string. In such a case, the variable representing the receiving argument will contain the address of the cell (or range of cells), and not the contents of that cell.

Excel's Event-Driven Mechanics

From an architectural standpoint, the spreadsheet is the quintessential event-driven application. In fact, if you think about it, most everything that Excel 2000 does is in *response* to something. Whereas the first PC programs gave the user numbered menus, drawing responses from the user, spreadsheets turn the tables, and compel the user to assemble a functional device from a wide assortment of calculation tools. In a very real sense, the designer of a working spreadsheet is the builder of a machine. The energy it consumes is data, and its work product is solutions.

When the user enters data into an Excel worksheet cell, she sets a complex process into motion, not unlike dropping the steel ball into the "Start" chute of a Rube Goldberg device. The calculation engine resolves the matter of which formulas have precedent over others, based on their chain of dependencies. In so doing, the application gains a clearer picture of the layout of this virtual machine, if you will. The engine provides power to the chain of calculations, and the work product shows up as solution data. It is the same process which required 1960s programmers to devote years of research and development, all completed by the everyday 1990s desktop computer user in a matter of minutes.

If you can imagine the Excel worksheet as a machine, then it should be easy for you to extend that image to include plug-in points, where planned and prerouted access to this machine is granted to the prospective programmer. The worksheet is already geared to respond to user events. Certain events among these are made accessible to the VBA programmer, as extensions of Excel's own event signals triggering the calculation engine into operation. VBA procedures may be "plugged into" these points of access, resulting in the user's natural actions triggering these procedures the same way they trigger the calculation engine.

Excel VBA procedures are geared to respond to events

When I talk about *events*, I'm referring to occurrences that an Office 2000 application is programmed to recognize. Excel relies upon these events to determine just what it is the user is doing. Because Excel doesn't specifically ask the user to do anything, and Excel also cannot "know" what it is a particular workbook or worksheet is having the user do, nearly all of its operations are contingent upon user interaction.

In trying to make the components of Excel programming seem more sensible to the programmer – more tangible, something upon which the programmer's mind can get a grasp – Microsoft has developed an environment of sorts in which these components reside and, in a less-than-fictional sense, interact with one another. For these components to be addressable by VBA, Microsoft has engineered them to be *objects*. In this context, an Excel object is a grouping of the program's own functions, addressable as though it were an independent entity. The most common, and perhaps most crucial, event that an object recognizes is being "clicked on," which VBA interprets as "receiving the `_Click` event."

All events recognized by Excel and the Chart object

What follows is a list of the events that the main objects in the Excel environment recognize. When you write a VBA module that gives the appearance of being tightly integrated into the active worksheet, you will want to take advantage of the VBA event procedures that respond to these events. Also in this list are some terms that I call "resonant events," which are recognized by higher class objects once the event procedure for the lower class object has terminated.

_ACTIVATE
Recognized by: Worksheet, Workbook, Chart

Description: Occurs when the object receives the focus. For a `Worksheet` class object, for instance, this happens when the cell pointer that indicates where newly typed data will appear, enters the area of the worksheet. For a `Workbook` class object, this occurs when a workbook is first loaded into the Excel workspace, or when the user has used the Window menu, or other means, to bring up an already loaded workbook. For a `Chart` class object that is a chart *sheet* and not an embedded chart, this occurs when the sheet becomes visible. For a `Chart` class object that is an embedded object in a worksheet, this occurs in either of these conditions: (a) when the user has clicked once on the chart (which, of course, assumes that the chart is already visible), just before the focus is given to the chart; or (b) when a VBA process gives the focus to the chart (although the `.Activate` method does not work for embedded charts).

RESONANT EVENTS `Workbook_SheetActivate Application_ =SheetActivate`
These echo events are recognized when both standard worksheets and chart sheets are made active, by the objects that contain them.

_ADDININSTALL
Recognized by: `Workbook`
   Description: Occurs when the workbook is marked as an *add-in* (its `.IsAddIn` property is set to `True`), and the user has loaded the workbook from the Tools→ Add-Ins menu. (See sidebar below.)

RESONANT EVENT   *Application_*`AddInInstall`

At Present: Adding in add-ins that aren't add-ins

Excel 2000, as well as other Microsoft applications including Office 2000, make available to the user certain functionality capsules called *add-ins*. These extension programs make it possible for a user to customize her copy of Excel. Perhaps more important, though, is that add-ins do not have to be loaded in. They enable certain functionality to be appended to the Excel package without all of that extra executable code having to be in memory, all the time, for every user.

Originally all add-ins, including one for ODBC links and another for data modeling and analysis, were written and compiled in C++ or Visual Basic Professional Edition. In other words, add-ins were all binary at first. Now, perhaps as an intriguing last-minute enhancement (that not all the documentation was caught up on), Excel workbook files with VBA modules built-in, can be loaded into memory as though they were Excel add-ins. These workbooks do not contain any visible sheets or charts, yet their VBA code remains executable, and addressable from within Excel formulas or other VBA modules in loaded workbooks.

Continued

At Present: Adding in add-ins that aren't add-ins
(continued)

Are these VBA workbooks really add-ins? An add-in workbook at first doesn't appear in the Add-ins list when the user first tries to load it from the Tools menu. To find the add-in workbook, the user has to click the Browse button on the Add-ins dialog box. VBA cannot automatically register "Add-in" workbooks within Excel's `AddIns` collection object, which lists all of the add-in components available to Excel whether they're loaded or not. But choosing an add-in file from a file selector does result in the add-in workbook being formally and permanently appended to the list. But when an add-in workbook is loaded into memory, it also gets registered as a member of Excel's `Workbooks` collection. What distinguishes it from the other workbooks is that its `.IsAddIn` property is set to `True`, so that it shows no visible worksheets.

_ADDINUNINSTALL
Recognized by: `Workbook`

Description: Occurs when the add-in workbook is checked off of the Add-Ins list and Excel is about to remove it from memory.

RESONANT EVENT   *Application*`_AddInUninstall`

_BEFORECLOSE
Recognized by: `Workbook`

Description: Occurs immediately after the user, or some other process, has directed Excel to close the antecedent workbook. The `Private Sub Workbook_BeforeClose()` event procedure gives your VBA program the opportunity to "tidy up" and save the workbook prior to closing, as well as enable the user the option of canceling the close process entirely.

ARGUMENTS

`Cancel`   A Boolean flag that, when set to `True` over the course of the procedure for this event, results in the workbook being left open. **Default value:** `False`.

RESONANT EVENT   *Application*`_BeforeClose`

_BEFOREDOUBLECLICK
Recognized by: `Worksheet`

Description: Recognized *when* the user double-clicks the worksheet (not before).

ARGUMENTS

Target   A Range class object that specifies the address of the cell in the approximate location of the double-click.

Cancel   A Boolean flag that, when set to True, results in whatever action that normally results from double-clicking on that portion of the worksheet that is being canceled. Generally, the resulting action is that the cursor is entered into the cell so that its contents may be edited; setting Cancel to True prevents this from happening, and may thus be used to "protect" the worksheet or regions of it.

RESONANT EVENT   Workbook_SheetBeforeDoubleClick
This resonant event is recognized for both Worksheet and Chart class objects.

_BEFOREDOUBLECLICK
Recognized by: Chart
   Description: Recognized *when* the user double-clicks the chart (not before).

ARGUMENTS

ElementID   One of 28 constants stating the category of the portion of the chart that was double-clicked on.

Arg1   A long integer that serves as an index pointing to which element, among others in its category, was double-clicked on (where applicable).

Arg2   A second long integer that is used by certain element categories as a secondary index. Unused by elements that do not require this index.

Cancel   A Boolean flag that, when set to True, results in whatever action that normally results from double-clicking on that portion of the chart being canceled.

RESONANT EVENT   Workbook_SheetBeforeDoubleClick

_BEFOREPRINT
Recognized by: Workbook
   Description: Recognized just prior to the commencement of a print process for the workbook.

ARGUMENT

Cancel   A Boolean flag that, when set to True, results in the print process
         being canceled.

RESONANT EVENT *Application*_SheetBeforePrint

_BEFORERIGHTCLICK
Recognized by: Worksheet, Chart
  Description: Recognized *when* the user right-clicks on the object (not before).

ARGUMENTS

Target   (Worksheet class only) A Range class object that specifies the address
         of the cell in the approximate location of the right-click.

Cancel   A Boolean flag that, when set to True, results in whatever action that
         normally results from right-clicking on that portion of the worksheet
         being canceled. Generally, the resulting action is the context menu
         popping up.

RESONANT EVENT Workbook_SheetBeforeRightClick

_BEFORESAVE
Recognized by: Workbook
  Description: Recognized just prior to the commencement of a save process for
the workbook.

ARGUMENTS

SaveAsUi   A Boolean flag that, when set to True over the course of the event
         procedure, results in the file selector for this workbook being
         displayed. **Default value:** Dependent on whether the workbook
         contents have changed since the last save.

Cancel   A Boolean flag that, when set to True over the course of the event
         procedure, results in the save process being canceled. **Default value:**
         False.

RESONANT EVENT *Application*_SheetBeforeSave

_CALCULATE
Recognized by: Worksheet, Chart

Description: Occurs whenever the calculation engine updates the current data for the object. For a `Worksheet` class object, this happens after the user has entered new contents into a cell, and has moved the cell pointer to a new location. For a `Chart` class object, this happens when the chart page is made visible once again, after the worksheet data on which the page is based has been updated.

RESONANT EVENT   *Application*_SheetCalculate

_CHANGE
Recognized by: Worksheet

Description: Occurs when the *contents* of at least one cell in the worksheet have been added or replaced, or when the cell pointer has moved from one location to another within the same worksheet. Changes to the *style* of a cell do not trigger the _Change event.

Exception: When a formula within a cell is edited or replaced with another formula, the _Change event *is not recognized*.

ARGUMENT

Target   A `Range` class object denoting the address of the cell or cells whose contents have changed. When multiple cells have been dragged or pasted to new locations, this argument reflects the entire area where the change takes place.

RESONANT EVENT   Workbook_SheetChange

_DEACTIVATE
Recognized by: Worksheet, Workbook, Chart

Description: Recognized by an object when the focus passes from it to another object, either in Excel or elsewhere in Windows.

RESONANT EVENTS

Workbook_SheetDeactivate
*Application*_SheetDeactivate

_DRAGOVER
Recognized by: Chart

Description: Recognized when a range of cells is being dragged over an embedded chart in a worksheet.

Embedded charts can only recognize events when a class module has been added to the module for that chart's containing workbook. The event procedure for the chart becomes part of its class module, as opposed to the ThisWorkbook module for the workbook containing the chart. It's a complicated matter, which will be discussed later in this chapter.

_DRAGPLOT

Recognized by: Chart

Description: Recognized when a range of cells is being dropped into an embedded chart in a worksheet.

_MOUSEDOWN

Recognized by: Chart

Description: Occurs when a mouse button is pressed while the pointer resides over the area of an embedded chart, after the chart has been given the focus.

ARGUMENTS

Button	A bitwise short integer that indicates which mouse button was pressed. Bit 0 – left; bit 1 – right; bit 2 – middle. These three base-2 values are added together for the final value; so if the left and right buttons were pressed simultaneously, the final value would be .
Shift	A bitwise short integer that indicates which extender key was pressed on the keyboard. Bit 0 – Shift; bit 1 – Ctrl; bit 2 – Alt. Again, base-2 values are combined for the final value.
X	A single-precision value representing the horizontal distance in points 1/72 of an inch) between the upper left corner of the chart and the mouse pointer's x-axis coordinate.
Y	A single-precision value representing the vertical distance in points between the upper left corner of the chart and the mouse pointer's y-axis coordinate.

_MOUSEMOVE

Recognized by: Chart

Description: Occurs when a change of position is registered for the mouse pointer while its "hot spot" resides over the embedded chart area. Arguments are the same as for the _MouseDown event.

_MOUSEUP

Recognized by: Chart

Description: Occurs when the mouse button is released while the pointer resides over the area of an embedded chart, after the chart has already been given the focus (the chart's _Activate event will already have fired). Arguments are the same as for the _MouseDown event.

_NEWSHEET

Recognized by: Workbook

Description: Occurs when the user has pulled up a new, blank worksheet from Excel's File → New menu.

ARGUMENT

Sh   An object reference to the new worksheet, which can either be a Worksheet class or Chart class object.

RESONANT EVENT   *Application_*WorkbookNewSheet

_NEWWORKBOOK

Recognized by: Application

Description: Occurs when the user has pulled up a new workbook with blank worksheets from Excel's File → New menu.

ARGUMENT

Wb   An object reference to the newly created Workbook class object.

_OPEN

Recognized by: Workbook

Description: Recognized immediately after all of the files, whose data comprise a workbook, have been loaded into memory. At this time, the contents of the workbook have yet to be made visible to the user. This gives a Private Sub Workbook_Open() event procedure the opportunity to make adjustments to those contents "behind the curtain."

For Excel 2000, Private Sub Workbook_Open() is the rough equivalent of the "AUTOEXEC" macro for a workbook, to borrow an old term from DOS.

RESONANT EVENT   *Application_WorkbookOpen*

_RESIZE
Recognized by: Chart

   Description: Occurs immediately after the user, or some other process, has altered the size of an embedded chart. This event does not occur when the *position* of the chart is changed.

_SELECT
Recognized by: Chart

   Description: Occurs after an element of a chart, such as the plot area, one of the axes, the legend, or a data series, has been "selected," or indicated with a series of square handles along its perimeter.

ARGUMENTS

ElementID	One of 28 constants stating the category of the portion of the chart that was selected.
Arg1	A long integer that serves as an index which points to which element, among others in its category, was selected (where applicable).
Arg2	A second long integer that is used by certain element categories as a secondary index. Unused by elements that do not require this index.

_SELECTIONCHANGE
Recognized by: Worksheet

   Description: Occurs when the range of cells indicated by a cell pointer changes, either by moving from one cell to another, or by expanding to indicate multiple cells.

ARGUMENT

Target A Range class object that specifies the address for the new selected cell or range.

RESONANT EVENT   Workbook_SheetSelectionChange

_SERIESCHANGE
Recognized by: Chart

   Description: Recognized when the value of a point represented on the chart is changed through the chart, not through the worksheet.

ARGUMENTS

SeriesIndex   A long integer that represents the series in the Series collection that is being changed, where 1 is the first series in the collection. Most charts generally plot one series against one set of values; charts, however, may plot more than one series (set of bars or graph line).

PointsIndex   A long integer that represents the point in the Points collection that is being changed, where 1 is the first point in the collection. A point represents a value on a chart.

_WINDOWACTIVATE

Recognized by: Workbook, Application

   Description: Occurs when a window belonging to the workbook is given the focus.

ARGUMENTS

Wb   (Application class only) A Workbook class object reference to the workbook associated with the window that has just been activated.

Wn   A Window class object reference to the window that has just been activated.

_WINDOWDEACTIVATE

Recognized by: Workbook, Application

   Description: Occurs when a window belonging to the workbook loses the focus. Arguments are the same as for the _WindowActivate event.

_WINDOWRESIZE

Recognized by: Workbook, Application

   Description: Occurs when a window belonging to the workbook has been resized. Arguments are the same as for the _WindowActivate event.

Considerations when working with Excel events

As mentioned previously, **arguments are passed to an event procedure not by a VBA procedure call, but by the VBA interpreter itself.** Think of them as messages from Excel, or whatever application owns the interpreter. So the names that are given to arguments, such as Target and SeriesIndex, may be safely changed, though their declared types may not be.

By "resonant events," we're referring to events with pretty much the same purposes as those that precede them, and that are handled by objects higher up in the object model, after the lower objects have had their turn at bat. For instance, the `Worksheet_SelectionChange` event is followed by a resonant event, `Workbook_SheetSelectionChange`. In this case, as with the others, the resonant event takes one more argument at the beginning of its list: a reference to the object that originally received the event. For `Private Sub Worksheet_SelectionChange()`, the first argument becomes `Sh`, a `Worksheet` class reference to the worksheet in which the selection change took place.

Why are there resonant events in the first place? Because there may be certain processes you will need to program that only make sense in the context of one worksheet, as well as others that make sense in the broader context of an entire workbook. In the case of the changed selection event pair, you might have a process that checks over the contents of all changed cells, for purposes of validation or transaction recording. If the process only matters insofar as a certain worksheet is concerned, then it should be assigned to the `_SelectionChange` event procedure of that worksheet. However, if the validation process should extend over the entire workbook, you would use the *workbook's* `_SheetSelectionChange` event instead. You would still have the `Sh` reference available to you. This is so you can have a single workbook event procedure that can ascertain what change was made and why, while maintaining access to a pointer showing you *where* it was made. If your process is immaterial to the workbook at large, it doesn't belong in the workbook's VBA module.

An example of a reactionary procedure

For quite some time, I've used Excel worksheets in which I embedded the basic color of the digits that make up the values for the cells inside the cell format descriptor. When I'm tracking changes in stock prices, for instance, the number format I use for the change in value column is this:

```
[Green]+# ?/?;[Red]-# ?/?;[Black]"UNCH"
```

Excel divides format descriptors into as many as three segments, with a semicolon used as the segment delimiter. When two segments exist, the first describes the formatting that Excel will apply to positive values or zero, and the second describes formatting applied to negative values. When three segments exist, the third describes how Excel will treat true zero values. By "true zero," I mean not null or not empty, when the value in the cell is zero *for a reason* as opposed to by default.

The main purpose for number formats is to represent the appearance of the data, not the appearance of the area in which it appears. Yet, in the example above, positive fractions show up as green text, negative fractions in red, and all zeroes are changed to the abbreviation `UNCH` in black. Whenever a worksheet calculates the value for a cell with this number format, the color is automatically applied.

At Present: Excel's more conservative styles

In Word 2000, a style describes the attributes used for a paragraph of text, or for characters typed into a paragraph. Word defines a style by building a complete set of attributes and calling that set Normal. From there, any other style may be an extension of the attributes given to Normal, or an extension of some other extension of Normal, and so on.

Excel 2000's implementation of styles is less similar to Word's than you might expect. Every style is a list of changes made to the existing format of the cell, *but not necessarily a complete list.* The Normal style in Excel generally takes into account the main six attribute categories: number format, alignment, font, perimeter borders, interior shading, and protection status in case the worksheet is ever locked. But neither Normal nor any other style has to take these categories into account if you so deem. **Those attributes of a cell or range that an applied style does not take into account, it leaves as they are.** So if a cell contained a percentage that included the %, and a style applied to that cell did not take into account the number format category, then the percentage would remain. On the other side of the equation, a user can change the attributes of a cell formatted with a particular style, and the cell will continue to be registered as having that style.

Suppose we wanted to take this idea a few steps further. For a long column of cells that reads + 1/2, + 1 3/8, - 1/4, UNCH, and so on, it would help the human reader if the *background* color of these cells were tinted in accordance with the "weight" of their value changes. For example, + 1/2 would show up on a slightly greenish background, while + 1 3/8 would show up in a bright green cell. Cells with negative values would be tinted more toward red. There's no way to embed the background color for a cell into its number format. A VBA procedure can set the background color, but we want it set immediately after the value of the cell changes.

Listing 17-2 is a self-contained event procedure that handles the background formatting. It uses the _Change event of a worksheet as an indicator of whether a value has changed anywhere in that worksheet. From there, it relies upon a specific style name as an indicator of which cells in the worksheet hold fractional value changes.

Listing 17-2: An automatic cell color tinter.

```
Private Sub Worksheet_Change(ByVal Target As Excel.Range)
    Dim sAmt As Single, iAmt As Integer, iBlend As Integer
    Dim iRHue As Integer, iGHue As Integer, iBHue As Integer
    Dim iRBld As Integer, iGBld As Integer, iBBld As Integer
    Dim celThis As Range
```

Continued

Listing 17-2: An automatic cell color tinter. *(continued)*

```
For Each celThis In Target.Cells
    If celThis.Value <> "" Then
        If IsNumeric(celThis.Value) And celThis.Style = _
        "StockChange" Then
            sAmt = celThis.Value
            If Abs(sAmt) > 2.5 Then
                sAmt = 2.5 * Sgn(sAmt)
            End If
            iAmt = Abs(Int(sAmt * 50))
            iBlend = Abs(Int(sAmt * 100))
            If sAmt > 0 Then
                iGHue = 255
                iGBld = 192
                iRHue = 255 - iAmt
                iRBld = 255 - iBlend
                iBHue = 255 - iAmt
                iBBld = 255 - iBlend
            ElseIf sAmt < 0 Then
                iRHue = 255
                iRBld = 192
                iGHue = 255 - iAmt
                iGBld = 255 - iBlend
                iBHue = 255 - iAmt
                iBBld = 255 - iBlend
            Else
                iRHue = 255
                iGHue = 255
                iBHue = 255
                iRBld = 255
                iGBld = 255
                iBBld = 255
            End If
            Select Case Abs(sAmt)
                Case Is > 2
                    celThis.Interior.Pattern = xlPatternSolid
                Case Is > 1.5
                    celThis.Interior.Pattern = xlPatternGray75
                Case Is > 1
                    celThis.Interior.Pattern = xlPatternGray50
                Case Is > 0.75
                    celThis.Interior.Pattern = xlPatternGray25
                Case Is > 0.5
                    celThis.Interior.Pattern = xlPatternGray16
                Case Is > 0.25
                    celThis.Interior.Pattern = xlPatternGray8
```

```
                End Select
                celThis.Interior.Color = RGB(iRHue, iGHue, iBHue)
                celThis.Interior.PatternColor = RGB(iRBld, _
                iGBld, iBBld)
            End If
        Else
            If celThis.Style = "StockChange" Then celThis.Style _
              ="StockChange"
        End If
    Next celThis
End Sub
```

A majority of the variables in this procedure are for mixing colors, which even on the most color-capable displays is not an easy process. As you'll see a bit later, Excel's background colors are mixtures of two simple solid colors in bitmapped patterns.

The _Change event procedure's single incoming argument is Target, which is a Range class object. On entering this procedure, Target represents all of the cells whose contents may have, or probably have, changed. A user can't type data into more than one cell at the same time (at least, not without some help with a very sophisticated VBA procedure), but a paste or drag-and-drop operation can change a set of cells simultaneously. So the cell range represented by Target can be a plurality. For this reason, a For Each...Next loop is employed to count through the Cells collection belonging to Target. Similar to the way a Range object in Word 2000 has constituent Paragraphs and Sentences, a Range object in Excel 2000 has constituent Cells.

This may seem peculiar, but by addressing the members of the Cells collection individually, we avoid having to refer to them by their worksheet cell address, such as E17 or QW45. In fact, nowhere in this entire procedure do we ever refer to any specific cell address; yet in worksheet formulas, cell addresses are the only way you can refer to cells. Addresses act in place of variables in cell formulas. This brings us to a crucial realization about the nature of Excel 2000 VBA modules and projects: **Excel worksheets are adept enough at calculation that they do not require VBA to assist them in that department.** Frankly, VBA is a far less capable calculation engine than Excel itself. What VBA can do is automate processes, to move and change things that math alone cannot do.

In our For...Each loop of Listing 17-2, variable celThis acts as a reference to each member of Target.Cells in turn. For a cell to qualify for a background change, it must pass three tests: First, it has to contain something – or, to characterize it the way VBA seems to imply, "not to contain nothing." The "not nothing" test here is If celThis.Value <> "". Here the .Value property is actually referring to the *visible contents* of the cell, as I explain in more detail in a few paragraphs. The contents of the cell are assessed *now*; which means that the change made to the cell contents have officially taken place at this point. If there's no visible contents ("") in the cell, it could be because the user deleted whatever contents were there before.

The second test a cell must pass is whether the value has *value*. Excel provides a function of its own for this test, `IsNumeric()`, which returns a Boolean True or False reflecting whether the single argument is a number and not a string. This is important here, because the background pattern the procedure builds for each cell is dependent entirely upon the *numeric* value of its contents. The third test, and perhaps the most important, is whether the name of the style applied to the cell or range is `StockChange`. Cells with any other style name should be left alone.

 The job of responding to an entry into a cell by painting the cell an appropriate color, can only be handled by an event procedure such as `Private Sub Worksheet_Change()`. If you try to use a custom function procedure for this purpose, your color-changing instructions will not generate an error — they just won't work. The contents of a worksheet are on "lockdown" while Excel evaluates the cell formula. These contents come off "lockdown" immediately afterwards; and at that point, VBA begins recognizing events.

Color mixtures and the Interior object

Excel 2000, no matter how many colors your copy of Windows uses, recognizes only 64 colors by number, some of which actually end up being the same shade of gray. As a result, true color gradation with Excel is a tricky business. Excel builds a background out of two separate hues from its 64-color palette. One of these hues is painted on solidly then the second is painted on top using a bitmap pattern – not unlike airbrushing through a stencil full of polka dots.

The background appearance for any `Range` class object is addressable through its constituent `Interior` object. Think of `Interior` as the representative for the graphical portion of the cell range. The three properties of `Interior` that are of interest to us here are `.Color` (the solid first coat), `.PatternColor` (the stenciled second coat), and `.Pattern` (the style of the bitmap used for the stencil). The two color properties may be expressed as results of the `RGB()` function, whose arguments are intensity values for red, green, and blue, ranging from 0 to 255. Unfortunately, Excel applies the hue from its 64-color palette that most closely approximates (to it) the 1-in-16.7 million color result of the `RGB()` function, otherwise we wouldn't be bothering with this color mixing scheme in the first place.

Next, the numeric value of the cell is copied into a single-precision variable `sAmt`. From this, two integer values are generated, `iAmt` and `iBlend`, which are used in mixing the solid color and the pattern color, respectively. Both colors are mixtures of triplets of intensity values. With 255 being as light – as close to white – as possible, a color is mixed closer to one of the major hues by *removing* light from the other two hues. The equations for `iAmt` and `iBlend` calculate the amount of light to remove, to vary the light from white back toward green (positive values) or red (negative values). Remember that color values for graphical displays are mixed using the laws of optics, not pigment; so green is a primary color, which when mixed with red makes yellow.

The `Select Case` clause in Listing 17-2 selects the "stencil," to continue the analogy, used in mixing the pattern color against the solid color. There is no logical scale for the patterns in Excel's repertoire; they're just all given numbers, and those numbers are each given constants, and who cares what the values of those constants are as long as the constants are always available to you? The "blend" color is a little darker than the "solid" color for any one mixture; so the higher the `sAmt` value, the heavier the pattern is for the blend color.

Near the end of Listing 17-2, the `Else` side of the conditional clause describes what Excel is to do when it encounters a cell that failed the first test: whether it was not empty. If it is empty, then perhaps the cell or range had contents a while ago, so we should interpret this as a user's directive to delete cell contents. When the user does that, we don't want to leave the backgrounds of these cells colored as they are.

Earlier I mentioned how cells formatted with a particular style but which have had their attributes altered somehow, continue to be registered as having the original style name. This partly explains the curious instruction `If celThis.Style = "StockChange" Then celThis.Style = "StockChange"`. At first glance, it seems pointless — almost like saying, "If it dies, it dies." The instruction does not give away its true intention, however: I want all cells in the range that were formatted with style `StockChange` to begin with, to revert to the original form of that style. Doing so would cancel out through the `.Color`, `.Pattern`, and `.PatternColor` properties. So the same equation that tests whether a range was formatted with a certain style originally, changes or no, is used to assign the original style back to the range. At this point, I have definitely failed the Kemeny & Kurtz test for a BASIC program's human legibility, but such is the price of progress.

How Excel's Range class works

If you're a veteran of Chapters 12 through 14, you may remember how Word 2000 used a `Range` class to refer to any given passage of text. At this point, you may as well disavow any memory of those chapters, because Excel 2000's own `Range` class object is identical in name only. Notice how Excel applies the antecedent of the `Range` class in the argument `Excel.Range`. An Excel `Range` is precisely what an Excel user would expect it to be: a range of cells. But in the Excel 2000 object library, a range can be *one or more* cells. All the important characteristics of those cells — their contents, their addresses, their formulas, the style of text, the style of background — are all encapsulated by the `Range` class. Mind you, `Range` is not the variable; in and of itself, `Range` does not have any value, contents, or constituents. Instead, `Range` is used to cast a new object variable into a specific mold. What is sometimes difficult to remember in the course of programming, though, is the fact that ranges in VBA are not necessarily pluralities. In other words, **any object that can represent the characteristics of just one cell may still qualify as a member of** Excel's `Range` **class.**

Just as certain words in the English language, such as "move" and "play," have definitions both as nouns and as verbs, the term Range in Excel 2000 has definitions both as a class and as an object of its own. As a constituent object, Range serves to draw a box of sorts around a group of cells, and then represent the shared characteristics of those cells as a Range class object. Yes, this makes Range a Range class object.

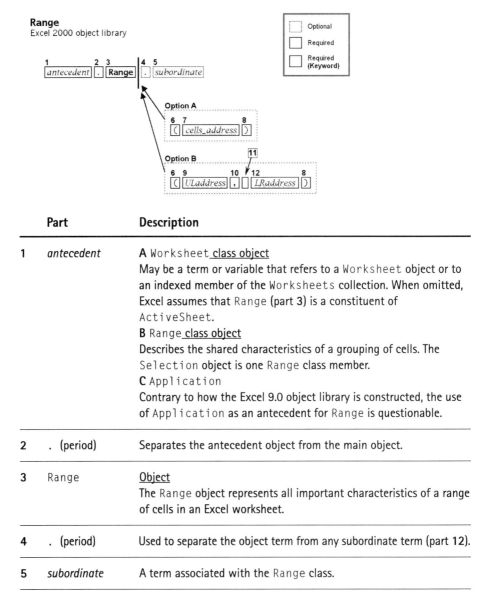

Part		Description
1	*antecedent*	A Worksheet <u>class object</u> May be a term or variable that refers to a Worksheet object or to an indexed member of the Worksheets collection. When omitted, Excel assumes that Range (part **3**) is a constituent of ActiveSheet. **B** Range <u>class object</u> Describes the shared characteristics of a grouping of cells. The Selection object is one Range class member. **C** Application Contrary to how the Excel 9.0 object library is constructed, the use of Application as an antecedent for Range is questionable.
2	. (period)	Separates the antecedent object from the main object.
3	Range	<u>Object</u> The Range object represents all important characteristics of a range of cells in an Excel worksheet.
4	. (period)	Used to separate the object term from any subordinate term (part **12**).
5	*subordinate*	A term associated with the Range class.

Part		Description
6	((left parenthesis)	Begins an optional segment where the range in question is defined specifically, either by means of a cell address or two ranges that represent the upper left and lower right corners of a block of cells.
7	*cells_address*	<u>String</u> Evaluates to an Excel range address. Here, a range is defined as any grouping of cells that can be represented using a single address, as in A1:G17. When the *antecedent* (part 1) is a Worksheet class object, this range refers to a regulated location on that worksheet. However, when part 1 is a Range class object, this range specifies an address relative to the construction of the range itself, where A1 points to the upper-left corner of the range, regardless of its location in any worksheet to which the range may belong.
8	) (right parenthesis)	Terminates the optional index.
9	*ULaddress*	**A** Range <u>class object</u> Represents the cell at the upper left corner of this range. Here, a member of the Cells collection could be used to refer to the cell, where Cells(2, 6) would refer to the worksheet cell F2.
B <u>String</u>		Represents the location of a cell in the worksheet — generally one cell. If this range is a plurality, then Excel "pays attention" only to the cell in the upper left corner of this range.
10	\, (comma)	
11	(space)	
12	*LRaddress*	**A** Range <u>class object</u> Represents the cell at the lower right corner of this range. **B** <u>String</u> Denotes the cell address of the lower right corner of this range in the worksheet. If this range is a plurality, then Excel "pays attention" only to the cell in the lower right corner of this range. **Examples:** Range(Cells(1, 1), Cells (4, 2)) is the equivalent of A1:B4. Range("A1:B4", "N5:Q6") is the equivalent of A1:Q6.

The true value of a cell

The .Value property of a cell represents its *visible* contents – the data which the user sees on the face of the worksheet. Its meaning is a bit blurry, because a cell's "value" can be textual. The rules for this property are as follows:

◆ If the true contents of a cell are numeric – for example, input data as opposed to a formula – then its .Value property evaluates to that number, excluding the format in which it appears. So a cell containing the "3.14159" has a .Value property of 3.14159, while "$34.95" evaluates to 34.95, and "12%" to 0.12. The exception involves dates on the calendar. **If a cell's number format is for the printing of dates (for instance, d mmm yy) then the .Value property for that cell evaluates to a date rather than a raw number.** So a cell showing "12/2/96" has a .Value property of 12/2/96. Excel maintains a mirror property .Value2 in case you actually require the raw numeral that represents that date in Excel (if you ever do, please write and tell me why). So for "12/2/96," the .Value2 property of the cell is 35401.

◆ If a cell's true contents are textual, then the .Value property for that cell will be a string.

◆ If a cell contains a formula, then the .Value property for that cell will contain the results of that formula. Meanwhile, the .Formula property for that cell will contain the text of that formula.

The Parts of an Excel Project

Table 17-1 dealt with four classes of objects that make up the backbone of Excel programming. As with the other Office 2000 applications, the Application object is near the top of the order, just beneath the Excel object. Within Excel itself, the Excel term isn't specified; but if you were addressing the Excel object library from within another application, you would need to specify Excel.Application explicitly.

The upper tiers of the Excel object hierarchy

In Excel 2000, so-called worksheets (Microsoft doesn't call them "spreadsheets") are contained within so-called workbooks; thus a Workbook class object is said to contain a Worksheet class object as its constituent. Separate VBA code modules exist for both workbooks and worksheets. Figure 17-1 shows a fully extended Project window from an Excel VBA workspace so you can get a better idea of how the Excel component parts are organized.

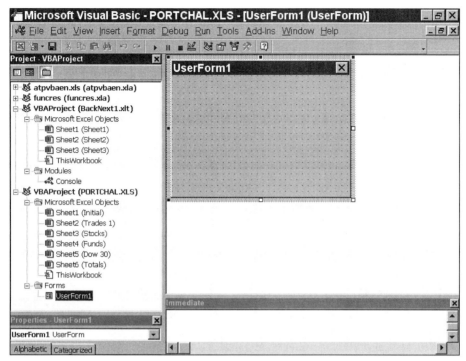

Figure 17-1: A fully loaded Excel 2000 VBA Project window.

In Figure 17-1, each open workbook has its own boldfaced listing in the first tier. The listing shows the name of the workbook as VBA expects to see it (`VBAProject` by default), followed by its filename – how the Excel application expects to see it – in parentheses. The four subordinate categories are as follows:

◆ **Microsoft Excel Objects** (always present) contain the VBA modules for all objects *native to the Excel application* that can receive their own events. Workbooks, worksheets, and chart *sheets* (not embedded charts) are objects that the Excel application knows how to deal with on an equal footing. As for everything else, VBA has to give Excel a little education. Each group so-named contains as many worksheet modules as there are worksheets, and as many chart sheet modules as there are chart sheets. There is also one module, referred to by VBA and by the Projects window as `ThisWorkbook`, that contains event procedures for the `Workbook` class plus any other procedures that may be contacted by those event procedures.

◆ **Modules** is a poorly named category (since all the contained objects are modules anyway) that consists of general procedure modules. These contain VBA procedures that do not pertain to any specific object nor respond to any recognized event. Instead, they are callable in the standard fashion by whatever names you've arbitrarily given them. General procedures intended to be called from outside of their given module – for instance, by another module, or by the Excel user through a toolbar button or the Macros list – are declared `Public`.

♦ **Forms** are `UserForm` modules that contain procedures specific to the execution of a custom window or dialog box. A VBA form is made up of graphical controls, all of which receive events and some of which receive direct input from the user. These controls are based around a form component whose object class is `UserForm`.

♦ **Class modules** are separate modules that define for Excel's purposes the behavior of a *redefined* class of object. Object types that are not native to the Excel application (believe it or not, embedded charts are one example) require class modules in order to give the workbook and worksheet modules a handle on what these classes are.

Why only the higher class objects receive events

Not all of the Excel objects – for instance, worksheet cells – recognize their own events. This is not a problem, because the user can only click one cell at a time anyway. To be conservative, rather than make VBA maintain a series of individual objects for the most indivisible of sensitive objects – in this case, cells – Excel gives event procedures arguments that point to the index number of the object in question in its given collection, or if the object is a cell or cells, to its worksheet range address when it's possible for the event to involve more than one cell.

In Depth: The extra control in the Toolbox

If you've been programming with the VBA environment for more than one O2K application, you may have noticed there's one extra control in the Toolbox for Excel than there is for other applications. The RefEdit control, as it has unfortunately been dubbed, is not a member of the Forms 2.0 suite; it's provided by a separate ActiveX control. However, its functionality is based entirely on the text box control in Forms 2.0 – a superset of the text box.

In many Excel dialog boxes, the user has the option of clicking on a button to the right of a text box. In response, the dialog collapses to show just the RefEdit control, and drops to a *modeless* state that allows the user an opportunity to select a range from the active workbook. The address of the selected range is immediately echoed into the control. Then to bring the dialog box back, the user clicks on the same button. This saves the user having to drop out of the dialog box to recall a needed range address, or to have to recall that address from memory.

The RefEdit control you can drop into your own form modules is exactly this control — it isn't something made to work *like* the control, it *is* that control. You do not have to write any code yourself to make the collapsing effect work; RefEdit takes care of this behavior automatically. However, it does no type checking to make certain anything that the user types into it is a range address — your code will need to perform that job. Think of RefEdit as a text box that has this one extraordinary ability. By the way, this ability is recognized by RefEdit as one exclusive event, `DropButtonClick`. This event is recognized exclusively for the drop button, while its `_Click` event applies to the remainder of the area of the control. The `DropButtonClick` event term is the only member of the RefEdit vocabulary that you need to know, besides those terms that it already shares with the text box control.

Linking Excel to Shared Objects

A chart, like a worksheet, is a registered type of data component. Although it appears to the user to be produced by Microsoft Excel, it is actually a product of a separate shared component. The workbook as an object is really a container that brings worksheets and charts together. From the point of view of Object Linking and Embedding, Excel charts and Excel worksheets are on equal footing with one another. The Excel application, however, views them differently, because while a chart does allow itself to be contained by a workbook, it may also be embedded in a worksheet, and the converse is not true.

The strange truth about charts

This results in the chart mechanism finding itself in an odd situation with regard to VBA. As you saw earlier, `Chart` class objects do receive events, just like the other major objects in the Excel library. But to get VBA to recognize them, since a chart is an object, you need to enlist the services of a class module. It is much too cumbersome to use an ordinary object module like `ThisWorkbook`, because even though you can declare an object reference such as `Private WithEvents chartThis As Chart`, your reference can only refer to one chart, and for each other chart in your workbook, you'd need a separate reference. This is because you can't declare an array `WithEvents`. Then each chart reference could be set, using the `Set` statement, as early as possible — probably within `Private Sub Workbook_Open()` — to refer to each chart specifically. Each chart would have its own exclusive set of event procedures — which is probably not what you want, because when you want to define new functionality for charts, you're probably thinking of "charts" as plural, not singular.

By contrast, you can devise a class module that contains one set of event procedures — and even property and method procedures, if you want to go that far with it — that may pertain to any number of charts in your workbook. You may then add a procedure that cycles through all the existing charts by number, and "attaches" them, if you will, to your extended chart class.

The process of introducing a chart class module to a project is not exactly simple, and more than a bit cumbersome:

1. Using the Projects window, right-click on the name of the project where the workbook that contains the chart is located, and from the popup menu select Insert, followed by Class Module. VBA will add a new class module to the Projects window, and a blank code window will appear in the VBA workspace.

2. In the Properties window, change the .Name property of the class module from Class1 to a unique name that will identify the chart class among other classes available to the project. **This will be the name that identifies the chart class to the other VBA modules.**

3. In the code window, add one instruction to the Declarations section. This instruction will declare that the class being defined here is really a chart. Here's an example:

```
Public WithEvents chartClass As Chart
```

Yes, we're breaking the rule about object modules not declaring public references. This is an exception, because your class module is extending the existing functionality of the Chart class; and other outside procedures will need to declare objects that connect to the Chart class that's supported by your class module. The Public declaration makes the class module officially visible to all the other modules. WithEvents is important because it enables the class module to notify the other modules to count its internal event procedures as part of the class, not just properties and methods. (You can define properties and methods for class modules, but that's for another time.) As Chart denotes that this class module is based on Excel's Chart class. The name chosen for this example is chartClass, though you can apply your own name here. **This will be the name that identifies the chart class to *this* class module, and that will be used as the class name within the module.** No other modules will recognize this name.

4. Write a procedure that the workbook's VBA module will execute early on, that enrolls all existing embedded charts and/or chart sheets as members of your new class.

You will be thankful that I did not leave Step 4 for you as an exercise. The way Microsoft would have you approach Step 4, you would have to write new VBA code each time the user added a new chart to any point in the workbook. This is because the Microsoft methodology advises you to specify each chart to be enrolled by its specific index number, which is a fact that you as programmer cannot know unless and until all of the charts exist. Since it's preferable for the VBA code for a workbook to exist prior to the advent of all the other data in the workbook, what you need is a VBA procedure that ascertains how many charts there are, and enrolls them wherever they may be. What I came up with isn't pretty, but what I had to start with was quite ugly, to say the least.

To start, you insert a class module into your current project. For this example, I named this class module `ChartEnhanced` in the Properties window. Next, you write this instruction in the Declarations section of the `ThisWorkbook` module where all your charts utilizing the enhanced class will be located:

```
Dim ChartEmbeds() As New ChartEnhanced, ChartSheets() As New _
   ChartEnhanced
```

Notice we're declaring dynamic arrays, which are currently of indeterminate size, full of objects of a `New` class. Here `New` does not refer to the fact that the class is new. It means that you are invoking objects of this class *right now*, rather than just building references to objects that will be assigned to them later. At this point, the arrays officially contain objects of type `ChartEnhanced`. Seem sensible? Absolutely not! Recall that declaring variables with closed parentheses ( ) is a signal to VBA that the number of elements in the array will be determined *later*. But the `New` parts of this instruction state to VBA that we're calling real objects, not references to objects, into existence *now*, for what Microsoft calls "early binding." It should not be possible, were common sense to be employed evenly over all of VBA programming, for you to be able to dynamically invoke an *indeterminate* amount of any given class, let alone one defined by the project itself. If you read the documentation literally, you'd conclude that the above instruction is entirely impossible. But here it is, and it works fine.

Why do we need this instruction the way it's written, with the `New` keyword? Because these variables will be used in `Set` statements that refer to these object variables' *constituents*, not just to the variables themselves. For the variables to have constituents, they must be real objects and not just references to objects.

In case you've forgotten, or joined us late, our intention here is to enroll all the charts in an Excel workbook as members of a class defined by VBA code, so that `Chart` events can be recognized. There's no other way to go about this. The procedure that does the job of making the `Chart` objects sensitive to events needs to go in a position where it can be executed early, and automatically. This means that you need an event procedure.

Could you conceivably write a procedure that enrolls a chart in a new class whenever it's activated? No, because for that to be possible the `_Activate` event for `Chart` class objects would need to be recognized, and for that you'd need the class module — which would leave us in an infinite loop. In addition to the fact that including an event procedure within the VBA module for each *worksheet* would be inconvenient, there is the more important fact that it is also impossible; there is no "AUTOEXEC" event for a *worksheet*. There is one, however, for a *workbook*. Such an event procedure would make the `Workbook` class the default, which is not bad because that gives you a way to address each worksheet in a workbook individually. Listing 17-3 shows the procedure I came up with, which you can copy into any workbook module (listed at the bottom of the group beneath the "Microsoft Excel Objects" tier in the Projects window) and leave as is, without any need for modification or customization.

Listing 17-3: Enrolling existing charts as enhanced chart objects.

```
Private Sub Workbook_Open()
    Dim iCount As Integer, iTotal As Integer
    Dim wksThis As Worksheet

    For Each wksThis In Me.Worksheets
        For iCount = 1 To wksThis.ChartObjects.Count
            iTotal = iTotal + 1
            ReDim Preserve ChartEmbeds(iTotal)
            Set ChartEmbeds(iTotal).chartClass = _
            wksThis.ChartObjects(iCount).Chart
        Next iCount
    Next wksThis

    ReDim ChartSheets(Me.Charts.Count)
    For iCount = 1 To Me.Charts.Count
        Set ChartSheets(iCount).chartClass = Me.Charts(iCount)
    Next iCount
End Sub
```

In short, this procedure enrolls all of the embedded charts in all of the worksheets in the workbook first, then enrolls all of the stand-alone chart sheets. The first For Each...Next loop counts through all of the Worksheet class constituents of the Workbook class object that is the default for this procedure. Which one is that? Me, of course. Me is VBA's internal *reflexive reference* to the default object of a procedure. Here it refers back to whatever Workbook class object to which this procedure belongs.

The embedded For...Next loop counts by index number through all of the ChartObject class objects associated with the worksheet. A ChartObject class object is a container for an embedded chart; it is not the chart itself. Why isn't a Chart class object contained directly by a worksheet? Because a chart is really designed to stand alone as a sheet in and of itself, not to interlock with a worksheet. The ChartObject class acts as a sort of converter, making the Chart class compatible with the Worksheet class. There is always a correspondence of one ChartObject per Chart, and that Chart class object is a formal constituent of the ChartObject class object.

Indexing each ChartObject is a tricky matter. A worksheet may have any number of embedded charts. We could have declared ChartEmbeds() as a two-dimensional array, with the first index referring to the worksheet number and the second referring to the ChartObject number. But all two-dimensional arrays in VBA are "square;"

which is to say, the highest-numbered second index is shared among all members of the first index, or rather, each row is always so many columns wide. The second index would have to have been declared as large as the largest number of ChartObject class objects for any one worksheet, which would have resulted in several unused array entries that referred to non-existent charts.

The alternative we chose here is not optimal, but it will work for now. A ticker variable iTotal counts each new ChartObject it runs across throughout the entire workbook. Each time a new ChartObject is found, the .chartClass constituent of the next available ChartEmbeds() entry is assigned to point to the Chart constituent of the ChartObject. This is confusing, so I'll write it out slowly: The embedded loop looks for embedded charts, and when it finds one, it increments iTotal. This number is then used as an index that identifies the entry in ChartEmbeds() with which the loop is concerned at the time. So what's .chartClass? Look back at Step 3 in the numbered list a few pages back. It's the same as the variable used in the class module to refer to the instance of that object class throughout that module. Notice that the variable chartClass was declared there As Chart. This makes .chartClass (with the period) a Chart class constituent of whatever variable is declared As ChartEnhanced.

The second loop clause in Listing 17-3 is simpler; it assigns the .chartClass constituents of all the members of the ChartSheets() array to refer to all of the Chart class constituents of the workbook. **A direct Chart class constituent of a workbook is a stand-alone sheet, not an embedded chart.**

To summarize, here are the connections that needed to be drawn between terms in order to link events to the Chart class objects:

◆ The .Name property of the class module that will contain chart events becomes the class name used to declare object variables in other modules.

◆ The variable name declared within the class module to refer to the class, becomes the name of the constituent of the class name within those other modules.

◆ A chart within an Excel workbook is "made live" by using the Set statement to equate the constituent name associated with a declared object variable with the chart name.

What happens to the array variables from here? Frankly, not necessarily anything at all. Equating the variables' .chartClass constituents with the Chart class objects made it possible for event procedures to be executed from within the class module. But it probably isn't realistic for you to use these variables any further to refer to the charts, since Excel makes the Charts collection available to you persistently anyway.

Now that we've gone through all this trouble, what's a good example of an event procedure for a chart? Excel 2000 already echoes changes in the plot points of a chart within their associated data in the worksheets, so that functionality has already been accomplished. One very simple, but perhaps very important, response to an event may be to prevent a chart from being edited by the user, by canceling the double-click:

```
Private Sub chartClass_BeforeDoubleClick(ByVal ElementID As _
  Long, ByVal Arg1 As Long, ByVal Arg2 As Long, Cancel As Boolean)
    Cancel = True
End Sub
```

How an Application is like a Chart

It might surprise you to know that Excel's own `Application` object faces the same dilemma as does `Chart` class objects: Its events need to be introduced to a VBA project by way of a class module.

What am I talking about? Suppose your Excel workbook was getting its data from an outside source, such as an Access database. Rather than bring in an entire table, which may take up a lot of room in a worksheet, this workbook generates fresh queries or filters, and updates the sheet accordingly with more concise data. This would turn the worksheet into something like a very elaborate dialog box for the Excel database, which means that you need some core code that is sensitive to user events, not unlike the event procedures for a `UserForm` object.

Excel's `Application` object does not present its events to a workbook automatically. The formal way to introduce an application to its events is by constructing another class module (separate from the `Chart` class module) that contains event procedures for an `Application` class object. The process this time is somewhat simpler:

1. Using the Projects window, right-click on the name of the project where the class module for application events will be located, and from the popup menu select Insert, followed by Class Module.

2. In the Properties window, change the `.Name` property of the new class module from `Class1` to a unique name that will identify the `Application` class module. You might want to use Hungarian Notation here to help you distinguish the locally enhanced application from the `Application` object itself, or else give your class module a name that Excel's programmers would never have used — for instance, `OneClassApp`. You'll recognize this name as something *you* did rather than Microsoft.

3. In the blank code window for the class module, add one instruction to the Declarations section, such as:

   ```
   Public WithEvents AppGrabber As Application
   ```

   This variable `AppGrabber` will represent the `Application` class within the class module, and will also serve as `OneClassApp`'s `Application` class constituent for the other modules in the project. This constituent is needed to act as a "plug-in," if you will, for the `Application` that the other modules in the project will recognize.

4. Within a module whose code will be executed early – I prefer the workbook module under "Microsoft Excel Objects" – in its Declarations section, declare an object variable as a member of the newly created class. For instance:

```
Dim YourApp As New OneClassApp
```

5. Within an early procedure, such as `Private Sub Workbook_Open()`, connect the `.AppGrabber` constituent of `YourApp` to the real Excel `Application` object; for instance:

```
Set YourApp.AppGrabber = Application
```

Now, within the `OneClassApp` class module, you'll be able to write event procedures that apply to the `Application` class,for events generated by all of the worksheets in the project to which the class module belongs.

Making Application events available to one module

There is a simpler method for introducing an application to its own events, one that does not involve class modules at all: Choose a module that will contain event procedures that will be recognized by the `Application` class object while the workbook is running – preferably the workbook module for the project. Within the Declarations section for that module (at the top), declare an object variable like this:

```
Private WithEvents appThis As Excel.Application
```

Yes, we did not break the object-export rule here, thank you very much. It's important that this declaration include `WithEvents` because it makes the events associated with the `Application` class (or here, the `Excel.Application` class for added clarity) available to this module. When you pull down the Object drop-down list (the one on the left) above the code window, you'll see the variable that you declared – in this case, `appThis` – as one of the objects. After you choose that, the Procedure list on the right will show all the events available to that object variable, just as though that variable were a native part of Excel.

There is, however, one more step to making those event procedures actually be executed; although you can write event procedures this way just fine, they won't run until VBA sees that the object variable `appThis` and the running application really are the same. You see, you only declared the variable's *type* As `Excel.Application`, but you haven't yet assigned to it the `Application` object. So in `Private Sub Workbook_Open()`, as near the top of the procedure as possible, add an instruction like this:

```
Set appThis = Excel.Application
```

Now the events recognized by Excel will actually trigger your event procedures.

Making someone else's events available to a module

From our Mad Sorcery Department: Notice how deftly I added the identifier `Excel` to the object `Application` to distinguish it from other possible `Application` objects. Could I have grafted some other Office 2000 object identifier to the declaration and assignment, and *make the events of some other open Office 2000 application accessible to Excel?*

Believe it or not, I can. However, there's one more step in the process: When you open the code for one of the modules into VBA's active window and then select References from VBA's Tools menu, you see a list of object libraries installed on your local system. Under "M" for "Microsoft," you'll find references to the other object libraries in O2KOM.

By checking the reference for "Microsoft Word 9.0 Object Library," you open a once-locked drawer and uncover the barren, unassembled mechanism for some devilish potential lab experiments. The way you establish links for these references is very similar to the shorthand process for `Excel.Application` just described: In the Declarations section of the workbook module that will house the Excel procedures for the Word events, add an instruction like this:

```
Public WithEvents appWord2K As Word.Application
```

Next, in the `Public Sub Workbook_Open()` event procedure of the same module, insert an instruction like this:

```
Set appNotThis = Word.Application
```

Because we checked Word's object library in the References list, we can use `Word` as an identifier; omitting this identifier from the assignment and from the declaration before it has the same effect as writing `Excel`. Now we can use Word's own events to notify Excel of what's happening within Word.

Globalizing class modules, as much as possible

Unfortunately, a VBA class module is only accessible to the project in which it appears. In other words, just because a class module exists within the VBA workspace does not render it available to every open workbook. For the functionality of a class module to be usable by more than one project, its code must be imported into more than one class module.

This is not too difficult a process. Once you've fully programmed a class module, you can right-click its name in the Projects window, select Export File from the context menu, and designate a separate file where you want the source code for the object library to be stored for the future. From then on, you can import that source code into a newly created class module for any project in which you require the same functionality. Once you've inserted the blank class module, right-click its title in the Projects window, and from the Context menu select Import File. From the file selector point to the location of the .CLS file where the class module's source code is stored.

On Point

Excel 2000 is a far more event-driven application than the other applications in the Office 2000 suite, primarily because the purpose of a spreadsheet is to ascertain functionality directly from its user through interaction. Excel has four main objects that are sensitive to events: Application, which represents Excel's primary automation server; Workbook, which represents a grouping of worksheets and chart sheets; Worksheet, which represents the functionality built into one sheet; and Chart, which may represent either a chart sheet or the functions of an embedded chart.

The Application and Chart objects do not have modules of their own in Excel. For that reason, their functionality has to be linked into workbook, worksheet, and independent modules through outside means. For Chart class objects, a class module may be constructed that presents the event procedures and other instructions for one or more Excel charts, embedded or stand-alone. Linking these class modules is accomplished by declaring a Public variable with the WithEvents qualifier, within the Declarations section of the module that will be utilizing this chart class, then using the Set statement to assign the chart class to all the charts that qualify. For linking in Application events, a similar process is required: Declare a Public variable of Application class, then assign it to point to Excel.Application. Curiously enough, this process can be used to "graft" one automation server to another, or at least give the appearance of doing so, by changing Excel.Application to Word.Application or PowerPoint.Application, or to the name of any other automation server that recognizes an Application object.

 VBA procedures can be linked directly to new or existing Excel toolbars. The Excel object library maintains a CommandBars collection that describes all of the toolbars the application has ever used. An .Add method brings in a new toolbar that can be described entirely in code. Handler procedures, instead of event procedures, are employed to respond to the user operating added toolbars or toolbar controls; this replaces the need for the user to link controls to macros. The names of these handler procedures are assigned as string literals to the .OnAction properties of the indexed Controls contained within the CommandBars collection.

In Theory: The Very First Argument

The need for programs to make contact with other programs did not present itself, logically enough, until it became feasible for more than one program to share the same processor. UNIX was the operating system that formalized the concept of multiple concurrent processes, and that defined "true multitasking" for the world. Prior to the widespread adoption of UNIX, interprocess communication did exist, but only within the limited confines of laboratories and universities – which in the United States in the 1960s and 1970s were generally the same place.

But the engineers who made UNIX work (perhaps I should capitalize all the words in that phrase) did not commence their job with the original idea, "Hey, let's make many programs run asynchronously on the same processor!" Instead, as they were developing UNIX's built-in programming language that is now known as C, the lead engineers realized that running function x concurrently with function y would be a convenience. Imagine a C program like one long ribbon. UNIX engineers realized this ribbon might flow more efficiently and not unravel itself out of control if it were folded into segments that overlapped one another at points. The way C works in UNIX, multiple C functions from several files grouped together form, from the point of view of the C *linker*, one long program anyway. So the fact that there really are multiple programs ends up being a trick of observation in UNIX; if you imagine all the functions unlinked, you really do see separate programs, but the linker doesn't see them that way.

Considered in that light, there are several incarnations of programming languages that preceded C, which, if the UNIX paradigm applied to them, would be multitasking systems to one degree or another. So at what point did it first become conceivable for programs to become concurrent and asynchronous?

It became conceivable when the framework of formal mathematics was first introduced to programming, once programming languages became complex enough that mathematical principles could be applied to them. The idea of formal functions that had names, that operated on a set of arguments separated by commas, and that represented their own result values within a formula, predates computers by perhaps a few centuries. But the first signal that these principles could be applied to computing flickered into existence in 1955 in Darmstadt, West Germany, at a conference attended by members of five major consortia assembled by what was then called the German Association for Applied Mathematics and Mechanics (which was called GAAMM or GAMM by English-speaking members, though among citizens of *Deutscheland* was called. . . well, something else). To be honest, the conference became formal after it was realized that the mathematicians who threw the party, and the engineers who attended the party, had something in common.

The conference came to this conclusion: Since math was an international language, but written language was not, computing language can be made more international by making it more *conventional* – that is to say, make it follow established mathematical principles. With that goal in mind, in 1957, the committee suggested to the president of the Association for Computing Machinery, Professor John W. Carr, III, that a joint conference be formed with the intention of developing a single international computing language that everyone in the world could embrace.

Which is not at all what they ended up doing. You see, while the name "ACM" at that time commanded the prestige and respect among colleges and universities that such names as Nike and Adidas command among colleges and universities today, ACM and its subordinate organizations were all *nonprofit*. They required funding from the outside world. Perhaps the occasional donation from the computing giants (IBM, GE, RCA, Sperry) were accepted, but not too large, and not enough for any one company to hold title to the products of their work. Instead, they relied upon one organization, recognized everywhere as the one source of funds that would not place undue, unfair, or self-serving demands on the individuals responsible for producing a final product: The United Nations.

You see, one of the UN's charter missions was the establishment of committees that enabled member countries to share their peaceful technologies with one another peacefully. But the United Nations (at one time, if you can believe it, the moral equivalent of the World Bank) did not fund mathematics. From the UN's perspective, math was already well funded, thank you very much, by the universities of the world, which, after all, charged their students literally *hundreds* of dollars in tuition fees. In order for UNESCO to approve funding for this international programming language, it could not look too much like math, even though German mathematicians were responsible for the idea. The *mechanical* aspects of the new language had to be advertised. Because the UN has always maintained a tight budget, the committees responsible for approving or rejecting funding for this computing project were made up mainly of mechanical and electrical engineers . . . with backgrounds in communications.

So the reason why computing principles were originally seeded into the first programming languages where named functions were employed was partly to advance the art of programming, and partly to acquire the funding to produce the thing in the first place. ALGOL (Algorithmic Language), developed by the UN-funded conference co-headed by GAMM and the ACM, never actually ended up as a full-fledged programming language. Its keywords, in keeping with the principles of *communications*, were English; after all, the international language of the airwaves for pilots and amateur radio operators was English. ALGOL became a *platform* for the construction of programming languages and systems, rather than a programming language in its own right. But *several hundred* programming languages were formed that were based on the principles of ALGOL. FORTRAN, officially the first true formula translator, was one of them. BASIC was another. And so was C. And C++. And Java.

The impact of the United Nations on the way we as a people communicate with one another using machines, and on the way we compute, is far greater than may ever be attained by Microsoft, Compaq, IBM, Intel, or The Artisans Formerly Known as Bell Labs. Because international organizations once funded the fundamental ideas responsible for the development of a technology, there had to be a convergence of mindsets among proponents from different fields in order for their ideas to address the broadest body of potential yes-voters. Today, the UN still funds some developments, but far fewer than before because it is now a widely held belief that Private Enterprise (perhaps I should not capitalize the words in that phrase) holds the key to all ingenuity.

Which brings me to this progress report on the state of technology: The next generation of internetworking technology is crawling along, mainly due to the fact that government agencies are unwilling to fund private projects that yield too little obvious political benefit, and private agencies are unwilling to fund revolutionary technologies that may too rapidly obsolete those that still reap significant returns on their investment. The communications system that links the world's computers is susceptible to threats from pre-teens in their basements with the capability to jeopardize the financial accounts of entire countries, as well as the occasional Ditch-Witch that accidentally drills into a backbone line in search of the source of a gas leak. The time between the idea for it being tossed around at a skiing party and the first implementation of ALGOL 58, is one-half the span of time between the first line of code written for the Windows 95 operating system, and the last line of code written for its final bug fix prior to Windows 98.

In 1955, somebody realized that communications was the key to computing. For the record, his name was John W. Backus. In the intervening decades, that realization has had to come to light again, and again, and yet again. It makes one wonder if the complete privatization of an inherently public enterprise is such a good idea after all.

In Brief

♦ The simplest Excel VBA procedures are Public Function procedures geared to accept their input from worksheet cells, and to present their output to at least one cell if not many.

♦ Much of Excel's VBA functionality is geared to respond to events recognized by the `Workbook` class.

♦ The Interior object represents the nonanalytical, nonformulaic content of any and all cells in a worksheet – for instance, its background and border colors.

♦ Excel's version of the `Range` class object refers to a block of cells. The properties of the `Range` class object represent the uniform characteristics of all of the cells in that range; and if two or more cells in the range do not share those characteristics, the property setting for the range may be `Null`.

♦ The `Chart` object is provided by a shared library, but is maintained by Excel. Still, it does not have its own object module in VBA, although with a little work, a class module for charts can be developed.

Chapter 18

Automating Access Transactions

IN THIS CHAPTER

♦ The differences with programming in the Access/VBA environment

♦ Defining the schema of a database

♦ Conceptualization of databases with the goal of normalization

♦ The constituent collections of Data Access Objects

♦ The member objects of ActiveX Data Objects

♦ The constitution of an Access/VBA module

♦ Access' exclusive terminology

♦ Logging onto database sessions or workspaces

♦ Determining when to rely upon Jet, and when to circumvent it with ODBCDirect

VBA MODULES AND projects serve as the basis for extending the functionality of Word, Excel, and PowerPoint. By contrast, a VBA module may act as the core process of an Access 2000 application. Or not.

The novice Access user is taught that the general automation of the database system is accomplished through the Access macro language. As you may recall from earlier in the book, Access macros and VBA modules are separate entities, as a shopping list is separate from a sonnet. Ordinary storage and retrieval operations, and simple form-based operations, can indeed be automated entirely through Access macros. The "language" of this system includes the everyday Access commands, which are phrased in tokenized form, and written in sequence on a device that looks curiously like an Excel worksheet. These macros can place calls and pass arguments to VBA procedures, so Access VBA procedures can continue to play the limited role that they play in other Office 2000 applications. But VBA can assume the entire database automation and management role. The majority of this chapter deals with VBA as the core process provider for Access 2000.

On Point

Modern databases are composed of tables that provide regulated mechanisms for logically relating data. Information that applies to multiple items in a finite number of given ways can be stored as records, using that same number of fields per record. A record may be likened to a row in a table, whereas a category of information may be likened to a column. A category of item that may appear in a record is called a field.

A query generates a separate set of records, or an informal table, based on the contents of other tables or sets of records to which it refers. The records in the product set contain data that meet criteria put forth in the query, as expressions or parameters. The Structured Query Language (SQL) poses query criteria in an expression-like manner called a predicate. Any number of such predicates may be found in SQL's SELECT statement, which is its only statement for record retrieval, and whose syntax is extremely versatile and simple to read, if not always to write.

The Access VBA Work Environment

Unlike the other Office 2000 applications, with Access, VBA is seated at the front of the table. While it's entirely possible to generate a reasonable data-in/data-out application using Access and conventional macros, the need for a truly interactive database application makes Access into a thinner shell wrapped around VBA functionality.

The six categories of Access objects represented here are as follows:

Tables   Lists the source data for the application. The contents of queries and views are produced by data retrieved from these tables.

Queries   Lists the views of records and tables whose data is produced as the results of processed queries. The Queries list is not a list of queries. Go figure.

Forms   Lists forms (I'd better be explicit about that now) produced with the database controls provided by Access. These are *not* the Forms 2.0 controls used by VBA with other O2K applications.

Reports   Lists documents formatted for printing, which may also contain Access controls when shown in an on-screen context.

Pages	Shows all forms associated with the database that are geared for deployment over the Web or an intranet, and that are stored as HTML pages. Called "Data Access Pages" by Microsoft, these are basically Web pages that utilize the new XML standard for isolating and identifying data fields on a page.
Macros	Shows all of the *macro sheets*, which are data sheets (not unlike Excel worksheets) into which Access macro instructions are written. The language here is a tokenized form of the commands executed by an everyday Access user, with some parameters added to bypass the use of dialog boxes.
Modules	Shows the names for VBA modules addressed by the objects and macros in the schema.

Notice that macros and modules are given two separate tabs in the Database window. Macro instructions can place calls to VBA modules, and even pass arguments to them. Yet they are separate entities from one another, presumably because macros are supposed to be easier to develop to the programming newcomer. (Why limited systems are necessarily deemed easier has always been a mystery to me.)

The Access application and Access, the application

If you think about it, an Access 2000 VBA project is truly an *Access application*, so that is what I will call it in this context. The interpreter of an Access application is actually Jet, which is a small and portable relational database management system (RDBMS). Jet serves as the engine for processing and managing the data associated with the Access application.

As a true application, the Access VBA program follows the rules with which any such body of code is constructed. The first rule is that the application's data is constructed first; and with Access, that fact is placed in front of our noses. The Access application should have a core process that outlines when data is to be retrieved and stored; that process is constructed next. Patterns of user interaction are modeled and *then* they are implemented as forms.

Access has its own forms, reports, and data sheets that are all used as both input and output devices. Access' own object library is responsible for representing these visual devices, not some dynamic link library from the outside world such as Forms 2.0. In order for a VBA program to utilize Access' intrinsic forms, the container application for Access (ACCESS.EXE) must be active. But you do not have to be "in" Access to use Jet; any other O2K application — or any other programming environment, for that matter — may build forms to use with Jet using the Forms 2.0 library. The differences between using Access and Jet and using Jet and Forms 2.0, are surprisingly slight.

What goes into an Access VBA program

In place of the "project" concept, each Access database maintains its own less regulated set of modules. Here, there are only two types of modules. A *general module*, which contains procedures accessible by name explicitly, and a *class module*, which contains event procedures that respond to user interaction with forms, reports, or controls. All of these modules are listed under the Modules tab in Access' Database window, and the names for these modules are entirely arbitrary.

Procedures that pertain to Access graphic objects, such as controls, are automatically located in class modules. These so-called *event procedures* respond to the behavior of these controls and to what the user does with them, and also change their content and general appearance. Class modules are the only containers that are designated to contain certain types of object-oriented procedures. Event procedures within a class module are triggered in response to user events that take place with respect to the controls on an Access form or report. Each form or report is apportioned no more than one class module, and may not have a class module at all if its events are handled by macros instead. **Access expects its controls' events to be handled by macros, not VBA procedures.** Because of this "either/or" state of affairs, Access has to be informed as to which system is responsible for handling the event.

Figure 18-1 shows Access in the midst of the design process for its own native forms. Next to the form under construction is Access' version of the Properties window. Here the third tab from the left is the Events tab. **Access controls have properties that designate which process is responsible for handling particular events.** The names of all of the events recognized by the indicated control in the form appear in the Events tab. Each field beside the name is a combo box which, when you give it the cursor and click on the down arrow, lists the names of all of the macros addressable within this schema. Access macros do not have to be named in any particular manner to qualify as event handlers; they just have to be named *something*.

At the top of this list, however, is an entry marked **[Event Procedure]**. When you choose this, Access knows not to look for a macro as the event handler for this control, and instead to look in the class module for the appropriately named VBA procedure. Access event procedures *do* follow the naming convention of event procedures throughout VBA. The name, or `.Name` property, of the control or class of object that contains these controls (usually the form or report) makes up the first part of the event procedure name, and is then followed by the name of the event, separated by an underscore character. The procedure is declared as a `Private Sub`, and may receive arguments passed to it by the VBA interpreter. These arguments serve as parameters, designating how VBA should handle the event.

Figure 18-1: Designating the event handler process in Access.

Access manages its own forms and controls

Access 2000's native forms are not UserForm objects of the type used by the VBA interpreters of other O2K applications. Likewise, the controls in an Access form are not provided by the Forms 2.0 object library. Controls and their containers used within Access are supplied by Access. You can develop UserForm-based form modules within Access VBA, but their functionality will not be quite as specialized as Access' native forms. Thankfully, the terms associated with Access forms and controls are much the same as those used throughout the rest of VBA, with some exceptions worth noting. Mainly, **Access forms and controls are so-called bound objects.** Rather than simply assigning a string literal or variable to a text box, an Access text box is directly associated with a field in a data table. This way, when the local view of the data changes, so does the field, and so then does the text box associated with that field.

When you start designing a new form, a dialog box presents you with a combo box that lists the tables and query result sets, or views, in the current schema. You choose the source data from this combo box before you can even begin building the form; so **all Access forms are bound to source data.** This makes all of the fields in the source tables and views accessible to all of the textual controls.

The Properties window in Access has five tabbed categories, the second of which is Data. You bind a textual or data output control to a field in a table by setting the `.ControlSource` property to the name of the field. If you leave this setting blank, VBA instructions may still be responsible for generating the contents of this field. But once you have bound a control to a field, updates to that control's contents become automatic. Binding of this nature frees a control from the need for macro- or VBA-initiated updates. Forms 2.0 controls also support their own `.Control Source` property, which does permit binding between control and data to take place. As I stated, the differences are slight, if sometimes non-existent.

The loose nature of general procedures

There are very few specific rules or restrictions pertaining to the nature or number of VBA procedures that may comprise a general module. Clustering procedures together within a single general module does make it possible for procedures to place calls to one another, and to share module-level variables with one another. Declaring a variable `Public` within the Declarations section of one module does make that variable accessible to all modules, so there is a cross-modular scope for Access applications. If two or more module-level variables, each in its own module, share the same name, then whenever your code needs to access the specific variable with the conflicting name belonging to the *other* module, it can identify that variable by stating the name of its module before the variable name, separated from it by a period; for instance, `Module2.lTop` as opposed to just `lTop`.

For the purposes of a database application, the benefits of separating non-event procedures among multiple modules do not make themselves obvious to the new programmer. In some cases, the source code of certain modules whose functionality might be useful to more than one Access application could be exported from one application and imported into others, as a single, separate module. But even then, you could cut the text of the procedures from the imported module and paste it into some other general module. As long as your non-imported code knows how to contact the imported procedures, there are no other rules governing where general procedures must or should be located.

Designing the Database Schema

If you're accustomed to working with databases outside of the Access 2000 environment, especially those engineered for access through SQL, you may have noticed a slight disparity between what Access calls things and what the rest of the world calls them. Table 18-1 attempts to clarify this and other variations, slight and not so slight, between the vocabulary of database engineers and that of Access.

TABLE 18-1 ACCESS' VOCABULARY TRANSLATED TO GENERAL DATABASE
          TERMINOLOGY

Access 2000 term	Definition	Common term
Database	The collection of tables and derivative sets that share a mutual context.	Catalog Schema
Data source	The location for all regulated data accessible by a client.	Database
Table	A collection of identically related data.	Table
Record set Recordset	A presentation of given attributes of data in a table or tables.	View
Record	A grouping of related data described by the attributes of a table.	Record
Relationship	Describes the association between data in a record.	Relation
Relation Relationship (on the menu bar)	A binding association between columns among two or more tables.	Relationship
Dynaset	A derivative set whose sources may be updated as a result of updating that derivative.	Updateable view
Workspace	A series of transactions between a client and the RDBMS.	Session

Database engineers have asked why it is that Microsoft chose not to apply standard terminology to its database system and documentation. Curiously enough, Microsoft's own engineers have asked precisely the converse question. Yet the majority of database users and programmers are not Access users, so a relearning of the language of database mechanics becomes necessary.

A table is not a database

The problem with the idea of designing a database around a model of a spreadsheet is that it compels the designer to write out his entire data definition in one big table. A table residing on an Excel worksheet, where several records reside on individual rows marked by field names along the top row, is what Excel calls a "database." Excel 2000 even gives automatically any cell region that has listings of like-formatted data in equally sized rows with titles at the top, the region name `Database`. Looking back further in history, the dBASE table file was long ago given the filename extender .DBF for "data base file." All of these nomenclatural disparities derive from the false notion that a table is a database. The truth is, a table is no more a database than a hammer is a building.

What a table truly is, is a set of equivalent relations. (As opposed to a dysfunctional family.) By "relations" in this context, I mean that the items in one record of the table are related to one another in precisely the same way as those items in the same position for every other record in the table. There is no one record in a table that contains any more fields or relations than any other record – no one record that stands out and has more to say about itself than any other. If a field is only pertinent to some records in a table but not all, then that field continues to exist even for the records that don't require it, although its contents for the records where it's unnecessary are blank or null. In a true relational database, "blank" and "null" are real logical values. They don't tell the RDBMS, "Don't pay attention to me;" instead they tell it, "Pay attention to the fact that I have nothing to say about this field."

Where your skill at doodling comes into play

When you're designing the database for your business, the best tool to use in the beginning is paper. Write a list of the *subjects* with which your business deals, and make the subjects you choose as indivisible as possible. By "indivisible," I mean information that doesn't appear to be derived from other information. Work toward a list of information that describes the *basis* of your business. Then take that list and using those time-tested graphical objects, boxes and arrows, compartmentalize the subjects that have direct bearing upon one another, then use arrows to symbolize the cause-and-effect relationships that subjects have on other subjects.

Some subjects you may write down that seem of prime importance at first may end up being incidental, because the data that describes them are in reality comprised of several sets of relations rather than just one. For instance, if your business is the production of periodicals, it might seem at first that a table of individual editions (what the press calls "numbers") would be a viable subject. But whether you consider a magazine as a product of several combined stories, or as a product of data or other news items compiled from various sources, or as a vehicle for the distribution of revenue-generating advertisements, or as a product of several dozen reams of a particular grade of stock newsprint, that magazine is a *product*. Even though the very product of your business – which takes into account the categories of items that you create or manufacture, or services that you provide – may define that business to your customers from an informational perspective, it is also a product, namely of the relationships of other basis elements to one another. The resources that go into the production, creation, distribution, or sale of those products truly are the basis of your operation.

If you think "backwards" now, and work toward isolating the factors that coalesce in the expedition of your particular business venture, you can arrive at a database model that itself works "forwards" just as your business does, modeling reality as it records information. In so doing, your data becomes more efficient. You can ascertain derivative information, such as how many worker-hours were required from all departments to build a line of products, or one unit in that line of products, and how many worker-hours it will take to maintain that one unit. Because your database models reality, its factors can be made to coalesce the same way human factors coalesce in your business.

Adapting to a more complex business model

Access 2000 comes with a well-stocked sample database that models a retail clothier. A retail operation uses a business model that is relatively simple to understand, and that is why Microsoft included this model with Access. But sometimes simplicity belies reality. Let's go back for a moment to the periodical publishing industry, whose business model is a bit more prismatic than a retail operation. The nature of the publishing business varies depending upon the angle from which you perceive it. Editorial, advertising, printing, sales, and distribution may each be perceived as "production," especially from the angle of the person assigned to that department. Someone in this business involved in promotion or human resources would argue — correctly — that her position is crucial to the enterprise as well, even though on the organizational charts such positions are notoriously chalked in later as ancillary branches.

Yet perhaps in no other business does one aspect of the operation more adeptly mask the other aspects when one focuses his attention exclusively upon it, than in the case of publishing. In fact, the person who would have the staff of one department pay closer attention and respect to the work of another, is often criticized for disrupting the sanctity and isolation so often perceived to be necessary for that department to truly do its work. If you think about the best dramatic works whose plots revolve around publishing (in print or other media), the dilemma the characters face is quite often centered around the conscience of the hero reporter who must refuse to "sell out" to the revenue-generating end of the business, in the face of pressure from the antagonistic producer, or publishing manager, or CFO. Rarely has the story been written where the hero budget-cruncher must face the persistent haranguing of the pompous antagonist holier-than-thou authors or reporters, mainly because of the false notion among authors that few would identify with the position of the person who runs the "business end" of the operation.

All right, why the long digression? As the programmer of a business database, you are performing a task around which few playwrights will center any master plots. Yet while it is the goal of your forms and reports to appear *dramatic* (after all, the company did spend dozens of dollars on fancy graphics software), the players on the stage of your database will most often be constructed around those aspects about which the world at large does not care. Do not let the drawing of your database schematics be motivated by dramatics or appearances. Know that your reports will make sense only when it is possible for them to present a view of *any* aspect of your business.

One who can masterfully perceive all matters, both respective of themselves and with respect to the business as a whole, is a true publisher. So a true publisher's database must model the individual aspects of his or her enterprise and be capable of regarding the products of that enterprise as derivative information.

Most forms and reports you will build with Access will present derivative information. A simple example: A form showing you the freelancer responsible for a story in progress might also show his or her e-mail address. But if the database were designed efficiently, the e-mail address and other personal information about the assigned author did not all come from the same table. If it had, all of that personal data would have to have been replicated among several records that were supposed to pertain not to personal data in the first place.

Here's a more complex example: A report of the contents of a particular issue of a magazine should not be a recitation of the contents of just one database table. The numbers of articles and advertisements that comprise any issue are variables, and the characteristics of the two categories are divergent. A report can still show this information, but its underlying data can and should be gathered from several tables. Certain null or logically incongruous data, such as the ad rates for an item that happens to be an article, or the name of the author of an item that happens to be an ad, can be left out of the report; but where relationships exist, such as the amount of space the items consume or what page they start on, are still of value when both categories are considered jointly. This type of joining together of divergent tables with key relationships has been termed by database engineers a *join*, and not a "dyna-plex" or a "mega-struct" or some other mutation of English. This joining takes place in memory as the result of a query.

When constructing a model of your business database, putting as much information as possible into a single table generally ends up being inefficient. E. F. Codd showed that as the number of relations per row (the mathematical term for which is *tuple*) grows, the number of rows or tuples necessary to represent those relations as one table increases multiplicatively over the number of rows necessary to represent that same information in multiple tables. Eventually, a database user will construct a view in which information from these tables are joined anyway—to use a frequent example, a list of customers *and* suppliers, or a list of suppliers *who are* customers. But joining this information manually during the creation of the data itself wastes storage space, and even wastes time on the part of the person entering all this data into the system. **The merger of divergent categories of information into a basis data table results in unnecessary redundancies and inefficient storage.** Or to put it another way, simply because *relationships* exist between elements of data does not mean that data should be permanently *related* by virtue of a mutual context or category.

Building towards normalization

The act of reducing the data in a database to its most basic form, increasing the number of tables and relationships if necessary, but reducing the number of relations per table, is called *normalization*. Most manuals on database programming gloss over the topic of normalization to some extent. Then many of them go right ahead and demonstrate some table attached to a form where each item of inventory is contained within a record which may include the name of a customer who may or may not have pre-purchased that item. You can generally tell that a database structure is not yet normalized when a table performs a function that could otherwise have been achieved through a query. Remember, the result of a query is a set of records, and Access treats these queries as though they were record sets and not requests. When you study the structure of an Access database, and you pull up a query from the list, it shows up at first as a record set, looking just like a table and listing the field names pertaining to the query. Depending upon whom you ask, there are several stages to true database normalization. The names "First Normal Form" and "Third Normal Form" have been used to refer to the stages of database normalization. There are several contradictory definitions of the enumerated "normal forms" propagated of late; but the best way I've found to describe the first three are as follows:

1. No two data fields in a single table should contain identical information.

2. No two data fields in a single table should contain information so similar to one another that one field could easily be derived from the other without significant use of arithmetic or logical operators (for instance, a "last name" and a "full name" field; or a "date of birth" and an "age" field).

3. No two tables in a database schema should contain the same information – that is, data whose meaning and purpose are exactly the same, although they are duplicated – the sole exception being that a unique identifier or *key field* may be used as a way to cross-reference information from a separate table that would otherwise be duplicated.

There are three more major forms of normalization, two of which are called the "fourth;" so as you can imagine, if database engineers have trouble numbering the laws themselves, their level of esoterics must be above average. E. F. Codd recently pointed out that such grand laws as put forth by the Normal Forms tend to overlook some of the eccentricities of the relational model, such as planning for undefined values. That said, Codd proposed a replacement, five-point system for accomplishing true normalization:

◆ A table should represent a distinct type so that the table's name and the name of the type can be viewed identically.

- ◆ Every record within a table must be uniquely identifiable by one field, called the *primary key*.

- ◆ A property that relates to the primary key value is considered a *fact*.

- ◆ Every fact pertaining to a recorded item must be explainable using single-valued properties.

- ◆ When a fact pertains directly to an item, it should be contained within the main record for that item, forming its main relation; whereas indirect facts may be contained in separate relations (records) that refer back to that item by way of its primary key.

Access, like any database manager, can display derivative data as though it had originated from a single table. Actually, the user should not be concerned with the source of the data in the first place. So the user can still see a list or form that shows product data, such as date of publication, number of pages, page one topic, cost of production. But the factors that lead to this information should be derived from independent sources, and joined together through a properly phrased query.

Access is the best tool for defining a schema

This chapter could spend several pages telling you how the schema of a database may be defined with a VBA program; and indeed, that can be done. But there's no clear reason why. First of all, the definition of a schema only needs to take place once, ever. If your database is part of an application that you'll be distributing to multiple users, then if the database is networked, the schema definition only needs to take place on the server anyway. If each user will be running his own local database with your application, then you can still define the schema with Access, and distribute a blank local database with each copy of your VBA program.

Access is better than VBA for this purpose because it gives you an environment for graphically establishing the formats for your tables, the data types for the fields in your tables' records, and just as importantly, the *relationships* between fields in your tables. In fact, Access' Relationships view of a schema is almost a work of art. It enables you to visualize each table as a block and each field as a row within that block. From there, you literally draw lines from table to table, thereby establishing the necessary relationships between tables. By "relationships" in this context, I'm referring to the correlations between fields whose purposes are identical – a way of telling Access and Jet, "*This* field in one table and *that* field in another table mean the same thing."

Through the Relationships view, you get a bird's eye view of normalization in action. What you learn immediately is that **normalization of a database is by no means simplification**, at least from the perspective of human beings. Normalizing a database schema may render it almost mind-numbingly complex, by separating data into isolated tables and replacing redundancies with relationships. (You'll see what I mean by this in a bit.) But the dynamics you will have created as a result of thorough normalization will make the database almost foolproof in its operation.

For this chapter's example of normalization, I've developed a database based around a form of information with which almost everyone who has ever had to write a thesis or a term paper will be instantly familiar, especially a business model may be difficult for you to grasp if you don't happen to be in that business at the time (case in point, my hypothetical magazine publisher from earlier in this chapter). A bibliography is comprised of very common data – the printed data from which information has been gathered. A word processor such as Word 2000 could conceivably maintain a table of references pertinent to a bibliography, and you might think this would be as simple to accomplish as an automated table of contents or index. But when you read the rules in the *Chicago Manual of Style* regarding how a bibliography entry should appear in a formal document when it refers to such diverse items as books belonging to anthologies, articles belonging to books, articles cited from magazines, and unpublished works found along the side of the curb, you begin to realize how difficult a task this would be to manage from *one* table.

Here are the first few entries from a real bibliography table which I used in generate the sample source code for this chapter. Note that this table is set up for formal *references*, which are notations added to the body of the book's text which point to the bibliography entry stating the source of the text's information.

[ABRA] N. Abramson, "The Aloha System," in *Computer Networks*, N. Abramson and F. Kuo, eds., Prentice-Hall, Englewood Cliffs, N.J., 1973.

[AHO] A. V. Aho, J. E. Hopcroft, and J. D. Ullman, *The Design and Analysis of Computer Algorithms*, Addison-Wesley, Reading, Mass., 1974.

[AHUJ] V. Ahuja, "Routing and Flow Control in Systems Network Architecture," *IBM Syst. J.*, vol. 18, no. 2, 1979, 298-314.

Even though the source of these few references was a formal publication, even these did not follow the *Chicago Manual of Style* to the letter. (Here, commas separate the data elements; the *Manual* suggests periods instead.) However, they do demonstrate the form of bibliography entries as they appear in a trusted source. From these examples, you can gather a certain order to the way data is presented in a bibliography reference table: reference mark, followed by authors' names, then the title of the work, the title of the work where it appears, the names of any other contributors to that work, then either the publisher information (if it's a book) or the volume number (if it's a periodical).

Suppose a VBA program with an underlying Jet database were to manage a system whereby all of the data pertinent to all of your information sources for a project could be easily entered and maintained. You could then have the program digest this data and produce a bibliography or references page for you automatically.

The conventional way in which a "macro" would approach the representation of bibliography data would involve a single table of references, whose general structure would be similar to a mail merge table of names and addresses, or a table of index entries. Among the fields in this single bibliography table might be the following:

◆ Author's name

◆ Name of book (if book is referenced)

◆ Name of article (if magazine is referenced)

◆ Name of magazine (if reference is an article)

◆ Date of publication

◆ Date of issue (if magazine)

◆ Name of anthology to which book may belong (if book is referenced)

◆ Other author's name (if more than one)

◆ Other author's name (if more than two)

◆ Editor's name (if editor is different from author)

Perhaps now you're starting to see the difference between a "simple" table and a normalized database. A single-table database such as the one alluded to above would need to support a field for each possible contingency, even when the meaning of that field might not apply in the context of most of the records in that table. "Name of anthology," for instance, would be blank most of the time. Furthermore, certain fields whose purposes are similar though not quite identical (Date of publication and Date of issue, for instance) would have to remain separate. And how many fields should be reserved for auxiliary authors, editors, and contributors? With each and every field you require enrolled into this single table, imagine the programming job you would have to perform if your program required just a list of all editors.

The job of normalizing a database table compels you to do the following:

♦ **Isolate and identify the basic elements about which the data is concerned.** For our example, articles, books, magazines in which articles may appear, and people who may have some role in the creation or production of these items, would all be separate elements. These elements will be the subjects of the tables in the normalized schema.

♦ **Gather next to these elements only those fields that have direct bearing on those elements.** A person, for our example, may be described by his name. All of the fields relating to that name have direct bearing on the identity of the person. However, what that person may have written does not directly identify him. Any one person in our database may have written or contributed to *zero or more* different works; so what a person wrote is not directly material to the record that describes who that person is. (Relationships will help us define pertinent indirect relations later.)

♦ **Devise a means for uniquely identifying each record in the normalized table.** With Access, you don't have to develop such a *primary key* for every table you make; but if you don't, Access will certainly gripe at you about it. A primary key is generally a unique ID number for every entry.

♦ **Develop tables so that, whenever a record in one table needs to refer to the element defined by some other table, the first table may borrow the primary key of the other table's record.** For our example, suppose an article appears in a magazine. Since several articles may also appear in the same magazine, it would be prudent to have the magazine defined once in its own table, and then give the primary key value for that magazine to the separate records for all the referenced articles contained in that magazine.

Figure 18-2 shows Access' Relationships view for the bibliography database schema I devised. At first, this view looks like the remains of a Paul Klée exhibition after having been raided by spiders. What look like spiders' webs in this view are actually representative of relationships between fields in the various tables.

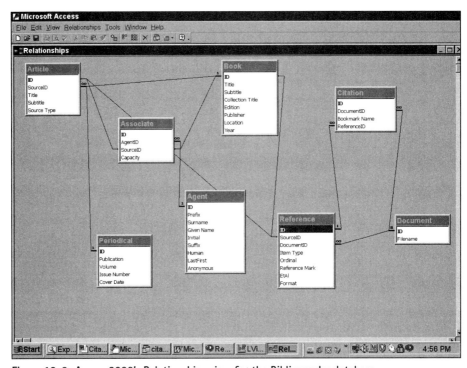

Figure 18-2: Access 2000's Relationships view for the Bibliography database.

The database I devised, dubbed Citation, takes into account far more than just the bibliography entries themselves. It also accounts for each document in which a bibliography may appear, as well as the individual reference codes (represented as Word 2000 bookmarks) scattered throughout those documents. Table 18-2 breaks down these tables and their constituent fields in a point size legible to the unassisted eye.

TABLE 18-2 NORMALIZED TABLES AND FIELDS FOR THE CITATION DATABASE

Table name	Field names	Description of table
Reference	ID	This is the table around which most everything revolves. It represents the *fact* that a document contains information that refers to something. That something is represented by SourceID, which is a copy of the primary key field for the record that describes the thing that is being referenced. The notation inserted throughout the document leading to this reference, is represented by Reference Mark.

Table name	Field names	Description of table
	SourceID	
	DocumentID	
	Item Type	
	Ordinal	
	Reference Mark	
	EtAl	
	Format	
Book	ID	Represents only the cited books among the items in the bibliography, and not the articles. Each table in this schema is uniquely identified by a primary key field, here called ID. When a reference cites a book and not an article, the SourceID field for that record in the Reference table will be set to the ID field that identifies this book. Notice the other fields here describe books, whereas they would not describe articles if all cited sources were to belong to the same table.
	Title	
	Subtitle	
	Collection Title	
	Edition	
	Publisher	
	Location	
	Year	
Article	ID	Represents only the cited articles among the items in the bibliography and not the books. Notice there's nothing in this table that directly describes the *magazine* or *newspaper* where the article appears. This is because such a publication may contain more than one cited article.
	SourceID	

Continued

TABLE 18-2 NORMALIZED TABLES AND FIELDS FOR THE CITATION DATABASE
(Continued)

Table name	Field names	Description of table
Article	Title	
	Subtitle	
	Source Type	
Periodical	ID	Represents only the magazines or newspapers whose cited articles appear in the bibliography. An article is attributed to a periodical by assigning the `ID` value of that periodical to the `SourceID` field for the record of the article.
	Publication	
	Volume	
	Issue Number	
	Cover Date	
Agent	ID	This table is reserved for describing any party who may be responsible in whole or part for any of the referenced works, be it book or article. Generally, this responsible party is human, in which case the Boolean value of the field `Human` is set to True. However, the responsible party may be listed as an organization; in which case, its title appears in `Surname` and the other fields are left blank. `LastFirst` indicates whether surnames are to be printed first rather than last, as in Asian names.
	Prefix	
	Surname	
	Given Name	
	Initial	
	Suffix	
	Human	
	LastFirst	
	Anonymous	

Table name	Field names	Description of table
Associate	ID	Since *any* cited work may be written or edited by *any* number of people, the `Associate` table becomes necessary to link the responsible party `AgentID` to the referenced work `SourceID`. The result is a junction of sorts.
	AgentID	
	SourceID	
	Capacity	
Citation	ID	Represents a place in the document where the referenced work is cited. Word 2000 can recall the textual range where the citation appears, since it already associates that range with the given `Bookmark Name`.
	DocumentID	
	Bookmark Name	
	ReferenceID	
Document	ID	Represents the Word document containing the citations.
	Filename	

The reason why relationships are formally defined

When either developing or addressing a database using SQL alone, the existence of any relationships between tables is only implied. SQL doesn't define the relationships, although they tend to exist by virtue of the way the database is queried – for instance, having the DBMS search for the name of the author whose ID number was pulled up in an `Associate` record.

There is no governing rule in Access or Jet that states you should formally define your relationships between queries; but if you do not, you miss out on a very valuable feature of the DBMS that you can only discover at the database's run time: Jet **enforces the rules of relationships so that no action may take place that is inconsistent with the way fields are related to one another.** Practically, one of the fields in a relationship is a primary key in one of the tables. Consider the sharing of a primary key the database equivalent of a salesperson handing a client his card. It exclusively identifies the salesperson to the client. When one table contains a copy of another table's primary key, any of the data in that other table may easily be cross-referenced. The result is virtually the same as having all the data from the cross-referenced record from the second table, written into the first table. So if you design two tables in such a way that two of their fields share a relationship (this is beginning to sound like a self-help guide to romance), Jet can recognize this relationship formally and ensure that all data in the record sharing the primary key ID is reflected in the table that's the source of the ID. In other words, a shared ID field may only reference a source ID field that presently exists – it can only refer to *real* data.

Access and Jet recognize four types of relationships between two tables' fields:

♦ A **one-to-many relationship** is a state whereby a field in the first table – especially a primary key – may be shared with multiple records in the second table, but the data shared with the second table pertains to only one record in the first table. This is the most common type of relationship, and is established for a record that exclusively identifies itself to many other records in other tables. (The definition for this term in Access' on-line help is not quite accurate; it implies that entire *records* are shared between tables, which is incorrect.)

♦ A **many-to-many relationship** may be established between two tables in such a way that any number of records in one table may share a field with any number of records in another table, and vice versa. This cut-and-dried definition is by no means self-evident, so I'll use the bibliography table as an example: There, any number of authors ("agents") may have written a book; and any one author may have written any number of books. In essence, a many-to-many relationship is a product of at least two one-to-many relationships. The facilitator of a many-to-many relationship is a *junction table*, which in Access is an explicit table. (Other DBMS systems permit junction tables to be implied using gathered fields from other tables.) In our example database, an "association," as I chose to call it, is a single record in a separate Association table that links one person to one source (a book or article), and then specifies the way in which that person is related to that source (as an author, editor, contributor, or translator). One-to-many relationships exist between the Agent and Association tables and between both "source tables" (Book and Article) and Association.

♦ A **one-to-one relationship** is supported by Access for two tables, for which the data in a record in one table relates exclusively to the data in another record in another table. Such a relationship is not conducive to true normalization, since the data in both tables could conceivably have been stored in one table with the result being a *gain* of efficiency rather than a loss.

♦ An **"express relationship"** (there actually is no name for it in Access) may exist between fields in two tables, without some of the rules which Access enforces for the other types of relationships. For example, Access presumes that a standard one-to-many relationship may only exist between one table and *one* other table. In our bibliography database, a referenced work or "source" may be either a book or an article, both of which are represented in separate tables. In order to allow the SourceID field of Associate to refer to *either* a book or an article, express relationships were established between Associate and Book and between Associate and Article. This way, the otherwise rigid enforcement governing which record receives the shared primary key, is relaxed. (Express relationships are not covered by Access' online help.)

In Access' wonderfully revealing Relationships map of a database schema, lines link the various linked fields in a relationship like wires on an old telephone circuit switchboard. A one-to-many relationship is symbolized with a 1 next to the source field and an infinity symbol (∞) next to the shared field. Express relationships are symbolized with just dots next to both linked fields.

The Citation database in our example contains ten formal relationships with varying degrees of enforcement, which are listed in Table 18-3.

TABLE **18-3** FORMAL RELATIONSHIPS IN THE CITATION EXAMPLE DATABASE.

Source field	Shared field	Relationship type
Book!ID	Reference!SourceID	**Express** — Represents the work to which information in a document refers.
Article!ID	Reference!SourceID	**Express** — Because the SourceID field may refer to either of two tables, an express relationship had to be established instead of a one-to-many.
Book!ID	Associate!SourceID	**Express** — Represents the work with which any number of people or institutions ("agents") may be associated.
Article!ID	Associate!SourceID	**Express** — Because the SourceID field may refer to either of two tables, an express relationship had to be established instead of a one-to-many.
Agent!ID	Associate!AgentID	**One-to-many** — Represents the one person or institution being associated with the one work cited in this record.

Continued

TABLE 18-3 FORMAL RELATIONSHIPS IN THE CITATION EXAMPLE DATABASE
(Continued).

Source field	Shared field	Relationship type
`Periodical!ID`	`Article!SourceID`	**One-to-many** — Represents a printed magazine or newspaper in which this article may appear, since a magazine may contain any number of articles.
`Book!ID`	`Article!SourceID`	**One-to-many** — Represents a book or bound collection of articles in which this article may appear. Notice that several fields may serve as the "many" in a one-to-many relationship, but only one field may serve as the "one."
`Reference!ID`	`Citation!ReferenceID`	**One-to-many** — Represents the links between several *citations* of a referenced work within a document, and the single record of the work being referenced.
`Document!ID`	`Citation!DocumentID`	**One-to-many** — Represents the links between several citations of a referenced work, and the single record for the document in which they appear.
`Document!ID`	`Reference!DocumentID`	**One-to-many** — Represents the vital link between a work referenced by a document, and the database's internal record of that document.

When you use VBA to address the contents of a field in a record, the name of the field is separated from the name of variable representing the table or record set that contains it by an exclamation mark, as in the examples shown in Table 18-3. However, when you use SQL to address the contents of a field in a record, the name of the field is separated from the name of the table by a period. This may appear on the surface to be a discrepancy; however, there is a good reason for this distinction: In VBA, you declare a separate object variable either As Table to refer specifically to an established table, or As

Recordset to refer to the results of an SQL query. This variable name is not the table name. As a VBA variable, its associated properties and methods are separated from it by a period, as in rstNames.RecordCount. So to identify a name as a member of a field rather than a property or method, the exclamation mark is used instead, as in rstNames!Surname.

With these relationships having been established, Jet may now be enlisted to enforce what it refers to as *referential integrity*. While this may sound at first like something a starship loses after an attack by the Klingons, the term actually refers to the reliability of the relationships presently established within the database. **With referential integrity being enforced for a one-to-many relationship, by default, a record may not be deleted if its primary key is referred to by any outstanding records in the table sharing the relationship.** These outstanding records would need to be deleted first. Now, recall from Chapter 16 that the SQL DELETE statement only deletes records from a single listed table, not from multiple tables based on criteria relating to the first table. With referential integrity being enforced, Access gives you the following options:

- **Cascade update related fields** refers to Jet's capability to make subsequent updates to the shared field contents of all records in a table sharing a relationship with a table whose source field is likewise being updated. So if a primary key field for a record has its value changed, all records containing a shared copy of that key field will be equally changed.

- **Cascade delete related records** refers to Jet's capability to delete all records in a table sharing a relationship whose shared fields refer to a record being deleted. This is Jet's alternative to simply not allowing the deletion to take place at all. In either event, the result is a database where no records refer to any non-existent sources.

When your Access VBA program poses an SQL query to delete a record that's protected by referential integrity enforcement (there's three words you never thought you'd see adjacent to one another), it is up to VBA, not SQL, to handle the resulting error.

How DAO and ADO Address the Database

Access 2000 is a database system on training wheels. One generally doesn't consider matters of performance and efficiency when selecting his son's next Big

Wheel. The underlying DBMS, Jet, isn't too shabby, but it is not FoxPro. Access' programmers have built a lot of handholding and wizards into the front end of the application. But when you first confront the issue of programming Access with an understanding of both VBA and SQL, much of Access' mechanics become entirely unnecessary. Access suddenly becomes an adequate front end tying together the Jet database engine, DAO, and ODBC. But then you realize that Excel can also function efficiently in that role if you utilize its own VBA system with UserForm objects rather than Access forms. Forms 2.0 controls are not bound to data like Access controls, and that is an inconvenience, yet one that can be overcome through the skillful use of event procedures.

Now that you have a better understanding of the constitution of a database schema, the meanings and contents of the collection objects that comprise Data Access Objects and ActiveX Data Objects, DAO's would-be successor, should now make some immediate sense.

Data Access Objects

With the exception of DBEngine, the top-level object in the DAO hierarchy (and the presumed global object for Access VBA projects), all DAO objects are represented as members of collections. There is no subordinate object in DAO that is not part of a collection.

Table 16-4 lists all of the collections in DAO 3.6 that are employed for sessions that involve both the Jet engine and ODBCDirect. All of these collection names are plural nouns, for which the names of all collection members are singular.

TABLE 16-4 COLLECTION NAMES FOR ALL DAO OBJECTS

Collection name	Constituent of	Description
Workspaces	DBEngine	Represents an active database session between client and server, which may involve any number of users and any number of databases.
Errors	DBEngine	Records an error reported by ODBC, not by the database server.
Databases	Workspace	Represents all of the active databases currently accessible by the client. Data tables are included by databases.

Collection name	Constituent of	Description
Groups†	Workspace User	Represents a cluster of users with identical database server access rights, as determined by the administrator of the database server. As a constituent of a User class object, such as a member of the Users collection, a Group object represents the cluster to which the user may belong, if any.
Users†	Workspace Group	Represents a registered user of the database server, as determined by the administrator of the database server. As a constituent of a Group class object, such as a member of the Groups collection, a User object identifies a user who is a member of an indexed group.
Connections‡	Workspace	Represents the separate dialogs between client and server in an ODBCDirect situation, where interchanges are made and data transactions are conducted.
TableDefs†	Database	Represents all of the regulated tables that are elements of the antecedent database.
QueryDefs	Database	Represents all of the SQL queries, persistent or otherwise, that are currently active and being responded to within the schema of the antecedent database.
Containers†	Database	A collection of certain permissions and restrictions given to sets of a database, indexed by the name of the collection to which these permissions are granted. Valid indexes are: Databases, Tables, and Relations.
Recordsets	Database	A collection of all active sets of records associated with the antecedent table, including the entirety of table records themselves, plus the results of all queries processed with regard to the database thus far.

Continued

TABLE 16-4 COLLECTION NAMES FOR ALL DAO OBJECTS *(Continued)*

Collection name	Constituent of	Description
Relations†	Database	Represents the characteristics of a *relationship* (technically **not a relation**) between fields belonging to record sets. In an Access 2000 schema, a field in a table may be mirrored by a field in another table. For instance, a customer listed in one table may have a pending order listed in another table, for items whose identities are listed in another table. A customer identifier featured in the customer table may be mirrored in the pending order table, and an inventory item identifier in the order table may be mirrored by an identifier in the inventory table. Relationships (not relations) are said to exist between these two pairs of tables, and it is the characteristics of these relationships that are represented by the (poorly named) Relations collection.
Fields	TableDef Recordset Relation Index	Represents all fields that comprise a record in the antecedent record object.
Indexes†	TableDef	Represents the state of, and records belonging to, all index tables associated with the antecedent table.
Parameters	QueryDef	Represents all of the variables acquired from the outside world (in this case, from VBA) whose values or contents play roles in the processing of the antecedent query.
Documents†	Container	A collection of certain permissions and restrictions given to particular elements of a Container class object, such as a member of the Containers collection.

† Indicates that the term applies to Jet database sessions only.
‡ Indicates that the term applies to ODBCDirect database sessions only.

ActiveX Data Objects

What makes ActiveX Data Objects an improvement over Data Access Objects — although DAO is a relatively stable technology — is that ADO cuts a lot of the overhead from the transaction process. The ADO object model has been pared down substantially, rerouting disparate DAO processes into fewer, more object-oriented methods with an abundance of properties. Unlike DAO, ADO objects are not all gathered into collections that have uniform names, with their members addressable through indexes. Instead, many of the members of the ADO model are classes, and you declare references using the `Dim`, `Public`, `Private`, or `Static` statement as instances of those classes. What Microsoft realized was that the DAO collections primarily existed for the sake of DAO, without necessarily providing anything of convenience to the programmer. Table 16-5 presents the major objects and object classes in the ADO scheme.

TABLE 16-5 PRINCIPAL OBJECTS IN ADO

Object name	Constituent of	Description
ADODB		Library The root object of ADO, representing its object library.
Connection	ADODB	Class Represents the separate dialogs between client and server where interchanges are made and data transactions are conducted.
Object name	**Constituent of**	**Description**
Errors	Connection	Collection Records an error reported by the data *provider*, not by the database server. Here, the provider may be ODBC or OLE DB, or both.
Command	Connection	Class Represents a directive to be given to the server along the current connection. This directive may be a retrieval query using an SQL `SELECT` statement, or a parameter query programmed by appending to the `Parameters` collection, or an SQL action query (`INSERT`, `UPDATE`, `DELETE`) that makes some change to the database contents.

Continued

TABLE 16-5 PRINCIPAL OBJECTS IN ADO *(Continued)*

Object name	Constituent of	Description
Recordset	Connection	<u>Class</u> Represents the set of all records processed.
Parameters	Command	<u>Collection</u> Contains search criteria to be matched against records in the database, for retrieval processes in which SQL is not used.
Fields	Recordset	<u>Collection</u> Represents all fields that comprise a record in the antecedent record object.
Properties	Connection Command Recordset Field	<u>Collection</u> Represents those aspects or characteristics of the transaction process that are made available through the data access provider in the Microsoft UDA scheme (ODBC, OLE DB, or any future acronym). Providers such as these do not utilize object libraries, because most database environments to which the ADO database application may pertain, do not involve the Windows operating system.

Comparing the two models, and why there are two

The most sweeping change in ADO is in how a database is always queried. A persistent query, as we mentioned earlier, is a permanent part of a database. A DAO persistent query may be stored and used over again, for instance, to update the contents of a form. But a DAO direct query, by contrast, may be placed immediately for any given database, data table, or record set, with the result being that a set of records matching the given criteria is immediately returned, and the text of the query itself is tossed out.

ADO lifts the distinction between persistent and direct queries. As a result, **ADO queries are always permanent parts of a database**. At first, this might seem like an omission or a fuzzification on ADO's part; but in practice, this new model for conceptualizing queries proves quite convenient. The reason is not obvious, so I'll explain it in detail:

Although the SQL text of a query represents the "question" in our own mind, to the database, it actually represents the "answer," or the response that meets the specified criteria. So a stored persistent query is made up of the criteria which matches a subset of the contained data. In the DAO structure, a query made to a database through Jet is set up as a *query definition*, or QueryDef object. This object becomes stored with the database, and assigned to a reference within the VBA (or other language) program that represents the query, using the .CreateQueryDef method of DAO's Database class object. This reference is a QueryDef class object in DAO. This query is then executed by means of the .Execute method.

The original idea for how queries would work in DAO was that .CreateQueryDef would only be necessary once for any particular query. When the query is needed again, it could be located within the QueryDefs collection and re-executed from there. This idea is simpler in theory than in practice. **DAO contains no methods or functions for locating any particular query.** As a result, the only way for you to find a query in QueryDefs is to render the entire query as a string variable, then search for a matching copy of it using a For Each...Next loop clause, comparing the text of the recorded queries against the text of the query you want to execute. The only alternative in DAO is to go ahead and define the new QueryDef and run the risk of redefining a query that already exists. There's nothing in DAO to keep you from defining the same query multiple times in the QueryDefs collection. Doing so affects nothing adversely but the size of the database, and thus the relative efficiency of the database file as a whole.

ADO cuts to the chase. With it, you always define a query within a Command class object, as though it were to be stored with the database. ADO completely hides the fact that a query you're defining may already exist as part of that database. Because you'd have to generate the query in order to look for it, ADO lets you go ahead, generate it, and then *use* it, and if the query already exists, big deal. You engage an ADO query by means of the .Execute method of the Commmand class object. The method returns results that are already representable by a Recordset class object.

Gone is DAO's separate TableDef class, which represented a single table in the database schema. There simply wasn't anything compelling about the capability to confine queries to referring to a single table. In ADO, all queries are directed toward the database as a whole. SQL SELECT queries tend to specify the tables in question anyway within their own WHERE clauses.

ADO has also ceded responsibility for maintaining the security of the database and its content to whatever the database server may be, since the ideal of client-based security is a little dubious anyway. Microsoft does supply an extension to ADO 2.1 – available from the Tools → References menu of VBA – that adds some security-oriented objects for situations in which the server (for instance, Jet) does not provide security on its own. By "security," I mean mostly the capability to protect some records from being overwritten or deleted, especially in a multi-user situation where two or more users may have simultaneous access to the same data. But the general notion that the server should be responsible for security (a correct one, if I may offer an opinion) is partly responsible for the removal of the Workspace object from Microsoft's data access model. In its place, the Connection object — originally devised for DAO and ODBCDirect — takes center stage as the representative of ADO's client/server transaction process.

Perhaps you're wondering, what has ActiveX Data Objects to do with ActiveX, the remote component operations system? The only certain similarity between them is their mutual trademark. At one time in ADO's development, the "X" was removed from "ActiveX," only to be replaced eight months later.

Creating dedicated workspaces, and other hobbies

Access 2000 maintains its own list of active sessions with data sources. The Jet engine, which actually does the work, calls those sessions *workspaces*. In DAO, their associated objects are represented by the Workspaces collection. The workspaces that Access initiates for its own purposes, without VBA's intervention, are each numbered but have no name. When you use VBA to address data that is not currently loaded into the active Access database (the one whose components are featured in the Database window), one of your VBA procedures will initiate a new workspace. The method term used for this part of the process, simply enough, is .CreateWorkspace.

On Point

A Visual Basic for Applications module for Access 2000 is separate and distinct from a macro. At any one time, this module may make references to two object libraries. The Access 2000 object library does not define the structure of a database, but instead defines the visual elements from which the contents of a database are displayed. Both Data Access Objects and ActiveX Data Objects present objects that represent the components of a Windows database communications process.

Access is not a manager of a database. Moreover, it is an environment for the staging of processes that are managed by the Jet database engine. VBA is just one provider of processes to the Access environment, though it is not the only one; the Access macro system is the other provider. The macro language for the most part mirrors the commands that an Access user might give to that application. VBA, by contrast, may act as an alternate provider of extended functionality to Access, or it may act as the provider of the core processes of a database manager system, utilizing Jet as its engine and Access as its front end.

You may give workspaces initiated through VBA their own names, so that you can refer to them later in the `Workspaces` collection by name. Whether you choose to make your newly created workspace a part of the formal `Workspaces` collection depends on whether you need this workspace – this session – to be persistent. In other words, if the database you will be contacting through DAO needs to be present at all times even while you are using the other database in Access' Database window, then by using the `.Append` method to attach the `Workspace` class object to the `Workspaces` collection, the session is presumed to continue even after you exit and restart Access. The session may be terminated with the `.Close` method. `Workspace` class objects not appended to the collection are automatically terminated when Access is closed.

Initiating a workspace truly is the start of a session because, as with the beginning of any other digital communications process, you log on. The `.Create Workspace` method requires a user ID and password. These are the identifiers maintained by Access, not by ODBC, not by your database source, and not by your network. Since you will rarely need a VBA procedure to act in the role of an Access user (what's the point of Access tracking user transactions that the user did not make?) the user ID for creating a workspace is generally `Admin`, and the password is generally a null string, unless you have set up Access to recognize a special administrator password.

There are two types of workspace sessions: those that use the Jet engine, and those that do not. Both types may utilize ODBC as a conduit for linking to your stored data, although for a Jet session that reads .MDB files, ODBC is not required. **You always use ODBC when you need to make contact with databases that are not available through the storage devices attached to your processor.** For any data whose source is elsewhere on the network, you need ODBC.

For locally available data, you need ODBC to retrieve data that is not in Jet's .MDB format, and for which you have drivers installed. These drivers may either handle the data files themselves or pass control to other programs or data managers that are responsible for the data, such as Oracle or SQL Server.

Whether you require Jet within your workspace depends on what component you expect to handle queries. Jet is devised to be able to use a subset of SQL for querying Access databases. The SQL interpreter in Jet may also be used to query the contents of local databases from other formats, as long as ODBC drivers for translating those formats on Jet's behalf are installed on your system. However, some ODBC drivers, including the dBASE driver, have their own SQL-subset parsers built in anyway. This is not the case with all ODBC parsers that you'll run across; the Oracle and Paradox drivers, for instance, assume that ODBC is connecting with the database *manager*, not with the database, so SQL queries can be passed through to the RDBMS – making a separate query handler unnecessary. There is also no query system provided with the Excel driver, which cannot apply SQL to a worksheet since that worksheet might not be formatted like a table anyway.

Who interprets the SQL code?

Access does not maintain the SQL interpreter for executing or checking the validity of SQL instructions. The Jet engine does have its own SQL interpreter, but it is significantly limited, especially with comparison to the level and breadth of instructions that Microsoft SQL Server, or Oracle, or IBM DB2 expects. Depending on the application at hand, you might not even require Jet's SQL interpreter.

Jet acts as a client-end query generator, generally for databases that are stored files rather than managed, active databases. It then serves as the mechanism for contacting data files and retrieving their contents, whether through logic or blind acquisition.

So who ends up being responsible for the queries? Here are some possible scenarios:

♦ A database formatted for Access 2000 (.MDB file) should be contacted through the Jet engine if the file is local, and if you intend to retrieve data based on a query. In such cases, Jet itself is the database server, and Jet is responsible for the queries.

♦ A local database stored using some format other than .MDB may be contacted through the Jet engine if you need for the SQL `SELECT` query you use to be monitored by Access as a transaction.

♦ Single queries that involve local data from two or more tables stored in different formats, require Jet to perform the join operation, since **ODBC drivers cannot make contact with one another.** Here, again, the Jet engine is required to handle queries.

♦ Connections to all remote databases require ODBC. However, if these databases are stored files rather than actively managed data, the same rules for whether to use Jet apply to these databases remotely as they do locally. If your ODBC driver has `SELECT` query capability, a system called ODBCDirect can be used in place of Jet to link VBA directly to the ODBC driver without using Jet as a go-between. In this case, the driver has responsibility for the query. If the driver doesn't have an SQL parser, then it acts as a simple Indexed Sequential Access Manager (ISAM) system, which is geared to return only one record at a time, either from the top of the table down, or cross-referenced by its index number.

♦ **If you intend to bind your data to Access forms and controls, you must use Jet to retrieve this data.** The Access environment looks to Jet for the contents of its text, list, and combo boxes. The Access object library — which does not include Jet — has no way to address ODBC drivers directly. So data retrieved by ODBC has a layover at Jet before it can get to its destination Access form.

◆ If your SQL query involves an instruction other than SELECT – for instance, UPDATE, INSERT, or DELETE – then your ODBC driver alone will not be capable of supporting it. If you use ODBCDirect, the query will need to pass through to an active RDBMS; otherwise, you will need to use Jet.

◆ If your VBA procedure creates new data, either by SQL's CREATE TABLE directive or through other means, your ODBC driver alone will not be capable of executing the data-creating directive. If your workspace uses ODBCDirect, then DAO's table definition object, TableDef, becomes unavailable to that workspace. So, again, you either need to use Jet or be able to pass a query through to an active RDBMS such as Microsoft SQL Server. **Using VBA code and ODBC drivers, you can create data that is stored in a format other than Jet.** It is a tricky maneuver that sometimes fails to work, but it can be done.

◆ If your data source is managed by an active RDBMS, then by all means, let it handle the SQL query and leave Jet alone. Use ODBCDirect to make a connection with the data source, then pass the SQL query directly through to the source and let it handle the retrieval process. The entire process will probably be faster anyway.

On Point

There are only two types of modules in an Access 2000 VBA application: a class module, which responds to events that take place regarding Access forms and controls, and a general module, which provides all the functionality that does not belong to a class module.

In designing an Access VBA application, your initial goal should be the proper design of the data. A database schema often involves many tables, and you shouldn't hesitate to build many tables with a smaller number of fields per record, if it means that the relations in your tables are tighter and the total number of records in your database becomes smaller. A properly normalized database schema takes into account that only tightly and directly related subjects should be bound together in a record. Indirectly related subjects can be split among two or more tables that share a common key field, making joins between related records easier.

An Access form represents a persistent query's results

When you begin to design a new form in the Access environment, a dialog box asks you to choose the "table or query" on which the form's data will be based. At this point, the stored queries belonging to the current schema are, at the very least, statements of certain desired fields that will appear in the view representing the query, with criteria regulating the contents from the source tables that will appear in these fields. In Access' Relationships window, the views produced by queries are treated equally with base tables.

With any database manager — Access being no exception — a view is a display of query results, and a form is the front end for a view. So when Access asks you for the "table or query" for a form, it is actually asking whether you want the new form's underlying query to be taken from an existing query definition, or instead based on a new and simple (criteria-less) SELECT * FROM... query.

Chapter 16 introduced you to the Structured Query Language, and focused in large part upon its SELECT statement, which is the basis of all of SQL's data retrieval instructions. **Every record set (view) in Access is based, one way or another, on a query represented by a SELECT statement.** The connection between a form and its underlying query may take any of the following routes:

♦ The Access Form object representing a form based on a table (from the user's perspective) has a .RecordSource property that is set to the name of that table, in effect making the underlying query SELECT * FROM, plus the name of that table.

♦ The Form object representing a form based on an existing query has a .RecordSource property that is set to the name of that query in the Access schema.

♦ A Form object declared, built, and executed entirely in VBA code has a .RecordSource property that is set directly to the text of the SQL query that produces the record set attributed to the form.

When you're using a VBA interpreter other than Access VBA, a form module — which is based on the UserForm object — is not bound to any particular query. It therefore becomes the responsibility of your VBA code to acquire user input from each textual control, and update the contents of those controls when the user is browsing through the database. At first, this may seem like an inconvenience. But as you saw earlier in this chapter, the act of normalizing a database can radically reshape a well regulated structure to appear something more like the plot to the *Mission: Impossible* movie. As a result, **few forms assigned to normalized databases will pertain to queries of single tables.**

Huh? Okay, follow along with me for a minute: The everyday Access form is generally bound either to a single table, or to a query that retrieves records from a single table. This one-to-one correlation between form and table preserves the user's perception of being able to modify an entire record on one screen. Earlier in the book, I mentioned that one goal of good programming is to effectively mask the dynamics of the program from the user. With a fully normalized database schema, almost any complete assembly of information on screen at any one time will be a composite of records from several tables. When a user sees a form full of data, he naturally assumes that any alterations he makes to the form may be committed to the database with a single button. If a strict single-form-to-single-table correlation to be adhered to, one button would not be enough to do the job. There would need to be separate forms, or at least separate "Insert" buttons, for each individual record. Conceivably, an Access form could be bound to a complex SELECT query that addresses multiple source tables by means of an INNER JOIN clause. Whenever the form was updated, the SELECT query could be re-executed. But an INSERT query in SQL can only address a single table at a time. So if there's a button on the form that essentially means "Save this" or "Insert this" or "Done," the event procedure triggered by that button will have to trigger as many INSERT statements as necessary to bring every table of the database up to date.

Here is where enforced relationships prove their worth: Suppose for our example bibliography program, a form or group of concurrent forms are used to enter the data for a work being referenced, the source of that work (if there is one), and the names of all pertinent people associated with the work, especially authors. Already, the event procedure for the "Insert" button on this form would be responsible for triggering at least three, and perhaps four, INSERT statements that address separate tables. With referential integrity enforced, the existence of a record representing an author would be ensured prior to the insertion of another record referring to that author in another table. This eliminates the possibility of a program being interrupted, thereby leaving a dangling reference in the database.

How VBA Manages a Database Through SQL

In the development of examples for this book, I produced an experiment to create a class module for Word that manages a bibliography database using Jet and SQL. The main objective of this class module is to provide any programmer with the raw functionality required for any project that involves recording information sources by name. But there is a second objective that is a bit more esoteric, but whose inspiration is easy to explain:

The class module should hide the intricacies of managing the database from the programmer that imports the class module into his VBA application. As you've seen explained to you (if not fully demonstrated in code to this point), SQL is a relational language that uses set logic to address one or more elements of data holistically. By contrast, the access scheme of Access and Jet is ISAM, which "thumbs" through each record in a set the way one browses through a telephone directory. Mathematically, the two schemes are incompatible with one another; but through the magic that is Microsoft's acronym soup, SQL manages to pass the baton to the ISAM scheme with dexterity and grace.

A random access scheme for addressing fields or records *by number* is generally more convenient to the programmer than stepping a cursor over a record set the way one kicks a soccer ball across Wembeley Stadium. Unfortunately, there is no way to convert the access scheme for any given database through Jet from ISAM to something more rational like random access or B-trieve. However, there is a way to develop a service-based architecture for a database from the very beginning, in which the underlying structure is fully normalized, but the data within that structure is provided to an interface to a second service tier that functions – or so it appears – like random access.

There's so much about a DBMS you don't have to know

Both DAO and ADO have extensive object libraries with which you address the ISAM portion of Jet directly. This book covers only portions of those libraries. There is a clear and convincing reason for this omission which I hope you appreciate even if one or two published reviewers will not: **You do not need to know the details of addressing ISAM if you are adept at using SQL.** Although the phraseology of a VBA instruction that passes an SQL query is arguably rather awkward, the underlying SQL is straightforward – in fact, more so than the direct-access methodologies which DAO and ADO would have you use instead.

In the development of the Citation class module (which uses the relationships model shown earlier in Figure 18-2), my goal was to completely hide the query-and-retrieval mechanism of the underlying data access library beneath a cloak of objects and properties that are purely consistent with the way VBA addresses items in everyday programming. So if you want to build a form module that utilizes this class module (a handful of form modules are included in the sample project), the code within that module can address the database's key data fields (book title, author's last name, date of publication, and the like) as though they were members of an established VBA collection. All the normalization issues, all the querying, and all the inner joining and outer joining are kept completely hidden, so they never get in the way of you developing a bibliography application.

Of course, to give you an idea of what I wanted to hide, I need to give you a peek here in this chapter. The size of the source code for the entire Citation class module would spill over this chapter into the previous *four*; there isn't space in this book to cover it all. However, much of the source code is made up of procedures which provide the same general functionality in the same way for different features, so it is possible here to demonstrate how Citation works.

The principal element of Citation's architecture is the envelopment of its key database fields within *properties*. When you instantiate the class module in your

VBA program, you make all of these properties available to you. There is no hierarchy to these properties; they're all one big list. You address one of these properties
by attaching it to the variable representing the instance of Citation, like this:

```
XCiter.SourceTitle(lRefID)
```

Here, XCiter is the name of a variable declared with the type classCitation.
The .SourceTitle property is reflected within the class module by a field in a
database. Depending on whether the source being referenced is a book or an article
appearing in a periodical, this field may be in the Book or Article table. But what's
important is that you don't have to know or care about this fact; the .SourceTitle
property always refers to the table you need it to refer to. When you're retrieving
existing data, the .SourceItemType property reveals whether the referenced work
is (1) a book, (2) an article, or (3) an unpublished work, such as a Web page. When
you're entering new data into the database, you let the class module know what
type of data to expect by invoking a method such as .NewBook or .NewArticle;
the class module handles the necessary distinctions from there.

The subscript lRefID in this example is a record ID number, the identity of
which you never have to know while you're using classCitation. If you want to
address multiple records within the same application, simply address your references to the properties of those records with different ID variables. The subscript
here provides you with the illusion of a *random access* scheme rather than the
indexed sequential scheme that the underlying database actually uses. If you had to
adapt your application to the sequential scheme, each table you address would
maintain its own *cursor*, which is an internal pointer to the "current record." So if
you want your application to address multiple records, you would have to move
this pointer around like an oxcart across a plantation, between one record and the
other. The Citation class module hides these details—it handles the movement of
the proverbial oxcart for you.

Figure 18-3 shows two of the forms that come with the sample application,
which enables you to enter data relating to the sources of information you'll be referencing. The list in the middle of the Reference dialog at left shows all the people
attributed to this work; though you enter each person in this list by way of a subordinate Agent dialog box at right.

Both of these forms are provided by conventional Forms 2.0 UserForm objects,
not Access Form objects. The data in the text and combo boxes for these forms are
supplied by properties of the classCitation class object, which for this application is called XCiter. These forms are designed so that the author of a Word document that formally references multiple information sources, can enter the data
about those sources as he goes along. Whenever he's ready, the user can have
classCitation produce a formal bibliography or endnotes table in the format prescribed by the Chicago Manual of Style.

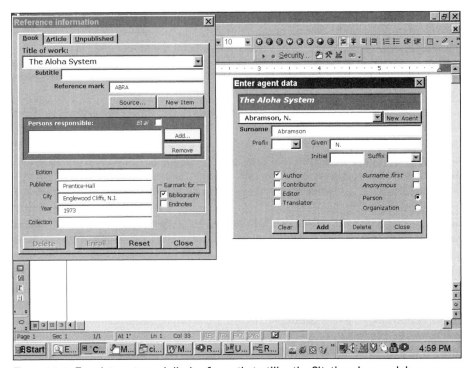

Figure 18-3: Two data entry and display forms that utilize the Citation class module.

For the sake of this particular program, I've introduced some compromise terminology that attempts to bridge the gap between the realm of professional research
and the realm of programming:

AGENT (N.)

A person responsible for all or part of a referenced work. Generally this person is an
author, but editors, contributing writers, and translators also play active roles.
These are the four categories of people covered by the Chicago Manual of Style in
its doctrine specifying how formal references are formatted.

REFERENCE (N.)

A formal accreditation of a literary work as a source of information appearing in
the document. A document references such a work no more than twice: once in the
Bibliography table, and perhaps a second time within an Endnotes table, whose format is slightly different.

CITATION (N.)

An abbreviated annotation that points to a reference. A document may contain any
number of citations in the course of its text.

SOURCE (N.)

A book, an article from a magazine, or an unpublished work such as a Web page. Here's how `classCitation` works in summary; you'll see some of the details momentarily: In keeping with the ISAM access scheme, the class "pays attention to" one record at a time from each table. This record is identified and indexed by its primary key field. In the reference `XCiter.SourceTitle(lRefID)`, the subscript `lRefID` equates with that key field. As long as the module that declared `XCiter` continues to supply the same value for `lRefID`, `classCitation` will continue to reference the same record from the source table. The first thing `classCitation` checks is whether this single argument is different from the one it received before. If it's the same, `classCitation` sticks with the record with which it's currently working. If it's different, `classCitation` dumps its current record to the database, either with an `INSERT` or an `UPDATE` SQL statement depending on whether the record formally exists. It then uses a `SELECT` statement to load the record whose ID is equal to the newly acquired argument. If it can't find this record, simply enough, it closes all records and flushes its memory of any record it's seen in that database. The `classCitation` module does have to be explicitly told when it is to expect information for a new record to be inserted into the database. But even then, `classCitation` is responsible for generating the new record's ID number and passing it to its owner – the instantiator of `XCiter` never has responsibility for the underlying database. So if `classCitation` is supplied with a non-existent ID number for a record, it simply stops. It's a blunt way of handling things, but it protects the database against improper access.

The following deceptively small procedure responds to the instruction `XCiter.SourceTitle(lRefID) = "The Aloha System"`. On the surface, this is assignment of the string `"The Aloha System"` to the `.SourceTitle` property. In actuality, it is a filtered insertion of the data in this string to the `SourceTitle` property. It is a `Property Let` procedure that triggers an analysis of the subscript `lRefID` – *not* the setting `"The Aloha System"` – before assigning the string to the private variable that supports the `.SourceTitle` property.

```
Public Property Let SourceTitle(lItemNo As Long, strEntry _
  As String)
    If ValidateOutgoingWhateverID(lItemNo) Then
        strRIPx_Title = strEntry
    End If
End Property
```

The support variable for the `.SourceTitle` property is `strRIPx_Title`. Here, the incoming data in `strEntry` is assigned to the support variable `strRIPx_Title` if the subscript value `lItemNo` – which receives the value from `lRefID` – passes the test presented by function `ValidateWhateverID()`. The listing for that function procedure appears below:

```
Private Function ValidateWhateverID(lItemNo As Long) As Boolean
    Select Case GetTableNo(lItemNo)
        Case BIB_REFERENCE
            ValidateWhateverID = ValidateReferenceID(lItemNo)
        Case BIB_BOOK
            ValidateWhateverID = ValidateSourceID(lItemNo)
        Case BIB_ARTICLE
            ValidateWhateverID = ValidateSourceID(lItemNo)
        Case BIB_UNPUBLISHED
            ValidateWhateverID = ValidateSourceID(lItemNo)
        Case BIB_DOCUMENT
            ValidateWhateverID = ValidateDocumentID(lItemNo)
        Case BIB_CITATION
            ValidateWhateverID = ValidateCitationID(lItemNo)
        Case BIB_AGENT
            ValidateWhateverID = ValidateAgentID(lItemNo)
    End Select
End Function
```

To ensure that each ID number used by `classCitation` throughout the database is unique, each ID number is generated with an exclusive "prefix digit" that applies to its record's table of origin. This way, it's easy to spot whether an ID refers to a record in the Book table or a record in the Agent table, simply by stripping and examining that prefix digit. The procedure which isolates this digit is mentioned at the top of the `Select Case` clause above, and is presented below:

```
Private Function GetTableNo(lItemNo As Long) As Integer
    GetTableNo = lItemNo \ 1000000
End Function
```

Simply enough, `Function GetTableNo()` strips the first digit from the seven-digit ID number. Back in `Function ValidateWhateverID()`, this digit is tested against a list of constants representing the various table prefixes, which were declared at the beginning of the class module as follows:

```
Private Const BIB_AGENT = 1
Private Const BIB_ARTICLE = 2
Private Const BIB_ASSOCIATE = 3
Private Const BIB_BOOK = 4
Private Const BIB_CITATION = 5
Private Const BIB_DOCUMENT = 6
Private Const BIB_PERIODICAL = 7
Private Const BIB_REFERENCE = 8
Private Const BIB_UNPUBLISHED = 9
```

Here, each of the tables is given its own exclusive prefix digit, and
"Unpublished" is given its own digit even though its data also belong to the Book
table. The ID number lItemNo received by the Property Let procedure could trigger a reference to the Book table (4), the Article table (2), or the Book table by virtue
of being an unpublished work (9). Because only the six prefixes listed in
ValidateWhateverID() could ever be the subject of some doubt, they are tested
here in order to direct VBA to execute the proper *real* validation procedure in each
case. Let's assume the retrieved prefix digit is 4, or BIB_BOOK. Listing 18-1 shows
the procedure that performs one of this class module's most critical tasks: switching
between active records.

Listing 18-1: How classCitation triggers the changeover to a new active record.

```
Private Function ValidateSourceID(lItemNo As Long) _
 As Boolean
Dim iTableNo As Integer
    Static lLastSeen As Long

    lItemNo = CLng(Abs(lItemNo))
    If lItemNo = lLastSeen Then
        ValidateSourceID = True
        Exit Function
    Else
        lLastSeen = lItemNo
        iTableNo = GetTableNo(lItemNo)
        If iTableNo = BIB_BOOK Or iTableNo = BIB_ARTICLE _
         Or iTableNo = BIB_UNPUBLISHED Then
            If lItemNo = lRIP_SourceID Then
                ValidateSourceID = True
            Else
                If bSourceIP Then
                    If bAgentIP Then
                        If WriteAgent() Then
                            ClearAgent
                            lAIP_ID = GenerateID(BIB_AGENT)
                        Else
                            ValidateSourceID = False
                            Exit Function
                        End If
                    End If
                    If bReferenceIP Then
                        If WriteReference() Then
                            ClearReference
                            lRIP_ID = GenerateID(BIB_REFERENCE)
                        Else
```

```
                              ValidateSourceID = False
                              Exit Function
                        End If
                  End If
                  If WriteSource() Then
                        lRIP_SourceID = lItemNo
                        If ReadSource() Then
                              ValidateSourceID = True
                        Else
                              ValidateSourceID = False
                        End If
                  Else
                        ValidateSourceID = False
                  End If
            End If
      End If
Else
      ValidateSourceID = False
End If
   End If
End Function
```

The purposes of this procedure are to determine whether lItemNo is different and, if so, formalize all changes being made to the record in memory before loading the requested record into memory. This procedure maintains a static variable lLastSeen. If the ID number being tested lItemNo is the same as the one recorded by this procedure during its last run, it already passes the test and the procedure is exited. Think of lLastSeen as a cache of sorts for the last polled source ID number; the rest of the procedure can be skipped if this number has been seen before. If the ID number is new, however, the next test it must pass is whether it's an ID for a valid source.

To understand what happens next, you need to be introduced first to classCitation's internal "cursors," to use the term as it applies to databases as opposed to word processors. **A cursor in an ISAM scheme is a pointer to the "current" record in a table or view (record set).** Each record in classCitation's tables are uniquely keyed, with respect both to their own tables and to each other's. This class maintains variables that point to the unique ID numbers for records currently under examination. Variable lRIP_SourceID — featured in Listing 18-1, as well as throughout the class module — points to the ID number for the referenced work, whether it is in the Book or Article table. The class can distinguish between the two because of their unique prefix numbers (Book is 4, Article is 2).

In Private Function ValidateSourceID(), the local argument lItemNo is compared against the module-level "cursor" variable lRIP_SourceID. While the *apparent* objective of this procedure is to confirm for other parts of the class whether this is a valid number for its implied purpose, its *concealed* objective is to determine whether this number is a different argument than the one it's seen before. A difference is to be interpreted as a signal to the database to change records and load in a different one – namely, the one pointed to by the new argument ID number `lItemNo`. This is how the indexed sequential access scheme is masked to appear like random access; any change in the sea of subscripts that these procedures are being fed trigger procedures which formalize any changes currently held in memory, by storing those changes to the database.

You'll recall that each important field in this database is addressed through this class module like a property. So an assignment to a field is phrased like a setting to a property, such as `XCiter.SourceTitle(lRefNo) = "The Aloha System"`. Whenever such an assignment is made, a module-level flag variable `bSourceIP` is set to `True`. You'll find several "IP" variables throughout `classCitation`, all of which act as signals that there is data in memory that has yet to be stored to the database. (The "IP" stands for "In Progress.") A simple change to a property setting does not trigger an immediate `INSERT` or `UPDATE` directive to the database; if it did, Jet would literally be flooded with such directives, and this author has noted the fragileness of Jet under pressure. So alterations to the record pointed to by `lRIP_SourceID` or one of its counterparts are held in memory until that cursor variable is to be changed, whereupon the changes are formally stored. (A side benefit of this architecture is that recent changes are easier to "undo" by simply having the class ignore them.)

The meat of Listing 18-1 is in the `Else` portion of the conditional clause that checks `If lItemNo = lRIP_SourceID` – of course, this portion will only be executed if the condition evaluates False. A source (a work being referenced) is a peculiar thing in `classCitation` because it is contingent upon two other main elements of the database: any author or other agent responsible for that source and to which that source is related, and any formal reference (the linking of a document with that work) which specifies that source. When you change the record for the source being examined to point to some other record or to some new record, the current reference record and the current agent record immediately become "disowned" because they no longer relate to the current source record.

So it only makes sense to cut the ties now. This is why `ValidateSourceID()` checks the "in progress" flag variables `bAgentIP` and `bReferenceIP`; if either is True, the contents of the record in progress is written to the database. The two cursor variables for the Agent and Reference tables are `lAIP_ID` and `lRIP_ID`, respectively. After their records in progress are written, they are wiped from memory and replaced with blank records with all new ID numbers generated for them.

With that housekeeping out of the way, Listing 18-1 can finally get down to business. The current source record either is inserted into the database (if it's new) or has its present contents updated (if it already exists) by means of the `WriteSource()` function procedure. Both `WriteSource()` and `ReadSource()` are structured in the conventional C-language fashion, where their return values are Boolean True/False error codes indicating success or failure. Listing 18-2 shows

Private Function WriteSource(), which commits to the database the current
contents of memory for the source record:

Listing 18-2: The Citation class module's wrapper around SQL's INSERT and DELETE.

```
Private Function WriteSource() As Boolean
    Dim rstVerify As DAO.Recordset
    Dim rstUnion As DAO.Recordset
    Dim strQuery As String, strErr As String, _
     strCriteria As String

    On Error GoTo WriteSourceErr

    If lRIP_SourceID = 0 Or strRIPx_Title = "" Then
        WriteSource = False
        Exit Function
    End If

    If iRIP_ItemType = 1 Or iRIP_ItemType = 3 Then
        strQuery = "SELECT DISTINCTROW * FROM Book WHERE ID = " _
                & Str$(lRIP_SourceID) & ";"
    ElseIf iRIP_ItemType = 2 Then
        strQuery = _
         "SELECT DISTINCTROW * FROM Article WHERE ID = " _
         & Str$(lRIP_SourceID) & ";"
    Else
        WriteSource = False
        Exit Function
    End If
    Set rstVerify = dbCitation.OpenRecordset(strQuery)
    If rstVerify.RecordCount > 0 Then
        rstVerify.MoveLast
        If iRIP_ItemType = 1 Or iRIP_ItemType = 3 Then
            'Verify that the book exists
            strQuery = "SELECT DISTINCTROW ID FROM BOOK " _
                    & "WHERE ID = " & Str$(lRIP_SourceID) & ";"
            Set rstVerify = dbCitation.OpenRecordset(strQuery)
            rstVerify.MoveLast
            If rstVerify.RecordCount > 0 Then
                strQuery = "UPDATE Book SET Title = '" _
                    & strRIPx_Title & "', " _
                    & "Subtitle = '" & strRIPx_Subtitle & "', " _
                    & "[Collection Title] = '" _
                    & strRIPx_CollectionTitle & "', " _
                    & "Edition =" & Str$(iRIPx_Edition) & ", " _
```

```
            & "Publisher = '" & strRIPx_Publisher & "', " _
            & "Location = '" & strRIPx_Location & "', " _
            & "Year = #" & datRIPx_Year & "# " _
            & "WHERE ID =" & Str$(lRIP_SourceID) & ";"
    Else
        strQuery = "INSERT INTO Book (ID, Title, " _
        & "Subtitle, [Collection Title], Edition, " _
        & "Publisher, Location, Year) VALUES (" _
        & LTrim$(Str$(lRIP_SourceID)) & ", '" _
        & strRIPx_Title & "', '" _
        & strRIPx_Subtitle & "', '" _
        & strRIPx_CollectionTitle & "'," _
        & Str$(iRIPx_Edition) & ", '" _
        & strRIPx_Publisher & "', '" _
        & strRIPx_Location & "', #" _
        & datRIPx_Year & "#);"
    End If
    dbCitation.Execute strQuery, dbConsistent _
     Or dbFailOnError
ElseIf iRIP_ItemType = 2 Then
    Set rstUnion = UnionBookPeriodical()
    strCriteria = "ID =" & Str$(lAIP_ID)
    With rstUnion
        .FindFirst strCriteria
        If .NoMatch Then
            strQuery = "INSERT INTO Article (ID, " _
            & "SourceID, Title, Subtitle, " _
            & "[Source Type]) " _
            & "VALUES (" & LTrim$(Str$(lRIP_SourceID)) _
            & ", " & Str$(lRIPx_SourceID) & ", '" _
            & strRIPx_Title & "', '" & strRIPx_Subtitle _
            & "'," & Str$(iRIPx_SourceType) & ");"
        Else
            strQuery = "UPDATE Article SET SourceID = " _
            & Str$(lRIPx_SourceID) & ", " _
            & "Title = '" & strRIPx_Title & "', " _
            & "Subtitle = '" & strRIPx_Subtitle & "', " _
            & "[Source Type] = " _
            & Str$(iRIPx_SourceType) _
            & " WHERE ID = " & Str$(lRIP_SourceID) & ";"
        End If
    End With

    dbCitation.Execute strQuery, dbConsistent _
```

Continued

Listing 18-2: The Citation class module's wrapper around SQL's INSERT and DELETE.
(Continued)

```
        Or dbFailOnError

        'Now update the periodical information
        strQuery = "SELECT DISTINCTROW ID FROM Periodical " _
        & "WHERE ID =" & Str$(lRIPx_SourceID) & ";"
        Set rstVerify = dbCitation.OpenRecordset(strQuery)
        rstVerify.MoveLast
        If rstVerify.RecordCount > 0 Then
            strQuery = _
             "UPDATE Periodical SET Publication = '" _
            & strRIPx_Publication & "', " _
            & "Volume = " & Str$(lRIPx_Volume) & ", " _
            & "[Issue Number] = " & Str$(lRIPx_IssueNumber) _
            & ", " & "[Cover Date] = #" _
            & Str$(datRIPx_CoverDate) & "# " _
            & "WHERE ID = " & Str$(lRIPx_SourceID) & ";"
        Else
            strQuery = _
             "INSERT INTO Periodical (ID, Publication, " _
            & "Volume, [Issue Number], [Cover Date]) " _
            VALUES (" & Str$(lRIPx_SourceID) & ", '" _
            & strRIPx_Publication & "', " _
            & Str$(lRIPx_Volume) & ", " _
            & Str$(lRIPx_IssueNumber) & ", #" _
            & CDate(datRIPx_CoverDate) & "#);"
        End If
        dbCitation.Execute strQuery, dbConsistent _
         Or dbFailOnError
    End If
Else
    If iRIP_ItemType = 1 Or iRIP_ItemType = 3 Then
        strQuery = "INSERT INTO Book (ID, Title, Subtitle, " _
        & "[Collection Title], Edition, " _
        & "Publisher, Location, Year) VALUES (" _
        & LTrim$(Str$(lRIP_SourceID)) & ", '" _
        & strRIPx_Title & "', '" _
        & strRIPx_Subtitle & "', '" _
        & strRIPx_CollectionTitle & "'," _
        & Str$(iRIPx_Edition) & ", '" _
        & strRIPx_Publisher & "', '" _
        & strRIPx_Location & "', #" & datRIPx_Year & "#);"
```

```
        ElseIf iRIP_ItemType = 2 Then
            strQuery = "INSERT INTO Article _"
            & "(ID, SourceID, Title, Subtitle, [Source Type])" _
            & " VALUES (" & Str$(lRIP_SourceID) & ", " _
            & Str$(lRIPx_SourceID) & ", '" _
            & strRIPx_Title & "', '" & strRIPx_Subtitle & "', " _
            & Str$(iRIPx_SourceType) & ");"
        End If
        dbCitation.Execute strQuery, dbConsistent Or dbFailOnError
    End If

    bSourceIP = False
    rstVerify.Close
    Set rstVerify = Nothing

    WriteSource = True
    CleanSources
    Exit Function

WriteSourceErr:
    strErr = "Trouble writing to one of the source tables:" _
    & Chr$(13) & Err.Description
    MsgBox strErr, vbCritical Or vbMsgBoxHelpButton, _
     "Citation Error", Err.HelpFile, Err.HelpContext
    Debug.Print strQuery
    On Error GoTo 0
    WriteSource = False
End Function
```

First, let's go over what Listing 18-2 accomplishes: It determines which is the right table to be receiving the written record, and then determines whether a record with the same ID number already exists. If it does not, an INSERT query is generated for the appropriate table; if it does exist, an UPDATE query is generated instead.

VBA assembles SQL queries into strings on the fly

Private Function WriteSource() looks longer than it is, by virtue of the fact that the many SQL queries it utilizes take up so much room. In the form in which these queries appear in this procedure, you might not recognize them. This is because **SQL queries must be supplied to DAO (or ADO) in their entirety as arguments to the method which retrieves the records or executes the requested changes.** Because SQL queries are generally longer than the average VBA instruction, they have to be broken up on multiple lines – which also means breaking up the string used to create the argument into segments joined with one another using the & concatenation operator. I arranged these broken up segments so that some of the & operators can be easily spotted, and so they can help the human eye to better ascertain that they're being used to join a chain of segments together.

The first SQL query posed by this procedure could appear to the Jet interpreter like this:

```
SELECT DISTINCTROW * FROM Book WHERE ID = 4000000;
```

The meaning of this query in SQL is essentially, "Select every field in the one row of the Book table whose ID number is 4000000." By itself, this SQL query isn't too difficult for the human eye to translate. But VBA has to assemble this query out of parts of strings, plus translated text of variables currently in play. Number 4000000 is an example of a valid ID number for the Book table, such as the kind represented by variable lRIP_SourceID. The way this query must be assembled through VBA, it ends up looking like this in the source code:

```
strQuery = "SELECT DISTINCTROW * FROM Book WHERE ID = " _
           & Str$(lRIP_SourceID) & ";"
```

For VBA's purposes, the underscore character (_) breaks up an instruction into multiple lines. The VBA intrinsic function Str$() (which may also be phrased as Str()) generates a copy of the contents of variable lRIP_SourceID converted from a real value into a series of seven digits. As you read this VBA instruction from left to right, where the double-quotes *begin* is where a string of characters belonging to the SQL instruction begins; and where the double-quotes *end* is where the SQL instruction is put on pause, if you will, and where VBA picks up by attaching the data in some variable or the result of some function. Where the double-quotes *begin* again is where the SQL instruction resumes. (This is the reverse of the situation with HTML code, in which the <angle brackets> are used to denote the beginning and end of the *code*, and all the text that falls outside of the brackets belongs to the Web page.)

Later in the procedure, an SQL UPDATE statement is generated which changes the field contents of an existing record in the Book table. The SQL interpreter in Jet might see a statement that looks like this:

```
UPDATE Book SET Title = 'The Aloha System', Subtitle = '',
[Collection Title] = '', Edition = 0, Publisher = 'Prentice-Hall',
Location = 'Englewood Cliffs, N.J.', Year = #1/1/73#
WHERE ID = 4000000;
```

All of the data which fill in the blanks after the = operators are supplied by the various VBA variables you find in the VBA instruction that assembles the query:

```
strQuery = "UPDATE Book SET Title = '" _
    & strRIPx_Title & "', " _
    & "Subtitle = '" & strRIPx_Subtitle & "', " _
    & "[Collection Title] = '" _
    & strRIPx_CollectionTitle & "', " _
    & "Edition =" & Str$(iRIPx_Edition) & ", " _
    & "Publisher = '" & strRIPx_Publisher & "', " _
    & "Location = '" & strRIPx_Location & "', " _
    & "Year = #" & datRIPx_Year & "# " _
    & "WHERE ID =" & Str$(lRIP_SourceID) & ";"
```

All the numeral values are converted into string form with the Str$() function, while the data that are already strings and dates are written into the VBA instruction as they are.

In Depth: Literals in SQL queries require 'single quotes'

If you can remember to say to yourself, "SeQueL queries require single quotes" (but not too fast), you could just save Access, if not Windows, from crashing on you entirely. Although not all SQL interpreters abide by the rule that string literals, such as those used in WHERE criteria for SELECT statements, should appear in 'single quotes' rather than "double quotes," the Jet engine does follow this rule. If you were to attach double quotes directly to the query text (you'd have to use Chr$(34) to represent the character), the SQL interpreter would stop parsing the query when it reached the first double quote, resulting in a half-statement that ends with WHERE =. On more than one occasion, a certain author who on more than one occasion applied double quotes where single ones belonged, found that the ODBC driver would try on its own to correct the error, fail, and place a call back to Access that was "out of frame," so that Access could not interpret the error. Sometimes the error message would be illegible, but most often Access would just crash, at times taking Windows with it. For quite some time, this author was uncertain of the actual cause of the crash, until in a brainstorm he corrected his query assembly methodology. Don't let yourself fall into this same trap.

How DAO presents the SQL query to Jet

There are many complex schemes made possible by DAO 3.6 for querying a database, none of which ever really have to be used as long as you're writing your queries in SQL rather than Access. The methodology used by Listing 18-2, as well as the entire `classCitation` module, is by far the simplest way to go. It is a three-step process which is actually easier to understand than it is to actually do:

1. For the result set of an SQL `SELECT` query, declare a variable as class `DAO.Recordset`. (Note: Don't declare the variable `As New DAO.Recordset`, because we don't want the actual record set to exist yet until after the SQL `SELECT` query has been executed.)

2. Assemble the segments of a SQL query from pieces of literal text and converted data, and assign those segments to a string variable such as `strQuery`. You've just seen two examples of this step demonstrated.

3. For a `SELECT` query, generate the record set using the `OpenRecordset` method for the `DAO.Database` class object declared earlier in your program. An example from Listing 18-2:

   ```
   Set rstVerify = dbCitation.OpenRecordset(strQuery)
   ```

   Here, `rstVerify` is the `DAO.Recordset` class object declared in Step 1. Variable `dbCitation` is declared at the beginning of the class module as type `DAO.Database`. Its `.OpenRecordset` method has the job of posing the query to Jet. Here, variable `strQuery` is the only argument the method requires. There are other optional arguments; but if you used the Access environment to normalize your database and establish your relationships between tables, chances are that you won't ever need any of these arguments. Also, one of the `.OpenRecordset` method's optional arguments refers to the *type* of record set it generates; but again, since you're using strictly SQL and won't be using ISAM to plow through each returned record one-at-a-time, the type of record set returned will be immaterial. (It's safe to say that most of the complexities of DAO and ADO are self-supporting, and may be almost entirely avoided.)

   For an SQL action query such as `INSERT`, `UPDATE`, or `DELETE`, the method you will want to use instead is `.Execute`, which simply "commits" the instruction to the database. Here is one example from Listing 18-2:

   ```
   dbCitation.Execute strQuery, dbConsistent Or dbFailOnError
   ```

   Again, the antecedent is the `DAO.Database` class object. In the second argument, two bitwise settings are supplied which engage the special referential integrity enforcement features deployed when the database was designed in Access. First, `dbConsistent` assures that any changes made to the database are in keeping with the rules established by the relationships.

So for instance, a record cannot be deleted if another record in another table refers to its primary key; and another record cannot have its references to a primary key changed as long as the record in another table which owns that primary key continues to exist. Secondly, `dbFailOnError` has any error resulting from SQL or Jet result in an error in VBA which can be trapped, identified, and perhaps remedied. **By default, VBA ignores any errors generated by Jet.** Strange, but true. This setting makes certain that cannot happen. The `Or` term here is a Boolean operator which joins `dbConsistent` and `dbFailOnError` into a single argument; it does *not* mean "one *or* the other."

Now that you have an idea of what's going on here, we can walk you through Listing 18-2 from the top. The purpose of `Public Function WriteSource()` is to formalize any changes made to the record of a book, article, or unpublished work in memory. As a security measure, if the ID number of the source record in memory `lRIP_SourceID` is 0, or if the record in memory has no title, the Boolean result of `WriteSource()` is set to `False`, and the procedure is exited.

The first real job the procedure has is to check for the existence of a record within the Book or Article table whose ID equates with the one in memory. **Because Access' referential integrity rules are enforced by this class module, sometimes a record has to be written to a database before all of its fields have been entered, in order that another record in another table that shares a relationship with this record's table, may exist.** While this enforces the *integrity* of the database, it places its *validity* in jeopardy. The database could end up being full of half-records (and in several previous builds of the class module, that's indeed what happened). The way `classCitation` avoids this occurrence is by maintaining a constant handle on whenever fields in memory have been changed, by setting module-level variable `bSourceIP` to `True`. `Private Function WriteSource()` will be executed if that variable is `True`. It will also be executed if it needs to use an `INSERT` query to generate a half-record in order not to violate referential integrity. Later on, the half-record in memory may be completed, making it into a full record whose ID number equates with that of the stored half-record. To respond to that contingency, this procedure always checks for the existence of a record with the same ID number. If it does exist, the procedure will generate an `UPDATE` query instead of an `INSERT` query, which would fail and generate an error (thanks to our telling it to in advance) if it tried to insert a record with an existing ID number. The `UPDATE` action query turns the half-record into a full record.

So all that Listing 18-2 does after verifying the existence/non-existence of the record, is determine the appropriate table, and `INSERT` the record if it doesn't exist yet or `UPDATE` the record if it does. It takes several instructions (and parts of instructions) to accomplish this, but that's truly all that it does. Within `classCitation`, similar procedures for the Reference, Agent, and Citation tables perform the same job in the same way.

Earlier in Listing 18-1, `Private Function ValidateSourceID()` had the job of determining whether the ID number it had been receiving had changed, and if it had, writing the record in memory to the database and reading the record with the new ID. You just saw the procedure that writes the record to the database. Listing 18-3 shows the procedure that reads in the newly requested record:

Listing 18-3: Using SQL's SELECT statement to read a single record into memory.

```
Private Function ReadSource(Optional lSourceNo As Long) As Boolean
    Dim rstSourceRead As DAO.Recordset
    Dim rstExtendRead As DAO.Recordset
    Dim strQuery As String, strErr As String
    Static lLastSeen As Long

    On Error GoTo ReadSourceErr

    If lSourceNo <> 0 Then
        If lSourceNo = lLastSeen Then
            ReadSource = True
            Exit Function
        End If
        If Not ValidateSourceID(lSourceNo) Then
            ReadSource = False
            ClearSource
            Exit Function
        Else
            lLastSeen = lSourceNo
            If bSourceIP Then
                WriteSource
            End If
        End If
    Else
        lSourceNo = lRIP_SourceID
    End If

    Select Case GetTableNo(lSourceNo)
        Case BIB_BOOK
            iRIP_ItemType = 1
        Case BIB_ARTICLE
            iRIP_ItemType = 2
        Case BIB_UNPUBLISHED
            iRIP_ItemType = 3
    End Select

    If iRIP_ItemType = 1 Or iRIP_ItemType = 3 Then
```

```
    strQuery = "SELECT DISTINCTROW * FROM Book WHERE ID = " _
            & Str$(lRIP_SourceID) & ";"
    Set rstSourceRead = dbCitation.OpenRecordset(strQuery)
    If rstSourceRead.RecordCount > 0 Then
        strRIPx_Title = rstSourceRead!Title
        strRIPx_Subtitle = rstSourceRead!Subtitle
        strRIPx_CollectionTitle = _
         rstSourceRead![Collection Title]
        iRIPx_Edition = rstSourceRead!Edition
        strRIPx_Publisher = rstSourceRead!Publisher
        strRIPx_Location = rstSourceRead!Location
        datRIPx_Year = rstSourceRead!Year
    Else
        ReadSource = False
        ClearSource
        Exit Function
    End If
ElseIf iRIP_ItemType = 2 Then
    strQuery = "SELECT DISTINCTROW * FROM Article " _
            & "WHERE ID = " & Str$(lRIP_SourceID) & ";"
    Set rstSourceRead = dbCitation.OpenRecordset(strQuery)
    rstSourceRead.MoveLast
    If rstSourceRead.RecordCount > 0 Then
        strRIPx_Title = rstSourceRead!Title
        strRIPx_Subtitle = rstSourceRead!Subtitle
        lRIPx_SourceID = rstSourceRead!SourceID
        iRIPx_SourceType = rstSourceRead![Source Type]
    Else
        ReadSource = False
        ClearSource
        Exit Function
    End If
    If iRIPx_SourceType = 1 Then
        strQuery = "SELECT DISTINCTROW * FROM Book " _
                & "WHERE ID = " & Str$(lRIPx_SourceID) & ";"
        Set rstExtendRead = dbCitation.OpenRecordset(strQuery)
        rstExtendRead.MoveLast
        If rstExtendRead.RecordCount > 0 Then
            strRIPx2_Title = rstSourceRead!Title
            strRIPx2_Subtitle = rstSourceRead!Subtitle
            iRIPx_Edition = rstSourceRead!Edition
            strRIPx_Publisher = rstSourceRead!Publisher
            strRIPx_Location = rstSourceRead!Location
            datRIPx_Year = rstSourceRead!Year
```

Continued

Listing 18-3: Using SQL's SELECT statement to read a single record into memory. *(Continued)*

```
            Else
                ReadSource = False
                ClearSource
                Exit Function
            End If
        ElseIf iRIPx_SourceType = 2 Then
            strQuery = "SELECT DISTINCTROW * FROM Periodical " _
                    & "WHERE ID =" & Str$(lRIPx_SourceID) & ";"
            Set rstExtendRead = dbCitation.OpenRecordset(strQuery)
            rstExtendRead.MoveLast
            If rstExtendRead.RecordCount > 0 Then
                strRIPx_Publication = rstExtendRead!Publication
                lRIPx_Volume = rstExtendRead!Volume
                lRIPx_IssueNumber = rstExtendRead![Issue Number]
                datRIPx_CoverDate = rstExtendRead![Cover Date]
            End If
            strRIPx2_Title = ""
            strRIPx2_Subtitle = ""

            rstExtendRead.Close
            Set rstExtendRead = Nothing
        End If
        RetrieveAgentsAssociated lRIP_SourceID

        ReadSource = True
    End If

    rstSourceRead.Close
    Set rstSourceRead = Nothing
    bSourceIP = False
    Exit Function

ReadSourceErr:
    strErr = "Trouble reading source data:" & Chr$(13) & _
     Err.Description
    MsgBox strErr, vbCritical Or vbMsgBoxHelpButton, _
     "Citation Error", Err.HelpFile, Err.HelpContext
    Debug.Print strQuery
    On Error GoTo 0
    ReadSource = False
End Function
```

By default, this procedure reads the record currently represented by lRIP_SourceID, unless an optional ID number lSourceNo is supplied. If it is, then it has to be verified through ValidateSourceID(lSourceNo).

If the source refers to a book or unpublished work, a query is assembled for it which might look like this:

```
SELECT DISTINCTROW * FROM Book WHERE ID = 4000000;
```

If the source is an article from a magazine or newspaper, the query instead might look like this:

```
SELECT DISTINCTROW * FROM Article WHERE ID = 2000000;
```

Just after these queries, the rstSourceRead.MoveLast instructions are a throwback to DAO 3.5, which could not get a current record count unless it first moved its ISAM cursor to the end of the record set; DAO 3.6 does not have this problem.

If the source is an article, then the data for the source *of* the article (a magazine or perhaps a book) must subsequently be loaded into memory. Since an article's own source may be a magazine, and a single magazine may contain more than one referenced article, this fully normalized database stores information about the magazine separately from the information about each article, and uses a relationship to link the two together. The SQL query that loads the Periodical table information doesn't look much different:

```
SELECT DISTINCTROW * FROM Periodical WHERE ID = 7000000;
```

Whenever data is written to a property of classCitation using a new ID number as the argument for that property, the class dumps whatever data it currently has in memory for the entire record, and loads the entire record with the new ID number into memory, *before* it assigns that property setting to the record. The same switchover happens whenever data is *polled* from a property of classCitation. The Property Get procedure which responds to a poll of the .SourceTitle property is quite simple: It assigns the property term the setting of the Title field, held in memory by strRIPx_Title as long as the ID number supplied as an argument is valid; otherwise, it assigns a blank string:

```
Public Property Get SourceTitle(lItemNo As Long) As String
    If ValidateWhateverID(lItemNo) Then
        SourceTitle = strRIPx_Title
    Else
        SourceTitle = ""
    End If
End Property
```

Now all a form module needs to do to retrieve the field contents from the database is to poll the properties of the `classCitation` class object, as you can see numerous times from this example from one of the form modules in my test project, presented in Listing 18-4:

Listing 18-4: How a form module addresses the Citation class to update itself.

```
Private Sub RefreshForm()
    Dim iCount As Integer, lGather As Long
    Dim strPubNames() As String, lPubNames() As Long

    If lRefID = 0 Then
        lRefID = XCiter.ReferenceID
    End If

    tabSourceType.Value = XCiter.ReferenceItemType(lRefID) - 1
    CorrectFlexLabels

    If cboTitle.Text = "" Then
        cboTitle.Text = XCiter.SourceTitle(lRefID)
    End If
    If txtSubtitle.Text = "" Then
        txtSubtitle.Text = XCiter.SourceSubtitle(lRefID)
    End If
    If txtReferenceMark.Text = "" Then
        txtReferenceMark.Text = XCiter.ReferenceMark(lRefID)
    End If

    Select Case tabSourceType.Value
        Case 0
            lGather = CLng(XCiter.SourceEdition(lRefID))
            txtFlex1.Text = IIf(lGather > 0, Str$(lGather), "")
            txtFlex2.Text = XCiter.SourcePublisher(lRefID)
            txtFlex3.Text = XCiter.SourceLocation(lRefID)
            lGather = CLng(XCiter.SourceYear(lRefID))
            txtFlex4.Text = IIf(lGather > CLng(#1/1/100#), _
             CDate(lGather), "")
            txtFlex5.Text = XCiter.SourceCollectionTitle(lRefID)
            lblSourceTitle.Caption = _
             XCiter.SourceBookTitle(lRefID)
        Case 1
            If XCiter.RetrievePeriodicalLabels(strPubNames(), _
             lPubNames()) Then
                cboFlex1.Clear
                If UBound(strPubNames) > 0 Then
```

```
                    For iCount = 1 To UBound(strPubNames)
                        cboFlex1.AddItem strPubNames(iCount)
                    Next iCount
                End If
            End If
            cboFlex1.Text = XCiter.SourcePublication(lRefID)
            lGather = XCiter.SourceVolume(lRefID)
            txtFlex2.Text = IIf(lGather > 0, Str$(lGather), "")
            lGather = XCiter.SourceIssueNumber(lRefID)
            txtFlex3.Text = IIf(lGather > 0, Str$(lGather), "")
            lGather = CLng(XCiter.SourceCoverDate(lRefID))
            txtFlex4.Text = IIf(lGather > CLng(#1/1/100#), _
             CDate(lGather), "")
            txtFlex5.Text = ""
            lblSourceTitle.Caption = _
             XCiter.SourceBookTitle(lRefID)
        Case 2
            txtFlex1.Text = XCiter.SourceLocation(lRefID)
            lGather = CLng(XCiter.SourceYear(lRefID))
            txtFlex2.Text = IIf(lGather > CLng(#1/1/100#), _
             CDate(lGather), "")
            txtFlex3.Text = ""
            txtFlex4.Text = ""
            txtFlex5.Text = ""
    End Select

    chkEtAl.Value = XCiter.ReferenceEtAl(lRefID)

    RefreshAgentsList

    lGather = XCiter.ReferenceFormat(lRefID)
    If lGather And 1 Then
        chkBibliography.Value = True
    End If
    If lGather And 2 Then
        chkEndnotes.Value = True
    End If
End Sub
```

Here, the classCitation class object XCiter is polled no fewer than 20 times, with the subscript lRefID pointing to the current ID number for the record in the Reference table each time. The return data is assigned to the various Forms 2.0 controls that make up this form. The trick here is that the value of lRefID never changes throughout the course of Private Sub RefreshForm(). *Not changing* is a signal to `classCitation` to maintain its focus on the same record, and not to execute a `SELECT` query to retrieve some other record.

Much ADO about . . . very little

And now for the real payoff in using SQL as opposed to either ISAM access method prescribed by DAO or ADO: The preceding examples used DAO 3.6 to achieve their purpose (though some code was left in to remain compatible with DAO 3.5). If for some reason you wanted to use ADO instead, you would need to declare and set up your database objects differently. Here's how the DAO version of `classCitation` declares its module-level database object variables:

```
Private dbCitation As DAO.Database
Private wkSpace As DAO.Workspace
```

Next, here is how DAO sets up its module-level database objects within its `Private Sub Class_Initialize()` procedure:

```
Set wkSpace = DAO.DBEngine.CreateWorkspace(Name:="", _
 UserName:="admin", Password:="", UseType:=dbUseJet)
Set dbCitation = wkSpace.OpenDatabase(Name:=strBaseFile, _
 Options:=False, ReadOnly:=False)
```

Here you see DAO setting up its "workspace" for the database in question, and "logging you in" as the administrator (as if the database really did care who you were). This `Workspace` class object `wkSpace` will rarely be used for any other purpose in DAO except for the very next instruction, which uses the `OpenDatabase` method to bring up the database – whose filename at this point has already been ascertained and loaded into variable `strBaseFile`.

For ADO, the two module-level variables are replaced with the following single one:

```
Private connCitation As ADODB.Connection
```

The "workspace" metaphor is effectively abolished; as you can see, it serves little purpose for DAO in practice. Next, ADO's connection to the database is established with the following instructions that are clearly easier for *humans* to read:

```
Set connCitation = New ADODB.Connection
connCitation.Open strBaseFile, "admin", ""
```

In ADO, the `Connection` class object is your program's single link between VBA and the database – which has some clear architectural advantages, although admittedly you only have a few instructions per project with which you may enjoy them.

After you've made these simple changes, here is how the three-step query method I outlined earlier for querying the database would need to change:

1. After making sure your VBA environment has "ActiveX Data Objects 2.1 Library" as an active reference in its References dialog, you would declare your record set objects `As ADODB.Recordset` rather than `As DAO.Recordset`.

2. You would change absolutely nothing about the way you assemble your SQL query strings.

3. For a `SELECT` query, you would change instructions such as this:

   `Set rstVerify = dbCitation.OpenRecordset(strQuery)`

   to read as follows:

   `rstVerify.Open strQuery`

   The references to your field contents, such as `rstVerify![Given Name]`, remain as they are.

   Each procedure which utilizes an action query, such as `INSERT`, `UPDATE`, or `DELETE`, will require you to declare a separate `ADODB.Command` class variable, like the following:

   `Dim commSource As New ADODB.Command`

   The text of your completed SQL action query will need to be assigned to this variable in the following manner:

   `commSource.CommandText = strQuery`

   The instruction which executes the action query becomes the following:

   `commSource.Execute`

You have just witnessed the entire transition from DAO 3.6 to ADO 2.1. That, as they say, is it. (For this, they throw a convention.)

Utilizing ODBC to Connect to the Database

As you've just seen, once a DAO workspace or ADO connection is established, the next step for your VBA program is to address and open a specific database. When you're addressing a local Access/Jet database file, you don't need ODBC. For DAO, you use the `.OpenDatabase` method belonging to the `Workspace` object you've declared. Generally, the only argument you need for this method is the name of the database. For ADO, you open your database with the same instruction you use to set up the connection, by way of the `.Open` method of the `Connection` class object. You have just read the single simplest portion of this chapter.

When you do use ODBC, the process of connecting to the database, and the process of connecting to the ODBC driver that will present the database to your VBA procedure, is made into the same step. With Jet in play, you use the `.OpenDatabase` method to point both to the database you're linking to, as well as to the ODBC driver that will be handling the connection. When you're using ODBCDirect to circumvent Jet, you'll instead be using an entirely different method, `.OpenConnection`. This method directly addresses only the ODBC driver used in the connection, but embedded in the information that you pass to this driver is the name of the data or database to which your VBA procedure will be connecting.

Where ODBC drivers come into play

The ODBC system supplies Jet and VBA with a series of database *drivers* – something less than managers but something more than data filters. These drivers are intended for what Microsoft calls "desktop use," meaning that the user application and the database share the same processor. These drivers are necessary for your VBA module, for whatever O2K application it may be designed, to address Access, dBASE, Excel, FoxPro, and delimited text files that are not directly managed through an active RDBMS. Remember that an "Access file" is really a Jet database file.

Office 2000 Setup does not install all of these desktop database drivers for you. If your data originates from Informix or Oracle, or if you intend for ODBC to import a simple text file, you need to install drivers for that purpose yourself. You can find the "ODBC Desktop Driver Pack" on Microsoft's Web site, in its Technical Support department.

The Access database driver may be unnecessary if your VBA module is geared to run within the Access workspace itself. Since Access utilizes Jet anyway, data that is open within an Access workspace is addressable through VBA automatically. However, Jet also has access to database files and active databases that are not loaded into the Access workspace. Furthermore, using a VBA module to address these other database files does not bring them into the Access workspace. Your VBA module may generate data that is added to whatever Access database is already open. But your module cannot open a table, a record set, or a query and add that to Access' Database window.

VBA and Access don't make contact the same way

The way you make contact with a database through VBA is not the same way you make contact with that same database through Access. In other words, **VBA instructions do not model how Access, or any other Office 2000 application, naturally accesses regulated data.** So when you set up a VBA workspace (session) using the Jet database engine, or when you set up an ODBC process that either uses or does not use Jet, what your procedure does is not at all equivalent to what Access does when a user gives commands to it.

Why is this important? Because the circumstances or error conditions you might expect to find with an ordinary Access operation will not be the same as with a VBA module. Access considers the data that you address through VBA as either data about to be linked into an existing Access table, or ancillary data. So what was all this about a VBA module being at the center of an Access application? If your VBA module does perform the core data operations, then how Access "considers" the data it uses is immaterial. You'll notice it, as Access' programmer, but if you build your application well, the user won't.

Whose data is it anyway?

The ODBC system muddies the conceptual waters a bit by maintaining three departments of so-called *data sources* with which your DAO workspace connects. A data source, or DSN (the "N" stands for "name," although the abbreviation has come to mean "data source"), is an address for an ODBC driver, installed either locally or on your network. The four categories are as follows:

◆ **System DSN** refers to an ODBC driver addressable by all users on all processors in the network, granted that these users are able to log in.

◆ **User DSN** refers to an ODBC driver installed locally that is (at least, once they get this part working) only addressable by a single user.

◆ **Machine DSN** refers to an ODBC driver installed locally on a client machine, and that is addressable by all users of that client.

◆ **File DSN** refers to an initialization file with the same general format as other .INI files in Windows, and that contains the general parameters necessary to log onto and engage an ODBC driver.

Now that those distinctions have been made – at least on paper – what's the *real* difference between these four DSNs? The simple answer – and I just love simple answers – is *none*. All DSNs for any one particular format or source of data lead to the engagement of the ODBC driver for specifically that data. The distinguishing factor between a system and user DSN – that a system DSN should be accessible to all users on a network whereas a user DSN should be accessible to one user on one system – is cast mercilessly to the wolves once we discover that a system DSN can be installed locally and that a user DSN refers to an ODBC driver that can be logged onto by anyone. Windows 98 attempts to address this latter problem by making the login information contingent upon each user's profile on the machine; but so far, this key distinction has yet to be made concrete in any sense other than the purely conceptual one. Meanwhile, the initialization file through which a file DSN is invoked so far contains one and only one parameter: the name of the ODBC driver being contacted. The DSN is complexity for complexity's sake.

When you use the `.OpenDatabase` or `.OpenConnection` method to make contact with a database through ODBC, one of the parameters in ODBC's complex connection string is marked `DSN=`. The name to which that marking refers is the name of the ODBC driver handling the data. In other words, **the parameter that asks for the data source name is actually expecting the driver name.** As long as you remember that, you can safely forget what DSN stands for — maybe you could pretend it's one of those upstart TV networks.

When your VBA procedure contacts an ODBC driver, yet another communications process begins, and the procedure "logs onto" that driver. A user ID and password are involved, separate from the user ID and password used to "log onto" the workspace. If the driver is just a local process that handles the query in lieu of an active RDBMS, then the user ID is generally `admin`, and the password is again a null string. But if the driver gives DAO an entry into a network database manager or a local RDBMS, then these identifiers are the ones that a user or administrator requires to gain entry to the database.

Retrieving records from the database or query

The main objective of a VBA procedure that utilizes DAO is to retrieve a certain specified set of records, whether it is directly from a table or as a compiled result of a query. The container for the retrieved records is the DAO `Recordset` class object. The DAO method that passes the query to its designated target and begins retrieval of the records is `.OpenRecordset`. It is an easy enough method to remember, although its arguments can cause pain to several sensitive vertebrae, as you'll soon witness for yourself. The return value of the `.OpenRecordset` method is this `Recordset` class object. You need an object variable at the ready that points to this returned object so that you may read the records (or more accurately, the first record) once it becomes available.

There is more than one way to make contact with a set of records, and which way you choose depends on the task at hand. **The chief limitation of an ODBC driver is that its data access scheme either is, or is modeled after, ISAM, where records are read one-at-a-time rather than as a set.** So, if your intention is to open an entire table, and not to retrieve a subset of the records in that table, then you declare an object variable that references the table (a `TableDef` class object) and invoke the `.OpenRecordset` method on that variable. When would you ever do this? Suppose your Access form lets the user browse through the entire table, or that you're using Excel to dynamically import the table into a worksheet. If you're simply opening a table and reading in the contents from front to back, you don't require a query. You might be presenting the user with a complete list of records that she could query or filter herself later. The `.OpenRecordset` method may link directly to the `TableDef` class object in such cases where a logical query is not required, at least not at the outset.

If the record set you're looking for is a logical subset of a table (for instance, all employees who earn over $45,000 annually) or a join product of the information in more than one normalized table (such as, the contents of all issues that contain more than ten articles), then you have an option: You can attach the SQL query that produces this subset as a parameter to the `.OpenRecordset` method, making that the automatic query for the method. Or, you can declare a `QueryDef` class object variable, which will contain an SQL query, and assign it to point to the database that will be queried. To be accurate, you may declare more than one `QueryDef` class variable for several queries regarding the database; so the real benefit of declaring `QueryDef` class objects in the first place is to enable multiple queries.

Coping with the ISAM-restricted nature of ODBC

If you use ODBC, with or without the aid of Jet, to retrieve records from a database — query or no query — when you first execute the `.OpenRecordset` method, the maximum number of records that will be retrieved is one. This is true even if more than one record in the queried table or tables match the criteria. Why is this the case? Because no matter what scheme was used to retrieve records from the database, or by whom or what, the scheme used to relate these records back to VBA through ODBC is *sequential* (the "S" in "ISAM"). A database manager or database-handling component (like an ODBC driver) that utilizes an ISAM scheme is only capable of "seeing" one record at any one time. The position of that record in the retrieval set, or in the table that is the source of the record, is maintained by the ISAM driver as what is called a *cursor.*

The fact that there may be more than one record, existing in a table or assembled through a field subset or join, that matches the query criteria does not mean that the final DAO `Recordset` class object will only have one record to its name. The way to coax the ISAM driver into "dripping," if you will, each record into the record set is to flush it, in a sense, using the `.MoveLast` method of the `Recordset` class. This directs the ISAM driver to scoot its cursor toward the final record in its set of *retrievable* records, wherever that may be located, and along the way insert all matching records it finds into the set of *retrieved* records — the set maintained by DAO. At that point, the `Recordset` class object has a full set of retrieved records matching the query criteria. This methodology holds true regardless of whether or not your procedure utilizes Jet, and regardless of whether or not it utilizes ODBC.

Constituents of permanent workspaces are permanent

When you use the `.Append` method to formally attach a newly declared and assigned `Workspace` class variable to DAO's `Workspaces` collection, the workspace becomes persistent and will not be shut down even if Access itself is shut down — even if your computer is shut down — until the `.Close` method is executed for the workspace.

Because a container object is nothing without its constituents, the constituents of a persistent workspace — for instance, table definitions (`TableDef` class objects) and query definitions (`QueryDef` class objects) – are automatically persistent. (The exception is `Connection` class objects, which are used only with ODBCDirect, and which are automatically closed when Access is exited.) However, **the object reference variables assigned to refer to any of these persistent objects do not themselves become persistent.** In other words, the VBA rules of scope do not change simply because DAO's constituency setup transcends that scope.

All persistent objects are members of their respective collections. So when your freshly started VBA module needs to assign new variables to refer to persistent collection members, rather than plow through each member of a collection by index number in search of some defining characteristic, your VBA code can refer to members by the names you gave them at the time of their creation. For example, the `.CreateQueryDef` method accepts an optional `Name:` argument.

Connecting the Database to the Outside World

The database used to make certain these examples would work under pressure, is a huge single table that wastranslated into several formats. The source is the Penn World Table, an annually updated table of comparative economic data for countries around the world, compiled by a team of scholars presently led by a group at the University of Pennsylvania. I chose this table because it contains quite a bit of statistical data, and also because it's huge.

Addressing an .MDB database through Jet

Our first example is the simplest: Jet is used to query the contents of an Access/Jet .MDB database. ODBC is not involved. Listing 18-5 shows a common procedure. This `Function` procedure takes a single argument: the name of a country. The Penn World table contains records pertaining to the economic performance of countries. Each record tracks the performance for a given year, so there are as many records for a country as there are years that the University of Pennsylvania has tracked that country.

Listing 18-5: Querying a local .MDB database through Jet.

```
Function GetCountryHistoryMDB(Optional strCountry As String) _
  As DAO.Recordset
    Dim dbThis As DAO.Database, rstThis As DAO.Recordset, _
    qdfMDB As DAO.QueryDef, prpMDB As DAO.Property
    Dim strQuery As String, bFound As Boolean

    For Each wrkThis In Workspaces
        If wrkThis.Name = "MDB" Then
```

```
            bFound = True
            Exit For
        End If
    Next wrkThis
    If bFound = False Then
        Set wrkThis = CreateWorkspace(Name:="MDB", _
         UserName:="admin", Password:="", UseType:=dbUseJet)
        Workspaces.Append wrkThis
    End If
    Set dbThis = wrkThis.OpenDatabase _
     (Name:="D:\DFS\Databases\WorldData.mdb")
    For Each qdfMDB In dbThis.QueryDefs
        If qdfMDB.Name = "Q-MDB" Then
            bFound = True
            Exit For
        End If
    Next qdfMDB
    If strCountry <> "" Then
        strCountry = UCase$(strCountry)
    Else
        strCountry = "U.S.A."
    End If
    If bFound = False Then
        Set qdfMDB = dbThis.CreateQueryDef(Name:="Q-MDB")
        With qdfMDB
            Set prpMDB = .CreateProperty(Name:="Country", _
             Type:=dbText, Value:=strCountry)
            .Properties.Append prpMDB
            strQuery = "SELECT * FROM PWT56 WHERE Country = '" _
             & strCountry & "';"
            .SQL = strQuery
        End With
    Else
        If UCase$(strCountry) <> qdfMDB.Properties("Country") Then
            strQuery = "SELECT * FROM PWT56 WHERE Country = '" _
             & strCountry & "';"
            qdfMDB.SQL = strQuery
        End If
        dbThis.QueryDefs.Refresh
    End If
    Set rstThis = qdfMDB.OpenRecordset(Options:=dbFailOnError)
    rstThis.MoveLast

    Set GetCountryHistoryMDB = rstThis
End Function
```

The path for the file "D:\DFS\Databases\WorldData.mdb" in the above listing may need to be altered to reflect the location where you install this database. For your own testing, WorldData.mdb is included on the CD-ROM that accompanies this book. Future listings that also include explicit paths, may need to be changed to reflect your particular installation locations.

The first For Each...Next loop searches to see if the workspace named MDB (the one created by this procedure) already exists and, if it does, sets a Boolean flag bFound, which prevents it from being "created" again. Looping through all of the members of the Workspaces collection in search of a familiar name, is the only way you can ascertain whether a workspace exists, other than risking an error-trap routine within this procedure that is executed whenever the procedure makes reference to MDB before it officially exists.

If the workspace does not exist (If bFound = False) then the CreateWork space function is invoked. Note its four arguments; besides the Name: argument is UserName: and Password:, which are necessary at all times, though only important when Access is monitoring the transactions of its own set of users. The UseType: argument sets whether Jet is used or not used; the alternate setting is dbUseODBC, which invokes ODBCDirect. Once a workspace is created, it is not a member of Jet's persistent collection until the .Append method is used to add it to Workspaces.

Database class objects are never persistent

Whether or not a Workspace class object is persistent, **a workspace invoked by a VBA module never points to any database until that database is explicitly opened.** In other words, even if your procedure picks up a persistent workspace from an earlier Access session, you cannot presume the databases to which that workspace referred before are open now. You must explicitly open any and all databases that a workspace will use using the .OpenDatabase method. Each time you invoke this method, a Database class object is added to the Databases collection. But this collection will always be empty whenever you address a workspace, persistent or not, for the first time. Meanwhile, queries (QueryDef class objects) that contain SQL code that references these databases, open or not, are made persistent when the workspace to which they belong is persistent.

Why is this the case? Because opening a database is the beginning of a communications process between the user and the database, which involves the user logging in (or VBA logging in on the user's behalf) and which is a formal transaction that Access might need to monitor and record. A workspace is just a piece of self-serving symbology, whereas a database is a real-world entity whose invocation and dismissal are real, everyday processes no matter how they're modeled.

QueryDef objects have amendable properties

In processing the query, this procedure needs to determine first of all whether an SQL instruction exists yet, and then if it does, whether the country passed to this `Function` procedure as an argument is the same country mentioned in the persistent query. The SQL query used by this procedure looks like this:

```
SELECT * FROM PWT56 WHERE Country = 'ANGOLA';
```

The asterisk here designates "all fields," so that the construction of the retrieved records does not have to be listed here field by field. What does `PWT56` mean? It's the name of the table being scanned, from SQL's point of view; it is also, by no coincidence, the filename of the file being scanned, minus the extender.

In Listing 18-5, I could have concocted a function that parses the existing query in search of the country; but what I did instead involves an interesting feature of `QueryDef` class objects: the capability for their intrinsic properties to be amended. After a `For Each...Next` loop clause determines that a query named Q-MDB (my arbitrary name) has yet to be created, the `.CreateQueryDef` method is used to construct the new query. Here, the object is created first, and its intrinsic properties are set later. The query that is the subject of this procedure is assigned to the object reference `qdfMDB`. Within a `With` clause that names `qdfMDB` as the default object, a `.CreateProperty` method builds an entirely new property for this `QueryDef` class object, in this case called `"Country"`. Granted, this property does not become a formal member of the DAO library, so you can't say "qdfMDB.Country." But the new property object (first there were "object properties," now there are "property objects") does become a member of the `QueryDef` class object's `Properties` collection. So the procedure can check later for this property with the term `qdfMDB.Properties("Country")`. This way, the name of the last *new* country supplied to this procedure will be remembered for next time, when the procedure checks whether the SQL query should be reassembled.

The newly created SQL query is assigned to the `.SQL` property of `qdfMDF`. In the `Else` side of the main conditional clause – the side that is executed if the `QueryDef` object was found in the persistent collection – a subordinate clause checks whether the stored `"Country"` property for the query is the same as the one passed to this procedure. If it isn't, the query is reassembled and reassigned to `qdfMDB.SQL`. The `.Refresh` method belongs to the `QueryDefs` collection, not to any one member, and instructs Jet to process all of the queries for this database over again, with new contents in case the database has changed.

Towards the end of Listing 18-5, the `.OpenRecordSet` method is finally invoked. In this particular case, the query reference `qdfMDB` gets to do the honors, since it is the query maintained by that object through which all of the records being scanned must pass. The resulting record set is assigned to variable `rstThis`; but as you may recall from earlier, the number of records in this set at first will always be 1 or 0, no matter how many matches there truly are. To retrieve all the matches, the

`.MoveLast` method is invoked, bringing the internal cursor of the ISAM manager to the end of its own set of retrieved records, and flushing them into DAO's record set along the way.

Finally in Listing 18-5, the complete record set is assigned to `GetCountry HistoryMDB`, the name of the `Function` procedure.

Addressing non-Jet databases through Jet

For Listing 18-6, ODBC is brought into the mix. Our objective here is to query the same information from the same database, but this time it's not a Jet database but a dBASE file. The dBASE ODBC driver is required for this operation whether the file is remote or local, but Jet will still serve as the manager.

With the release of Office 2000, Microsoft has announced that it has ceased its support for all ODBC drivers that pertain to Borland (Inprise) brand products, including dBASE and Paradox. Such drivers will continue to exist, though they will probably have to be manufactured solely by Inprise. This could, of course, mean these drivers will work just fine.

Listing 18-6: ODBC makes a dBASE file accessible to Jet.

```
Function GetCountryHistoryDBF(Optional strCountry As String) _
  As DAO.Recordset
    Dim wrkThis As DAO.Workspace
    Dim rstThis As DAO.Recordset, qdfDBF As DAO.QueryDef
    Dim strType As String, strPathname As String, strQuery _
    As String

    Set wrkThis = CreateWorkspace(Name:="DBF", _
    UserName:="admin", Password:="", UseType:=dbUseJet)
    strType = "dBASE IV;DATABASE=D:\DFS\Databases\pwt56.dbf"
    strPathname = "D:\DFS\Databases\"
    Set dbThis = wrkThis.OpenDatabase(Name:=strPathname, _
    Options:=dbDriverNoPrompt, ReadOnly:=False, Connect:=strType)
    If strCountry <> "" Then
        strCountry = UCase$(strCountry)
    Else
        strCountry = "U.S.A."
    End If
    strQuery = "SELECT * FROM PWT56 WHERE Country = '" _
    & strCountry & "';"
```

```
    Set qdfDBF = dbThis.CreateQueryDef(Name:="", _
     SQLText:=strQuery)
    Set rstThis = qdfDBF.OpenRecordset(Type:=dbOpenSnapshot)
    rstThis.MoveLast
    Set GetCountryHistoryDBF = rstThis
End Function
```

I streamlined this version of the procedure somewhat, because I don't intend for the workspace created here to be persistent. The theory here is that addressing the dBASE file may be a one-time occurrence, so the workspace involved in this process does not need to be maintained. The upshot of this is that this procedure does not need to analyze any persistent queries as was done in Listing 18-5.

Here in Listing 18-6, a Workspace class object wrkThis is declared local; it's not going to be persistent, so it the variable that refers to it does not need to be Public. Notice in the CreateWorkspace() function, that the argument UseType:=dbUseJet remains.

In order for Jet to make the link with ODBC, it needs to be able to tell ODBC two things: the name of the data format that ODBC should expect for the database or table file, and the name of that file along with its path. Both of these items of information are crammed into a *connection string*, which in this example is assigned to strType for safekeeping. Connection strings for ODBCDirect are far more complicated, as you'll soon see.

When the file is a table and not a database

This time around, the Name: argument passed to the .OpenDatabase method contains not the full name of a database file, but just the path in which it may be located, represented here by strPathname. How come? Because in instances such as this one, and especially where dBASE files are involved, the true schema for the database combines several files, which hopefully have some relationships to one another. To keep .DBF, .DBT, and indexing files in order, they are generally all stored in the same directory. So indeed, the path name of this directory becomes the name of the database.

Notice later in the arguments list for the .OpenDatabase method, the constant dbDriverNoPrompt. When the logon process for the ODBC driver begins, by default, any information that is not supplied by the connection string or anyone else is requested from the user by a dialog box. This setting turns off the dialog box. If you want the dialog box to appear in all cases, the appropriate setting is dbDriverPrompt. On the other hand, if you want the dialog box to appear only if the information set by the connection string is incomplete for ODBC to initiate the connection, the setting is dbDriverComplete. Notice also the final argument, Connect:, which is set to the connection string strType.

Def jam

In creating and executing the QueryDef class object for Listing 18-6, I didn't waste any time. Rather than create a large With clause — which wasn't needed here since none of the database objects are to be persistent — I simply passed the query text strQuery as the optional SQLText: argument to the .CreateQueryDef method. Immediately after assigning variable qdfDBF to point to the QueryDef class object, I invoked the .OpenRecordset method on that variable.

The single argument used in this rendition of .OpenRecordset is Type:=dbOpenSnapshot. This constant refers to one of several types of record sets, their classifications having mainly to do with their degree of accessibility and malleability. A *snapshot* is a record set whose contents are not expected to change during the course of its use. The contents of the source data on which it was based may change, but this will not affect the snapshot contents.

Connecting to a .DBF file through ODBCDirect

For our third example of remote access, we set Jet aside and deal with the alternate method for retrieving data from outside of Access 2000, ODBCDirect. Listing 18-7 shows how the connection and retrieval may be made. However, I offer this caveat: **The following listing will most likely not work on your system. It will need to be adjusted in some way so that it does work.** How come? Because the parameters which are necessary for ODBC to connect to the data source on your computer are bound to be different from the same parameters on my computer. Following Listing 18-7, you'll see a process which outlines the most painless way for you to make this adjustment for yourself.

Listing 18-7: Connecting to the Penn World table through ODBCDirect.

```
Function GetRemoteCountryHistoryDBF(Optional strCountry _
 As String) As DAO.Recordset
    Dim wrkThis As DAO.Workspace, cnnThis As DAO.Connection, _
     rstODBC As DAO.Recordset, qdODBC As DAO.QueryDef
    Dim strConnect As String, strQuery As String
    Dim bFound As Boolean

    On Error GoTo ODBCErr
ProcTop:
    Set wrkThis = CreateWorkspace(Name:="ODBC-DBF", _
     UserName:="admin", Password:="", UseType:=dbUseODBC)
    strConnect = "ODBC;DSN=dBASE Files;DBQ=d:\DFS\DATABASES;" _
                & "DefaultDir=d:\DFS\DATABASES;DriverId=533;" _
                & "MaxBufferSize=2048;PageTimeout=5;UID=admin;"
    If strCountry <> "" Then
        strCountry = UCase$(strCountry)
```

```
    Else
        strCountry = "U.S.A."
    End If
    strQuery = "SELECT * FROM PWT56 WHERE Country = '" & _
     strCountry & "';"
    Set cnnThis = wrkThis.OpenConnection(Name:="ODBC-dBASE", _
     Options:=dbDriverCompleteRequired, ReadOnly:=False, _
     Connect:=strConnect)
    Set rstODBC = cnnThis.OpenRecordset(Name:=strQuery, _
     Type:=dbOpenDynamic, Options:=0, LockEdit:=dbOptimistic)
    Set GetRemoteCountryHistoryDBF = rstODBC
    GoTo ProcOut
ODBCErr:
    On Error GoTo 0
    MsgBox Err.Description, vbInformation, "Official ODBC Screwup
Report"
ProcOut:
    cnnThis.Close
    Set cnnThis = Nothing
End Function
```

The major difference in this particular procedure is the inclusion of the error trap routine, which will be discussed in detail in a few paragraphs. Error traps aren't necessary for ODBCDirect connections, but since ODBC errors are an entirely separate matter from DAO and VBA errors, and there is no Jet engine in this procedure to handle ODBC errors, at the very least it is a convenience to have an error trap just to report what the problem is.

The details of an ODBCDirect connection

The CreateWorkspace() function in Listing 18-7 bears little difference here than in its previous two incarnations, except for the argument UseType:=dbUseODBC. This is the parameter that tells VBA that the connection will circumvent Jet. But from there, things do not get easier. Take a good look at the connection string assigned to variable strConnect. It is huge and it is a mess. I could spend several pages here discussing every possible parameter that you might find in an ODBCDirect connection string; those shown here don't even scratch the surface. But I appreciate your sanity at least as much as you, and are happy to inform you that there is an easier way to go about deriving a proper string for any particular ODBCDirect connection:

1. Build a prototype of your procedure where the Options: argument of your .OpenConnection method is set to dbDriverPrompt. This makes a prompt appear for logging onto the ODBC driver in all circumstances,

regardless of what the connection string may contain, or even if there is one.

2. Place a breakpoint at the instruction just following the `.OpenConnection` instruction. If you haven't done this before, point to the gray bar at the left of the code window, at a spot aligned with the row containing the instruction, and click once. A brown dot will show up there, and the instruction will be highlighted in brown, indicating that execution of the procedure will pause at that point.

3. Run the procedure as it stands, and use the dialog box to log onto the ODBC driver in the same way that the procedure will log on once it's complete.

4. When execution stops at the breakpoint, bring up the Immediate window and, in the lower pane where the blinking prompt is contained, have VBA execute a direct command to print the `.Connect` property of the object reference variable to which the ODBCDirect connection is assigned. For Listing 18-7, an example would look like this:

```
?cnnThis.Connect
```

The response to this command will be the complete connection string that a revised form of your procedure will need to log onto the ODBC driver exactly the way you just did.

5. Using the Immediate window as though it were Notepad, highlight the entire connection string, right-click it, and select Cut from the pop-up menu, then paste the string directly into your code window, at a convenient position above the `.OpenConnection` instruction.

6. Amend the line where the connection string now appears, so that the string is surrounded by quotation marks (double quotes, not single) and assigned to a string variable such as `strConnect` in Listing 18-7.

7. Rewrite the `.OpenConnection` instruction, making certain that it includes an argument like `Connect:=strConnect`, and changing the `Options:` setting to either `dbDriverNoPrompt` (which bypasses the dialog box in all cases) or `dbDriverCompleteRequired`, as in Listing 18-7. With the latter choice, should the ODBC driver ever be upgraded and the connection parameters change as a result, you'll know it when the log-on dialog box shows up, instead of Windows crashing all around you.

The `.OpenConnection` method is very much like the `.OpenDatabase` method used by Jet, except that it does not require the name of the database to be passed to it in any way. The connection represented here is between VBA and ODBC, not VBA and the database. The connection string, represented here by `strConnect`, contains all the information that the ODBC driver will need for it – not VBA – to make contact with the database.

At this point, perhaps you may recall something you may have read about in Access called the "ODBC Connection Wizard," and are wondering, why didn't I include mention of it here instead of this strange seven-step process? It is this author's experience that the Connection Wizard may either (a) conjure an ODBC connection string from the planet Neptune, or (b) fail to work altogether. Meanwhile, the process outlined above never fails. So much for wizardry.

Making sense of the ODBC connection strings

The title of this segment implies that the act is indeed possible. True, we can strive toward this goal, and perhaps come closer in the journey.

The *connection string* is a literal that ODBC requires for it to identify which ISAM driver to pull up, which database to scan, and generally the user ID and password of the user of the driver if not its underlying database manager. This string is necessary to make contact with ODBC, because **ODBC is not an OLE process.** (Neither is OLE DB, but that's a very long story, and this book is fast running out of space.) This means that there are no channels that Windows makes available to VBA, or Jet, or anything else for transparent communication with ODBC. Instead, everything ODBC needs to know to do its job is encrypted in a language comprehensible perhaps by the inhabitants of another galaxy, then shipped quite overtly to the ODBC manager process.

Like all connection strings, the one in Listing 18-7 begins with the characters `ODBC;`. All connection strings are segmented, with semicolons serving as delimiters between segments, and, occasionally, though not always, terminating the string. The six most common elements of an ODBC connection string are as follows:

- The characters `ODBC;` which always begins a connection string.

- The name of the ODBC driver used in the connection, which is marked with the indicator `DSN=`. The abbreviation stands for "data source name." However, the text that goes here is not actually a data source name, but instead a separate string reserved for the specific ODBC driver.

- The user ID or username of the "person" logging onto the ODBC driver process. This may be the Access user, but often it's just `admin`. This segment is indicated with `UID=`

- The password of the "person" logging on. Where a password is indicated, no characters separate the `PWD=` indicator and the next semicolon, or the end of the string.

- The filename of the database being scanned, which may include the path as well. In Listing 18-6, the path is not included in the string because it is supplied elsewhere. The indicator here is `DATABASE=`

◆ The path where any and all databases being scanned by the ODBC driver for this process are to be located. This is especially helpful if the process is scanning more than one database or table. (Recall that a .DBF file is a table, not a database by the conventional definition.) The indicator for this segment (not shown in Listing 18-6) is DBQ=

In Depth: Setting the error trap

Listing 18-7 utilized an old BASIC programming technique that is not necessarily related to ODBC or databases, but which is crucial here nonetheless: the *error trap*. Notice the way I sectioned this procedure, using line labels that referenced GoTo statements. This segmentation of the procedure is necessary in order to embed within it this curiously foreign object known as the error trap routine.

GoTo is that pesky little statement that has pervaded high-level languages since FORTRAN, and which modern "modular" programmers have worked for years to rid themselves of. Its purpose is to redirect execution to a named or labeled portion of the program. This type of redirection is called a *forced branch*. With all of the members of the Visual Basic family, the scope of forced branches is limited to within the same procedure; you can't have a GoTo statement that points to a line outside of the procedure that contains that statement. At the same time, the only mechanism that VB6 provides for exception handling is old-style error trapping, which is done with the all-errors-considered branching statement On Error GoTo. With all GoTo branches limited to the most local scope there is, each procedure where errors are vital must maintain their own error trap routines. There are no other instructions in VB that *react* to errors; in other words, there's nothing that can automatically trigger execution of a procedure when an error has been registered. You're left instead to post guards at every gate, as it were, which is not exactly a "professional" way to program.

Once the trap is set, one line label ProcTop: marks the functional "Top" of the procedure. The region skipped over is marked ODBCErr: and contains my version of an error handler. Since VBA is, for the most part, powerless to fix whatever ODBC might have fouled up, all that can be done here is to report to the user what ODBC is reporting to VBA. (At the time of this writing, all ODBC error codes were spitting out *blank* strings. Sometimes silence is golden, but there's no sign of gold here.) The error handler routine has an "open bottom," which drops out to a point labeled ProcOut: where the top section of the procedure would jump if no error occurred. From here, I can close the procedure. The most convenient location for an error trap routine is near the end of a procedure, though not at the end. This is because cleanup instructions, such as cnnThis.Close, may be necessary in both erroneous and nonerroneous cases.

On Point

DAO's representation of a database session is called a workspace, for what reason this author is incapable of fathoming. In order to begin retrieving records, VBA has to connect itself to a workspace through DAO. Access always has one workspace of its own, numbered `Workspaces(0)` in the collection. VBA may connect itself to that workspace and link new data to it, or it may launch any number of new workspaces with the `CreateWorkspace()` function. A workspace represents a communications process between a user and Access; and in the case of `Workspace` class objects, VBA acts as the role of the user, not as Access. So VBA finds itself logging onto a workspace, signing in as a user.

Communication with a database of any format may or may not involve the Jet database engine. When Jet is involved, it serves as the interpreter for SQL queries. When Jet is not involved, and ODBC drivers are contacted directly (ODBCDirect), the driver could serve as the SQL interpreter if it is so endowed. But for greater efficiency, SQL queries could be passed through the ODBC driver to the active RDBMS that is managing the database on the network or local processor. When ODBC is involved — and it does not have to be if Jet is managing the query and the database is of Jet's native format — the VBA procedure has to log onto the driver. This is a separate process from logging onto the workspace.

Since an SQL query specifies the tables from which records are to be scanned, VBA procedures that are based on such queries do not have to declare variables to represent tables, even though `TableDef` class objects are available. Instead, a `QueryDef` object may be created whose `.SQL` property both handles the query and names the tables involved in the query. The `RecordSet` class constituent of a `QueryDef` object is assumed to contain the results of the `QueryDef` object's query. The `.OpenRecordset` method initiates the process of loading the `RecordSet` class variable with results of the query. Because the address scheme of Jet and ODBC is inherently sequential (ISAM) and not "set-logical," the method will only retrieve the first record in the set of matching records. So the `.MoveLast` method is required to flush out the retrieval set into the `RecordSet` variable.

In Theory: The Global View of Data

All queries from clients and all transfers of data between server and client are considered transactions, not unlike the events that take place everyday at a bank. As does a bank manager, a database server monitors and accounts for all transactions, both in progress and completed. While bank officials like to put forth that all this accounting is to protect your resources, we all have surmised, and even come to understand to some extent (on those days when the lines are shorter), that this accounting is to protect the bank's own interests.

The need for transaction accounting in database management becomes more evident as you come to realize that data – in essence, the topic of the conversation between all parties in the model – is never a very stable entity in and of itself. Like cash, it is a liquid asset. It is susceptible to alteration not only by people, but also by the programs whose job it is to keep the information in a database up-to-date. Oftentimes the work of these programs goes entirely unseen by individuals. The world's public financial information is, in a holistic sense, one big database with several million clients, relatively few of whom are people.

When it comes time for those of us in the computing business to describe what it is that makes up a database, we tend to find metaphors in much simpler structures. Book authors have a tendency to equate databases with dictionaries, encyclopedias, or telephone directories – volumes that themselves are not subject to change, even though their publishers often print new editions every year. More accurately, these volumes represent *views* of the databases they represent. Although the data itself changes – people change their phone numbers, the boundaries of the West Bank change from week to week, Microsoft adds another word to the language – the views themselves do not, although they can be replaced from time to time with fresher editions. The distributions of these views of databases are communications processes. Although they may happen annually, which is not enough to qualify as "fast" by the standards of anyone whose job is data processing, they still involve parties whose exchanges of data follow specified protocols. Granted, people tend to use dictionaries and telephone books without much regard to their publishers; there doesn't seem to be much of a bond between these parties, at least in the social sense. But communications is not necessarily a social science. A television advertisement communicates with you, because it provides you with a message that is engineered to invoke a response; yet that process is entirely impersonal. Impersonal communication does take place every day between entities and people, and between entities and other entities. But it is still communication.

Databases are not static entities by definition because, primarily, they exist in *time.* A database's internal variables involve not so much states of being as states of change, or states that are subject to change. Rather than examine data as things, the relational model proposed by E. F. Codd has you observe the periodic states of data in flux. When one observes data, one is looking at a *view* of it, at a snapshot that represents the state of that data at a particular time. Because multiple people are ultimately responsible for the creation of data and their actions take place in time, the changes that they make to this data are likely based on their own unique views of it. And because these changes are likely to take place at *any* time, an arbiter must be enabled to ascertain which changes directed by the people using this data can logically apply to the database. Otherwise, someone looking at an older view could conceivably request a change that might, in the intervening time, have been superseded by some other change that the previous view did not take into account.

In Brief

◆ Access 2000 utilizes its own native forms, although with this edition, it is now capable of making use of `UserForm`-based form modules, like those used in Word, Excel, and PowerPoint. These modules will not have the same specialized functionality found in Access' native form modules, since Access' own forms utilize bound controls that maintain links to fields, columns, and records in databases.

◆ In developing the database foundation for an application, the act of normalization consists of reducing the amount of logic required to symbolize the relations and execute transactions to a minimum.

◆ A record set is Access' version of a view. Both DAO and ADO recognize a `Recordset` class object as a set of records retrieved from one or more tables in a database, whose contents or relations match a specified set of criteria in a query.

◆ The relationship is Jet's most important contribution to the structure of a database schema. It enables a fully normalized database to be capable of governing itself in such a manner that data in one record will never refer directly to data in a non-existent or non-updated record.

◆ Microsoft currently supports two data access models with varying degrees of simultaneity. Data Access Objects is the older model, while ActiveX Data Objects – devised originally as DAO's replacement – reduces much of the overhead required by DAO.

Appendix

What's on the CD-ROM

The CD-ROM that accompanies *Microsoft Office 2000 Developer's Guide* contains the source code of all of the VBA applications with which we experimented in this book, as well as two of John Walkenbach's add-ins: Power Utility Pak and Sound-Proof.

Source Code

Here's how I organized the files: There are subdirectories named for each of the core Office 2000 applications. Within those subdirectories are templates, add-ins, or databases that contain the modules you need. This way, you don't have to import the text yourself. For Word, Excel, and PowerPoint, you can use the Macro Organizer to move these modules into any other add-in or template – such as the Normal template in Word 2000.

Here are the contents of the core subdirectories of `\O2KGuide`:

◆ `\Word2K` contains a document template, `O2KGuide_Word.dot`. In that template are the sorting algorithms with which we experimented in the first three chapters, plus the Jerry Pournelle-inspired true document statistics form module, named `frmJerryStats`, which was featured in Chapter 14. **Bonus:** You'll also find a document template called **LetterManager** that gives you your choice of stationery and embedded graphical signature, all in a single template. This example was cut from the book for lack of space.

◆ `\Excel2K` contains a worksheet `CellTinter.xls`, which has a general module with the code that tints the background color of your cell based on the numeric value you enter into it. Also, `CellShadow.xls` contains the cell navigation tool we developed in Chapter 17. This worksheet is suitable for conversion into an add-in.

◆ `\Access2K` contains a database stored in two formats, Access and xBase/dBASE. Both represent data from the Penn World table from Chapter 18. This database contains economic and social statistics compiled in a study of the major countries of the world over the last several decades. You can learn more about this data and the people who compile it by visiting `http://www.epas.utoronto.ca:5680/pwt /pwt.html`. The VBA modules with which you make remote contact with either of these database formats, are contained in the database file `ODBC2000.mdb`.

◆ `\PowerPoint2K` contains the automated presentation generator that was the focus of Chapter 15. This module involves both PowerPoint 2000 and Word 2000.

◆ `\ClassOf2000` contains this book's real gems:

   ■ **DiagramMatic**, the wrapper class around Word 2000 special diagrams presented in Chapter 9

   ■ **INIControl**, which automates the process of saving persistent settings and parameters for your VBA programs, from Chapter 10

   ■ **Jukebox**, which enables VBA to play .WAV sound files in response to events you designate, also from Chapter 10

   ■ **Citation.dot**, the class module that automates the storage and retrieval of lists of information sources, featured in Chapter 18

JWalk Power Utility Pak and Sound-Proof

By special arrangement with my fellow IDG author, John Walkenbach of JWalk and Associates, the CD-ROM also includes the fully working shareware edition of his award-winning Power Utility Pak for Excel 97.

Power Utility Pak is an Excel add-in that consists of general purpose Excel utilities, custom worksheet functions, and enhanced shortcut menus. The shareware version on the CD-ROM does not include the complete feature set. The complete VBA source code is also available for a small fee.

 The CD-ROM contains PUP97, which works with both Excel 97 and Excel 2000. A significantly enhanced version, PUP 2000, was being finalized as this book went to press. If you would like to try the shareware version of PUP 2000, you can download a copy from `http://www.j-walk.com/ss`.

Sound-Proof is an Excel add-in that uses a synthesized voice to read the contents of selected cells. It's the perfect proofreading tool for anyone who performs data entry in Excel. Options include straight digits (for example, "one two three point five") or natural language ("one hundred twenty-three point five") and cell order (by rows or columns). The pause between cells is adjustable. The shareware is fully functional but, until you register it with the author, it will only let you read a range of 12 cells.

To install the Power Utility Pak, look on the CD-ROM in the subdirectory \JWalk for the file PUP97R3.EXE. Copy this file to a blank directory of your hard disk, and double-click on the file to execute it. Instructions on how to proceed from there will appear on-screen. The Sound-Proof demo may be found in the same directory as file SPDEMO.EXE. My thanks to John for his generosity. I think you'll appreciate the effort he undertook to make Excel work better. (You can contact John at: **JWalk and Associates,** via e-mail at: support@j-walk.com. Or check out his Web site at: http://www.j-walk.com.)

Look for *Excel 2000 Power Programming with VBA* by John Walkenbach (IDG Books Worldwide, 1999).

Index

continued

G

continued

continued

IDG BOOKS WORLDWIDE, INC.
END-USER LICENSE AGREEMENT

<u>READ THIS</u>. You should carefully read these terms and conditions before opening the software packet(s) included with this book ("Book"). This is a license agreement ("Agreement") between you and IDG Books Worldwide, Inc. ("IDGB"). By opening the accompanying software packet(s), you acknowledge that you have read and accept the following terms and conditions. If you do not agree and do not want to be bound by such terms and conditions, promptly return the Book and the unopened software packet(s) to the place you obtained them for a full refund.

1. <u>License Grant</u>. IDGB grants to you (either an individual or entity) a nonexclusive license to use one copy of the enclosed software program(s) (collectively, the "Software") solely for your own personal or business purposes on a single computer (whether a standard computer or a workstation component of a multiuser network). The Software is in use on a computer when it is loaded into temporary memory (RAM) or installed into permanent memory (hard disk, CD-ROM, or other storage device). IDGB reserves all rights not expressly granted herein.

2. <u>Ownership</u>. IDGB is the owner of all right, title, and interest, including copyright, in and to the compilation of the Software recorded on the disk(s) or CD-ROM ("Software Media"). Copyright to the individual programs recorded on the Software Media is owned by the author or other authorized copyright owner of each program. Ownership of the Software and all proprietary rights relating thereto remain with IDGB and its licensers.

3. <u>Restrictions on Use and Transfer</u>.

   (a) You may only (i) make one copy of the Software for backup or archival purposes, or (ii) transfer the Software to a single hard disk, provided that you keep the original for backup or archival purposes. You may not (i) rent or lease the Software, (ii) copy or reproduce the Software through a LAN or other network system or through any computer subscriber system or bulletin-board system, or (iii) modify, adapt, or create derivative works based on the Software.

   (b) You may not reverse engineer, decompile, or disassemble the Software. You may transfer the Software and user documentation on a permanent basis, provided that the transferee agrees to accept the terms and conditions of this Agreement and you retain no copies. If the Software is an update or has been updated, any transfer must include the most recent update and all prior versions.

4. <u>Restrictions on Use of Individual Programs</u>. You must follow the individual requirements and restrictions detailed for each individual program in the "What's on the CD-ROM" appendix of this Book. These limitations are also contained in the individual license agreements recorded on the Software Media. These limitations may include a requirement that after using the program for a specified period of time, the user must pay a registration fee or discontinue use. By opening the Software packet(s), you will be agreeing to abide by the licenses and restrictions for these individual programs that are detailed in the "What's on the CD-ROM" appendix and on the Software Media. None of the material on this Software Media or listed in this Book may ever be redistributed, in original or modified form, for commercial purposes.

5. <u>Limited Warranty</u>.

(a) IDGB warrants that the Software and Software Media are free from defects in materials and workmanship under normal use for a period of sixty (60) days from the date of purchase of this Book. If IDGB receives notification within the warranty period of defects in materials or workmanship, IDGB will replace the defective Software Media.

(b) IDGB AND THE AUTHOR OF THE BOOK DISCLAIM ALL OTHER WARRANTIES, EXPRESS OR IMPLIED, INCLUDING WITHOUT LIMITATION IMPLIED WARRANTIES OF MERCHANTABILITY AND FITNESS FOR A PARTICULAR PURPOSE, WITH RESPECT TO THE SOFTWARE, THE PROGRAMS, THE SOURCE CODE CONTAINED THEREIN, AND/OR THE TECHNIQUES DESCRIBED IN THIS BOOK. IDGB DOES NOT WARRANT THAT THE FUNCTIONS CONTAINED IN THE SOFTWARE WILL MEET YOUR REQUIREMENTS OR THAT THE OPERATION OF THE SOFTWARE WILL BE ERROR FREE.

(c) This limited warranty gives you specific legal rights, and you may have other rights that vary from jurisdiction to jurisdiction.

6. <u>Remedies</u>.

(a) IDGB's entire liability and your exclusive remedy for defects in materials and workmanship shall be limited to replacement of the Software Media, which may be returned to IDGB with a copy of your receipt at the following address: Software Media Fulfillment Department, Attn.: *Microsoft(r) Office 2000 Developer's Guide*, IDG Books Worldwide, Inc., 7260 Shadeland Station, Ste. 100, Indianapolis, IN 46256, or call 1-800-762-2974. Please allow three to four weeks for delivery. This Limited Warranty is void if failure of the Software Media has resulted from accident, abuse, or misapplication. Any replacement Software Media will be warranted for the remainder of the original warranty period or thirty (30) days, whichever is longer.

(b) In no event shall IDGB or the authors be liable for any damages whatsoever (including without limitation damages for loss of business profits, business interruption, loss of business information, or any other pecuniary loss) arising from the use of or inability to use the Book or the Software, even if IDGB has been advised of the possibility of such damages.

(c) Because some jurisdictions do not allow the exclusion or limitation of liability for consequential or incidental damages, the above limitation or exclusion may not apply to you.

7. <u>U.S. Government Restricted Rights</u>. Use, duplication, or disclosure of the Software by the U.S. Government is subject to restrictions stated in paragraph (c)(1)(ii) of the Rights in Technical Data and Computer Software clause of DFARS 252.227-7013, and in subparagraphs (a) through (d) of the Commercial Computer – Restricted Rights clause at FAR 52.227-19, and in similar clauses in the NASA FAR supplement, when applicable.

8. <u>General</u>. This Agreement constitutes the entire understanding of the parties and revokes and supersedes all prior agreements, oral or written, between them and may not be modified or amended except in a writing signed by both parties hereto that specifically refers to this Agreement. This Agreement shall take precedence over any other documents that may be in conflict herewith. If any one or more provisions contained in this Agreement are held by any court or tribunal to be invalid, illegal, or otherwise unenforceable, each and every other provision shall remain in full force and effect.

my2cents.idgbooks.com

Register This Book — And Win!

Visit **http://my2cents.idgbooks.com** to register this book and we'll automatically enter you in our fantastic monthly prize giveaway. It's also your opportunity to give us feedback: let us know what you thought of this book and how you would like to see other topics covered.

Discover IDG Books Online!

The IDG Books Online Web site is your online resource for tackling technology — at home and at the office. Frequently updated, the IDG Books Online Web site features exclusive software, insider information, online books, and live events!

10 Productive & Career-Enhancing Things You Can Do at www.idgbooks.com

- Nab source code for your own programming projects.

- Download software.

- Read Web exclusives: special articles and book excerpts by IDG Books Worldwide authors.

- Take advantage of resources to help you advance your career as a Novell or Microsoft professional.

- Buy IDG Books Worldwide titles or find a convenient bookstore that carries them.

- Register your book and win a prize.

- Chat live online with authors.

- Sign up for regular e-mail updates about our latest books.

- Suggest a book you'd like to read or write.

- Give us your 2¢ about our books and about our Web site.

You say you're not on the Web yet? It's easy to get started with IDG Books' *Discover the Internet,* available at local retailers everywhere.

CD-ROM Installation Instructions

The CD-ROM that accompanies this contains the source code, as well as two add-ins: Power Utility Pak and Sound-Proof. Refer to the appendix "What's on the CD-ROM" for complete information.

Source Code

\O2KGuide is comprised of subdirectories that are named for each of the core Office 2000 applications and within these are templates, add-ins, or databases that contain the modules you need. This way, you don't have to import the text yourself. For Word, Excel, and PowerPoint, you can use the Macro Organizer to move these modules into any other add-in or template, such as the Normal template in Word 2000.

The core subdirectories of \O2KGuide are: \Word2K, \Excel2K, \Access2K, \Power Point2K, and \ClassOf2000 (which contains **DiagramMatic, INIControl, Jukebox,** and **Citation.dot**).

JWalk Power Utility Pak and Sound-Proof

To install the Power Utility Pak, look on the CD-ROM in the subdirectory \JWalk for the file PUP97R3.EXE. Copy this file to a blank directory of your hard disk, and double-click on the file to execute it. Instructions on how to proceed from there will appear on-screen. The Sound-Proof demo is found in the same directory as file SPDEMO.EXE.